MACROECONOMIC THEORY

Edited by
HAROLD R. WILLIAMS
and
JOHN D. HUFFNAGLE
Both of Kent State University

MACROECONOMIC THEORY
Selected Readings

New York

APPLETON-CENTURY-CROFTS
EDUCATIONAL DIVISION
MEREDITH CORPORATION

PREFACE

Macroeconomic theory encompasses a wide range of subject areas. Although each topic is a component in a generally accepted aggregate model, the properties and distinctions peculiar to each have been widely debated. Differences of opinion exist not only with regard to the pertinent variables and the nature of functional relationships but also with respect to the relative importance of different variables. Given these circumstances, it is difficult to do justice to the broad scope of economic theory in a textbook *per se*. The textbook exposes the student to a skeleton of most of the material, but often the brevity of such exposure does not permit adequate assimilation and appreciation of the outstanding contributions to economic analysis. In addition, the student should have the edification of savoring in the original the enthusiasm and style, combined with the analytical subtleties of model building, of the fine academicians, past and present, in the field of economics. To accomplish these ends, the instructors must invariably assign outside readings.

This compilation of readings brings together and makes readily accessible some of the articles in which economists have made outstanding contributions to macroeconomic theory. The collection does not pretend to be exhaustive, but we believe it includes some of the more important contributions which should be read by students taking upper-level courses in macrotheory. Although many instructors may prefer to use this volume as a supplement to a textbook in income and employment analysis, it is also possible to use *Macroeconomic Theory* as the basic book around which the course is organized. We have used both approaches. When using the latter alternative, we add various articles on the topics that are to be emphasized.

The articles contained in this volume were selected on the basis of their theoretical significance, empirical contributions, or interpretative importance. In addition to these broad criteria, articles were selected whenever possible to demonstrate the transition from classical to Keynesian economics. These latter readings bring out the evolutionary and revolutionary character of Keynesian analysis.

The readings in *Macroeconomic Theory* are divided into three parts. Part One includes articles which give the background and assumptions (both implicit and explicit) of classical and Keynesian economics, as well as an overall comparison of the two theories. These comparisons present a good view of much of the classical tradition and its points of agreement and disagreement with Keynes. Part Two pertains to the major components of aggregate economics and is divided into four sections: *Theory of consumption, Theory of investment, Theory of money, interest, and employment,* and *Theory of the price level, money wage rates, and employment.* The papers contained in each section deal with the classical view (where relevant), and extensions, modifications, and testing of the components and models. *Macroeconomic Theory*'s last part, Part Three, comprises readings on economic growth. These theories make use of a variety of tools and assumptions in their analysis of the many facets of economic growth. Although not nearly as wide in scope as classical growth models, the more recent contributions are imposing in their construction and insights into the problem of economic growth.

For standardization and to provide additional information we have often supplemented or expanded bibliographical information given in the articles' footnotes. Where this has been done, the material is enclosed in brackets.

We wish to express our appreciation to all the authors and publishers who permitted us to reprint their works. It is they who deserve the credit for any merit this compilation of readings may have. A special note of acknowledgment goes to Professors Milton Friedman and Robert Solow for helpful suggestions on the preparation of their articles, and to Professor Wallace C. Peterson for helpful comments in the early development of this reader. We wish also to thank the manuscript's reviewer, Professor Howard Sherman, for his valuable comments and suggestions. To the others who assisted in this project we express our appreciation. It was with much regret that we had to exclude many excellent papers from this collection in order to keep the text to a reasonable size.

H. R. W.
J. D. H.

CONTENTS

THREE. Theory of Economic Growth

MACROECONOMIC THEORY

INTRODUCTION

In the analysis of income and employment theory it is customary to distinguish between the *classical, Keynesian,* and *modern* theories. The classical approach, which is generally thought of as a synthesis of the ideas of many economists, among whom Keynes included Ricardo, J. S. Mill, Marshall, Edgeworth, and Pigou, was widely accepted by laymen and economists prior to the mid-1930's. The mass unemployment and economic stagnation of the 30's, however, combined with the appearance in 1936 of Keynes' systematic analysis of income and employment determination, raised grave doubts about the validity of the classical analysis. Disenchantment grew and Keynesian theory gradually displaced the classical theory in the late 30's and early 40's. Modern income analysis is the Keynesian model modified by the many refinements and extensions of economic analysis since the *General Theory.*

There can be no doubt of the impetus and direction given modern income and employment theory by the Keynesian aggregative model. The basic framework of modern theory has clearly evolved from the formulations of Keynes, as the readings in this volume illustrate. However, the relationship between Keynes' theoretical model and that of the classics is not as easily discernible. In fact, there is considerable controversy as to whether any significant ties exist at all. Keynes himself felt that he had sounded the death knell of the classical theory (which to Keynes was epitomized by the writings of his former teacher, A. C. Pigou), although he recognized the earlier theory was valid under certain restrictive conditions. Notwithstanding Keynes' view, economists have continuously debated whether Keynes' model is basically a complete break with, or merely an extension of, the classical tradition.

The papers in Part One, *Classical Economics and Keynes,* provide insights into the background and assumptions of the classical and Keynesian theories, as well as an overall comparison. The articles by Harris, Streeten, Leontief, and Klein provide the student with general knowledge needed to understand and compare the different systems. Keynes' pre-*General Theory* attitude toward laissez faire and his attack on classical, as well as Marxian, economics is aptly presented by Harris. Leontief discusses classical and Keynesian postulates and points to what he feels are Keynes' outstanding

1

contributions. Streeten examines some philosophical traditions of classical economics and Keynes' relation to these traditions. The paper by Klein compares the classical, Keynesian, and Marxian theories of employment. Is Keynes' theory basically a complete break with the classical tradition as some economists allege, or is Keynesian theory merely an extension of the earlier analysis? While the student may not yet have sufficient knowledge about the intricate subtleties and complexities of the Keynesian model to formulate his opinion on this and many other questions, the readings in this text should provide ample resources with which he can begin to formulate his own synthesis. Of course, one should be aware that simple answers do not exist.

Part Two, *Keynesian Economics, the Classics, and the Keynesians,* relates to the major components of aggregate economic analysis. Modern income and employment analysis, although Keynesian in nature, has progressed beyond the model found in the *General Theory.* Of course, in some respects subsequent investigation has entailed merely an elaboration of Keynes' basic ideas. In other respects, however, theoretical and empirical research has led to significant alterations and advancements of the Keynesian system. The articles in Part Two were selected essentially on the basis of their extension, modification, and testing of the various components and models of aggregate economics. However, where possible, papers were incorporated to show the classical view relative to each major aspect of modern theory. The readings are classified by whether they deal primarily with consumption, investment, money and interest, or the price level and money wage rates.

Three articles on consumption theory are included in the first section of Part Two. The articles, by Duesenberry, Modigliani and Brumberg, and Friedman, deal primarily with reconciliation of the short-run and long-run consumption functions. Duesenberry accomplishes this reconciliation by developing a relative income hypothesis. According to his view consumption depends not only on current income — the Keynesian view — but also on the relationship between current income and the peak income realized by consumers in the past, and on the spending units' relative income position. Modigliani and Brumberg espouse an income hypothesis which is analytically similar to Duesenberry's, but their explanation differs in some important aspects. Friedman advocates a permanent income hypothesis that is significantly different in nature from the two preceding explanations. He explains the long-run proportionality between consumption and income in terms of the relationship between permanent consumption and permanent income.

The second section, on investment theory, contains five papers. Although many excellent articles have been written on the various aspects of investment theory, the lack of significant movement toward reasonably wide agreement makes it difficult to tie these writings into a neat and carefully structured package. Nonetheless, the papers included here strike at several important aspects of the theory of investment. Samuelson's classic article skillfully shows the interaction between the multiplier and accelerator. Eckaus discusses the acceleration principle in various forms and points out why he believes it has considerable merit, even though it appears to lack empirical validity. Witte and Jorgenson, while using different approaches, are both basically concerned with the relationship between the stock of capital and investment. Witte examines the underlying microfoundation of the Keynesian aggregate investment function and the relationship of the investment function to the stock of capital. Jorgenson, using neoclassical optimal capital stock analysis, explains and develops the connection between the stock of capital and investment theory. He then contrasts the neoclassical investment demand theory with other investment theories. Brems discusses several aspects of investment theory in order to discover what factors underlie induced investment. After studying the current state of investment theory, the reader should understand why some economists believe the theory of investment requires much theoretical rethinking and further empirical investigation.

The basic theory of money, interest, and employment is set forth in the third section's articles by Hicks, Modigliani, and Tobin. Hicks' paper is the foundation on which the well-known and widely utilized "Hicks-Hansen" IS-LM model is anchored. The paper by Modigliani considers several theories of interest and money and skillfully uses the vital aspects of each analysis to formulate a more general model. Tobin discusses some of the problems associated with Keynes's explanation of the liquidity preference function and presents an alternative explanation based on risk-averting behavior.

The last section of Part Two contains four articles on the price level, money wage rates, and employment. In the first article, Pigou argues that given constant technology, the economy must *ultimately* move to a stationary level — the classical stationary state; and, in opposition to the Keynesian view, Pigou maintains that this level must be one of full employment. He implies here, as he has emphasized in other places (for example, his *Employment and Equilibrium*, [London: Macmillan & Co., 1941]pp. 85-98), that the classical theory is generally misconstrued to mean that full employment will always exist, whereas the classical theory really maintains only that there is a *tendency* toward full employment. Metzler contrasts a modern version of classical theory which incorporates a wealth-saving relation, with classical theory, which emphasizes the interest rate. Tobin analyzes the impact of alterations in money wage rates on the volume of employment according to the classical and Keynesian analyses. Patinkin's paper investigates the relationship between price flexibility and full employment, a relationship which has been much debated because of the apparently polar positions taken by Keynesians and the classical defenders. The relationship is analyzed both statically and dynamically with considerable emphasis on the Pigou, or Real Balance, Effect.

Part Three, *Theory of Economic Growth*, contains some of the outstanding contributions to growth theory. The models and ideas of the classical economists, presented in Parts One and Two, are omitted and Part Three begins with more recent articles, all of which have been written since World War II. The papers presented are purely theoretical. They attempt to explain the nature and causes of economic growth, but they do not purport to explain particular historical growth patterns.

The earliest models of growth presented are those of Harrod (1948, but originally published in a slightly different version in 1939) and Domar (1947). Despite important differences, these theories reach basically the same conclusion because of a crucial common feature: both are based on a production function with fixed factor proportions. Therefore, the models imply that the economy must move along a particular path of advance from which any deviation in either direction will cause secular exhilaration and inflation or secular deflation. The subsequent articles challenge this gloomy interpretation of economic growth by altering the assumptions upon which the Harrod-Domar models are based and by presenting different models.

The remaining papers are basically neoclassical in nature. Their models are characterized by a production function which allows a continuum of alternative capital-output ratios, thus averting the razor's edge equilibrium associated with diverging growth rates in the Harrod-Domar models. The papers of Solow, Swan, and Tobin place the neoclassical model in a prominent position in the study of economic growth. Swan's discussion ranges from classical and neoclassical to the Harrodian model of growth. As a starting point Solow uses the assumptions of the Harrod-Domar models except that of fixed proportions. He then analyzes the implications for economic growth of variable factor proportions, monetary factors, and technological change. In addition to considering factors in variable proportions, Tobin analyzes monetary factors associated with growth. Unlike the Harrod-Domar models, these neoclassical theories conclude that, with variable factor proportions and flexible prices, the economy can adjust to whatever rate of growth is necessary to maintain full employment.

The growth model by Kaldor and Mirrlees is basically Keynesian. Most important here is the crucial role played by the "technical progress function," which replaces the usual production function. However, complications such as imperfect competition and the relevance of the distribution of income to the stability of the system are also investigated.

ONE

Classical Economics and Keynes

SEYMOUR E. HARRIS 1

Introduction: Keynes' attack on laissez faire and classical economics and wage theory

In this introduction, I shall deal primarily with the attitude of Keynes towards laissez faire and classical economics as revealed in the pre-*General Theory* period.

As Dr. Smithies observes, supporters and detractors of Keynesian economics in the popular press will find little support for high wage theories in the *General Theory*. In fact the thesis of Keynes' book, subject to reservations, is that a change in money wages will not influence real wage rates, employment, or output. Association of Keynes' name with high wage theories rests on his earlier writings and particularly on his antagonism to wage cutting in the inter-war period.

Laissez faire

In his biography of Marshall, Keynes noted both that the former was aware of the conflict between the social and private interest, and that Professor Pigou had elaborated on this theme.[1] The lesson was not lost on Keynes, who also emphasized this conflict, and, following Bentham, he would

From THE NEW ECONOMICS: KEYNES' INFLUENCE ON THEORY AND PUBLIC POLICY, edited by Seymour E. Harris. Copyright 1947 by Alfred A. Knopf, Inc. Reprinted by permission. Pp. 541–557. [Footnotes renumbered and expanded — *Eds.*]
[1] *Essays in Biography* [New York: Harcourt, Brace & Co., 1933], p. 227.

distinguish (but anew) the *agenda of government* from the *non-agenda*, and he would be sympathetic with a political system within a democratic framework which would be capable of accomplishing the agenda — and a broader one than that supported by Bentham.[2]

In many fields of economic activity, laissez faire had broken down.
*   First, there is the area of money, which is discussed fully elsewhere. In that area, Keynes' main complaint was that the monetary system tended to operate in a manner which yielded a smaller income than intelligence, industry, and resources made possible.[3] The difficulty was in part the fear of management of interference, which stemmed from the laissez faire philosophy, and in part from the fear of poor management.[4] In his early writings, Keynes had stressed the need of monetary stability, lamenting with equal eloquence those inflationary episodes which destroyed savings — at that time considered a desideratum — and those deflationary episodes which tended to increase risks and reduce business enterprise.[5] Yet even in 1923 he saw in the depreciation of money a "weighty counterpoise against the cumulative results of compound interest and the inheritance of fortunes," as well as a loosening influence "against the rigid distribution of old-won wealth and the separation of ownership from activity."[6] His general position, and especially in the last 20 years, was that monetary authorities were not disposed to interfere aggressively, and thus to shackle the forces tending to deflate the economy. It was the right of the State to control vested interests and revise contracts that had become intolerable. The task of the monetary authority was to free a country from outside forces that tended to raise interest rates and restrict monetary supplies and, if necessary, to introduce controls (e.g., ban on capital exports) which would preclude the export of money from having unsettling effects on the international position. Above all, correct monetary policy stipulated a monetary system sufficiently elastic to keep the rate of interest low enough to assure investment at an adequate level — even in the *General Theory*, when he had lost some of his early enthusiasm for monetary policy, he still supported expansionist monetary policies.[7]

*   Second, laissez faire policies were bound to result in deficient demand, unemployment, wasted resources, etc. Keynes' analysis of the classical system, which was the foundation of his own, led him to reject the laissez faire philosophy. Although he was prepared to admit that the modern

[2]*Essays in Persuasion* [New York: Harcourt, Brace & Co., 1932], pp. 312-313.

[3][*The*] *General Theory* [*of Employment, Interest, and Money* (New York: Harcourt, Brace & Co., 1936], pp. 217-220, 339.

[4]Cf. [*A*] *Tract* [*on Monetary Reform* (New York: Harcourt, Brace & Co., 1924)], pp. 164-167.

[5]*A Tract on Monetary Reform, ibid.*, pp. 34–37; *Essays in Persuasion, op. cit.*, pp. 90–92.

[6]*A Tract on Monetary Reform, op. cit.*, p. 87.

[7]*A Treatise on Money* (New York: Harcourt, Brace & Co., 1930), II, 188–189; *Tract, op. cit.*, p. 67; *General Theory, op. cit.*, pp. 235–236.

classicist did not embrace Say's Law in its crude form, he nevertheless insisted that classical economics was primarily interested in the distribution of the product, and not in the employment of resources, and that in general it was assumed that all income earned in producing output would also be used to purchase it. At any rate, no adequate attempt had been made to study effective demand and its relation to the supply function.[8]

In quarters where Say's Law was accepted, there would be no obstacle to full employment. Keynes, however, found in the failure to spend current income on consumption and investment goods the cause of unemployment. It was, therefore, necessary to control consumption, savings, and investment. Most of the proposals to flout the laws of the market place originated in the quest for adequacy of demand. It was necessary to control and reduce savings, and to raise consumption in conditions of less than full employment — through taxation and deficit spending *inter alia* — to increase investment through reductions in the rate of interest, stimulation of consumption, and public programs of investment. Keynes was even prepared to give serious consideration to usury laws, which were directed to discouraging use of capital to finance transfers, and to stamped money, as a means of forcing money into productive channels.[9]

• Third, Keynes considered the application of laissez faire principles to some sectors of the economy (e.g., exchange markets) may be especially injurious when other parts (e.g., the labor markets) are inflexible. Wages might move upwards too rapidly and thus interfere with the growth of an economy — he contended that in Spain, for example, the planned expansion following the gold discoveries of the sixteenth century was nipped by wage inflation. Falling wages in response to declining prices and rising exchange rates might not yield an equilibrium position short of complete economic exhaustion; and besides, modern trade-unionism precludes the required downward adjustment of wages. At any rate, Keynes was not inclined to allow the threat of the economic Juggernaut — that wages should be determined by economic pressures and the economic machine should crash along, irrespective of what was done to individual groups.[10]

Capitalism or socialism

Although Keynes was critical of the excesses of the capitalist system, he was far from friendly to Marxism or to any form of socialism. He could not accept a doctrine based entirely on an economic textbook which he knew

[8]*General Theory, op. cit.,* especially, pp. 18–22, 26.
[9]*General Theory, op. cit.,* pp. 351–358 and Chap. 24.
[10]*Essays in Persuasion, op. cit.,* pp. 261–262; *Treatise, op. cit.,* I, 176–178, 273, and II, 155–156. Keynes' attacks on the classical postulate that the marginal disutility of labor = the real wage will be discussed later.

"to be not only scientifically erroneous but without interest or application in the modern world." Nevertheless, he had much in common with Marx. They both were aware of exploitation by capitalists, of deficient demand and over-savings, of declining marginal efficiency of capital, and the unwisdom of capital exportation. Marx, of course, considered the last an attempt of capitalist nations to find an outlet for their surplus commodities, whereas Keynes was critical, not because exploitation of borrowing nations was involved, but rather because the uncontrolled flow of capital abroad reduced the gains of capitalism for Great Britain vis-à-vis the debtor nations and imposed upon the British economy monetary contraction and unemployment.[11]

Keynes would indeed try to preserve capitalism by ridding it of its parasitic elements. Excess savings; high rates of interest; the hereditary principle and its debilitating effect on capitalism; the preference of the future over the present — these were the special targets of his criticism.[12]

Money-making and the quest for profits were indeed acceptable pursuits in Keynes' views: it was better to tyrannize over pocketbooks than over lives. In fact a large part of the Treatise is devoted to a defense of money-making and enterprise against thrift. It was the quest for profits and its ensuing profit inflation which, in the years 1500–1700, produced modern capitalism. Keynes, however, envisaged the day when, with continued accumulation of capital and improvements in technology, the pursuit of monetary gains would become a much less important feature of everyday life, the problem then becoming one of effectively using leisure time. And one of the few features of the Russian experiment that appealed to Keynes was its attempt to reduce the importance of money-making.[13]

In 1926, he concluded that capitalism could still "be made more efficient for attaining economic ends than any alternative system yet in sight," but it was nevertheless in many ways extremely objectionable. At this time, he was not yet prepared to give the State as much authority or right to intervene as he was ten years later. The State should concern itself with the amount of savings, the population problem, central banking policy, and provide information for business decisions — thus making capitalism more efficient.[14] In later years, the breakdown of capitalism undoubtedly contributed to a revision of his views concerning the province of the State. In particular, its responsibility for underwriting demand became a central part of his program.

Yet it is far from the truth to classify Keynes as a socialist or even as a destroyer of capitalism. In his attacks on the Labor Party, on the tyranny of trade unionism, on socialism and communism, in his unwillingness even in

[11]Essays in Persuasion, op. cit., p. 300; Treatise, op. cit., I, Chap. 21, and II, 184–196, 312–313; cf. the essay by P. Sweezy, [The New Economics (New York: Alfred A. Knopf, Inc., 1947), pp. 102–109].
[12]Treatise, op. cit., II, 313; and General Theory, op. cit., pp. 220–221 and Chap. 24.
[13]General Theory, op. cit., p. 374; Treatise, op. cit., chap. 30; Essays in Persuasion, op. cit., pp. 302–303, 366–373.
[14]Essays in Persuasion, op. cit., pp. 312–322.

wartimes to deprive consumers of their rights to choose among alternative commodities, Keynes showed that to the very end he remained a defender of capitalism, of a system of private enterprise, but that this was to be adapted to modern institutional requirements. Keynes' faith in capitalism is well revealed in his brilliant essay on "Economic Possibilities for our Grandchildren" (1930). Here Keynes contrasted the pessimists of the left who would save us by revolution and the pessimists of the right who considered "the balance of our economic and social life so precarious that we must risk no experiments." It was the forces of compound interest, the accumulation of gold and profits, which had yielded the modern economic society. A further annual rise of capital by 2 per cent per year would increase capital equipment by 7½ times in one hundred years. He concluded that, if the problems of war and population could be solved, then the *economic problem* might be solved within one hundred years. Man's problem, then, would be to learn how to use his freedom from material cares and how to enjoy and profit from his leisure.[15]

To many, the *General Theory* may seem to be a frontal attack on capitalism. Yet what are Keynes' final words on the issue of statism *vs.* liberalism?

Our criticism of the accepted classical theory of economics has consisted not so much in finding logical flaws in its analysis as in pointing out that its tacit assumptions are seldom or never satisfied, with the result that it cannot solve the economic problems of the actual world. But if our central controls succeed in establishing an aggregate volume of output corresponding to full employment as nearly as is practicable, the classical theory comes into its own again from this point onwards. If we suppose the volume of output to be given, i.e., to be determined by forces outside the classical scheme of thought, then there is no objection to be raised against the classical analysis of the manner in which private self-interest will determine what in particular is produced, in what proportions the factors of production will be combined to produce it, and how the value of the final product will be distributed between them. . . . Thus, apart from the necessity of central controls to bring about an adjustment between the propensity to consume and the inducement to invest, there is no more reason to socialize economic life than there was before.[16]

Keynes then goes on to argue that the present system has broken down, not in the *direction* of its employment, but rather in the actual *amounts* of employment made available.[17] In his view, the advantages of the system are the efficiency of decentralization, the play of self-interest. Individualism, if it can be purged of its excesses and defects, will greatly widen the field for the

[15]Keynes' views on issues raised in this paragraph may be found, for example, in *Persuasion, op. cit.*, pp. 312-322, 358-369; *How to Pay for the War* [New York: Harcourt, Brace & Co., 1940], pp. 7, 52, 55; *Treatise, op. cit.*, II, 163.
[16]*General Theory, op. cit.*, pp. 378–379.
[17]Cf. P. Sweezy, *op. cit.*, pp. 102–109.

exercise of formal choice; and the proposed controls are the only manner of salvaging private enterprise and assuring the exercise of individual initiative.[18]

Variants of Keynesianism

Keynes was particularly critical of socialist economics. It is difficult to understand his rather extreme and unfair attack on both Marxian and Russian economics. In his view, there was nothing to be learned from Russian economics.[19] Perhaps Keynes would not take this extreme position today, in view of the remarkable accomplishments of the Soviet, and particularly since 1928. Over a period of twelve years (1928–1940), individual output rose by 650 per cent and real per capita income by 350 per cent; and there were significant rises in productivity. (Russian figures indeed are not thoroughly reliable, and corrections for price changes offer many difficulties; but all competent observers agree that there has been no significant attempt to manipulate the figures.) The gains indeed were absorbed primarily in the production of capital goods and war goods and did not contribute adequately to an improved standard of living. Capitalist nations may not approve of Russian methods, nor did Keynes: control of the allocation of economic resources, serious infringements on private liberty, etc. But the Russians nevertheless have shown that if a country is prepared to pay the price in curtailment of personal liberty, then rapid rates of industrialization, very rapid advance from a low level of output, and full employment without the large inflationary pressures that seem to accompany full employment in democratic countries, and particularly the United States — all of these can be achieved. The Soviet has shown the capitalist world that through co-ordinated rationing, allocation, taxing, pricing, and saving policies, the State can achieve a balanced growth of the economy, and can largely determine the distribution of goods.[20]

This brings me to the variations of the Keynesian theme that now prevail. All groups involved accept one fundamental feature of Keynesian economics: the imperative necessity of underwriting, subsidizing, socializing, or guaranteeing, demand, that is, the responsibility of the Government to assure an adequacy of demand.

At one extreme is the Beveridge group.[21] Beveridge and his followers

[18]*General Theory*, *op. cit.*, pp. 379–380.

[19]*Essays in Persuasion*, *op. cit.*, pp. 297–311, especially, p. 306.

[20]See especially A. Baykov, *The Development of the Soviet Economic System*, pp. 290, 384; A. Yugow, *Russia's Economic Front in Peace and War* (1942), p. 199; L. H. Bean, "International Industrialization and Per Capita Income" in NBER [National Bureau of Economic Research], Conference on Research in National Income and Wealth, *Studies in Income and Wealth*, VIII (1946), 732.

[21]Sir W. Beveridge, *Full Employment in a Free Society* ([London: Allen & Unwin, Ltd.,] 1944), especially Parts I, IV, V, VI; and *The Economics of Full Employment*, Studies Prepared by the Oxford University Institute of Statistics (1944), especially Chaps. 3 and 4.

would not only socialize demand; they would also control the distribution of labor and capital, take strong measures to curb inflation, even to the extent of restricting activities of trade unionism, discouraging make-work practices, etc.; and they might even impose upon the public, through control of allocation of economic resources, proper consumption standards. In the international field, they are prepared, if necessary, to have recourse to bilateralism, minute control of foreign trade, bulk commodity agreements, etc. The most extreme position is taken by Dr. Balogh in the Oxford volume noted.

At the other extreme, Polanyi would rely exclusively on monetary manipulation — his work is based more on the *Treatise* than on the *General Theory*. According to Polanyi, the Government should manufacture enough money to assure a demand adequate to exclude spilled savings, that is, the gap between savings and investment must be filled. At some point in this expansionary process, the public will begin to disgorge its hoards. Once the monetary supplies become excessive (i.e., the gap becomes negative), the government can reverse its policies by withdrawing cash through a proper tax policy. Above all, it is not the job of the government to waste resources on public works or to interfere in any manner with the allocation of economic resources. Polanyi undoubtedly overestimates the effectiveness of purely monetary measures and underestimates the institutional difficulties of reversing inflationary or deflationary policies.[22] Lerner, in his functional finance theories, approaches the Polanyi position, but in other respects comes closer to the Beveridge position.

In the middle we shall find the doctrines of Keynes and perhaps of a majority of his followers. They are content to rely primarily on monetary expansion and socialization of demand. They are aware of structural maladjustment, but are impressed by the practical difficulties, within the time available, to treat these sore spots effectively — though, of course, they would make earnest efforts to do so. In the London *Times*, Keynes emphasized, for example, the difficulties involved in dealing with distressed areas through specific measures.[23]

Wages and demand

Few economists and few businessmen are now unaware of the relation of wages and demand. That this relationship is a matter of common knowledge, and general acceptance, is a reflection of Keynes' influence on both economic theory and practice. As has been noted, this popular association of wage rates and demand originates in his earlier writings. Long before the days of the *General Theory*, Marx had put forth a theory of exploitation, inadequate

[22]M. Polanyi, *Full Employment and Free Trade* ([Cambridge: Cambridge University Press] 1945), Chap. 1, especially pp. 64–66.
[23]LT, January 12, 1937.

wages, and deficiency of demand. But theories associated with Socialism were not palatable in a free enterprise system. It remained for a bourgeois economist, whose views would command some respect among economic practitioners in a capitalist society, whose presentation could more readily be understood than Marx's, and whose views might more easily percolate, to convince the economist first, and the lay public second, of the dependence of demand on wages.

Keynes' views on wages evolved gradually. In his *Tract*, he had little to say about wages: his main point was that real wages had risen both during the war and the early post-war period.[24] In the second half of the twenties, he began to pay more attention to the wage problem. The decision to return to gold at pre-war parity had made necessary a deflationary policy which encountered its greatest difficulties, particularly of an institutional kind, in the assault on wage rates, and particularly in export industries. At first, indeed, Keynes was inclined to emphasize justice against the laws of supply and demand, the former suggesting maintenance of wages against the pressure of a rising £ sterling.[25] But it was not long before he had contrasted the cost *vs.* demand aspects of wage-cutting. A reduction of money wages brings a corresponding decline of demand; the analogy of favorable effects of general wage reductions with those of wage cutting by one employer does not hold; reduction of wages in export industries might increase export trade, but it might be countered by similar reductions elsewhere; a better attack in the international field would be a re-allocation of economic resources and an international program for increasing prices; and finally, Keynes contended in 1930–31 that money wages in Great Britain were not too high, given the British output potential and allowing for the severe cyclical decline, which would presently run out.[26]

Wages in the "General Theory"

In general, Keynes' discussion of wages revolved around the effects of a reduction of wages upon demand and output. There is relatively little said about rises in wage rates. In the *Treatise*, indeed, Keynes had been careful to point out that wage inflation had brought an early end to a profit inflation in Spain stimulated by the inflow of gold.[27] In the *General Theory* he urged that, in periods of technical progress, rising wages and stable prices, as against the alternative of stable wages and falling prices, would bring the gains of progress largely to the active members of society, and proper incentives would be assured to stimulate the transfers of workers from less

[24]*Tract, op. cit.*, pp. 27–30.
[25]*Essays in Persuasion, op. cit.*, pp. 257–262.
[26]*Treatise, op. cit.*, I, 176–178 and chap. 21; *Macmillan Report*, Addendum I, 193–199.
[27]*Treatise, op. cit.*, II, chap. 30, 155–156.

to more productive occupations.[28] These discussions of rising wages were rare, however; and they related to the long run.

What was Keynes' theory of wages? Since the determinants of effective demand, employment, and output, were the marginal efficiency of capital, the rate of interest, and the propensity to consume, changes in wage rates could not influence output unless they affected one or more of these variables.[29] The general presumption is against a change in money wage rates influencing output; or at least that the net effect was not easy to predict.

Keynes could envisage conditions under which a reduction of money wages might have favorable effects; but this was not the likely outcome. First, there was the adverse effect of the transfer of income from workers to capitalists, the former having a higher marginal propensity to consume. Keynes was particularly critical of the classical economists, who were too quick to assume that demand would rise with a reduction of wages and prices and with the ensuing increased purchases by non-wage-earners. They were disposed to leave out of account the effect on output of the decline in wages, without which consideration the assumption of expanded demand by non-wage-earners was not very meaningful. The crucial point in this discussion of demand is that, even if entrepreneurs should mistakenly expand their output in response to a decline in the wage rates, their expectations would be disappointed — unless the marginal propensity to consume were unity[30] or unless the difference between the actual propensity and unity were made up by a rise in investment. This would only happen if the marginal efficiency of capital should rise relatively to the rate of interest. No reason is adduced for this to happen.

Second, would the marginal efficiency of capital react favorably to a reduction in the wage rate? Entrepreneurs might indeed expand output on the assumption that wage-cutting would help them; but their expectations, as was just pointed out, are bound to be disappointed. Keynes also points out that one decisive wage cut, on the understanding that this would be the one and only cut, might stimulate investment. A reduction of these proportions is not, however, practical; and a series of downward revisions would be the signal for entrepreneurs to wait until wages had reached rock bottom. Marginal efficiency of capital is then not likely to rise.

Third, what of effects via the rate of interest? Here Keynes is hopeful, because, with wage and price reductions, the demand for cash might well be reduced. (Labor, dissatisfied and fearful of the consequences of wage-cutting, might, however, increase its hoards.) If the favorable effects are to be had through what amounts to an expansion in monetary supplies, then Keynes, spurning wage-cutting and its unfortunate social and economic

---

[28] *General Theory, op. cit.*, pp. 269–271.
[29] *General Theory, ibid.*, pp. 260–261.
[30] If the marginal propensity were less than unity, then the reduction of demand by workers would not be offset by a corresponding rise of demand by other groups.

consequences, would directly expand monetary supplies, though at the same time warning the reader of the limitations of monetary expansion as a weapon for expanding output and employment.[31]

The attack on the classical theory of wages and employment

Classical economics, in Keynes' view, assumes that the marginal disutility of labor is equal to the real wage. Against this postulate, Keynes contends that involuntary unemployment generally prevails, a condition associated with an excess of the real wage over the marginal disutility of labor. Involuntary unemployment prevails when demand is deficient. Unemployed workers are prepared to work at current real wage rates or at reduced real wage rates (i.e., at higher than current money wage rates but not rising as much as the cost of living); but they are unable to bring about the required reduction in real wage rates. In short, though a large proportion of the unemployed are prepared to work at lower real wages, they are unable to depress the real wage rate; and hence they remain involuntarily unemployed. As Mr. Tobin puts it, labor is beset by a money illusion and hence will work at a lower real wage rate, and yet labor is powerless to take advantage of the potential demand for its services at lower real wage rates, because a reduction in the money wage rate will not bring about a decline in the real wage rate.

Messrs. Leontief, Smithies, and Tobin all discuss the classical and Keynesian postulates. In Professor Leontief's view,[32] for example, the classicist, in starting with the general nature of consumers' choice, relied much more on experience than did Keynes, who built on three postulates, (1) the demand schedule for consumers' goods, (2) the slope of the labor supply schedule, and (3) the relation of income and savings. According to Professor Leontief, the postulate that labor supply was a function of the real wage rate was not the fundamental one of classical economics. Dr. Smithies points out that in the Keynesian system *real income is determined independently of changes in money and income;* that the main factors determining the distribution of income are independent of wages and prices; that real output and employment are not dependent on conditions of labor supply; and that real wages are independent of the money bargain — they depend on the relative equilibrium value of prices and wages. Mr. Tobin shows clearly the relation of Keynes' consumption function — that *real* consumption expenditure is a unique function of *real* income with a positive value of less than unity — to changes in wage rates. So far as consumption expenditure is concerned, a change in money wage rates could not affect the volume of employment and output.

---

[31]Cf. *General Theory, op. cit.,* especially pp. 257–260, 265–271.
[32]See his essay [in *The New Economics, op. cit.,* pp. 345-364].

None of these authors is prepared to accept Keynes' discussion as the final word on the relation of wage rates and employment, though they all agree that Keynes made important contributions. Even Professor Leontief, who is the most critical of the three towards Keynes, sees in Keynes' treatment an improvement over classical short-run theory; and he finds that Keynes, like Marx before him and unlike the classicists whom Keynes criticized, made important contributions to the distributive aspects of economics. (In contrast, Keynes was inclined to criticize the classicists for their concentration on distribution and their failure to deal with the level of employment. Keynes and Leontief are not necessarily in disagreement here, for to some extent the level of employment and output is a problem of distribution.)

In the three essays under consideration, the authors attempt to reconcile Keynes' economics with classical economics. Professor Leontief, for example, critical of the universality given to involuntary unemployment by Keynes, suggests the manner in which classical economics might deal with the problem. It would only be necessary to obtain an upward shift in the classical monetary supply and demand curve — prices would rise and real wages decline. Unfortunately, Keynes' liquidity preference stops the proposed expansion of money from bringing about the required rise of prices and the elimination of involuntary unemployment.

Keynes built his system on over-simplified assumptions; and therefore it is necessary to relax some of the unrealistic assumptions. Both Smithies and Tobin deal with this problem in some detail. Smithies, for example, relaxes the assumptions of constancy of techniques and equipment; of perfect competition; of non-interference by Government; of a closed system; of irrelevance of relative wages and prices; of static analysis. Even in short periods, he holds, techniques change, and, therefore, average productivity may continue to rise and marginal productivity of labor to decline (and therefore labor's share to fall). The removal of the assumption of perfect competition suggests the possibility of expanding employment, rising real wage rates (as Tobin says in criticism of Keynes, real wages are not a declining function of output) and a reduction of supply price. Government fiscal policy in an inflationary period would bring a greater rise of receipts than expenditures, and, therefore, employment and output would not be determined independently of wage and price levels. Again, the reintroduction of international trade under a system where trade is important, exchanges fixed, domestic and foreign trade industries closely related, would bring about a situation in which wage rates would seriously influence employment and output.

Tobin also suggests the limitations of Keynes' assumptions. He deals with monopoly and considers the effects of monopoly on distribution and demand. He does not see (nor does Leontief) why the effects of the money illusion should be restricted to a discussion of the effects on the supply schedule of labor. The money illusion may also influence the consumption function. Keynes' failure to consider factors of production other than labor is also a subject for criticism. In attacking the problem in this manner, Keynes fails to take into account the possibility of changes in wage rates resulting in substitution for labor of other factors, or vice versa. And why should not the money illusion relate to the prices acceptable by owners of non-labor factors?

Wage theory and wage policy

In a simplified discussion, Keynes showed that the presumption was against wage-cutting, and primarily because favorable effects upon employment via the propensity to consume and the marginal efficiency of capital were not anticipated, and any favorable effects through a reduction in the rate of interest could more easily be achieved through monetary expansion. In developing a theory of wages which was integrated especially with demand as against the classical concentration on costs, Keynes made a notable advance. Even though he did not consider all relevant variables, and even though, as the contributors to this volume show, this involved making heroic assumptions, the theory was much more nearly adequate than earlier classical theories with their emphasis on costs, their neglect of demand, their assumptions of a fixed supply of money, their assumptions (or, as Leontief says, their goal) of full employment, and hence their concern with the availability of wage-goods, and in general with their failure to deal with important variables.[33]

Other virtues can be found in Keynes' wage theory, not the least of which is that it fitted in well with institutional requirements. That Keynes' wage theory was the outgrowth of the economic history of the inter-war period is not in my opinion a black mark against it. The case against wage-flexibility or wage-cutting stemmed from, *inter alia*, the difficulties of cutting wages, and from the injustices that resulted. Once the authorities became aware of wage rigidities, moreover, they would be less disposed to impose exchange rates, which in turn might require downward wage adjustments. Above all, Keynes, in contrast to Professor Pigou, would not attempt to stabilize wage rates in terms of wage goods; for every small fluctuation in the propensity to consume or inducement to invest would cause prices to rush violently between zero (should output rise) and infinity (should output fall).[34]

Keynes was not by any means unaware of the imperfections of markets and the need for taking measures to attain the optimum allocation of economic resources. His theory that marginal disutility of labor was not

---

[33]Cf. *General Theory, op. cit.,* pp. 272–279; and S. E. Harris, "Professor Pigou's Theory of Unemployment," *Quarterly Journal of Economics,* [XLIX] (Feb. 1935), 286-324.
[34]*General Theory, op. cit.,* pp. 238–239.

equal to the real wage originated in his concern with market imperfections and irrational behavior. He defended his long-run policy of stable prices and rising wage rates on the grounds, *inter alia*, that the wage incentive would then attract workers into the more productive occupations. And he devoted a whole chapter to the employment function, concerning himself especially with the problem of the varying effects upon employment of a given rise in effective demand.[35] The last is some evidence that his discussions were not limited to over-all demand.

Keynes' main concern over the years was with the relation of wage changes and demand; and he gave much more attention to downward than to upward revision of money wages. His attitude towards our *current* wage problems would indeed be an interesting matter for speculation. In *How to Pay for the War*, he made clear his opposition to wages rising with the cost of living in a war period when taxes, employment, and output were rising.[36] With the Government requiring a large part of current output, he proposed forced loans and relative wage stability as programs for *excluding* inflation. His views since the days of the *Treatise* had changed: at that time he urged an *inflationary* program as the only way to assure the State adequate resources in war — prices and wages both rising but the latter with a lag.[37]

Undoubtedly Keynes in 1946–47 would object to wage increases which were not related to rising productivity, although he looked with favor upon a rise of money wages in the United States which would tend to bring the supply and demand for dollars once more in equilibrium.[38] It would be interesting to conjecture how he would deal with the problem of sterilization of purchasing power. Workers now are not only interested in the relation of money wages and the cost of living index — a concern with real wages which, as Leontief suggests, Keynes was inclined to underestimate — but their decisions concerning offer of work are related to the extent to which their dollar claims on goods can be validated. Finally, would Keynes continue to stump for a policy of advancing wages and stable prices in a world where the *organized* workers arrogate to themselves the main gains of progress, and one-half or three-quarters of the population are squeezed? The latter may not only not share in the gains but may actually lose, whilst organized workers, farmers, and businessmen gain.

Conclusions on wages

In the pre-*General Theory* era, Keynes stressed the relation of wage rates, demand, and output. His discussion of inter-war British economic policy

[35]Chap. 20; cf. A. Smithies [*The New Economics, op. cit.*, pp. 558-571].
[36]*How to Pay for the War, op. cit.*, pp. 72–74.
[37]*Treatise, op. cit.*, II, 173–174.
[38]Lord Keynes, "The Balance of Payments of the United States," *Economic Journal*, [XLVI] (June 1946), 185.

might well be interpreted as one supporting high wages, or at least against falling wage rates. From these early discussions, the modern supporter of Keynesian economics in the public arena undoubtedly finds support for high wage theories. Yet Keynes had little to say in favor of rising wage rates; and, as has been noted, he was critical of wage inflations which brought an end to expansion in the years 1500–1700. That the proponents of high wage theories still find support in the *General Theory* for their theories can be explained by their failure to understand the *General Theory*, by *their* improvement on the *General Theory* through the introduction of more realistic assumptions which to some extent point to favorable effects of rising wages, and perhaps by their confusion of Keynes' general emphasis on the marginal propensity to consume and the desirability of raising it with the relation of rising wage rates and the propensity to consume.[39] Perhaps their support is also found in his effective attack, in the *General Theory*, on the classical theory that unemployment is associated with excessive wage rates. It was a great contribution of Keynes to show that employment depends on effective demand, and that rises in effective demand come via changes in consumption, the marginal efficiency of capital, and the rate of interest — even if the shift of emphasis from wage rates to effective demand was carried too far.

[39]Cf. S. H. Slichter, "Wage-Price Policy and Employment," and comments by A. P. Lerner, *Papers and Proceedings of American Economic Association* [XXXVI] (May 1946), 304–318, 330–335. Here Lerner, adhering closely to the *General Theory* version of wage theory, contends against Slichter that a rise of wage rates leads to a reduction of employment in Slichter's formulation only because the latter fails to take into account the rise of prices following the rise in wage rates.

PAUL P. STREETEN **2**

Keynes and the classical tradition

The purpose of this essay is to bring out some of the value premises implicit in Keynes's analysis and recommendations, and to relate these premises to the great classical tradition of British economic thought.

The harmony of interests

The doctrine that there is a harmony of interests in society was one of the main inspirations for the formulation of economic laws. Like a leitmotif it runs through the whole of economic theory. It is so deep-rooted that some of the fiercest critics of the harmony theory were themselves its victims. The terminology changed and numerous qualifications and modifications were introduced in the course of time. Nevertheless, the common origin is clearly recognizable.

The economists inherited the doctrine from the philosophers of natural law. For Adam Smith economic laws were the decrees of a benevolent and beneficent natural order which turns man's stupid and selfish interests into the common good. Bentham no longer had Adam Smith's faith in the natural order. For him the ends which the economic system pursues are

Reprinted from Kenneth K. Kurihara (ed.), *Post-Keynesian Economics* (New Brunswick: Rutgers University Press, 1954), pp. 345–364, by permission of the publisher and author. [Footnotes expanded — *Eds.*]

21

the ends of men, not of Nature. The market is a mechanism (not an organism) designed by men to serve their will.[1]

At first sight it would seem that utilitarianism made the harmony doctrine redundant. The felicific calculus should have made it possible to compare pleasures and pains and to compute them in social sum. Recommendations could thus be formulated in spite of interest clashes. This appearance seems to be confirmed by the fact that Bentham attacked violently the doctrine of natural law.

Recently, Professor Viner has stressed again that Bentham was not a crude harmony theorist. Although his utilitarianism was, in spite of his protestations, inspired by, and a development of, natural law philosophy, it was a modified version. Many passages show that Bentham did not believe in the actual existence of a harmony of interests. His doctrine of legislation is an attempt to harmonize divergent interests by setting sanctions. Professor Viner has emphasized that Bentham was aware of the gulf between private and public interest, and that he believed that it could be bridged only through education, legislation, and religion. Bentham "did prescribe limits for the field of governmental intervention in economic matters, but these limits were not . . . very narrow ones, and in any case were not so narrow as to give scope to the doctrine of the natural harmony of interests, in the sense of a harmony preordained or inherent in the nature of man living in a society unregulated by government."[2]

Yet, it would be false to conclude that Bentham recognized fully the implications of interest conflicts. He believed in harmony, though in a different sense from that used by Professor Viner.

It is useful to distinguish between a *crude* and the various versions of a *modified* harmony doctrine. According to the crude harmony doctrine the free play of self-interests automatically promotes the interest of society. There is no need for government regulation. Each, by promoting his own interest, simultaneously promotes the interest of "all" (in some significant sense).

According to the modified harmony doctrine the "interest of society,"

---

[1] It would be easy to quote numerous passages from Adam Smith's *Wealth of Nations* which could show that this contrast between his own belief in a *natural* harmony with Bentham's view of a *contrived* harmony is false. Adam Smith clearly recognized the necessity of a good deal of legislation and was certainly not naïvely optimistic about the power of uncontrolled self-interest. But, taking Smith's writings as a whole, and in particular his more general reflections, the difference in emphasis is clearly noticeable. The toughness of this belief is illustrated by the following quotation from Marshall: "This doctrine (Adam Smith's) of natural organization contains more truth of the highest importance to humanity than almost any other which is equally likely to evade the comprehension of those who discuss grave social problems without adequate study; and it has a singular fascination for earnest and thoughtful minds." (*Principles [of Economics*, 6th ed., London: Macmillan & Co., 1910),] p. 246.)

[2] J. Viner, "Bentham and J. S. Mill," *American Economic Review*, [XXXIX] Mar. 1949, p. 369. Professor L. Robbins too has again stressed that the classical economists did not believe in harmony in the sense in which the Physiocrats did. *The Theory of Economic Policy in English Classical Political Economy* ([London: Macmillan & Co.], 1952).

or the "interest of *all*," does not automatically coincide with the interests of each of its members, although it is in the interest of all, and in some sense also in the interest of *each*, to promote the social interest. The theory assumes different degrees or layers of self-interest, only one of which leads to harmony. The most commonly discussed obstacle to the realization of this kind of self-interest is ignorance, but there are others. Conflicts can arise if we think we want to follow certain courses which would not really be to our advantage.

The characteristic feature of this doctrine is that society is held to be some kind of unified body with a purpose and an interest, which are identical with private purposes and interests after the latter have been corrected and disturbing influences eliminated. The modified version of the harmony doctrine is compatible with strong authoritarian interventions and even with despotism. Individuals may be too stupid or too lazy or too misguided, too much bound by habit or enticed by temptation, to pursue their true interests (and hence the common interest) and therefore must be forced to do so.

Thus the crude version of the harmony doctrine tends to lead to a liberal laissez-faire view of policy,[3] whereas the modified version *may* provide reasons for government regulations. Harmony may have to be engineered. But according to both versions there is, actually or potentially, behind the manifold activities of individuals and groups, a coordination of activities towards a purpose. Both imply that there is a subject, a will, a plan and a rational adaptation of means towards an end in society. Society is looked upon as a super-individual[4] or a large family[5] with a unified goal which is simultaneously the (properly defined) goal of each of its members. Hence

[3]But the liberal, laissez-faire view can also be justified on grounds of *absence* of harmony. Distrust of politics and politicians, resulting from a conviction of the selfishness and corruptibility of human beings is perhaps a sounder basis for liberalism than purely economic arguments. The laissez-faire world, to paraphrase F. H. Bradley, is the best of all possible worlds, and everything in it is a necessary evil.

[4]The social-harmony doctrine has its equivalent in the personal sphere. The liberal view of the single human being is often blind to the tensions and conflicts which give rise to morality and overemphasizes order and consistency. This lack of imagination characteristic of the more rationalistic forms of liberalism has been analyzed by Lionel Trilling, *The Liberal Imagination*. What Noel Annan says of the moralist is also true of the economist: "... a humanist is always being surprised by human beings in the right way — they are always more curious and diverse than he has yet foreseen and his surprise keeps his imagination supple. The moralist who is not a humanist is always being surprised in the wrong way; he finds his moral categories too narrow to contain the variety of experience, he is shocked by what he finds...." (*Leslie Stephen*, pp. 239 ff.)

[5]It is obvious that conflicts exist also within the family, and even inside an individual. Some of the criticisms therefore also apply to any view that looks upon the latter as unified systems. But there is the difference that individual actions and those of a family *are* often directed towards a purpose, whereas "the market" is not. The analogy holds only for absolute monarchies where the will of the ruler is identified with the will of the state.

On the other hand it is equally obvious that there may be interest harmony in some respects over wider areas, *e.g.*, the neighborhood, the class, the nation, perhaps even the world. The objection to the harmony doctrine is not that harmony cannot exist, but that a social analysis of interest groupings and interest conflicts is excluded by a question-begging assumption.

the teleological implications of such terms as "the economy," "social welfare," "economic organization," "economic function," "equilibrium," "maximum social welfare," "economic laws," etc.

Many versions of utilitarianism, in their transition from the proposition that each seeks his own happiness, to the postulate that he ought to seek the happiness of all, introduce a modified harmony doctrine. It is clear that an authoritarian, antiliberal version of utilitarianism is possible, as Bentham's views testify. But it still contains the basic assumption of interest harmony.

The rule that social happiness should be maximized requires: (1) comparisons between the happiness of different people, and (2) the imperative that whatever increases happiness on balance, subtracting losses from gains, ought to be done. The imperative (2) implies that there is always a *rational* way (which, in some interpretations means a way based on cool, enlightened self-interest) of resolving conflicts. Harmony is not automatic, but it can be contrived by careful calculation and manipulation. The "interest of society" is maximum social happiness.

More conscientious writers who felt scruples about the manner in which the promotion of the greatest social happiness could be justified to those who would suffer from it, frequently reinforced their case by an argument of which the following passage is typical:

Moreover, each party may reflect that, in the long run of various cases, the maximum sum-total utility corresponds to the maximum individual utility. He cannot expect in the long run to obtain the larger share of the total welfare. But of all principles of distribution which would afford him now a greater, now a smaller proportion of the sum-total utility obtainable on each occasion, the principle that the collective utility should be on each occasion a maximum is most likely to afford the greatest utility in the long run to him individually.[6]

Two difficulties inherent in the utilitarian philosophy have strengthened the need to have recourse to a cruder version of the harmony doctrine with its liberal policy implications, particularly in economics. The first is the impossibility to calculate and compare *in practice* the effects on happiness of a particular measure. It seems both simpler and safer to rely on the spontaneous harmony of egoisms than to perform an impossible calculation. This argument for noninterference from the complete ignorance of the effects of interference can still be found in the most up-to-date controversies.

The second aid to the cruder harmony version is the already mentioned difficulty of deriving both actual (hedonistically determined) and moral behavior from the all-powerful motives of pleasure and pain. The dangerous logical jump from "we must do what we think will please us" to "we ought to do what pleases others" is greatly eased if identity of interests can be

[6]F. Y. Edgeworth, *Papers Relating to Political Economy*, Vol. II [London: Macmillan and Co., 1925] pp. 102–103.

postulated. In discussions of economic matters the otherwise helpful concept of "sympathy" is usually dropped.

What then, in the light of the above distinction, was Bentham's attitude to interest harmony? In spite of rejecting the crude version, and in spite of admitting the necessity for government intervention to enforce the greatest happiness, Bentham remained faithful to the tradition of the harmony doctrine. In his view private and sectional interests are not ultimate forces, but are the result of imperfect insight and foresight. "Vice may be defined as a miscalculation of chances," he said. Even the natural law philosophers had envisaged interest clashes which may arise from error and ignorance. Unless Bentham makes the assumption of harmony, the "public interest" which the legislator is to promote could not be objectively determined nor advanced by threats and cajoleries which reinforce self-interest. It would be impossible to say that it is desirable for each to aim at "the greatest happiness" unless harmony is assumed to start with.[7]

The quest for recommendations which can be based on a harmony of interests is as old as economic thought, and as keenly pursued today as 150 years ago. It found its crudest expression in the Physiocrats and has, in the course of time, been modified and qualified. Yet, economists have endeavored to avoid controversial judgments and to give "scientific," "objective," "unequivocal" advice, just as the natural law philosophers recommended policies because they arose "from the nature of things." When people were less sceptical about the objectivity of values, value and fact were simply equated without further discussion. Later, some justification was thought to be necessary and the distance from factual premise to value conclusion was lengthened. But it amounted merely to a widening of the diameter of a vicious circle. The utilitarian reasoning from the desired to the desirable is an example of this process. Eventually, with growing scepticism about the capacity of facts to yield imperatives, the factual side only was stressed, the value aspect was suppressed, and one hears of "scientific" advice about how to increase welfare.

Yet, at least since Jevons,[8] renunciation of the possibility to resolve

---

[7]This, at least, would have to be the interpretation if Bentham's views are to be consistent. One could also argue that they were inconsistent. He argued both (1) that the maximization of individual happiness by each involves conflict, and (2) that it is desirable for each, and particularly the task of the legislators, to maximize the social sum of happiness. Marx made Benthamism consistent by rejecting its harmony doctrine: legislators, like businessmen, run their affairs (the state, the firms) in their own interests.

[8]"The reader will find, again, that there is never, in any single instance, an attempt made to compare the amount of feeling in one mind with that in another. I see no means by which such comparison can be accomplished. . . . Every mind is thus inscrutable to every other mind, and no common denominator of feeling seems to be possible. . . . Motives in the mind of A may give rise to phenomena which may be represented by motives in the mind of B; but between A and B there is a gulf. Hence the weighing of motives must always be confined to the bosom of the individual." Jevons, *Theory of Political Economy* [London: Macmillan & Co.,], 1871, (4th ed., 1924), p. 14.

conflicts by "objective" tests accompanied scientific "recommendations." Jevons, Bohm-Bawerk, Walras, Pareto, Fisher,[9] among many others, and, more recently Professor Lionel Robbins[10] rejected at some place in their writings the possibility of objective interpersonal comparisons of utility or satisfactors.

Such denials, however, did not prevent these writers from continuing to make recommendations "on economic grounds," even though it is clear that the measures recommended would involve losses for some people. Attempts were made to remove this contradiction. They usually took the form of a distinction between production (including exchange) and distribution, and thus between "efficiency" and "social justice." Pronouncements on "efficiency" (i.e., the sphere of production) were held to be noncontroversial (i.e., subject to interest harmony) while the concern for "justice" was left to the politicians, moralists, governments, etc.

The critics, on the other hand, ever since Godwin, Thompson and Hodgskin pointed out, though they were not consistent in this, that such a separation involves a circular argument, and that production cannot be conceptually separated from distribution.

Income distribution

Keynesian theory strengthened the utilitarian tradition because it resolved one of the great moral dilemmas of the neoutilitarians. Since Bentham it was held that a more egalitarian income distribution would raise general welfare. But inequality, it was thought, is required in order to safeguard sufficient savings. Saving is the source of investment and investment is an essential condition of economic progress and of a rising standard of living of all, including the poor. Equality would defeat its own purpose by reducing the wealth not only of the rich but also of the poor.

Keynes showed that a more equal distribution raises welfare not only on the Benthamite argument that a pound transferred from a rich to a poor man reduces the utility of the former by less than it increases the utility of the latter. It would also in certain conditions speed up investment and economic progress (at any rate in the short run). He thus removed, in his own words, "one of the chief social justifications of great inequality of wealth" and thus, in the words of Schumpeter, he "smashed . . . the last pillar of the bourgeois argument . . . into dust."[11]

[9]Fisher regarded comparisons between the pleasures of different individuals as "mysterious" matters which "do not belong here." (*Mathematical Investigations in the Theory of Value and Prices*, 1892, pp. 99, 87). "Philosophic doubt is right and proper but the problems of life cannot and do not wait." (*Economic Essay in Honour of John Bates Clark*, p. 180).

[10]L. Robbins, *Essay on the Nature and Significance of Economic Science* [London: Macmillan & Co., 1935].

[11]J. M. Keynes, [*The*] *General Theory* [*of Employment, Interest, and Money* (New York: Harcourt, Brace & Co., 1936)], p. 373; Joseph A. Schumpeter, ["Keynes the Economist,"] in *The New Economics*, ed. by Seymour E. Harris [New York: Alfred A. Knopf, Inc., 1947], p. 99.

This argument has its forerunners among the early critics of liberal-utilitarian economics. William Thompson, whose pleas are typical of those of other socialist critics before Marx, wrote that "production would be increased, and capital accumulated with a rapidity, and to an extent, hitherto unknown"[12] if workers received the whole product of their labor and if free exchange were allowed to take place. A system in which workers receive less is restrictive, generates unemployment and waste, as well as all kinds of other vices. Greater equality, on the other hand, would set free vast productive powers, as well as all kinds of other virtues.

These early critics, like Keynes and some modern "Liberal-Socialists" (*e.g.*, Lerner, Meade) had no sympathy for detailed planning. They believed as strongly as the liberals whom they attacked in the virtues of the free market and the pricing system. What distinguished the critics from the orthodox liberals is their conviction that if only some particular institutional arrangement which causes an "artificial disturbance" could be corrected, free exchange could be relied upon to produce a social optimum.[13] The difference between the classical liberals and their critics lay in their conception of the "natural state" in which all works out for the best. The socialists, from Godwin, Thompson and Hodgskin on, attempted to show that the liberal argument, by which actual distribution was justified by competition, is circular; that legal institutions like property, contract enforcement, inheritance, and the distribution resulting from these institutions were historical, arbitrary and unjust. They argued that the "natural laws of distribution" ought to be allowed to reign. Their policies aimed at restraining restraints and thus safeguarding "real" freedom.

To the demand to reform property and inheritance laws, other critics added monopoly and the concentration of economic power. Veblen thought that if only financiers could be got out of the way the engineers could be relied upon to produce a social optimum. List, in a somewhat different tradition, believed that once manufacturing industry had been developed behind a protective tariff free trade would maximize income. Wicksell and Keynes stressed the possibility that the natural rate may diverge from the market rate of interest and that this may cause trouble. Others have emphasized wage rigidities. The common feature of all these criticisms is that the classical scheme comes into its own as soon as certain institutional "disturbances," which the classics were supposed to have ignored, were removed. The purpose of economic policy is conceived to be the removal of brakes on the free-wheeling economic process, not the provision of active power.

Like ignorance in Bentham's scheme, these obstacles were thought to

---

[12]William Thompson, *An Inquiry into the Principles of the Distribution of Wealth Most Conducive to Human Happiness*, 1822, ed. by William Pare [London: W. S. Orr & Co., 1850], p. 175.

[13]The more cautious writers usually set out a series of conditions which would have to be met before one could say that competition maximizes output.

prevent the achievement of an underlying harmony of interests. But once they are removed, the elegant and anonymous operation of free competition could be relied upon to maximize the common welfare. Thus some of the fiercest critics of liberal doctrine tacitly accepted its fundamental tenet.

Social security measures as they are practiced today, or detailed quantitative economic planning would have been rejected by the early English socialists. On similar grounds, Keynes and some Keynesians took no great interest in the former and rejected the latter.

It may seem that Keynesian measures of regulating investment as a means of achieving and maintaining full employment represent a break with the liberal-utilitarian tradition for two reasons: first, they appear to violate the *liberal* tradition because they are interferences not only with the *distribution* but also with the *production* sphere.[14] Second, they seem to make the canons of *utilitarianism* redundant, because they appear to promote the interests of all at the expense of none.

Interference with the sphere of production

The unqualified laissez-faire dogma was first modified for the sphere of distribution, particularly clearly by J. S. Mill. Adam Smith and Ricardo already had drawn a sharp distinction between production (always to be understood as including exchange) and distribution. Their proof of the liberal doctrine was much more successful in relation to production than to distribution. Adam Smith's well-known theory of the division of labor was a convincing demonstration that specialization and free exchange reduce costs and increase benefits. But this proof was frequently considered to apply also without further discussion to the sphere of income and property distribution.

J. S. Mill, who was influenced by the socialist critics, challenged the principle of *laissez faire* for the sphere of distribution. But production, he still believed, should, on the whole, be left to look after itself.[15] With this

---

[14]See above, p. 34.

[15]"The laws and conditions of the Production of wealth partake of the character of physical truths. There is nothing optional or arbitrary in them. Whatever mankind produces, must be produced in the modes, and under the conditions, imposed by the constitution of external things, and by the inherent properties of their own bodily and mental structure. . . . It is not so with the Distribution of wealth. That is a matter of human institution solely. The things once there, mankind, individually or collectively, can do with them as they like. . . . The distribution of wealth, therefore, depends on the laws and customs of society. The rules by which it is determined are what the opinions and feelings of the ruling portion of the community make them, and are very different in different ages and countries; and might be still more different, if mankind so chose." *Principles of Political Economy*, 1848, ed. by Ashley [(London: Longmans, Green and Co.] 1920), II, I, 1, Adherence to the labor theory of value facilitated, of course, faith in this distinction. Computation in labor units makes possible to give meaning to "physical output" and avoids the crucial index number problem.

qualification the doctrine entered into British welfare economics and is still widely accepted today.

Seen against this background, Keynes appears as a proponent of a different tradition. In some respects his views resemble those of Continental and American critics of liberalism who tried to show that production will not "look after itself." According to Keynes, government action is necessary, not only and not mainly in order to correct undesirable distributional results, but also and largely in order to maintain total effective demand and thus full employment and production.

In this respect Keynes has more in common with conservative advocates of production policies like Friedrich List than with the British classics or socialists. Both List and Keynes held that productive powers would lie stagnant unless released by certain types of state action. Both saw in the state not an agency whose activity is confined to (usually undesirable forms of) consumption and redistribution, but a powerful stimulant to production. But both also believed that, once the productive forces were released, the liberal system would work well.

Yet, from a different point of view, Keynes appears much more closely aligned with the liberals than with the antiliberals. Although List and other advocates of production policy on the one hand, and Keynes on the other, share the belief that the state has to take certain actions in order to create the right environment for private self-interest to work beneficially, there is an important difference. The Protectionists advocate interference with particular branches of production and regulation of the composition of output, whereas Keynes believed that if "we suppose the volume of output to be given, *i.e.*, to be determined by forces outside the classical scheme of thought, then there is no objection to be raised against the classical analysis of the manner in which private self-interest will determine what in particular is produced, in what proportions the factors of production will be combined to produce it, and how the value of the final product will be distributed between them. . . . It is in determining the volume, not the direction, of actual employment that the existing system has broken down."[16]

There were, of course, many Keyneses. The Keynes of the *General Theory* has, in spite of his production policies, greater faith in *laissez faire* than the Keynes of *The End of Laissez-Faire*. We have already noticed that their preoccupation with "artificial disturbances" was the hallmark of those critics who remained steeped in liberal thought in spite of their criticism of the classical arguments. They pilloried such evils as the maldistribution of income (the liberal socialists), monopoly, and financial ill-management (radical liberals, Veblen), etc. Keynes's analysis, faithful to this tradition, brings to light another type of obstacle to what is believed would otherwise be the successful operation of the market. The rigidity of the rate of interest

[16]*General Theory, op. cit.*, pp. 178-179.

(together, possibly, with the rigidity of wage rates) due to speculation is another distorting element. State interference is necessary in order to establish, according to the *Treatise*, coincidence of the market rate with the natural rate[17] and, according to the *General Theory*, the full-employment rate. At the same time, a series of other "complications" are ignored.[18]

In spite of his unorthodox views on production policy, Keynes, particularly later in life, stood faithfully in the liberal-utilitarian tradition.[19] He was not, of course, a laissez-faire utilitarian. But then neither was Bentham, Mill, Sidgwick or Pigou. One can believe in the greatest happiness principle without believing that the greatest happiness is the automatic result of free market forces. Positive government action is necessary in order to safeguard the great happiness or general welfare. The characteristic *utilitarian* feature and the relic of the harmony doctrine is the belief, which Keynes shared with Bentham and Mill, that the economic welfare of a nation is something that the government can and should discover and promote.[20]

---

[17]"Natural" echoes the vocabulary of eighteenth-century natural law philosophers. Analogously, the early socialists believed that the correction of the maldistribution of wealth would re-establish the "natural" state.

[18]He never discusses "the complications which arise — (*1*) when the efficient units of production are large relatively to the units of consumption, (2) when overhead costs or joint costs are present, (*3*) when internal economies tend to the aggregation of production, (*4*) when time required for adjustments is long, (*5*) when ignorance prevails over knowledge, and (*6*) when monopolies and combinations interfere with equality in bargaining." *The End of Laissez-Faire* (1926), *op. cit.*, p. 33. ". . . I see no reason to suppose that the existing system seriously misemploys the factors of production which are in use." *General Theory, op. cit.*, p. 379.

[19]"Thus I agree with Gesell that the result of filling in the gaps in the classical theory is not to dispose of the 'Manchester System,' but to indicate the nature of the environment which the free play of the economic forces requires if it is to realize the full potentialities of production." *General Theory, ibid.* Of Bretton Woods and the Anglo-American Loan Agreement he said: "Here is an attempt to use what we have learnt from modern experience and modern analysis, not to defeat, but to implement the wisdom of Adam Smith." *Economic Journal,* [LVI] 1946, p. 186.

[20]Keynes was not, of course, a utilitarian in the strict philosophical sense but only in a much looser sense. He was certainly not guilty of attempting to derive ethical propositions from descriptive propositions. Keynes's philosophical views were greatly influenced by the teaching of G. E. Moore about the naturalistic fallacy. Cf. "My Early Beliefs," in *Two Memoirs.* "I do not regard [the Benthamite tradition] as the worm which has been gnawing at the insides of modern civilisation and is responsible for its present moral decay." And ". . . we are amongst the first of our generation, perhaps alone amongst our generation, to escape from the Benthamite tradition." *op. cit.*, p. 96.

Professor Smithies considers Keynes as a "lineal descendant of the English Utilitarians" because "he regarded worth-while theory as a basis for programmes of action." Arthur Smithies, "Schumpeter and Keynes," *Review of Economics and Statistics,* [XXXIII] May 1951, p. 164. In this sense very many are, of course, utilitarians. Professor Smithies quotes Schumpeter's views that Mill "might have been saddened by evidence of disbelief in the fundamentals of Utilitarianism, but he would surely have been reconciled by still stronger evidence of firm adherence to its spirit and to some of its most important practical consequences. Philosophical radicalism is obviously not dead as yet — spreading among us as it does its generous hopes for humanity and its stout refusal to see in life but a little intermezzo of irritating nonsense between eternities of death." Joseph A. Schumpeter, *Economic Journal,* [XLIII] 1933, p. 657.

The *liberal* feature is the conviction that the promotion of economic welfare requires only a little tampering here and there, and that, for the rest, the automatic play of self-interest is a better driving force than any practical alternative.

Neither the utilitarian nor the liberal component of this conviction is shared, *e.g.*, by some members of the historical school, by the Marxists, or by the Schumpeterians, who reject the notion of a "common well-being" and who look upon government policies as the outcome of the struggle between different interests. The conviction that national well-being is something analogous to individual or family well-being is so deeply embedded in the Anglo-Saxon utilitarian tradition that one tends to overlook its metaphysical character. Antihedonist thinkers have criticized it on logical, psychological and sociological grounds,[21] but its hold remains strong.

Interest harmony and antidepression policies

If the first objection to looking upon Keynes as a liberal and a utilitarian was that his recommendations *violate liberal* canons, the second is that they do *not require* utilitarian canons. It may appear at first sight that the whole dispute about distribution and its relation to economic welfare, which is at the heart of recent controversies in welfare economics, is irrelevant for the policies with which Keynesian economics is concerned.

In some spheres, interests seem to coincide and there, at any rate, quasi objective recommendations[22] would appear to be possible. Monetary policy is occasionally quoted as an example. Thus it might seem quite safe to say that prosperity and stability are better than depression and fluctuations, and that measures which increase and prolong general prosperity are in the general interest. Professor Frank H. Knight wrote recently: "The business cycle . . . is not a problem of conflict of interests, since practically no one profits from depressions."[23] Many of the quibbles of welfare economics about how to achieve the best allocation of given and already fully, though not optimally, employed resources may appear trivial in comparison with the problem of how to increase the employment of resources, to reduce unemployment of men and promote prosperity.

It may seem that Keynesian measures are designed to promote the "interests of all" in a sense which makes it unnecessary to compare and weight interests, since nobody is harmed. Thus even those who believe that

[21]Cf. Gunnar Myrdal, *The Political Element in the Development of Economic Thought.* [Trans. P. Streeten, Cambridge, Mass.: Harvard University Press, 1955].

[22]They would require the value judgment that what is in the interest of each and hurts no one ought to be done.

[23]Frank H. Knight, "Economic and Social Policy in Democratic Society," *Journal of Political Economy,* [LVIII] Dec. 1950, p. 520.

every man's enjoyment is unique and incommensurable with any other man's could still subscribe to Keynesian measures. Surely everyone prefers prosperity to depression and stability to fluctuations, except possibly for a few speculators. If this were true, the utilitarian assumption of the comparability of individual utilities could be dropped. Measures to achieve full employment would not present any of the awkward problems of comparing and weighting which a policy of "tightening up," *i.e.*, of rendering more efficient an already fully employed economy, would have to face. It would seem that we could increase the national cake without reducing anybody's slice.

Yet, this appearance is deceptive for at least three reasons. (1) Some people are bound to lose in any case. (2) Harmony would not prevail even if nobody were to lose pecuniarily. (3) Even if problems of redistribution could be side-stepped in the short run, they might become urgent in any long-run policy to maintain full employment. Moreover, the acceptance of Keynesian policies would, once again, bring allocative and thus distributional problems into the foreground.

In the first place, some people are bound to lose even through antidepression policies. Fixed income receivers will be worse off. It is, of course, true that they could be compensated or, if not, that their losses are negligible in comparison with the gains (which is a value judgment and involves interpersonal comparisons). There is therefore a greater degree of harmony here than in policies designed to restore, say, free trade or competition. Yet, there is hardly ever complete harmony.[24]

Second, and perhaps more important, post-Keynesian experience and controversy suggest that there is neither general agreement on Keynes's analysis nor a general harmony of those interests which are affected by Keynesian measures, quite apart from the disharmony which arises from the reduced incomes of fixed income receivers.

Opposition may arise from misunderstanding. This is possible even in the Benthamite scheme. It could, in principle, be cleared up and harmony be established. But opposition may arise in spite of, or rather because of, a full understanding of the implications of Keynesian measures. Some people oppose them because they do not want full employment, either because they believe it undermines the discipline of workers, or because they fear that, if trade unions are strengthened through full employment, the share of profits will fall; or even if it is not expected to fall, entrepreneurs may fear that their power and status in society would be reduced.[25]

Keynes himself believed more strongly in a harmony of interests in this respect than the later experience of full-employment conditions would warrant. He ascribed the opposition to antidepression policies to the stupidity

[24]T. Scitovsky, "The State of Welfare Economics," *American Economic Review*, [XLI] June 1951, [pp. 303–315].

[25]Cf. Sidney Alexander, "Opposition to Deficit Spending," in *Essays in Honour of Alvin Hansen* [New York: W. W. Norton & Co., Inc., 1948, pp. 177–198].

of bankers and believed that the removal of risks and the increase in profits would commend these policies to entrepreneurs. In fact, their opposition is perfectly rational, both on economic and political grounds. These policies undermine their bargaining power. Decisions which in slump conditions would have been in their power become in conditions of full employment matters of government policy, such as redistribution, the rate of investment and progress.[26]

The problem has been put succinctly in a recent series of articles in *The Economist*.[27] It is argued there that the objectives of (a) full employment, (b) a stable price level, and (c) free collective bargaining, are incompatible. Full employment and stable prices can only be had with a loss of freedom. Stable prices and free bargaining involve unemployment, and free bargaining together with full employment spell inflation. Moreover, even if any one of these three objectives is sacrificed to the two others, in the end none may be attained.

The argument may be extended from free bargaining to freedom from state controls generally. Many consider full employment an objective which involves a sacrifice, a "price," foregone opportunities.[28] Some of these costs cannot be expressed in money terms (*e.g.*, the anticipated loss of liberty) and are, perhaps, not strictly economic. But the crucial point is that there is no harmony of interests. The situation is complicated by the necessity to compare not only the tastes of different individuals as expressed in their market choices but also their value systems. Even in the short run, a dilemma between unemployment and controls may arise, if inflation is ruled out.

A measure of agreement might perhaps be reached by drawing a distinction between antidepression policies and full-employment policies. Many who would reject the latter might accept the former, though it would be difficult to reach agreement on where the line between the two should be drawn. But there is more wide-spread agreement on the desirability of avoiding very high, long-term unemployment than on the desirability of maintaining full employment.

Even if there were complete national harmony on antidepression policies, conflict will still arise with the interests of other nations and hence with the value systems of those who have international welfare at heart. Changes in the balance of payments and changes in the terms of trade resulting from antidepression policies will have repercussions abroad. Some of these changes may be welcomed by foreigners, but others will require adjustments which they may not be willing to make. The harmony doctrine is even less plausible if we attempt to apply it to the world economy. A nation has a government which, in some conditions, might act as if the fiction of a

---

[26]T. Balogh, [*The*] *Dollar Crisis* [Oxford: Blackwell, 1949], pp. 79–80, 105–106.

[27]"The Uneasy Triangle," *The Economist*, August 9th, 16th, 23rd, 1952.

[28]Cf., *e.g.*, J. Viner, "Full Employment at Whatever Cost," *Quarterly Journal of Economics*, [LXIV] Aug. 1950, [pp. 385–407].

unified body of interests were true. There is no similar international institution. In the absence of international compensation for losses the conflict of interests is sharpened and the chance to reach agreement reduced.

The third reason why Keynesian policies do not avoid interest conflicts is this: Keynes's own analysis applies to the short run. It is easier to stimulate investment sufficiently to *attain* full employment, than it is to sustain this level of investment, and thus full employment, over a prolonged period of time. In the short run investment generates income but not consumption output. In the long run, however, investment also yields increased consumption output. If the investment required to generate full-employment *income* is the same as the investment required to yield the *output* which is demanded under continued full employment, full employment will be maintained. But this would be an odd coincidence. It is quite possible that the investment required to generate full-employment income is larger than (a) the investment required to meet effective demand or (b) the investment which can be worked profitably with a given population (or a given rate of population increase). In other words, full-employment investment may fall off, either (a) because there is insufficient consumption demand for the goods which it helps to produce indirectly, or (b) because the labor force required to work in conjunction with the fixed capital equipment is too small. In either case excess capacity will emerge and investment will be reduced. It will be impossible to maintain full employment. In order to avoid case (a) consumption would have to be raised, and in order to avoid both (a) and (b) policies designed to transfer labor from the investment goods industries to the consumption goods trades would have to be carried out. In such a situation a redistribution of income from the wealthier to the poorer might have to play an essential part. Such a redistribution would reduce the investment required to generate income and would help to prevent the generation of excess capacity in relation to either demand or the available labor force.[29] It appears therefore that the distribution of income may play an important part in maintaining full employment over a period of time.

This type of prognosis must, however, remain highly speculative and unreliable. Policies of redistribution inevitably change not merely relative incomes but also consumption and saving habits. It is impossible to foresee the psychological and sociological factors which would influence the amount and the direction of expenditure in a society whose social structure is different from that of the existing one.

Finally, even if full agreement could be reached on antidepression

---

[29]Against this, one could argue that the required transfer of resources from investment into consumption could be brought about without such drastic measures of redistribution. Alternatively, one might argue that a good deal of new investment is not geared to consumption demand and this type of investment could always be expanded. Sufficiently laborsaving investment would remove the danger of excess capacity from either cause. Investment in housing could always be increased and would reduce the danger of demand deficiency. The rate of growth of output could also be reduced by the enjoyment of more leisure.

policies, the wide-spread *knowledge* of Keynesian *analysis,* and the *adoption* of Keynesian *remedies* would bring the problem of interest conflicts into the forefront again, even if one could assume that it lies dormant in a world of undiagnosed and uncured unemployment.

In conditions of large-scale unemployment one group's gain need not spell another's loss. But with the adoption of antidepression policies, and a fortiori with full-employment policies, conflicts become once again acute. Measures which were before socially costless, or had a negative social cost, now involve genuine sacrifices. The question how to weigh gains against losses arises as a result of the adoption of policies which might meet with unanimous approval.

But this is not the only ground for sharpened conflicts to which a society more fully aware of its workings and more strongly determined to decide its economic fate may give rise. The conditions which most nearly approach the successful working of a harmony of egoisms were those of early and mid-Victorian society. Quasi-harmony existed then, because in their economic activities as in other departments of life the Victorians accepted without much questioning certain taboos and ancient rules. The conventionalism and traditionalism characteristic of the heyday of Victorian society contributed to the formation of a tacit consensus of opinion which made for the successful working of the economic system. The mythology which fostered the idea that this was "rational" and "economic" behavior par excellence only shows how deep-seated and unconscious the acceptance of the taboos was. The gold standard, a free money market, balanced budgets, the pursuit of free competition, the acceptance of unemployment, the belief in hard work and saving, all testify to this submission to external unquestioned rules and conventions.

The quasi-harmony broke down, not because people lost their heads and indulged in a wave of irrationalism, but because they became more rational, more conscious of the working of the economic system. Less prepared to accept ancient beliefs, they stripped the structure of economic relations of the superstitions which had cemented them. With knowledge came the desire for conscious manipulation. By breaking down the tacit consensus based on convention and superstition, the conflict of interests stood more clearly revealed.

The absorption of Keynes's view is part of this process of awakening. It helped to destroy the barriers which prevented the full pursuit of a selfish manipulation of society, thus brought clashes into the open, and made government action inevitable.

Summary

We have singled out three components of the classical tradition, namely, liberalism, utilitarianism, and the harmony doctrine.

1. Liberals are those who advocate a minimum of government interference, particularly (a) with production, both (i) in the aggregate and (ii) in particular branches; but also, to a smaller or greater extent, (b) with distribution. Critics have maintained that the distinction between production and distribution is logically invalid. In the course of time liberals have admitted increasing interference with distribution, particularly since J. S. Mill, although they insisted that "production" ought not to be thereby impaired. In a sense, even the earliest liberals advocated some government action in the field of production (things that would otherwise not get done, *e.g.*, education, lighthouses).

2. Utilitarians believe that social happiness (or, more generally, welfare) should be maximized. They may be (a) liberals, *i.e.*, hold that maximization can be brought about with a minimum of government interference; or they may be (b) authoritarians, *i.e.*, believe that regulations of various kinds are necessary.

3. Adherents of the harmony doctrine hold that social or public interest can be objectively determined by a careful examination of private interests. They may believe either (a) that harmony is established automatically, or (b) that it has to be engineered.

One might say that all the preceding discussion amounts to is this: If we were to draw up an *Agenda* and a *Non-Agenda* for government action, different people would, for various reasons, put different items on the one and on the other, and there are many intermediate stages between putting nothing and putting everything on the *Agenda*. Any given recommendation can be viewed in contrast to opinions on either side of this alignment, and would appear in a different light, according to whether we contrast it with extreme *laissez faire* or with extreme planning.

Although this is true, the philosophical assumptions which underlie such programs do not shade into each other with similar continuity and present more suitable criteria of distinction than the policy conclusions derived from them. These assumptions would have to form the basis of discussion, when disagreement arises.

What, then, is Keynes's position in the classical tradition?

1. Keynes's thought is unmistakably in the classical liberal-utilitarian tradition. He can be considered as a harmony theorist in the sense that he looked upon the economic activities of a nation as if they were those of an individual or a family, *i.e.*, as if they had a common purpose which, properly understood, is also the purpose of each individual. The common good, public welfare, maximum output, etc., are for him meaningful concepts and desirable objectives.

2. It may appear that Keynes's recommendations represent a break with the classical tradition for the paradoxical reasons (a) that they involve interference with *production*, not merely with distribution; and (b) that, by apparently promoting the interests of each and all they

seem to make the *utilitarian* calculus superfluous. But (a) does not represent a break with the *harmony* tradition and the appearance of (b) is deceptive, for losses of some kinds are bound to occur.

3. Advocates of production policies have often accepted the meaningfulness and desirability of maximizing the common welfare, in particular in the light of consideration 2 (b). Keynes, in particular, advocated the regulation of *aggregates* only. He stood in the *liberal* tradition in the sense that the interferences which he advocated aim at the removal of particular breaks on the free pursuit of the common good.

4. For several reasons, Keynesian measures do not in fact meet with applause from all and each. (a) Some are bound to lose in any case. (b) Nonmaterial considerations may cause opposition even where there is no strictly economic loss. (c) Long-run maintenance of full employment may require redistribution.

5. In a country, or in a world, pledged to full employment not only the classical problems of interest conflicts come into their own again, but new problems of the distribution of economic power and its conscious manipulation arise.

WASSILY LEONTIEF **3**

Postulates: Keynes' *General Theory* and the classicists[1]

> Yet after all there is no harm in being sometimes wrong — especially if one is promptly found out.
>
> Keynes in "Alfred Marshall, 1842–1924," *Economic Journal*, 1924, p. 345.

1.

In staging his assault against orthodox theory, Keynes did not attack the internal consistency of its logical structure; he rather attempted to demonstrate the unreality of its fundamental empirical assumptions by showing up what he considered to be the obvious falsity of its factual conclusions. The orthodox theory proves that involuntary unemployment can not exist, but we know that it actually does exist. Since the formal logic of the orthodox proof is essentially correct, the fault must be sought in its choice of the basic empirical premises. This is the general plan of the Keynesian attack.[2] It took

From THE NEW ECONOMICS: KEYNES' INFLUENCE ON THEORY AND PUBLIC POLICY, edited by Seymour E. Harris. Copyright 1947 by Alfred A. Knopf, Inc. Reprinted by permission. Pp. 232–242.

[1] For comments on this essay, see Introduction to Part Eight, and cf. also the essays by Messrs. Smithies and Tobin, [*The New Economics* (New York: Alfred A. Knopf, Inc., 1947), pp. 541-587.]

[2] Its peculiar indirect nature is clearly revealed in Keynes' willingness to accept the orthodox analysis as a valid, albeit practically unimportant, special case of his own general theory.

the overzealous enthusiasm of numerous neophytes to confuse the elegant outlines of the master's enveloping strategy by opening a non-discriminating sniping at the orthodox adversary all along the line of the argument.

Since it is the question of factual premises on which Keynes chooses to base his criticism of the traditional theory, an examination of these assumptions and of those substituted by him in their place can serve as a convenient starting point for a comparative study of the two systems.

The nature of the supply of labor and that of the demand for money are the two principal points of divergence between the basic postulates of the *General Theory* and the teachings of the classical doctrine. The departure from orthodox analysis in the treatment of these two particular issues enables Keynes to lift the traditional theory off its hinges and develop his own peculiar theory of effective demand and involuntary unemployment. The problem of labor supply is technically the less intricate one of the two and we will follow Keynes' own example in taking it up first.

2.

Traditional analysis considers the aggregate quantity of labor supplied, in the case where this supply is a competitive one, to be a function of the *real* wage rates; Keynes on the contrary assumes that up to a certain point — defined by him as the point of full employment — one particular level of *money* wages exists at which the supply of labor is perfectly elastic and below which no labor can be hired at all. The deliberate exclusion of the cost of living as a determinant of labor supply makes the latter independent of the level of *real* wages.[3]

Not only are the two statements describing the nature of the labor supply incompatible, but the positions occupied by them within the theoretical structures to which they respectively belong are also different. The monetary supply curve of labor is a fundamental postulate of the *General Theory* in the true sense of the term. A starting point of a long chain of deductive reasoning, it is itself not theoretically derived within the body of the Keynesian system; if it were, if the salient properties of his labor supply function had been derived from some other, more general, propositions of the Keynesian theory, the statement of these properties itself could not have been considered to constitute a fundamental postulate. It would become one of the many deductively demonstrable theorems. A truly fundamental postulate by its very nature cannot be verified by deductive reasoning, in empirical science it must be accepted or rejected on the basis of direct reference to facts. In keeping with this principle, the author of the *General*

---

[3]Keynes himself did not consider in any detail the conditions of a labor supply possibly exceeding full employment level. Most of his interpreters assume, however, that beyond that critical point the nature of the supply schedule changes and the quantity of labor offered for hire becomes a function of the real wage rate alone.

Theory justifies his own assumptions concerning the nature of the labor supply curve through direct reference to immediate experience of the mechanism of actual labor markets. Taking up the criticism of the alternative, orthodox approach — which explains the magnitude of labor supply in terms of real rather than money wages — Keynes by analogy refers to it as a fundamental postulate, which it obviously is not. The extreme form of this Keynesian interpretation of the classical position is expressed in the often repeated statement that the orthodox theory assumes the existence of full employment, a statement which obviously reveals confusion between the conclusions to which an argument leads and the assumptions with which it begins.

Far from being directly assumed, the real supply curve of labor is derived by the modern non-Keynesian theory from a set of other much more general propositions. The truly fundamental postulates of the orthodox theory deal with the general nature of economic choice. Without embarking upon a technical discussion of this familiar piece of analysis, it is sufficient to make here two observations on the particular aspect of this theory which has a direct bearing upon the issue at hand: in sinking its foundations deeper in the ground of experience than does the Keynesian analysis, the traditional theory is able to use a smaller number of separate assumptions and thus to achieve a more integrated system of theoretical conclusions. Instead, for example, of making one separate assumption describing the shape of the labor supply schedule, another defining the properties of the demand schedule for consumers' goods, and yet a third stating the nature of the relationship between the income of an individual and his propensity to save, the classical economist derives all three kinds of relationship from the same set of more general assumptions. This, incidentally, enables him also to reveal the mutual interdependence of the three kinds of schedules.

In making the phenomena, which the orthodox theorist thinks himself able to explain in terms of some common principle, objects of separate fundamental postulates, Keynes imparts to his system the freedom to deal with assumed situations which from the point of view of the orthodox approach are clearly logically impossible and thus theoretically unmanageable. This characteristic double-jointedness of his analytical apparatus gives Keynes a good reason to claim that his theory is more general than that of the orthodox economists. If, on the other hand, the ability to explain a given set of phenomena on the basis of a smallest possible set of independent assumptions were used as the criterion of generality, the Keynesian approach would clearly appear less general than the classical.

3.

It is only natural that attempts have been made to place under the Keynesian postulate some kind of theoretical underpinnings which would bring the foundation of his analytical structure to the level of orthodox argument. One approach would follow very closely the line of classical procedure in deriving the monetary supply curve of labor from a general utility function. In contrast to the classical, this Keynesian utility function would include, among the ultimate constituents of an individual's preference varieties, not only the physical quantities of (future and present) commodities and services but also the money prices of at least some of them. In particular the *money* wage rate would be considered as entering directly the worker's utility function: confronted with a choice between two or more situations in both of which his real income and his real effort are the same, but in one of which both the money wage rates (and, consequently, also the prices of consumers' goods) are higher than in the other, he would show a definite preference for the former. A classical *homo economicus* would find neither of the two alternatives to be more attractive than the other.

From such a monetary utility function, a monetary supply curve of labor can be easily derived. In contrast to its classical counterpart, it will show the labor supply as dependent not only on the relative but also on the absolute prices and wage rates.[4]

The same is true of all the other demand and supply curves derived from a basic monetary preference function. In particular the propensity to save — which Keynes considers as depending only on the size of the real income — will necessarily vary with even a proportional rise or fall in prices and wages.[5]

Although neat and internally consistent, such "psychological" interpretations of the monetary element of the Keynesian theory of wages are hardly appropriate. They contradict the common sense of economic behavior. The reference to the fact that no worker has ever been seen bargaining for real wages — even if true — is obviously beside the point, since while bargaining in terms of dollars the worker, as any one else, can still be guided in his behavior by the real purchasing power of his income. Moreover, the "psychological" interpretation of the monetary element in consumers' behavior deprives Keynes' unemployment concept of its principal attribute. Why should any given rate of employment or unemployment be called "involuntary," if it is determined through conscious preference for higher money wages as against larger real income?

4.

Much more in keeping with the spirit of the *General Theory* is an interpretation which ascribes the monetary bias of the Keynesian supply curve of

---

[4]In mathematical language, that means that all the classical supply and demand schedules are homogeneous functions (of all the present and expected future prices and wage rate) of the zero degree, while the corresponding Keynesian supply and demand curves are not.

[5][See Tobin's essay, "Money Wage Rates and Employment," *The New Economics, op. cit.*, pp. 572–587.]

labor to the influence of some outside factors, that is, factors clearly distinguishable from the preference system of the workers. A minimum wage law offers a good example of such an outside factor. Whatever the shape of the intrinsic or potential supply curve (curve S_1S_2 in the adjoining

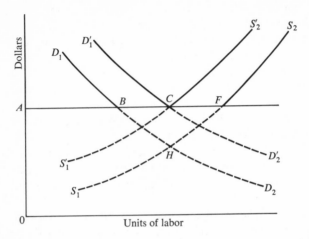

graph) no workers can be hired in this case at a wage rate which is lower than the legal minimum, OA. In other words, the effective supply curve would be strictly horizontal up to the point, F, in which the potential supply curve S_1S_2 crosses it from below. From that point on, a further addition to the labor supply can be obtained only at a price exceeding the legal minimum, and the effective supply curve thus coincides with the potential. That is precisely the type of a supply curve described by Keynes in the first chapters of the *General Theory*. If the position of the demand curve, say D_1D_2, happened to be such that it intersects the effective supply curve to the left of point F, say at B, the amount of employment, AB, is determined by the level, OA, of the minimum wage rate. The difference, BF, between this actual employment and the maximum amount, AF, which could be achieved without any change in the wage rate, provided the demand curve had shifted so as to cross the effective supply curve at F rather than at B, has been defined by Keynes as involuntary unemployment.

Although Keynes' labor market functions as if it were operating under a strictly enforced minimum wage law, the author of the *General Theory* explicitly refuses to limit the application of his theoretical scheme to obvious instances of such outside influence. The real reason for this obstinate insistence on universal validity of an apparently quite special assumption will become clearer after examination of the monetary determinants of effective demand. Keynes treats this issue as a problem of the demand for money; the orthodox economists describe it as the question of the velocity of circulation of money.

5.

The existence of a reservation price for labor would not lead to involuntary unemployment, if the relative position of the classical supply curve of labor and of the corresponding demand curve happened to be such that they intersected on or above the level of the minimum wage rate. So, for example, the supply curve $S_1'S_2'$ intersects the demand curve $D_1'D_2'$ in point C, establishing the equilibrium wage rate OA and employment AC. The corresponding Keynesian supply curve $ABCS_2'$ gives in combination with the demand curve D_1D_2 the same equilibrium position C.

Involuntary unemployment could thus always be eliminated through an upward shift of the classical monetary supply and demand curves, a shift which necessarily would follow a general rise of all prices (excluding the price of labor). Additional employment (BC) created by a reduction in the purchasing power of money which, for example, would have lifted the submerged classical equilibrium point H up to the effective minimum wage level OA, must — as can be easily noted on the diagram — be smaller than the amount of unemployment (BC) defined as being involuntary in the original situation. With a higher cost of living and a positively inclined classical supply curve of labor, the amount of labor seeking employment at the prescribed minimum wage rate will be necessarily reduced.[6]

It hardly needs to be added that any further inflation, raising the classical equilibrium point above this minimum level, can have no additional effect on the amount of employment.

6.

The theory of liquidity preference provides the Keynesian system with a deflationary mechanism which defeats, through the process of automatic hoarding, every tendency toward inflationary reduction of involuntary unemployment. The outstanding characteristic of this particular part of the *General Theory* is its exclusively dynamic character. The speculative motive — which is the very heart of this deflationary mechanism — reacts not to the absolute magnitudes of the relevant variables, which are the rate of interest and the present and expected prices, but only to the rates of change of these variables.

Keynes does not deny the possibility of maintaining a quantity of money great enough to support any given level of prices, once this quantity is already in circulation and the corresponding price level actually established. In this respect, his theory of liquidity preference does not differ in its assumptions and conclusions, although it does in formulation, from the

[6]In case of a negatively inclined supply curve of labor, additional employment achieved through a general price rise would on the contrary exceed the original amount of involuntary idleness.

simple quantity theory of money. In particular it can not and does not refute the classical proposition that with a given money rate of interest a proportional change in all prices will leave the *real* demand for money exactly the same as before.

It is the transition from one price level to another which according to Keynes might prove to be impossible. Without entering into the details of the argument, it is sufficient to indicate that it runs in terms of the effects of a potential change in the price level on the velocity of circulation.

Having centered his attention on the problem of change, Keynes does not, however, treat it in explicitly dynamic terms. True to the Cambridge tradition, he resorts to the Marshallian substitute for dynamic theory — the "short-run" analysis. The short-run analysis is related to a truly dynamic approach in the same way as the, also Marshallian, partial equilibrium theory stands in respect to the Walrasian general equilibrium analysis. In both instances the problem at hand is simplified by selective omission of some of the relevant relationships, on the one hand, and treatment as independent of some of the really dependent variables, on the other. The theory of liquidity preference considers the effects which a deviation of the interest rate from its long-run equilibrium level would have on the short-run demand for money. This relationship is analyzed on the assumption of a given price level. The conclusion that under these conditions the price level cannot be raised through an increase in the supply of money is analogous to the conclusion that one cannot walk up a flight of stairs since, if one considers the position of the left foot at the first step as given, the right foot cannot possibly reach the upper platform of the stairway. For the analytical purpose at hand, this short-run argument is hardly more adequate than a static theory satisfied with description of the two hypothetical long-run equilibria, one preceding and the other succeeding the actual ascent.

7.

Having observed the dynamic element in the Keynesian theory of money, one might turn back to his theory of wages and ask to which extent his assumption of rigid money rates possibly also represents a first awkward move in the direction of dynamic analysis. Indeed, a short-run interpretation of a time lag leads easily to treatment of the lagging variable as if it were a constant. A dynamic relationship between money wages and the cost of living, considered from the point of view of supply of labor, implies the existence of a definite lag between the former and the latter. Hence the short-run assumption that the wage rates are constant. This interpretation of the Keynesian monetary supply curve of labor seems to harmonize with the obvious reluctance of the author of the *General Theory* to commit himself to some specific institutional explanation of this particular assumption. Moreover it points the way to a further generalization of this type of reasoning which, although not advocated by the master himself, found universal acceptance among the great majority of his followers: if the stickiness assumption is a legitimate device in treatment of dynamic relationship, there is no reason why its use should be limited to the analysis of the labor market. Thus in the newer Keynesian literature not only money wage rates but also all the other prices are more often than not assumed to be fixed throughout the argument.

The limited usefulness of this simplified approach to the problem of change is unwittingly demonstrated by those authors who, on top of the typical short-run assumption of sticky money wages and fixed prices, also introduce genuine dynamic relationships into their theoretical models. The incongruity of conclusions, in which the short-run cyclical fluctuations are derived from explicitly stated dynamic relationships and long-run unemployment is explained on the basis of the short-run postulate of universal stickiness, can hardly remain unnoticed.

In the light of the foregoing observations, the principal difference between the Keynesian and the orthodox type of analysis would appear to be procedural rather than substantial. With its set of basic assumptions formulated without reference to the dynamic aspects of the problem, the classical approach suffers from what might be called theoretical farsightedness — the ability to appraise correctly the long-run trends, coupled with a singular inability to explain or even to describe the short-run changes and fluctuations. The Keynesian lenses improve somewhat but do not really correct the analytical vision so far as the short-run phenomena are concerned. However they put entirely out of focus the longer views of economic development. Only a careful reformulation of the basic postulates of the traditional theory in explicitly dynamic terms would make it applicable to the study of short-run changes without subjecting the long-run conclusion to the distorting influence of the artificial conventions of Marshallian short-run analysis.

8.

Interwoven with short-run and monetary analysis, there runs through the fabric of the *General Theory* the thread of an argument which, although at first it seems to be quite unorthodox, proves on closer inspection to be entirely in line with the basic postulates of traditional doctrine. Its subject is the relationship between the level of employment and the rate of investment, and its conclusion is the proposition that an increased rate of investment means a higher, and a reduced rate of investment a lower, rate of employment.

The orthodox demonstration of this relationship would in its simplest form run in terms of comparative utility of leisure (or disutility of labor), on the one hand, and of the products of labor — in this instance of investment goods — on the other. Increased demand for housing, machinery or any other new commodity could easily induce the society to redouble its labor efforts in the same way and for the same reason that causes the aborigines to crowd the employment offices of colonial plantation enterprises after they have been acquainted with and acquired a new "need" for imported glass beads and gaily colored cloth squares. A more artificial but not less mandatory need of paying taxes with money which cannot be secured by any other means but longer hours of work can obviously lead to the same result, as does compulsory labor service or, say, a program of planned industrialization.

The second set of examples fits the Keynesian line of thought obviously better than the first, the reason being that it inserts into the argument what might be called the distributive element. In a society as closely integrated and at the same time as greatly differentiated as ours, any particular set of new needs or, say, of new investment opportunities more often than not appears as a problem of free economic choice only to some relatively small section of the community; the rest is confronted with the indirect results of this choice in the form of "changed circumstances," favorable or otherwise. The demand for labor in particular is often expanded and contracted because of some primary change in tastes or opportunities other than those of the worker himself.

The apparent paradox of the situation lies not in the mechanics of economic interdependence — which can readily be described and explained without departure from classical postulates — but rather in its welfare implications. If all members of society were equally situated in respect to all the relevant choices and economic decisions, if each was employee and employer, saver and investor, farmer and city dweller, all at the same time, the distributive problem could not possibly arise: the fall in employment resulting from everybody's reduced demand for housing could (except in some special cases of external economies or diseconomies or of market imperfections) not be called involuntary any more than a morning headache could be called an involuntary result of a late party on the night before.

The liberal economist of the past century was prone to overlook the troublesome distributive aspects of economic change. Keynes, as Karl Marx before him, did well in pointing out this indeed most serious omission. He seemed to press, however, for reconstruction of the whole foundation in order to mend a leaky roof.

LAWRENCE R. KLEIN **4**

Theories of effective demand and employment[1]

There is much talk about such matters as the downward rigidity of wage rates, the relationship of wages to employment and output, the influence of liquid assets on the level of economic activity, and the stage of maturity of the American economy. The various theories of employment must be examined in the light of these concepts in order to get some clear answers to important economic problems. The Keynesian theories are often accused of being based on assumptions of rigid wage rates or interest-elastic liquidity preferences, but there may be much less truth in these assertions than is commonly thought to be the case. The purpose of this paper will be to study three theories of employment — (1) the classical, (2) the Keynesian, and (3) the Marxian — in order to attempt to clear up some confusions that still exist. One of the main objectives will be to try to show the distinctions between necessary and sufficient assumptions that underlie each theory.

Reprinted from Lawrence R. Klein, "Theories of Effective Demand and Employment," *The Journal of Political Economy*, Vol. 55 (April 1947), pp. 108–131, by permission of The University of Chicago Press. Copyright 1947 by The University of Chicago Press. [Footnotes expanded — Eds.]

[1]Some of the ideas on Keynesian economics contained in this article are more fully discussed in the author's book, *The Keynesian Revolution* ([2nd ed.,] New York: Macmillan Co., [1966]).

I. The classical theory

Since the publication of the *General Theory*, there have been numerous discussions in the professional literature comparing Keynes and the Classics. As a result of these discussions, we now have a good idea as to the form of the classical model. The simplest version is as follows: (1) The supply of and demand for labor determine the real wage rate and the level of employment. (2) The technological input-output relationship determines the level of real output since the input of labor services has been determined by step 1. It is, of course, assumed that the stock of fixed capital is given. (3) The equation of savings and investment determines the rate of interest. (4) Given output from step 2, the constant velocity of circulation and the given supply of cash determine the absolute price level (quantity theory).

The mathematical version of this system is

$$M = kpY \text{ (quantity equation)}, \tag{1.1}$$

$$S(i) = I(i) \text{ (savings-investment equation)}, \tag{1.2}$$

$$Y = Y(N) \text{ (production function)}, \tag{1.3}$$

$$\frac{dY}{dN} = \frac{w}{p} \text{ (demand for labor)}, \tag{1.4}$$

$$N = f\left(\frac{w}{p}\right) \text{ (supply of labor)}, \tag{1.5}$$

where M = cash balances, p = price, Y = output, i = interest rate, N = employment, w = wage rate. Given the amount of money, there are five equations to determine p, Y, i, N, and w.

The classical economists not only counted relations and variables; they also assumed that the forms of their relations were such that a unique solution was possible. This solution will always be one of full employment because all who want to work at the going real wage rate can find a job; equation (1.5) tells us that. This equation shows how much employment will be offered at any real wage rate. If all the equations of the system are consistent, as was classically assumed, equation (1.5) must hold, i.e., all who offer their services at prevailing real wages can find employment. In this model, since all equations hold simultaneously, the solution must be on the supply curve of labor, which is what is meant by full employment.

It is easy to make a slight generalization of this model and still get the same results. Those defending the classical doctrine against Keynes's 1936 attack were quick to point out that the classical economists did not neglect the fact that the demand for money depends on the rate of interest or that savings and investment depend on income. The same results, so far as the level of employment is concerned, follow even if the quantity equation and the savings-investment equation are modified. Steps 1 and 2 of the process of solving the classical model remain as before. Steps 3 and 4 become: (3′) Given the level of output from step 2, the equation of savings and investment determines the rate of interest. (4′) Given the level of output from step 2 and the level of the interest rate from step 3′, the given supply of cash determines the absolute price level.

Equations (1.1) and (1.2) are replaced by

$$\frac{M}{p} = L(i,Y), \tag{1.1′}$$

$$S(i,Y) = I(i,Y). \tag{1.2′}$$

The other equations remain as before.

As presented here, the classical system is static and should be looked upon as the equilibrium solution of a more general dynamical system. It is evident that the equilibrium will always be one of full employment. In the general case — when the system is not at its equilibrium position — there may be unemployment, but this unemployment will be only temporary if the dynamic movements are damped, as the classical economists implicitly assumed. When unemployment does occur in the state of disequilibrium, there is always an appropriate remedial policy available — namely, an increase in the amount of money or (its equivalent) a cut in prices or in wages. Every variable in the classical system can be expressed in terms of the autonomous supply of money as a parameter, and it is easy to calculate the effect upon the system of varying the quantity of money. The assumptions of the structure of the classical system are such that variations in the quantity of money tend to raise the level of output and employment when there is a deviation from the full-employment equilibrium.

II. The Keynesian theory

The Keynesian theory is quite different from the classical theory. The basic hypothesis of the Keynesian theory is that people make two kinds of decisions in our present type of economy. They decide, on the basis of their income, whether to spend or save; and they decide, on the basis of the rate of interest, the form in which they want to hold their accumulated savings — cash or securities. In the classical theory income is the strategic variable in the money equation (1.1), and interest is the strategic variable in the savings-investment equation (1.2). Exactly the reverse is true in the Keynesian system. Keynes's great contribution was to replace the classical savings-investment theory of interest with a savings-investment theory of the determination of income.

The simplest Keynesian theory is the following: Savings as a function of the level of income equals autonomous investment. This is one equation in one variable, namely, the level of income. Investment is considered to be autonomous because it depends upon such factors as the expectations of future market demand, innovations, fiscal policy, etc. It is obvious, however, that the validity of the Keynesian theory does not depend on the fact that investment is autonomous, for, if investment is also a function of income, the Keynesian theory of the savings-investment determination of the level of income still holds.

One pillar of support for the simplest Keynesian model is that it is not contradicted by the data. If the hypothesis is that savings as a function of income equals autonomous investment, there should be a close correlation between income and investment. The published data (United States) on disposable income (constant dollars, per capita) are very highly correlated with investment — defined as the difference between disposable income and consumer expenditures (constant dollars, per capita) — and lagged disposable income during the interwar period. There is nothing artificial in this high correlation, and statisticians have never found a similar confirmation of the alternative classical theories from the available data.

The Keynesian revision of the savings-investment theory is of profound importance. Since the Keynesian theory does not involve the introduction of any new variables and since it merely involves a change of form of some of the classical equations, it would seem natural that the system (1.1)–(1.5) could be re-written with the suggested revisions, so that we would again have a model of full-employment equilibrium. However, this supposition is not correct. The revised model would be

$$\frac{M}{p} = L(i) \text{ (liquidity-preference equation)}, \qquad (2.1)$$

$$S(Y) = I(Y) \text{ (savings-investment equation)}, \qquad (2.2)$$

$$Y = Y(N) \text{ (production function)}, \qquad (2.3)$$

$$\frac{dY}{dN} = \frac{w}{p} \text{ (demand for labor)}, \qquad (2.4)$$

$$N = f\left(\frac{w}{p}\right) \text{ (supply of labor)}. \qquad (2.5)$$

There is a basic contradiction and indeterminacy in this system. The supply of and demand for labor, plus the production function, determine the level of output. But the savings-investment equation also determines the level of output, and there is no obvious mechanism to insure that these two levels of output will be the same. Furthermore, the liquidity-preference equation cannot determine both the price level and the rate of interest.

There are various ways out of the difficulties that arise in the system (2.1)–(2.5). The liquidity-preference and savings-investment equations can be generalized; the supply-of-labor equation can be changed; or possibly other changes may be suggested. It should be pointed out, however, that there is little that can be done to either the production function or the demand for labor. The production function cannot be changed, because it is a technological phenomenon. The laws of nature cannot be tampered with, while the hypotheses of economic behavior can. Many empirical studies have shown that the aggregate production function can be closely approximated by a linear-logarithmic relation. From the theories of profit maximization it follows that a linear-logarithmic production function implies a demand equation for labor such that the wage bill is proportional to the aggregate value of output. This constancy of labor's share of the national product is precisely what the data show. In dynamic econometric models this relation can be improved by saying that the wage bill is a linear function of the value of current output, lagged output, and a time trend. A demand equation for labor, of this generalized dynamic type, can be easily derived from empirical production functions. In various econometric models that the author has constructed, there is no relation that is more stable than the demand for labor; hence it seems unwise to attempt to clear up the theoretical difficulties of the above model by altering (2.3) or (2.4). We must concentrate our attention on (2.1), (2.2), and (2.5). This is precisely the Keynesian approach.

If the generalized forms of the money equation and the savings-investment equation presented in the previous section — (1.1′) and (1.2′) — were substituted for (2.1) and (2.2), the Keynesian theory would appear to be coincident with the classical theory. But such a conclusion would be hasty. Suppose that (2.1) and (2.2) are replaced by (1.1′) and (1.2′). If there was formerly a contradiction between the level of output determined from one part of the model, (2.3)–(2.5), and from another part of the model, (2.2), a classical economist would argue that the contradiction is now avoided because the interest rate would adjust itself so that investment would offset savings out of the same income that is determined by (2.3)–(2.5). But, according to the Keynesian theory, an interest-rate adjustment is not generally possible. There is no assurance that the equation

$$S(i, Y_0) = I(i, Y_0) \qquad (2.6)$$

has a solution in $i > 0$ when Y_0 is the full-employment level of income determined from (2.3)–(2.5). In fact, if savings and investment are both interest-inelastic, the chances are very great that there will be no solution to this equation. Interest-inelasticity of these schedules is one of the fundamental assumptions of modern Keynesian theory. The extreme case occurs when i is omitted as a variable from the savings and investment schedules.

Econometric and questionnaire investigations have always shown the influence of the interest rate on savings and investment to be small or absent; it remains for the opponents of Keynes to show that there is high interest-elasticity in these schedules.

One of the main reasons why savings are interest-inelastic is that some savings respond positively to variations in the interest rate (savings for wealth accumulation), while other savings respond negatively to variations in the interest rate (savings for annuities). On balance, the total effect is in doubt in regard to sign. In the modern society, savings are regulated largely by habits and considerations of economic security and have little to do with the rate of interest.

On the side of investment, it is well known that businessmen make capital outlays on the basis of a very short horizon (one to five years) and that the shorter the horizon the smaller is the effect of interest rates.[2] Furthermore, the increased use of internal financing — coupled with a failure to charge imputed interest — have intensified the neglect of the interest rate in the formation of investment decisions. These are two of the main reasons why the investment schedule is interest-inelastic.

There is a method of assuring a full-employment solution to the system, although it is highly artificial and unobserved in the real world. Professor Knight has suggested that the investment schedule be made infinitely interest-elastic. If this were assumed, there would always be full-employment equilibrium. Knight has written, "The heart of a correct theory of interest is the fact, corresponding more or less to infinite 'elasticity of demand for capital,' that the investment market is capable of absorbing savings at the maximum rate at which they are forthcoming, ..."[3] If the investment schedule possessed infinite interest-elasticity, equation (2.6) would always have a solution and the contradiction would be solved. However, Knight's assumption — which comes to exactly the same thing as Say's law — is untenable in the light of statistical data or any other knowledge that we have of the facts in the savings-investment market.

Supporters of Knight's views on capital theory may point out that the foregoing quotation applies only to a long-run situation. In this event, the term "elasticity of demand for capital" must take on a new connotation. Elasticities are ordinarily computed as logarithmic partial derivatives, which means that other variables are held constant. In the long run these other variables are not constant. If Knight is referring only to long-run processes in the quotation, his remarks are not related to the problem that we are discussing.

Professor Pigou[4] was one of the first classically minded economists to

[2]See G. L. S. Shackle, "Interest Rates and the Pace of Investment," *Economic Journal* LVI ([March] 1946), 1–17.

[3]Frank H. Knight, "Capital, Time, and Interest Rate," *Economica*, N.S., I ([Aug.] 1934), 285.

[4]A. C. Pigou, "The Classical Stationary State," *Economic Journal*, LIII ([Dec.] 1943), 343–351.

point out clearly that the amended system may be overdetermined with the added condition $i > 0$. Pigou acknowledged that savings and investment may be sufficiently interest-inelastic that the interest rate cannot be relied upon to bring them into balance at full employment. He suggested a further alteration in the savings-investment equation in order to salvage the classical doctrine of full-employment equilibrium. His suggestion would mean replacing the savings-investment equation by

$$S\left(i, Y, \frac{M}{p}\right) = I(i, Y), \qquad (2.2')$$

with the assumption that savings vary inversely with the real stock of cash.[5] The solution to an unemployment disequilibrium is now obvious. If wages are cut with M held constant by the banking system, M/p can be pushed to sufficiently high levels so that savings and investment are in balance at full employment. Since prices (equally well, wages) enter as a denominator in real cash balances, there is no limit to the size of M/p as a result of wage cuts and hence no limit to the extent to which savings can be lowered.[6] Thus, by always restoring the system toward its full-employment equilibrium, competitive wage cuts during periods of unemployment solve the problem for Pigou.

Equation (2.2') rests on an unconfirmed hypothesis, namely, that savings vary inversely with the real stock of cash balances. Just as the classical assumptions about the influence of interest rates on savings and investment have never been discovered to hold empirically, so has it never been discovered that consumption or savings patterns are significantly influenced by the stock of cash balances. The data of the interwar period show that cash balances, at best, had a very mild influence on consumption. If we adopt the following simple model for purposes of statistical investigation,[7]

$$S = \alpha_0 + \alpha_1 Y + \alpha_2 Y_{-1} + \alpha_3 \left(\frac{M}{p}\right)_{-1} = I = \text{autonomous} \qquad (2.7)$$

or

$$Y = \frac{-\alpha_0}{\alpha_1} - \frac{\alpha_2}{\alpha_1} Y_{-1} - \frac{\alpha_3}{\alpha_1}\left(\frac{M}{p}\right)_{-1} + \frac{1}{\alpha_1} I,$$

[5] Other economists, notably Professor Haberler, have made the same suggestion, although none has been so explicit as Pigou.

[6] The "real" models of this paper have been constructed in terms of the price level, p, as a deflator, but we could just as easily have constructed the system in wage units with w as the deflator. If the system is written in wage units, the appropriate variable for (2.2') is M/w. This form makes it possible to see more directly how wage cuts are used as a lever to raise the level of real balances.

[7] All variables are per capita in 1935–39 dollars. The time period is 1922–41. The figures in parentheses below the estimated parameters are standard errors of the estimates. Y = disposable income, S = personal savings, I = net investment, M = total cash balances (current dollars).

the least-squares estimates of the parameters are

$$Y = 186.53 + .30Y_{-1} + .13 \left(\frac{M}{p}\right)_{-1} + 2.36I.$$
$$\quad\quad\quad (.13) \quad\quad (.10) \quad\quad\quad\quad (.34)$$

The standard error of the estimate of $1/\alpha_1$ is relatively small, .34. On the other hand, the standard error of the estimate of α_3/α_1 is relatively large. The coefficient of M/p could easily be close to zero, but since $1/\alpha_1$ is definitely not zero, it follows that α_3 could be zero. Pigou's hypothesis is not confirmed. Even if the true value of α_3 is not zero, it may not be very large. The main point, however, is that the size (and sign) of α_3 is very uncertain. There is no "proof" of Pigou's hypothesis.

The size of the coefficient relating savings to cash balances is very important for Pigou's theory. Recall that the systems of this paper are regarded as equilibrium solutions of more complex dynamical systems. The classical theory implicitly assumes that the system returns rapidly to its equilibrium when it is displaced to a position of disequilibrium. This implies that the dynamical system is damped. But do wage-and-price cuts always lead to damped processes in time? In order to insure that the classical assumption of dampening is correct, it will be necessary to assume that a small cut in wages, for example, will tend to restore the system immediately to its position of equilibrium. Thus it is required that the multiplier effect of wage cuts (or increases in the real stock of cash) be very large. The statistical calculations of (2.7) do not show this. There exists the possibility, but not the necessity, that the increase may be practically zero. Instability may develop in a model like this. There is an initial position of unemployment. Wages fall, but employment and income increase little or not at all. Wages fall still further, but unemployment is still not eradicated. This is a perfect setting for expectations of further wage cuts, the very conditions that make the system unstable and make it likely that wage cuts will push the system away from rather than toward its full-employment equilibrium.

If there are expectations of falling wages, entrepreneurs will postpone production until a time when labor costs will be lower yet. Wage-earners will feel very insecure and spend as little as possible. Hyperdeflation will never cure unemployment. The only way that unstable situations of hyperdeflation can be stopped is by direct, autonomous action on the part of the state or some other authoritative agency, as was the case in the period 1929–33 in the United States. Admittedly, the process of hyperdeflation is the worst set of circumstances that can arise in Pigou's system, yet — on the basis of the available data — an assumption of such unfavorable conditions is legitimate even though other assumptions can safely be made also. The problem, as yet, remains unsettled.

In the most general model — in which the savings-investment equation is (2.2′) and the liquidity-preference equation is (1.1′) — the expression for the rate of change of real income with respect to real cash balances is more complicated. Without going into the mathematics of this expression, it is possible to present certain results on an intuitive basis. If savings are insensitive to variations in i and M/p and if investment is insensitive to variations of i, then it will follow that real income will not be greatly stimulated by increases in real cash balances. These are the properties of the savings-investment equation that have already been discussed in the preceding pages. The conclusion about small variations in real income associated with variations in real balances is *reinforced* if we appeal to the Keynesian assumptions about the shape of the liquidity-preference equation. Keynes put forth the hypothesis that the demand for cash is infinitely elastic with respect to the interest rate in the neighborhood of low interest rates. Some economists have singled out this hypothesis of Keynes as his strategic assumption which is necessary for the validity of his theories. The truth of the matter is that high interest-elasticity of liquidity preferences is sufficient in many cases but never necessary. The validity of the theory of employment does not depend on the validity of the assumption about the form of liquidity preferences. It is obvious that the simplest version of the Keynesian theory (savings as a function of income equals autonomous investment) has nothing to do with the theory of interest.

It is instructive to examine the empirical relationship between the interest rate and cash balances to see whether or not the Keynesian hypothesis is correct. If we identify active cash balances as circulating currency plus demand deposits, and idle cash balances as savings deposits, we find for the interwar period very strong linear correlations (a) between active balances, net national product and trend and (b) between idle balances, corporate-bond yield, lagged corporate-bond yield, lagged idle balances, and trend. The data also show that the corporate-bond yield is not a statistically significant variable in (a) and that net national product is not a statistically significant variable in (b). These latter findings imply that the empirical split between active and idle balances is not bad.

The fact that idle balances are linearly related to the interest rate in the interwar period implies that the Keynesian hypothesis of infinite elasticity cannot be correct. But the postwar data show something different. The current data are consistent with Keynes's hypothesis. While the interwar demand relation for active balances is close to the postwar facts, the interwar demand relation for idle balances gives a computed level of idle balances, for observed interest rates, much lower than the actual level. There are several explanations for the breakdown of this empirical function in the postwar years. One explanation is that the whole relation has shifted. Another explanation is that some variable, which was relatively unimportant in the past, is now important and accounts for the discrepancy. A third explanation, which is very appealing, is that the Keynesian hypothesis is correct. If the liquidity-preference function were approximately linear for interest rates above 3 per cent and asymptotic to the line, interest rate = 2.5

per cent, it would fit the interwar data, the postwar data, and the Keynesian hypothesis. There are a variety of simple mathematical functions which have the required properties.

The intuitive significance of the various assumptions about interest-elasticities can be summed up briefly. Assuming that the mechanism to maintain full-employment equilibrium is a fluctuating stock of real balances, it follows that these fluctuations will have little influence on the interest rate if the liquidity preferences are highly elastic, and it follows further that they will have little influence on savings and investment if these schedules are interest-inelastic. It may seem that much weight is attached to the interest rate, but the opposite is the case. The complex of elasticities assumed in the Keynesian theory makes the interest rate extremely unimportant. The same results can be obtained by altogether dropping interest as an independent variable from the system.

The other available alternative by which the contradictions of the system may be reconciled is the modification of the supply curve of labor. This is the alternative that Keynes chose for himself. Before discussing this alternative, however, several points should be made clear. We have been able to demonstrate a basic contradiction in the working of the capitalist system when the traditional supply curve of labor is used. The recognition of this contradiction represents a great step forward in economic theory, and this contribution has nothing to do with any special assumptions about wages. The truly important ideas of Keynes, contrary to much of popular belief, are independent of any special assumptions about the labor market. Keynesian theories of the savings-investment process superimposed on the classical theory of the labor market show that full employment is not automatic under capitalism.

Keynes recognized that full employment was not the equilibrium position for the real world, and he set about to develop a theory of an unemployment equilibrium by changing the classical supply curve of labor and by adopting a new definition of unemployment. It is this part of his theory that many of the modern Keynesians would like to give up while still retaining the savings-investment theory of income determination. The strict Keynesian approach amounts to replacing (2.5) by

$$N = F(w) \tag{2.8}$$

and adopting the well-known definition of involuntary unemployment found in the early pages of the *General Theory*. It is assumed that the new supply curve of labor has infinite wage-elasticity up to the full-employment point. This system is rigged to get an unemployment equilibrium as much as the classical system is rigged to get a full-employment equilibrium. Neither approach is entirely acceptable.

There are at least two criticisms of the Keynesian solution. In the first place, Keynes's definition of unemployment has the unsavory implication that the cause of unemployment is a money-illusion on the part of workers;

if workers would only bargain in terms of real wages instead of in terms of money wages, there would be no problem of unemployment, other than the frictional variety. Surely, a small thing like a money-illusion cannot be responsible for the existence of unemployment. Second, the supply curve of labor given by (2.8) has never been tested against the facts and may not hold if it is tested. The behavior patterns of recent years (since the Little Steel Formula) give the impression that workers do not bargain exclusively in terms of money wages. They are very conscious of the relation between wages and the cost of living, and it does not seem correct to assume that they are fooled by any money-illusion. Many of the parts of the Keynesian system have withstood the test of being consistent with observed data, but all that we can say about equation (2.8) is that we do not know about its validity. It must be re-emphasized, however, that the important parts of the Keynesian theory are independent of Keynes's own theories of wages and the labor market.

Joan Robinson has made a very important remark that holds the key to an answer to the problem. She said: "Again, the orthodox conception of wages tending to equal the *marginal disutility* of labour, which has its origin in the picture of a peasant farmer leaning on his hoe in the evening and deciding whether the extra product of another hour's work will repay the extra backache, is projected into the modern labour market, where the individual worker has no opportunity to decide anything except whether it is better to work or to starve."[8] The essence of capitalism is that there exists a definite legal respect for private ownership of the means of production. The owners of the means of production, the capitalists, make all the final decisions with regard to the use of the means of production. The workers have nothing to say about the amount of employment that will be forthcoming at any point of time. Either the entire concept of the supply curve of labor must be dropped, or the supply curve of labor must become a curve of *virtual* points on which observations do not occur. The first alternative means that the demand for labor is given by profit maximization (marginal-productivity theory); the supply of labor is an exogenous variable represented by the labor force and determined by demographic factors; the wage rate is determined by a market adjustment between demand and supply (collective bargaining). The mathematical model would be

$$\frac{dY}{dN} = \frac{w}{p} \text{ (demand for labor)}, \qquad (2.4)$$

$$\bar{N} = \text{labor supply}, \qquad (2.9)$$

$$\frac{d\left(\frac{w}{p}\right)}{dt} = g(\bar{N} - N). \qquad (2.10)$$

[8]Joan Robinson, *An Essay on Marxian Economics* (London: Macmillan & Co., 1942), pp. 2–3.

Equation (2.10) could be replaced by

$$\frac{dw}{dt} = h(\bar{N} - N) \tag{2.10'}$$

if all the other equations of the system are used also. The same arguments about expectations and damping apply to the path by which this system approaches or diverges from equilibrium. If the system is damped and $g(0) = 0$ or $h(0) = 0$, we have a model of full-employment equilibrium.

It was pointed out above that equation (2.4) is based on sound empirical verification. Similarly, market adjustment equations like (2.10') are also consistent with the data. First differences in the general wage rate (U.S.A., interwar period) are highly correlated (inversely) with unemployment and the lagged wage rate. The parameters of this empirical equation suggest that small wage cuts are not associated with large increases in employment and that $h(0) \neq 0$, from which we conclude that the system does not have a stable equilibrium of full employment.

If the concept of a supply curve of labor is to be retained, it must be interpreted in a new way. We can say that the supply curve of labor shows how much the people would *like* to work at any given real wage. It does not mean, as in the classical system, that people's desires become effective. In this situation the supply curve of labor exists as a set of virtual points which are never observed. However, it is known that the demand curve for labor represents a set of observed points. This means that we shall have an observed point on the demand curve and off the supply curve. If this point is such that supply exceeds demand (at the same wage) there is unemployment, and if this point is such that demand exceeds supply (at the same wage) there is overemployment. This concept of unemployment is not easily measurable, however, since it involves virtual, unobserved points. In order to measure unemployment in this model, we would have to sample the population, questioning them on the amount of employment that they would like to supply at prevailing wage rates.

Thus far we have attempted to point out the main differences between Keynesian and classical economics. But there is also an important aspect of similarity, namely, methodology. For both types of systems, macroeconomic models have been studied in this paper. The macroeconomic models are similar except for emphasis. A single model with one set of parameters yields the classical theory and with another set of parameters yields the Keynesian theory. However, the macroeconomic models are not the basic elements of either system. It is necessary to analyze the considerations that lie behind the macrosystem, i.e., the microsystem. It will be found here, too, that the methodologies of classical and Keynesian economics do not differ. There are two steps in the formation of the macroeconomic systems. First, it is necessary to formulate the behavior pattern of individuals. Both theories are based on household utility-maximization to get the demand for consumer goods and household cash-holdings, and on business-firm profit- (or utility-) maximization to get the demand for producer goods, labor, and business cash-holdings. The second step is to show how to pass from a theory involving individual firms, households, factors, and commodities to a theory involving communities of individuals, composite factors, and composite commodities. This step involves the index-number problem. The discussion of both these subjects is important but lengthy. The reader is referred to other works for more extensive analysis.[9] The point to be emphasized at this stage is that the methodology is the same for classical and Keynesian economics at all steps in the process of deriving the macrosystems.

III. The Marxian theory[10]

There are two important subsections of the modern theories of employment which need to be clarified. One subsection is the stagnation thesis, and the other is the relation between wages, profits, and employment. The modern version of the stagnation thesis is an outgrowth of the Keynesian developments in American economic thinking. The opposite theory of the stationary state is a natural outgrowth of the classical system. But neither model, as usually stated, gives an adequate analysis of the theory of economic development. It is possible to modify these theories with the introduction of trend variables, the stock of capital, etc., in order to get some information about the economic laws of motion of society; but it seems preferable to go to a theory which deals directly with this subject. From a historical point of view it is also fitting to use the theory which first tackled the problems related to the stagnation thesis. The Marxian theory of the falling rate of profit is one of the first, and probably one of the best, tools for analyzing the stagnation theory. Since Marxian theory comes to conclusions similar to those of the modern stagnationists, but for different reasons, it will also be instructive to study it in some detail.

The other problem of the relation between wages, profits, and employ-

[9]On the problem of the theories underlying the Keynesian and classical macroeconomic systems see Klein, *op. cit.* On the problem of aggregation see Francis W. Dresch, "Index Numbers and the General Economic Equilibrium," *Bulletin of the American Mathematical Society*, XL (Feb. 1938), 134–141; Lawrence R. Klein, "Macroeconomics and the Theory of Rational Behavior," *Econometrica*, XIV (April 1946), 93–108; and "Remarks on the Theory of Aggregation," *Econometrica*, XIV (Oct. 1946), 303–312; Kenneth May, "The Aggregation Problem for a One-Industry Model," *Econometrica*, XIV (Oct. 1946), 285–298; Shou Shan Pu, "A Note on Macro economics," *Econometrica*, XIV (Oct. 1946), 299–302.

[10]The author is indebted to Professor Kenneth May for helpful criticisms in this section.

ment is of great current interest but also cannot be properly analyzed within the customary frameworks of Keynesian and classical economics. These theories can also be modified by distinguishing in the consumption function between wage income and profit income. But the Marxian theory is based fundamentally on the interrelationships between wages and profits. The Marxian theories of reproduction are well suited for the study of this problem.

Here it will be necessary to digress for a few pages in order to show explicitly the structure of the Marxian model. This model will then be compared with the Keynesian model and used for the analysis of the stagnation theory and the relationship between wages, profits, and employment.

The methodology of the Marxian approach is quite different from that of Keynes and the Classics: Instead of studying the behavior of individuals, Marx studied the behavior of classes directly. His theory is probably the origin of macroeconomics. But the Marxian system of macroeconomics differs essentially from the Keynesian and classical systems. The macrounits in the latter systems are producers and consumers, and this overlapping fails to bring out some essentials. The macrounits of the Marxian system are not only producers and consumers but also workers and capitalists. The latter two groups are, practically speaking, exclusive, and their basic conflict of interests can more easily be singled out as one of the moving forces in the system.

The economic writings of Marx were not presented in the form of systems of simultaneous equations. The equation-system approach to economics came at a later date. There are various equations throughout Marx's writings, but these equations are mainly definitions. They state, for example, that total output can be broken up into three components: constant capital, variable capital, and surplus value. Various manipulations are carried out with these components, but complete systems of equations are not formulated. However, imbedded in Marx's literary discussion and numerical examples, there are several hypotheses and assumptions that can be used to build a system of equations. The validity of the equation system depends upon the validity of the hypotheses made. It is the function of the empirical studies to test the validity of these equations.

The supply-and-demand equations of orthodox economics also are based upon some assumptions the validity of which cannot be assumed a priori. The systems of supply-and-demand equations are usually based on the assumptions that households maximize their individual utility functions subject to certain constraints. The assumptions produce the maximization equations which are essentially the supply-and-demand equations. In the same way, we shall have to introduce Marxian assumptions in order to construct an equation system out of *Capital*.

A concrete example will demonstrate clearly the relation between definitional equations and behavior equations (or refutable hypotheses). Suppose we write, as did Marx,

$$c + v + s = \text{total value,} \tag{3.1}$$

$$\frac{s}{v} = \text{rate of surplus value,} \tag{3.2}$$

$$\frac{c}{c + v} = \text{organic composition of capital,} \tag{3.3}$$

$$\frac{s}{c + v} = \text{rate of profit,} \tag{3.4}$$

where c = constant capital, v = variable capital, s = surplus value.[11]

Equations (3.1)–(3.4) are definitions. They define four different terms and hold, regardless of any economic behavior patterns. We cannot test the validity of any of these equations because they must hold by definition They are not refutable hypotheses.

According to the simplest rules of algebra the following equation.

$$\frac{s}{c + v} = \frac{s}{v}\left(1 - \frac{c}{c + v}\right), \tag{3.5}$$

must hold[12] because

$$\frac{s}{v}\left(1 - \frac{c}{c + v}\right) = \frac{s}{v}\left(\frac{c + v - c}{c + v}\right) = \frac{s}{c + v}.$$

Equation (3.5) is not a refutable hypothesis either. It, too, must hold, regardless of the actual values of the variables c, v, s. Equation (3.5) merely states the truism that

$$\frac{s}{c + v} = \frac{s}{c + v}.$$

In so far as Marxian economics is based on equations (3.1)–(3.5) no real progress can be made. None of these equations tells us anything about fundamental economic behavior. The extensive use by Marx and the Marxists of equations similar to (3.1)–(3.5) has undoubtedly led Oscar Lange to remark: "This whole [Marxist] literature tries to solve the fundamental problems of economic equilibrium and disequilibrium without even

[11]For the individual firm, c consists of depreciation and raw materials; v consists of wage payments; and s consists of profit, interest, and rent.

[12]For the use of such equations in Marxian economics see Paul M. Sweezy, *The Theory of Capitalist Development* (New York: Oxford University Press, 1942), p. 68.

attempting to make use of the mathematical concept of functional relationship."[13]

But Marx was probably not so guilty as Lange's remark implies. In Volume III of *Capital*, when discussing the theory of the falling rate of profit, Marx[14] made specific assumptions in his numerical examples. He assumed that s/v in equation (3.5) is constant. Thus he was able to say that the rate of profit, $s/(c + v)$, varies inversely with the organic composition of capital, $c/(c + v)$. Here is a refutable hypothesis, namely, $s/v =$ constant. This is an economic hypothesis that can be tested. We can examine data on wages, profits, interest, and rent to see whether or not s and v have a constant ratio. By making this assumption, Marx was able to develop the theory of the falling rate of profit which states that the rate of profit falls as the organic composition of capital rises. From equations (3.1)–(3.5) we can say nothing about the behavior of the economic system, but from equations (3.1)–(3.5) and the assumption $s/v =$ constant we can say very much. However, the system is not yet complete even at this stage.

It is worth pointing out that this confusion is not peculiar to Marxian economics. It has arisen in non-Marxian economics in connection with the quantity theory of money. Let us define $M =$ total stock of money; $V =$ average number of times a monetary unit is spent in a given period on newly produced goods and services; $p =$ average price of newly produced goods and services; $X =$ aggregate output of newly produced goods and services.[15] It follows by definition that

$$MV = pX. \tag{3.6}$$

Equation (3.6) tells us nothing about economic behavior. In its present form it is of the same nature as equation (3.5). There is no refutable hypothesis contained in either (3.5) or (3.6).

The classical economists did the same thing about (3.6) that Marx did about (3.5). They assumed that certain variables in (3.6) were known numbers. Specifically, they assumed $V =$ constant and $X =$ full-employment output. For them, V was determined by institutional and psychological phenomena such as the frequency of wage payments, attitudes toward holding cash, etc. With V and X known, the classical economists could say that the price level varies directly with the amount of money. The validity of this theory depends upon the validity of the assumptions about V and X.

These examples illustrate our method. We shall search through Marx's literary explanations and numerical examples for the strategic hypotheses that will produce a determinate system of equations.

[13]Oscar Lange, "Marxian Economics and Modern Economic Theory," *Review of Economic Studies*, II (June 1935), 196.

[14]Karl Marx, *Capital*, III (Chicago: Charles H. Kerr & Co., 1909), 247.

[15]The aggregates p and X are constructed so that their product, pX, is exactly equal to the total value of newly produced output.

First we must define the variables carefully. We shall retain Marx's notation of c, v, s. When referring to the individual firm, c consists of depreciation and purchases of raw materials, v consists of wage payments, and s consists of profit plus interest plus rent. The aggregate value of output for the individual firm is $c + v + s$. When referring to the economy as a whole, we must redefine constant capital in order to avoid double counting. For the entire system, constant capital, denoted by C, is defined as the value of depreciation charges. Constant capital does not include raw materials for the system as a whole because such an inclusion would lead to excessive double counting in determining the value of output. Variable capital for the entire system will be denoted by V and will include all wage payments. Surplus value for the entire system will be denoted by S and will include total profits, interest, and rents. In modern terminology, we have

$$C + V + S = \text{gross national income,}$$

$$V + S = \text{net national income.}$$

National income can be considered from two sides — production and factor payments. National income as the sum $V + S$ represents total factor payments.[16] From the side of production, national income can be considered as equal to the total production of two types of goods and services — consumption and investment (consumer goods and producer goods). Consumer goods are those that flow to households and producer goods those that flow to business firms. We shall denote consumption by R and net investment by I. Net national income will be denoted, as usual, by Y. We have, thus far, the two following definitional equations:

$$V + S = Y, \tag{3.7}$$

$$R + I = Y. \tag{3.8}$$

The variables V, S, Y, R, I, are all measured in real terms, for example, constant dollars.

It is now necessary to develop behavior equations to show how these variables are determined. First consider R, consumption. Marx divided consumers into two strategic groups — workers and capitalists. He *assumed* that workers spend all their incomes on consumer goods and services. In fact, he wrote: ". . . . the variable capital advanced in the payment of the labor-power of the laborers is mostly spent by them for articles of consumption; . . . ."[17] This assumption is also carried through in a purer form in his

---

[16]It is only in orthodox economics that S represents a factor payment. In Marxian terminology, S represents expropriation. The term "factor payment" is used in the text only because it is customarily used today in discussions of national income statistics.

[17]Karl Marx, *op. cit.*, II, 466.

numerical examples of reproduction schemes in Part III, Volume II of *Capital*. In the numerical examples he always put workers' consumption exactly equal to wages (not approximately equal). In the quotation he said that wages are "mostly spent" (but not entirely spent) on consumer goods and services. As a matter of fact, empirical data suggest that Marx's quoted assumption is the correct one. The marginal propensity to consume out of wages is not unity, although it is very close to unity.

It is less obvious how to determine the behavior pattern for capitalist consumption in the Marxian system. The main clue comes from a study of numerical examples that Marx used to analyze capitalist reproduction schemes. The theory of simple reproduction is not much of a clue, for in that scheme a steady state is assumed in which variable capital (wages) and surplus value are always exactly spent on consumer goods and capital is replaced without any net investment taking place. The schemes of accumulation and reproduction on an enlarged scale, found at the end of Volume II of *Capital*, provide the basis for a theory of capitalist consumption.

In his examples on accumulation, Marx divided the economic system into two departments — the department (I) producing producer goods and the department (II) producing consumer goods. In the first department, workers were assumed to spend all their wage income on consumer goods produced by the second department, while capitalists were assumed to spend only a part of their surplus-value income on consumer goods. The exact relation for capitalist behavior in Department I was

$$\text{consumption} = \tfrac{1}{2}(\text{surplus value}).$$

This is the consumption function for capitalists in Department I. In a consistent theory it should be expected that capitalists in Department II would also behave in a similar fashion, their consumption being a function of their surplus-value income. True, Marx assumed that the capitalists in Department II consumed out of their surplus-value income, but he did not assume that there existed an independent relation between consumption and surplus value for capitalists in Department II. The behavior of capitalists in the consumer-goods industry was entirely passive in the sense that their consumption was calculated as a residual. This residual consumption was taken to be the difference between total surplus value in Department II and that part of surplus value which was transferred to expenditure on constant and variable capital. The latter expenditure was calculated by Marx so that the reproduction scheme could work smoothly without a glut of the market. Marx did not assume, by any means, that capitalism works smoothly; but he set down in his reproduction schemes the conditions under which capitalism could work smoothly. He argued that if his conditions were not met a crash would occur. One step in a possible method of introducing fluctuations into the model, with recurring crises and recovery, is to make capitalist consumption in Department II also a function of surplus value. We can even simplify the entire system by doing away with the distinction between departments I and II. Let us assume instead that capitalists behave the same way in both departments. Identical behavior is assumed for workers in these two departments, and it seems reasonable to assume that capitalists should not have different consumption habits according as they produce consumer goods or producer goods. Hence we shall assume that the consumption of capitalists is a function of surplus value.

Denoting the consumption of workers by R_1 and the consumption of capitalists by R_2 we have the two consumption functions[18]

$$R_1 = V, \tag{3.9}$$

$$R_2 = \alpha_0 + \alpha_1 S, \qquad 0 < \alpha_1 < 1. \tag{3.10}$$

The total consumption function is given by

$$R_1 + R_2 = R = \alpha_0 + \alpha_1 S + V. \tag{3.11}$$

In a more general formulation, where the workers' marginal propensity to consume is not unity, we have

$$R_1 = \alpha_2 + \alpha_3 V, \qquad 0 < \alpha_3 < 1, \tag{3.9'}$$

$$R = (\alpha_0 + \alpha_2) + \alpha_1 S + \alpha_3 V, \alpha_3 > \alpha_1. \tag{3.11'}$$

The next step is to derive the demand for the other type of good in the system — investment or producer goods. We shall first derive the demand relation for constant capital (capital used up) according to Marx and then transform the demand for constant capital into investment. Workers buy only consumer goods in the Marxian system, for that is what distinguishes workers from capitalists. The demand for constant capital will be based entirely on the behavior of capitalists. Again, we rely on the examples of expanded reproduction in order to discover the variables influencing capitalists' demand for constant capital.

In Volume II, Marx assumed that capitalists in Department I (the producer-goods industry) spend from surplus value on constant capital. His relation was

$$\text{constant capital} = C_0 + k \,(\text{surplus value}), \qquad 0 < k < 1,$$

where $C_0 = $ the initial level of constant capital and $k = $ a fraction which is the product of the fraction of surplus value to be accumulated in both

[18]As a first approximation, we shall assume a linear system.

variable and constant capital and the fraction of total capital represented by constant capital.

The expenditures on constant capital in Department II were like the expenditures by capitalists on consumer goods in that department in the sense that both expenditures were calculated as a residual. The capitalists in Department II did not decide, independently, to accumulate capital but based their decision entirely on the relationship between expenditures in both departments so that the process would run smoothly without a glut of the market. We can again do away with the assumption of a smooth-working capitalist system by supposing that capitalists behave the same way in both departments in so far as the demand for constant capital is concerned. We shall assume that capitalists in both departments demand constant capital as a fraction of surplus value.

There is one condition, implicit in Marx's example, which must be avoided for our model. Marx assumed that whatever capitalists do not spend out of surplus value on consumer goods they spend on constant or variable capital. We shall assume, instead, an independence between the marginal propensity to consume and the marginal propensity to invest. We must point out, however, that Marx made this assumption only to obtain the conditions for a smooth-working system. He did not imply that these conditions held in the real world. Our alternative assumption is one way of achieving the conditions of the real world in the Marxian spirit.

We now have the equation

$$C = \beta_0 + \beta_1 S. \tag{3.12}$$

Since we are going to work with the variable I instead of C, it will be necessary to carry out a transformation of variables. The transformation involves common-sense technological relations which are constructed by the present author and do not appear in *Capital*.[19]

The variable C represents the amount of fixed capital used up in the production process. The amount of capital used up (depreciation) will depend upon the stock of fixed capital in existence. The capital in existence will, in turn, be made up of the elements of durable capital, plant, and equipment — acquired at various stages of past history. Denoting the capital acquired during the pth preceding time period by x_{-p}, we have

$$C = C(x, x_{-1}, x_{-2}, x_{-3}, \ldots) \tag{3.13}$$

or in a linear approximation[20]

$$C = \delta_0 + \delta_1 x + \delta_2 x_{-1} + \delta_3 x_{-2} + \ldots \tag{3.14}$$

---

[19]These transformations are so obvious that it is assumed that anybody wishing to work with I instead of C would use approximately the same transformations.

[20]Since the linear function is an approximation, we shall not assume the constant term equal to zero, although logically there should be no constant term in this equation.

In statistical work we cannot measure separately the capital purchased during every preceding time period, but we can approximate all these variables with a proxy variable which represents all the capital accumulated up to the time period under consideration. Instead of (3.14), let us write

$$C = \delta_0 + \delta_1 x + \delta_2' Z_{-1}. \tag{3.14'}$$

The stock of existing fixed capital, Z_{-1}, can be written in terms of the net investment of all preceding periods as

$$Z_{-1} = \sum_{t=-1}^{-\infty} I_t. \tag{3.15}$$

Equation (3.14') at least makes the distinction between new and old capital, but it is not so complete as (3.14), which makes the distinction between capital of all different age groups. This distinction is useful because the capital in different age groups has different productivities, the newest capital being technologically superior.

It is net investment rather than gross investment which is of primary importance for the particular model of this paper. We can obviously write

$$x = I + C. \tag{3.16}$$

Substituting (3.16) into (3.14') we get

$$C = \delta_0 + \delta_1(I + C) + \delta_2' Z_{-1} \tag{3.17}$$

or

$$C = \frac{\delta_0}{1 - \delta_1} + \frac{\delta_1}{1 - \delta_1} I + \frac{\delta_2'}{1 - \delta_1} Z_{-1}.$$

We can now eliminate C between (3.12) and (3.17) to get

$$I = \beta_2 + \beta_3 S + \beta_4 Z_{-1}. \tag{3.18}$$

This is the final form of our investment function.

There is now lacking one more equation for the completion of the system. Capitalists demand commodities in the form not only of producer and consumer goods but also in the form of labor power. Our equation of the demand for labor power will appear in a disguised form. We shall develop an equation which serves to determine the aggregate amount of variable capital, V. But this variable represents the total remuneration paid out by capitalists for labor power. The equation which serves to determine V in our system is the same thing as the demand equation for labor power.

Those familiar with Marx will recall that he regarded the surplus value as transformed into variable and constant capital in his schemes of expanded reproduction. We could have made $C + V$ a function of S instead of making C alone a function of S. However, since Marx always assumed a definite relation between C and V, we were able to eliminate V in the above relation. He imposed the condition that variable and constant capital be used in the same proportions throughout the production process; hence we were able to develop a relation between C and S not involving V. While Marx assumed a definite relation between C and V, he also assumed a definite relation between S and V. It may appear that we are getting too many equations, but both these relations (that between C and V, and that between S and V) are not independent. Suppose that total capital is a function of surplus value

$$C + V = f(S) \tag{3.19}$$

and that variable capital is also a function of surplus value

$$C + V(S) = f(S) \tag{3.20}$$

or

$$C = f^*(S).$$

This forms the basis of equation (3.12). It is evident that there must also be a relation between C and V, since

$$S = V^{-1}(V) \tag{3.21}$$

and

$$C = f^*(V^{-1}[V]) = f^{**}(V).$$

This simple demonstration shows that a relation between C and S and a relation between V and S imply a relation between C and V. The latter relation is not independent of the other two; hence there are not too many equations.[21]

As was seen above in the brief discussion of the theory of the falling rate of profit, the assumption, $S/V =$ constant, led to very important conclusions. In the numerical examples of expanded reproduction, Marx maintained a constant ratio between S and V. This assumption implies that labor will receive a constant fraction of net national income. Economists have long been puzzled by the fact that national-income statistics have shown labor's share of total income to be nearly constant over a long time period. There has possibly been some trend in these data which show that labor's share has

[21]The above demonstration is a method of keeping the system from becoming overdetermined. However, it is questionable whether Marx intended the relation between C and V to be dependent on other relations or whether he intended it to be an independent technological phenomenon. From a technological point of view, there is no reason why labor and capital should be used in a fixed relation during the entire production process; hence we have not made use of an independent technological relation between C and V.

been gradually increasing. This trend term could be explained by the institutional phenomenon of a growing labor movement in the United States.
The next equation is thus

$$V = \gamma_1 S. \tag{3.22}$$

We may introduce the trend by a modification to

$$V = \gamma_0 + \gamma_1 S + \gamma_2 t. \tag{3.22'}$$

Since $V + S = Y$, it is equivalent to say that V and S are proportional or that V and Y are proportional. In recent years the stability of labor's share has usually been discussed in terms of V and Y rather than V and S. As an alternative formulation, we could write

$$V = \gamma_3 + \gamma_4 Y + \gamma_5 t. \tag{3.23}$$

The Marxian system is now complete. The entire set of equations is[22]

$$R = \alpha_0 + \alpha_1 S + \alpha_2 V, \tag{3.24}$$

$$I = \beta_0 + \beta_1 S + \beta_2 Z_{-1}, \tag{3.25}$$

$$V = \gamma_0 + \gamma_1 Y + \gamma_2 t \tag{3.26}$$

$$Y = S + V, \tag{3.27}$$

$$Y = R + I, \tag{3.28}$$

$$\Delta Z = I. \tag{3.29}$$

Equation (3.24) follows from (3.11'), (3.25) from (3.18), (3.26) from (3.23), (3.27) from (3.7), (3.28) from (3.8), and (3.29) from (3.15). We have, in (3.24)–(3.29), six equations and six endogenous variables R, V, S, I, Z, Y. All variables are measured in "real" units, and we have been able to complete the system without introducing the quantity of money.

Several observations are called for before we go on to some problems of economic analysis based upon this model. While it is true that this version of the Marxian theory has been developed largely through an examination of Marx's writings and by a slight generalization of his own methods (i.e., a generalization of his numerical examples into functional relationships), the same model can readily be developed from other considerations. By assuming certain behavior patterns for workers and capitalists, like utility- and profit-maximization, we can obtain the same mathematical model.

[22]We have renumbered all subscripts on the parameters for purely aesthetic reasons.

The reader will also notice that the model (3.24)–(3.29) is very similar to Kalecki's theories. Practically no model implies a unique theoretical basis. Furthermore, we have not utilized Marx's methods to their fullest extent. Only those aspects of Marx's theories are used that are necessary to build a complete system of equations. Many Marxian theories are unrelated to the principle of effective demand, but even some of those parts of his theory that are related to effective demand have been left out. It was necessary to make the latter omission in order to keep from getting an overdetermined model. For example, Marx assumed that the wage *rate* would be determined by the value of the means of subsistence of a worker, where the means of subsistence, in turn, depends upon the traditional standard of life in the particular region where the worker lives. But it is easy to show that the model cannot contain this theory of an autonomous wage rate as well as the theory underlying equation (3.26). Suppose that equation (3.26) is accepted as a correct theory. The model then enables us to determine the real wage bill and the level of output. Every system must contain a technological input-output relationship. In the Marxian system, input is given by the employment of labor power and the depreciation of fixed capital, C. From our discussion there are enough relations to determine output and C; hence the other type of input, employment of labor power, is uniquely determined. Since the real wage bill and employment are known, the real wage rate is also known. There is no room in this system for an autonomously determined wage rate. The strong empirical foundation behind equation (3.26) is an argument for using this Marxian hypothesis rather than the other hypothesis of a given wage rate. It is certain that both hypotheses cannot be used simultaneously within the framework of our model. This example serves to show that the above model is not the only mathematization of *Capital*. There are a variety of models that can be developed from the Marxian theories, and we have chosen one that is plausible, simple, and useful for the analysis of specific problems.

It is interesting to make certain comparisons between the Keynesian and the Marxian models. A simple version of the Keynesian theory — in which the quantity of money and the interest rate do not appear as variables — is a special case of the Marxian model. By substitution from (3.26) and (3.27) into (3.24), it is possible to make consumption a function of income; and, by substitution from (3.26) and (3.27) into (3.25), it is possible to make investment a function of income and the stock of capital. For the short-run theories, Keynes took the stock of capital as given; thus, such a reduced version of the Marxian model comes to the same thing as the simple Keynesian model. The primary advantage of the Marxian model is that it provides more information than does the Keynesian system. In the former model the complete solution always gives the demand for consumer goods, producer goods, and employment, while in some forms[23] of the latter model,

[23]This is true in those forms of the Keynesian theory in which the savings-investment equation alone is used to determine the level of output.

the complete solution gives only the demand for consumer goods and the demand for producer goods. The demand for factors of production (employment and producer goods) determines supply; hence the Marxian model has the virtue of always giving the full conditions of demand and supply. This cannot be said, in general, of the Keynesian model.

It is not meant to imply that Marx fully anticipated the Keynesian theory of effective demand. Our model is intended as an extension of the Marxian analysis to a logical conclusion in terms of a theory of effective demand. Actually, Marx laid the groundwork for a complete equation system to determine the level of income (effective demand) but did not build the complete system. In his discussions of the reproduction schemes in Volume II of *Capital*, Marx set forth some conditions under which there would not be excessive savings in the system, conditions under which all savings are offset. He then showed that these conditions are very complex and that it is not reasonable to assume that they will always be met, hence the crisis. But he did not offer an exact theory to show the quantitative extent to which they will not be met. Keynes's theory also shows the conditions for full employment and argues that they will not always be met, but Keynes went one step further: He provided a general theory to determine the level of employment when it is not one of full employment. The Keynesian model shows how any level of employment is determined. Our procedure in this paper has been to introduce mathematical extensions of the Marxian theory to show how any level of income (or employment) is determined. In case the conditions for full employment — or for no glut of the market in Marx's sense — are not met, our mathematical model shows precisely what level of employment will ensue under the less-than-full-employment conditions.

It should be pointed out that the author has applied various methods of statistical estimation to the Marxian model and has found the estimated parameters to be very reasonable in size. Moreover, the model fits the observed data very closely. Except for small random error, workers and capitalists have, in fact, behaved as the Marxian model says they behave. Lags, government investment, taxes, etc., were introduced in the statistical models in order to depict the real world more exactly. A discussion of the statistical results is too lengthy to be included in this paper, and the conclusions are mentioned only to inform the reader that the model is not purely hypothetical.

IV. The stagnation thesis

It has become very popular of late to criticize the stagnation thesis severely and to assert that ours is still a young, vigorous, expanding economy. The critics have been quick to forget the lesson of the thirties and have misunderstood the thesis. Negative though most criticism has been, the spirit of this section is one of constructive criticism, by which some new ideas that support the thesis may be injected into the argument.

Despite the fact that the stagnation thesis grew out of the discussions of Keynesian economics of the past decade, the foundations of the theory are much older, going back to Marx's theory of the falling rate of profit. The critics would have had a much more difficult time finding evidence against a mature-economy doctrine based on the theory of the falling rate of profit than against the doctrine based on such factors as population growth, disappearance of the frontier, and growth of depreciation reserves. They were quick to point out that population growth slowed down and the frontier disappeared long before the decade of the thirties, yet stagnation did not then set in.

The Marxian theory states that, with a constant rate of surplus value (S/V), the rate of profit will vary inversely with capital accumulation. Equation (3.5) shows that the rate of profit is the product of "the rate of surplus value" and "one minus the organic composition of capital." Capital accumulation implies a rising organic composition of capital and, hence, a falling rate of profit from (3.5). The main hypothesis of this theory, the constancy of the rate of surplus value, is known to be valid, as shown by the available data. This theory can easily be applied to the interwar period. The application runs as follows: After World War I the profit outlook in manufacturing (especially automobile), utilities, and housing appeared to be good and persistent. Capitalists accumulated all during the twenties. They built so many plants and houses and so much equipment that the rate of return on the expanded volume began to fall. The rate of return on the greatly expanded capital structure was so small during the thirties that there was little capital investment and the system was depressed for a decade. It was the capital accumulation of the twenties which led to the fall in the rate of profit and the consequent stagnation of the thirties. The theory does not say that the stagnation or maturity is permanent. It is no contradiction of the theory to observe that housing capital, *relative to the population*, declined during World War II, thus generating a high rate of return on housing capital and a building boom again. Similarly, the present capital expansion in other industries is no contradiction of the theory. However, the theory indicates specifically that the capital expansion will not continue indefinitely. Once a large stock of capital has been accumulated again, the mature-economy doctrine should predict another stagnant period of a decade or more.

In the Marxian model, (3.24)–(3.29), it will be observed that the demand for investment goods depends upon two variables — profits and the stock of capital. The essence of the Marxian theory is that both variables must be in this relation. The dependence on profit is positive, and the dependence on capital is negative. The stock of capital becomes a very serious drag upon the system. Many of the present author's statistical investigations in separate industries, as well as for the economy as a whole, have shown that the stock of fixed capital is negatively related to investment. The more capital there is, other things unchanged, the less is the desire for new capital. The consequences of capital accumulation have never been fully explored. For example, if we drop the capital variable from the Marxian model or if we use the customary forms of the Keynesian model, the multiplier equation for the whole system usually takes the form:

$$Y + \alpha_1 Y_{-1} + \alpha_2 Y_{-2} + \ldots + \alpha_n Y_{-n} = \beta G, \qquad (4.1)$$

where Y = real income and G = real exogenous investment. If, on the other hand, the variable, Z_{-1} = stock of fixed capital, is introduced in the equation of demand for producer goods, the multiplier equation will have the form:

$$Y + \alpha_1 Y_{-1} + \alpha_2 Y_{-2} + \ldots + \alpha_n Y_{-n} = \beta_1 G + \beta_2 G_{-1}. \qquad (4.2)$$

The difference between (4.1) and (4.2) is significant. The values of β and β_1 will be positive, but if capital has a depressing influence on investment, the value of β_2 will be negative. Both the truncated and the untruncated multipliers from (4.2) will be smaller, the larger is the negative value of β_2. The depressing influence of capital accumulation operates not only partially in the demand equation for producer goods but also permeates the entire system with a depressing influence. The stimulative shocks given to the system by exogenous investment, such as new industries and government spending, will be cushioned by the depressing influence of capital accumulation.

The reason for introducing the stock of fixed capital in the investment-demand equation of the Marxian system is that in this form the equation fits in so well with the theory of the falling rate of profit. It is also possible to argue that an implied "theory of the declining marginal efficiency of capital" in the Keynesian theory would call for the introduction of a variable representing capital accumulation in the Keynesian investment schedule. In the past, economists have modified the Keynesian investment function in this way, but only for the long-run theory in which investment is zero. The real world, however, is not one of long-run equilibrium in which investment is zero or one of short-run equilibrium in which the stock of capital is taken as given. The real world falls between these extremes, and the Marxian model of this paper is a representation of the compromise.

V. Redistribution of income

No theory has received more vulgarizations than has the theory of the effect on employment of the redistribution of income. The correct results need to be systematized with all assumptions stated explicitly. For simplicity, we shall consider redistribution between only two types of income, wages and nonwages (= profits). One type of vulgarization is to look at wages only as a demand factor and not at wages as a cost factor. The argument is that a redistribution from profits into wages will always increase income and employment.

Many old-fashioned trade-unionists argue that the only way to cure a condition of unemployment is to redistribute income from profits into wages. They see faulty distribution as the principal flaw in the economic system and regard its correction as a sufficient policy to insure smooth working of the social mechanism. Many economists who call themselves Keynesians have also relied very heavily on redistribution of income as a powerful antidepression policy. They have often overemphasized the demand aspects of wages to the neglect of the cost aspects.

There is another group of economists who look at wages purely as a cost factor and neglect the influence of wages as a demand factor. Most of the supporters of wage cuts as a policy for curing depressions are in this category. They argue that, if wages are cut, capitalists will have lower costs and hence will be able to expand their plants. This argument is wrong not only because it is based on an incorrect analysis of redistribution but also because it does not take into account the possibility that falling wages may generate adverse expectations.

Obviously, the most proper type of model for analyzing the effects of redistribution is one that gives full effect to wages as a cost factor and to wages as a demand factor. The Marxian model is very well suited for this purpose. The consumption function distinguishes between wages and profits as separate demand factors, while the investment function — an equation of capitalist behavior alone — depends on profits, which means that wages enter as a cost factor. If our analysis is limited to the instantaneous effect on output of redistribution of income *within a given period*, we can neglect the influence of capital accumulation as a variable in the investment function. The term $\beta_2 Z_{-1}$, in (3.25), can be incorporated with the constant term because $\beta_2 Z_{-1}$ is predetermined and thus given for any single time period.

The following result can be stated for our model: If the capitalists' marginal propensity to spend (consume and invest) is greater than the workers' marginal propensity to consume, redistribution from profits into wages will decrease income. If the two marginal propensities are the same, income will be unaffected by the redistribution, and if the latter marginal propensity is greater than the former, redistribution from profits into wages will increase the level of income. It is by no means certain, a priori, which propensity is greater. Capitalists like to accumulate, and workers like to consume. Only by making accurate quantitative measurements of the propensities can the final result be determined. The author has found that some methods of statistical estimation give one result, and some methods give another. By any method of estimation used thus far, the confidence intervals for the parameters are so large that no definite conclusion can be drawn.

The intuitive explanation of the foregoing propositions is very simple. If a dollar is taken away from a capitalist, he will cut expenditures by the amount of his marginal propensity to spend, and, if this dollar is given to a worker, he will increase expenditures by the amount of his marginal propensity to consume. The quantitative effect on income depends on the extent to which these marginal propensities diverge. The data upon which the statistical models are based show that the marginal propensities are, at least, close together. If we take into account the capitalists' marginal propensity to spend on producer goods as well as the marginal propensity to spend on consumer goods, we find that the total marginal propensity to spend is probably between .7 and .9. The workers' marginal propensity to spend is also in the same neighborhood, between .8 and .9. In the discussion of redistribution, economists often tend to consider only the two groups' marginal propensities to consume, which are, of course, much farther apart.

There are special cases in which unequivocal results can be obtained. Marx has been interpreted as having claimed that the workers spend all their income, i.e., have a marginal propensity to consume equal to unity. If, as seems reasonable, the capitalists have a marginal propensity to spend which is less than unity, it follows by assumption that redistribution from profits into wages will always stimulate production. It can be shown that, for this case in the Marxian model, the increase in income is always greater than twice the amount redistributed. This is not a realistic case, however, because time-series and family-budget data both show that the marginal propensity to consume out of wages is not so great as unity. The budget data show little or no aggregate savings in the low-income classes, but some investigators have wrongly interpreted this to mean that the marginal propensity to consume is unity. The thing to look at is not the aggregate savings in the low-income groups but the slope of the savings or consumption function in this income range. The slope is definitely not unity throughout the range $0–$3,000 income per year. In this income range there are both dissaving and saving, which cancel each other to a large extent and make the total appear small. But the dissaving can always be more or less than the observed amount, and it is not correct to infer that the existence of dissaving means that low-income families consume exactly 100 per cent of every extra dollar of income that they receive.

Another special case in which the effects of redistribution can be more exactly assessed is that of exogenous investment. If it is believed that investment decisions of businessmen are unrelated to variables internal to the system — depending instead on innovations, psychological expectations, legislative decisions, etc. — the only relevant parameters for the redistribution problem are the marginal propensities to consume of workers and capitalists. The data show definitely that the marginal propensity to consume of the former class is greater than that of the latter class; therefore, within the framework of the model of exogenous investment, redistribution from profits into wages will always stimulate income.

There are also special models where redistribution from profits into wages certainly decreases income. For example, there is a tendency on the part of many model-builders to assume that total income (wages plus profits) is the relevant variable in the consumption function. This assumption gives equal weight to wages and profits on the side of demand for consumer goods. If, to this assumption, is added the assumption that investment expenditures depend on profits, the marginal propensity to spend out of profits will be greater than the marginal propensity to consume out of wages, and redistribution will have the above-stated effect.

There is nothing in the uncertainty of the conclusions of this section to contradict either the Marxian or Keynesian theoretical systems. This point must be made clear because many supporters of these theories make more extravagant claims about redistribution than can be justified on the grounds of the theories of employment alone, convincing though these claims may be from the point of view of economic welfare, equity, and justice.

In the Marxian theory, to state matters mildly, there is no hint that redistribution of income is a sufficient policy to insure that capitalism will always provide uninterrupted full production and employment. This is consistent with the findings that the marginal propensity to spend out of profits is not very different from the marginal propensity to spend out of wages, so that the redistribution effect is minimized. If the system is such that the latter marginal propensity exceeds the former, one must conclude that workers are kept so close to physical subsistence that they are forced to spend practically all their income. This is the situation which calls for redistribution from profits into wages as an employment-creating policy. If the former marginal propensity exceeds the latter, the Marxian explanation is that capitalism generates such fears and uncertainties about the future in the minds of the workers that they are forced to save for the "rainy day." Precautionary saving of this type is enough to drive their marginal propensity to consume below the marginal propensity to spend out of profits. Under such circumstances, redistribution from profits into wages which does not alleviate the fear of the future[24] will not create employment. In the Marxian theory, redistribution policies which do not alter the mode of production are not adequate to solve the problem of the occurrence of crises.

---

[24]Social security planning is a type of redistribution which does alleviate the fear of the future.

TWO

Keynesian Economics, the Classics, and the Keynesians

Theory of consumption

JAMES S. DUESENBERRY **5**

Income-consumption relations and their implications

Of all the new ideas introduced by Keynes in *The General Theory*, the concept of the "consumption function" was the easiest to accept. Few wished to deny that consumption expenditures are primarily determined by income; Keynes' arguments for the stability of the relationship were cogent enough to convince a great number of economists. The opportunities for empirical work opened up by the introduction of the new concept were at once apparent. Here, for once, was a theoretical relationship which involved magnitudes which could be measured not merely theoretically but practically. Econometricians went to work with a will and their efforts were amply rewarded. They were not only able to find a relationship between income and consumption, but they found that virtually all of the variation in consumer expenditures was explained by variations in income.

Yet, in spite of these empirical successes, the consumption function is a more controversial subject today than it was ten years ago. For empirical investigation has yielded not one consumption function but many, and each of them explains all the variations in consumption.

Like most economic magnitudes the literature on the consumption function seems to grow according to the compound-interest law. This would be easy to understand if the literature appeared as the result of the discovery

Reprinted from INCOME, EMPLOYMENT AND PUBLIC POLICY, Essays in Honor of Alvin H. Hansen. By permission of W. W. Norton & Company, Inc. Copyright 1948 by W. W. Norton & Company, Inc. Pp. 54–81. [Footnotes expanded — *Eds.*]

of new data. But no fundamental changes in our knowledge of the facts about income and consumption have occurred in the past five years.

Most of the articles on the consumption function present hypotheses about the relation between consumption, income, and some other variable such as time, the price level, or the degree of unemployment. The hypothesis is presented in the form of an equation which makes consumption a function of the other variables. The appropriate regression is fitted to the data, and the correlation between the observed and calculated values of consumption or saving is computed. The correlation is invariably high, and most writers seem to be satisfied that a high correlation coefficient provides an adequate test of their hypothesis. But a test which is passed by so many different hypotheses is not a very satisfactory one. Before any more consumption functions are introduced it seems desirable to give some consideration to our methods of testing hypotheses.

In Section I it is shown that aggregate hypotheses cannot be adequately tested by the use of correlation analysis. The general principles on which appropriate testing methods can be developed are then discussed. Section II is devoted to a consideration of the possibility that the relation between saving and income is different at different points of the trade cycle. A test based on the principles developed in Section I shows that we must reject the hypothesis that the saving-income relation is invariant with respect to measures of position in the trade cycle.

In Section III hypotheses which explain both cyclical and secular movements of savings are developed. It is shown that these hypotheses are consistent with: (1) the long-run data on income and consumption given by Kuznets, (2) the annual data on income and consumption in the period 1923–1940, (3) the budget study data collected in 1935–1936 and 1941. These hypotheses lead to the conclusion that aggregate saving out of disposable income can be estimated by the equation $\frac{s_t}{y_t} = .165 \frac{y_t}{y_0} - .066$, where s_t = current savings, y_t = current disposable income, y_0 = highest disposable income ever attained, with all variables corrected for population and price changes.[1]

I. Tests of aggregate hypothesis

When we deal with a problem in aggregate economics we usually seek for relationships which are, in some sense, invariant. By invariance we do not mean a historical invariance like the Pareto law. Rather, we mean that the relationship between a certain set of variables is unaffected by changes in

---

[1] Part of this paper was presented at the meeting of the Econometric Society in January, 1947. At the same meeting Prof. Franco Modigliani presented a paper containing an almost identical income-saving relation.

some other variables. The concept of an invariant relationship is therefore a relative one; a relation may be invariant with respect to one set of variables, but not with respect to some others. Indeed it might be said that hardly any economic relationship can be regarded as completely invariant. For no economic relation is likely to continue to hold good both before and after a fundamental change in social organization. In fact, one of the objects of economic policy is the modification of social organization in such a way as to produce relations of a desirable type among economic variables.

Our idea of invariance is somewhat as follows: We conceive that at any one moment certain variables within the control of households or firms are related in a definite way to certain other variables not within their control. For example, we suppose that the consumption expenditure of families depends on their income. The form of these relations is governed by the behavior characteristics of individuals and by institutional factors such as laws or customs. The relations we seek are invariant with respect to all variables except these psychological or institutional factors. A relation which satisfies that criterion may be said to be more or less stable according as these factors are more or less constant. We can make satisfactory predictions if we can find invariant relations of this type which are highly stable.[2]

If an invariant relation of this type holds for the variables associated with individual households or firms, then a corresponding invariant relation must hold among some functions (not necessarily sums) of all the household or firm variables of the same kind. If we can write $y_i = f_i(x_i)$ for every household (when x_i and y_i are variables applying to the ith household), then we can write $\emptyset(x_1, x_2 \ldots x_n, y_1, y_2, \ldots y_n) = O$. The invariance of the second relation will depend on the constancy of the behaviour characteristics

---

[2]Finding invariant relations of this sort actually helps in only one kind of policy problem. We may conceive of the "structure" of the economy as being described by a certain set of invariant relations. Then one kind of policy consists in fixing the values of certain of the variables which enter into these equations without otherwise disturbing any of the relations. Fixing an interest rate or tax rate is a policy of this sort. If we know all the invariant relations necessary to describe the structure, we can predict the effect of this sort of policy (at least in the sense that we can assign a probability to any values of any economic variable at each point in the future).

On the other hand, many of the most important policies involve changes in the structure. If a law is changed which has never been changed before, then we may know that certain structural equations will be changed, but we may not be able to foretell exactly what the new equations will be like. Or, to take a simple example, if the Treasury undertakes a campaign to get people to save more, it will be difficult to know what its effect will be. For this is an attempt to induce changes in behaviour patterns, and we have comparatively little experience with this kind of change. The kind of data with which economists deal is not likely to reveal anything about the possible effects of the Treasury's campaign. On the other hand, a sufficiently general theory of behaviour ought to make a prediction possible, but this would be entirely a question of social psychology.

As a matter of fact, it seems probable that most of the economic policies of really fundamental importance involve structural changes of this sort. To the extent that this is true, economists can be regarded as competent to judge the effect of these policies only by default on the part of the social psychologists.

and institutional elements which determine the invariance of the original relations, and in some cases on the constancy of the distribution of the x's. Aggregate relations which can be deduced from household or firm relations, I shall call fundamental aggregate relations. (There are of course some additional fundamental aggregate relations which are definitional and need not be deduced from anything.)

Now consider a pair of such fundamental aggregate relations:

$$\emptyset_1(x_1 \, x_2 \ldots x_n) = \psi_1(y_1 \, y_2 \ldots y_n) \tag{1}$$

$$\emptyset_2(x_1 \, x_2 \ldots x_n) = \psi_2(z_1 \, z_2 \ldots z_n) \tag{2}$$

where the x's are exogenous variables.

It is clear that a further relation (3) $x_1(y_1 \, y_2 \ldots y_n) = x_2(z_1 \, z_2 \ldots z_n)$ may be derived from the first two. Further, this relation will be invariant so long as (1) and (2) are invariant. This type of relation I shall call a derived aggregate relation.[3]

Now suppose that we observe the historical invariance of the relation (3) and conclude that it is a fundamental relation. We might then conclude that by changing the z's we could manipulate the y's. But we might find instead that we had merely invalidated the relation (2) without having any effect at all on the y's or x's. Derived relations like (3) may break down either as a consequence of policy changes or of structural changes in the economy. In addition there is an important class of derived relations which are likely to hold good only during the course of a single trade cycle. For example, a certain variable z may be partly dependent on the level of unemployment. Within the course of a single trade cycle, income is very closely associated with the level of unemployment. If we have data covering only a single trade cycle, we might conclude from the empirical evidence that z is determined by income. Actually we have a derived relation between z and income, which is bound to break up because the upward trend in income will ultimately change the association between income and unemployment. It is clear from these considerations that many of the relations observed empirically may be only derived relations which will break down because of a structural change in one of the fundamental relations on which they are based. This is particularly true of relations whose existence has been tested against the data of only a single trade cycle. Whether we are concerned with policy or with prediction, we shall often make errors if we treat derived relations as though they were fundamental ones. The difficulty of distinguishing between these two kinds of relations is one of the fundamental difficulties in testing economic hypotheses.

Let us now return to a consideration of the adequacy of correlation

[3]Cf. T. Haavelmo, "The Probability Approach to Econometrics," *Econometrica*, *Supplement*, [XII] July 1944 [1-115.]

methods of hypothesis testing. Suppose we have a hypothesis which asserts that total consumer expenditure is dependent on disposable income. We can fit a regression to the data for income and consumption and compute the correlation coefficient. When we find a significant correlation, what, exactly, have we found? We have not shown that the "data are consistent with the hypothesis." We have merely disproved the null hypothesis. That is, we have shown that the association between income and consumption was too strong to allow us to ascribe it to chance. Then we should be reasonably confident in asserting that we have found either (a) a fundamental relation between income and consumption, or (b) a derived relation between them. We might exploit our results a little further. If it could be shown that the lower confidence limit on the correlation was (say) .95, we could assert that during the period income was linearly related to all the variables fundamentally related to consumption. But this is about as far as we can safely go. It can be argued, of course, that a derived relation will tend to produce lower correlations than a fundamental relation. But, when our data cover only short periods, the connections between economic variables may be so close that the differences in correlations between the two sorts of relations may be too small to be statistically significant. Moreover, if the variables in a derived relation have a lower observational error than those in the fundamental relations, the correlation in the derived relation may be the higher one.

A very simple example of a derived relation is that which appears to have existed between consumer expenditures in dollars and disposable income in dollars during the period 1929–1940. Just as good a correlation is obtained by using undeflated as deflated data. This can be true only because the price level was related to income during the period. If real consumption is fundamentally related to real income, the money relationship is a derived one and will break down in the postwar period. Conversely, if money consumption is fundamentally related to money income the relation between the real variables is a derived one and will break down. Now it is obviously of vital importance to know which is the fundamental relation, but the correlation test is not very helpful.

The difficulties we have just been discussing arise because of the existence of derived relations among aggregate variables. But, ordinarily, such derived relations will not hold for individual firms or households. This suggests that in testing hypotheses we ought to operate on the following principles. First, every hypothesis ought to be stated in terms of the behaviour of individual firms or households, even when we are only interested in aggregate results. This does not, of course, prevent us from considering interactions among individuals, any more than the use of the theory of the firm in analysis of monopolistic competition prevents us from dealing with interactions among firms. Second, in so far as it is possible, we ought to test our hypotheses against data which indicate the behaviour of individual households or firms. This does not mean that we ought to abandon statistical procedures. Nearly every hypothesis has to allow for random elements in behaviour so that in making tests we have to measure the average behaviour of groups. But by dealing with relatively small groups we may escape the net of interrelations which makes it impossible to test aggregate hypotheses.

Suppose we are faced with the following situation: One hypothesis asserts that saving varies with income and the price level, another asserts that saving depends on income alone. Aggregate income and the price level are related in the period for which data are available. Then, if one of these hypotheses is true, it will be impossible to disprove the other by means of aggregate data alone. But, while movements of aggregate income may have been correlated with those of the price level, there are certainly some individuals whose incomes moved in a different way. By studying the behaviour of those individuals it will be possible to disprove one of the hypotheses. When this has been done the parameters in the chosen relation may be fitted. by the use of aggregate data (though in some cases this may still be difficult because of multicollinearity).

Of course it will not always be possible to find the data necessary to test every hypothesis. But there is a great deal of microeconomic data, which has never been properly exploited because of the tendency of econometricians to emphasize parameter fitting rather than hypothesis testing. Actually it is much more important to work with a true hypothesis than to make extremely precise estimates of parameters.

II. Changes in income and the rate of saving

In this section we shall apply the method just suggested to some questions about the consumption function. In the view of a number of writers, notably Smithies and Mosak,[4] consumer expenditures are essentially dependent on the prevailing level of disposable income. The effect on consumption of an increase in income is supposed to be the same whether the increase comes about through a rise of employment during recovery from a depression or through a rise in productivity in a period of sustained full employment like that of the twenties. Professor Hansen[5] and Professor Samuelson[6] have maintained for some time that the relation between income and consumption varies through the trade cycle. Mr. Woytinski[7] and Mr. Bean[8] have made similar statements and have tried to test them empirically. They

[4]"Forecasting Postwar Demand, I, III," *Econometrica*, [XIII] Jan. 1945, [pp. 1–14]

[5]*Business Cycles and Fiscal Policy* (New York: W. W. Norton & Company, 1941), pp. 225–249.

[6]"Full Employment after the War," in *Postwar Economic Problems*, edited by S. E. Harris (New York: McGraw Hill, 1943).

[7]"Relationship between Consumer's Expenditure, Savings and Disposable Income," *Review of Economic Statistics*, Jan. 1946, [pp. 1–12].

[8]"Relationship of Disposable Income and the Business Cycle to Expenditure," *Review of Economic Statistics*, [XXVIII] Nov. 1946, [pp. 199–207].

obtained correlations just as good as the others but no better, and certainly cannot claim to have disproved the alternative hypothesis. There is, however, some evidence which proves nearly conclusively that the consumption function is cyclically variable though not quite in the ways suggested by Bean or Woytinski.

This evidence is provided by the budget studies made in 1935–36[9] and 1941.[10] One of the remarkable results of the Study of Consumer Purchases of 1935–36 was that a great number of families reported expenditures in excess of income for the year. The average deficit of the under $500 a year group amounted to 50 per cent of income, while the average deficit of the $500–$1000 group was 10 per cent of income.[11] The results of the 1935–36 study are not above criticism, of course, but the fact that deficits were reported in every city and every area, together with the independent evidence of studies like those of Gilboy, Clague, and Powell, makes it clear that very substantial deficits did occur during the depression.[12]

The total deficits of urban and rural non-farm families (who were white and not on relief) alone amounted to 593 million dollars for 1935–36. Since total net savings of consumers during the twenties and thirties varied from $7.6 to $2.0 billion, an explanation of the deficits can contribute a good deal to our understanding of variations in saving.

But the real significance of the deficits does not lie in their magnitude but in what they reveal about the relations between income and saving. We shall first show that the deficits arose largely because families whose income fell in the depression tried to preserve their pre-depression living standards. Families in the higher income groups did the same thing but accomplished it by reducing their rate of saving rather than by dissaving. The analysis of the deficits is important chiefly because it helps us to analyze variations in the positive savings of higher income groups.

Let us first consider what kind of people were in the low income groups in 1935–36. While there is little direct information about the low income families in 1935–36, a rough estimate of their composition can be made from the data on income and employment in 1939 contained in the Census of 1940. Table 1 shows the result of this estimate.[13]

[9]Summarized by the National Resources Committee in *Consumer Expenditures in the United States*, Washington, 1938; *Consumer Incomes in the United States*, Washington, 1939; *Family Expenditures in the United States*, Washington, 1941.

[10]Bureau of Labor Statistics, Bulletins 723 and 724.

[11]*Family Expenditures in the United States, op. cit.*, p. 1.

[12]Elizabeth Gilboy, *Applicants for Work Relief* (Cambridge: Harvard University Press, 1940). E. Clague and W. Powell, *Ten Thousand Out of Work* (Philadelphia: University of Pennsylvania, 1933).

[13]This estimate was obtained by reconciling the data given by the National Resources Committee on numbers of families with incomes under $1000 in 1935–36 with the data in the Census of 1940 on the family wage and salary income and employment in 1939. See *Family Expenditures in the United States, op. cit.*, pp. 123, 127, 130; and Census of 1940, *The Labor Force (Sample Statistics)*, *Wage or Salary Income in 1939* and *Family Wage or Salary Income in 1939*.

Table 1

White urban and rural non-farm families
with incomes under $1000 in 1935–36

	RELIEF	NON-RELIEF
Retired	600,000	600,000
Independent business and professional	100,000	600,000
Partially or fully unemployed	2,100,000	1,900,000
Fully employed	—	2,400,000
Total	2,800,000	5,500,000

In the nature of the case this estimate can be only a rough one since it has to be based on a number of unverified assumptions. Yet there does not seem to be much doubt that the non-relief low-income families included a high proportion of families whose incomes were low because of unemployment and whose incomes were much higher in periods of full employment. Moreover, some of the families in the independent business and professional group would have higher incomes in more prosperous periods. Finally, some of the fully employed wage and salary workers were downgraded from higher wage jobs so that their normal incomes were higher than the incomes reported in 1935–36.

1. Keeping these considerations in mind, let us now ask what is the significance of the deficits for the theory of saving. A supporter of the view that saving depends on real income would say, presumably, that $c/y = f(y)$ and that c/y exceeds 1 for some positive value of y (where y is in constant prices). When that value of y is reached, those who have assets or credit will have deficits; the others will have to be content with spending all of their income.

In its simple form this position is untenable, for the break-even point (the income at which consumption just equals income) stood at about $800 in 1917 and $1500 in 1935–36, using 1941 prices in both cases.[14] If consumption were merely a function of current income the break-even level of income should have remained the same. To this the sophisticated Keynesian will reply by introducing a trend factor. Consumption at a given level of income can be changed by the introduction of new goods (this is about the only factor likely to cause a trend in the consumption of urban families, and these are the families included in the budget studies in question). For the sake of the argument let us agree that introduction of new goods in itself increases consumption at a given level of income. We know too that families in the low income groups were driving automobiles and using various recently

---

[14]See G. Cornfield, W. D. Evans, and M. Hoffenberg, "Full Employment Patterns in 1950, Part I," *Monthly Labor Review*, [LXX] Feb. 1947, p. 181.

introduced household appliances. This does not advance the argument much, however, for the families in question were for the most part using these things rather than buying them. We can turn to other new goods, movies and silk stockings (say), which were also consumed by the low-income groups in the thirties. Let us grant that a family with an $800 income did not buy these things in 1917 and did in 1935. Then it follows that at least part of the deficits in the thirties were due to the fact that low income families bought new goods which did not exist in the earlier period. But this is not the whole story. We can say on the one hand that families at an $800 income level in the thirties spent more than families with that income in 1917 because they had become used to a high standard of living (including silk stockings and movies) in the twenties and found it difficult to give up. Or we can say that even if income had remained constant from 1917 to 1935 the attraction of these new goods was so irresistible that they incurred deficits to get them (or at least that they would have done so if they had had the necessary assets or credit). The latter position seems to be a somewhat untenable one. But, if we argue that consumption depends on current real income and trend, that is the position which must be maintained in order to explain the facts. For, if we write $c/y = f(y,t)$, nothing has been said about the influence of past living standards on current consumption.

This does not disprove the proposition that consumption at a given moment is dependent on real income alone; but it does require the supporters of that proposition to subscribe to some very strong propositions about the influence of new products and similar trend factors.

2. We can make a further test if we compare the deficits reported in 1935–36 with those reported in 1941. Deficits at given levels of income were much smaller in 1941 than in 1935–36. At every level deficits were less than one half as great in 1941 as in 1935–36. How is this shift to be explained? Suppose the deficits, in both cases, were due to the fact that families whose incomes had fallen as a result of unemployment found it hard to reduce their living standards. Then the explanation is easy. The low income group consists primarily of two subgroups: families whose earners are normally fully employed at low wages, and families whose incomes have been reduced by unemployment. The second group will run deficits to protect the high living standard attained when they were fully employed. The first group balances its budget. Suppose now that we have complete data on families in the $1000 income group in two periods. Suppose that the situation is as follows:

	NUMBER	DEFICIT
Fully employed families (with normal incomes)	5000	0
Partially employed families	5000	$300
Average		$150

Suppose that in a second period we obtain reports from the same group but that half of the families in the $1000 group have increased their incomes. The situation in the $1000 group now is as follows:

	NUMBER	DEFICIT
Fully employed families	5000	0
Partially employed families	2500	$300
Average		$100

Now suppose that instead of subdividing the families in this way our report had shown only the average deficit of the $1000 income families. We would have observed a reduction in the average deficit from $150 to $100 per family without knowing why. The differences in the 1935–36 and 1941 studies seem to correspond very clearly to the examples just given. In 1935–36 there were about 8 million unemployed, in 1941 there were only 3 million. In 1935–36 a much higher proportion of families in the low income groups were there because of unemployment than in 1941. If, therefore, we accept the proposition that the deficits were due to unemployment, or to incomes low by comparison with previous ones, the difference between the two studies is easily explained.

If we try to support the view that consumption depends on absolute income, how shall we explain the difference? The trend explanation cannot be used in this case. For the break-even point moves in the wrong direction.

We can suppose that the families left in the low income groups would like to have run deficits but were unable to do so because they lacked the necessary assets or credit. But we have argued that a higher proportion of the low income group in 1941 were permanent members of that group than in 1935–36. It follows that the higher deficits in 1935–36 must have been incurred by the group whose incomes had fallen. For those permanently in the low income group were in more or less the same position in both years. Then we have to explain the differences in the reactions of the two groups. There are three possible explanations. (1) The families with temporarily low incomes were technically in a better position to have deficits. That is, they were not more willing to run deficits, but more able to get the resources to do so. (2) The families with temporarily low incomes had expectations of reëmployment and higher income in the future. (3) These families had had higher living standards in the past and were therefore more willing to have deficits to protect their living standards.

If either of the last two factors is influential, then consumption must depend on past income (since this governs the expected level of income at full employment) as well as on current income. In this case a general rise in income to levels above the 1929 peak followed by a fall would bring about a recurrence of the deficits, for the standard of living and expectations of income would be based on the new peak. If income declined from this peak by the same percentage as 1935 income had declined from the 1929 peak, deficits of a relative magnitude as large as those of 1935 would occur. This would be true even if the absolute level of income were as high as the 1929 level. On the other hand if the break-even point is independent of past levels of income no deficits would occur unless income were absolutely low.

The budget study data do not tell us anything directly about which of the three factors just mentioned are actually relevant. We must leave the question open for the moment. However, it should be noted that the hypothesis that consumption depends on past as well as on current income is consistent with all the data discussed so far. The alternative hypothesis that consumption depends only on current income can be made consistent with the data only if we are willing to accept some rather doubtful subsidiary propositions.

3. One further piece of evidence is available for testing these two hypotheses. The 1941 budget study reported income for the first quarter of 1942 as well as for 1941. Families at each income level were classified by the changes in their income. Savings for the first quarter of 1942 were separately reported for those whose incomes had changed less than 5 per cent, for those whose incomes had increased more than 5 per cent, and those whose incomes had decreased more than 5 per cent from the 1941 level. The results are shown in Table 2. Families whose incomes rose had about the same savings or deficits as those whose incomes stayed the same.

Table 2

Average yearly savings in 1942 for city families by income change from 1941 to 1942

	CONSUMERS WHOSE INCOMES IN 1942		
MONEY INCOME CLASS IN 1942	DECREASED OVER 5 PER CENT	CHANGED LESS THAN 5 PER CENT	INCREASED OVER 5 PER CENT
0 to $1000	−337	−35	−15
$1000 to $1500	−181	−34	62
$1500 to $2000	− 81	126	157
$2000 to $3000	0	242	290
$3000 and over	143	1228	1059

Annual rate for 1942 based on first quarter.
Based on B.L.S. Bulletin 724.

On the other hand, families whose incomes fell had much smaller savings or larger deficits than those whose incomes stayed constant. Now these facts can be interpreted in two ways. On the one hand we can say that they show that a rate of change factor is important in the determination of saving. That is, we write $c/y = f(y,y')$ where y' is the rate of change of income. On the other hand we can say that saving is low when income is low relative to past income. The two explanations are not the same. In a year when income is declining, either explanation would lead to the same result. But suppose that income declines and then remains at a (more or less constant) low level. After the decline has stopped, the rate of change is zero but income is still low relative to its pre-depression level.

It is fairly easy to tell which of the two hypotheses is correct. If the rate of change of income is an important factor it should show up in regressions of aggregate data. But it is well known that when the equation $c = f(y,t,y')$ is fitted to aggregate data for the twenties and thirties the addition of the factor y' contributes very little to the correlation. In the face of the budget study data this is difficult to explain unless we accept relative income instead of rate of change as the explanation of the differences in saving at the same level of income.

The asymmetry in the results is also important. If we take the view that rate of change of income is a determinant of saving, then there are strong reasons for supposing that the adjustment lag works in both directions. On the other hand, if we argue that people whose incomes are low relative to their past incomes reduce saving to protect their living standard, the asymmetry is easy to understand. Those whose incomes rose were for the most part getting back to levels of incomes which they had previously experienced. In these circumstances they merely returned to the expenditure patterns of the past and no adjustment lag is involved.

The data just discussed seem to show fairly conclusively that consumption at a given level of income does depend on past income. This hypothesis is consistent with the existence of deficits in 1935–36 and 1941, with the changes in deficits (at given levels of income) from 1935–36 to 1941, with the upward movement of the break-even point from 1917 to 1935–36 and 1941, and with the differences in saving among families whose incomes had changed in different ways. It is difficult to explain all of these facts on any other hypothesis.

Psychological foundation

So far our argument has been a strictly empirical one. But it must be clear that it also has a strong psychological foundation. The fundamental psychological postulate underlying our argument is that it is harder for a family to reduce its expenditures from a high level than for a family to refrain from making high expenditures in the first place. Consider two families who have incomes of $1000 per year at a particular time. Now suppose one of these families has an income of $1000 per year for ten years thereafter. Suppose the other family gets an increase in income from $1000 to $1500, retains this position for nine years, and then has its income reduced to $1000 so that in the last year it is in the same position as the other family. Initially both families might have exactly balanced their budgets at $1000, and the first family might continue in this way for the whole ten-year period. But when the second family had its income increased it would increase its consumption by (say) $400 and its saving by $100. When the reduction in income occurred it would certainly find it difficult to cut its consumption to the $1000 level. The first family had only to refrain from increasing its consumption expenditures to balance its budget. The second family had actually to give up consumption of $400 per year to achieve the same result. It would be surprising if a family in these circumstances succeeded in reducing its consumption sufficiently to balance its budget after the loss in income.

Since all of the data are consistent with the view that this does happen, there does not seem to be much doubt that past income has an influence on current consumption and saving.

The argument so far has been devoted to explaining the deficits reported in the budget studies. But the significant result of this argument is not the conclusion that deficits will occur when income falls below previously attained levels but the more general proposition that families are willing to sacrifice saving in order to protect their living standard. This proposition applies to all income groups who have suffered losses in income. We can argue in the following way. If a family has a certain income y_o and this income is higher than any previously attained, it will save some amount. This amount will be a function of income $s_o = f(y_o)$. If its income increases the same function will hold. But if after an increase income falls to the original level its saving will be less than $f(y_o)$. If the family's income and saving are low throughout, it will have a deficit after the fall in income. If the family is in a higher bracket it will simply save less after the fall in income than it did before the increase. This view is checked by the fact that savings in the last five years of the twenties averaged 10.2 per cent of disposable income while from 1936 to 1940 they averaged only 9.0 per cent. Real disposable income per capita was almost the same in the two periods.

A base year for downward adjustments of consumption

We have now shown that consumption is dependent on current income relative to past income as well as on the absolute level of current income. The problem now is to find just which past incomes are relevant. In view of the argument just given we appear to be safe in supposing that past incomes lower than the current one are not very relevant. This is pretty well demonstrated by the 1941–42 budget figures cited above. Families whose incomes rose to a given level saved about the same amount as those whose incomes had been at that level in the previous year. At first glance then it would seem reasonable to suppose that current consumption depends on the ratio of current income to some weighted average of past higher incomes, with weights decreasing as the time interval involved grows longer. There are, however, some fairly strong arguments against this position. The declines in income which occur in the depression are not uniformly distributed even though the size distribution of income remains more or less unchanged.

Income losses will be of three kinds: (1) reductions in property incomes, (2) reductions in wage rates, (3) losses due to underemployment. Since real wage rates did not decline very much in the depression (and were even higher in the late years of the depression than in the twenties), losses of income are mostly of types (1) and (3). (A fourth class results from downgrading of workers either within or between industries, but for our purposes this can be regarded as underemployment.)

Let us first consider the effect of losses of income in the upper income groups. It is not important here whether the losses are due to reductions in property incomes or to salary reductions. It can be assumed, however, that unemployment among the upper income groups is not important. The upper 10 per cent of the income distribution produces almost all of the positive saving for the whole economy. Moreover, families in this group save a high proportion of their income. This means that they have a good deal of leeway in maintaining consumption standards without running into deficits; also they have more free (non-contractual) saving. When high income families suffer a loss in income, therefore, they continue to live in the same kind of neighborhoods and maintain their contacts with others of the same socio-economic status. In general they maintain the way of life which was established before the onset of the depression. They will, of course, cut expenditures on some lines, particularly on durable goods. But in view of the high rate of savings maintained in prosperity they can absorb a considerable reduction of income by reducing saving without cutting consumption too deeply. Moreover, there is no reason why they should not continue in this position for several years. Suppose now that income falls sharply from a cyclical peak and then remains constant for several years. The peak year's consumption sets the standard from which cuts are made (provided the peak did not represent a mere spurt in income). The higher the peak consumption, the more difficult it will be to reduce consumption to any given level. After the initial reductions are made the situation becomes static. The peak year does not lose its influence because the consumption of the following years depends on the peak consumption. Of course, if income began to fall again further consumption cuts would take place, and the intermediate level of income would be important in determining the extent of the cuts as well as the previous peak income. But if the depression consists in a fall of income lasting only a couple of years followed by a rise or a low plateau, the consumption of the peak year is likely to have very heavy weight in determining consumption in the depression. The influence of the peak consumption will not "fade away" unless income continues to fall steadily.

All of the above argument applies only to the upper income groups. Those who were in the lower 90 per cent of the distribution in prosperity are in a different situation. For this group, reductions in individual income are usually associated with unemployment. These people probably save very little even in prosperous times. In a depression they can only influence saving by having deficits. A considerable number of families in this group go nearly unscathed by the depression. Their real wages do not fall and they never have serious losses of employment. These we may leave out of account since their savings are simply zero throughout. The remaining families suffer serious loss of employment at some point during the depression. These may also be divided into two groups. Some will remain employed up to a certain point, then lose their jobs and never get steady employment again until a high level of prosperity is reached. These families will presumably run substantial deficits immediately after they become unemployed, but as their assets become smaller they will have to adjust to the new situation and presumably balance budgets in which relief is the principal source of income. They may continue to have deficits for a long time, but in any case the influence of the prosperity living standard will certainly "fade away" as time passes. However, it should be noted that not all of the persons who will eventually constitute the "hard core" of unemployment get there at once. The result is that a certain number of families are going through the initial stages of long-term unemployment at any time during the depression. Presumably, however, there are rather more families in this position during the downturn in the early years than later on. We should expect, therefore, to find somewhat greater deficits and lower aggregate savings at a given income in the downturn than in the upturn. However, the total number of families in this group was not very large in the thirties, and the differences in the numbers entering cannot have been great enough to cause numerically important reductions in aggregate savings.

The remainder of the unemployment is widely spread so that a large number of workers "take turns" being unemployed. Families lose income through unemployment and accordingly cut consumption; they also run a deficit. When they get reëmployed they may return to something very close to the prosperity consumption standard. Sometime later unemployment may reoccur and the process repeats. Those families who are very frequently in and out of employment will presumably gradually reduce consumption (even when employed) because of the decrease in their assets and the accumulation of debt. The influence of the peak standard will therefore gradually lose its effect. But a great part of the total unemployment can be accounted for by families who have only one or two stretches of prolonged unemployment during the depression. For these families the influence of the peak consumption standard will not fade away because it renews itself with each stretch of full employment.

We can conclude then that the income or consumption of the last cyclical peak will carry a special and very heavy weight in determining consumption at a given (lower) level of income during a depression. In principle a weighted average of all the incomes from the peak year to the current year ought to be used. But with only a few observations it would be impossible to estimate the weights. In what follows we shall consider the relation of current consumption to the ratio $\dfrac{\text{current income}}{\text{highest previously attained income}}$ but the results are to be taken as an approximation to the true relation.

If the argument just given is correct, then there is a cyclical component in the explanation of saving. Savings at a given level of income, when income is the highest ever attained, as in the late twenties, will be higher than savings at a similar income level reached in a decline from a still higher level. I conclude, therefore, that in a general way at least the propositions of those who have argued that saving varies with the trade cycle as well as with income are supported by the evidence of the budget studies.

III. Aggregate income-saving relationships

So far it has been shown that saving depends on the level of current incomes relative to higher incomes in previous years. But saving also depends on the absolute level of income. We may write then, $s_t = f(y_t, y_t/y_o)$ where y_o is the highest income attained previous to the year t. Then

$$\frac{ds_t}{dy_t} = \frac{df}{dy_t} + \frac{df}{d\frac{(y_t)}{y_o}} \cdot \frac{d(y_t/y_o)}{dy_t}$$

If we plot out the long period relation of saving and income considering only periods of approximately full employment, the term $\dfrac{dy_t/y_o}{dy_t}$ will be 0 so that $ds_t/dy_t = df/dy_t$. But, with data covering a trade cycle, $\dfrac{dy_t/y_o}{dy_t}$ will have a positive value, and, if we use cyclical data to estimate the secular marginal propensity to consume, our estimates will be too high.

If data covering a number of cycles were available, we could take the regression of saving on y_t/y_o and y_t and estimate simultaneously the secular and cyclical components in saving. Unfortunately the period 1923–1940 covers only one major cycle, so that we are forced to estimate the influence of the two factors separately. First, it should be noted that there are strong grounds for supposing that (in the absence of cyclical fluctuations) aggregate saving remains a constant proportion of aggregate income.

This position can be best understood by a consideration of the apparent contradictions in the relations between saving and income. On the one hand, we have the Keynesian dictum that "apart from short period changes in the level of income, it is also obvious that a higher absolute income will tend to widen the gap between income and consumption. For the satisfaction of the immediate primary needs of a man and his family is usually a stronger motive than the motives toward accumulation, which only acquire effective sway after a margin of comfort has been attained. These reasons will lead as a rule to a greater proportion of income being saved as income increases."[15] This argument which, at first glance at any rate, appears very plausible, has had wide acceptance. Moreover, it seems to be supported by important empirical evidence. Every budget study supports the view that families with high incomes save a greater proportion of income than those with low incomes. It is also known that, in the period 1923–1940, saving fluctuated more than in proportion to income. On the other hand, the data given by Kuznets indicate that aggregate saving has been an approximately constant proportion of income for a long time.[16]

From a psychological viewpoint, Keynes' argument about the relative importance of saving and accumulation at different income levels does not throw much light on the situation to which it is supposed to apply. It is no doubt true that a family will not save when its income is so low that it cannot satisfy its immediate primary needs. But in the United States, at least, the problem of getting an income high enough to maintain physical existence has hardly existed (for families whose workers are employed) for many years. The problem is not one of saving vs. consuming enough to maintain existence. It is one of choosing between an immediate comfort and security. Any psychological theory of saving must give an explanation of the resolution of the conflict between the desire for security and the desire for comfort. When the problem is put in this way the conclusion that saving rises more than in proportion to income is not at all obvious. Moreover, in view of the paucity and ambiguity of the empirical evidence a psychological basis is necessary if an adequate theory of saving is to be constructed.

Such a theory already exists in the form of marginal utility and "indifference map" analysis, but it is hardly adequate for our purposes. The whole structure of preference analysis is based on the assumption that one individual's preferences are independent of the actual consumption patterns of another individual's. It is this assumption which permits us to add up the demand functions of individuals to get a market-demand function.

[15]J. M. Keynes, *The General Theory of Employment, Interest, and Money* (New York: Harcourt, Brace and Co., 1936), p. 97.

[16]Simon Kuznets, *Uses of National Income in Peace and War* (New York: National Bureau of Economic Research, 1942), p. 30.

Yet consumption preferences can hardly be regarded as innate characteristics of individuals. Nor can they be regarded, in a society as dynamic as ours, as being determined by tradition. There is a great deal of evidence to show that consumer tastes are socially determined. This does not mean that consumer tastes are governed by considerations of conspicuous consumption. Rather, it means that any individual's desire to increase his expenditure is governed by the extent to which the goods consumed by others are demonstrably superior to the ones which he consumes. If we can assume that the degree of superiority of one set of goods over another is highly correlated with the relative costs of obtaining these goods, we are led to the following proposition. The strength of any individual's desire to increase his consumption expenditure is a function of the ratio of his expenditure to some weighted average of the expenditures of others with whom he comes in contact. The weights are determined by the social character of these contacts. If the distribution of income is constant (in the Lorenz curve sense) this weighted average can be regarded as a function of an individual's percentile position in the income distribution. The proportion of income saved is set by balancing the desire to increase current consumption against the desire to increase assets relative to current consumption (that is, to have a greater assurance of continued maintenance of the existing standard). We may therefore conclude that if the strength of the desire to increase consumption is a function of percentile position in the income distribution, the proportion of income saved will be a function of the same variable. It is also easy to see that it will be a rising function.[17]

This hypothesis leads to the following conclusions:

(a) At any one moment the proportion of income saved will be higher for the higher income groups than for low income groups.
(b) If income increases, while the proportional distribution remains constant, the ratio of aggregate saving to aggregate income will be constant.

Both of these conclusions are in accord with known facts.

If we accept the hypothesis just given, then secularly consumer saving will be a constant proportion of disposable income.

This hypothesis, together with the cyclical relation, considered in Section II, should give a complete explanation of variations in saving.

If the secular relation between savings and income makes for a constant income-saving ratio, the *proportion* of income saved will depend only on cyclical factors.[18] Then we may write $s_t/y_t = F(y_t/y_o)$. There is not much

---

[17]In a paper of this length it is impossible to go too deeply into the theory of consumer behaviour underlying the above propositions. This theory together with some empirical tests of its adequacy will be developed more fully in a forthcoming paper.

[18]If we accept the proposition that the high marginal propensity to consume indicated by linear income consumption relationships is largely due to cyclical factors, there is no *evidence* of the existence of any powerful trend in consumption. Various factors which might have caused either an upward or a downward trend can be cited. But when we have a hypothesis which explains all the data there is no point in introducing a trend unless some evidence of its operation can be given.

basis for selecting any particular functional form for $F(y_t/y_o)$. However, a linear approximation, which fits the data well, is always satisfactory, provided that we do not have to make predictions involving values of the variable outside the range of the data used in fitting the approximation. In the period 1923–1940 values of y_t/y_o ranged from about 1.1 to .5. It seems unlikely that income will ever decline to less than 50 per cent of full employment levels, so that we can be safe in using a linear form for $F(y_t/y_o)$ for prediction. When the relation $\dfrac{s_t}{y_t} = a\dfrac{y_t}{y_o} + b$ is fitted to the data for the period 1923–1940, we obtain a = .165, b = .066.[19] The correlation is .9, which is as good as that usually obtained for relations between savings and income.

However, the correlation is not the test of the adequacy of the relation. The test is based on the fact that the secular average propensity to consume is predicted by the relation just given. In a period when income is slowly rising with only minor cyclical fluctuations, each year's income should be slightly above that of the preceding year. y_t/y_o should be about 1.02 in each year. If we put $y_t/y_o = 1.02$ in the relation $\dfrac{s_t}{y_t} = .165\dfrac{y_t}{y_o} - .066$ we obtain $s_t/y_t = .102$ which is very close to Kuznets' estimate of the (stable) savings ratio in the period 1879–1919. Since the regression was based on the period 1923–1940 we may say that the regression "predicted" the Kuznets' results.

All three major sources of data about income and consumption are consistent with the two hypotheses, (1) that secularly an individual's propensity to consume is a function of his position in the income distribution (which implies that aggregate saving tends in the long run to be a constant proportion of income) and (2) that, cyclically, the aggregate propensity to consume depends on the ratio of current income to the highest income previously achieved. They are also consistent with the internal evidence of the budget studies and with the results of intertemporal comparisons of budget studies. So far as I am aware there are no data about saving and income which are inconsistent with these hypotheses.

There is, however, another important class of hypotheses which has not been considered here. These are the hypotheses which introduce variables other than income into the consumption function. In particular it has been suggested that saving may vary with the price level (when the price level is considered as a separate variable and not as a mere deflator) and with the value of assets. There is, of course, no real conflict between these hypotheses and the ones presented here. The two variables just mentioned are highly correlated with income, so that it is quite possible that they may be important contributors to the variance of saving, even though a high correlation

---

[19]The data used are those given by E. G. Bennion, "The Consumption Function Cyclically Variable," *Review of Economic Statistics*, [XXVIII] Nov. 1946, [pp. 219–224]. Disposable income and savings are both corrected for price and population changes.

can be obtained without considering them. These hypotheses will have to be tested by methods similar to those used in Section II of this paper.

The implications of the hypotheses developed here are fairly obvious. We may expect that, when the transition period is completed, consumer savings will fall to around 10 per cent of disposable income. This may be compared with the estimate of 14 per cent given by Smithies for consumer savings out of a disposable income of 158.2 billion dollars in 1943 prices.[20] The volume of offsets to savings required to maintain full employment is therefore considerably smaller than would be expected from estimates based on simple income-consumption regressions.

The relation $\dfrac{s_t}{y_t} = .166\dfrac{y_t}{y_0} - .066$ has the property that the marginal propensity to save out of disposable income is fairly high with respect to cyclical movements of income, but the average propensity to save is much lower and does not tend to rise with secular increases in income. During the trough of a cycle (from the time income falls below the peak value for one cycle until it rises above that value in the next cycle) y_t/y_0 is dependent entirely on y_t (since y_0 is constant). We have then $s_t = \dfrac{.166}{y_0} y_t{}^2 - .066y_t$;

then $\dfrac{ds_t}{dy_t} = .332\dfrac{y_t}{y_0} - .066$. The marginal propensity to save with respect to decreases in income is therefore about .26 at the peak of a cycle. As income declines ds_t/dy_t falls until it reaches zero at an income equal to one-fifth that of the last cyclical peak.

On the other hand, the average propensity to save does not rise as income rises secularly. For in the upswing of a cycle after full employment is reached, y_0 and y_t move together. If income increases steadily at an annual rate of 3 per cent, y_t/y_0 is constant at a value of 1.03. The long-run savings function is therefore $s_t = .166(1.03)y_t - .066y_t$ or simply $s_t = .102y_t$. Thus the cyclical marginal propensity to save is (in the relevant range) higher than the long-run propensity to save, and the use of cyclical data to estimate the long-period relationship leads to invalid conclusions.

[20]*Vide* A. Smithies, "Forecasting Postwar Demand," *Econometrica*, [XIII] Jan. 1945 [pp. 1–14].

FRANCO MODIGLIANI[2]
RICHARD BRUMBERG

6

Utility analysis and the consumption function: an interpretation of cross-section data[1]

Introduction

Of John Maynard Keynes' many hypotheses, the one that has been subject to the most intensive empirical study is the relation between income and consumption. By now, his generalization is familiar to all:

> The fundamental psychological law, upon which we are entitled to depend with great confidence both *a priori* from our knowledge of human nature and from the detailed facts of experience, is that men are disposed, as a rule and on the average, to increase their consumption as their income increases, but not by as much as the increase in their income.[3]

Reprinted from Kenneth K. Kurihara (ed.), *Post-Keynesian Economics* (New Brunswick: Rutgers University Press, 1954), pp. 388–436, by permission of the publisher. [Footnotes expanded — *Eds.*]

[1]We are indebted to several colleagues, and especially to Messrs. R. Cyert, of Carnegie Institute of Technology, and C. Christ, of the Johns Hopkins University, for reading the manuscript and making valuable suggestions.

[2]My contribution to this paper is a direct outgrowth of the research carried out as director of the project on "Expectations and Business Fluctuations" financed by a grant of the Merrill Foundation for the Advancement of Financial Knowledge. I should particularly like to call attention to the relation between consumption, assets, income expectations, and the life cycle of income as developed in this paper and the relation between production, inventories, sales expectations, and the seasonal cycle of sales as developed in my joint paper with O. H. Sauerlender, "The Use of Expectations and Plans of Firms for Short Term Forecasting," *Studies in Income and Wealth*, Vol. XVII [Princeton: Princeton University Press, 1955].

[3]John Maynard Keynes, *The General Theory of Employment, Interest, and Money*, ([New York: Harcourt, Brace & Co.,] 1936), p. 96.

The study of the consumption function has undoubtedly yielded some of the highest correlations as well as some of the most embarrassing forecasts in the history of economics. Yet the interest in the subject continues unabated since, if it were possible to establish the existence of a stable relation between consumption, income, and other relevant variables and to estimate its parameters, such a relation would represent an invaluable tool for economic policy and forecasting.

The work done in this area during the last few years has taken two directions.[4] One has consisted in extensive correlations of data on aggregate consumption, or saving, with income and a large collection of additional miscellaneous variables. The second direction has been the exploitation of cross-section data. Old material has been reworked and new information collected. The most elaborate of the new studies have been those of the Survey Research Center of the University of Michigan. As in the time series analysis, more and more variables have been included, or are proposed for inclusion, in order to discover stable relations.[5]

By now the amount of empirical facts that has been collected is truly impressive; if anything, we seem to be in imminent danger of being smothered under them. What is, however, still conspicuously missing is a general analytical framework which will link together these facts, reconcile the apparent contradictions, and provide a satisfactory bridge between cross-sectional findings and the findings of aggregative time series analysis.

It is our purpose to attempt to provide such an analytical framework through the use of the well-developed tools of marginal utility analysis. We have shown elsewhere[6] that the application of this instrument proves of great help in integrating and reconciling most of the known findings of aggregative time series analysis. In this paper, we shall attempt to show how the same model of individual behavior can be applied to the analysis of cross-section data. We hope to demonstrate that this model provides a consistent, if somewhat novel, interpretation of the existing data and suggests promising directions for further empirical work.

[4]For two excellent bibliographies in this field, see: G. H. Orcutt and A. D. Roy, "A Bibliography of the Consumption Function," University of Cambridge, Department of Applied Economics, mimeographed release, 1949; and *Bibliography on Income and Wealth, 1937–1947*, edited by Daniel Creamer, International Association for Research in Income and Wealth, 1952.

[5]For example, see Lawrence R. Klein, "Savings Concepts and Their Relation to Economic Policy: The Viewpoint of a User of Savings Statistics," paper delivered at the Conference on Savings, Inflation, and Economic Progress, University of Minnesota, 1952.

[6]Franco Modigliani and Richard Brumberg, "Utility Analysis and Aggregate Consumption Functions: An Attempt at Integration," a forthcoming study.

I. Theoretical foundations

I.1 Utility analysis and the motives for saving

Our starting point will be the accepted theory of consumer's choice. The implications of this theory have been so incompletely recognized in the empirically-oriented literature of recent years, that it will be useful to retrace briefly the received doctrine.[7]

Consider the following variables:

c_t consumption of the individual during the t-th year (or other specified interval) of his life, where t is measured from the beginning of the earning span;

y_t income (other than interest) in the t-th year (for an individual of age t, y_t and c_t denote current income and consumption, while y_τ and c_τ, for $\tau > t$, denote expected income and planned consumption in the τ-th year):

s_t saving in the t-th year;

a_t assets at beginning of age period t;

r the rate of interest;

N the earning span;

M the retirement span; and

L the life span of economic significance in this context, that is, $N + M$

It is assumed that the individual receives utility only from present and prospective consumption and from assets to be bequeathed. If we assume further that the price level of consumables is not expected to change appreciably over the balance of the life span, so that the volume of consumption is uniquely related to its value, then for an individual of age t, the utility function can be written as

$$U = U(c_t, c_{t+1}, \cdots c_L, a_{L+1}). \tag{1.1}$$

This function is to be maximized subject to the budget constraint, which, if the rate of interest, r, is not expected to change appreciably over the balance of the life span, can be expressed by means of the equation

$$a_t + \sum_{\tau=t}^{N} \frac{y_\tau}{(1+r)^{\tau+1-t}} = \frac{a_{L+1}}{(1+r)^{L+1-t}} + \sum_{\tau=t}^{L} \frac{c_\tau}{(1+r)^{\tau+1-t}}. \tag{1.2}$$

[7]For an extensive application of marginal utility analysis to the theory of saving see the valuable contributions of Umberto Ricci, dating almost thirty years back: "L'offerta del Risparmio," Part I, *Giornale degli Economisti*, Feb. 1926, pp. 73–101; Part II, *ibid.*, March 1926, pp. 117–147; and "Ancora Sull'Offerta del Risparmio," *ibid.*, Sept. 1927, pp. 481–504.

[8]See, for instance, J. Mosak, *General Equilibrium Theory in International Trade* [Bloomington, Ind.: Principia Press, 1944], Ch. 6, especially pp. 116–117.

For the utility function (1.1) to be maximized, the quantities c_τ and a_{L+1} must be such as to satisfy the first order conditions:

$$\frac{\partial U}{\partial c_\tau} = \frac{\lambda}{(1 + r)^{\tau+1-t}}; \quad \tau = t, t + 1, \cdots, L$$

$$\frac{\partial U}{\partial a_{L+1}} = \frac{\lambda}{(1 + r)^{L+1-t}}$$

(1.3)

where λ represents a Lagrange multiplier. The equation (1.3), together with (1.2), yields a system of $L - t + 3$ simultaneous equations to determine $L - t + 1$ $\bar{c}_\tau$'s, $\bar{a}_{L+1}$ and $\bar{\lambda}$, the barred symbols being used to characterize the maximizing value of the corresponding variable.

If current income, $y_t + ra_t$, is unequal to c_t, the individual will be currently saving (or dissaving); and similarly, if $y_\tau + ra_\tau$ is not equal to $\bar{c}_\tau$, the individual will be planning to save (or dissave) at age τ. The traditional model suggests that we may usefully distinguish two separate reasons for such inequalities to arise. We refer to these reasons as the "motives for saving."[9]

I. The first of these motives is the desire to add to the estate for the benefit of one's heirs; it arises when $\bar{a}_{L+1}$ is greater than a_t. Under this condition $y_\tau + ra_\tau$ must exceed $\bar{c}_\tau$ for at least some $\tau \geq t$.

II. The second motive arises out of the fact that the pattern of current and prospective income receipts will generally not coincide with the preferred consumption, $\bar{c}_\tau$, for all $\tau \geq t$. This clearly represents an independent motive in that it can account for positive (or negative) saving in any subinterval of the life span, even in the absence of the first motive.

It is precisely on this point that a really important lesson can be learned by taking a fresh look at the traditional theory of the household; according to this theory there need not be any close and simple relation between consumption in a given short period and income in the same period. The rate of consumption in any given period is a facet of a plan which extends over the balance of the individual's life, while the income accruing within the same period is but one element which contributes to the shaping of such a plan. This lesson seems to have been largely lost in much of the empirically-oriented discussion of recent years, in the course of which an overwhelming stress has been placed on the role of current income, or of income during a short interval centering on the corresponding consumption interval, almost to the exclusion of any other variable.

Before proceeding further with the implications of our model, it is necessary to devote brief attention to one conceivably important element that we have neglected so far, namely, the phenomenon of uncertainty. No attempt will be made in this paper to introduce uncertainty in the analysis in a really rigorous fashion. The reason for this procedure is simple; we

[9]Cf. Keynes, op. cit., p. 107

believe that for the purposes in which we are interested, a satisfactory theory can be developed without seriously coming to grips with this rather formidable problem. An examination of the considerations that support this conclusion, however, is best postponed until we have fully explored the implications of our model under certainty. We may simply note at this point that the presence of uncertainty might be expected to give rise to two additional motives for saving:

III. The precautionary motive, *i.e.*, the desire to accumulate assets through saving to meet possible emergencies, whose occurrence, nature, and timing cannot be perfectly foreseen. Such emergencies might take the form of a temporary fall in income below the planned level or of temporary consumption requirements over and above the anticipated level. In both cases the achievement of the optimum consumption level might depend on the availability of previously acquired assets.

IV. Finally, as a result of the presence of uncertainty, it is necessary, or at least cheaper, to have an equity in certain kinds of assets before an individual can receive services from them. These assets are consumers' durable goods. If there were no uncertainty, a person could borrow the whole sum necessary to purchase the assets (the debt cancelling the increase in real asset holdings), and pay off the loans as the assets are consumed. In the real world, however, the uncertainty as to the individual's ability to pay forces the individual to hold at least a partial equity in these assets.

While we have thus come to distinguish four separate motives for saving, we should not forget that any one asset in the individual's "portfolio" may, and usually will, satisfy more than one motive simultaneously. For example, the ownership of a house is a source of current services; it may be used to satisfy part of the consumption planned for after retirement; it may be bequeathed; and, finally, it is a source of funds in emergencies. It follows that any possession which can be turned into cash will serve at least one of the four motives and should accordingly be treated as an asset. These possessions include, in particular, equities in unconsumed durable goods.

Saving and dissaving can then usefully be defined as the positive, or negative, change in the net worth of an individual during a specified time period. Correspondingly, consumption will be defined as the expenditure on nondurable goods and services — adjusted for changes in consumers' inventories — plus current depreciations of direct-service-yielding durable goods.[10]

[10]Quite recently, many others have advocated this definition. See, for instance, Kenneth Boulding, *A Reconstruction of Economics* [New York: John Wiley & Sons, Inc., 1950], Ch. 8; Mary W. Smelker, "The Problem of Estimating Spending and Saving in Long-Range Projections," Conference on Research in Income and Wealth (preliminary), p. 35; Raymond W. Goldsmith, "Trends and Structural Changes in Saving in the 20th Century," Conference on Savings, Inflation, and Economic Progress, University of Minnesota, 1951; James N. Morgan, "The Structure of Aggregate Personal Saving," *Journal of Political Economy*, [LIX] Dec. 1951; and William Hamburger, "Consumption and Wealth," unpublished Ph.D. dissertation, The University of Chicago, 1951.

As we shall see, the fact that assets are capable of satisfying more than one motive simultaneously provides the foundation for our earlier statement that it should be possible to neglect the phenomenon of uncertainty without too serious consequences. But a fuller development of this point will have to wait until later.

I.2   Some further assumptions and their implications

The currently accepted theory of the household, even in the very general formulation used so far, has begun to broaden our view of saving behavior. It is, however, too general to be really useful in empirical research. If we are to derive from it some propositions specific enough to be amenable to at least indirect empirical tests, it will be necessary to narrow it down by introducing some further assumptions about the nature of the utility function (see Assumption II below). For convenience of exposition, however, we shall also find it useful to introduce several additional assumptions whose only purpose is to simplify the problem by reducing it to its essentials. These assumptions will enable us to derive some very simple relations between saving, income, and other relevant variables, and it will appear that the implications of these relations are consistent with much of the available empirical evidence. While some of the simplifying assumptions we are about to introduce are obviously unrealistic, the reader should not be unduly disturbed by them. In the first place we have shown elsewhere[11] that most of these assumptions (except Assumption II) can be greatly relaxed or eliminated altogether, complicating the algebra but without significantly affecting the conclusions. In the second place, the question of just which aspects of reality are essential to the construction of a theory is primarily a pragmatic one. If the theory proves useful in explaining the essential features of the phenomena under consideration in spite of the simplifications assumed, then these simplifications are thereby justified.

It may be well to recall, first, that one simplifying assumption has already been made use of in developing our basic model of equation (1.1) to (1.3); this is the assumption that (on the average) the price level of consumables is not expected to change appreciably over time. The first of our remaining assumptions will consist in disregarding altogether what we have called the "estate motive." Specifically, we shall assume that the typical household, whose behavior is described by equations (1.1) to (1.3), does not inherit assets to any significant extent and in turn does not plan on leaving assets to its heirs. These conditions can be formally stated as:

[11]Modigliani and Brumberg, *op. cit.*

ASSUMPTION I. $a_1 = 0,$ $\bar{a}_{L+1} = 0.$[12]

Assumption I, together with equation (1.2), implies that our household, in addition to having no inherited assets at the beginning of its life, also does not receive any gift or inheritance at any other point of its life; it can only accumulate assets through its own saving.

From Assumption I and equation (1.2), it follows immediately that current and future planned consumption must be functions of current and expected (discounted) income plus initial assets, *i.e.*,

$$\bar{c}_\tau = f(v_t, t, \tau), \qquad \tau = t, t + 1, \cdots, L;$$

where

$$v_t = \sum_{\tau=t}^{N} \frac{y_\tau}{(1 + r)^{\tau+1-t}} + a_t,$$

and t denotes again the present age of the individual.[13]

Now what can be said about the nature of the function f? Or, to re-formulate the question, suppose that, on the expectation that his total resources would amount to v_t, and with a given interest rate, our individual had decided to distribute his consumption according to the pattern represented by $\bar{c}_\tau$. Suppose further that, before carrying out his plan, he is led to expect that his resources will amount not to v_t but, say, to $v_t + \Delta v_t$. Should we then expect him to allocate the additional income to increase consumption in any specific period of his remaining life (*e.g.*, his early years, or his late years, or his middle years), relative to all other periods, or can we expect him to allocate it so as to increase all consumptions roughly in the same proportion?

We are inclined to feel that the second alternative is fairly reasonable; or, at any rate, we are unable to think of any systematic factor that would tend to favor any particular period relative to any other. And for this reason we are willing to assume that the second answer, even if it is not true for every individual, is true on the average.[14] This gives rise to our second

---

[12]The assumption $\bar{a}_{L+1} = 0$ might be stated more elegantly in terms of the following two:

$$\text{(a)} \quad \frac{\partial U}{\partial a_{L+1}} \equiv 0; \qquad \text{(b)} \quad a_{L+1} \geqq 0.$$

The first of these equations specifies certain properties of the utility function U; the second states an institutional fact the individual must take into account in his planning, namely that our economic, legal, and ethical system is set up so as to make it rather difficult to get away without paying one's debts. The addition of these two equations to our previous system implies $\bar{a}_{L+1} = 0$.

[13]The fact that $a_1 = 0$ by Assumption I of course does not imply $a_t = 0$.

[14]The expression "on the average" here means that if we aggregate a large number of individuals chosen at random, their aggregate consumption will behave approximately as though each individual behaved in the postulated way.

assumption, the only one that is really fundamental for our entire construction, namely:

ASSUMPTION II. The utility function is such that the *proportion* of his total resources that an individual plans to devote to consumption in any given year τ of his remaining life is determined only by his tastes and not by the size of his resources. Symbolically, this assumption can be represented by the following equation:

$$\bar{c}_\tau = \gamma_\tau^t v_t, \qquad \tau = t, t + 1, \cdots, L \tag{1.4}$$

where, for given t and τ the quantity γ_τ^t depends on the specific form of the function U and on the rate of interest r, but *is independent of "total resources,"* v_t.

As a result of well-known properties of homogeneous functions, it can readily be shown that a sufficient condition for Assumption II to hold is that the utility function U be homogeneous (of any positive degree) in the variables $c_t, c_{t-1}, \cdots, c_L$.[15]

The remaining two assumptions are not essential to the argument, but are introduced for convenience of exposition.[16]

ASSUMPTION III. The interest rate is zero, *i.e.*, $r = 0$.

As a result of this assumption, the expression

$$v_t = \sum_{\tau=t}^{N} \frac{y_\tau}{(1 + r)^{\tau+1-t}} + a_t$$

can be rewritten as $y_t + (N - t)y_t^e + a_t$, where

$$y_t^e = \left(\sum_{\tau=t+1}^{N} y_t \right) \Big/ (N - t),$$

represents the average income expected over the balance of the earning span.

---

[15]More generally, it is sufficient that the utility index be any monotonic increasing function of a function U homogeneous in $c_t, \ldots, c_L$. This assumption can also be stated in terms of properties of the indifference map relating consumption in different periods. The postulated map has the property that tangents to successive indifference curves through the points where such curves are pierced by any one arbitrary radius vector are parallel to each other.

It may also be worth noting that a simple form of the utility index U satisfying our assumption is the following:

$$U = \log U = \alpha_0 + \sum_{\tau=t}^{L} \alpha_\tau \log c_\tau$$

since U is clearly homogeneous in $c_t, \ldots, c_L$. The above expression in turn has the same form as the well-known Weber Law of psychophysics, if we regard U as a measure of the intensity of the sensation and c as the intensity of the stimulus. One may well speculate whether we have here something of deeper significance than a mere formal analogy.

[16]For a discussion of the effects of removing them, see Modigliani and Brumberg, *op. cit.* Also, see various footnotes below.

Equation (1.4) now reduces to:

$$\bar{c}_\tau = \gamma_\tau^t[y_t + (N - t)y_t^e + a_t] \tag{1.4'}$$

which implies

$$\sum_{\tau=t}^{L} c_\tau = [y_t + (N - t)y_t^e + a_t] \sum_{\tau=t}^{L} \gamma_\tau^t.$$

Furthermore, taking into account Assumption I ($\bar{a}_{L+1} = 0$) we also have

$$\sum_{\tau=t}^{L} c_\tau = y_t + (N - t)y_t^e + a_t. \tag{1.5}$$

From (1.4') and (1.5) it then follows that

$$\sum_{\tau=t}^{L} \gamma_\tau^t = 1. \tag{1.6}$$

ASSUMPTION IV.   All the γ_τ^t are equal; *i.e.*, our hypothetical proto-type plans to consume his income at an even rate throughout the balance of his life.

Let γ_t denote the common values of the γ_τ^t for an individual of age t. From (1.6) we then have

$$\sum_{\tau=t}^{L} \gamma_\tau^t = (L + 1 - t)\gamma_t = 1; \tag{1.7}$$

or,

$$\gamma_\tau^t = \gamma_t = \frac{1}{L + 1 - t} \equiv \frac{1}{L_t},$$

where $L_t \equiv L + 1 - t$ denotes the remaining life span at age t.

II. Implications of the theory and the empirical evidence

II.1   The individual consumption function and the cross-section consumption-income relation

Substituting for γ_τ^t in equations (1.4') the value given by (1.7), we establish immediately the individual consumption function, *i.e.*, the relation between *current* consumption and the factors determining it:

$$c = c(y, y^e, a, t) = \frac{1}{L_t} y + \frac{(N - t)}{L_t} y^e + \frac{1}{L_t} a; \tag{2.1}$$

where the undated variables are understood to relate to the current period.[17]

---

[17]For an individual of age $t > N$, by assumption, $y = y^e = 0$ and only the last term on the right-hand side of (2.1) remains.

According to equation (2.1), current consumption is a linear and homogeneous function of current income, expected average income, and initial assets, with coefficients depending on the age of the household.

The corresponding expression for saving is

$$s = y - c = \frac{L-t}{L_t} y - \frac{N-t}{L_t} y^e - \frac{1}{L_t} a. \tag{2.2}$$

In principle, equations (2.1) and (2.2) could be directly tested; but they cannot easily be checked against existing published data because, to our knowledge, data providing joint information on age, assets (which here means *net worth and not just liquid assets*), and average expected income, do not exist.[18] We must, therefore, see whether we can derive from our model some further implications of a type suitable for at least indirect testing in terms of the available data. Since most of these data give us information about the relation between consumption in a given short interval and income over the same interval (or some small neighborhood thereof) we must seek what implications can be deduced as to the relations between these variables.

If the marginal propensity to consume is defined literally as the increment in the current consumption of the household accompanying an increment in its current income, divided by the increment in income, keeping other things constant, then, according to equation (2.1), this quantity would be $\partial c/\partial y = 1/L_t$, which is independent of income but dependent on age. The consumption function (2.1) would be represented by a straight line with the above slope and an intercept $\dfrac{(N-t)y^e + a}{L_t}$; and, since this intercept can be assumed positive,[19] the proportion of income saved should tend to rise with income.

In order to get some feeling as to the quantitative implications of our results, let us say that the earning span, N, is of the order of 40 years, the retirement span, M, 10 years, and therefore the total active life span, L, of the order of 50 years. These figures are not supposed to be anything more than a very rough guess and their only purpose is to give us some notion of the magnitudes involved. On the basis of these figures, the marginal propensity to consume would lie somewhere between a minimum of 1/50, or 2 per cent, and a maximum of 1/11, or 9 per cent, depending on age.

These figures seem unreasonably small. This is because the above definition of the marginal propensity to consume is clearly not a very reasonable one. A change in the current income of the household will generally

---

[18]The valuable work in progress at the Survey Research Center of the University of Michigan gives hope that the variety of data required for such a test may sometime become available. Clearly, the problem of measuring average expected future income may prove a serious challenge. On this point, however, see text below and the Appendix.

[19]Obviously, both y^e and a will generally be nonnegative.

tend to be accompanied by a change in its expected income, y^e, so that there is little sense in including ye among the things that are supposed to be constant as y changes. Note, however, that the same objection does not apply to a, for a denotes initial assets and, for a given household, assets at the beginning of the current period necessarily represent a constant.

Once we recognize that y^e is generally a function of y, the marginal propensity to consume at age t may be defined as

$$\frac{dc}{dy} = \frac{1}{L_t} + \frac{N-t}{L_t}\frac{dy^e}{dy}. \tag{2.3}$$

Since dy^e/dy would generally tend to lie between 0 and 1,[20] the marginal propensity to consume would fall for different individuals between a minimum of 1/50 and a maximum of 4/5, depending both on age and on the value of dy^e/dy.

Unfortunately, the empirical validity of these statements cannot be tested from observations of actual individual behavior. The reason is that consumption and income can only have a *single* value for a *given individual at a given age*. To be sure, we might be able to observe the behavior of an individual whose income had changed in time; but, even if we could control the value of y^e, we could not keep constant his age nor probably his initial assets (*i.e.*, assets at the beginning of each consumption period). The only way we could possibly check these conclusions is by observing the behavior of (average) consumption of *different* households at different income levels, *i.e.*, by observing the "cross-section" average and marginal rate of consumption with respect to income.[21]

Suppose we make these observations and, for the sake of simplicity, suppose further that all the households we examine have approximately the same age and in every case $y = y^e$. Should we then expect the marginal rate of consumption to be $\dfrac{N-t+1}{L_t}$, as equation (2.3) would seem to imply? The answer is no; the individual marginal propensity to consume cannot be simply identified with the cross-section marginal rate of consumption. Turning back to equation (2.1), we can easily see that (if all individuals behave according to this equation) the cross-section marginal rate of consumption should be

$$\frac{d'c}{d'y} = \frac{N+1-t}{L_t} + \frac{1}{L_t}\frac{d'a}{d'y}, \tag{2.4}$$

---

[20]See below, Section 3, especially footnote 39.

[21]We speak here advisedly of average and marginal rate of consumption, rather than of "cross-section marginal propensity to consume," for, as will become clear, the use of the latter term is likely only to encourage a serious and already too frequent type of confusion. The word "propensity" denotes a psychological disposition and should refer to the way in which a *given* individual reacts to different stimuli, and not to the way in which *different* individuals react to different stimuli. The differential reaction of different individuals in relation to different stimuli may give us information about the individual propensity, but it is not, in itself, a propensity.

where the differential operator d' is used to denote cross-section differentials. Although da/dy must be zero for an individual, there is no reason why the cross-section rate of change, $d'a/d'y$, should also be zero. Quite the contrary. Our model leads us to expect a very definite relation between the (average) net worth of households at a given income level and the income level itself, which relation we now proceed to explore.

II.2 The equilibrium income-asset-age relation and the consumption-income relation in a stationary and nonstationary cross section

To see clearly the implications of our model it will be useful to examine at first the nature of the cross-section relation between consumption and income in a special case which we shall call a cross section of "stationary" households. A household will be said to be in stationary position if it satisfies the following two conditions: (a) at the beginning of its active life it expects a constant income throughout its earning span; and (b) at every point of its life cycle it finds that its original expectations are completely fulfilled in the sense that its past and current income are as originally expected and its expectations for the future also coincide with its original expectations.[22] From equations (1.4) and (1.7) (since by assumption $y_1^e = y_1$ and $a_1 = 0$) we see that for such a household the consumption plan at age 1, which we denote by $\bar{c}_\tau^1$, must be

$$\bar{c}_\tau^1 = \frac{N}{L} y_1, \qquad\qquad \tau = 1, 2, \cdots, L; \qquad\qquad (2.5')$$

and the saving plan

$$\bar{s}_\tau^1 = \begin{cases} \dfrac{M}{L} y_1, & \tau = 1, 2, \cdots, N \\[2ex] -\dfrac{N}{L} y_1, & \tau = N + 1, N + 2, \cdots, L. \end{cases} \qquad (2.5'')$$

Finally, the asset plan, which is the sum of planned savings, must be

$$\bar{a}_\tau^1 = \begin{cases} \dfrac{(\tau - 1)M}{L} y_1, & \tau = 1, 2, \cdots, N \\[2ex] \dfrac{N(L + 1 - \tau)}{L} y_1, & \tau = N + 1, N + 2, \cdots, L. \end{cases} \qquad (2.5''')$$

We will make use of equation (2.5''') to define the notion of "stationary

[22]For a generalization of the notion of stationary household, see below footnote 25.

equilibrium" assets. We say that initial asset holdings at age t, a_t, are in equilibrium relative to any given level of income, y, if

$$a_t = a(y,t) = \begin{cases} \dfrac{(t-1)M}{L}\, y, & t = 1, 2, \cdots, N \\[2ex] \dfrac{N(L+1-t)}{L}\, y, & t = N+1, N+2, \cdots, L. \end{cases} \qquad (2.6)$$

Now it can readily be shown that for households fulfilling the stationary conditions and behaving according to equation (2.1), assets, at any age, will coincide precisely with those planned at age 1.[23] But, by definition, for a household of age $t \leq N$ in stationary position, current income, y, equals y_1; it follows that its assets at the beginning of the current period must be

$$a = \bar{a}_t^1 = a(y_1,t) = a(y,t) = \frac{(t-1)M}{L}\, y, \qquad t \leq N \qquad (2.8)$$

which exhibits explicitly the relation between current initial assets, income, and age. Substituting from (2.8) into (2.1) and (2.2) and remembering that, by assumption, income expectations coincide with current income, we find for any age $t \leq N$,

$$c = \frac{N}{L}\, y, \qquad s = \frac{M}{L}\, y; \qquad (2.9)$$

i.e., for households fulfilling the stationary conditions and within the earning

---

[23]This proposition may be established by mathematical induction. Suppose that the proposition holds for t, *i.e.*, that

$$a_t = \bar{a}_t^1 = \frac{(t-1)M}{L}\, y_1;$$

then, since by assumption

$$y_t = y_t^e = y_1, \qquad t \leq N - 1,$$

we have, from (2.2),

$$s_t = \frac{M}{L}\, y_1$$

and

$$a_{t+1} = a_t + s_t = \frac{(t-1)M}{L}\, y_1 + \frac{M}{L}\, y_1 = \frac{tM}{L}\, y_1 = \bar{a}_{t+1}^1$$

Thus, if equation (2.7) holds for t it holds also for $t + 1$. But equation (11.7) holds for $t = 1$, since

$$a_1 = 0 = \frac{(L-1)M}{L}\, y_1 = \bar{a}_1^1.$$

Hence, equation (2.7) holds for all $t \leq N$. By similar reasoning, it can be shown that it holds also for $N + 1 \leq t \leq L$.

span, current consumption and saving are proportional to the current income.[24]

At first sight this conclusion may appear to have little empirical meaning, since the notion of a stationary household is a theoretical limiting concept with little operational content. But our result need not be interpreted literally. Clearly our model has the following very significant implication: if we take a cross section of households within their earning span, which are reasonably well adjusted to the current level of income (in the sense, that, for each household, current income is close to the level the household has received in the past and it expects to receive in the future), then we should find that the proportion of income saved is substantially the same at all levels of income.[25] Even this more general conclusion is not easy to test from available data. Yet we shall be able to show presently that some rather striking evidence in support of this implication of our model is provided by certain recent studies.

From the result just established it follows directly that, if our sample consisted primarily of households in stationary position, then the cross-section rate of change of consumption with respect to income, $d'c/d'y$, is entirely different from the individual marginal propensity to consume defined by equation (2.3). According to equation (2.9) the cross-section rate of change must be N/L, a result which can also be derived from equation (2.4), by observing that, for stationary households, equation (2.8) holds so that, for given age t, $\dfrac{d'a}{d'y} = \dfrac{(t-1)M}{L}$. Note, in particular, that (*a*) the individual marginal propensity varies with age, whereas the cross-section

---

[24]While this result implies that, at zero income, consumption itself would have to be zero, it should be remembered that, under our stationary assumptions, the current level of income coincides with the level received in the past and expected in the future. A household whose income is permanently zero could hardly survive as a separate unit. Or, to put it differently, a household, within its earning span, whose current income is zero or negative cannot possibly be in stationary equilibrium.

[25]It can be shown that if we eliminate Assumption III, our model still implies that, for a stationary cross section, the proportion of income saved is independent of income; however, this proportion will tend to rise with age, up to retirement. The conclusion that the proportion of income saved is independent of income, given age, also continues to hold if we relax our Assumption IV and assume only that there exists a typical pattern of allocation of resources to current and future consumption which does not necessarily involve a constant planned rate of consumption over time. Finally this conclusion also remains valid if we recognize the existence of a typical life pattern of income and redefine a stationary household as one who expects its income not to be constant over time but rather to follow the normal life pattern, and whose expectations are continuously fulfilled in the sense stated in part (b) of the original definition in the text. Just what effects these two relaxations would have on the relation between the proportion of income saved and age depends, of course, on the specific shape of the pattern of allocation of resources to consumption over the life cycle and on the shape of the life pattern of income. Note, however, that since the line of relation between saving and income *for each* age group is supposed, in any event, to go through the origin, even if we fail to stratify by age, the regression of consumption on income should tend to be linear (though not homoscedastic) and a regression line fitted to the data should tend to go approximately through the origin.

rate of change is independent of the age composition of the sample (provided all households are within the earning span); and (b) the slope of the cross-section line could not even be expected to represent some average of the marginal propensities at various ages. Indeed, even under unity elasticity of expectations, the marginal propensity at any age (except age 1) is less than N/L.[26]

In general, however, a random sample would not consist entirely, or even primarily, of households in stationary position. Let us therefore proceed to the more general case and see what we can learn from our model about the behavior of households who are not in stationary equilibrium.

Making use of the definition of $a(y,t)$ given in (2.6), the individual saving function (2.2) can be rewritten in the following useful form:

$$s = \frac{M}{L} y^e + \frac{L - t}{L_t} (y - y^e) - \frac{1}{L_t} [a - a(y^e,t)] \qquad (2.2')$$

$$= \frac{M}{L} y + \frac{N(L - t) - M}{LL_t} (y - y^e) - \frac{1}{L_t} [a - a(y^e,t)].$$

The quantity $(y - y^e)$, representing the excess of current income over the average level expected in the future, may be called the "nonpermanent component of income"[27] (which may be positive or negative). Similarly, the quantity $[a - a(y^e,t)]$, representing the difference between actual initial assets and the volume of assets which would be carried by an individual fully adjusted to the "permanent" component of income y^e, may be called the "imbalance in initial assets" or also "excess assets" relative to the permanent component of income.

The first form of equation (2.2') states the proposition that saving is equal to: (1) a constant fraction of the permanent component of income (independent of both age and income) which fraction is precisely the stationary equilibrium saving ratio; plus (2) a fraction of the nonpermanent component of income [this fraction is independent of income but depends on age and is larger, in fact much larger, than the fraction under (1)]; minus (3) a fraction, depending only on age, of excess assets. A similar interpretation can be given to the second form of (2.2').

Equation (2.2') is useful for examining the behavior of an individual, who, after having been in stationary equilibrium up to age $t - 1$, experiences an unexpected increase in income at age t so that $y_t > y_{t-1}^e = y_{t-1}$. Here we must distinguish two possibilities. Suppose, first, the increase is viewed as

26As we have seen, under the assumption $y^e = y$ (and therefore $dy^e/dy = 1$) the individual marginal propensity to consume is $\dfrac{N - t + 1}{L_t}$, which reaches a maximum for $t = 1$, the maximum being N/L.

27Cf. M. Friedman and S. Kuznets, *Income from Independent Professional Practice* [New York: National Bureau of Economic Research, 1945], pp. 325 ff.

being strictly temporary so that $y_t^e = y_{t-1}^e = y_{t-1}$. In this case $a_t = a(y_t^e, t)$.[28] There is no imbalance in assets and, therefore, the third term is zero. But the second term will be positive since a share of current income, amounting to $y_t - y_{t-1}$, represents a nonpermanent component. Because our individual will be saving an abnormally large share of this portion of his income, his saving ratio will rise above the normal figure M/L. This ratio will in fact be higher, the higher the share of current income which is nonpermanent, or, which is equivalent in this case, the higher the percentage increase in income.[29] Let us next suppose that the current increase in income causes him to raise his expectations; and consider the limiting case where $y_t^e = y_t$, i.e., the elasticity of expectations is unity.

In this case the transitory component is, of course, zero; but now the third term becomes positive, reflecting an insufficiency of assets relative to the new and higher income expectation. Accordingly, the saving ratio rises again above the normal level M/L by an extent which is greater the greater the percentage increase in income. Moreover, as we might expect, the fact that expectations have followed income causes the increase in the saving ratio to be somewhat smaller than in the previous case.[30]

Our model implies, then, that a household whose current income unexpectedly rises above the previous "accustomed" level (where the term "accustomed" refers to the average expected income to which the household was adjusted), will save a proportion of its income larger than it was saving before the change and also larger than is presently saved by the permanent inhabitants of the income bracket into which the household now enters. The statement, of course, holds in reverse for a fall in income.[31]

II.3   A reinterpretation of the cross-section relation between consumption and income

The propositions we have just established are not easy to test directly with existing data, since such data do not usually provide information on the

[28]Since the individual was in stationary equilibrium up to the end of period $t - 1$, we must have $a_t = a(y_{t-1}, t)$ and, by assumption, $y_{t-1} = y_t^e$.

[29]From the last equality in equation (2.2') and with $y_t^e = y_{t-1}$, we derive immediately

$$\frac{s_t}{y_t} = \frac{M}{L} + \frac{N(L - t) - M}{LL_t}\left(\frac{y_t - y_{t-1}}{y_t}\right).$$

[30]From equation (2.2'), with $y_t^e = y_{t-1}$ and since $a_t = \frac{(t - 1)M}{L}y_{t-1}$, we derive,

$$\frac{s_t}{y_t} = \frac{M}{L} + \frac{(t - 1)M}{LL_t}\left(\frac{y_t - y_{t-1}}{y_t}\right).$$

It is easily verified that the right-hand side of this expression is necessarily smaller than the corresponding expression given in the preceding note.

[31]This conclusion fails to hold only if the elasticity of expectations is substantially greater than unity.

"accustomed" level but, at best, only on the level of income during a previous short period. However, even this type of information should be useful, at least for an indirect test of our conclusions. For, suppose we divide all the households into three groups: (1) those whose income has increased in the current year; (2) those whose income is approximately unchanged; and (3) those whose income has fallen. Then, unless most of the income changes just happen to be such as to return the recipients to an accustomed level from which they had earlier departed,[32] group (1) should contain a greater proportion of people whose income is above the accustomed level than group (2) and, a fortiori, than group (3). Hence, according to our model, the households in group (1) whose income has risen should save, on the average, a larger proportion of income than those in group (2), which in turn should save a larger proportion than those in group (3). It is well known that this proposition is overwhelmingly supported by empirical evidence.[33] Even where some apparent exceptions have been reported, these have occurred largely because of the inclusion in expenditure of current outlays for durable goods which we do not include in consumption as far as they result in an increase in net worth.[34]

We will readily recognize that the proposition we have just derived is far from novel; but notice that our model suggests an explanation that is quite different from the one usually advanced. According to the usual explanation, which is already to be found in the *General Theory* (p. 97), consumer expenditure habits are sticky and only adjust with a lag to the changed circumstances; in the meantime, savings, which are considered as a passive residual, absorb a large share of the changed income. In our model, on the other hand, savings tend to go up either because the new level of income is regarded as (partly or wholly) transitory or, to the extent that it is regarded as permanent, because the initial asset holdings are now out of line with the revised outlook. If the outlook has improved, assets are too low to enable the household to live for the rest of its expected life on a scale commensurate with the new level of income; if the income outlook has deteriorated, then, in order for the household to achieve the optimum consumption plan consistent with the new outlook, it is not necessary to add to assets at

[32]More precisely, unless there is a very strong correlation between the current change in income, $y - y_{-1}$, on the one hand, and the difference between the previous "accustomed" level and the previous year income, $y^e_{-1} - y_{-1}$, on the other.

[33]See, for instance, G. Katona and J. Fisher, "Postwar Changes in the Income of Identical Consumer Units," *Studies in Income and Wealth* [New York: National Bureau of Economic Research, 1951], XIII, 62–122; G. Katona, "Effect of Income Changes on the Rate of Saving," *The Review of Economics and Statistics*, XXXI (May 1949), 95–103; W. W. Cochrane, "Family Budgets — A Moving Picture," [*The Review of Economics and Statistics*, XXIX] (Aug. 1947), 189–198; R. P. Mack, "The Direction of Change in Income and the Consumption Function," [*The Review of Economics and Statistics*, XXX] (Nov. 1948), 239-258.

[34]Katona and Fisher, *op. cit.*, especially Section D, pp. 97–101; and Katona, *op. cit.*, pp. 95–103.

the same rate as before, and perhaps even an immediate drawing-down of assets to support consumption may be called for.

We feel that this alternative interpretation has merits. While not denying that the conventional explanation in terms of habit persistence may have some validity, we feel that it has been made to bear too heavy a weight. We all know that there are hundreds of things that we would be eager to buy, or do, "if only we could afford them," and nearly as many places where we could "cut corners" if it were really necessary. Therefore, as long as we are dealing with moderate variations in income (variations whose possibility we had already envisaged at least in our day-dreams), there is not likely to be any significant lag in the adjustment of total expenditure. Of course, there may be significant lags (and leads) in certain types of expenditures: moving to a more exclusive neighborhood may take years to be realized, but meanwhile that dreamed-of vacation trip may come off at once.[35]

Our discussion of the effect of income changes enables us to proceed to an analysis of the cross-section relation between current consumption and current income that we should expect to find, and actually do find, in a random sample which does not consist primarily of households in stationary position.

As is well known, budget studies typically show that the proportion of income saved, far from being constant, tends to rise from a very low or even negative figure at low levels of income to a large positive figure in the highest brackets. These findings are by no means inconsistent with our earlier results concerning the saving-income relation for a stationary cross section. Quite the contrary; the observed relation is precisely what we should expect on the basis of our model when we remember that, in the type of economies to which these budget data mostly refer, individual incomes are subject to short-term fluctuations, so that current income generally will tend to differ more or less markedly from the previous accustomed level and from current

[35]It is, in principle, possible to design an experiment to test which of the two hypotheses represents a better explanation of the observed behavior. One possible test might be as follows. Select the set of households whose income has changed unexpectedly in the given year T, and who expect the change to be permanent. Consider next the subset whose income in the immediately following years remains at the new level and whose expectations are therefore fulfilled. If the traditional explanation is the correct one, then by the year $T + 1$ saving should revert to the average level prevailing for all households who have saved for two or more years in the income brackets into which our households have moved. On the other hand, if our hypothesis is correct, the saving of our subset of households should, in the years following T, continue to remain higher, on the average, than the saving of the households who have been *permanent* inhabitants of the relevant brackets. Furthermore, under our model, the difference between the saving of the new and the original inhabitants should tend to remain greater the more advanced the age of the household in the year T. Needless to say, the data for such a test are not available at this time and the case for our explanation must rest for the moment on the evidence that supports our model as a whole. The purpose of describing a possible experiment is to emphasize the fact that the two alternative hypotheses have implications that are, in principle, observationally distinguishable. Some of these implications are, in fact, of immediate relevance for aggregative time series analysis.

income expectations. Such fluctuations may vary in intensity according to time, place, occupation, and other characteristics of the sample covered, but they will never be entirely absent and frequently will be substantial.

The very same reasoning we have used in the discussion of the effect of income changes leads to the conclusion that, in the presence of short-term fluctuations, the highest income brackets may be expected to contain the largest proportion of households whose current income is above the accustomed level and whose saving is, therefore, abnormally large. Conversely, the lowest income brackets may be expected to contain the largest proportion of people whose current income is below the accustomed level and whose saving is, therefore, abnormally low. As a result of the presence of these groups, which are not fully adjusted to the current level of income, in the lowest brackets the proportion of income saved will be lower, and in the highest brackets it will be higher than the normal figure (M/L in our model) which we should expect to be saved by the permanent inhabitants of these respective brackets. Thus, the proportion of income saved will tend to rise with income, and the cross-section relation between consumption and income will tend to be represented by a line obtained by rotating the stationary line clockwise around a fixed point whose x and y coordinates coincide approximately with the average value of income and consumption respectively.

While the general line of argument developed above is not new,[36] it may be useful to clarify it by means of a graphical illustration developed in Figures 1 and 2. We will start out by analyzing a cross section of households all belonging to a single age group within the earning span, and will examine first the consumption-income relation; once we have established this relation, the saving-income relation can easily be derived from it.

Our consumption function (2.1) can be rewritten in a form analogous to the saving function (2.2′), namely:

$$c = \frac{N}{L} y^e + \frac{1}{L_t} (y - y^e) + \frac{1}{L_t} [a - a(y^e,t)] \qquad (2.1')$$

$$= \frac{N}{L} \left\{ y^e + \frac{L}{NL_t} (y - y^e) + y \frac{L}{NL_t} [a - a(y^e,t)] \right\}$$

In the construction of our figures, we shall find it convenient to have a symbol to represent the expression in braces; let us denote it by $p = p(y,y^e,t,a)$. This expression may be regarded as the stationary equivalent income of the current set of values y, y^e, t and a, for the household, in the sense that, if the household were fully adjusted to a level of income $p =$

[36]See, for instance, the brilliant paper of William Vickrey, "Resource Distribution Patterns and the Classification of Families," *Studies in Income and Wealth*, [*op. cit.*,] Vol. X, pp. 260–329; Ruth P. Mack, *op. cit.*, and the contributions of Margaret G. Reid quoted in the next section.

$p(y,y^e,t,a)$, then it would behave in the same way as it currently does. Let us further denote by the symbol $\bar{x}(y)$ the average value of any variable x for all the members of a given income bracket, y. Then the proportion of income consumed by the aggregate of all households whose current income is y is,

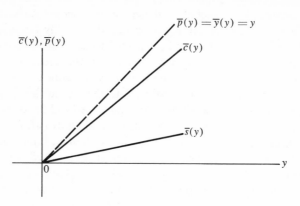

Figure 1

clearly, $\bar{c}(y)/y$. Our problem is, therefore, that of establishing the relation between $\bar{c}(y)$ and y. But, according to (2.1'), $\bar{c}(y)$ is proportional to $\bar{p}(y)$ whose behavior, in turn, as we see, depends on that of $\bar{y}^e(y)$ and $\bar{a}(y)$. We must therefore fix our attention on the behavior of these last two quantities.

In the case of a *stationary* cross section, illustrated in Figure 1, we know that for *every* household, $y^e = y$ and also $a = a(y^e,t)$. It follows that, for *every* household, $p = y$, and therefore the average value of p in any income

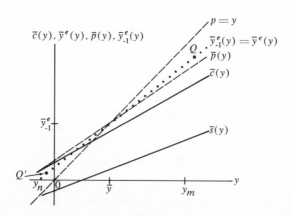

Figure 2

bracket y, $\bar{p}(y)$, is also equal to y, i.e., $\bar{p}(y) = y$. Thus, the cross-section relation between $\bar{p}(y)$ and y is represented by a line of slope one through the origin — the dashed line of our Figure 1. The consumption-income relation is now obtained by multiplying each ordinate of this line by the constant N/L, with the result represented by the upper solid line. Because the $\bar{p}(y)$ line goes through the origin, so does the consumption-income relation, $\bar{c}(y)$, and the elasticity of consumption with respect to income is unity. These same propositions hold equally for the saving-income relation, $\bar{s}(y)$ (lower solid line of Figure 1), obtained by subtracting $\bar{c}(y)$ from y. This merely illustrates a result established in the preceding section.

Let us consider now what we may expect to happen if income is subject to short-term fluctuations, a case illustrated in Figure 2. We may assume for expository convenience that on the average these fluctuations cancel out so that average current income, $\bar{y}$, is the same as the average future income expected in the year before by the sample as a whole, $\bar{y}^e_{-1}$. But, because of the presence of short-term variations, this equality will not hold for individual households; for some households current income will be higher than y_{-1}^e, while for others it will be lower. As a result of these fluctuations, as we have already argued, in the highest income brackets there will be a predominance of households whose current income is above y^e_{-1}. This, in turn, means that in these brackets the average value of $y^e_{-1}, \bar{y}^e_{-1}(y)$, will be less than y itself;[37] in terms of our graph, $\bar{y}^e_{-1}(y)$ will fall below the dashed line, which represents the line of slope one through the origin. For instance, corresponding to the highest income bracket shown, $y_m, \bar{y}^e_{-1}(\bar{y}_m)$ may be represented by a point such as q in our graph. Conversely, in the lowest income bracket shown, y_n, there will tend to be a preponderance of people whose current income is below y^e_{-1}, and therefore the average value of y^e_{-1} in this bracket, $\bar{y}^e_{-1}(y_n)$ will be greater than y_n and above the dashed line, as shown by the point q', in the figure. Extending this reasoning to all values of y, we conclude that the relation between $\bar{y}^e_{-1}(y)$ and y will tend to be

---

[37]The specific "technical" assumption underlying the entire discussion can be formulated thus:

$$y_i = y^e_{-1i} + \epsilon_i \tag{2.10}$$

where the subscript i denotes the i-th household and the random term ϵ is assumed to have zero mean and to be independent of y_{-1}. From (2.10), making use of a well-known proposition of correlation theory, we deduce

$$\bar{y}^e_{-1}(y) = \alpha + \beta y; \qquad \beta = r^2_y y^e_{-1}, \quad \alpha = \bar{y}^e_{-1} - \beta \bar{y} \tag{2.10'}$$

Clearly, β is necessarily less than one and α is necessarily positive (since, by assumption, $\bar{y}^e_{-1} = \bar{y}$). A more general and realistic stochastic assumption than the one just formulated would be the following:

$$y_i = ky^e_{-1i}(1 + \epsilon_i^*),$$

ϵ' having the same properties as ϵ in (2.10). Since this assumption would complicate the analysis considerably (e.g., it would destroy the linearity of (2.10') without affecting the essence of our argument), it has seemed preferable to base our discussion in this paper on equation (2.10).

represented by a curve having the following essential properties: (a) it will intercept the dashed line in the neighborhood of a point with abscissa $\bar{y}$; and (b) to the right of this point, it will fall progressively below the dashed line, while to the left of it, it will stand increasingly above this line. In our graph this relation is represented by the dotted straight line joining the points q' and q; in general, the relation need not be a linear one, although the assumption of linearity may not be altogether unrealistic. What is essential, however, is that the $\bar{y}^e_{-1}(y)$ curve may be expected to have everywhere a slope smaller than unity and to exhibit a positive intercept; and that its slope will tend to be smaller, and its intercept larger, the greater the short-term variability of income.

From the behavior of $\bar{y}^e_{-1}(y)$, we can now readily derive that of $\bar{y}^e(y)$, which is the quantity we are really interested in. The latter variable is related to $\bar{y}^e_{-1}(y)$ and to y itself through the elasticity of income expectations. The elasticity of expectations relevant to our analysis can be defined as the percentage change in income expectation over the two years in question, $\dfrac{y^e - y^e_{-1}}{y^e_{-1}}$, divided by the corresponding percentage difference between current income and the previous year's expectation, $\dfrac{y - y^e_{-1}}{y^e_{-1}}$.

If we denote this elasticity by the symbol E, we have

$$E = \frac{y^e - y^e_{-1}}{y - y^e_{-1}},^{38} \qquad (2.11)$$

which in turn implies:

$$y^e = y^e_{-1} + E(y - y^e_{-1}) = (1 - E)y^e_{-1} + Ey; \qquad (2.11')$$

i.e., the current income expectation is a weighted average of the previous expectation and current income, with weights depending on the elasticity of expectation. If E is close to zero, current income will have little influence in reshaping expectations and y^e will be close to y^e_{-1}; if, at the other extreme, E is close to unity then current expectations will be determined primarily by

---

[38]This definition is not altogether satisfactory for an individual household since y may have been expected to be different from y^e_{-1} (which is the average income expected over the entire balance of the earning span); in this case the fact that y differs from y^e_{-1} need not generate any revision of expectations, *i.e.*, y^e may be equal to y^e_{-1}. As an alternative definition that would give more adequate recognition to the causal relation between the behavior of current income and changes in expectations, we may suggest the following:

$$E = \frac{y^e - y^e_{-1}}{y^e_{-1}} \bigg/ \frac{y - y^{e(t)}_{t-1}}{y^{e(t)}_{t-e}},$$

where $y^{e(t)}_{t-t}$ denotes the income expected in the previous year for the current year. However, when we aggregate a large number of households, it is not unreasonable to expect that, on the average $y^{e(t)}_{t-1} = y^e_{-1}$, in which case our alternative definition leads back to equation (2.11) in the text.

the recent behavior of income. From (2.11′) we readily deduce the relation between $\bar{y}^e(y)$ and $y^e_{-1}(y)$, namely:

$$\bar{y}^e(y) = \bar{y}^e_{-1}(y) + E[y - \bar{y}^e_{-1}(y)]. \tag{2.12}$$

Equation (2.12) admits of a very simple graphical interpretation. Suppose, first, that E is zero: then $\bar{y}^e(y)$ coincides with $y^e_{-1}(y)$, the dotted line of Figure 2. Next, suppose E is positive but less than one; then, for any value of y, $\bar{y}^e(y)$, if it were drawn, would lie between y and $\bar{y}^e_{-1}(y)$, i.e., between the dashed and the dotted line and precisely E per cent of the way from the dotted to the dashed line. Finally, if E is greater than one, or less than zero, then $\bar{y}^e(y)$ will fall outside the band marked off by our two lines. The last two cases, however, may be regarded as extremely unlikely, when one remembers that y^e and y^e_{-1} are defined as expectations about the average level of income over the entire balance of the earning span.[40] In our graph we have assumed a zero value for E so that $\bar{y}^e(y)$ coincides with $\bar{y}^e_{-1}(y)$; this assumption has been chosen not because we think it is realistic but only

[39]In deriving (2.12) from (2.11), we are implicitly assuming that the average value of E is approximately the same at all levels of income, an assumption that does not seem unreasonable for the specific stochastic model with which we are presently dealing. A more general formulation of (2.12), which may be especially useful in establishing a connection between cross-section and aggregative time-series analysis, might be as follows:

$$\bar{y}^e(y) = \bar{y}^e_{-1}(y) + E_1[y - \bar{y}^e_{-1}(y)] + E_2(\bar{y} - \bar{y}^e_{-1}), \tag{2.12′}$$

which states that individual expectations depend not only on the behavior of individual income but also on that of average income for the entire community, $\bar{y}$. This hypothesis is supported by the consideration that changes in aggregate income may well represent a more reliable indicator for the future than just a change in individual income. It follows from (2.12′) that the elasticity of expectation for the community as a whole is

$$\frac{\bar{y}^e - \bar{y}^e_{-1}}{\bar{y} - \bar{y}^e_{-1}} = E_1 + E_2,$$

an expression that could be close to unity even if, as seems likely, E_1 is much smaller than one. On the other hand, it can be easily verified that if (2.12′) holds, with $E_2 \neq 0$, the elasticity of expectation as defined by (2.11) will generally change from income bracket to income bracket unless $\bar{y} = \bar{y}^e_{-1}$, an equality which has been explicitly assumed for the purposes of our discussion in the text and which makes (2.12′) identical with (2.12).

[40]Such cases are of course not impossible for an individual household; all we claim is that they are unlikely for the average of all households falling in a given income bracket. (See, however, footnote 38.)

There is, of course, no opportunity to test the above statement fom available data, since no attempt has yet been made, to our knowledge, to secure information on y^e and y^e_{-1}. Data such as those collected by the Survey Research Center on income expectations for the following year, and presented, for example, in G. Katona, *Psychological Analysis of Economic Behavior*, p. 120, have only a rather remote connection with our concepts. In terms of our notation, these data refer to y_{iT}, y_{iT-1}, and $y_{iT}^{e(T+1)}$, where T denotes the calendar year of the survey. If one is willing to make the rather risky assumption that $y_{iT}^{e(T+1)} = y_{iT}^e$, and the even more risky one that $y_{iT-1} = y_{iT-1}^e$, then it can be inferred from Katona's tabulations that the proportion of households with E greater than one has been somewhat under 20 per cent, and fairly stable, in the surveys for which data are presented.

because it eliminates the necessity of showing a separate curve in our figure. In general, we should rather expect E to be positive but less than one, so that the $\bar{y}^e(y)$ curve would fall between the dotted and the dashed line. *The slope and intercept of this curve will thus depend on the degree of short-term variability of income* [which determines the shape of $\bar{y}^e_{-1}(y)$] *and on the elasticity of expectations.* But note that where short-run fluctuations play a large role, as might be the case, say, for a sample of farmers, the elasticity of expectations may, itself, be expected to be small on the average, since current income will contain little new reliable information on the basis of which to reshape the previous expectation about average future income, y^e_{-1}. Hence, a large short-term variability of income will tend to depress the slope, and raise the intercept, of $\bar{y}^e(y)$ for two reasons: (1) because it pulls the $\bar{y}^e(y)$ closer to $\bar{y}^e_{-1}(y)$, and (2) because it diminishes the slope of $\bar{y}^e_{-1}(y)$.

We have thus exhibited the behavior of the first component of $\bar{p}(y)$. As we see from (2.1'), the second component is very simple to handle; it represents again a fraction, L/NL_t, of the difference between y and $\bar{y}^e(y)$, *i.e.*, of the distance from the dotted to the dashed line. Furthermore, for any reasonable assumption about the values of L and N, this fraction is quite small within the earning span. Thus, the sum of the first two terms of $\bar{p}(y)$ could be represented by a new line falling somewhere between the dashed and the dotted line but very close to the latter. Since it would be so close, this new line is not shown separately in our figure and we will assume that the line $\overline{q'q}$ represents already the sum of the first two components.

We may now proceed to the last component of $\bar{p}(y)$ which measures the (average) unbalance in assets at each current income level. A repetition of the familiar reasoning suggests once more that in the highest income brackets there should tend to be an abnormally large proportion of households whose current income expectation is higher than it had been in the past and for whom, accordingly, current assets are low relative to the current expectation y^e; and that the opposite should be true in the lowest income brackets. Hence, the last term will again be negative for sufficiently large values of y and positive for sufficiently small values. The zero point is again likely to occur for a value of y close to $\bar{y}$, although its location may vary depending on the previous history of the economy (especially the history of the last t years).[41] In any event $\bar{p}(y)$, which is obtained by adding this last term to the

---

[41]The average gap between initial assets, a, and the stationary equilibrium value,

$$a(y^e,t) = \frac{(t-1)M}{L} y^e,$$

at any given level of income, can be derived from the stochastic assumption introduced in footnote 36, with the addition of an analogous stochastic assumption as to the relation between a and y^e_{-1}, namely

$$y^e_{-1i} = \lambda x_i + \omega_i, \tag{2.13}$$

where $\qquad x_i \equiv a_i \Big/ \dfrac{(t-1)M}{L}, \qquad E(\omega_i) = 0, \quad E(\omega_i x_i) = 0.$

previous two, will tend to have a slope everywhere smaller than our dotted line and a larger intercept; its graph may therefore look something like the dashed-dotted line of Figure 2.

We are now ready to exhibit the consumption-income relation $\bar{c}(y)$, which is obtained simply by multiplying the ordinates of $\bar{p}(y)$ by the constant, N/L. The result is represented by the upper solid line. As we intended to show, it is a line much flatter than the stationary cross-section line of Figure 1 (from which it can be obtained by rotation around its point $(\bar{y}, \bar{y}^e)$) and it exhibits the large positive intercept characteristic of budget data. In other words, in the presence of short-term fluctuations in income, the proportion of income consumed will tend to fall with income and the elasticity of consumption with respect to income will be less than one. Another important result we have established is that the elasticity of consumption with respect to income should depend, according to our theory, on three major factors which are capable of variation in different samples. This elasticity depends, inversely, on (a) the degree of short-term variability of income; (b) the magnitude of variations over time in the permanent component of income that give rise to unbalances in the relation between assets holdings and the permanent component itself; and (c) directly, on the elasticity of

---

x_i may be regarded as a function of the income expectations held by the household during all previous years of its active life.

From (2.13), we derive

$$\bar{x}(y^e_{-1}) = \mu + \nu y^e_{-1}; \qquad \nu = r^2 x^e_{y-1}/\lambda, \quad \mu = \bar{x} - \nu \bar{y}^e_{-1}. \qquad (2.14$$

Since in a growing economy $\lambda = \bar{y}^e_{-1}/\bar{x}_i$ may be expected to be at least as high as unity, we must have $0 \leq \nu \leq 1$, $\mu \geq 0$. From (2.14) and the definition of x_i, we obtain

$$\bar{a}(y) = \frac{(t-1)M}{L} \bar{x}(y) = \frac{(t-1)M}{L} [\mu + \nu \bar{y}^e_{-1}(y)].$$

Finally, taking into consideration the definition of $a(y^e,t)$, and using equation (2.12), we derive

$$E\{[a - a(y^e,t)]|y\} = \bar{a}(y) - \frac{(t-1)M}{L} \bar{y}^e(y)$$

$$= \frac{(t-1)M}{L} [\mu + (\nu - 1 + E)\bar{y}^e_{-1}(y) - Ey],$$

which can be expressed entirely in terms of y by making use of equation (2.10′). The above expression must fall as income rises, as stated in the text, since its derivative with respect to y is proportional to $-[E(1 - \beta) + \beta(1 - \nu)]$, which is necessarily negative (provided $E > 0$, which is assumed). In fact, we can establish that

$$E\{[a - a(y^e,t)]|y\} \gtreqqless 0$$

as

$$y \lesseqqgtr \bar{y} \left[1 - \frac{\lambda - 1}{\lambda[E(1 - \beta + \beta(1 - \nu))]}\right],$$

which shows explicitly the level of income at which the average gap between a and $a(y^e,t)$ is zero.

income expectations.[42] Given the magnitude of these three factors, the elasticity should depend also on the age of the households in the sample since, as we see from equation (2.1′) the coefficient of the second and third components of p vary with age. This point, however, will receive proper attention in the next section.

In our discussion so far we have been concerned with a cross section of households within the earning span. The effect of the inclusion of retired households in the sample can readily be established. According to our model, these households should have, on the average, levels of consumption not very different from the over-all average,[43] while, at the same time, earning incomes well below average (in our present simplified version, no income at all). The inclusion of these households, therefore, will have the effect of raising still further the $\bar{c}(y)$ curves for low levels of y, thereby increasing its general tilting and possibly making it convex to the income axis.[44]

Summing up, the typical findings of budget studies as to the relation between consumption, saving, and income in a given year, or some other short interval of time, are precisely what they should be according to our model. But, as we see, the interpretation of these findings that follows from our model is radically different from the one generally accepted. According to the usual interpretation, these findings show that the proportion of income saved rises with the economic status of the household. According to

[42]We have seen that a high elasticity of expectations tends to pull $\bar{y}^e(y)$ closer to the 45-degree line; at the same time, however, it will tend to flatten the $\bar{p}(y)$ curve relative to the $\bar{y}^e(y)$ curve, for, if assets are approximately adjusted to y^e_{-1}, then the larger the gap between y^e and y_{-1}, the larger will tend to be the unbalance in assets. Since, however, the second effect does not quite offset the first (see the discussion of Section 2.2, especially page 121), a high value of E will, on the whole, increase the slope and reduce the intercept of $\bar{p}(y)$ and thus of $\bar{c}(y)$.

[43]They may, in fact, have an average consumption level below the over-all average for two reasons: (a) because it seems likely that the level of consumption planned for after retirement will, on the whole, tend to be smaller than the average level during the earning span; (b) because of the secular rise in income per capita which characterizes most of the economies for which we have budget data. See, on this point, Modigliani and Brumberg, *op. cit.*

[44]Our statements about retired households find strong support in the data on the size distribution of income by age, reported by Janet A. Fisher, in "Income, Spending, and Saving Patterns of Consumer Units in Different Age Groups," *Studies in Income and Wealth*, [*op. cit.*,] Vol. XV, especially Tables 1 and 2, pp. 81 and 82. Actually, these tables are likely to overestimate the income (used in our sense) of elderly people, since income, there, is defined to include such items as pensions and retirement pay (p. 81, footnote 6). These inclusions also reduce the usefulness of the information on saving and dissaving by age groups presented in Table 11 (p. 93). Even with the upward-biased definition of income, the proportion of positive savers is smaller in the age group 65 and over than in any other group except the group 18 to 24. For this latter group, of course, the figures are seriously affected by the inclusion of durable goods purchases in consumption. Presumably, had our definitions of income and saving been adopted, the relative scarcity of savers and predominance of dissavers in the elderly group would be much more pronounced.

our model, on the other hand, they only show that households whose income is above the level to which they are adjusted save an abnormally large proportion and those whose income is below this level save an abnormally low proportion, or even dissave.

To be sure, up to this point, we have done little more than to show that the findings of budget data are consistent with either interpretation. It may be objected that this demonstration is an insufficient ground for discarding the old and widely accepted explanation for our new and radically different one. It would seem that, to support our claims, we should be able to produce some crucial tests, the result of which will enable us to discriminate between the two competing explanations. We believe that the remarkable piece of research recently reported on by Margaret G. Reid, discussed in the next section, comes as close to providing such a test as seems feasible with the kind of data that are presently available.[45]

II.4   Some evidence on the constancy of the saving ratio
for a stationary cross section

In order to understand the foundations of Reid's highly ingenious techniques and the meaning of her results, we must turn back to our Figures 1 and 2, and to the reasoning underlying their construction. Suppose that, somehow, we had been able to locate a sample of households, within their earning span, each of which fulfilled completely our stationary specifications. For *every* member of this sample, because of the complete absence of short-term income fluctuations, we would have the chain of equalities $y = y^e = y^e_{-1} = y_{-1}$ so that the correlation between current and previous income, r_{yy-1}, would be unity. Furthermore, if our theory is correct, the elasticity of consumption with respect to current income, η_{cy}, would also be unity. Moreover, this conclusion would continue to hold if the above chain of equalities were replaced by "proportionality," *i.e.*, $y = \dfrac{y^e}{k_1} = \dfrac{y_{-1}^e}{k_2} = \dfrac{y_{-1}}{k_3}$. In this case, all the households are out of stationary equilibrium but, so to speak, by the same proportion; this would affect the slope of the $\bar{c}(y)$ curve

[45]These results were first reported in a brief communication presented at the Conference on Saving, Inflation and Economic Progress, University of Minnesota, in May, 1952. The authors have also had the opportunity to consult a preliminary draft on "The Relation of the Within-Group Permanent Component of Income to the Income Elasticity of Expenditures," and have had the benefit of extensive discussion and consultations with Miss Reid. The hypothesis tested in the above-mentioned paper had already been partly anticipated in Reid's earlier contribution, "Effect of Income Concept upon Expenditure Curves of Farm Families," *Studies in Income and Wealth*, [*op. cit.*,] Vol. XV, especially pp. 133–139.

of Figure 1, but not its intercept, so that the consumption-income elasticity would remain unity.[46]

Now, since information on the permanent component of income and the degree of adjustment to it is not available, it is impossible to locate a sample fulfilling exactly our specifications. On the other hand, it may not be impossible to find one for which short-term fluctuations are of relatively minor importance and current income is relatively close to the level to which the household is adjusted. These conditions might be satisfied, for instance, by a sample of government employees or of college professors. For such a sample we would expect to find a correlation between current and previous income, r_{yy-1}, close to unity and, *if our model is correct*, an elasticity of consumption with respect to income, η_{cy}, close to unity. At the other extreme, for a group of households for which random short-term fluctuations play a dominant role, say, a sample of farmers over a wide geographical region, we would have a low value of r_{yy-1} and, as we know from the analysis of Figure 2, a low elasticity of consumption with respect to income. This implication of our model clearly forms the basis for a crucial experiment; this experiment has not been carried out as such, although we look forward to its being performed in the near future by anyone having the resources and interest. Meanwhile, Reid's method is very similar to the comparison we have just proposed. The discussion that has led us to the formulation of our crucial experiment suggests that the correlation between current and previous income can be taken as indirect, approximate measure of the degree to which the current income of each household is close to the level to which the household is adjusted (or to a constant multiple of this level — see previous paragraph). In the first place, this correlation is a very good direct measure of strictly short-term fluctuations which, as we have seen, control the relation between $\bar{y}^e(y)$ and y. Secondly, it seems reasonable to expect that the gap between $\bar{p}(y)$ and $\bar{y}^e(y)$ will, itself, tend to be smaller the

----

[46]If the equalities are replaced by proportionality, the correlation r_{yy-1} remains unity. Furthermore, replacing in (2.1) y^e by $k_i y$, and a by

$$\frac{(t-1)M}{L} vy^e_{-1} = \frac{(t-1)Mvk_2}{L} y,$$

(since by assumption, up to the beginning of the current year the assets of every household are proportional to the stationary equilibrium value, v being the proportionality factor and having the same meaning as in note 41), we obtain

$$c = \frac{L + L(N-t)k_1 + M(t-1)vk_2}{LL_t} y,$$

so that, for any given age t, the consumption-income relation is still a straight line through the origin and therefore η_{cy} is still unity. Since, however, the slope varies with age, if we fail to stratify by age, we may find that the computed value of η_{cy} is not exactly one, even for a stationary cross section. On the other hand, it can be verified, from the above expression, that the variation in slope with age is likely to be rather small so that, in fact, η_{cy} should be quite close to unity, unless k_2 and v are substantially different from unity, an unlikely case except in deep depression or at the peak of a boom.

smaller the short-run variability of income; for, when incomes are basically stable, there should also be less opportunity for significant discrepancies between the permanent component of income and assets to develop. Thus, when the correlation between current and previous income is high, $\bar{p}(y)$ itself should tend to be close to y. The $\bar{p}(y)$ and $\bar{c}(y)$ curves should, therefore, be similar to those of Figure 1, and the elasticity of consumption with respect to income should be close to unity. Conversely, when the correlation between current and previous income is small, evidencing the presence of pronounced short-term fluctuations, the $\bar{y}^e(y)$, $\bar{p}(y)$, and $\bar{c}(y)$ curves should be similar to those shown in Figure 2, and the elasticity of consumption with respect to income should be well below unity.

Hence, if we take several samples of households and, for each of these samples, we compute (a) the correlation between current and previous income, r_{yy-1} and (b) the elasticity of consumption with respect to income, we should find a clear positive rank correlation between the two above-mentioned statistics and, furthermore, η_{cy} should approach unity as r_{yy-1} approaches unity. In essence, this is precisely the test Reid has carried out and her results clearly confirm our inference. The fact that for none of her groups r_{yy-1} is, or could be expected to be, as high as unity prevents η_{cy} from ever reaching the theoretical stationary value of unity; but her data do show that, in the few cases where r comes close to one, η_{cy} is also impressively close to unity. According to Reid's results η_{cy} ranges from a value as low as .1 for r in the order of .2 to values as high as .8 for the highest values of r, which are in the order of .8.[47]

The above discussion is, of course, not intended as an exhaustive account of Reid's techniques and many valuable results; for this purpose the reader is referred to her forthcoming publications. Nevertheless, the brief sketch presented should be sufficient to indicate why her results seem to us to represent as impressive a confirmation of one important implication of our theory, at the micro-economic level, as one may hope to find at this time.

In addition to the test just described, there are several other, partly older, findings that support our model and acquire new meaning in the light of it.

According to our model the typical findings of budget studies as to the relation between consumption and income are basically due to the fact that, in the presence of short-term fluctuations, income over a short interval is a poor and *seriously biased* measure of the accustomed level. In the previous test the extent of this bias was measured by the correlation r_{yy-1}; the higher the correlation, the smaller the bias and, therefore, the higher the elasticity

---

[47]The figures just quoted are in part approximate since Reid has not used the statistic r_{yy-1} but, instead, one closely related to it. Although we do not have specific information on the age composition of the samples, we understand that retired households, if any, represent a negligible proportion of the samples.

of consumption with respect to income. Margaret Reid and a few others have suggested and tested alternative methods of getting a more reliable index of the accustomed level than current income and, invariably, it is found that when consumption is related to such a measure, the elasticity of consumption with respect to it rises markedly above the consumption-current income elasticity, and comes close, frequently remarkably close, to unity.[48]

Another set of results that supports our model is that reported in the classical contribution of Dorothy S. Brady and Rose D. Friedman, "Savings and the Income Distribution."[49] As is well known, their major finding is that the saving ratio appears to bear a much more stable relation to the position of the income recipient in the income distribution than to the absolute level of income itself. In other words, the proportion of income saved in a *given decile* varies much less over time and space than the proportion of income saved at a *given level of income*. It is not difficult to see that these results are what one would expect if our model is correct. As should be clear from the reasoning we have followed in developing our Figure 2, the relative frequency of households in a given income bracket whose income is below or above their accustomed level, depends, not on the absolute level of income, but, rather, on the position of the income bracket relative to the average income. For example, in a given income bracket, say $10,000, we should expect to find a large proportion of people whose accustomed level is less than $10,000 if, say, the average income is $2,000 and the level $10,000

---

[48]See, for instance, Josephine H. Staab, "Income-Expenditure Relations of Farm Families Using Three Bases of Classification," Ph.D. dissertation, The University of Chicago, 1952; Reid, *op. cit.* (several new experiments are also reported in Reid's preliminary draft quoted above); Vickrey, *op. cit.* In essence Vickrey's point is that consumption is more reliable than current income as a measure of the permanent component of income (p. 273) and he suggests, accordingly, that the individual marginal propensity to consume (with respect to the permanent component) can be estimated more reliably by relating consumption (per equivalent adult), c, to $\bar{y}(c)$ than by relating $\bar{c}(y)$ to y, as has been usually done. It can be shown that Vickrey's suggestions receive a good deal of support from our model (with the addition of the stochastic assumptions introduced in various footnotes above) in that the relation between c and $\bar{y}(c)$ should be very similar to that between c and our quantity p. In particular, c should be nearly proportional to $\bar{y}(c)$, a conclusion that Vickrey himself did not reach but which is well supported by his own tabulations. A double logarithmic plot of c against $\bar{y}(c)$, based on his data, reveals an extremely close linear relationship with a slope remarkably close to unity. (We have estimated this slope, by graphical methods, at .97.) On the other hand, using the conventional plot, $\bar{c}(y)$ against y, the slope for the same data can be estimated at somewhat below .85, and, in addition, the scatter around the line of relationship is distinctly wider than for the first mentioned plot.

In the contribution under discussion Vickrey has also been very much concerned with the influence of the size composition of the household on saving behavior. This is a point which, because of limitations of space, we have been forced to neglect in the present paper. We will merely indicate, at this point, that our central hypothesis (that the essential purpose of saving is the smoothing of the major and minor variations that occur in the income stream in the course of the life cycle) provides a framework within which the influence of family size can be readily analyzed. We hope to develop this point in later contributions.

[49]*Studies in Income and Wealth*, [*op. cit.*,] Vol. X, pp. 247–265.

is in the top decile; while, in this same bracket, we should expect to find a small proportion of people whose accustomed level is below $10,000 if the community average income were, say, $50,000 so that the $10,000 bracket is in the lowest income decile. More generally, it can be shown that provided, as seems likely, there is a fairly stable relation between average income in a given decile and the over-all average income, then the saving ratio, in a given decile, would depend primarily on the (relative) short-term variability of income.[50] Thus, if we compare, over time or space, groups for which the (relative) variability of income is not very different, the proportion of income saved in any given decile should be roughly the same for every group. As an example, we can compare the behavior of nonfarm families in different regions and at different points in time (see Brady and Friedman, Charts 1 through 4) and we find our inference confirmed. Furthermore, within a group, the greater the variability in income, the greater should be the variation in the saving ratio as between the lower and the upper deciles. This inference, too, is supported by comparison of nonfarm and farm groups (compare Chart 2 with Chart 5).

It will be recognized that our theory offers an explanation for the Brady-Friedman findings that is fundamentally different from the social-psychological explanation that has been advanced heretofore.[51] Although our current interpretation is much simpler and integrates these findings with

---

[50]Making use of equations (2.10′), (2.12) and the expression for $\bar{a}(y)$ derived in note 41, our cross-section income-consumption relation can be reduced to the form

$$\bar{c}(y) = A + By = A^*\bar{y} + By,$$

where A^* and B depend on the coefficients E, α, β, λ, μ, ν we have introduced earlier, and on age. These coefficients, in turn, depend primarily on the variability of income as measured by $r_{yy}e_{-1}$ and $r_{xy}e_{-1}$, and, probably to a lesser extent, on the long-term trend of income (which affects λ, μ and ν) and on the cyclical position of the economy (which affects α and β and possibly E). Hence, if we have various samples of households for each of which the variability of income is approximately the same, the coefficients A^* and B should also be approximately the same for each sample, especially if the samples in question do not differ too markedly with respect to age, composition and the cyclical position of total income. Denoting by $\bar{c}_i$ and $\bar{y}_i$ the average value of consumption and income for all households falling in the i-th quantile of a given sample, we must have

$$c_i = A^*\bar{y} + B\bar{y}_i.$$

If, furthermore, for each of the samples compared $\bar{y}_i/\bar{y}$ is approximately constant, so that we can write $\bar{y}_i = k_i\bar{y}$, we obtain

$$\bar{c}_i/\bar{y}_i = \overline{(c/y)}_i = \frac{A^*}{k_i} + B,$$

i.e., the proportion of income consumed in a given quantile, i, should be approximately the same for all samples compared, as stated in the text. We may add that, if we replace our simple stochastic assumption (2.10) by the more realistic one suggested at the end of note 37, the conclusion stated in the text would still stand, although the relation between $\overline{(c/y)}_i$ and i would be more complex than indicated by the right-hand side of the above equation.

[51]For example, see James Duesenberry, *Income, Saving and the Theory of Consumer Behavior* [Cambridge, Mass.: Harvard University Press, 1949].

many others without recourse to additional postulates, we do not wish to deny that the earlier explanation may have some validity.

One more finding of some significance has to do with the relation between the elasticity of consumption with respect to income on the one hand and age on the other, to which reference has been made earlier. It can be shown that the slope of $\bar{c}(y)$ should tend to fall, and its intercept to rise, with age, unless, on the average, the elasticity of income expectations is extremely low, say, in the neighborhood of zero.[52] Since such a low average elasticity of expectations is rather unlikely to prevail, especially in a basically growing economy, we should generally expect the elasticity of consumption with respect to income to fall with age. This conclusion finds empirical support in the findings reported by Janet Fisher.[53] Our theory provides a common-sense explanation for her empirical finding. The increase in expected income, y^e, which accompanies the change in current income, produces a relatively larger increase in the anticipated total resources of a younger than of an older household, if E is above the minimal value, because of the greater number of years over which the higher level of income will be received. To give a specific illustration, suppose that $E = 1$, and that y, and therefore also y^e, increase by one unit. For a household of age $N - 1$, which has only one year to go before retirement, total resources, v_{N-1}, increase by only two units, and these two units have to be spread over the remaining two years of earning and M years of retirement. Therefore consumption rises by only $\dfrac{2}{M + 1}$. At the other extreme, if the household had age 1, its total anticipated resources rise by N units, to be spread over $N + M$ years. Hence, current consumption rises by $\dfrac{N}{N + M}$ units. By a similar reasoning, one can conclude that the depressing effect on current consumption of the unbalance in assets that has been created by the change in income is greater the older the household, because of the smaller number of years available to the household to redress the unbalance.

In conclusion then, there is already ample evidence, and from widely

---

[52]Making use of equations (2.10'), (2.12) and of the expression for $\bar{a}(y)$ of note 41, it can be verified that

$$\frac{\partial^2 \bar{c}(y)}{\partial y\, \partial t} < 0,$$

i.e., the slope of the cross-section consumption-income relation falls with age, provided

$$E > \frac{1}{M + 1} - \frac{M\beta(1 - \nu)}{(M + 1)(1 - \beta)}.$$

A very similar condition on E must be satisfied in order for the constant term to rise with age. Since $1/(M + 1)$ should be in the order of 0.1, and β and ν are typically smaller than unity, the right-hand side of the above inequality cannot significantly exceed zero and is, in fact, likely to be negative.

[53]Op. cit., p. 90 and p. 99.

different, sources which is consistent with the most distinctive implications we have derived so far from our theory and which is not equally consistent or, at any rate, readily explainable in terms of any other single set of hypotheses that, to our knowledge, has been advanced so far.

II.5 Individual saving, assets, and age

In recent years a good deal of attention has been devoted to the influence of assets on consumption, and attempts have been made at estimating the cross-section relation between these variables on the expectation that the parameters obtained would yield information on the time-series relation. Our theory has something to contribute as to the pitfalls of such an attempt. To begin with, it suggests that the relevant concept of assets is *net worth;* unfortunately, most of the recent empirical work has concentrated instead on liquid assets, a variable which, according to our model, bears no definite relation to consumption, except perhaps as a very imperfect proxy for net worth.

But even if information on net worth were available, knowledge of the variation in consumption as between different households having different asset holdings, would give very little (and that little would be biased) information as to how a household would react if its assets were increased unexpectedly by a given amount, say, by an anonymous gift of the usual benevolent millionaire or, to take a more fashionable example, by an unexpected fall in the price level of consumables. This failing occurs because the observed asset holdings do not just happen to be there; instead, they reflect the life plan of the individual, which in turn depends on income and income expectations.

To interpret the positive correlation between assets and consumption as implying that people consume more *because* they have more assets would be only slightly less inaccurate than the inverse inference that people have higher assets because they consume more. The point is that both consumption and assets are greatly affected by the other variables: income, income expectations,[54] and age.

It may be objected that we are destroying a straw man; anyone studying the effect of assets would have sense enough to control the effect of, say, income. This may well be true, yet we feel that the above paragraph contains a useful lesson as to the relation between assets and consumption plans that one may too easily forget. For instance, the statement which has been repeated *ad nauseam* that in the early postwar years people bought durable goods lavishly *because* they had such large holdings of liquid assets (which

---

[54]There is ample evidence of a very pronounced correlation between assets and income‘ at least as far as liquid assets are concerned. See, for example, Lawrence Klein, "Assets, Debts, and Economic Behavior," *Studies in Income and Wealth*, [*op. cit.*,] Vol. XIV, Table 1, p. 209; and Fisher, *op. cit.*, Table 6, p. 86.

may even find some apparent confirmation in survey results) might well stand a good deal of re-examination along the lines indicated above.

But our model tells us that it is not enough to control income or even income expectations. As it is brought out clearly by our analysis of the stationary case, assets depend also on age (see equation (2.8); and this implication of our model is one for which scattered supporting empirical information is available.[55] Furthermore, as we have seen, our hypothetical household goes on consuming a constant fraction of income (equation 2.9) even though its assets continue to rise, and reach their peak just before retirement; the rise in assets relative to income does not depress saving because it is part and parcel of the life plan. In other words, higher assets do not necessarily affect saving; they do so only if, on account of unexpected variations, assets turn out to be out of line with income and age: it is only an excess (or shortage) of assets that affects the saving ratio (see equation 2.2′).[56]

Finally, we can see from our equation (2.1) that the cross-section marginal rate of change of consumption (or saving) with respect to asset holdings (income and income expectations constant) could not yield a reliable estimate of the marginal propensity to consume with respect to assets. The reason is simple. From (2.1), it follows that this marginal propensity is

$$\frac{\partial c}{\partial a} = -\frac{\partial s}{\partial a} = \frac{1}{L_t}. \tag{2.15}$$

This expression is independent of assets and income but depends on age.

---

[55]Gustave Cassel, *The Theory of Social Economy* [New York: Harcourt, Brace & Co.,] 1932 ed., p. 244; Horst Menderhausen and Raymond W. Goldsmith, "Measuring Estate Tax Wealth," *Studies in Income and Wealth*, [*op. cit.*,] Vol. XIV, Table 4. p. 140; and Fisher, *loc. cit.* The most systematic information we have found on this subject is that presented by Janet Fisher, although, unfortunately, her most interesting tabulations relate to liquid assets. For this reason we will not attempt an extensive comparison of her findings with our theory. We may point out, however, that in terms of liquid assets, her data agree remarkably well with our theory in several respects. For example, a comparison of the mean income ratio (Table 1, p. 81) with the mean ratio of liquid asset holdings (Table 4, p. 84) by age groups, reveals that the ratio of assets per spending unit to income per spending unit rises steadily with age. For the age group 45-64, which is her oldest group wherein active households presumably predominate, this ratio is nearly three times as large as for her youngest group, 18–24. For the age group 65-and-over, wherein, presumably, retired people predominate, the ratio nearly doubles again. This very high ratio is precisely what should be expected from our model where assets are drawn down slowly but income falls much faster with retirement. In terms of assets, rather than of the income/asset ratio, the peak should be reached just before retirement. Confirmation of this inference is found in the tabulations of Table 5 (p. 85).

Also suggestive of this relation is the complaint by Lawrence Klein, "Assets, Debts, and Economic Behavior," that: "There is some indication that the influence of age on savings may be obscured by a significant positive correlation between (L/Y) and a (where Y = income, L = liquid assets, and a = age of the spending-unit head in years)."

[56]All this has, of course, some significant implications about the "Pigou effect" which are developed in Modigliani and Brumberg, *op. cit.*

We cannot, therefore, properly speak of *the* marginal propensity to consume with respect to assets, as this quantity will vary substantially from age group to age group, tending to increase with age.

Let us finally remember that, in order to compute the individual marginal propensity from cross-section data, it is also not sufficient to control age by introducing this variable linearly in a linear regression of consumption on income and assets,[57] for, according to our model, age does not enter in a linear fashion. The only way of estimating the marginal propensity at various ages and, in the process, test equation (2.15) is to carry out a full stratification by age groups (or some equivalent procedure). It is to be hoped that data for such a test may sometime be available.[58]

II.6   Uncertainty, saving, and the composition of assets

The analysis of the previous sections is helpful in providing a justification for our earlier contention that the phenomenon of uncertainty can be neglected without seriously affecting the usefulness of the analysis.

As we have seen, even under the assumption of certainty there are sufficient incentives for the household to accumulate assets at a rapid rate during the early years of its life. Since the assets thus accumulated can be used to acquire durable goods and are also available as a general reserve against emergency, it would appear that the last two motives (p. 392), which are the result of uncertainty, need not affect significantly the saving behavior.[59]

To be sure, though assets can satisfy several purposes, their efficiency will not be the same in this respect. For instance, those assets which are best suited to satisfy the fourth motive are frequently not very well suited to satisfy the third. Accordingly, variations in the relative urgency of our four motives as between different individuals, and at various points of the life cycle for the same individual, will be reflected in the composition of the balance-sheet. This composition will also be affected by the current and prospective total resources, by the nature of the available alternatives, and, last butnot least, by "social" pressures. Cautious individuals will hold relatively more liquid assets. Individuals with large means will tend to hold more durable goods. Examples of social pressure on the type of assets held

---

[57]Cf. Klein, *op. cit.*, pp. 220 ff.

[58]More generally, the essential implication of our theory that should be tested is that the (average) relation between consumption and net worth, given income and income expectations, is linear and with a slope which tends to grow with the age of the household. The specific value of the slope given by (2.15) depends on Assumptions III and IV which are convenient for exposition but are not essential to the theory.

[59]In the very early years these motives might possibly lead to a somewhat faster rate of accumulation than might occur otherwise. On the other hand, in his early years, an individual may feel less of a need for precautionary assets since, being a better risk, he will be in a better position to borrow, and may also be able to rely, for emergencies, on his relatives.

are also not far to seek; witness the scramble for common stock during the 'twenties and the adoption of television after the Second World War.[60]

As to the effect of the life cycle on the composition of the "portfolio," one might expect that during the period of family formation people will put most of their savings into durables. Automobiles, refrigerators, stoves, and other appliances are felt to be essential to the establishment of an American household. After the initial purchase of durables, although depreciated goods are to be replaced and some additional goods are to be bought, savings flow into other kinds of assets. Various liquid assets may be acquired. The acquisition of a house, which requires (except for the recent G.I. housing) a prior large stock of cash, can be expected to occur throughout the life span. These generalizations are borne out by the existing data.[61]

In conclusion, uncertainty as well as many other factors must be recognized as being of great importance if one is interested in developing a satisfactory theory of the composition of the "portfolio" or, which is equivalent, of the rate of addition to the specific assets. They do not seem to be essential, however, for the development of a useful theory of the factors controlling the over-all rate of saving. Needless to say, the final justification of this statement must rest on whether or not our theory proves helpful in explaining facts which are presently known or will be revealed by further empirical work. The results so far are encouraging.

II.7   Summary

On the basis of the received theory of consumer's choice, plus one major assumption as to the properties of the utility function, we have been able to derive a simple model of individual saving behavior which is capable of accounting for the most significant findings of many cross-section studies. Inasmuch as this model has been shown elsewhere to be equally consistent with the major findings of time-series analysis, we seem to be near the ultimate goal of a unified, and yet simple, theory of the consumption function.

The results of our labor basically confirm the propositions put forward by Keynes in *The General Theory*. At the same time, we take some satisfac-

---

[60]Cf. Boulding, *op. cit.*, Ch. 3 and Ch. 5 for a novel approach to the choice of asset combinations. See also J. Marshack, "Money and the Theory of Assets," *Econometrica*, [VI], Oct. 1938, pp. 311–325.

Because durable goods generally seem more vulnerable to social pressure than the forms of saving that make up the ordinary (*e.g.*, Department of Commerce) definition, it is easy to see why they have been thought of as consumption. Keynes enforced the definition only by his interest in the modes of saving not necessarily matched by investment. However, the idea of ostentatious durables typifying "conspicuous consumption" preceded the *General Theory* by many years.

[61]See: Dorothy S. Brady, "An Analysis of Saving on the Basis of Consumer Expenditure Data," *Saving and Capital Market Study*, Section 3, R. W. Goldsmith, Director, preliminary; and Fisher, *op. cit.*, Tables 4, 5, and 6, pp. 85–89.

tion in having been able to tie this aspect of his analysis into the mainstream of economic theory by replacing his mysterious psychological law with the principle that men are disposed, as a rule and on the average, to be forward-looking animals.[62] We depart from Keynes, however, on his contention of "a greater *proportion* of income being saved as real income increases" (p. 97, italics his). We claim instead that the *proportion of income saved is essentially independent of income;* and that systematic deviations of the saving ratio from the normal level are largely accounted for by the fact that short-term fluctuations of income around the basic earning capacity of the household, as well as gradual changes in this earning capacity, may cause accumulated savings to get out of line with current income and age. The common sense of our claim rests largely on two propositions: (a) that the major purpose of saving is to provide a cushion against the major variations in income that typically occur during the life cycle of the household as well as against less systematic short-term fluctuations in income and needs; (b) that the provisions the household would wish to make, and can afford to make, for retirement as well as for emergencies, must be basically proportional, on the average, to its basic earning capacity, while the number of years over which these provisions can be made is largely independent of income levels. We have shown that our claim is strongly supported by budget data when these data are properly analyzed.

In *The General Theory*, Keynes did not put much emphasis on the proposition quoted above. But in the literature that followed, the assumption that the proportion of income saved must rise with income has frequently been regarded as one of the essential aspects of his theory and, as such, it has played an important role in Keynesian analysis and its applications to economic policy and forecasting.

The task of developing the policy implications of our analysis falls outside the scope of this paper. We may, nonetheless, point out, as an example, that our new understanding of the determinants of saving behavior casts some doubts on the effectiveness of a policy of income redistribution for the purpose of reducing the average propensity to save.

Finally, we hope our study has proved useful in pointing out the many pitfalls inherent in inferences derived from cross-section data without the guidance of a clear theoretical framework. For instance, we must take a dim view of the attempts that have been made at deriving the time-series average and marginal propensity to save from the cross-section relation between saving and income. *The individual marginal propensity cannot, generally, be identified with the cross-section rate of change;* in fact, as we have seen, these two parameters need not bear any definite and stable relation to one another.

---

[62]Our conclusions are also in complete agreement with B. Ohlin's brief but illuminating remarks and criticism of Keynes developed in "Some Notes on the Stockholm Theory of Savings and Investment," reprinted in [American Economic Association] *Readings in Business Cycle Theory* [Homewood, Ill.: Richard D. Irwin, Inc., 1944] see especially pp. 98–100.

We have further shown elsewhere[63] that the individual marginal propensity to save bears, in turn, a very complex relation to the time-series marginal propensity and hardly any relation at all to the time-series average propensity.

Needless to say, many implications of our theory remain to be tested. In fact, it is a merit of our hypothesis that it leads to many deductions that are subject to empirical tests and therefore to contradiction. We would be the first to be surprised if all the implications of the theory turned out to be supported by future tests. We are confident, however, that a sufficient number will find confirmation to show that we have succeeded in isolating a major determinant of a very complex phenomenon.

APPENDIX

Some suggestions for the adaptation of our model to quantitative tests and some further empirical evidence

Of the many cross-section studies of saving behavior in recent years, the one that comes closest to testing the hypothesis represented by our equations (2.1) and (2.2) is the extensive quantitative analysis reported by Lawrence R. Klein in "Assets, Debts and Economic Behavior," *op. cit.* (see especially pp. 220–227 and the brief but illuminating comment of A. Hart, *ibid.,* p. 228). In this appendix we shall attempt to provide a brief systematic comparison of his quantitative findings with the quantitative implications of our theory.

We have already pointed out the many shortcomings of his analysis for the purpose of testing our theory, both in terms of definitions of variables and of the form of the equation finally tested. Because of these shortcomings, the result of our comparison can have at best only a symptomatic value. In fact, the major justification for what follows is its possible usefulness in indicating the type of adaptations that might be required for the purpose of carrying out statistical tests of our model.

Making use of the identity $N - t \equiv \dfrac{N(L - t)}{L} - \dfrac{Mt}{L}$, our equation (2.2) can be altered to the form

$$s_i = \frac{L - t_i}{L_i} y_i - \frac{N(L - t_i)}{LL_i} y_i^e - \frac{a_i}{L_i} + \frac{M}{LL_i} t_i y_i^e, \qquad (A.1)$$

where the subscript i denotes the i-th household, and L_i is an abbreviation for $L + 1 - t_i$.

Unfortunately, the variable y_i^e is usually unknown. Some information

---

[63]Modigliani and Brumberg, *op. cit.*

on it might be gathered by appropriate questions analogous to the question on short-term income expectations which has already been asked in the past. Klein himself, however, has not made use of this possible source of information in the study in progress. We must, therefore, find some way of relating y_i^e to the variables actually used by Klein, which are also those most commonly available.

It is clear that y^e must bear a fairly close and reasonably stable relation to current income, y. In fact, at various points in the text we have suggested that the relation between these two variables may be expressed by the equation

$$y^e = (1 - E)y_{-1}^e + Ey + A + U \tag{A.2}$$
$$= (1 - E)(\alpha + \beta y) + Ey + U',$$

where A is a constant for a given sample (though subject to variation over time); E is the elasticity of income expectations defined by equation (2.11); U and $U' = (1 - E)\epsilon' + U$ are random errors; α, β are defined by equations (2.10'); and ϵ' is the random component of that equation.

If we also have information on previous year's income, y_{-1}, we can clearly exploit this information to get a better estimate of y_{-1}^e, and (A.2) then takes the form

$$y^e = \alpha^* + \beta_1 y + \beta_2 y_{-1} + U^*. \tag{A.3}$$

The coefficients of this equation, as well as the random component U^*, depend again on the short-term variability of income as measured by the correlation $r_{yy_{-1}}$, on the variance of U and on the elasticity of expectations E. It is not worth-while, however, to derive here this relation explicitly.

Substituting for y^e from (A.3) into (A.1), and rearranging terms (and neglecting the error term which is proportional to U^*) we get:

$$s_i = -\frac{(N - t_i)\alpha^*}{L_i} + \frac{(L - t_i)(L - N\beta_1) - L(N - t_i)\beta_2}{LL_i} y_i \tag{A.4}$$

$$- \frac{a_i}{L_i} + \frac{(N - t_i)\beta_2}{L_i} (y_i - y_{-1i}) + \frac{M\beta_1}{LL_i} t_i y_i.$$

Finally, dividing through by y_i and making use of the identity $L \equiv M + N$, we obtain the result[64]

$$\frac{s_i}{y_i} = \frac{(L_i - 1)(L - N\beta_1) - L(L_i - M - 1)\beta_2}{LL_i} \tag{A.5}$$

$$- \frac{(L_i - M - 1)\alpha^*}{L_i} \frac{1}{y_i} - \frac{1}{L_i} \frac{a_i}{y_i}$$

$$+ \frac{(N - t_i)\beta_2}{L_i} (y_i - y_{-1i})/y_i + \frac{M\beta_1}{LL_i} t_i.$$

[64]The division by y_i creates certain statistical problems in connection with the random term; this difficulty can be handled by an appropriate modification of equation (A.2) or (A.3) which need not be discussed here since it would greatly complicate the presentation without basically affecting the conclusions.

If the quantity L_i were a constant, this equation would be identical in form with the equation Klein proposed to test;[65] although, in the actual statistical test he has found it convenient to approximate the first two terms by an expression of the form $\lambda + \mu \log y_i$, and the variable $\dfrac{y_i - y_{-1i}}{y_i}$ by $\dfrac{y_i - y_{-1i}}{y_{-1i}}$.

If we now look at Klein's results, we can take courage from the fact that all his coefficients have at least the sign required by our model; namely, a positive sign for income, income change, and age (t in our notation, a in Klein's) and negative for assets (a/y in our notation, L/Y in Klein's). This result is of some significance, especially in the case of the age variable. According to our model, the positive sign of this coefficient reflects the fact that within the earning span, for a given level of income and assets, the older the household the smaller will tend to be its resources per remaining year of life, and therefore the smaller the consumption (*i.e.*, the higher the saving).

It would be interesting to compare the size of Klein's coefficients with the values implied by our model. At this point, however, we must remember that the analogy between Klein's equation and our equation (A.5) is more formal than real; for Klein treats his coefficients as if they were constant, whereas, according to our model, they are all functions of age since they all involve the quantity L_i. Consideration of the sensitivity of the coefficients of our equation to variations in t suggests that the error involved in treating them as constants might be quite serious. We must further remember that the specific value of the coefficients in (A.5) is based on Assumptions III and IV. As we have repeatedly indicated, these Assumptions are introduced for expository convenience but are not an essential part of our model. With the elimination of Assumption III and the relaxation of IV, along the lines suggested in footnote 25, the form of our equations and the sign of the coefficients are unchanged, but the value of these coefficients is not necessarily that given in equation (A.5), nor is it possible to deduce these values entirely on a priori grounds, except within broad limits.

We might, nonetheless, attempt a comparison, for whatever it is worth, by replacing the variable t_i in the expression L_i by a constant, say, by its average value in Klein's sample. Unfortunately, this average is not published, but we should not go far wrong by putting it at between 15 and 25 and computing a range for each coefficient using these two values." We must also take a guess at the value of β_1 and β_2. These quantities, it will be noted, are not observable. On the basis of an analysis of factors controlling these coefficients we suggest, however, that a value in the order of .5 to .6 for β_1 and of .2 and .3 for β_2, is not likely to be far from the mark. Using our standard assumption as to the value of L and N, we then get the following comparison:

---

[65]*Klein, op. cit.*, p. 220.

COEFFICIENT OF	KLEIN'S ESTIMATES[66]		OUR MODEL (LINEAR APPROXIMATION)		
<u>Assets</u>	−.21;	−.25	−.04	to	−.03
Income	(.02)	(.03)			
Income change	.03;	.07	.1	to	.2
	(.05)	(.06)			
Age	.0013;	.0055	.003	to	.0045
	(.0022)	(.0024)			

The age coefficient falls squarely within the range of Klein's results and nothing further need be said about it. The coefficient of income change estimated from the sample is lower than we should have expected, although, at least in one case, the difference from our estimate is well within the range of the standard error.[67] In the case of assets, however, the statistical coefficient is clearly far too great. A large part of this disparity is due, we suggest, to the fact that Klein's variable L represents liquid assets whereas our variable a represents net worth, which is clearly, on the average, several times as large as liquid assets. Hence, if liquid assets holdings are a reasonably good index of total net worth, Klein's coefficient would have to be a large multiple of ours.[68] While it is doubtful that this multiple could be as large as 6 or 7, there seems little doubt that this correction would cut the excess of Klein's coefficient over the theoretical value very substantially, probably to well within one half.[69]

Unfortunately, no definite statement can be made about the coefficient of income and the constant term on account of the logarithmic transformation introduced by Klein. However, approximate computations we have

[66]Figures in parentheses represent the standard errors. The two figures in this column represent the parameters of the equation for "Home Owners" and "Renters," respectively (*op. cit.*, p. 221). Since the completion of this Appendix, Mr. Klein has kindly informed us that the average age for the two samples combined is 46 years; this implies an average age, since entering the labor force, in the order of 20 to 25 years, which is within the assumed range.

[67]We suspect that expressing income change in terms of y_{-1} instead of y may also contribute to the discrepancy.

[68]If this explanation is correct, it would also follow that Klein's coefficient greatly overestimates the effect on consumption of an increase in assets due, say, to an unanticipated fall in the price level of consumables. In any event, as already pointed out, the relation between the cross section and the time-series marginal propensity is a complex one. In the companion paper quoted earlier, we have shown that the time-series marginal propensity to consume with respect to net worth should be in the order of 0.1.

[69]There is also reason to believe that failure to take into account properly the age variable may lead to an appreciable upward bias in the asset coefficient if the cross section includes retired people. Since we do not know whether Klein's sample does have a significant representation of retired households we cannot say whether this explanation is relevant.

made suggest that these coefficients are in line with our theory in the case of his first equation and somewhat too large (in absolute terms) for the second.

It would thus appear that, at least in terms of orders of magnitude,

Klein's findings agree with the implications of our model. We hasten to repeat that the comparison has very limited significance and its results must be taken with a good deal of salt; yet Klein's estimates, just as the many other empirical data we have been able to locate, would seem to warrant the feeling that we are on the right track.

MILTON FRIEDMAN **7**

The permanent income hypothesis

The magnitudes termed "permanent income" and "permanent consumption"* that play such a critical role in the theoretical analysis cannot be observed directly for any individual consumer unit. The most that can be observed are actual receipts and expenditures during some finite period,

From Milton Friedman, *A Theory of the Consumption Function*, National Bureau of Economic Research (Princeton: Princeton University Press, 1957), pp. 20–37. Reprinted by permission of Princeton University Press, Published 1957 by Princeton University Press. All rights reserved. [Footnotes expanded — *Eds.*]

*[In *A Theory of the Consumption Function* (NBER; Princeton: Princeton University Press, 1957), Friedman discusses the meanings of these two terms as follows:

"The designation of current receipts as 'income' in statistical studies is an expedient enforced by limitations of data. On a theoretical level, income is generally defined as the amount a consumer unit could consume (or believes that it could) while maintaining its wealth intact. (The well-known problems raised by this definition are not relevant to the analysis that follows. For a discussion of some of them see J. R. Hicks, *Value and Capital*, Oxford: Oxford University Press, 1939, pp. 171–188.) On our analysis, consumption is a function of income so defined. . . . .

"A similar problem arises about the meaning of "consumption." We have been using the term consumption to designate the value of the *services* that it is *planned* to consume during the period in question, which, under conditions of certainty, would also equal the value of the services actually consumed. The term is generally used in statistical studies to designate actual expenditures on goods and services. It therefore differs from the value of services it is planned to consume on two counts: first, because of additions to or subtractions from the stock of consumer goods, second, because of divergencies between plans and their realization.

"Let us use the terms 'permanent income' and 'permanent consumption' to refer to the concepts relevant to the theoretical analysis, so as to avoid confusion with the frequent usage of income as synonymous with current receipts and consumption as synonymous with current expenditures, and let us designate them by y_p and c_p respectively, with an additional numerical subscript to denote the year in question." (pp. 10-11) — *Eds.*]

141

supplemented, perhaps, by some verbal statements about expectations for the future. The theoretical constructs are *ex ante* magnitudes; the empirical data are *ex post*. Yet in order to use the theoretical analysis to interpret empirical data, a correspondence must be established between the theoretical constructs and the observed magnitudes.

The most direct way to do so, and the one that has generally been followed in similar contexts, is to construct estimates of permanent income and permanent consumption for each consumer unit separately by adjusting the cruder receipts and expenditure data for some of their more obvious defects, and then to treat the adjusted *ex post* magnitudes as if they were also the desired *ex ante* magnitudes. Cash expenditures during a particular time period that are regarded as expenses of earning income can be deducted from cash receipts during the corresponding time period; accrual methods of accounting can be substituted for cash accounting for some or all income items; expenditures on durable consumer goods can be regarded as capital expenditures and only the imputed value of services rendered included as consumption; and so on. These adjustments clearly reduce the difference between the statistical estimates and the theoretical constructs and are therefore highly desirable. But even when they are carried as far as is at all feasible, the resulting magnitudes, interpreted as estimates of permanent income and permanent consumption, are not consistent with equation (2.6)†: measured consumption turns out to be a smaller fraction of measured income for high than for low measured incomes even for groups of consumer units for whom it does not seem reasonable to attribute this result to differences in the values of i, w, or u.

We are thus driven either to reject equation (2.6), which is what earlier workers have done, or to resort to more indirect means of establishing a correspondence between the theoretical constructs and the observed magnitudes, which is what I propose to do. One indirect means is to use evidence for other time periods and other consumer units to interpret data for one consumer unit for one period. For example, if Mr. A's measured income fluctuates widely from year to year while Mr. B's is highly stable, it seems reasonable that Mr. A's measured income is a poorer index of his permanent income than Mr. B's is of his. Again, suppose Mr. A's measured income in any period is decidedly lower than the average measured income of a group of individuals who are similar to him in characteristics that we have reason to believe affect potential earnings significantly — for example, age, occupation, race, and location. It then seems reasonable to suppose that Mr. A's measured income understates his permanent income.

†[Equation (2.6) is

$$c_p = k(i,w,u,)y_p = k(i,w,u)iW,$$

where w stands for the ratio of nonhuman wealth to permanent income; u for utility factors such as age, family composition, and the like as well as any objective factors that affect anticipations; i for the rate of interest; and W for wealth of a consumer unit. All variables refer to the same point in time. See Friedman, *op. cit.*, p. 17 — *Eds.*]

The following formalization of the relation between the theoretical constructs and observed magnitudes is designed to facilitate the use of such evidence. Its central idea is to interpret empirical data as observable manifestations of theoretical constructs that are themselves regarded as not directly observable.

1. The interpretation of data on the income and consumption of consumer units

Let y represent a consumer unit's measured income for some time period, say a year. I propose to treat this income as the sum of two components: a permanent component (y_p), corresponding to the permanent income of the theoretical analysis, and a transitory component (y_t),[1] or

$$y = y_p + y_t. \tag{3.1}$$

The permanent component is to be interpreted as reflecting the effect of those factors that the unit regards as determining its capital value or wealth: the nonhuman wealth it owns; the personal attributes of the earners in the unit, such as their training, ability, personality; the attributes of the economic activity of the earners, such as the occupation followed, the location of the economic activity, and so on. It is analogous to the "expected" value of a probability distribution. The transitory component is to be interpreted as reflecting all "other" factors, factors that are likely to be treated by the unit affected as "accidental" or "chance" occurrences, though they may, from another point of view, be the predictable effect of specifiable forces, for example, cyclical fluctuations in economic activity.[2] In statistical data, the transitory component includes also chance errors of measurement; unfortunately, there is in general no way to separate these from the transitory component as viewed by the consumer unit.

Some of the factors that give rise to transitory components of income are specific to particular consumer units, for example, illness, a bad guess about when to buy or sell, and the like; and, similarly, chance errors of measurement. For any considerable group of consumer units, the resulting transitory components tend to average out, so that if they alone accounted for the discrepancies between permanent and measured income, the mean measured income of the group would equal the mean permanent component, and the mean transitory component would be zero. But not all factors giving rise to transitory components need be of this kind. Some may be

[1]The terminology, and much of the subsequent analysis, is taken from Friedman and Kuznets, *Income from Independent Professional Practice* [New York: National Bureau of Economic Research, 1945], pp. 325–338, 352–364.

[2]This division is, of course, in part arbitrary, and just where to draw the line may well depend on the particular application. Similarly, the dichotomy between permanent and transitory components is a highly special case. See *ibid.*, pp. 352–364, for a generalization to a larger number of components.

largely common to the members of the group, for example, unusually good or bad weather, if the group consists of farmers in the same locality; or a sudden shift in the demand for some product, if the group consists of consumer units whose earners are employed in producing this product. If such factors are favorable for any period, the mean transitory component is positive; if they are unfavorable, it is negative.[3] Similarly, a systematic bias in measurement may produce a nonzero mean transitory component in recorded data even though the transitory factors affecting consumer units have a zero effect on the average.

Similarly, let c represent a consumer unit's expenditures for some time period, and let it be regarded as the sum of a permanent component (c_p) and a transitory component (c_t), so that

$$c = c_p + c_t. \tag{3.2}$$

Again, some of the factors producing transitory components of consumption are specific to particular consumer units, such as unusual sickness, a specially favorable opportunity to purchase, and the like; others affect groups of consumer units in the same way, such as an unusually cold spell, a bountiful harvest, and the like. The effects of the former tend to average out; the effects of the latter produce positive or negative mean transitory components for groups of consumer units; the same is true with chance and systematic errors of measurement.

It is tempting to interpret the permanent components as corresponding to average lifetime values and the transitory components as the difference between such lifetime averages and the measured values in a specific time period. It would, however, be a serious mistake to accept such an interpretation, for two reasons. In the first place, the experience of one unit is itself but a small sample from a more extensive hypothetical universe, so there is no reason to suppose that transitory components average out to zero over the unit's lifetime. In the second place, and more important, it seems neither necessary nor desirable to decide in advance the precise meaning to be attached to "permanent." The distinction between permanent and transitory is intended to interpret actual behavior. We are going to treat consumer units *as if* they regarded their income and their consumption as the sum of two such components, and *as if* the relation between the permanent components is the one suggested by our theoretical analysis. The precise line to be drawn between permanent and transitory components is best left to be determined by the data themselves, to be whatever seems to correspond to consumer behavior.

---

[3]Note the difference from *ibid.*, p. 326, where the mean transitory component can be taken to be zero without loss of generality. The difference reflects a narrower definition of transitory component in *ibid.* plus the use of the concept to compare the same group in two years.

Figure 2 is designed to bring out more explicitly the wide range of possible interpretations of permanent income. This figure refers to a single consumer unit, the head of which is assumed to be 30 years of age on the date in 1956 for which the figure is drawn. We may suppose the unit to have

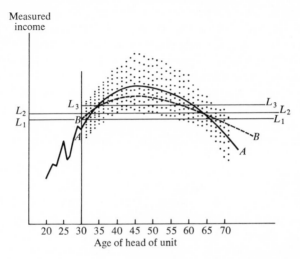

Figure 2

Illustration of alternative interpretations of permanent income. Lifetime income experience as viewed in 1956 by a consumer unit with head aged 30

been formed when the head was aged 20. Measured income experience from 20 to 30, as recorded in the solid jagged line, is a datum; so also, of course, are other items not recorded in the figure, such as the amount of nonhuman wealth possessed, the occupation of the head and of other members of the unit, location, and so on. Future measured income experience is uncertain. The scatter of dots for later ages is intended to represent the possibilities as *viewed* by the unit; for each future date, there is some anticipated probability distribution of measured income. Because of the limitations of a two-dimensional figure, this scatter diagram seriously misrepresents the situation in one important respect. It suggests that the probability distributions at different ages are independent, whereas in general they might be expected to be interdependent. The distribution anticipated for age 40, for example, if a high measured income is realized at age 31 would presumably be different from the distribution expected if a low measured income is realized.[4] But this defect of the figure is not serious for our present limited purpose.

[4]The most general description would be in terms of a probability distribution of alternative age-measured-income functions. It should be noted that the generalized analytical formulation in *ibid.*, pp. 352–364, allows fully for interdependence.

The scatter in the figure should not be confused conceptually with the corresponding scatter that would be generated by plotting the contemporaneous incomes of a large number of units with heads of different age. The scatter in the figure is the anticipated experience of one unit, not the realized experience of many. In forming its anticipations, the one unit may well take into account the contemporaneous experience of units which are of different age but alike in respect to other factors such as occupation, nonhuman wealth, etc.; and it may for some purposes usefully be regarded as doing so by simply accepting the contemporaneous differences as describing its own future possibilities. On the conceptual level, however, there is no need to foreclose the possibility that the unit will take other information into account as well.[5]

The solid curve AA in Figure 2 is the mean of the probability distributions anticipated for future years. It is one possible interpretation of the permanent income to which consumption is adapted. The horizontal line L_1L_1 is the mean lifetime income as anticipated at age 20; L_2L_2, as anticipated at age 30, taking into account realized experience from age 20 to age 30; L_3L_3, mean income anticipated at age 30 for the remaining lifetime of the unit. Each of these is another possible interpretation of permanent income, and almost at the opposite extreme of the spectrum from AA. No one of these has very great intuitive appeal as *the* permanent income to which consumption is adapted; AA, because it implies an exceedingly short time horizon; L_1L_1, L_2L_2, and L_3L_3, not only because they imply an extremely long time horizon, but also because they imply that units can borrow on the basis of anticipated receipts from both human and nonhuman wealth at the same interest rate at which they can lend accumulated nonhuman wealth. L_3L_3 has the further objection that it supposes no carry-over into the present of past adaptations. The dashed curve BB is an intermediate interpretation, intended to be something of an average of AA and L_1L_1 or L_2L_2. Something like this seems intuitively the most plausible interpretation, but intuitive plausibility gives little guidance to the exact kind of average, or length of horizon. For this, we must rely on the empirical evidence. (See Chapter VII, where a tentative estimate is made on the basis of existing evidence.)

Figure 2 is drawn for a particular date. There is nothing about the concept of permanent income that requires the relevant parts of the figure to remain the same for any later date. Aside from the point already made, that in advance the probability distribution for any future date depends on the measured income actually experienced, the whole joint probability distribution may be shifted by occurrences that were entirely unanticipated at the date in question. In our empirical work, we shall sometimes find it desirable

---

[5]For example, in sec. 3 of Chap. 4 below [Friedman, *op. cit.*], the unit is interpreted as modifying contemporaneous experience by information on the secular trend of income.

to suppose that permanent income, or the age pattern of permanent income, remains unchanged over a period of years, but it should be clear that this is an empirical specialization of a more general concept.

2. A formal statement of the permanent income hypothesis

In its most general form our hypothesis about the consumption function, which we shall hereafter refer to as the permanent income hypothesis, is given by the three equations (2.6), (3.1), and (3.2):

$$c_p = k(i, w, u)y_p, \tag{2.6}$$

$$y = y_p + y_t, \tag{3.1}$$

$$c = c_p + c_t. \tag{3.2}$$

Equation (2.6) defines a relation between permanent income and permanent consumption. It specifies that the ratio between them is independent of the size of permanent income but does depend on other variables, in particular: (1) the rate of interest (i) or sets of rates of interest at which the consumer unit can borrow or lend; (2) the relative importance of property and non-property income, symbolized by the ratio of nonhuman wealth to income (w); and (3) the factors symbolized by the portmanteau variable u determining the consumer unit's tastes and preferences for consumption versus additions to wealth. The most significant of the latter factors probably are (a) the number of members of the consumer unit and their characteristics, particularly their ages, and (b) the importance of transitory factors affecting income and consumption, measured, for example, by the "spread" or standard deviation of the probability distributions of the transitory components relative to the size of the corresponding permanent components. Equations (3.1) and (3.2) define the connection between the permanent components and the measured magnitudes.

In this most general form the hypothesis is empty, in the sense that no empirical data could contradict it. Equations (3.1) and (3.2) are purely definitional; they add two equations but also two additional unknowns, the transitory components. There are a variety of ways to specialize the hypothesis so that it is capable of being contradicted by observed data. The one I shall use is to specify some of the characteristics of the probability distributions of the transitory components. A particularly simple specification, yet one that seems adequate to explain existing evidence, is to suppose that the transitory components of income and consumption are uncorrelated with one another and with the corresponding permanent components, or

$$\rho_{y_t y_p} = \rho_{c_t c_p} = \rho_{y_t c_t} = 0, \tag{3.3}$$

where ρ stands for the correlation coefficient between the variables designated by the subscripts.

The assumptions that the first two correlations in (3.3) — between the permanent and transitory components of income and of consumption — are zero seem very mild and highly plausible. Indeed, by themselves, they have little substantive content and can almost be regarded as simply completing or translating the definitions of transitory and permanent components; the qualitative notion that the transitory component is intended to embody is of an accidental and transient addition to or subtraction from income, which is almost equivalent to saying an addition or subtraction that is not correlated with the rest of income. The merging of errors of measurement with transitory components contributes further to the plausibility that these correlations are zero.

For a group of individuals, it is plausible to suppose that the absolute size of the transitory component varies with the size of the permanent component: that a given random event produces the same percentage rather than the same absolute increase or decrease in the incomes of units with different permanent components. This may make more convenient an alternative definition of transitory component that is suggested below; it is not, however, inconsistent with zero correlation. Zero correlation implies only that the *average* transitory component — the algebraic average in which positive and negative components offset one another — is the same for all values of the permanent component. For example, suppose that the transitory component is equally likely to be plus or minus 10 per cent of the permanent component. The average transitory component is then zero for all values of the permanent component, although the average absolute value, which disregards the sign of the components, is directly proportional to the permanent component.

The plausibility of taking our definition of transitory components to imply a zero correlation for a group of consumer units depends somewhat on the criteria determining membership in the group. The clearest example is a classification of units by the size of their measured income. For each such group, the correlation between permanent and transitory components is necessarily negative, since with a common measured income the permanent component can be relatively high only if the transitory component is relatively low, and conversely.[6]

The assumption that the third correlation in (3.3) — between the transitory components of income and consumption — is zero is a much stronger assumption. It is primarily this assumption that introduces important substantive content into the hypothesis and makes it susceptible of contradiction by a wide range of phenomena capable of being observed. The ultimate test of its acceptability is of course whether such phenomena are in fact observed, and most of what follows is devoted to this question.

[6]See [Friedman and Kuznets, *op. cit.,*] pp. 326 and 327.

It is hardly worth proceeding to such more refined tests, however, unless the assumption can pass — or at least not fail miserably — the much cruder test of consistency with casual observation of one's self and one's neighbors, so some comments on the intuitive plausibility of the assumption are not out of order.

The common notion that savings, or at least certain components of savings, are a "residual" speaks strongly for the plausibility of the assumption. For this notion implies that consumption is determined by rather long-term considerations, so that any transitory changes in income lead primarily to additions to assets or to the use of previously accumulated balances rather than to corresponding changes in consumption.

Yet from another point of view, the assumption seems highly implausible. Will not a man who receives an unexpected windfall use at least some part of it in "riotous living," i.e. in consumption expenditures? Would he be likely to add the whole of it to his wealth? The answer to these questions depends greatly on how "consumption" is defined. The offhand affirmative answer reflects in large measure, I believe, an implicit definition of consumption in terms of purchases, including durable goods, rather than in terms of the value of services. If the latter definition is adopted, as seems highly desirable in applying the hypothesis to empirical data — though unfortunately I have been able to do so to only a limited extent — much that one classifies offhand as consumption is reclassified as savings. Is not the windfall likely to be used for the purchase of durable goods? Or, to put it differently, is not the timing of the replacement of durable goods and of additions to the stock of such goods likely to some extent to be adjusted so as to coincide with windfalls?

Two other considerations argue for the plausibility of the assumption that transitory components of income and consumption are uncorrelated. First, the above identification of a windfall with transitory income is not precise. Suppose, for example, inheritances are included in a particular concept of measured income. Consider a consumer unit whose receipts remain unchanged over a succession of time periods except that it receives an inheritance in the final period. If the inheritance was expected to occur some time or other, it will already have been allowed for in permanent income; the transitory component of income is only the excess of the inheritance over this element of permanent income. There seems no reason why the receipt of the inheritance should make consumption in the final period different from that of preceding periods, except through inability to borrow in advance on the strength of the inheritance. But this implies that the receipt of the inheritance changes w (the ratio of wealth to income) in (2.6); it is therefore already taken into account in the hypothesis. There is no essential difference if the inheritance is unexpected. The effect of the inheritance is then to increase the permanent income of the unit, and this will justify a higher consumption in the final period; again the transitory component is only the excess of the windfall over this element of permanent income, and it is no longer intuitively obvious that it should lead to an increase in current consumption.[7] The second consideration is that just as there are instances in which one would expect a transitory increase in income to produce a transitory increase in consumption, so also there are instances in which one would expect the reverse. The simplest example is when a transitory increase in income reduces opportunities for consumption as when it is obtained by working longer hours or going to a backward country. Such negative and positive correlations will tend to offset one another.

The preceding remarks abstract from errors of measurement. Yet, as noted, in any statistical analysis errors of measurement will in general be indissolubly merged with the correctly measured transitory components. The effect on the correlation between statistically recorded transitory components of income and consumption depends critically on how the statistical data are obtained. If income and consumption are measured independently, the errors of estimate might be expected to be independent as well and therefore to contribute toward a small or zero observed correlation between transitory components of income and consumption. On the other hand, if consumption is estimated, as it frequently is, by measuring independently savings and income and subtracting the former from the latter, then measured consumption and measured income have common errors of measurement. This tends toward a positive observed correlation between transitory components of income and consumption.

The purpose of these remarks is not to demonstrate that a zero correlation is the *only* plausible assumption — neither evidence like that alluded to nor any other can justify such a conclusion. Its purpose is rather to show that common observation does not render it absurd to suppose that a hypothesis embodying a zero correlation can yield a fairly close approximation to observed consumer behavior. The assumption that the correlation between transitory components of income and consumption is zero could, of course, be replaced by the less restrictive assumption that it is a positive number between zero and unity, but this would greatly weaken the hypothesis and reduce its potential usefulness for predicting behavior. It seems highly undesirable to do so until and unless a significant contradiction arises between the stronger hypothesis and empirical evidence on consumer behavior.

A particularly simple special case of the hypothesis arises if, in addition to (3.3), it is assumed that the mean transitory components of consumption and income are zero, or

$$\mu_{y_t} = \mu_{c_t} = 0, \tag{3.4}$$

[7]I owe this point to Modigliani and Brumberg, "Utility Analysis and the Consumption Function [An Interpretation of Cross-Section Data," *Post-Keynesian Economics*, ed. by Kenneth K. Kurihara (New Brunswick: Rutgers University Press,] 1954), pp. 405-406. [Friedman develops this point further in "Windfalls, the 'Horizon' and Related Concepts in the Permanent-Income Hypothesis," in Carl Christ et al., *Measurement in Economics*, (Stanford, Calif.: Stanford University Press, 1963).—*Eds.*]

where μ stands for the mean of the variable designated by its subscript. This assumption is eminently reasonable if the probability distribution in question is sufficiently comprehensive. In general, however, we shall want to use conditional probability distributions, for example, the distribution of transitory components in a particular year, or for members of a particular group. In such cases, it will generally be undesirable to assume that (3.4) holds, just as for the single consumer unit viewed *ex post* it is undesirable to assume that the transitory components themselves are necessarily zero.

It may be desirable or necessary to impose additional conditions on the probability distributions to facilitate the estimation of the parameters of the system from observed data. I shall, however, largely neglect the problem of statistical estimation, and so we need not go into such conditions.

A more important qualification is that, for simplicity of exposition, equations (3.1) and (3.2) express the relation between observed income and its permanent and transitory components as additive. The form of the relation is important because it may affect the empirical validity of such specifications of the characteristics of the probability distributions as (3.3) and (3.4), as well as the validity of using specifications of other characteristics of the distribution that are convenient statistically. From this point of view, I conjecture that a multiplicative specification is preferable for income and consumption data. If we let capital letters stand for the logarithms of the variables designated by the corresponding lower case letters, the equations defining the hypothesis then take the following alternative form:

$$C_p = K(i, w, u) + Y_p, \tag{2.6'}$$

$$Y = Y_p + Y_t, \tag{3.1'}$$

$$C = C_p + C_t, \tag{3.2'}$$

$$\rho_{Y_t Y_p} = \rho_{C_t C_p} = \rho_{Y_t C_t} = 0. \tag{3.3'}$$

Many of the results that follow apply equally to both forms of the hypothesis, requiring only that the same symbol be interpreted in one case as an absolute value, in the other, as a logarithm. For any significant results for which this is not true, the logarithmic expressions are given in footnotes.

3. The relation between measured consumption and measured income

Suppose we have observations on consumption and income for a number of consumer units, for all of whom the k of equation (2.6) can be taken to be numerically the same. Let us proceed, as is usually done in family budget studies, to estimate from these data a relation between consumption and income. For simplicity, let the relation to be estimated be linear, say:

$$c = \alpha + \beta y, \tag{3.5}$$

where c is to be interpreted as the mean consumption for a given value of y, it being understood that the consumption of individual units deviates from this value by chance.[8] The least squares estimates of α and β (call these a and b), computed from the regression of c on y, are

$$b = \frac{\Sigma(c - \bar{c})(y - \bar{y})}{\Sigma(y - \bar{y})^2}, \tag{3.6}$$

$$a = \bar{c} - b\bar{y}, \tag{3.7}$$

where $\bar{c}$ and $\bar{y}$ stand for the mean consumption and income respectively of the group of consumer units, and the summation is over the group. In the numerator of the expression for b, replace y and c by the right-hand sides of (3.1) and (3.2), and $\bar{y}$ and $\bar{c}$ by the corresponding sums of means. This gives

$$\Sigma(c - \bar{c})(y - \bar{y}) = \Sigma(c_p + c_t - \bar{c}_p - \bar{c}_t)(y_p + y_t - \bar{y}_p - \bar{y}_t) \tag{3.8}$$

$$= \Sigma(c_p - \bar{c}_p)(y_p - \bar{y}_p) + \Sigma(c_p - \bar{c}_p)(y_t - \bar{y}_t)$$

$$+ \Sigma(c_t - \bar{c}_t)(y_p - \bar{y}_p) + \Sigma(c_t - \bar{c}_t)(y_t - \bar{y}_t).$$

From (2.6),

$$c_p = ky_p. \tag{2.6}$$

Inserting (2.6) in (3.8) yields

$$\Sigma(c - \bar{c})(y - \bar{y}) = k\,\Sigma(y_p - \bar{y}_p)^2 + k\,\Sigma(y_p - \bar{y}_p)(y_t - \bar{y}_t) \tag{3.9}$$

$$+ \frac{1}{k}\Sigma(c_t - \bar{c}_t)(c_p - \bar{c}_p) + \Sigma(c_t - \bar{c}_t)(y_t - \bar{y}_t).$$

Given the zero correlations specified in (3.3), the final three terms will differ from zero only because of sampling fluctuations: they will approach zero as the sample size is increased, or average zero over many similar samples. Since our present concern is not with the problem of statistical estimation but with the interpretation of the results, let us suppose the sample to be sufficiently large so that sampling error can be neglected. In that case

$$b = k\,\frac{\Sigma(y_p - \bar{y}_p)^2}{\Sigma(y - \bar{y})^2} = k \cdot P_y, \tag{3.10}$$

[8]On our hypothesis, the relation between the mean value of c and y will be linear only under special conditions. For example, it will be if y_p, y_t, and c_t are distributed according to a trivariate normal distribution. See D. V. Lindley, "Regression Lines and the Linear Functional Relationship," *Journal of the Royal Statistical Society, Supplement,* IX (1947), 218–244.

where P_y is the fraction of the total variance of income in the group contributed by the permanent component of income. More generally, of course, b can be regarded as an estimate of the righthand side of (3.10).[9]

The algebraic relation in (3.10) lends itself directly to meaningful interpretation in terms of the permanent income hypothesis. The regression coefficient b measures the difference in consumption associated, on the average, with a one dollar difference between consumer units in measured income. On our hypothesis, the size of this difference in consumption depends on two things: first, how much of the difference in measured income is also a difference in permanent income, since only differences in permanent income are regarded as affecting consumption systematically; second, how much of permanent income is devoted to consumption. P_y measures the first; k, the second; so their product equals b. If P_y is unity, transient factors are either entirely absent or affect the incomes of all members of the group by the same amount; a one dollar difference in measured income means a one dollar difference in permanent income and so produces a difference of k in consumption; b is therefore equal to k. If P_y is zero, there are no differences in permanent income; a one dollar difference in measured income means a one dollar difference in the transitory component of income, which is taken to be uncorrelated with consumption; in consequence, this difference in measured income is associated with no systematic difference in consumption; b is therefore zero. As this explanation suggests, P_y, though *defined* by the ratio of the variance of the permanent component of income to the variance of total income, can be *interpreted* as the fraction of any difference in measured income that on the average is contributed by a difference in the permanent component. This point is developed more fully below.

Substitute (3.10) in (3.7), replace $\bar{c}$ by $\bar{c}_p + \bar{c}_t$, $\bar{y}$ by $\bar{y}_p + \bar{y}_t$, and $\bar{c}_p$ by $k\bar{y}_p$. The resulting expression can then be written:

$$a = \bar{c}_t - kP_y\bar{y}_t + k(1 - P_y)\bar{y}_p. \tag{3.11}$$

The elasticity of consumption with respect to income at the point (c, y) is

$$\eta_{cy} = \frac{dc}{dy} \cdot \frac{y}{c} = b \cdot \frac{y}{c} = kP_y \cdot \frac{y}{c}. \tag{3.12}$$

Suppose that the mean transitory components of both income and consumption are equal to zero, so that $\bar{y} = \bar{y}_p$, $\bar{c} = \bar{c}_p$. In this special case

$$\frac{\bar{y}}{\bar{c}} = \frac{1}{k}. \tag{3.13}$$

[9]In the special case of the preceding footnote, $\beta = kP_y$.

It follows that if the elasticity is computed at the point corresponding to the sample mean:

$$\eta_{cy} = P_y. \tag{3.14}$$

Consider, now, the regression of y on c, say

$$y = a' + b'c. \tag{3.15}$$

By the same reasoning it can be shown that, sampling errors aside,

$$b' = \frac{1}{k} P_c, \tag{3.16}$$

where P_c is the fraction of the variance of consumption contributed by the permanent component, and

$$a' = \bar{y}_t - \frac{1}{k} P_c \bar{c}_t + \frac{1}{k}(1 - P_c)\bar{c}_p. \tag{3.17}$$

The elasticity of consumption with respect to income computed from this regression is

$$\eta_{cy}' = \frac{dc}{dy} \cdot \frac{y}{c} = \frac{1}{b'} \cdot \frac{y}{c} = \frac{k}{P_c} \cdot \frac{y}{c}. \tag{3.18}$$

Again, if $\bar{y}_t = \bar{c}_t = 0$,

$$\eta_{cy}' = \frac{1}{P_c}, \tag{3.19}$$

if evaluated at the point corresponding to the sample mean.[10]

[10]For the logarithmic alternative described by (2.6′), (3.1′), (3.2′), and (3.3′) the analogues to the results given in the text are

$$B = P_Y, \tag{3.10′}$$

$$A = K + \bar{C}_t - \bar{Y}_t P_Y + \bar{Y}_P(1 - P_Y), \tag{3.11′}$$

$$\eta_{cy} = \frac{dC}{dY} = B = P_Y, \tag{3.12′}$$

$$B' = P_C, \tag{3.16′}$$

$$A' = -K + \bar{Y}_t - \bar{C}_t P_C + \bar{C}_p(1 - P_C), \tag{3.17′}$$

$$\eta_{cy}' = \frac{1}{P_C}. \tag{3.19′}$$

These results are in some ways simpler and more appealing than those in the text, since the elasticity of consumption with respect to income is the same everywhere and hence equal to P_Y or $1/P_C$ without the necessity of assuming the mean transitory components to be zero.

Some of these results are presented in graphic form in Figure 3 for the special case in which the mean transitory components of income and consumption are zero.

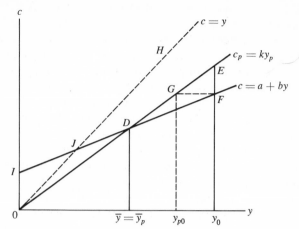

Figure 3

Hypothetical relation between measured consumption and measured income (mean transitory components equal zero)

Consider the consumer units with a particular measured income, say y_0, which is above the mean measured income for the group as a whole. Given zero correlation between the permanent and transitory components of income, the average permanent income of these units is less than y_0; that is, the average transitory component is positive. These units have been classified together precisely because their measured income is a certain amount *above* the average income of the group; such a relatively high measured income could have been received despite unfavorable transitory effects; clearly, it is more likely to have been received because of favorable transitory effects; the winners in any particular set of races may well be better on the average than the losers but they are also likely to have had more than their share of good luck. Put more rigorously, the transitory component of income is positively correlated with the sum of itself and a variable (the permanent component) with which it is itself uncorrelated.[11] What about the average transitory component of consumption for these units? The corresponding component of their income is positive because the transitory component of income helped to determine which units had a measured income of y_0 and so were classified together; given, however, that the transitory components of income and consumption are uncorrelated, a classifica-

[11]See Friedman and Kuznets, *op. cit.*, pp. 327–332, esp. footnotes 10 and 13.

tion by income is random with respect to transitory components of consumption; in consequence, the latter tend to average out to the average for the group as a whole, which is assumed to be zero. The average consumption of units with a measured income y_0 is therefore equal to their average permanent consumption. On our hypothesis, this is k times their average permanent income. If y_0 were not only the measured income of these units but also their permanent income, their mean consumption would be ky_0 or y_0E. Since their mean permanent income is less than their measured income, their average consumption, y_0F, is less than y_0E.

By the same reasoning, for consumer units with an income equal to the mean of the group as a whole, or $\bar{y}$, the average transitory component of income as well as of consumption is zero, so the ordinate of the regression line is equal to the ordinate of the line OE which gives the relation between permanent consumption and permanent income. For units with an income below the mean, the average transitory component of income is negative, so average measured consumption is greater than the ordinate of OE. The regression line therefore intersects OE at D, is above it to the left of D, and below it to the right of D.

Let us return to the income class y_0. Draw a horizontal line through F. The abscissa of the point G, where this line intersects OE, is the permanent income associated with a permanent consumption y_0F. This income, labelled y_{p0} on the figure, is therefore the average permanent component of the income of the members of the income class y_0, and $(y_0 - y_{p0})/(y_0 - \bar{y})$ is the fraction of the deviation of their average income from the average for the group attributable to the transitory component. If this fraction is the same for all income classes, IF is a straight line, and the common value of the fraction is $1 - P_y$.[12] The higher this fraction, the flatter IF and conversely. At one extreme, if P_y is zero, that is, if all members of the group have the same permanent component, average consumption is the same for all income classes and IF is horizontal. At the other extreme, if $P_y = 1$, so transitory components are all zero, IF coincides with OE.

If k is less than unity, permanent consumption is always less than permanent income. As is clear from the figure, however, it does not follow that measured consumption is necessarily less than measured income. The line OH on the figure is a 45 degree line along which $c = y$. The vertical distance between this line and IF is average measured savings. Point J is the "break even" point at which average measured savings are zero. To the left of J, average measured savings are negative, to the right, positive; as measured income increases, so does the ratio of average measured savings to measured income. Our hypothesis thus yields a relation between measured consumption and measured income that reproduces the broadest features of the

[12]See *ibid.* pp. 332–336, 358. Figure 3 is essentially the same as Chart 28 on p. 333.

corresponding regressions that have been computed from observed data.

For the special case for which Figure 3 is drawn, k could be readily computed from observed data on the measured consumption and measured income of a group of consumer units, since average measured consumption and average measured income then equal the corresponding average permanent components. The line OE in the figure therefore goes through the point describing the mean income and consumption of the group, so $k = \bar{c}/\bar{y}$. P_y could then be computed from the relation between the regression of c on y (the line IF) and the line OE, and P_c from the corresponding relation between the regression of y on c and the line OE.[13]

If the mean transitory component of consumption is not zero, the curve IF is shifted vertically by a corresponding amount — upwards, if the mean transitory component is positive, downwards, if it is negative. Clearly, there is no way of distinguishing such a shift from a change in k. Similarly, a positive mean transitory component of income shifts IF to the right, a negative mean, to the left. For a straight line, there is no way of distinguishing such horizontal shifts from vertical shifts produced by a mean transitory component of consumption. It follows that, if the mean transitory components cannot be set equal to zero, data for one group for one time period are inadequate to estimate all the parameters. Some other source of information is required as well.

Our hypothesis gives a major role to certain features of the income distribution generally neglected in consumption studies. It asserts that some of the most strikingly uniform characterisitics of computed regressions between consumption and income are simply a reflection of the inadequacy of measured income as an indicator of long-run income status. In consequence, differences among various groups of consumer units in observed marginal propensities to consume may not reflect differences in underlying preferences for consumption and wealth at all; they may reflect primarily the different strength of random forces, including errors of measurement, in determining measured income. Fortunately, considerable evidence is available on the importance of transitory components of income from studies of changes over time in the relative income status of individuals or consumer units. One of the attractive features of our hypothesis is that it enables us to bring this independent body of evidence to bear on the interpretation of consumption behavior; such evidence can provide some of the additional

---

[13]The estimation problem is the classical one of "mutual regression" or regression when "both variables are subject to error." See D. V. Lindley, *op. cit.*, for an excellent analysis of the problem and survey of the literature. Many of our equations duplicate equations in his paper. As Lindley points out, there are no efficient statistics for estimating all the parameters in the model from sample data. The method described in the text is therefore not statistically efficient. The usual solution is to assume the ratio of the variance of y_t to the variance of c_t known, in which case efficient statistical procedures do exist.

information required when transitory components of income and consumption cannot be supposed to be zero.

Before examining these data, however, we shall first examine the consistency of the hypothesis with some of the major general findings of empirical studies of consumption behavior and its relation to the relative income hypothesis suggested by Brady and Friedman, Duesenberry, and Modigliani. This will serve the double purpose of bringing out more fully the implications of the hypothesis and of suggesting the evidence that recommends its acceptance as a provisional working hypothesis.

Theory of investment

PAUL A. SAMUELSON **8**

Interactions between
the multiplier analysis and
the principle of acceleration

Few economists would deny that the "multiplier" analysis of the effects of governmental deficit spending has thrown some light upon this important problem. Nevertheless, there would seem to be some ground for the fear that this extremely simplified mechanism is in danger of hardening into a dogma, hindering progress and obscuring important subsidiary relations and processes. It is highly desirable, therefore, that model sequences, which operate under more general assumptions, be investigated, possibly including the conventional analysis as a special case.[1]

In particular, the "multiplier," using this term in its usual sense, does *not* pretend to give the relation between total national income induced by governmental spending and the original amount of money spent. This is clearly seen by a simple example. In any economy (not necessarily our own) where any dollar of governmental deficit spending would result in a hundred dollars less of private investment than would otherwise have been undertaken, the ratio of total induced national income to the initial expenditure is

Reprinted by permission of the publisers from Paul A. Samuelson THE REVIEW OF ECONOMICS AND STATISTICS Cambridge, Mass.: Harvard University Press, Copyright, 1939, 1967, by the President and Fellows of Harvard College. Vol. 21 (May 1939), pp. 75–78.

[1]The writer, who has made this study in connection with his research as a member of the Society of Fellows at Harvard University, wishes to express his indebtedness to Professor Alvin H. Hansen of Harvard University at whose suggestion the investigation was undertaken.

overwhelmingly negative, yet the "multiplier" in the strict sense must be positive. The answer to the puzzle is simple. What the multiplier does give is the ratio of the total increase in the national income to the total amount of investment, governmental and private. In other words, it does *not* tell us how much is to be multiplied. The effects upon private investment are often regarded as tertiary influences and receive little systematic attention.

In order to remedy the situation in some measure, Professor Hansen has developed a new model sequence which ingeniously combines the multiplier analysis with that of the *acceleration* principle or *relation*. This is done by making additions to the national income consist of three components: (1) governmental deficit spending, (2) private consumption expenditure induced by previous public expenditure, and (3) induced private investment, assumed according to the familiar acceleration principle to be proportional to the time increase of consumption. The introduction of the last component accounts for the novelty of the conclusions reached and also the increased complexity of the analysis.

A numerical example may be cited to illuminate the assumptions made. We assume governmental deficit spending of one dollar per unit period, beginning at some initial time and continuing thereafter. The marginal propensity to consume, α, is taken to be one-half. This is taken to mean that the consumption of any period is equal to one-half the national income of the previous period. Our last assumption is that induced private investment is proportional to the increase in consumption between the previous and the current period. This factor of proportionality or *relation*, β, is provisionally taken to be equal to unity; i.e., a time increase in consumption of one dollar will result in one dollar's worth of induced private investment.

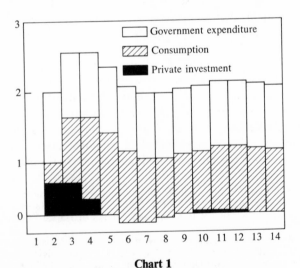

Chart 1

Graphic representation of data in Table 1 (unit: one dollar)

In the initial period when the government spends a dollar for the first time, there will be no consumption induced from previous periods, and hence the addition to the national income will equal the one dollar spent. This will yield fifty cents of consumption expenditure in the second period, an increase of fifty cents over the consumption of the first period, and so according to the *relation* we will have fifty cents worth of induced private investment. Finally, we must add the new dollar of expenditure by the government. The national income of the second period must therefore total two dollars. Similarly, in the third period the national income would be the sum of one dollar of consumption, fifty cents induced private investment, and one dollar current governmental expenditure. It is clear that given the values of the marginal propensity to consume, α, and the *relation*, β, all succeeding national income levels can be easily computed in succession. This is done in detail in Table 1 and illustrated in Chart 1. It will be noted

Table 1

The development of national income as a result of a continuous level of governmental expenditure when the marginal propensity to consume equals one half and the relation equals unity
(unit: one dollar)

PERIOD	CURRENT GOVERNMENTAL EXPENDITURE	CURRENT CONSUMPTION INDUCED BY PREVIOUS EXPENDITURE	CURRENT PRIVATE INVESTMENT PROPORTIONAL TO TIME INCREASE IN CONSUMPTION	TOTAL NATIONAL INCOME
1	1.00	0.00	0.00	1.00
2	1.00	0.50	0.50	2.00
3	1.00	1.00	0.50	2.50
4	1.00	1.25	0.25	2.50
5	1.00	1.25	0.00	2.25
6	1.00	1.125	−0.125*	2.00
7	1.00	1.00	−0.125	1.875
8	1.00	0.9375	−0.0625	1.875
9	1.00	0.9375	0.00	1.9375
10	1.00	0.96875	0.03125	2.00
11	1.00	1.00	0.03125	2.03125
12	1.00	1.015625	0.015625	2.03125
13	1.00	1.015625	0.00	2.015625
14	1.00	1.0078125	−0.0078125	2.00
—	—	—	—	—

*Negative induced private investment is interpreted to mean that for the system as a whole there is *less* investment in this period than there otherwise would have been. Since this is a marginal analysis, superimposed implicitly upon a going state of affairs, this concept causes no difficulty.

that the introduction of the acceleration principle causes our series to reach a peak at the 3rd year, a trough at the 7th, a peak at the 11th, etc. Such oscillatory behavior could not occur in the conventional model sequences, as will soon become evident.

For other chosen values of α and β similar model sequences can be developed. In Table 2 national income totals are given for various selected

Table 2

Model sequences of national income for selected values of marginal propensity to consume and relation (unit: one dollar)

PERIOD	$\alpha = .5$ $\beta = 0$	$\alpha = .5$ $\beta = 2$	$\alpha = .6$ $\beta = 2$	$\alpha = .8$ $\beta = 4$
1	1.00	1.00	1.00	1.00
2	1.50	2.50	2.80	5.00
3	1.75	3.75	4.84	17.80
4	1.875	4.125	6.352	56.20
5	1.9375	3.4375	6.6256	169.84
6	1.9688*	2.0313	5.3037	500.52
7	1.9844	.9141	2.5959	1,459.592
8	1.9922	− .1172	− .6918	4,227.704
9	1.9961	.2148	−3.3603	12,241.1216
—	—	—	—	—

*Table is correct to four decimal places.

values of these coefficients. In the first column, for example, the marginal propensity to consume is assumed to be one-half, and the *relation* to be equal to zero. This is of special interest because it shows the conventional multiplier sequences to be special cases of the more general Hansen analysis. For this case no oscillations are possible. In the second column the oscillations in the national income are undamped and regular. In column three things are still worse; the oscillations are explosive, becoming larger and larger but always fluctuating around an "average value." In the fourth column the behavior is no longer oscillatory but is explosive upward approaching a compound interest rate of growth.

By this time the investigator is inclined to feel somewhat disorganized. A variety of qualitatively different results emerge in a seemingly capricious manner from minor changes in hypotheses. Worse than this, how can we be sure that for still different selected values of our coefficients new and stronger types of behavior will not emerge? Is it not even possible that if Table 2 were extended to cover more periods, new types of behavior might result for these selected coefficients?

Fortunately, these questions can be given a definite negative answer. Arithmetical methods cannot do so since we cannot try all possible values of the coefficients nor compute the endless terms of each sequence. Nevertheless, comparatively simple algebraic analysis can be applied which will yield all possible qualitative types of behavior and enable us to unify our results.

The national income at time t, Y_t, can be written as the sum of three components: (1) governmental expenditure, g_t, (2) consumption expenditure, C_t, and (3) induced private investment, I_t.

$$Y_t = g_t + C_t + I_t$$

But according to the Hansen assumptions

$$C_t = \alpha Y_{t-1}$$

$$I_t = \beta[C_t - C_{t-1}] = \alpha\beta Y_{t-1} - \alpha\beta Y_{t-2}$$

and

$$g_t = 1$$

Therefore, our national income can be rewritten

$$Y_t = 1 + \alpha[1 + \beta]Y_{t-1} - \alpha\beta Y_{t-2}$$

In other words, if we know the national income for two periods, the national income for the following period can be simply derived by taking a weighted sum. The weights depend, of course, upon the values chosen for the marginal propensity to consume and for the *relation*.

This is one of the simplest types of difference equations, having constant coefficients and being of the second order. The mathematical details of its solution need not be entered upon here. Suffice it to say that its solution depends upon the roots — which in turn depend upon the coefficients α and β — of a certain equation.[2] It can be easily shown that the whole field of possible values of α and β can be divided into four regions, each of which gives qualitatively different types of behavior. In Chart 2 these regions are plotted. Each point in this diagram represents a selection of values for the

---

[2] Actually, the solution can be written in the form

$$Y_t = \frac{1}{1 - \alpha} + a_1[x_1]^t + a_2[x_2]^t$$

where x_1 and x_2 are roots of the quadratic equation

$$x^2 - \alpha[1 + \beta]x + \alpha\beta = 0,$$

and a_1 and a_2 are constants dependent upon the α's and β's chosen.

marginal propensity to consume and the *relation*. Corresponding to each point there will be a model sequence of national income through time. The qualitative properties of this sequence depend upon whether the point is in Region *A*, *B*, *C*, or *D*.[3] The properties of each region can be briefly summarized.

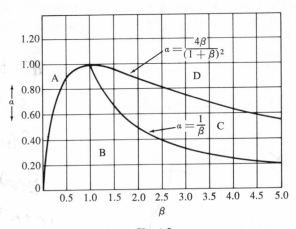

Chart 2

Diagram showing boundaries of regions yielding different qualitative behavior of national income

Region A (relatively small values of the relation)

If there is a constant level of governmental expenditure through time, the national income will approach asymptotically a value $(1/1 - \alpha)$ times the constant level of governmental expenditure. A single impulse of expenditure, or any amount of expenditure followed by a complete cessation, will result in a gradual approach to the original zero level of national income. (It will be noted that the asymptote approached is identically that given by the Keynes-Kahn-Clark formula. Their analysis applies to points along the α axis and is subsumed under the more general Hansen analysis.) Perfectly periodic net governmental expenditure will result eventually in perfectly periodic fluctuations in national income.

Region B

A constant continuing level of governmental expenditure will result in damped oscillatory movements of national income, gradually approaching

---

[3]Mathematically, the regions are demarcated by the conditions that the roots of the equation referred to in the previous footnote be real or complex, greater or less than unity in absolute value.

the asymptote $(1/1 - \alpha)$ times the constant level of government expenditure. (Cf. Table 1.) Governmental expenditure in a single or finite number of periods will result eventually in damped oscillations around the level of income zero. Perfectly regular periodic fluctuations in government expenditure will result eventually in fluctuations of income of the same period.

Region C

A constant level of governmental expenditure will result in *explosive*, ever increasing oscillations around an asymptote computed as above. (Cf. column 3 of Table 2.) A single impulse of expenditure or a finite number of expenditure impulses will result eventually in explosive oscillations around the level zero.

Region D (large values of the marginal propensity to consume and the relation)

A constant level of governmental expenditure will result in an ever increasing national income, eventually approaching a compound interest rate of growth. (Cf. column 4 of Table 2.) A single impulse of net investment will likewise send the system up to infinity at a compound interest rate of growth. On the other hand, a single infinitesimal unit of disinvestment will send the system ever downward at an increasing rate. This is a highly unstable situation, but corresponds most closely to the pure case of pump-priming, where the total increase in national income bears no finite ratio to the original stimulus.

The limitations inherent in so simplified a picture as that presented here should not be overlooked.[4] In particular, it assumes that the marginal propensity to consume and the *relation* are constants; actually these will change with the level of income, so that this representation is strictly a *marginal* analysis to be applied to the study of small oscillations. Nevertheless, it is more general than the usual analysis. Contrary to the impression commonly held, mathematical methods properly employed, far from making economic theory more abstract, actually serve as a powerful liberating device enabling the entertainment and analysis of ever more realistic and complicated hypotheses.

---

[4]It may be mentioned in passing that the formal structure of our problem is identical with the model sequences of Lundberg, and the dynamic theories of Tinbergen. The present problem is so simple that it provides a useful introduction to the mathematical theory of the latter's work.

R. S. ECKAUS **9**

The acceleration principle reconsidered*

I. Introduction

Old ideas seem to die hard. Perhaps it is this which explains continued use of the acceleration principle by some economists even after its considerable theoretical deficiencies as an explanation of investment expenditures and apparent lack of empirical verification have been repeatedly pointed out. On the other hand, it may not be tradition alone which supports the acceleration principle but also the opinion that it is a useful summarization of some economic truth. In this paper I shall set forth some of the fundamental reasons for such a favorable opinion of the principle and also indicate the similarity between the acceleration principle and other explanations of investment that have been considered quite different by their sponsors.

The central role given to the acceleration principle in recent years in theoretical models dealing with the growth and fluctuations of the economic system is a continuation of the revival of interest which started in the early 1930's in the well-known Clark-Frisch controversy. This revived interest led to the inclusion of the principle in business cyle theories and examination

Reprinted by permission of the publishers from Richard S. Eckaus THE QUARTERLY JOURNAL OF ECONOMICS Cambridge, Mass.: Harvard University Press, Copyright, 1953, by the President and Fellows of Harvard College. Vol. 67 (May 1953), pp. 209–230. [Footnotes renumbered and expanded — Eds.]

*The author wishes to acknowledge his indebtedness to Professors E. C. Brown, R. Solow, S. Laursen and P. A. Samuelson who read an early draft of this paper.

of the implications of its combination with multiplier theory; but intensive criticism also accompanied this renewed interest in the acceleration principle. Numerous vitiating theoretical objections were raised and various statistical tests were concluded with an opinion that the idea of acceleration-induced investment had been tried and generally found wanting.[1]

In spite of the criticism, most of the essential points of which had been covered by the beginning of World War II, the acceleration principle has continued to be used in recent years, e.g., in the noteworthy theoretical systems of Hicks, Harrod, and Domar.[2] The consequence has been further criticism and a virtual rejection of the ideas involved in the acceleration principle on the part of other economists. This has been apparent, for example, in the reviews of Hicks's book. According to Kaldor, the acceleration principle is "a crude and highly unsuitable tool for analysis," the use of which is the "real weakness" of Hicks's model.[3] A. F. Burns seems to take a very similar view.[4] In other connections Klein and Tsiang[5] have also explicitly rejected the acceleration principle as being an unsatisfactory explanation of investment behavior.

In view of the conflicting opinions as to the validity of the acceleration principle it seems desirable to set forth its underlying logic more explicitly than to my knowledge has yet been done. This will be done in Section II of this paper. Such a consideration will, I think, lead to further fundamental criticisms of the acceleration principle when the accelerator is considered as a constant coefficient. However, the analysis will also show the reasoning that has been in the back of the minds of those economists who have used the acceleration principle and will help to indicate the extent of the justification for its use. Rather than attempting mainly to justify or condemn the acceleration principle, I shall try to set out what I believe to be its foundations and prerequisites for usefulness.

Validity of the acceleration principle will be found, except in very special cases, to be limited to the use of a variable accelerator. Whether

---

[1] Since several comprehensive bibliographies of the acceleration principle exist there will be no attempt to provide another one. Extensive references are given in G. Haberler, *Prosperity and Depression* (3rd ed., [New York: Columbia University Press,] 1946), pp. 85–105; H. M. Somers, *Public Finance and National Income* (Philadelphia: [The Blakiston Co.,] 1949), pp. 67–116; and G. H. Fisher, "A Survey of the Theory of Induced Investment, 1900–1940," *Southern Economic Journal*, XVIII (April 1952), 474–494. The article by Fisher gives a useful survey of the historical development of the theory of the acceleration principle.

[2] J. R. Hicks, *A Contribution to the Theory of the Trade Cycle* (Oxford: [Oxford University Press,] 1950); R. F. Harrod, *Towards A Dynamic Economics* (London: [Macmillan, 1948]); E. D. Domar, "Capital Expansion, the Rate of Growth and Employment," *Econometrica*, XIV (Apr. 1946), 137–147.

[3] N. Kaldor, "Mr. Hicks on the Trade Cycle," *Economic Journal*, LXI (Dec. 1951), 837.

[4] A. F. Burns, "Hicks and the Real Cycle," *Journal of Political Economy*, LX (Feb. 1952), 24.

[5] L. R. Klein, "Studies in Investment Behavior," in *Conference on Business Cycles*, National Bureau of Economic Research (New York: [NBER,] 1951), p. 258; S. C. Tsiang, "Accelerator, Theory of the Firm and the Business Cycle," *Quarterly Journal of Economics*, LXV (Aug. 1951), 327.

sufficient theoretical justification for its inclusion in business cycle theories survives this evaluation of the acceleration principle will remain, at least partly, a matter of opinion. Section III will review the major criticisms of the acceleration principle and present briefly some of the elements involved in arriving at such an opinion and tentative evaluation.

In Section IV I shall show that the acceleration principle can be readily adjusted to meet some of the demands of its critics: in one case by a simple rewriting and in another case by broadening the concept of the acceleration coefficient to include the influence of expectations. By defining a coefficient of expectations similar to that used by Metzler in his paper on inventory cycles,[6] the effect of changing expectations can be included in the mathematical statement of the acceleration principle. The method of analysis used in Section II will then be employed to indicate the close relation between the acceleration principle, in which investment depends on the rate of change of the rate of output, and another type of investment relation in which the major variables are the rate of output itself and the level of capital stock. Since critics of the acceleration principle have often recommended this latter type of investment relation as a replacement for the acceleration principle, a comparison will help to clarify the validity of these two hypotheses.

II. Theoretical development of the acceleration principle[7]

In the history of the development of the theory of the acceleration principle illustrative, arithmetical examples have played an important role. Aftalion referred to a hypothetical textile industry, Bickerdike to a shipbuilding industry and J. M. Clark to an unspecified but supposedly typical manufacturing industry. These original examples, however, were not related explicitly to the theory of the firm but usually merely assumed the existence of a definite ratio between output and the capital stock needed for its production. On this basis it was shown, in a now familiar way, how increases in the rate of demand for a firm's output would result in magnified changes in the demand of the firm for capital equipment, with the maximum demand for durable producers' goods preceding the maximum point of demand for the final product. The applicability of this result for typical firms to aggregative business cycle analysis was then accomplished by a generalization of the particular instance to the general case on the basis of the implicit assumption that all firms or large segments of business faced generally similar conditions at each stage of the business cycle.

[6]L. A. Metzler, "The Nature and Stability of Inventory Cycles," *Review of Economics and Statistics*, XXIII ([Aug.] 1941), 113–129.
[7]Throughout this paper unless specified otherwise when I use the term investment I shall mean net investment only.

In the early writings on the acceleration principle there seems to be little emphasis on the possibility that the acceleration coefficient is strictly a constant. Rather, the original statements of the principle ran mainly in terms of tendencies without stressing a constant proportionality. This is particularly true of Clark's exposition. It is also interesting to note that Clark, himself, stated explicitly a number of basic qualifications to the acceleration principle.[8] In the 1930's the formulation of the acceleration principle was subjected to statistical testing by Kuznets, Tinbergen, and others and was used in the pathbreaking dynamic model of Frisch in 1933.[9] For statistical testing or for inclusion in a mathematical model, it is convenient to express the acceleration principle as a linear relation with constant coefficients; i.e., net investment is made equal to some parameter, called the accelerator or the relation, times the change in the rate of demand for output. However, such a formulation does not necessarily imply a lack of awareness that the accelerator is not constant and that there are considerable qualifications to its use.[10]

It does seem, however, that in the subsequent use of the acceleration principle there has been little further exposition of the underlying microeconomic logic beyond the arithmetical examples of the type originally used. Harrod, for example, who was one of the first to incorporate the acceleration principle into a full-fledged business cycle theory and even gave it the "pride of place" in this theory, did not go deeply into its logic.[11]

The point has been made by Fisher that in the history of the *use* of the acceleration principle there has been a "gradual shift from a micro- to a macro-economic orientation."[12] On the other hand, those who have *criticized* the use of the acceleration principle on theoretical bases have generally proceeded in the opposite direction, their analysis of behavior of firms in a world of fluctuations leading them to a denial of the principle's macroeconomic validity. The failure to analyze the basis of the acceleration principle on the micro-economic level more explicitly may have contributed to an overestimate of its potentialities by its proponents and has, perhaps, also led some of its critics to overstate their case. Therefore, I believe it will be useful to revert at least briefly to the basic theory of the firm under

[8]See p. 184 below.

[9]S. Kuznets, "Relation Between Capital Goods and Finished Products in the Business Cycle," *Economic Essays in Honor of Wesley Clair Mitchell* (New York: [Columbia University Press,] 1935), pp. 211–267; J. Tinbergen, "Statistical Evidence on the Acceleration Principle," *Economica*, New Series, V (May 1938), 164–176; R. Frisch, "Propagation Problems and Impulse Problems in Dynamic Economics," *Economic Essays in Honor of Gustav Cassel* (London: [George Allen & Unwin, Ltd.,] 1933), pp. 171–205.

[10]Thus, in his seminal article Professor Samuelson noted the limitations of a constant accelerator and the restrictions it placed on the analysis. "Interactions Between the Multiplier Analysis and the Principle of Acceleration," *Review of Economic Statistics*, XXI (May 1939), 78.

[11]R. F. Harrod, *The Trade Cycle* (Oxford: [Clarendon Press,] 1936), chap. 2.

[12]*Op. cit.*, p. 474.

drastically simplified conditions in order to lay bare the reasoning behind the acceleration principle. The truth which does exist in the acceleration principle will then come out more clearly and further relevant criticisms will also evolve.

To start, it will be assumed that we are dealing with a single firm that moves smoothly from one position of equilibrium to another with perfect foresight. We rule out all problems of availability of credit, nonhomogeneity and indivisibilities of capital equipment, inaccurate expectations, excess capacity, or full employment of capital goods industries. These drastic assumptions for a tool of business cycle analysis are made to facilitate a simple demonstration of the acceleration principle.

In Figure I the equal-product curves derived from the firm's production function, involving the use of two factors only, capital and labor, are repre-

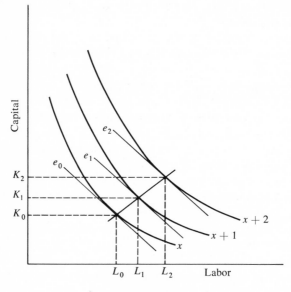

Figure I

sented by the heavy curved lines convex to the origin. Each equal-product line represents the various proportions in which capital and labor can be combined by this firm to produce the outputs x, $x + 1$, $x + 2$, etc.

The lighter lines in Figure I are equal-expenditure lines representing the various amounts of capital and labor which could be purchased at the constant costs e_0, e_1, e_2, etc.[13] If the firm has no excess capacity and wishes to

[13]While the drawing of the equal-expenditure curves as straight lines implies pure competition in the purchasing of factors, these lines could be considered as representing the slopes at the tangencies of concave equal-expenditure curves indicating some degree of monopsony, the only condition being that there be a unique tangency position for each expenditure line.

increase its output, say, from x to $x + 1$ and wants to minimize its costs in doing so, the well-known theory of the firm requires it to use additional capital and labor in a combination that is indicated by the tangency of an equal-expenditure line e_1, with the equal-product line $x + 1$. Satisfaction of this geometrical requirement is equivalent to the condition that the ratio of the marginal physical productivities of the two factors be equal to the ratio of their market prices.

The purpose of reverting to this elementary theory of the firm is to obtain a clear picture of the meaning of the accelerator under simple assumptions which, it is hoped, will provide some insights under more complicated conditions. Figure I indicates that, if the firm decides to increase its output from x to $x + 1$, or by Δx_1, it will increase its use of labor from L_0 to L_1, or by ΔL_1, and its use of capital from K_0 to K_1, or by ΔK_1. Expressing the increase in capital ΔK_1 as some factor, β_1, times Δx_1, the increase in output, we can obtain the following statement of the acceleration principle for the firm under these extremely simplified conditions.

$$\Delta K_1 = \beta_1 \cdot \Delta x_1, \tag{1}$$

where β_1 is now the acceleration coefficient. If Δx_1, the change in output, is considered to be a unit change. or $\Delta x_1 = 1$, then

$$\Delta K_1 = \beta_1. \tag{2}$$

Thus, in this case the accelerator for the firm, β_1, is equal in numerical value to the increase in capital required to increase output by one unit from x to $x + 1$.

If the firm should further expand its output by one unit from $x + 1$ to $x + 2$, there would again be additional capital required and again a coefficient, β_2, which could be called an accelerator; and so on for further increases in output. The line drawn through the points of tangency is the firm's "expansion path."

Before going on to utilize this simple demonstration it is necessary, even under the drastic assumptions being used, to settle the matter of the dimensional character of the accelerator, β. So far the time dimensions of the analysis have been almost completely suppressed. Actually the outputs x, $x + 1$, ... should be understood as flows per unit of time; by contrast $K_0, K_1, \ldots$ are stocks, not flows. The magnitude of the x's depends on the time units chosen; the magnitude of the K's does not. An increase in output means a change in the rate of output with respect to time and requires a change in the capital stock over time, or the undertaking of new net investment. The accelerator, itself, linking the stock of capital and the flow of output is measured dimensionally by the units in which time is measured, and its magnitude, therefore, depends on the time units chosen.

The major points resulting directly from this analysis can now be made quickly. Even more special assumptions would have to be added to all those already made for the firm's accelerator to be constant. For example, under the assumptions of constant returns to scale, if the factor price ratios remained constant, then $\beta_1 = \beta_2 = \ldots$, and the accelerator would be constant.[14] Or if the assumption of constant coefficients of production were added to that of constant returns to scale, the accelerator would remain constant even if the factor price ratios changed, or if the firm exercised some degree of monopsony in purchasing the factors. With production functions of a type other than linear and homogenous functions it can be easily seen that it would be quite unlikely that the firm's accelerator would be constant as it increased its output. But there would still be an expansion path for the firm which could be summarized by a variable accelerator.

If the drastically simplifying assumptions made at the start of this analysis are dropped, a host of difficulties come flooding back. The firm still will have an expansion path which could be plotted on a diagram with coordinates as in Figure I, but now this path would be irreversible. Each point on the expansion path would now be affected by all the influences previously assumed away: e.g., failure of business firms to try to minimize costs, stringencies in the financing of additional capital, indivisibilities and so on. Over sufficiently small ranges of output the expansion might be approximated by a straight line and a constant accelerator might still be utilized. With larger changes in output, the acceleration coefficient itself would change, and if the acceleration principle is to be meaningful it should be able to explain such changes. If this could be done, Kaldor's answer to the question which he poses, "In what sense can it be assumed that investment is a simple (and linear!) function of the *change* in the level of output?" would not have to be the one which he gives: "*as between alternative positions of long-period equilibria.*"[15] (His italics.) Limiting the applicability of the acceleration principle to long-run analysis would not overcome the problem of the variability of the accelerator. On the other hand, if the accelerator is explicitly considered a parameter whose variations require an independent

---

[14]This analysis above sets out in more detail Hicks's brief reference to the dependence of the acceleration principle on "a kind of *constant* returns," (*op. cit.*, p. 58) to which Tsiang takes exception. Tsiang's criticisms increase our appreciation of the care needed in stating and using the acceleration principle; still, several of these criticisms, I believe, are not well taken. It is true, of course, that in periods too short for capital stock to be increased a firm would not be able to move along its expansion path and that the acceleration principle would not operate. However, I do not believe it is true, as Tsiang holds, that the acceleration principle requires entrepreneurs to adjust their capital stock to short-run rather than long-run changes in output. (Cf. H. M. Somers, *op. cit.*, p. 83, on expectations.) Much of Tsiang's condemnation of the acceleration principle stems from his conception of the accelerator as a constant term. There are assumptions under which this is true, as indicated above, but it is not necessary to posit such cases to have a useful relation. (Cf. Tsiang, *op. cit.*, p. 329.)

[15]Kaldor, *op. cit.*, pp. 837–838.

explanation, use of the acceleration principle need not be limited to long-run analysis.[16]

As it now stands then the acceleration principle claims that, if excess capacity is at the lowest level desired by the firm, new investment is equal to some parameter times the increase in its output and that variations in the parameter must be explained separately. As a variable parameter the accelerator concept retains more general validity, I believe. Indeed, if one believed, for example, that there was capital deepening in the upward phases of the cycle, or increasing or decreasing returns to scale, the accelerator could be used to describe these different types of production functions and the growth of capital equipment during an expansion of output.[17]

[16]The concept of a variable or nonlinear accelerator has been explicitly proposed by many economists as, for example, in Samuelson, *op. cit.*, p. 269, Somers, *op. cit.*, p. 102 and S. Alexander, "Issues of Business Cycle Theory," *American Economic Review*, LXI (Dec. 1951), 861–878. The analyses of this problem by R. M. Goodwin are especially noteworthy, e.g., "The Nonlinear Accelerator and the Persistence of Business Cycles," *Econometrica*, XIX (Jan. 1951), 1–17. Even Hicks, who has been subjected to considerable criticism for his supposed commitment to a constant accelerator in his book on the trade cycle, explicitly discusses the possible variations in the accelerator during the upward phase of the cycle (*op. cit.*, p. 51).

[17]This can, perhaps, be seen more readily with another diagram derived from Figure I. Suppose Figure I is converted into a three dimensional surface by having an output axis rise vertically out of the page from the junction of the other two axes. Then project on the capital stock-output plane the outline of a curve running along the surface from one of the points of tangency to another. This would develop a curve something like the adjoining. The acceleration coefficient for the increase in output from x to $x + 1$ is now seen to be the tangent of the angle α_1. If there are increasing returns to scale, for example, α_2 will be less than α_1, and the tan α_2 will also be smaller than the tan α_1.

Figure I could also be utilized to clarify the distinctions between the natural, warranted, and actual rates of growth made by Harrod (*op. cit.*, chap. 3). At the natural, or full employment rate of growth, the yearly increments to output would be limited on the labor side by the annual increase in the labor force. If factor prices are assumed to remain constant, the annual increments to capital stock necessary for this rate of growth are also determined for any given production function of the type shown. The author is indebted to Professor Samuelson for this suggestion with respect to a similar diagram.

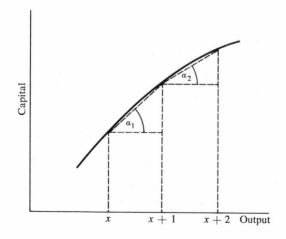

But an explanation of the variations in the accelerator must be given if the acceleration principle is to be meaningful.

III. Critical appraisal of the acceleration principle

If the validity of the acceleration principle is confined to the realm of abstraction, it can hardly be useful for business cycle theory. Having gone back to fundamentals to show the basic justification for the acceleration principle, it is now necessary to consider further to what extent the principle is vitiated by the qualifications which must be imposed, and to what extent it retains some usefulness for business cycle analysis in its flexible or non-linear form.

The criticisms of the acceleration principle as descriptive of a firm's investment behavior are well-known and numerous.[18] Many of the qualifications the acceleration principle requires, which its critics stressed in the 1930's and again recently, were recognized by its early proponents. Clark, in his original paper, discussed briefly the amendments to the theory necessitated if excess capacity existed, and the unsymmetrical operation of the accelerator on the downward phase of the cycle. He also mentioned other barriers to the action of the acceleration principle which have been stressed in recent writings: (1) the limitations imposed by the separate problems of financing additional capital equipment; (2) prohibitive changes in the relative prices of capital and other factors; (3) uncertainty of producers regarding permanency of an increase in demand leading to unwillingness to undertake capital expansion; (4) possible delay in acquiring additional capital stock due to lack of idle capacity in producers' goods industries.[19] In addition to the limitations mentioned by Clark a number of further qualifications are important of which the following list is meant to be more representative than exhaustive. Some of these were also at least touched on by Clark. Briefly, additional qualifications are: (1) Business firms do not always follow profit maximizing behavior or even act in such a way as to maintain their share of the market due to lack of motivation or knowledge of opportunities; (2) the existence of discontinuities or indivisibilities in the production function prevents smooth and continuous adjustments; (3) a separate and distinct influence is exerted by expectations based on factors other than demand for output, such as group psychological buoyancy or depression; (4) changed methods of production modify the reactions of firms to changes in demand for output; (5) changes in profits

---

[18]Haberler, *op. cit.*, pp. 85–105 and Somers, *op. cit.*, pp. 67–116 have comprehensive surveys.

[19]J. M. Clark, "Business Acceleration and the Law of Demand: A Technical Factor in Economic Cycles," *Journal of Political Economy*, XXV (Mar. 1917), 217–235; reprinted in *Readings in Business Cycle Theory* (Philadelphia: [The Blakiston Co.,] 1944), pp. 235–260.

may exert an influence on businessmen's investment decisions in a way which is, to some extent, distinct and different from the influence of changes in output.

The process of generalizing the acceleration principle from the level of a partial explanation of the investment behavior of the firm to a macroeconomic relation involves further possible pitfalls. In addition to the foregoing qualifications the macro-economic accelerator will also be modified by changing relations between the various sectors of the economy. For example, since the various sectors of the economy do not fluctuate simultaneously, variations in the size of the macro-economic accelerator will be introduced owing to the differences in the ratios of investment to changes in output in the various sectors. Moreover, nonrecurring shifts in the relative contribution of different sectors of the economy to total output and differential technological changes will again introduce variations in the acceleration principle.

In addition to these criticisms, deduced from theoretical considerations, the statistical tests of the acceleration principle, with some exceptions, have been generally unfavorable, although their conclusions have been somewhat tempered as the methods of some of the tests have been called into question.[20] The "testing" of the acceleration principle was started by Clark who found in his original article tentative support for the principle.[21] However, the conclusions of the later investigations of Kuznets and Tinbergen have been in the opposite direction.[22] More recent statistical investigations have not provided unequivocal results in verification or refutation of the hypothesis of the acceleration principle, although the results for the most part have been unfavorable.[23]

One point raised in criticism of the acceleration principle by Tsiang needs special consideration. Tsiang drew a parallel between the quantity theory of money and the acceleration principle and argued that:

just as the old-fashioned quantity theory of money is vitiated by the discovery that the velocity of circulation is not exogenous but is a pliable endogenous variable of the economic system, so may the theory of the business cycle, which is based on the mechanical interaction between a constant acceleration and a constant multiplier, be vitiated by the fact that the acceleration is probably not an exogenous constant, but is rather a pliable endogenous variable.[24]

The crucial issue for the velocity of circulation as well as for the accelerator,

[20]E.g., Somers, *op. cit.*, p. 111: "It appears that Tinbergen begins his statistical analysis with a confused notion of the nature of the acceleration principle, both in itself and in relation to other economic factors. As a result of this, the statistical results obtained are of no significance in determining the importance of the acceleration principle."

[21]*Op. cit.*, pp. 245–249.

[22]Kuznets, *op. cit.*, p. 263; Tinbergen, *op. cit.*, p. 176.

[23]E.g., H. B. Chenery, "Overcapacity and the Acceleration Principle," *Econometrica*, XX (Jan. 1952), 1–29.

[24]Tsiang, *op. cit.*, p. 327.

however, is not whether they are exogenous or endogenous variables. It is true that if they were exogenous neither concept would require an economic explanation. But, if the concepts can be given "dependable" economic explanations, it is not a damaging criticism to say that they are endogenous. The original hypothesis of the quantity theory was that the velocity of circulation is constant. The arguments which led to the abandonment of this hypothesis, however, opposed more generally the idea of a stable relationship explaining the holding of cash balances.[25] On the other hand, the acceleration principle need not be based on the hypothesis that the accelerator is constant, if, as some economists believe, other acceptable hypotheses can be advanced to explain its behavior. A mathematical model which uses a changing parameter for the accelerator has a limited autonomy for each value of the parameter but that does not necessarily make such a relation unusable unless the variations in the parameter are unpredictable.

The evidence and the deductions are conflicting. Although there seem to be more arguments against the acceleration principle than for it, informed opinion is not uniformly opposed to it. On the one hand, there are those who believe with Burns, Kaldor, and Klein that the acceleration principle is not a fruitful tool for analysis. And, on the other hand, there are those who, with Alexander and Somers, although recognizing the many necessary qualifications to the acceleration principle, still consider it a useful and valid tool.[26] Can these conflicting arguments and opinions be brought together and resolved in a final conclusion that the acceleration principle is or is not a useful tool for business cycle analysis? I think not. Such a final conclusion cannot be achieved as yet; individual judgments based on insufficient knowledge are still necessary for a balancing of opposing factors.

Although no very far-reaching statements can be made, the following conclusions, in my own opinion, are warranted on the information now available. In its qualified form, considered as a relation which changes under the impact of various forces, the acceleration principle has given useful insights into economic processes and presumably can give still more. It is clearly not the total explanation of investment. The criticisms of the acceleration principle are sufficiently significant so that relationships embodying some of the qualifications or stressing different interconnections can certainly add to our understanding. Since the acceleration coefficient does not seem likely to remain constant over very wide ranges of output, the acceleration principle using a constant coefficient can be used only for marginal analysis. For a complete business cycle analysis the acceleration coefficient

[25]Cf. W. Fellner, "Employment Theory and Business Cycles," in *A Survey of Contemporary Economics*, ed. H. S. Ellis (Philadelphia: [The Blakiston Co.,] 1949), p. 52.

[26]E.g., Somers, *op. cit.*, p. 116: "The acceleration principle as interpreted here nevertheless remains an important tool for the analysis of changes taking place in business investment at any particular time, when the numerous conditions involved are known or can be estimated."

should be viewed as a parameter for which a separate explanation must be provided.

These opinions are supported, I believe, by the example of the usefulness of the simple acceleration principle in economic analysis found in Samuelson's exposition of the implications of the synthesis of the multiplier and accelerator theories. Where more complicated expressions can be used for the determination of investment, which would require less "steering" by forces exogenous to the investment relation than does the simple acceleration principle, the self-sufficiency or autonomy of the relation would be increased. H. B. Chenery has found, for example, that a modification of the acceleration principle which contains adjustments for indivisibilities of capital equipment and the over or under capacity which develops, gives better results in some cases than the simple accelerator.

IV. Other forms of the acceleration principle

The time sequence in the acceleration principle, of changes in rate of output and of induced investment, is one aspect of the principle which has been the subject of some discussion. A very general formulation is given by Hicks, who makes investment in time t a weighted function of an indefinite number of previously experienced changes in output.[27] In another formulation new investment undertaken in period t is made to depend on the change in output which is experienced in that same period. It has also been suggested by at least one author that the acceleration principle should be altered in some circumstances so that investment is not dependent at all on past changes in output. The basis for this latter view is the belief that in periods of full or nearly full utilization of productive resources, an increase in the rate of production of capital equipment requires a diversion of resources from production of consumer goods. Only after these resources have been diverted and the additional increment of capital equipment produced and put to use can a higher rate of output be achieved. Thus, according to this view, any change in the rate of output under conditions of full utilization of productive resources must come after the new net investment.[28]

The purpose of the acceleration principle as used in models of income analysis is to provide a way of determining investment from changes in output, not vice-versa. The acceleration principle would not be a satisfactory relation for the determination of investment expenditures in a period analysis if investment in period t were used to explain increased output in later periods. To frame a relation which determines the change in output from a given investment would be a different task from that which the acceleration principle undertakes.

[27]Hicks, *op. cit.*, p. 182.
[28]Somers, *op. cit.*, p. 82.

A relation for the determination of investment in a dynamic period analysis must be made to depend on current and past events as the only way of judging what the future might be. This dependency in the acceleration principle might come about in several ways even in circumstances in which there is nearly full utilization of resources. For example, an increase in output in such a situation might be achieved by firms using their capital stock at a rate above that which is considered desirable over the long run. To redress this undesirable condition additional capital would be required in an amount which could be determined by the acceleration principle, in this instance from past changes in output. Or, instead of the above process, there might be an increase in the rate of sales which is made possible by a reduction in inventories. A higher rate of investment might be predicted on the basis of this higher rate of sales in the belief that it meant a permanently higher demand for output, and that new investment therefore would be justified in the sense that its capacity would be used. In this latter formulation, however, investment would depend on changes in the rate of sales rather than changes in the rate of output.

The procedure of relating new investment to changes in the rate of past output through the acceleration principle raises, of course, the problem of expectations. Usually it has been assumed in the use of the acceleration principle that business men extend the current or past changes in the rate of output into the future unchanged as a basis for making their decisions about the additional investment desirable.[29] That is, the acceleration principle is often formulated as follows:

$$I_t = \beta(X_{t-1} - X_{t-2}), \tag{3}$$

with I being investment, X output, and t time. β is the accelerator and usually is not explicitly considered to be affected by expectational influences. It would be possible to adapt this expression at least partially to include the effect of varying expectations by use of a coefficient of expectations, η, defined much like that used by Metzler in his paper on inventory cycles.[30] Instead of extending past changes in output $(X_{t-1} - X_{t-2})$ into the future unchanged, the collective expectation of demand for increased output would now be equal to η times the observed change in output from period $(t - 2)$ to period $(t - 1)$. Additional investment would then be considered necessary to increase output by the amount $\eta(X_{t-1} - X_{t-2})$ rather than by $(X_{t-1} - X_{t-2})$. Investment in period t due to a previous change in output would, therefore, be

$$I_t = \beta\eta(X_{t-1} - X_{t-2}). \tag{4}$$

The usual formulation of the acceleration principle is the case where $\eta = 1$. If, however, it is believed that η, the coefficient of expectations, is usually less than one, the effective accelerator, $\beta\eta$, would be somewhat less

[29]For a noteworthy exception see D. M. Wright, "A Neglected Approach to the Acceleration Principle," *Review of Economics and Statistics*, XXIII ([May] 1941), 100–101.
[30]*Op. cit.*, p. 116.

than β. If the coefficient of expectations were zero then no new investment would be undertaken in spite of past increases in output. If a past increase in output were expected to be reversed in the future into a decline in output then the coefficient of expectations would be negative and disinvestment would occur.

This formulation, incidentally, has interesting implications for the stability aspects of models using the acceleration principle. If the coefficient of expectations were less than one, the stability conditions applied to the "effective accelerator," $\beta\eta$, would be less restrictive than when applied to β alone, and, on the other hand, large values of η could introduce instability not otherwise present. It should be noted that in the form of equation (4) above, the coefficient of expectations occurs only as a multiplier of β, the acceleration coefficient. It can, therefore, be considered as absorbed into a modified β and no new mathematical analysis is necessary.

The flexibility of the acceleration principle as a partial explanation of investment is improved, I believe, by its formulation with explicit recognition of the role of expectations. However, it does require a separate theory for the variation of expectations.

Among the critics of the acceleration principle there has been an interesting amount of agreement as to a more suitable relation for the determination of investment. The replacement for the acceleration principle which has been suggested quite often in various forms is a relation in which the rate of investment is made to depend on the rate of output and the level of capital stock. This particular type of replacement for the acceleration principle will be considered now in order to place both the criticism of the acceleration principle and the formula suggested in its stead in a better perspective.[31]

Although the relations were generally derived by different methods there is a strong "family resemblance" among the investment-determining relations developed by Tinbergen, Klein, Kalecki, Kaldor, Chenery, and Goodwin. Inasmuch as it is the type of investment relation developed by these men which has gained wide support as a superior replacement for the acceleration principle, some of the various formulae will be presented briefly for comparison. I shall then show that by a simple restatement the acceleration principle can be made to contain very similar features.[32]

---

[31] If the nomenclature started by Clark were continued, in which the relation whereby investment depends on the rate of change of output is called the "acceleration principle," then the relation whereby investment depends on the level of output and the stock of capital should, perhaps, be called the "velocity principle."

[32] Goodwin and Chenery, of course, considered their formulae as modifications of the acceleration principle. Here, I shall show a more explicit derivation. It will be noticed that some of the examples of investment relations to be given run in terms of output while some are in terms of profits. This paper will not take up the question of whether the acceleration principle should most desirably be formulated in terms of profits or output except to note general agreement with Somers who takes the position that the "profit principle" and the acceleration principle in terms of output are not contrasting and separate theories (*op. cit.*, pp. 106–108).

Klein, one of the recent critics of the acceleration principle, has followed an approach much like that of Tinbergen and developed several types of investment relations which are generally similar. In Klein's relations investment is sometimes made a function of profits rather than output. The stock of capital enters with a lag and the profits or output variables are either or both current and lagged terms. Effects of other variables such as the interest rate or a price index of capital are also included in some of Klein's investment relations. The following equation will serve as an example of the type of investment relation with which Klein works. In his book, *Economic Fluctuations in the United States, 1921–1941*,[33] Klein develops three models in the first of which the investment relation is

$$I = \beta_0 + \beta_1 \frac{pX - E}{q} + \beta_2 \left(\frac{pX - E}{q}\right)_{-1} + \beta_3 K_{-1} + \beta_4 t + u_2. \qquad (5)$$

I is net investment in constant dollars; pX is the value of privately produced output; E stands for excise tax payments; K_{-1} is the stock of capital at the end of the previous year in constant dollars; q is the price of producer goods; t is time, introduced as a specific allowance for trend. The β's are constants, and u_2 is a random disturbance.

The general form of the investment relations developed by Tinbergen and Klein is in turn similar to that developed by Kalecki, as was noted by Klein with particular respect to the model from which equation (5) was drawn. One such investment relation of Kalecki's which contains modifications of an earlier formula, though omitting some other refinements, is

$$2\epsilon\frac{dI_{t+\epsilon}}{dt} = a\frac{dP_t}{dt} - (b + c)I_t .^{34} \qquad (6)$$

In this equation I is the rate of investment; P is profits and t is time. The letters a, b and c stand for parameters reflecting respectively the influence on investment of changes in the price of capital goods, the repressive influence on new investment of the existing capital stock, and the effects of risk, market imperfections and the degree of indebtedness of entrepreneurs. ϵ is the total lag of a change in the rate of investment behind changes in

[33](New York: [John Wiley & Sons, Inc.,] 1950), p. 87. Klein's equations are distinguished by a careful and explicit derivation from micro-economic theory. Another example of the type of investment relation with which Klein works is the following, derived for railroad investment.

$$I = 1596 + 0.75\pi_{-1} - 51i - 0.14K_{-1} + u$$

I is now gross investment in constant dollars; π is deflated new railway operating income before depreciation; K is road and equipment fixed capital in constant dollars, and i is the average yield on new railway bonds; u is again a random disturbance. ("Studies in Investment Behavior," in *Conference on Business Cycles*, National Bureau of Economic Research (New York: [NBER,] 1951), p. 250.)

[34]M. Kalecki, *Studies in Economic Dynamics* (London: [Farrar & Rinehart, Inc.,] 1943), p. 68.

the level of profits. If equation (6) is integrated, an equation for the level of investment is obtained as follows:

$$I_{t+\epsilon} = \frac{a}{2\epsilon} P_t - \frac{(b+c)}{2\epsilon} K_t + \text{a constant.} \tag{7}$$

Kaldor did not derive an investment relation in an explicitly algebraic form in his "Model of the Trade Cycle" paper.[35] Although he devoted an appendix to an explanation of the differences between himself and Kalecki on this matter, Kaldor has also testified as to the extent of agreement between them with respect to the important variables in the investment relation and the manner in which they affect investment. Thus, Kaldor, too, believes that the level of output and the level of capital stock are the important determinants of new investment.[36]

The examples which have been given of investment relations in which the rate of output or profits and the level of capital stock with appropriate lags are the important variables could probably be extended at length. Two more examples should be mentioned here at least briefly in order to indicate the ubiquity of this type of relation and the further modifications which are possible: the "capacity principle" of Chenery and the "flexible accelerator" of Goodwin. Neither Chenery nor Goodwin could be described as hostile to the general idea behind the acceleration principle, and each separately developed a modification in a form similar to the examples given above. Chenery's final modification of the acceleration principle[37] is written

$$\Delta K_{t+\theta} = b(\beta X_t - \lambda K_t). \tag{8}$$

K is capital stock so that ΔK is investment. X is output and t is time. β is the accelerator; b is a "reaction coefficient," and λ is a "capacity factor" indicating the optimum degree of utilization of plant at any particular time. Approaching from a quite different theoretical direction, Goodwin arrived at a very similar expression. By successive modifications of the theory of the marginal efficiency of capital Goodwin[38] derived the flexible accelerator in the form

$$K = \frac{1}{\xi} (\kappa y + \phi - K). \tag{9}$$

In this relation the notation is similar to that of Chenery's above with K

---

[35]*Economic Journal*, L (1940), 78–92.

[36]*Ibid.*, p. 89ff. As has been indicated above the acceleration principle was one of Kaldor's main targets for criticism in his review of Hicks's book. In this review the investment relation $I_{t+1} = Y_t f(Y_t/C_t)$ was recommended as avoiding most of the difficulties inherent in the acceleration principle. Here again I is investment; Y is output and C is capacity. "Mr. Hicks on the Trade Cycle," *Economic Journal*, LXI (Dec. 1951), 840.

[37]*Op. cit.*, p. 15.

[38]*Op. cit.*, p. 120.

now the time rate of change of capital stock, or investment. ϕ is an "innovational shift function"; $1/\xi$ is a constant similar to Chenery's b, and κ is the accelerator. This relation, although written in terms of differentials instead of differences, has the same family characteristics as the preceding examples in which investment is also made to depend primarily on the level of income and capital stock. The investment relations derived by Chenery and Goodwin are unique, however, as compared with the previous examples, in that they are intended to make the acceleration principle operate as a feedback mechanism. That is, the rate of investment is made to depend upon differences between the actual level of capital stock and the ideal level desired.

It is the type of investment relation as exemplified by the equations (5) to (9) in which the levels of output and capital stock play the most important roles, which I will call for convenience the velocity principle. In various forms it is this type of relation which has often been suggested recently as the most likely replacement for the acceleration principle. It is now interesting to revert to the acceleration principle, which depends on the rate of change of output, and ask how different it is from the velocity principle. For this purpose a diagram such as that of note [17] above will be used. The ordinate of this diagram is the level of capital stock and the abscissa is the level of output. The curve KK' drawn on this coordinate system indicates the aggregated capital equipment which businessmen would desire for each level of output. Time is implicit in the diagram which will be considered to be irreversible. Price changes, uncertainty, indivisibilities, and other factors affecting investment decisions may all be assumed to be reflected in the curve.

If initially, K_0, the level of capital stock, was in the aggregate exactly that desired to produce an output X_0, then K_1 indicates the higher level needed if output rises at time t_1 to output X_1 under some (changing) set of price and outlook influences. The line aa' is drawn through points 0 and 1 on the curve KK'. α_1 is the angle with the horizontal made by aa'.

It can be seen readily that the investment $K_1 - K_0$ necessary to raise output from X_0 to X_1 is

$$I_1 = K_1 - K_0 = (\tan \alpha_1)(X_1 - X_0). \tag{10}$$

This is the acceleration principle, and in this form $\tan \alpha_1$ is the accelerator. Rewriting equation (10), it can be put in the form

$$I_1 = (\tan \alpha_1) X_1 - K_0 + a. \tag{11}$$

Thus, the acceleration principle can be rewritten as the velocity principle. The resemblance of equation (11) to the examples given above of the investment relations developed by, say, Klein and Kalecki, in which the levels of output and capital were the important variables, is clear.

It is not mere coincidence that the relation in equation (11) derived from the acceleration principle looks so much like Klein's and Kalecki's relations. The acceleration principle and these other relations are derived from quite similar conceptions of investment by the firm. From each point of view the firm compares the future output which it wants to produce with its existing productive capacity, and invests if added productive capacity is needed to make up the difference. The future output which the firm wants to be able to produce is a decision based on expectations created by recent experiences of output and/or profits. Present productive capacity can be measured either by the existing stock of capital, as in, say, Klein's relations, or by current output with an appropriate adjustment if not all the capital stock is being used, as is done in the acceleration principle. The question now is really whether there is any difference between the acceleration principle and the velocity principle. The difference, I believe, is only in that the velocity principle includes in the formula for investment an allowance for the effect of the initial amount of capital equipment. In using the acceleration principle the effect of the initial stock of capital must be specified as a condition.

The diagram in Figure II can be used further to indicate how the acceleration principle can be adjusted to make allowance for certain other

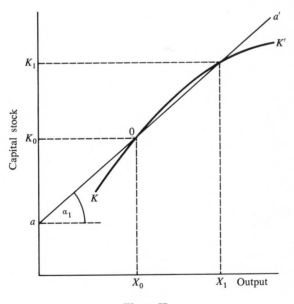

Figure II

qualifications and show even closer similarity to the equations of Klein, Kalecki, Chenery, and Goodwin. Should the initial level of capital not be just at K_0, the aggregate amount desired by businessmen to produce X_0, then equation (11) can take account of this by use of a parameter in front of K_0. The investment relation would then read

$$I_1 = (\tan \alpha_1)X_1 - cK_0 + a. \tag{12}$$

The similarity in form of equation (12), a restatement of the acceleration principle, and Kalecki's relation in equation (7) does not necessarily imply that they are now equally useful. Kalecki's relation has a temporary advantage in that it assigns to each of the coefficients particular roles in allowing for price changes, effects of risk, etc. However, it would be possible by analysis of the factors influencing the shape of the curve KK' in Figure II and thus of the economic significance of the coefficients of equation (12) also to make allowance for similar forces and, perhaps, in a manner as definite as in Kalecki's relation.

Figure II could be exploited still further to show how the acceleration principle can be put in a form very similar to that of Klein's investment relation in which current as well as lagged income and the lagged level of capital stock are the important variables. This could be done by substituting for the constant a a function of X.[39] Further manipulation of terms could also produce a relation similar to Tinbergen's "profit principle" except that it would be in terms of output. By additional assumptions modifications could be achieved with respect to lags and the effects of other variables. Multiplying the right hand side of equation (12) by an appropriate coefficient would produce a relation which could be interpreted similarly to Chenery's and Goodwin's investment functions.

One of the important qualifications to the simple acceleration principle is that it would give misleading results when applied to situations of decreasing output. As a result it is considered to apply only to the upward phase of the cycle. Hicks's use of the principle was, for example, subject to this consideration. Equation (12) provides another way of seeing how the acceleration principle will give an indication of when it should be "turned off." When $(\tan \alpha_1)X_1 < cK_0 + a$, then I_1 would be negative. Since the rate of disinvestment is limited by other factors than those in the equation, the occurrence of a negative figure for I_1 can be used as a signal for the suspension of the action of the acceleration principle.

This section has shown that, rewritten in a slightly different form, the acceleration principle correctly stated becomes the velocity principle and actually allows for the influence of the level of capital stock, the supposed neglect of which is one of the major criticisms often made against it. In this modified form of the velocity principle other qualifications can be imposed on the acceleration principle and it can take on a form quite similar to the

[39]Other variables than output and capital stock are often present in such equations as those of Klein's models. While not minimizing the added significance which these variables give to the investment relations, I wish to stress here the presence of the variables which represent levels of output and capital stock.

investment relations which some of its critics have proposed in its stead. A summarization should, perhaps, be confined to the limited observation that there is often more than one way of coming to the same conclusion. But even this bare observation is useful in counteracting some of the excessive criticism of the acceleration principle and in defining its range of usefulness. The acceleration principle, though it must be used carefully and with judicious qualifications, does, I believe, contain an important core of truth. This final section, by showing the connection of the acceleration principle to other forms of investment relations, has helped to demonstrate this truth.

JAMES G. WITTE, JR. **10**

The microfoundations of
the social investment function[1]

I. Introduction

In some theoretical discussions of the determinants of the rate of investment, emphasis has been placed on a continuous function relating the rate of investment of a firm to alternative levels of the rate of interest. From this view the Keynesian investment function is derived by a quite unspecified process of aggregation from the micro-investment functions. Such a view is questionable. Quite apart from the difficulties of aggregation, for example, the use of consistent assumptions as to the *ceteris paribus* conditions, the continuous function relating the rate of investment to the rate of interest at the micro level has no foundation in the ordinary theory of the firm. The reason for this is quite simple. The firm's demand is for the services of the capital goods it acquires. To maximize profits over a specified time interval it must secure at particular dates a specified flow of services of capital goods, and to secure these services, it must acquire the capital goods. Thus derived from its demands for a flow of capital services is a demand for a stock of capital goods and not for a continuous flow of these goods.

Reprinted from James G. Witte, Jr., "The Microfoundations of the Social Investment Function," *The Journal of Political Economy*, Vol. 71 (October 1963), pp. 441–456, by permission of The University of Chicago Press. Copyright 1963 by The University of Chicago Press. [Footnotes expanded — *Eds.*]

[1] I am indebted to Harry G. Johnson, Samuel M. Loescher, Henry M. Oliver, and Lloyd D. Orr for valuable criticisms and suggestions.

Once the firm has acquired its optimal flow of capital goods' services, its capital stock will not be augmented by new investment. Its net investment will remain equal to zero in the absence of a change in circumstances which renders its present stock of capital goods non-optimal. The firm's demand is for stock rather than for flow of capital goods because the services it wishes to have available are proportional to, or are at least functionally related to, the stock and not to the rate of change of the stock. Its optimum stock will change with the change of circumstances, and net investment (positive or negative) will be observed. But in the absence of such changes, the firm's optimal stock will remain constant. Even in the event of a change in circumstances, such as an increase in the demand for its product or a drop in the rate of interest, the firm's rate of investment will ordinarily be unpredictable. All that can be said is that the change in circumstances increases the size of the firm's optimum stock of capital, that is, a disequilibrium is created to which the firm will presumably adjust by acquiring more capital goods. The fact of positive capital accumulation says nothing, however, about the rate at which capital goods will be acquired. A given gap between the firm's actual and desired capital stock is literally consistent with an indefinitely large number of rates of investment, ranging from almost zero to almost infinity, depending upon, among many other things, the durability of its existing stock.[2] A theory of the rate of investment of the firm is an inter-equilibrium theory, a type of dynamic theory that is explicitly excluded by the ordinary comparative statics formulation of the theory of the firm. All of the factors that may be relevant to the interequilibrium dynamics, a topic which has hardly begun to be explored in a systematic way, would have to be considered. At the present time, in my opinion, a theory sufficiently broad to be capable of generalization would be devoid of empirical content and one sufficiently specific to explain the behavior of a particular real-world firm would be incapable of generalization. About one thing we can be quite certain, however. Within the context of the traditional comparative statics theory of the firm, a function relating the rate of investment to the rate of interest does not exist.[3] Questions about the elasticity of this function are, therefore, meaningless.

II. The dilemma for theory

Such a finding is somewhat discouraging because it appears to undermine attempts to integrate macro and micro theory. The seriousness of this can be seen by a reflection on what is perhaps the basic principle of macro theory, its fundamental law since at least the eighteenth century; that an increase in

[2]Cf. T. Haavelmo, *Studies in the Theory of Investment* (Chicago: University of Chicago Press, 1961), p. 216.
[3]*Ibid.*, p. 190.

the quantity of money tends to raise the level of money income by exerting at least a temporary downward pressure on the money rate of interest.[4] The fall in the rate of interest creates positive excess demands at current prices, which will generate a rise in money income and a rise in output and prices, the proportions of which will depend upon the extent of idle capacity existing at that moment of time. Under conditions of full employment, prices will rise in proportion to the increase in the quantity of money, and the rate of interest will return to its original level. There are, of course, many other possible variations, but the point is that this has been the central principle of orthodox macroeconomic theory from Hume to Keynes. It is still central today as is evident from an examination of the works of contemporary economists such as Friedman and Patinkin.[5] Central to this proposition is the existence of an interest-elastic function relating the aggregative rate of investment to the rate of interest. Apart from some recondite discussions of the Pigou effect, most theoretical discussions have related changes in the quantity of money to the level of income via changes in interest rates and investment. If economists were to conclude that an interest-elastic investment function could not exist, perhaps for microeconomic reasons, then this central principle would be without support. I suspect that most economists would not be willing to abandon the corpus of macroeconomic theory without considerable persuasion.

The other horn of the dilemma is no more inviting. If there exists no microeconomic foundation for the aggregate investment function, the economist who continues to employ the latter is implicitly rejecting the traditional theory of the firm as incorrect or, at least, as irrelevant. Yet the theory of the firm, or more properly the theory of resource allocation under competitive conditions, is as important a part of the economist's way of thinking as macroeconomics. A rejection of the theory of resource allocation, because it appears to conflict with macro theory, carries with it the danger of the economist becoming exclusively preoccupied with macroeconomic problems to the exclusion of all the others. Granted, the problems of unemployment and inflation are important. So are problems of monopoly, tariff rates, and the distribution of income. I doubt, for example, that the problems of encouraging and absorbing technological progress can be handled within an exclusively macroeconomic framework.

III. The conceptual framework at the micro level

As I have said, the relevant demand for capital goods at the micro level is derived from the firm's demand for the services that capital goods can

[4] D. Patinkin, *Money, Interest, and Prices* (Evanston, Ill.: Row, Peterson & Co., 1956), chap. 15.

[5] *Ibid.*; and M. Friedman, "The Lag in Effect of Monetary Policy," *Journal of Political Economy*, LXIX (Oct. 1961), 462.

provide. At this level of generality, there is no conceptual difference between the demand for capital goods and the demand for labor, except that we cannot employ the implicit identification between the source of the services and the services themselves which we make in the case of labor. If labor's services were purchased in stock form, as would be the case in a slave-owning society, even this distinction would disappear. With either labor or capital goods then, the theory of the firm can explain the quantity employed in a given set of circumstances. It is the quantity for which the value of the marginal product is equal to the purchase price of the unit acquired. The only difficulty in the case of capital goods is that, solely because of durability, a means must be found to relate the incremental flow of income (the marginal product) to the acquisition cost (the cost of several years' service flow). One such means of doing this is to relate the present value of the expected incremental income to the cost of acquisition; by discounting the expected profit annuity at the relevant rate of interest, this flow may be converted into a stock, which can then be compared with the purchase price of the unit of the capital stock to be acquired. In order to derive a demand function for capital goods on this basis, that is, the amount demanded as a function of purchase price, we must consider the consequence for the present value of the marginal expected profit annuity of alternative quantities of particular capital goods, prices of other inputs being held constant. What we should expect to observe is that the marginal expected profit annuity will diminish as the quantity of the capital good increases. The reasons are quite familiar: (a) as the scale of the enterprise increases, difficulties of control and communication may produce rising costs; (b) as the scale of the firm and its competitors increase, product selling prices may be expected to fall; (c) as the capacity of the enterprise and its competitors increase, the prices of certain resources not in perfectly elastic supply may be expected to rise. This does not necessarily mean that the enterprise expects product prices to fall and resource prices to rise because of the impact of its own increased outputs and increased inputs on the respective markets, but that the simultaneous expansion of a number of enterprises may be expected to produce this result. In other words the expectation of declining net income per unit of capital invested, because of falling product prices and rising resource prices, is not inconsistent with atomistic competition, because the firm is presumably aware of the fact that its competitors are expanding at the same time that its investment is taking place. The theory of competitive price determination would lead us to expect that the stimuli affecting investment, such as increases in product demand or decreases in interest rates, are common to a large number of firms at any particular moment of time. To the extent that the stimuli producing the investment response are normally common to entire groups of firms, the entrepreneur's own experience would lead him to predict some decline in his selling price and some rise in his resource prices.

For this reason I do not see the necessity of introducing market imperfections to explain limitations on the amount of capital employed by the firm.[6] To argue that there is no limit to the expansion of the firm under conditions of pure competition in output and input markets, as some economists have done, is to suggest that the stimulus to expansion is always peculiar to the individual firm in question and that its competitors are and remain in stationary equilibrium. Market imperfections may exist and may be important for certain problems, but I do not consider them essential to the proposition that the firm expects a decline in its marginal profit annuity to be associated with an increase in its stock of capital. If we plot the present value of the marginal expected profit annuity as a function of the quantity of capital goods employed, we can expect that the demand curve for a profit-maximizing enterprise slopes downward to the right. It must be remembered that there is one such demand curve for each rate of interest, because we are comparing the marginal present value, a stock concept, with the purchase price of capital goods. The vertical intercept of each stock demand curve is a function of the rate of interest. What this means is that, other things being equal, the firm's optimal capital quantity is greater, the lower is the rate of interest.

In addition to exogenous changes in the rate of interest, other environmental changes can be incorporated into this model. An increase in the demand for the firm's product will also shift the capital demand curve to the right for obvious reasons, that is, it increases the present value of the marginal profit annuity associated with any given quantity of capital goods. An increase in the firm's wage rates or in the expected rate of obsolescence of capital goods will have, presumably, the opposite effect.

Thus even if an investment function of the Keynesian type is inconsistent with the traditional theory of the firm, use can still be made of the rate of interest as a factor affecting the optimal quantity of capital goods. The questions on which the rate of interest bears are not, however, in an analysis employing the method of comparative statics, those relating to the rate of investment; instead, they are questions relating to the size of the optimal capital quantity — not to the speed of acquisition of capital goods but to the overall scale of operations. Therefore it seems that the wrong type of question was asked in the Oxford Inquiry.[7] Given the type of question asked, one should not be surprised that little information was gained concerning the determinants of a firm's rate of investment. A straightforward use of the stock demand concept at the micro level should lead to a new set of questions concerning the influence of the interest rate on the firm's behavior. There is no reason to think that the old questions could not

[6]For an alternative view see Tibor Scitovsky, *Welfare and Competition* (Homewood' Ill.: Richard D. Irwin, Inc., 1951), pp. 191-216.

[7]P. W. S. Andrews, "A Further Inquiry into the Effects of Rates of Interest," *Oxford Studies in the Price Mechanism* (Oxford: Oxford University Press, 1951).

be reformulated successfully with the help of an explicitly dynamic theory of the firm; but the development of such a theory has not proceeded very far.

One of the factors that has inhibited the use of my type of capital goods demand concept has been the popularity of a quasi-investment function, which I call an array-of-opportunities curve.[8] A finite number of things usually called investment "opportunities" or "projects" is typically arrayed in descending order of expected rate of return with a cut-off point or minimum acceptable rate of return juxtaposed. The cut-off point is designed to indicate that projects expected to yield less than some required minimum are not worthy candidates for some limited quantity of investible funds (limited usually by some unspecified constraints). Some such procedure is required for the rational allocation of funds, of course, but my contention is that an array-of-opportunities curve is in no sense an investment function. There is no way of using such a construct to estimate the rate of return as a function of the size of the capital stock or the rate of investment. This can be seen by posing this question: If one way of using capital goods is more profitable than others, why employ the other methods at all? I suspect that the answer to this question would lead us step by step through the analysis of this section to the kind of demand function used in this paper; I see no other way to explain the quantity of capital goods employed by the profit-maximizing enterprise — nor, for that matter, to explain the quantity of coal employed. Incidentally, I believe that the indiscriminate use of this array-of-opportunities curve has led many economists to believe that for the enterprise or for the economy as a whole a rate-of-return-on-capital function should be expected to be quite discontinuous, and that investment opportunities are kinds of things that exist in a sort of lump that may appear during certain time periods and be non-existent at others. This conclusion is unacceptable, because it results from an erroneous identification of the demand function for capital goods with the array-of-opportunities curve.

IV. Determination of the prices of capital goods

The aggregate demand curve for a particular type of capital good is derived by summation from the demand curves of all the firms which are actual or potential users of the type of capital good in question. The demand curve in Figure 1 relates quantity of the capital good desired to be held to the market price of the capital goods. I am employing a demand curve of the Wicksteed type, in which the reservation schedules of those firms with some initial

[8]Examples of this are legion. One such is the statement of Tarshis: "In the final analysis, the elasticity depends upon the pattern of yields expected from the various projects under active consideration. The closer to one another are the expected yields from different projects, the greater is the elasticity" (L. Tarshis, "The Elasticity of the Marginal Efficiency of Capital Function," *American Economic Review*, LI [Dec. 1961], 983).

endowment of the capital good are included in the demand curve. By this procedure the supply schedule of the capital good is inelastic with respect to price; the stock in existence is a given datum at any point in time. The

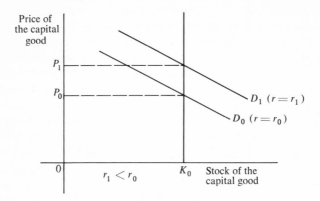

Figure 1

size of the stock will change over time unless the rates of depreciation and production are equal to one another, but at any particular moment of time the stock must be treated as a datum. This is particularly important if the annual increment to the stock, resulting from current production less capital consumption, is small relative to the total stock. In this case the influence of demand predominates over that of *flow* supply in the determination of the market price. This can be said without denying the fact that flow supply considerations must dominate the outcome in the long run. In the case of very durable goods, however, a relatively long time must elapse before positive or negative net production produces a significant alteration in the size of the total stock. This is only to say that Marshall's momentary-equilibrium analysis is probably more applicable to houses or office buildings than to special-purpose machinery and certainly more applicable to houses than to merchants' stocks. For clarity we assume that the annual increment to the stock of this type of capital good is so small that we can ignore any influence of the annual flow supply on the market price. Thus variations in demand will necessarily be associated with variations in the market price, for, as Clower has noted, price flexibility is necessary to reconcile the freedom of the individual firm to hold all it wishes with the restriction that the entire stock must be held by someone.[9]

In addition to the stock-supply schedule we also have a flow-supply schedule relating the rate of output of capital goods to producers' expecta-

[9] R. W. Clower, "An Investigation into the Dynamics of Investment," *American Economic Review*, XLIV (March 1954), 64–81. The analytic device employed in this paper is an adaptation of that originally developed by Clower.

tions of market price. This seems to be the ordinary Marshallian supply schedule in which the rate of output is a function of ex ante market price. With a given capacity in the capital goods industry at any time, the flow-supply schedule will be positively sloped, reflecting the law of variable proportions in the individual firms. There are two conditions of equilibrium in the market for capital goods at any time: the market price must be such as to induce firms to hold the entire stock of capital goods, and the rate of output of capital goods must be such as to equate the marginal supply price with the market price. This presupposes that the law of indifference holds: that is, that two units of the same economic good cannot sell at two different prices. In applying the law of indifference to the capital goods market some allowance must be made for the fact that identical goods of different chronological ages have different remaining economic life spans. We assume that price differentials are functionally related to differentials of expected economic life span. In Haavelmo's words: "The law of indifference of capital prices states that, for units of capital that are equivalent in any production function, the prices in a perfect capital market, without elements of price expectations or the like, can differ only because of differences in their durability properties."[10] We conclude that there is a unique rate of output of capital goods, a unique rate of gross investment, associated with each market price of capital goods.

V. Variations in the rate of interest

With the stock of capital goods given let the rate of interest fall. For a given level of firms' sales expectations this fall in the rate of interest raises the present value of the marginal expected profit annuity associated with its capital stock, creating excess firm demand for capital goods at the prevailing price. Thus, in Figure 2 the aggregate demand curve shifts to the right and the market price of capital goods must rise so that the market be cleared. The increase in the market price creates a flow disequilibrium, which is followed by a higher rate of output of new capital goods, the rate being that for which the marginal supply price is equal to the new market price. For any conjectural variation in the rate of interest a new rate of output, a new rate of gross investment, can be determined. The essential point is that the rate-of-investment decision, as opposed to the optimum-stock decision, is made by the capital-goods-producing firms, which determine how much they care to produce at the prevailing market price.[11] With the capital stock and the level of sales expectations given, what is determined is a set of rates

[10]*Op. cit.*, p. 183.
[11]*Ibid.*, p. 196. "Note that it is, actually, not the users of capital who 'demand' investment, it is the producers of capital goods who determine how much they want to produce at the current price of capital."

of gross investment uniquely associated with a corresponding set of interest rates. This set of equilibrium relationships traces out a social investment function that relates aggregate investment to the rate of interest. The point is that this social investment function, or marginal-efficiency-of-capital

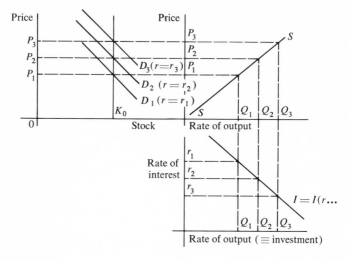

Figure 2

schedule, is not a demand curve for anything and is not derived by aggregation from similar micro-investment functions. In Patinkin's language, it is a market equilibrium curve rather than a demand curve.[12] Its micro foundations are not suspect, nor is it derived by any expectational *deus ex machina*. Its existence stems from the fact that the aggregate quantity of capital goods cannot be increased very rapidly. Whereas the individual firm can increase its stock of capital significantly within one year's time, when other enterprises are not increasing their demands for capital goods, all enterprises cannot do this simultaneously. The limitation is one of capacity and cost. Thus, the aggregative rate of investment can be regarded as a function of the rate of interest, whereas this would not be possible if there were no constraint on the rate of output of capital goods.[13] Once again, the rate-of-investment decision is the rate-of-output decision of supplying enterprises and not the rate-of-input decision of capital-using firms.

The interest elasticity of investment is really the interest elasticity of the rate of output of capital goods. Since both a demand and a supply response

[12]*Op. cit.*, pp. 103–104.
[13]Clower's conclusion is somewhat different from this, at least in terms of emphasis. He writes, "a once-over change in the rate of interest may permanently alter the level of the stock of durable goods and the levels of gross investment and disinvestment; but, *ceteris paribus*, the continuance of non-zero levels of net investment depends upon nonrecurring changes in the rate of interest" (*op. cit.*, p. 77).

are subsumed under this relationship, I say, following Shackle, that this elasticity is dependent upon two other elasticities.[14] These are (a) the elasticity of demand price with respect to the rate of interest, and (b) the elasticity of the rate of output of capital goods with respect to the market price of capital goods. From my assumption of no feedback from flow supply to stock supply in the relevant time period, I can identify market price with demand price. From this it follows that the elasticity of the rate of interest, *ceteris paribus*, is equal to the multiplicative product of the other two elasticities.

The first elasticity is that of the capitalized marginal profit annuity with respect to the rate of interest. This elasticity governs the extent of the movement in demand price consequent upon a change in the relevant market rate of interest. Shackle has shown that this elasticity varies within the limits of almost zero to minus one, with its absolute value a function of the length of the entrepreneur's time horizon.[15] Its absolute value reaches a maximum value of unity as the entrepreneur's time horizon approaches infinity, which it will if the entrepreneur plans periodic replacement of the capital good into the indefinite future. In all other cases the value of this elasticity is less than unity. An interesting implication of this is that this elasticity should be regarded as a function of the strength of the entrepreneur's expectations and not of the ephemeral expected life of a particular type of capital good. This much is clear as soon as we recognize the possibility of periodic replacement. Thus there is no necessity for the interest elasticity of the demand price for inventories to be less than that of the demand price for more durable capital goods; both are subject to periodic replacement. A short horizon is then seen as the entrepreneur's defense against uncertainty and not as a technological necessity. This is, of course, commonly recognized as the rationale of the short payoff periods on which many businessmen insist before they acquire new capital goods.[16]

The second elasticity is simply the ordinary supply elasticity of the capital-goods industry. The only restriction that can be imposed on its value is that it is less than plus infinity, which must be the case with a given productive capacity in the short run. This elasticity will probably vary inversely with the rate of capacity utilization in the capital-goods industry, being high for a low level of aggregate economic activity and vice versa. From this one should not conclude that the elasticity of the social investment function will tend to be relatively high in periods of recession, however, for the entrepreneur's degree of uncertainty might be relatively high in a period of low aggregative activity. Both elasticities determine the proportionate

[14]G. L. S. Shackle, "Interest Rates and the Pace of Investment," *Economic Journal*, LXI (March 1946), 1–17.

[15]*Ibid.*, pp. 4–14.

[16]Cf. V. L. Smith, *Investment and Production* (Cambridge, Mass.: Harvard University Press, 1962), pp. 232–241.

response of the rate of investment to the rate of interest, and both must be considered in such a judgment.

A necessary condition for there to be a determinate rate of output of new capital goods is that the flow supply curve have less than infinite elasticity. This raises an interesting question concerning the compatibility of this analysis with a model of underemployment equilibrium. If a state of excess capacity prevails throughout the economy during a recession, surely the capital-goods sector must experience some excess capacity. Indeed the durable-goods industries seem to have marked excess capacity in recession years. Does the existence of excess capacity threaten the validity of the assumption of a finitely-elastic flow-supply curve? If so, the consequence is serious, because the analysis developed in this paper would be inapplicable to periods of underemployment.

One way out of this problem is to assume, along with Keynes, that marginal costs of the individual firm rise with the rate of output over any relevant range of output.[17] In Stigler's terminology, Keynes assumed that industrial plant is adaptable and indivisible.[18] This assumption suffices to generate a supply curve of finite elasticity and a determinate rate of investment, but it is not consistent with many empirical studies of industrial cost behavior. However, a failure of individual firm marginal costs to rise with the rate of output when there is a great deal of excess capacity does not necessarily rule out the possibility of an industry supply curve of finite elasticity. If each firm's marginal cost curve is flat over ranges of outputs likely to be encountered in a recession, the industry supply curve may still be positively sloped if there is *temporary* exit from the industry. The existence of a flat range of the marginal cost curve implies that average variable cost is approximately equal to marginal cost over some of the range of flatness. Thus it would not be too surprising to observe that some firms would shut down in a recession when price falls to a level that approximates average variable cost. Those firms with relatively pessimistic expectations about the duration of the recession and those with relatively weak financial positions may be the ones expected to shut down. To the extent that temporary exit occurs in recessions, followed by re-entry when demand recovers, the industry supply curve would have a positive slope, and the rate of output would be determinate. Thus there is no necessary inconsistency between the required assumption of finite supply elasticity and conditions of underemployment equilibrium.[19]

[17]J. M. Keynes, *The General Theory of Employment, Interest, and Money* (New York: Harcourt-Brace & Co., 1936), chap. 21.

[18]G. J. Stigler, "Production and Distribution in the Short Run," American Economic Association, *Readings in the Theory of Income Distribution* (Philadelphia: Blakiston Co., 1951), p. 124.

[19]For an application of the thesis of temporary exit during recession and subsequent re-entry during recovery see S. M. Loescher, *Imperfect Collusion in the Cement Industry* (Cambridge, Mass.: Harvard University Press, 1959), pp. 61–72.

VI. Lerner on the marginal productivity of capital and the marginal efficiency of investment

An early attempt at stock-flow integration in the theory of investment is that of A. P. Lerner.[20] Central to Lerner's argument is the distinction between the marginal efficiency of investment and the marginal productivity of capital. The marginal efficiency of investment is the rate of return over cost at the margin of investment. More precisely, it is the ratio of the expected increment in annual net income to the cost of acquisition of the associated unit increment in the capital stock. The marginal productivity of capital is the rate of return over cost for a unit increase in the capital stock when the rate of net investment approaches zero. If the marginal cost of production of capital goods is positively associated with the rate of output of capital goods, the marginal efficiency of investment is less than the marginal productivity of capital for any quantity of the capital stock if the rate of investment is positive. The two rates of return are equal for any quantity of capital only as the rate of net investment approaches zero. Thus, following Keynes, Lerner concludes that the rate of return over cost diminishes with the size of the capital stock, and for any given quantity of capital, diminishes with increases in the rate of investment. There are, thus, two independent reasons for a declining rate of return.

In this paper I have reached a different conclusion. My conclusion that the current cost of production of capital goods does not affect the rate of return on capital is a corollary of the proposition that this cost of production is largely price-determined rather than price-determining. This is necessarily the case if the annual flow of new capital goods adds such a small quantity to the stock of capital goods that the rate of return is unaffected. In this case the price of capital goods is equal to the capitalized marginal profit annuity of the capital stock, and, because of the law of indifference, the price of newly produced capital goods must be the same. Profit-maximizing producers adjust their rates of output so that the marginal supply price of capital goods is equal to this price. What is determined by the cost schedules of capital-goods producers is the rate of output of new capital goods but not the rate of return over cost of the capital-goods users.

If the assumption of isolation of market price from the influence of flow supply is modified, the rate of return may be affected by the annual increment to the capital stock. An increase in the capital stock will reduce expected income per unit of capital and, at the prevailing market price of capital goods, will reduce the marginal rate of return over (acquisition) cost. At a given rate of interest the marginal present value of the capital stock will be less than the prevailing market price; if businessmen are to hold the larger capital stock, the price must fall so as to equate the marginal rate of return with the interest rate. Thus, an increase in the capital stock, *ceteris*

[20]*The Economics of Control* (New York: Macmillan Co., 1946), pp. 323–340.

paribus, tends to reduce the marginal rate of return over cost at the prevailing market price of capital goods. To the extent that the annual flow of capital-goods output produces a significant increase in the capital stock, the rate of return over cost will decline.

However, the effect of production costs on the value of capital goods is the opposite of that implied by the Lerner thesis. Production costs serve as a barrier to an increase in the capital stock. The more sharply marginal costs rise with the rate of output of capital goods, the less is the rate of increase of the capital stock, and the less rapidly does the rate of return decline. The greater is the elasticity of supply of new capital goods, or the less rapid the rise in marginal costs with the rate of output, the greater will be the impact of the annual output on the capital stock and the rate of return. For this reason I must differ with Lerner when he suggests that the rate of return on capital would be least affected by the rate of investment if marginal costs were constant. Rather the opposite would be true.[21]

This does not deny that, in the long run, the rate of return is profoundly influenced by, if not determined by, the cost of production of new capital goods. That is, positive net investment will increase the stock of capital until the price of capital goods falls to equality with the long-run marginal cost of capital goods. The cost of acquisition would be equal to the cost of production of new capital goods, which is true in the short run as well, but production costs would dominate the outcome in the long run. My contention is only that the cost of production has no such direct influence on the rate of return except in a long-run stationary equilibrium; what influence cost has is on the rate of capital accumulation. Costs tend to retard capital accumulation and, therefore, tend to maintain rather than depress the rate of return. Thus the Keynes-Lerner thesis that rising marginal costs constitute an independent factor tending to reduce the rate of return is incorrect.

VII. Keynes and the "Modus operandi of bank rate"

In his *Treatise on Money* Keynes developed a theory of the response of investment to changes in the interest rate that is quite similar to the central argument of this paper.[22] He argued that the principal impact of interest rate changes is not on the cost of production but on the demand price of capital goods. If an increase in the interest rate produced only an all-around rise in costs, there would not necessarily be any change in aggregate demand, at least in a closed economy, because interest is both a cost and an income. Rather a rise in the rate of interest tends to reduce investment because it reduces the demand price of capital goods.

The demand price is the capitalized value of future earnings expected to flow from the existing capital stock. Given the expectations of businessmen

[21]*Ibid.*, p. 339.
[22]J. M. Keynes, *A Treatise on Money* (London: Macmillan & Co., 1953), pp. 185–213.

with respect to these future earnings, a rise in the rate of interest will reduce the present value of these expected earnings. The demand price of capital goods will, therefore, vary inversely with the rate of interest. The market price of capital goods will also fall, since this is equal to demand price for a given capital stock. The fall in price will induce capital-goods producers to curtail their rates of output as it will be "impossible for producers of capital goods to market their output on terms as satisfactory as before in relation to their costs of production."[23] In the terminology of this paper, the rate of output of capital goods will be reduced until marginal cost is again equal to the market price. The extent of reduction in the rate of investment will depend upon (a) the response of demand price to the rate of interest and (b) the elasticity of supply of capital goods with respect to price. Concerning the former, Keynes assumed that the demand price would vary in inverse proportion to the rate of interest, which, as I have shown in an earlier section of this paper, presupposes that businessmen plan indefinite periodic replacement of existing capital goods. Concerning the latter his argument implies that the elasticity of supply of capital goods is positive but not infinite.

The statement of Keynes that changes in the interest rate operate on demand price rather than on costs is misleading. Granted that the response of investment to changes in the interest rate occurs because of changes in the demand price of capital goods, this change in demand price is, itself, a response to changes in cost. An increase in the rate of interest reduces the cost of obtaining a given income from the purchase of marketable securities. This increases the (opportunity) cost of obtaining a given income by direct investment within the business enterprise; the cost of transforming present inputs into future outputs is increased. The increase in cost reduces the attractiveness of holding the existing capital stock at its current market price. Thus the market price of capital goods must decline until the rate of return from holding the capital stock is again equal to the rate of return over the cost of acquisition of alternative assets. The fall in market price is the result of the market behavior of businessmen who are suddenly confronted with an increase in costs.

The argument of this paper is an extension and elaboration of that of the *Treatise*. Perhaps confusion over the relationship between the rate of investment and the rate of interest would not have developed had economists devoted more attention to the *Treatise*.

VIII. Income and investment

My approach to the theory of investment leads to a simple and direct inclusion of the level of national income as an independent variable in the social investment function. To any level of national income there corresponds a

[23]*Ibid.*, p. 205.

more-or-less unique pattern of sales expectations on the part of business-men; the imprecision of this statement results from the realization that more than one distribution of the pattern of over-all demand is probably consistent with any given level of national income — the importance of this reservation can only be determined empirically. In any event the level of sales expecta-tions should be expected to vary directly with the level of national income. For a given level of national income and a given interest rate there exists a particular demand curve for capital goods of any particular type. Given the existing stock of a type of capital good, an equilibrium market price is thus determined. Given the cost schedules of producers of the capital good, a unique rate of output is established for which the marginal supply price is equal to the market price. The rate of output of new capital, determined by similar factors in each market, is what is meant by the rate of gross invest-ment in constant dollars. To the extent that the vertical intercept of each stock demand curve is a function of the level of sales expectations, given the rate of interest, it is also a function of the level of income.

Given the stock of any particular type of capital good and the durability of that good, there exists a rate of output that would keep the stock un-changed, period after period. That is, there exists a rate of production that is equal to the rate of capital consumption. Given the cost schedules of the capital-good producers, there exists a particular market price that would induce that rate of output consistent with an unchanging capital stock. If the market price is higher than that which generates a rate of output equal to capital consumption, a portion of the annual output is net investment, and the capital stock will increase. If the market price is less than the price required for a constant stock, net investment will be negative, and the capital stock will shrink.

Whether the market price is greater than, equal to, or less than, that which induces a zero rate of net investment depends upon the vertical inter-cept of the demand curve for the capital good: that is, upon the rate of interest and the level of national income. For any given rate of interest, therefore, the existence of positive, negative, or zero net investment depends upon the level of national income. The higher the level of national income, *ceteris paribus*, the greater will be the rate of gross investment and the greater will be the rate of net investment in absolute value. Whether a given rate of gross investment is associated with positive or negative net investment depends upon the rate of capital consumption. The resulting interaction between income levels and rates of output of capital goods permits the derivation of a market-equilibrium curve relating the rate of gross invest-ment to the level of national income. More formally the conclusion is that the rate of gross investment is a function of the level of national income and the rate of interest. In terms of the stability properties of the function in a complete macro system, which have been explored by Modigliani among others, the *total* derivative of gross investment with respect to the rate of interest is negative, and the *total* derivative of gross investment with respect to income is positive.[24] All that I am adding to that discussion is the contention that there is nothing suspect about the inclusion of the level of income in the social investment function.

It may be useful to contrast this result with that reached by the use of the acceleration principle, because there are economists who contend that the level of income is not useful in explaining the rate of investment.[25] More specifically, the unlagged accelerator model tells us that the rate of *net* investment in period t is equal to the marginal capital-output ratio times the increase of income from period t-1 to period t. By implication, if income remains constant at the level realized in period t-1, the rate of net investment is zero in all subsequent periods. Thus the rate of net investment is a function of the rate of change of income with respect to time. In terms of the framework of this paper what this means is that the market price of capital goods corresponding to income in period t-1 is just sufficient to induce a rate of production equal to the rate of capital consumption; otherwise there would be positive or negative net investment even if the rate of change of income were zero. The unlagged accelerator model implies, therefore, that the rate of *replacement* investment is a function of the *level* of income, or that the rate of *gross* investment is a function of the level of national income when the rate of change of income is zero. With respect to its conclusions as to the rate of net investment, there are two fundamental defects in the unlagged accelerator model.

First, given the stock of capital the price of capital goods is jointly determined by the level of income and the rate of interest. If the unchanging level of income is sufficiently high for positive net saving to take place, downward pressure on the rate of interest will tend to raise the demand for capital goods, their market prices, and hence their rates of output. With some rigidity of factor prices, the level of income will tend to fall, tending to reduce the demand for capital goods. Thus two opposing forces tend to alter the rate of net investment away from the zero rate predicted by the model.

Second, if the market price of capital goods associated with a constant income level is higher than the long-run marginal cost of the same rate of output of capital goods, capacity expansion will ensue in the capital-goods sector. Not only does this mean a positive rate of net investment associated with a given level of income, but the enlargement of capital-goods capacity will mean that a higher rate of output of capital goods will be associated with each market price. The opposite will be true, given sufficient time for adjustment, for a market price below long-run industry marginal cost. Thus the

[24]F. Modigliani, "Liquidity-Preference and the Theory of Interest and Money" as reprinted in L. W. Mints and F. A. Lutz (eds.), *Readings in Monetary Theory* (Philadelphia: Blakiston Co., 1950), pp. 206–210.

[25]Cf. Daniel Hamberg, *Economic Growth and Instability* (New York: Norton, 1956), Appendix to chap. 8.

unlagged accelerator model presupposes that the market price of capital goods associated with a constant income level is equal to long-run marginal cost in the capital-goods industry for a rate of output equal to the rate of capital consumption.

In the lagged accelerator model the rate of net investment is a function of capital-stock deficiencies or backlogs that are the result of prior increases in the level of the national income.[26] In the model outlined in this paper the state of excess capital demand is a function of the rate of interest and the difference between the current level of income and that level for which the current capital stock would be optimal. In neither model is the rate of current net investment equal to the total of capital-stock deficiencies, because common to both models is a time lag between the recognition of stock deficiencies and their elimination by investment. The principal difference between the two models, apart from their different treatment of the rate of interest, is the explanation of the time lags. In the lagged accelerator model the delays are those of the capital users. Some time is required for businessmen to assure themselves that an observed increase in sales is permanent rather than ephemeral, there may have been a prior fall in demand so that the investment response to an increase in sales may be postponed or damped by the existence in excess capacity, there may be lags in arranging for financing, and some firms that lack access to money markets may have to accumulate internal savings before executing investment decisions.[27] Other delays in making and implementing the investment decision may occur, but these models implicitly identify changes in the demand for capital goods with the rate of net investment. This is a characteristic common to both the lagged and the unlagged versions of the acceleration principle.

Because of this implicit identification of changes in the amount of capital demanded with the rate of net investment, the acceleration principle in either version is not a theory of investment at all, but simply a theory of the demand for additions to the capital stock. Without explicit considerations of the supply of capital goods the acceleration principle is no more a theory of investment, than is the marginal productivity principle a theory of wages and employment. As Haavelmo has argued, the acceleration principle needs some hypothesis concerning the adjustment of supply to changes in demand, in order to explain variations in the rate of output of capital goods.[28]

The model employed in this paper seeks to do this by employing a different type of time lag. In this model the uncertainty, illiquidity, and internal-delay factors affect the response of the capital-goods demand curve

[26]Robert Eisner, "A Distributed Lag Investment Function," *Econometrica*, [XXVIII] Jan. 1960, pp. 1–29.

[27]On the reasons for these lags see *ibid.*, p. 2, and J. S. Duesenberry, *Business Cycles and Economic Growth* (New York: McGraw-Hill Book Co., 1958), chap. 5.

[28]Haavelmo, *op. cit.*, p. 8.

to changes in income and the rate of interest. There is no attempt to deny that these may be important. But for any state of demand for capital goods there is an intervening variable between demand and the rate of investment: namely, conditions of capital-goods supply. Any increase in the amount of capital goods demanded that results from a rise in income or a fall in the rate of interest will be partly damped by a rise in capital-goods prices. In addition the investment response to a rise in capital-goods prices will be governed by the state of capacity utilization in the capital-goods sector of the economy. Thus there is no simple identification, in this model, between the amount of excess demand at prices prevailing prior to some exogenous change, and the response of the rate of investment. In contrast to the lagged accelerator model, this model suggests that the investment response, that is, the change in the rate of output of capital goods, to a change in capital-goods demand would vary inversely with the level of activity over the course of the business cycle. The principal justification for regarding the level of income as more significant than its rate of change as a determinant of the rate of gross investment, is that the level of sales expectations is more likely to be associated with the former than the latter.

IX. Conclusion

The conclusion of this paper is somewhat at variance with the traditional view of the determinants of the rate of investment. I find no inconsistency between the view that there is no demand-for-investment function at the micro level and the view that the rate of aggregative investment is a function of the rate of interest and the level of national income. The theory of the firm, in its traditional comparative-statics form, yields only a capital-stock demand function and not a rate-of-investment demand function, because the firm's demand is for the services of capital goods, which services are proportional to a stock and not to the time rate of change of that stock. That is, the traditional theory of the firm permits the determination only of the optimum size of the capital stock and not of the optimum rate of adjustment of that stock to a change in the external environment of the firm.

The flow problem of investment theory, that is, the discovery of the determinants of the observed positive rate of capital accumulation, can be attacked at three levels, microdynamic, macrodynamic, and macrostatic. Concerning the first we have nothing to contribute beyond the statement that what must be determined are the factors responsible for the speed of adjustment of the firm's capital stock in response to disequilibrating changes in the firm's external environment. This is a problem in dynamics par excellence and is excluded by definition from comparative statics. The fact that the investment flow problem at the micro level can only be approached by dynamic considerations does not mean, however, that the macroeconomic investment flow problem will not yield to analysis of the comparative-statics type. In this respect my conclusions differ from those of traditional discussions.

I find that a sufficient condition for the existence of a market-equilibrium relationship between the aggregative rate of investment and the rate of interest (and the level of national income) is a capacity and cost constraint on the rate of output of capital goods. This constraint prevents the simultaneous adjustment of each firm's capital stock to a new optimum level following a disturbance, and permits us to demonstrate that the aggregative rate of gross investment is uniquely related to the rate of interest and the level of national income. While I would grant that a departure from a long-run stationary equilibrium would have to be explained in terms of changes in the rate of interest and level of national income I question the usefulness of the stationary state as a beginning or terminal point of macroeconomic theory.

DALE W. JORGENSON **11**

The theory of investment behavior

1. Introduction

Business investment behavior is one of the areas of modern economic research that is being studied most intensively; empirical studies are accumulating rapidly,[1] and at the same time important developments in the eco-

Reprinted from Robert Ferber (ed.), *Determinants of Investment Behavior* (New York: National Bureau of Economic Research, 1967), pp. 129–155, by permission of the publisher and author. [Footnotes expanded — *Eds.*]

[1] A very detailed review of the literature through 1960 has been provided by R. Eisner and R. Strotz, "The Determinants of Business Investment," in D. B. Suits, *et al.*, *Impacts of Monetary Policy* (Englewood Cliffs, [N.J.: Prentice-Hall,] 1963), pp. 60–338. A more concise review of developments through 1962 has been presented by E. Kuh, "Theory and Institutions in the Study of Investment Behavior," *American Economic Review*, [LIII] May 1963, pp. 260–268. Empirical studies published since 1962 include: S. Almon, "The Distributed Lag between Capital Appropriations and Expenditures," *Econometrica*, [XXXIII] Jan. 1965, 178–196; W. H. L. Anderson, *Corporate Finance and Fixed Investment*, (Boston: [Harvard Business School,] 1964); A. Bourneuf, "Investment, Excess Capacity, and Growth," *American Economic Review*, [LIV] Sept. 1964, pp. 607–625; R. Eisner, "Investment: Fact and Fancy," *American Economic Review*, [LIII] May 1963, pp. 237–246; Eisner, "Capital Expenditures, Profits, and the Acceleration Principle," *Models of Income Determination*, Studies in Income and Wealth 28, Princeton University Press for National Bureau of Economic Research, 1964, pp. 137–176; Eisner, "Realization of Investment Anticipations," in J. S. Duesenberry, E. Kuh, G. Fromm, and L. R. Klein, eds., *The Brookings Quarterly Econometric Model of the United States* (Chicago: [Rand McNally,] 1965); E. Greenberg, "A Stock-Adjustment Investment Model," *Econometrica*, [XXXII] July 1964, pp. 339–357; B. Hickman, *Investment Demand and U.S. Economic Growth* (Washington: [The Brookings Institution] 1965); D. W. Jorgenson, "Capital Theory and Investment Behavior," *American Economic Review*, [LIII] May 1963, pp. 247–259; Jorgenson, "Anticipations and Investment Behavior," in *Brookings Quarterly Econometric Model;* E. Kuh, *Capital Stock Growth: A Micro-Econometric Approach*, (Amsterdam: [North Holland Publ. Co.,] 1963); J. R. Meyer and R. R. Glauber, *Investment Decisions, Economic Forecasting and Public Policy* (Boston: [Harvard Business School,] 1964); G. J. Stigler, *Capital and Rates of Return in Manufacturing Industries*, Princeton for NBER, 1963.

nomic theory of investment behavior are taking place.[2] As yet, there is very little common ground between the empirical and theoretical approaches to this subject. From a certain point of view this is a desirable state of affairs.[3] Econometric studies of investment behavior date back no more than thirty years.[4] Only recently have data on investment expenditures suitable for analysis by econometric methods become available. If empirical studies are forced prematurely into a theoretical straitjacket, attention may be diverted from historical and institutional considerations that are essential to a complete understanding of investment behavior. On the other hand, if theoretical work is made to conform to "realistic" assumptions at too early a stage in the development of empirical work, the door may be closed to theoretical innovations that could lead to improvements in empirical work at a later stage.

While there is some surface plausibility in the view that empirical and theoretical research are best carried out in isolation from each other, this view is seriously incomplete. Econometric work is always based on highly simplified models. The number of possible explanations of investment behavior, which is limited only by the imagination of the investigator, is so large that, in any empirical investigation, all but a very few must be ruled out in advance. Insofar as the necessary simplifications restrict the possible explanations of investment behavior, these simplifications constitute, at least implicitly, a theory of investment behavior. Such theories can be compared with each other most expeditiously by reducing each to its basic underlying assumptions, after which empirical tests to discriminate among alternative theories can be designed. Far from forcing empirical studies into a theoretical straitjacket, judicious use of a theoretical framework is essential to the proper direction of empirical work.

---

[2]See, for example, the following papers: K. J. Arrow, "Optimal Capital Policy, The Cost of Capital, and Myopic Decision Rules," *Annals of the Institute of Statistical Mathematics*, 1964, pp. 21–30; "Optimal Capital Adjustment," in K. J. Arrow, S. Karlin, and H. Scarf, eds., *Studies in Applied Probability and Management Science*, (Stanford, [Calif.: Stanford University Press,] 1962); K. J. Arrow, M. Beckmann, and S. Karlin, "Optimal Expansion of the Capacity of the Firm," in K. J. Arrow, S. Karlin, and H. Scarf, eds., *Studies in the Mathematical Theory of Inventory and Production*, (Stanford, [Calif.: Stanford University Press,] 1958); A. S. Manne, "Capacity Expansion and Probabilistic Growth," *Econometrica*, [XXIX] Oct. 1961, pp. 632–649; E. Zabel, "Efficient Accumulation of Capital for the Firm," *Econometrica*, [XXXI] Jan.-April 1963, pp. 131–150; and the following books: T. Haavelmo, *A Study in the Theory of Investment*, (Chicago: [University of Chicago Press,] 1960); F. A. Lutz and D. G. Hague, eds., *The Theory of Capital*, (London: [Macmillan & Co.,] 1961); P. B. D. Massé, *Optimal Investment Decisions*, (Englewood Cliffs, [N.J.: Prentice-Hall,] 1962); V. L. Smith, *Investment and Production*, Cambridge, [Mass.: Harvard University Press,] 1961; B. Thalberg, "A Keynesian Model Extended by Explicit Demand and Supply Functions for Investment Goods," *Stockholm Economic Studies*, Pamphlet Series, No. 3, 1964.

[3]This point of view has been put forward by K. Borch, "Discussion," *American Economic Review*, [LIII] May 1963, pp. 272–274.

[4]J. Tinbergen, *Statistical Testing of Business Cycle Theories*, Part I, "A Method and its Application to Investment Activity," Geneva, 1939.

The view that theoretical and empirical research should be carried out in isolation is incomplete in a second respect. The use of economic theory as a source of possible explanations for investment behavior frees econometric work from reliance on empirical generalizations that have not been subjected to rigorous econometric tests. There is a very real danger that econometric models of investment behavior may be made to conform prematurely to assumptions that are "realistic" by the standards of empirical work not based on econometric methods. Just as premature reliance on "realistic" assumptions may be stultifying to the development of economic theory, so reliance on historical and institutional generalizations may restrict the development of econometric models unduly. The paramount test for "realism" of an econometric model is its performance in econometric work. If a model does not perform satisfactorily by the standards of econometrics, it must be rejected, however closely it parallels historical and institutional accounts of the same economic behavior.

The point of departure for this paper is that progress in the study of investment behavior can best be made by comparing econometric models of such behavior within a theoretical framework. Ideally, each model should be derived from a common set of assumptions about the objectives of the business firm. Differences among alternative models should be accounted for by alternative assumptions about the behavior of business firms in pursuing these objectives. It will undoubtedly be surprising to some that a theoretical framework is implicit in the econometric models of investment behavior currently under study. The objective of this paper is to make this framework explicit in order to provide a basis to evaluate evidence on the determinants of investment behavior. This objective can only be attained by a thoroughgoing reconstruction of the theory of investment. Once the theory of investment is placed in a proper setting, the arguments advanced for pessimism about combining theoretical and empirical work largely evaporate.

In providing a framework for the theory of investment behavior, the first problem is to choose an appropriate basis for the theory. Two alternative possibilities may be suggested. First, the theory of investment could be based on the neoclassical theory of optimal capital accumulation. There are three basic objections to this possibility, the first of which is that a substantial body of noneconometric work on the motivation of business firms, mainly surveys of businessmen, suggests that "marginalist" considerations are largely irrelevant to the making of business decisions. This evidence has been subjected to careful scrutiny by White,[5] who concludes that the data accumulated by the surveys are so defective, even by the standards of noneconometric empirical work, that no reliance can be placed on conclusions based on them. A second objection is that previous attempts to base the

[5] W. H. White, "Interest Inelasticity of Investment Demand," *American Economic Review*, [XLVI] Sept. 1956, pp. 565–587.

study of investment on neoclassical economic theory have been unsuccessful,[6] but this argument will not withstand critical scrutiny. First, none of the tests of the neoclassical theory reported in the early literature was based on a fully rigorous statement of the theory. Secondly, the assumptions made about the lag between changes in the demand for capital services and actual investment expenditures were highly restrictive. Frequently, the lag was assumed to be concentrated at a particular point or to be distributed over time in a very simple manner. Tests of the neoclassical theory were carried out prior to the important contribution of Koyck to the analysis of distributed lags and investment behavior.[7] Despite these deficiencies, the pioneering tests of the neoclassical theory reported by Tinbergen reveal substantial effects for the price of investment goods, the change in this price, and the rate of interest.[8] Similarly, tests reported by Roos reveal substantial effects for the price of investment goods and rate of interest.[9] Klein's studies of investment in the railroad and electric power industries reveal substantial effects for the rate of interest.[10]

A third and more fundamental objection has recently been restated by Haavelmo, who argues that a demand schedule for investment goods cannot be derived from neoclassical theory:[11]

What we should reject is the naive reasoning that there is a demand schedule for investment which could be derived from a classical scheme of producers' behavior in maximizing profit. The demand for investment cannot simply be derived from the demand for capital. Demand for a finite addition to the stock of capital can lead to any rate of investment, from almost zero to infinity, depending on the additional hypothesis we introduce regarding the speed of reaction of capital-users. I think that the sooner this naive, and unfounded, theory of the demand-for-investment schedule is abandoned, the sooner we shall have a chance of making some real progress in constructing more powerful theories to deal with the capricious short-run variations in the rate of private investment.

We will show that it is possible to derive a demand function for investment goods based on purely neoclassical considerations. While it is true that the conventional derivation of such a demand schedule, as in Keynes' construction of the marginal efficiency of investment schedule,[12] must be dismissed

[6]J. Meyer and E. Kuh, *The Investment Decision*, (Cambridge, Mass.: [Harvard University Press, 1957,]) pp. 7–14.

[7]L. M. Koyck, *Distributed Lags and Investment Analysis* (Amsterdam, 1954).

[8]Tinbergen, *Statistical Testing, op. cit.*, see also the discussion of Tinbergen's results by T. Haavelmo, "The Effect of the Rate of Interest on Investment: A Note," *Review of Economic Statistics*, [XXIII] Feb. 1941, pp. 49–52.

[9]C. F. Roos and V. S. Von Szeliski, "The Demand for Durable Goods," *Econometrica*, [XI] April 1943, pp. 97–122; Roos, "The Demand for Investment Goods," *American Economic Review*, [XXXVIII] May 1948, pp. 311–320; Roos, "Survey of Economic Forecasting Techniques," *Econometrica*, [XXIII] Oct. 1955, pp. 363–395.

[10]L. R. Klein, "Studies in Investment Behavior," in *Conference on Business Cycles* (New York: National Bureau of Economic Research, 1951).

[11]Haavelmo, *Theory of Investment, op. cit.*, p. 216.

[12]J. M. Keynes, *The General Theory of Employment, Interest and Money*, (New York: [Harcourt, Brace & Co.,] 1936), esp. Chapter 11, pp. 135–146.

as naive, there is a sense in which the demand for investment goods can be taken to depend on the cost of capital; such a theory of investment behavior can be derived from the neoclassical theory of optimal capital accumulation.

A second possible basis for the theory of investment is the assumption that business firms maximize utility defined more broadly than in the characterization of objectives of the firm in the neoclassical theory of optimal capital accumulation. This basis has been suggested by Meyer and Kuh:[13]

Partial recognition of institutional changes has led in recent years to shift the theory of the firm, and consequently of plant and equipment investment, from a profit maximization orientation to that of utility maximization. Primarily, this move represents a growing belief that profit maximization is too narrow to encompass the full scope of modern entrepreneurial motives, particularly once the previously assumed objective conditions are released from *ceteris paribus*, and the theory seeks to explain a much wider range of behavioral responses.

This position has recently been supported with much force by Simon: ". . . I should like to emphasize strongly that neither the classical theory of the firm nor any of the amendments to it or substitutes for it that have been proposed have had any substantial amount of empirical testing. If the classical theory appeals to us, it must be largely because it has a certain face validity . . . rather than because profit maximizing behavior has been observed."[14]

In putting forward this view, Simon ignores the entire econometric literature on cost and production functions, all of which is based on the neoclassical theory of the firm. A recent survey of this literature by Walters[15] enumerates 345 references, almost all presenting results of econometric tests of the neoclassical theory of the firm which are overwhelmingly favorable to the theory. The evidence is largely so favorable that current empirical research emphasizes such technical questions as the appropriate form for the production function and the appropriate statistical specification for econometric models of production based on this theory. We conclude that Simon's statement that the alternatives to the neoclassical theory of the firm have had no substantial amount of empirical testing is correct. However, his characterization of the empirical evidence on the neoclassical theory is completely erroneous.

One possible reaction to a proper assessment of the support for the neoclassical theory of the firm from econometric studies of cost and production functions is to reject out of hand studies of investment behavior not based explicitly on the neoclassical theory, such as the study of Meyer and Kuh. In fact, the theoretical basis for the econometric model of investment behavior proposed by Meyer and Kuh is consistent with the neo-

---

[13]Meyer and Kuh, *Investment Decision, op. cit.*, p. 9.

[14]H. A. Simon, "New Developments in the Theory of the Firm," *American Economic Review*, [LII] May 1962, p. 8.

[15]A. A. Walters, "Production and Cost Functions: An Econometric Survey," *Econometrica*, [XXXI] April 1963, pp. 1–66.

classical theory of optimal capital accumulation. Their appeal to a less narrow view of entrepreneurial objectives is not essential to the interpretation of the empirical results they present. We conclude that the objections to the neoclassical theory of the firm as a basis for the theory of investment behavior are ill-founded. Furthermore, the appeal to a broader view of entrepreneurial objectives than that which underlies this theory is not required by evidence either from econometric studies of cost and production functions or from studies of investment behavior. The neoclassical theory of optimal accumulation of capital is a far more powerful theory than the "broader view" suggested by Simon and others in the sense that a much narrower range of conceivable behavior is consistent with it than with the amorphous utility-maximizing theory. Accordingly, we will employ a theoretical framework based on the neoclassical theory of the firm for constructing a theory of investment behavior.

The objective of explaining investment behavior on the basis of the neoclassical theory of the firm cannot be described as novel. This objective is clearly in evidence in Tinbergen's pioneering monograph, *Statistical Testing of Business Cycle Theories*. Subsequently, a similar objective was adopted by Roos and by Klein.[16] In these early studies of investment behavior, the neoclassical theory was employed to provide a list of possible explanatory variables for investment expenditures. The rate of interest, the level of stock prices, the price of investment goods, and changes in the price of investment goods were used along with other variables such as profits, output, and changes in output. Little attention was paid to the manner in which the rate of interest and the price of investment goods enter the demand for capital services or the demand for investment goods. Both variables enter only through the *user cost* of capital services.[17] There is no effect of the price of investment goods except in combination with the rate of interest and vice versa. We conclude that, although the objective of explaining investment behavior on the basis of the neoclassical theory of the firm is not new, this objective remains to be fully realized.

2. The neoclassical framework

In formulating a theory of investment behavior based on the neoclassical theory of optimal capital accumulation, a great number of alternative versions of the theory could be considered. Reduced to its barest essentials,

[16]See footnotes 9 and 10. See also L. R. Klein, *The Keynesian Revolution*, (New York: [The Macmillan Co.,] 1947), esp. pp. 62–68, pp. 196–199; Klein, "Notes on the Theory of Investment," *Kyklos*, II, Fasc. 2, (1948), 97–117; Klein, *Economic Fluctuations in the United States, 1921–1941*, (New York: [John Wiley & Sons, Inc.,] 1950), esp. pp. 14–40.

[17]A complete discussion of the concept of user cost has been given by W. A. Lewis, "Depreciation and Obsolescence as Factors in Costing," in J. L. Meij, ed., *Depreciation and Replacement Policy*, Amsterdam, 1961, pp. 15–45. See also Keynes, *General Theory, op. cit.*, pp. 66–73; A. P. Lerner, "User Cost and Prime User Cost," *American Economic Review*, [XXXIII] March 1943, pp. 131–132; F. A. Lutz and V. Lutz, *The Theory of Investment of the Firm*, (Princeton: [Princeton University Press,] 1951); A. D. Scott, "Notes on User Cost," *Economic Journal*, [LXIII] June 1953, pp. 364–384.

the theory requires only that capital accumulation be based on the objective of maximizing the utility of a stream of consumption. This basic assumption may be combined with any number of technological possibilities for production and economic possibilities for transformation of the results of production into a stream of consumption. In selecting among alternative formulations, a subsidiary objective must be borne in mind. The resulting theory of capital accumulation must include the principal econometric models of investment behavior as specializations, but the theory need not encompass possibilities for the explanation of investment behavior not employed in econometric work.

The essentials of a theory of optimal capital accumulation that meets this basic objective are the following: The firm maximizes the utility of a consumption stream subject to a production function relating the flow of output to flows of labor and capital services. The firm supplies capital services to itself through the acquisition of investment goods; the rate of change in the flow of capital services is proportional to the rate of acquisition of investment goods less the rate of replacement of previously acquired investment goods. The results of the productive process are transformed into a stream of consumption under a fixed set of prices for output, labor services, investment goods, and consumption goods. These prices may be considered as current or "spot" prices together with forward prices for each commodity or, alternatively, as current and future prices together with a normalization factor, which may be identified with current and future values of the rate of time discount or interest rate. Both current and forward prices are taken as fixed by the firm. Alternatively, current and future prices together with current and future values of the rate of interest are taken as fixed. Under these conditions, the problem of maximizing utility may be solved in two stages. First, a production plan may be chosen so as to maximize the present value of the productive enterprise. Secondly, consumption is allocated over time so as to maximize utility subject to the present value of the firm. In view of our concern with the theory of business investment behavior, we will consider only the first of these problems. It should be noted that, under the assumption of fixed prices, the choice of a production plan is independent of the subsequent allocation of consumption over time. Two firms with different preferences among alternative consumption streams will choose the same plan for production.

This version of the neoclassical theory of the firm is not the only one available in the literature on capital theory. From a certain point of view, the objective of maximizing the present value of the firm is only one among many possible objectives for the firm. In a recent survey paper on the theory of capital, Lutz remarks that "It is one of the surprising things about capital theory that no agreement seems to have been reached as to what the entrepreneur should maximize."[18] Alternative criteria discussed in the literature

[18]F. A. Lutz, "The Essentials of Capital Theory," in Lutz and Hague, *Theory of Capital*, *op. cit.*, p. 6.

include maximization of the average internal rate of return, maximization of the rate of return on capital owned by the firm, investment in any project with an internal rate of return greater than the ruling market rate of interest, and so on. None of these criteria can be derived from maximization of the utility of a stream of consumption under the conditions we have outlined. Maximization of the present value of the firm is the only criterion consistent with utility maximization. This approach to the theory of optimal capital accumulation was originated by Fisher and has recently been revived and extended by Bailey and by Hirshleifer.[19] The essential justification for this approach is summarized by Hirshleifer, as follows:

Since Fisher, economists working in the theory of investment decision have tended to adopt a mechanical approach — some plumping for the use of this formula, some for that. From a Fisherian point of view, we can see that none of the formulas so far propounded is universally valid. Furthermore, even where the present-value rule, for example, is correct, few realize that its validity is conditional upon making certain associated financing decisions as the Fisherian analysis demonstrates. In short, the Fisherian approach permits us to define the range of applicability and the short-comings of all the proposed formulas — thus standing over against them as the general theoretical solution to the problem of investment decision under conditions of certainty.[20]

A second controversial aspect of the version of the neoclassical theory outlined above is the assumption that the set of technological possibilities confronted by the firm can be described by a production function, where the flow of output is a function of flows of labor and capital services and the flow of capital services is proportional to the stock of capital goods obtained by summing the stream of past net investments.[21] The concept of capital service is not essential to the neoclassical theory. A production function relating output at each point of time to inputs of labor and capital services at that point of time may be replaced by a production function relating output at every point of time to inputs of investment goods at every point of time; this description of the set of production possibilities is employed by Fisher; moreover, it may be characterized abstractly so that even the

[19]I. Fisher, *The Theory of Interest* (New York: [The Macmillan Co.,] 1930). M. J. Bailey, "Formal Criteria for Investment Decisions," *Journal of Political Economy*, [LXVII] Oct. 1959, pp. 476–488. J. Hirshleifer, "On the Theory of the Optimal Investment Decision," in E. Solomon, ed., *The Management of Corporate Capital* (Glencoe, [Ill.: Free Press,] 1959), pp. 205–228.

[20]*Ibid.*, p. 228.

[21]For a discussion of this assumption and some of its implications, see J. Robinson, "The Production Function and the Theory of Capital," *Review of Economic Studies*, [XXI] No. 54, (1953–54), 81–106; R. M. Solow, "The Production Function and the Theory of Capital," *Review of Economic Studies*, [XXIII] No. 61 (1955–56), 101–108; J. Robinson, "Reply," *Review of Economic Studies*, [XXIII], No. 62, (1955–56), 247; J. Robinson, "Some Problems of Definition and Measurement of Capital," *Oxford Economic Papers*, [XI] June 1959, pp. 157–166; K. J. Arrow *et al.*, "Symposium on Production Functions and Economic Growth," *Review of Economic Studies*, [XXIX] June 1962.

notion of a production function may be dispensed with, as is done by Malinvaud.[22] The description of the set of technological possibilities by means of a production function as presented by Fisher is a specialization of the description given by Malinvaud. The further assumption that the relationship between inputs of investment goods and levels of output may be reduced to a relationship between output at each point of time and a corresponding flow of capital services involves a specialization of the description of technological possibilities given by Fisher.

In the neoclassical literature, two basic models of the relationship between flows of investment goods and flows of capital services have been discussed, namely, a model of inventories and a model of durable goods. At the level of abstraction of Fisher's description of the set of production possibilities, no distinction between inventories and durable goods is required. For both inventories and durable goods, the acquisition of a stock of productive goods may be represented as an input to the productive process at the time of acquisition. For inventories, the individual items "used up" at different points of time may be represented as the output of a subprocess representing the holding of stocks; these outputs may be inputs into other subprocesses. For durable goods, the outputs of the corresponding stock-holding process are the services of the goods rather than the individual items of the stock; the services of the durable goods may be inputs into other parts of the productive process.

The basis for the distinction between inventories and durable goods lies in the relationship among the initial input and the various outputs from the stockholding process. For inventories, the outputs provided by the stockholding process are customarily treated as perfect substitutes. For each item held in stock, the ultimate consumption of that item can occur at one and only one point in time. By contrast, the outputs provided by durable goods are treated as if they were perfectly complementary. The output of the service of a durable good at any point of time is assumed to bear a fixed relation to the output of the same service at any other point of time. The assumptions that outputs provided by a given input of investment goods are perfectly complementary or perfectly substitutable are highly restrictive. Nevertheless, the simplification of the neoclassical theory for these limiting cases and the practical importance of these cases are very great. A far more substantial proportion of the literature on capital theory is devoted to these two limiting cases than to the theory of production at the level of abstraction of the descriptions of technology given by Fisher or by Malinvaud. In the following we assume that the conventional neoclassical description of a durable good is appropriate for each investment good considered.

A second assumption required for a relationship between output at each point of time and the corresponding flow of capital services is that the services of investment goods acquired at different points of time are perfect substitutes in production. Accordingly, the flow of capital services from each investment good is proportional to the stock of capital that may be obtained by simply adding together all past acquisitions less replacements. This assumption is highly restrictive; the assumption can be justified primarily by the resulting simplification of the neoclassical theory. We discuss only a single investment good. Under the assumptions outlined above, there is only a single capital service. This simplification is also completely inessential to neoclassical theory.

Finally, we assume that the flow of replacement generated by a given flow of investment goods is distributed over time in accord with an exponential distribution. This assumption implies that the flow of replacement investment at any point of time is proportional to the accumulated stock of investment goods. Again, this assumption is only one among many possibilities. Alternative assumptions employed in practice include the following: First, replacement is equal to investment goods acquired at some earlier point in time; second, replacement is equal to a weighted average of past investment flows, with weights derived from studies of the "survival curves" of individual pieces of equipment.[23] For empirical work the exponential distribution of replacements is of special interest. While empirical studies of "survival curves" for individual pieces of equipment reveal a wide variety of possible distributions, there is a deeper justification for use of the exponential distribution. This justification arises from a fundamental result of renewal theory, namely, that replacement approaches an amount proportional to the accumulated stock of capital whatever the distribution of replacements for an individual piece of equipment, provided that the size of the capital stock is constant or that the stock is growing at a constant rate (in the probabilistic sense).[24] This asymptotic result may be used as the basis for an approximation to the distribution of replacements; for any investment good, the stream of replacements eventually approaches a stream that would be generated by an exponential distribution of replacements. Accordingly, the exponential distribution may be used as an approximation to the distribution of replacements for the purpose of estimating the stream of replacements. A simple indirect test of the validity of this approximation has been carried out by Meyer and Kuh.[25] For any distribution of replacements except the exponential distribution, one would expect to observe an "echo effect" or bunching of replacements at lags corresponding to points of relatively

---

[23]A summary of research on the lifetimes of capital equipment as given by A. Marston, R. Winfrey, and J. C. Hempstead, *Engineering Evaluation and Depreciation* (2nd ed., New York: [McGraw-Hill,] 1953).

[24]For a statement of the basic theorem, see E. Parzen, *Stochastic Processes* (San Francisco: [Holden Day,] 1962), pp. 180–181.

[25]Meyer and Kuh, *Investment Decision, op. cit.*, pp. 91–94.

high density in the conditional distributions of replacements for individual types of equipment. Meyer and Kuh report no evidence for such an effect.

To summarize, we consider a version of the neoclassical theory in which the objective of the firm is maximization of its present value. This may be derived from the objective of maximizing the utility of a consumption stream subject to a fixed set of production possibilities and to fixed current and future prices and interest rates. Since the choice of a production plan is entirely independent of the corresponding choice of a consumption stream, two individuals with different preferences among consumption streams will choose the same production plan. Secondly, we consider a description of technological possibilities in which output at each point of time depends on the flow of labor and capital services at that point of time, the flow of capital services is proportional to the stock of capital goods, and replacements are also proportional to the stock of capital goods. This description of technology is a specialization of the descriptions given by Malinvaud and by Fisher. The essential justification for this specialization is that the resulting theory of optimal capital accumulation is sufficiently broad to include the principal econometric models of investment behavior as special cases.

3. Optimal capital accumulation

To develop the theory of investment behavior in more detail, we must first define the present value of the firm. For simplicity, we limit the analysis to a production process with a single output, a single variable input, and a single capital input. Where Q, L, and I represent levels of output, variable input, and investment in durable goods and p, w, and q represent the corresponding prices, the flow of net receipts at time t, say $R(t)$, is given by:

$$R(t) = p(t)Q(t) - w(t)L(t) - q(t)I(t). \tag{1}$$

Present value is defined as the integral of discounted net receipts; where $r(s)$ is the rate of time discount at time s, net worth (W) is given by the expression:

$$W = \int_0^\infty e^{-\int_0^t r(s)\,ds} R(t)\,dt. \tag{2}$$

For purposes of the following discussion, we may assume that the time rate of discount is a constant without loss of generality. Accordingly, the present value of the firm may be represented in the simpler form:

$$W = \int_0^\infty e^{-rt} R(t)\,dt.$$

Present value is maximized subject to two constraints. First, the rate of change of the flow of capital services is proportional to the flow of net investment. The constant of proportionality may be interpreted as the time rate of utilization of capital stock, that is, the number of units of capital service per unit of capital stock. We will assume that capital stock is fully utilized so that this constant may be taken to be unity. Net investment is equal to total investment less replacement; where replacement is proportional to capital stock, this constraint takes the form:

$$\dot{K}(t) = I(t) - \delta K(t) \tag{3}$$

where $\dot{K}(t)$ is the time rate of change of the flow of capital services at time t. This constraint holds at each point of time so that $\dot{K}$, K, and I are functions of time; to simplify notation, we will use K in place of $K(t)$, I in place of $I(t)$, and so on. Secondly, levels of output and levels of labor and capital services are constrained by a production function:

$$F(Q, L, K) = 0. \tag{4}$$

We assume that the production function is twice differentiable with positive marginal rates of substitution between inputs and positive marginal productivities of both inputs. Furthermore, we assume that the production function is strictly convex.

To maximize present value (2) subject to the constraints (3) and (4), we consider the Lagrangian expression:

$$\mathcal{L} = \int_0^\infty [e^{-rt}R(t) + \lambda_0(t)F(Q, L, K) + \lambda_1(t)(\dot{K} - I + \delta K)]\, dt, \tag{5}$$

$$= \int_0^\infty f(t)\, dt,$$

where

$$f(t) = e^{-rt}R(t) + \lambda_0(t)F(Q, L, K) + \lambda_1(t)(\dot{K} - I + \delta K).$$

The Euler necessary conditions for a maximum of present value subject to the constraints (3) and (4) are:

$$\frac{\partial f}{\partial Q} = e^{-rt}p + \lambda_0(t)\frac{\partial F}{\partial Q} = 0, \tag{6}$$

$$\frac{\partial f}{\partial L} = -e^{-rt}w + \lambda_0(t)\frac{\partial F}{\partial L} = 0,$$

$$\frac{\partial f}{\partial I} = -e^{-rt}q - \lambda_1(t) = 0,$$

$$\frac{\partial f}{\partial K} - \frac{d}{dt}\frac{\partial f}{\partial \dot{K}} = \lambda_0(t)\frac{\partial F}{\partial K} + \delta\lambda_1(t) - \frac{d}{dt}\lambda_1(t) = 0,$$

and also:

$$\frac{\partial f}{\partial \lambda_0} = F(Q, L, K) = 0,\tag{7}$$

$$\frac{\partial f}{\partial \lambda_1} = \dot{K} - I + \delta K = 0.$$

Combining the necessary conditions for labor and output, we obtain the marginal productivity condition for labor services:

$$\frac{\partial Q}{\partial L} = \frac{w}{p}.\tag{8}$$

Of course, output, labor, wages, and prices are all functions of time. The difference between this marginal productivity condition and the corresponding condition of the "static" theory of the firm is that condition (8) holds at every point of time over the indefinite future whereas the marginal productivity condition of the "static" theory of the firm holds only at a single point in time. A similar marginal productivity condition for capital services may be derived. First, solving the necessary conditions (6) for $\lambda_1(t)$:

$$\lambda_1(t) = -e^{-rt}q,$$

the necessary condition for capital services may be written:

$$\lambda_0(t)\frac{\partial F}{\partial K} - \delta e^{-rt}q - re^{-rt}q + e^{-rt}\dot{q} = 0.$$

Combining this condition with the necessary condition for output, we obtain the marginal productivity condition for capital services:

$$\left(\frac{\partial Q}{\partial K}\right) = \frac{q(r + \delta) - \dot{q}}{p}\left(\frac{c}{p},\right)\tag{9}$$

where:

$$c = q(r + \delta) - \dot{q}.\tag{10}$$

Again, output, capital, prices, and the rate of time discount are functions of time so that these conditions hold at every point of time over the indefinite future.

Expression (10) defines the implicit rental value of capital services supplied by the firm to itself. This interpretation of the price $c(t)$ may be justified by considering the relationship between the price of capital goods and the price of capital services. First, the flow of capital services over an interval of length dt beginning at time t from a unit of investment goods acquired at time s is:

$$e^{-\delta(t-s)} \, dt.$$

If $c(t)$ is the price of capital services at time t, then the discounted price of capital services is $e^{-rt}c(t)$, so that the value of the stream of capital services on the interval dt is:

$$e^{-rt}c(t)e^{-\delta(t-s)} \, dt.$$

Similarly, if $q(s)$ is the price of capital goods at time s, then the discounted price of capital goods is $e^{-rs}q(s)$, so that the value of a unit of investment goods acquired at time s is:

$$e^{-rs}q(s).$$

But the value of investment goods acquired at time s is equal to the integral of the discounted value of all future capital services derived from these investment goods:

$$e^{-rs}q(s) = \int_{s}^{\infty} e^{-rt}c(t)e^{-\delta(t-s)} \, dt,$$

$$= e^{\delta s} \int_{s}^{\infty} e^{-(r+\delta)t}c(t) \, dt.$$

Solving for the price of capital goods, we obtain:

$$q(s) = e^{(r+\delta)s} \int_{s}^{\infty} e^{-(r+\delta)t}c(t) \, dt,$$

$$= \int_{s}^{\infty} e^{-(r+\delta)(t-s)}c(t) \, dt.$$

To obtain the price of capital services implicit in this expression, we differentiate with respect to time:

$$\dot{q}(s) = [r(s) + \delta]q(s) - c(s),$$

so that:

$$c = q(r + \delta) - \dot{q},$$

which is expression (10) given above for the implicit rental value of capital services.

The conditions describing the neoclassical model of optimal capital accumulation may also be derived by maximization of the integral of discounted profits, where profit at each point of time, say, $P(t)$, is given by:

$$P(t) = p(t)Q(t) - w(t)L(t) - c(t)K(t). \tag{11}$$

The integral of discounted profits, say, W^+, is given by the expression:

$$W^+ = \int_0^\infty e^{-rt}P(t)\,dt. \tag{12}$$

The side condition for investment may be disregarded, since investment does not enter into the definition of profit (11); substituting the side condition for the shadow price of capital services into the profit function, we obtain:

$$W^+ = \int_0^\infty e^{-rt}[p(t)Q(t) - w(t)L(t) - \{q(t)[r(t) + \delta] - \dot{q}(t)\}K(t)]\,dt.$$

To maximize this function subject to the production function, it suffices to maximize profit at each point of time subject to the production function. But this yields the marginal productivity conditions (8) and (9) and the production function (4) itself. Reintroducing the side conditions (3) and (10), we obtain the complete neoclassical model of optimal capital accumulation.

The integral of discounted profits is not the same as the integral defining present value of the firm. The difference between the two is given by:

$$W - W^+ = \int_0^\infty e^{-rt}[R(t) - P(t)]\,dt$$

$$= \int_0^\infty e^{-rt}[\{q(t)[r(t) + \delta] - \dot{q}(t)\}K(t) - q(t)I(t)]\,dt$$

$$= \int_0^\infty e^{-rt}[q(t)\delta K(t) + q(t)r(t)K(t) - \dot{q}(t)K(t) - q(t)\dot{K}(t)$$

$$- q(t)\delta K(t)]\,dt$$

$$= q(0)K(0),$$

which is the value of capital stock on hand at the initial point of time. The present value of the firm is the sum of the integral of discounted profits and the market value of the assets of the firm. Since the market value of the assets of the firm is fixed, maximization of the integral of discounted profits results in the same path for accumulation of capital as maximization of present value of the firm. To summarize, the neoclassical model of optimal capital accumulation may be derived by maximizing present value of the firm, by maximizing the integral of discounted profits of the firm, or simply by maximizing profit at each point of time.

In taking maximization of profit as the objective of the firm, profit is defined in a special sense, namely, net receipts on current account less the implicit rental value of capital services. This concept of profit would agree with the usual accounting definition of profit only in rather unusual circumstances, for example, where the firm actually rents all the capital services it employs. The price of capital services is then a market price and the rental value of the services is an actual outlay. Where the firm supplies capital services to itself, the implicit rental value of capital services $c(t)$ is a shadow price which may be used by the firm in the computation of an optimal path for capital accumulation. For optimal capital accumulation, the firm should charge itself a price for capital services equal to the implicit rental value and should then maximize profit at each point of time in the usual way. It is very important to note that the conditions determining the values of each of the variables to be chosen by the firm — output, labor input, and investment in capital goods — depend only on prices, the rate of interest, and the rate of change of the price of capital goods for the current period. Accordingly, in the neoclassical theory of optimal capital accumulation, the firm behaves at each point of time as in the "static" theory of the firm, provided that the price of capital services is taken to be equal to the corresponding implicit rental value. Of course, in the "static" theory the marginal productivity condition (9) holds only at a single point in time.

The complete neoclassical model of optimal capital accumulation consists of the production function (4) and the two marginal productivity conditions (8) and (9):

$$F(Q, K, L) = 0, \qquad \frac{\partial Q}{\partial L} = \frac{w}{p}, \qquad \frac{\partial Q}{\partial K} = \frac{c}{p},$$

and the two side conditions (3) and (10):

$$I = \dot{K} + \delta K,$$

$$c = q(r + \delta) - \dot{q}.$$

The production function and marginal productivity conditions hold at each point of time. The side conditions are differential equations also holding at each point of time. Combined, these conditions determine the levels of output, labor input, and capital input, together with the level of investment and the shadow price for capital services.

The interpretation of condition (3) determining the level of investment is the source of some difficulty in the literature. If the level of investment is bounded, the derivative of the level of capital services must be bounded. But this implies that the level of capital services itself must be continuous. Since we have assumed that the production function is twice differentiable, a sufficient condition for continuity of the level of capital services is continuity of the prices — w, p, c.

One interpretation of condition (3) is that the initial value of the level of capital services may be chosen arbitrarily. This interpretation has been suggested by Haavelmo and by Arrow.[26] If the initial level of capital services is derived from the production function and the marginal productivity conditions and if the initial value of capital is fixed arbitrarily, optimal capital accumulation may require an unbounded initial level of investment. In management science, this interpretation of the problem may be of some interest, though even there the interpretation seems somewhat forced, as Arrow points out.[27] For empirical work this interpretation is completely artificial since firms are viewed as making new decisions to invest continuously over time. To maximize present value at each point of time, a firm following an optimal path for capital accumulation must maximize present value subject to the initial condition given by the optimal path up to that point. But this results in a new optimal path which is precisely the same as the old from that point forward. Accordingly, if the optimal path for capital accumulation is continuous, the initial value of the level of capital services may not be chosen arbitrarily in the maximization of the present value of the firm. At each point it is precisely that for which the initial level of investment is bounded, namely, the level of capital services derived from the production function and the marginal productivity conditions. A possible objection to this view is that firms must begin to accumulate capital at some point in time. But at such a point the initial level of capital services is not given arbitrarily; the initial level must be zero with a positive derivative.

4. The theory of investment behavior

Beginning with the neoclassical model of optimal capital accumulation, we may derive differentiable demand functions for labor and capital services and a differentiable supply function for output, say:

$$L = L(w, c, p), \qquad K = K(w, c, p), \qquad Q = Q(w, c, p). \qquad (13)$$

The problem of deriving the demand for investment goods as a function of the rate of interest is a subtle one. Haavelmo expresses the view that the demand for investment goods cannot be derived from the profit-maximizing

[26]Haavelmo, *Theory of Investment, op. cit.*, pp. 162–165. Arrow, "Optimal Capital Adjustment," in *Studies in Applied Probability, op. cit.*, p. 2.
[27]*Ibid.*, p. 6, fn. 1.

theory of the firm. This is a consequence of his interpretation of the demand function for capital services and condition (3) determining the level of investment from replacement and the rate of change of demand for capital services. According to this interpretation, finite variations in the rate of interest with all other prices held constant result in finite changes in the demand for capital services. As the rate of interest varies, demand for investment goods assumes only three possible values — negatively infinite, positively infinite, or the value obtained where the initial level of capital services is precisely equal to the demand for capital services. Investment demand has a finite value for only one rate of interest. In this interpretation, the demand function for capital services is analyzed by means of comparative statics, that is, by comparing alternative production plans at a given point of time. Any attempt to derive the demand for investment goods as a function of the rate of interest by such comparisons leads to nonsensical results, as Haavelmo correctly points out.

However, an alternative interpretation of the demand function for capital services and condition (3) determining the level of investment is possible. Under the hypothesis that the firm is following an optimal path for capital accumulation and that the optimal path is continuous, the initial level of capital is always equal to the demand for capital services. By imposing this condition at the outset, the demand for investment goods as a function of the rate of interest at any point of time may be analyzed by means of comparative dynamics, that is, by comparing alternative paths of capital accumulation, each identical up to that point of time and each continuous at that point. The demand for investment goods is given by condition (3):

$$I = \quad + \delta K,$$

where the level of capital services, K, is fixed; but from the demand function for capital services (13), this condition implies that for fixed values of the price of output and the price of labor services, the implicit price of capital services must remain unchanged. Holding the price of investment goods constant, the rate of change of the price of investment goods must vary as the rate of interest varies so as to leave the implicit price of capital services unchanged. Formally, the condition that variations in the rate of interest leave the implicit price of capital services unchanged may be represented as:

$$\frac{\partial c}{\partial r} = 0;$$

holding the price of investment goods constant, this condition implies that the own-rate of interest on investment goods, $r - \dot{q}/q$, must be left unchanged by variations in the rate of interest.

We assume that all changes in the rate of interest are precisely compensated by changes in the rate of change of the price of current and future investment goods so as to leave the own-rate of interest on investment goods unchanged. Under this condition the discounted value of all future capital services, which is equal to the current price of investment goods, is left unchanged by variations in the time path of the rate of interest. The condition that the time path of the own-rate of interest on investment goods is left unchanged by a change in the time path of the rate of interest implies that forward prices or discounted future prices of both investment goods and capital services are left unchanged by variations in the rate of interest. For a constant rate of interest, this condition may be represented in the form:

$$\frac{\partial^2 e^{-rt} c(t)}{\partial r \partial t} = 0.$$

Like the previous condition, this condition holds at every point of time.

To derive the demand for investment goods as a function of the rate of interest, we first differentiate the demand for capital services with respect to time, obtaining:

$$\dot{K} = \frac{\partial K}{\partial w} \cdot \frac{\partial w}{\partial t} + \frac{\partial K}{\partial c} \cdot \frac{\partial c}{\partial t} + \frac{\partial K}{\partial p} \cdot \frac{\partial p}{\partial t}.$$

For simplicity, we consider only the case in which $\partial w / \partial t = \partial p / \partial t = 0$, that is, the price of output and the price of labor services are not changed. In this case, we obtain:

$$\dot{K} = \frac{\partial K}{\partial c} \cdot \frac{\partial c}{\partial t}.$$

Differentiating the implicit price of capital services with respect to time, we have:

$$\frac{\partial c}{\partial t} = \frac{\partial q}{\partial t}(\delta + r) + q \frac{\partial r}{\partial t} - \frac{\partial^2 q}{\partial t^2}. \tag{14}$$

To derive the demand for investment goods, we combine expression (14) for the rate of change of capital services with condition (3) for the rate of investment, obtaining:

$$I = \frac{\partial K}{\partial c}\left[\frac{\partial q}{\partial t}(\delta + r) + q \frac{\partial r}{\partial t} - \frac{\partial^2 q}{\partial t^2}\right] + \delta K,$$

which depends on the rate of interest and the price of investment goods through the rate of change of capital services. Differentiating this investment demand function with respect to the rate of interest, we obtain:

$$\frac{\partial I}{\partial r} = \frac{\partial^2 K}{\partial c^2} \cdot \frac{\partial c}{\partial r} \cdot \frac{\partial c}{\partial t} + \frac{\partial K}{\partial c} \cdot \frac{\partial^2 c}{\partial t \partial r} + \delta \frac{\partial K}{\partial c} \cdot \frac{\partial c}{\partial r}.$$

But $\partial c / \partial r = 0$, since changes in the rate of interest are compensated by changes in the rate of change of the price of investment goods so as to leave the implicit price of capital services unchanged. This condition implies that:

$$\frac{\partial^2 q}{\partial t \partial r} = q.$$

Secondly, $\dfrac{\partial^2 e^{-rt} c(t)}{\partial r \partial t} = 0$, since changes in the time path of the rate of interest leave the time path of forward or discounted prices of capital services unchanged. This condition implies that:

$$\frac{\partial^2 c}{\partial t \partial r} = c.$$

Combining these two conditions, we obtain:

$$\frac{\partial I}{\partial r} = \frac{\partial K}{\partial c} \cdot c < 0,$$

so that the demand for investment goods is a decreasing function of the rate of interest.

We conclude that it is possible to derive the demand for investment goods as a function of the rate of interest on the basis of purely neoclassical considerations. However, the demand for investment goods depends on the rate of interest through a comparison of alternative paths of capital accumulation, each continuous and each depending on a time path of the rate of interest. Although this conclusion appears to be the reverse of that reached by Haavelmo, his approach to the demand for investment goods is through comparative statics, that is, through comparison of alternative production plans at a given point of time. The demand function for investment goods cannot be derived by means of such comparisons. As a proposition in comparative statics, any relation between variations in the rate of investment and changes in the rate of interest is nonsensical.

To summarize, the complete neoclassical model of optimal capital accumulation consists of the production function (4), the two marginal productivity conditions (8) and (9), and the side condition (10). An alternative form of this model consists of the demand functions for capital and labor services, the supply function for output:

$$L = L(w, c, p), \qquad K = K(w, c, p), \qquad Q = Q(w, c, p);$$

and the demand function for investment goods:

$$I = \frac{\partial K}{\partial c} \frac{\partial c}{\partial t} + \delta K,$$

$$= I\left(w, c, p, \frac{\partial c}{\partial t}\right).$$

The demand for investment goods depends on the change in the demand for capital with respect to a change in the implicit price of capital services, the time rate of change in the price of capital services, and the level of replacement demand. Where the time rates of change of the price of labor services and the price of output are not zero, the demand function for investment goods may be rewritten:

$$I = \frac{\partial K}{\partial w}\frac{\partial w}{\partial t} + \frac{\partial K}{\partial c}\frac{\partial c}{\partial t} + \frac{\partial K}{\partial p}\cdot\frac{\partial p}{\partial t} + \delta K,$$

$$= I\left(w, c, p, \frac{\partial w}{\partial t}, \frac{\partial c}{\partial t}, \frac{\partial p}{\partial t}\right).$$

5. Alternative theories of investment behavior

The neoclassical theory of demand for investment goods just outlined may be contrasted with the theory current in the literature. Most recent accounts of the theory of demand for investment are based on Keynes' *General Theory*, in which the criterion for optimal investment behavior is that any project with an internal rate of return greater than the ruling rate of interest is undertaken.[28] An investment demand schedule is constructed by varying the rate of interest and plotting the quantities of investment undertaken for each value of the rate of interest. The criterion for optimal investment behavior used by Keynes is inconsistent with maximization of the present value of the firm, as Alchian and Hirshleifer have pointed out.[29] Nevertheless, a substantial portion of the current literature on the investment demand function is based on a straightforward reproduction of Keynes' derivation. Alchian lists a number of examples from the literature prior to 1955; examples from the current literature are provided by the recent work of Duesenberry and Tarshis.[30] Keynes' construction of the demand function for investment must be dismissed as inconsistent with the neoclassical theory of optimal capital accumulation.

An alternative construction of the demand function for investment goods has been suggested by Fisher.[31] In Fisher's theory any project with positive present value is undertaken. Keynes appears to have identified his

[28]Keynes, *General Theory, op. cit.*, Chap. 11, see especially p. 136.

[29]A. A. Alchian, "The Rate of Interest, Fisher's Rate of Return over Costs and Keynes' Internal Rate of Return," in *Management of Corporate Capital, op. cit.*, p. 70; and J. Hirshleifer, in *ibid.*, pp. 222–227. This conclusion of Alchian and Hirshleifer contradicts the position taken by Klein in *The Keynesian Revolution, op. cit.*

[30]J. S. Duesenberry, *Business Cycles and Economic Growth*, (New York: [McGraw-Hill,] 1958), pp. 49–85. Duesenberry asserts that Keynes' derivation is based on "profit maximization" (p. 85). L. Tarshis, "The Marginal Efficiency Function," *American Economic Review*, [LI] Dec. 1961, pp. 958–985. Tarshis asserts that the Keynesian theory is based on that of the "profit-maximizing firm" (pp. 958–959).

[31]Fisher, *Theory of Interest, op. cit.*, pp. 159–176.

construction of the marginal efficiency of capital schedule with that of Fisher, as Alchian points out.[32] There are two difficulties with Fisher's construction. First, the construction is carried out by means of comparative statics so that the resulting schedule may be interpreted as a theory of demand for capital services for which no demand function for investment goods exists. Second, the construction is not internally consistent in a second sense pointed out by Alchian, since ". . . we cannot in full logical consistency draw up a demand curve for investment by varying only the rate of interest (holding all other prices in the impound of *ceteris paribus*)."[33] The relevant prices are forward prices of all commodities; but altering the rate of interest amounts to altering certain forward prices. It is inconsistent to vary the rate of interest while holding such prices fixed. This inconsistency may be eliminated by stipulating that variations in the rate of interest must be precisely compensated by changes in the time rate of change of the price of investment goods. The price of investment goods at a given point of time is held fixed; the rate of change of the price of investment goods varies with the rate of interest. The construction of the demand function for investment goods involves a comparison among alternative paths of optimal capital accumulation; all paths are identical up to the point of time for which the investment function is constructed. Such a theory of investment behavior is internally consistent and may be derived by means of comparative dynamics.

Klein has attempted to derive a demand function for investment goods on the basis of profit maximization. His treatment, though suggestive, is marred by a number of inconsistencies. In his first attempt, the stock of investment goods is defined as the integral of past flows of investment, but the flow of investment is employed as a stock in the production function and in the definition of "discounted profit."[34] A second attempt involves the identification of the flow of capital services with the flow of depreciation.[35] In both attempts, quantities measured as rates of capital service per unit of time are added to quantities measured as rates of investment per unit of time, which is self-contradictory. This inconsistency carries over to the empirical implementation of the resulting investment function, where the price of investment goods is identified with the price of capital services.[36] An internally consistent treatment of the theory of investment along the lines suggested by Klein leads to a comparative statics theory of demand for capital services in which no demand function for investment goods exists. Another branch of the current literature is based on the view that no

[32]Alchian, in *Management of Corporate Capital, op. cit.,* p. 67; Klein (*Keynesian Revolution, op. cit.,* p. 62) follows Keynes in identifying these two distinct approaches to the construction of the marginal efficiency schedule.

[33]Alchian, *Management of Corporate Capital, op. cit.,* p. 71.

[34]Klein, *Keynesian Revolution, op. cit.,* esp. pp. 196–199.

[35]Klein, in *Kyklos,* II, fasc. 2, (1948), 97–117; and his *Economic Fluctuations, op. cit.*

[36]*Ibid.* The price of investment goods (p. 21 and p. 85) is identified with the price of capital services (p. 15).

demand function for investment goods exists. We have already cited Haavelmo's support of this position. A similar view may be found in Lerner's *Economics of Control*. Lerner argues that, under diminishing returns, the firm has a downward sloping demand curve for capital services but that, except where there is no net investment, the rate of investment is unbounded:[37]

... there is no limit to the rate per unit of time at which [the individual] can acquire assets by buying them, borrowing money for the purpose if he has not enough of his own. This indefinitely great rate of "investment" means that he can move at once to the position ... which makes the (private) marginal productivity of capital equal to the rate of interest. Once he gets there, there is no tendency for further expansion. ...

This view is the same as that expressed by Haavelmo. A recent restatement of this position has been given by Witte, who concludes, with Lerner and Haavelmo, that "... the continuous function relating the rate of investment to the rate of interest at the micro level has no foundation in the ordinary theory of the firm."[38] We have demonstrated that it is possible to derive the demand for investment goods from the comparative dynamics applied to the ordinary neoclassical theory of the firm. The conclusion reached by Haavelmo, Lerner, and Witte concerning a demand function for investment goods derived on the basis of comparative statics is, of course, correct.

An attempt has been made by proponents of the view that the demand function for investment goods does not exist to rehabilitate the Keynesian marginal efficiency of investment schedule. Alternative versions of this rehabilitation are presented by Haavelmo, Lerner, and Witte.[39] The essentials of the argument are that, at a given rate of interest, a certain price for investment goods is required to equate the marginal productivity of capital with the implicit price of capital services; but the higher this price the lower the rate of interest, so that a rising supply curve for investment goods implies that the amount of investment goods produced will increase as the rate of interest falls. A fundamental difficulty with this view is that it fails to account for the purchase of new investment goods by the users of capital equipment.[40]

[37]A. P. Lerner, *The Economics of Control*, *op. cit.*, esp. pp. 330–338.
[38]James G. Witte, Jr., "The Microfoundations of the Social Investment Function," *Journal of Political Economy*, [LXXI] Oct. 1963, pp. 441–456.
[39]Haavelmo, *Theory of Investment*, *op. cit.*, pp. 194–197. See also: B. Thalberg, "An Analysis of a Market for Investment Goods," in Lutz and Hague, *Theory of Capital*, *op. cit.*, pp. 161–176, and "A Keynesian Model Extended by Explicit Demand and Supply Functions for Investment Goods," in *Stockholm Economic Studies*, Pamphlet Series No. 3, 1964. Lerner, *Economics of Control*, *op. cit.*, pp. 333–334. Witte, *op. cit.*, pp. 445–447.
[40]A second difficulty with this view is that an increase in the price of investment goods may result in a rise or a fall in the supply of investment goods, depending on the relative capital intensity of the investment goods and consumption goods industries. Lerner, for example, assumes implicitly that investment goods are produced with no capital services. This difficulty was pointed out to me by James Tobin.

Witte summarizes this consequence of the view as follows: ". . . the rate-of-investment decision is the rate-of-output decision of supplying enterprises and not the rate-of-input decision of capital-using firms."[41] In the same vein Haavelmo writes, ". . . it is, actually, not the users of capital who demand investment, it is the producers of capital goods who determine how much they want to produce at the current price of capital."[42] A further attempt along these lines of the rehabilitation of the Keynesian marginal efficiency of investment schedule has been presented by Clower.[43] His argument follows that of Haavelmo, Lerner, and Witte in assuming that demand for capital services is equal to supply. However, Clower introduces a demand for investment goods which is not necessarily equal to the supply of investment goods. The excess or deficiency of demand over supply is net accumulation of capital. This view also fails to account for the purchases of new investment goods by the users of capital equipment.

For internal consistency, the rehabilitation of the Keynesian marginal efficiency of investment schedule requires either a changing rate of interest, as suggested by Haavelmo, or a changing price of capital goods, as suggested by Lerner.[44] For if the rate of interest and the price of investment goods are fixed over time and the marginal productivity of capital is equal to the implicit price of capital services, the firm's demand for investment is determinate; this demand is precisely equal to replacement demand so that net investment is zero. Under these circumstances, the rate of investment demand by users of capital equipment is independent of the rate of interest so that the price of investment goods must be that at which this rate of investment will be supplied by investment goods producers. But then if the marginal productivity of capital is to be equal to the implicit price for capital services, the rate of interest is uniquely determined, which is inconsistent with variations in the rate of interest from whatever source.

To complete the rehabilitation of the Keynesian marginal efficiency of investment schedule, interpreted as the level of investment resulting from a market equilibrium in investment goods corresponding to a given rate of interest, market equilibrium must be studied in a fully dynamic setting. The demand for investment goods must be derived from a comparison among alternative paths of optimal capital accumulation. It remains to be seen whether such a rehabilitation can be carried out in an internally consistent way.

[41]*Op. cit.*, p. 448.
[42]Haavelmo, *Theory of Investment, op. cit.*, p. 196.
[43]R. W. Clower, "An Investigation into the Dynamics of Investment," *American Economic Review*, [XLIV] March 1954, pp. 64–81.
[44]Haavelmo, *Theory of Investment, op. cit.*, p. 196. Lerner, *Economics of Control, op. cit.*, diagram, p. 336.

HANS BREMS **12**

What induces induced investment?[1]

Two broad categories of cycle and growth theories may be distinguished: First, in Schumpeterian models technological progress induces investment in *better* producers' goods. Second, in a Harrod theory of growth or a Samuelson 'interaction' model, pure quantitative growth induces investment in *more* producers' goods *via* a rigid capital coefficient or accelerator.

By applying standard theory of the firm first to pure technological progress and then to pure quantitative growth, the present paper will examine the firm's response to the two inducements and search for a common measure of the inducements. But first some definitional groundwork will have to be done.

I. Defining net worth and internal rate of return ('marginal efficiency of capital')

Consider a firm producing consumers' goods by absorbing labor services as well as services rendered by durable producers' goods. Let b be the capital coefficient, i.e. number of physical units of producers' goods required per physical unit of consumers' goods produced per annum. Let π_c be the price of consumers' goods. Revenue per annum per physical unit of producers'

Reprinted from *Kyklos*, Vol. 16 (1963) FASC. 4, pp. 569–582, by permission of the publisher and author.

[1]For criticism and suggestions the author is indebted to Marvin Frankel and Donald R. Hodgman.

goods is then π_c/b. Let a be the number of man hours of direct labor per annum required to cooperate with one physical unit of producers' goods. Let π_l be the money wage rate. The direct labor cost per annum per unit of producers' goods is then $\pi_l a$, and revenue *minus* direct labor cost per annum per unit of producers' goods is $\pi_c/b - \pi_l a$. The present worth of revenue *minus* direct labor cost per small fraction dt of a year located t years away in the future is:

$$\left(\frac{\pi_c}{b} - \pi_l a\right)e^{-it}\, dt$$

where e is the base of the natural system of logarithms, and where i is a rate of interest to be defined in Section 3 and 4. All we say about it here is that it must be independent of the project now under consideration. Let L be the useful life of one unit of producers' goods. The present worth of the sum total of revenue *minus* direct labor cost for the entire useful life is, then:

$$\int_0^L \left(\frac{\pi_c}{b} - \pi_l a\right)e^{-it}\, dt = \left(\frac{\pi_c}{b} - \pi_l a\right)\frac{1 - e^{-iL}}{i}$$

Let the price of a new unit of producers' goods be π_p. The present net worth n of the acquisition of one such unit is, then:

$$n = \left(\frac{\pi_c}{b} - \pi_l a\right)\frac{1 - e^{-iL}}{i} - \pi_p \qquad (1)$$

Define the internal rate of return ι as that rate of interest which makes the present net worth n equal to zero:

$$\left(\frac{\pi_c}{b} - \pi_l a\right)\frac{1 - e^{-\iota L}}{\iota} - \pi_p = 0 \qquad (2)$$

II. Defining the amount of net profits

The amount of net profits is the amount the owner may consume and yet maintain his assets intact. Per annum per unit of producers' goods that amount may be alternatively specified either as $i(n + \pi_p)$ or as $\iota\pi_p$, depending on whether the interest rate i or the internal rate of return ι is adopted as a guide. The proof is this. Per annum per unit of producers' goods, revenue *minus* direct labor cost was seen to be $\pi_c/b - \pi_l a$. Out of this amount, let the owner consume alternatively $i(n + \pi_p)$ or $\iota\pi_p$ and consider the remainder his capital consumption allowances C_i or C_ι, respectively, per annum per unit of producers' goods:

$$C_i = \frac{\pi_c}{b} - \pi_I a - i(n + \pi_p) \tag{3}$$

$$C_\iota = \frac{\pi_c}{b} - \pi_I a - \iota\pi_p \tag{4}$$

Into (3) insert (1), and into (4) insert (2):

$$C_i = \frac{i(n + \pi_p)}{e^{iL} - 1} \tag{5}$$

$$C_\iota = \frac{\iota\pi_p}{e^{\iota L} - 1} \tag{6}$$

Let the owner invest his capital consumption allowance continuously at the rates i or ι, respectively. The future worth at scrapping time of the sum total of all capital consumption allowances during the entire useful life is:

$$\int_0^L C_i e^{it} \, dt = C_i \frac{e^{iL} - 1}{i} \tag{7}$$

$$\int_0^L C_\iota e^{\iota t} \, dt = C_\iota \frac{e^{\iota L} - 1}{\iota} \tag{8}$$

Into (7) insert (5), into (8) insert (6), and find the two integrals to be equal to $n + \pi_p$ and π_p, respectively. Depending on whether the interest rate i or the internal rate of return ι is adopted as a guide, $n + \pi_p$ and π_p respectively, represent the money value of the asset to its owner, hence the asset has been maintained intact over the useful life L years. On the entire capital stock of S physical units of producers' goods the amount of net profits per annum is, respectively:

$$p_i = i(n + \pi_p)S \tag{9}$$

$$p_\iota = \iota\pi_p S \tag{10}$$

The two amounts are not identical. If (1) is inserted into (9), p_i turns out to be $(\pi_c/b - \pi_I a)(1 - e^{-iL})S$; if (2) is inserted into (10), p_ι turns out $(\pi_c/b - \pi_I a)(1 - e^{-\iota L})S$. From this we can see that if ι is greater than i, then p_ι is greater than p_i. The reason why the latter is the more conservative view of profits is, of course, that once seen the net worth n is immediately considered part of the assets to be maintained intact; only the interest on it, calculated at the rate i, is consumable.

III. Neoclassical behavior assumptions

So far we have been merely defining concepts. A theory of the optimal capital stock also needs behavior assumptions. The neoclassical set of behavior assumptions was this. First, let there be diminishing physical productivity manifesting itself in a rising capital coefficient b as capital stock rises. Second, let the firm be selling under pure competition: Unlimited quantities of consumers' goods could be sold at the going price. Third, in a neoclassical theory the rate of interest i referred to above as being independent of the project under consideration and referred to in (1) would be the external rate of interest at which the firm is capable of borrowing funds in the open market. However, we shall develop our theory of the optimal capital stock on modern assumptions.

IV. Modern behavior assumptions

First, much modern theory would deemphasize diminishing returns. Let a, b, and L be technological parameters, then. Hence a rigid proportionality would hold between the number of physical units of producers' goods S and the output of consumers' goods X:

$$S = bX \tag{11}$$

Second, much modern theory would deemphasize pure competition. So while π_l and π_p are parameters beyond the control of the firm, let π_c, the price of consumers' goods, be controlled by the firm with quantity demanded σ adjusting to it. Quantity demanded at any price would be finite, and output should be equal to that quantity:

$$X = \sigma \tag{12}$$

Third, much modern theory would deemphasize external financing. Rather, in a modern theory the rate of interest i referred to above as being independent of the project under consideration and referred to in (1) would be the internal rate of return at which the firm is capable of investing internally elsewhere (in other projects, in subsidiaries etc.). No investment project will be executed unless it promises an internal rate of return ι greater than or equal to i thus defined:

$$\iota \geq i \tag{13}$$

Since $(1 - e^{-\iota L})/\iota$ is falling with rising ι, it follows from (1) and (2) taken together that if (13) is satisfied, then

$$n \geqq 0 \tag{14}$$

Now let the firm optimize its output X by maximizing the present net worth N of the entire project of acquiring S physical units of producers' goods:

$$N = nS \tag{15}$$

Insert (1) and (11) into (15), take the derivative of N with respect to X, set that derivative equal to zero, multiply it by $i/(1 - e^{-iL})$, and get:

$$\frac{d(\pi_c X)}{dX} = \left(\pi_l a + \frac{i\pi_p}{1 - e^{-iL}}\right)b \tag{16}$$

The left-hand side of (16) represents marginal revenue, the right-hand side represents marginal cost. Since the coefficients a and b are technological parameters, labor input and capital stock are always in direct proportion to output, and marginal cost is the cost of expanding output by expanding *all* inputs. Clearly the marginal cost curve is a horizontal line.

The firm optimizes output X and capital stock S by satisfying (16) taken in conjunction with (11). Given the optimal capital stock, the optimal volume of investment, to be carried out over an unspecified period of time, is the difference between the optimal capital stock and that part of it already owned by the firm.

How does this theory handle the two alternative inducements to invest, i.e., pure technological progress and pure quantitative growth?

V. Pure technological progress

Let there be no change in the quantity demanded σ of consumers' goods at a given price π_c. But let there be technological progress thought of as follows: At constant values of the other two technology parameters, either the direct labor input coefficient a falls, the capital coefficient b falls, or the useful life L rises. In all three cases marginal cost as defined by the right-hand side of (16) falls. For (16) to remain satisfied, a price reduction becomes necessary. But what does pure technological progress in these three forms do to the present net worth n, to the internal rate of return of the project as a whole ι, and to optimal capital stock S?

For each of the three forms we shall first assume the demand curve faced by the firm to have a constant elasticity η assumed to be finite, negative, and numerically greater than one. In these cases we shall find it convenient to write marginal revenue:

$$\frac{d(\pi_c X)}{dX} = \pi_c\left(1 + \frac{X}{\pi_c}\frac{d\pi_c}{dX}\right) = \pi_c\left(1 + \frac{1}{\eta}\right) \tag{17}$$

If η is finite and negative, so is $1/\eta$; hence by letting output X move closer to zero we can always raise price π_c above any finite value we care to mention, for example marginal cost as defined by the right-hand side of (16). Hence in optimum defined by (16), net worth n can never be nonpositive.

Then we shall assume the demand curve to have constant slope assumed to be finite and negative. In these cases we shall find it convenient to write marginal revenue:

$$\frac{d(\pi_c X)}{dX} = \pi_c + X\frac{d\pi_c}{dX} \tag{18}$$

If in a straight-line demand curve X equals zero π_c assumes a finite value. If marginal cost defined by the right-hand side of (16) equals or exceeds that value, n will be respectively zero or negative.

Demand curves convex to the origin but still having numerically declining elasticity should lead to results between those of the two extremes studied.

1. Automation

CASE A: CONSTANT DEMAND ELASTICITY.   Let the direct labor input coefficient a fall with price π_c adjusting to it. Use (1), (16), and (17) to find the derivative of net worth n with respect to a:

$$\frac{\partial n}{\partial a} = \pi_l\left(\frac{1}{1 + 1/\eta} - 1\right)\frac{1 - e^{-iL}}{i} \tag{19}$$

Under our assumptions about the elasticity η, $1 + 1/\eta$ is a positive proper fraction; hence (19) is positive, and n and ι are both down. But n cannot in this case be nonpositive; since before the technological progress (13) and (14) were satisfied, they will remain so. Optimal capital stock S is up, for X is up with b constant.

CASE B: CONSTANT DEMAND SLOPE.   Let the direct labor input coefficient a fall with price π_c adjusting to it. Use (1), (16), and (18) to find the derivative of net worth n with respect to a:

$$\frac{\partial n}{\partial a} = -\frac{\pi_l}{2}\frac{1 - e^{-iL}}{i} \tag{20}$$

which is negative, and n and ι are both up. If before the technological progress (13) and (14) were dissatisfied, they may now become satisfied; if they were satisfied, they will remain so. Optimal capital stock S is up, for X is up with b constant.

2. Lower capital coefficient

CASE C: CONSTANT DEMAND ELASTICITY.   Let the capital coefficient b fall with price π_c adjusting to it. Use (1), (16), and (17) to find the derivative of net worth n with respect to b:

$$\frac{\partial n}{\partial b} = 0 \tag{21}$$

So n and ι are both unaffected. n cannot in this case be nonpositive; since before the technological progress (13) and (14) were satisfied, they will remain so. As for optimal capital stock S, use (11), (16), and (17) to find the derivative of it with respect to b:

$$\frac{\partial S}{\partial b} = (1 + \eta)X \tag{22}$$

Under our assumptions about the elasticity η, (22) is negative, and S is up.

CASE D: CONSTANT DEMAND SLOPE.   Let the capital coefficient b fall with price π_c adjusting to it. Use (1), (16), and (18) to find the derivative of net worth n with respect to b:

$$\frac{\partial n}{\partial b} = \frac{-\pi_c + Xd\pi_c/dX}{2b^2} \frac{1 - e^{-iL}}{i} \tag{23}$$

Under our assumptions about the slope of the demand curve, (23) is negative, and n and ι are both up. If before the technological progress (13) and (14) were dissatisfied, they may now become satisfied; if they were satisfied, they will remain so. As for optimal capital stock S, use (11), (16), and (18) to find the derivative of it with respect to b:

$$\frac{\partial S}{\partial b} = \frac{3 + \eta}{2} X \tag{24}$$

so if elasticity η is numerically greater than 3, (24) is negative, and S is up; if η is numerically smaller than 3, (24) is positive, and S is down.

3. Longer useful life

CASE E: CONSTANT DEMAND ELASTICITY.   Let technological progress reduce vibration, friction, or corrosion so as to raise the useful life L of producers' goods, with price π_c adjusting to it. Use (1), (16), and (17) to find the derivative of net worth n with respect to L:

$$\frac{\partial n}{\partial L} = \pi_l a e^{-iL}\left(\frac{1}{1 + 1/\eta} - 1\right) \qquad (25)$$

Under our assumptions about the elasticity η, $1 + 1/\eta$ is a positive proper fraction; hence (25) is positive, and n and ι are both up. n cannot in this case be nonpositive; since before the technological progress (13) and (14) were satisfied, they will remain so. Optimal capital stock S is up, for X is up with b constant.

CASE F: CONSTANT DEMAND SLOPE.   Let the useful life L of producers' goods rise with price π_c adjusting to it. Use (1), (16), and (18) to find the derivative of net worth n with respect to L:

$$\frac{\partial n}{\partial L} = e^{-iL}\left[\frac{i\pi_p}{2(1 - e^{-iL})} - \frac{X}{b}\frac{d\pi_c}{dX}\right] \qquad (26)$$

Under our assumptions about the slope of the demand curve, (26) is positive, and n and ι are both up. If before the technological progress (13) and (14) were dissatisfied, they may now become satisfied; if they were satisfied, they will remain so. As for optimal capital stock S, it is up, for X is up with b constant.

VI. Pure quantitative growth

Let population increase raise the quantity demanded σ of consumers' goods at a given price π_c, thereby easing the constraint (12). But let there be no technological progress. Hence marginal cost as defined by the right-hand side of (16) is left unaffected. Demand and marginal revenue curves, however, shift to the right. What does this kind of pure quantitative growth do to the present net worth n, to the internal rate of return of the project as a whole ι, and to optimal capital stock S?

The answer lies in the specific way in which demand and marginal revenue curves shift to the right. At the same price assume the quantity demanded by each household, h, to be the same for all households. Let there be m households. At any price, then, common to all households, market demand σ is:

$$\sigma = mh \qquad (27)$$

Insert (12) and (27) into the definition of marginal revenue (18) and get:

$$\frac{d(\pi_c X)}{dX} = \pi_c + mh \frac{d\pi_c}{d(mh)} = \pi_c + h \frac{d\pi_c}{dh} \qquad (28)$$

The m is (28) cancelling out, we conclude that at the same price π_c, regardless of the value of m, marginal revenue remains the same. That is exactly what it should do to satisfy (16), for on the right-hand side of (16), population growth has changed nothing. So optimum price π_c does remain the same as population increases. But then no magnitude entering (1) or (2) has changed, so n and ι are both unaffected. Hence whether before the population started growing (13) and (14) were satisfied or dissatisfied, they will remain so. Optimal capital stock S is up, for X is rising with b constant.

VII. Conclusions

In each case of pure technological progress as well as pure quantitative growth, the present paper has determined the effects upon three strategic variables: (1) the present net worth per physical unit of producers' goods, called n; (2) the internal rate of return ('marginal efficiency of capital'), called ι; and (3) the optimal number of physical units of producers' goods to be held by the firm, called S. In all cases examined, n and ι moved together, so we may confine our attention to one of them, say n.

A basic assumption was inequality (14) saying that no investment project will be executed unless it promises a nonnegative present net worth per physical unit of producers' goods, n. Hence anything raising net worth n from a negative to a nonnegative value constitutes an inducement to execute the project. And, we may add, anything raising net worth n of a project not yet executed from a lower nonnegative value to a higher one, raises the urgency with which the project should be executed. Could one, in consequence, measure the inducement to invest simply by the net worth n? To begin with, in our cases B, E, and F net worth n and optimal capital stock S do move together. On the other hand, in the cases where net worth n was reduced or left constant but was still positive, i.e. in the cases A and C of pure technological progress as well as in the entire case of pure quantitative growth, optimal capital stock S was up. And in the one case, i.e. D, where optimal capital stock S was possibly down, net worth n was up. As a measure of the inducement to invest, then, net worth n alone will not do.

How large is the optimal capital stock of the firm? If the net worth n is negative, optimal capital stock S is zero. If the net worth n is nonnegative, optimal capital stock S is positive and determined by our condition (16) above. Anything giving rise to a positive optimal capital stock S constitutes an inducement to hold capital stock. Could one, then, measure the inducement to invest by the optimal capital stock S? Again let us see if our cases would provide an answer. To be sure, an effect upon optimal capital stock S without any effect upon net worth n was found on two occasions, i.e., our case C of pure technological progress and our entire case of pure quantitative growth. Furthermore, as we have already seen, in our cases B, E, and F net worth n and optimal capital stock S move together. But in case A, although optimal capital stock S is up, the urgency to invest is reduced by the net worth n being down, and in case D it is the other way around: Although optimal capital stock S is possibly down, the urgency to invest is increased by the net worth n being up. As a measure of the inducement to invest, then, optimal capital stock S is no doubt better than net worth n. But still, optimal capital stock S alone does not present the whole picture.

A more satisfactory measure of the inducement to invest would seem to be one which included net worth n *as well as* optimal capital stock S. One such measure would be the flow of earnings on the net worth of the entire capital stock, mathematically expressed as inS. Statistical data on this measure are not readily available. Readily available, however, are statistical data on the amount of net profits per annum. And the amount of net profits per annum, p_i, as defined by (9) might well represent inS by proxy: As the reader will easily verify by comparing (9) with inS, anything raising net worth n at constant optimal capital stock S will raise p_i and inS by the same *amount*. And anything raising optimal capital stock S at constant net worth n will raise p_i and inS in the same *proportion*.

Perhaps the amount of net profits per annum as defined and measured by the United States Department of Commerce might also represent inS by proxy. If so, we should expect the amount of net profits thus defined and measured to serve well as an explanation for investment in econometric work. Indeed it *has* served well[2] — far better than alternative explanations such as the accelerator or the rate of interest.

MATHEMATICAL APPENDIX

The results (19), (20), (21), (23), (25), and (26) are arrived at using elementary calculus. The present appendix provides a few stepping stones needed by some readers when crossing the creek.

[2]Lawrence R. Klein and Arthur S. Goldberger, *An Econometric Model of the United States 1929–1952.* (Amsterdam: [North-Holland], 1955), use capital stock, business liquid assets, and lagged profits as the independent variables in their investment function. But the coefficients of the first two are not significantly different from zero at the five per cent level. And Carl F. Christ, 'Aggregate Econometric Models,' *American Economic Review,* [XLVI] (June 1956), 385–408, says (392/393) that the current rather than the lagged value of the profit variable would serve even better in explaining investment. Current profits are used as the sole independent variable of the investment function in the much cruder model in Hans Brems, 'Wage, Price, and Tax Elasticities of Output and Distributive Shares,' *Journal of American Statistical Association,* [XLVII] Sept. 1962, 607–621, for the United States, as well as in the corresponding model in Hans Brems, 'Wages, Prices, and Profits in a Macroeconomic Model Illustrated by German Data,' *Weltwirtschaftliches Archiv,* [LXXXIX] Dec. 1962, 179–207.

In the constant-elasticity cases A, C, and E take (16) and (17) together and get:

$$\pi_c = \frac{[\pi_l a + i\pi_p/(1 - e^{-iL})]b}{1 + 1/\eta},$$

where the elasticity η is a constant. From this follows that:

$$\frac{\partial \pi_c}{\partial a} = \frac{\pi_l b}{1 + 1/\eta} \qquad (29)$$

$$\frac{\partial \pi_c}{\partial b} = \frac{\pi_c}{b} \qquad (30)$$

$$\frac{\partial \pi_c}{\partial L} = -\frac{bi\pi_p}{1 + 1/\eta} \frac{ie^{-iL}}{(1 - e^{-iL})^2} \qquad (31)$$

Use these three derivatives respectively when taking the derivatives of (1) and arrive at (19), (21), and (25), respectively.

In the constant-slope cases B, D, and F take (16) and (18) together and get:

$$\pi_c = \left(\pi_l a + \frac{i\pi_p}{1 - e^{-iL}}\right)b - X\frac{d\pi_c}{dX},$$

where the slope $d\pi_c/dX$ is a constant. From this follows that:

$$\frac{\partial \pi_c}{\partial a} = \frac{\pi_l b}{2} \qquad (32)$$

$$\frac{\partial \pi_c}{\partial b} = \frac{\pi_c + X d\pi_c/dX}{2b} \qquad (33)$$

$$\frac{\partial \pi_c}{\partial L} = -\frac{bi\pi_p}{2} \frac{ie^{-iL}}{(1 - e^{-iL})^2} \qquad (34)$$

Use these three derivatives respectively when taking the derivatives of (1) and arrive at (20), (23), and (26), respectively.

Summary

In Schumpeterian models technological progress induces investment in *better* producers' goods, whereas in a Harrod theory of growth or a Samuelson 'interaction' model, pure quantitative growth induces investment in *more* producers' goods *via* a rigid capital coefficient or accelerator. By applying standard theory of the firm the present paper examines the firm's response to the two inducements and searches for a common measure of the inducements. Pure technological progress is thought of as follows: At constant values of the other two technoolgy parameters, either a producer's good's direct labor input coefficient falls, its capital coefficient falls, or its useful life rises.

In each case of pure technological progress as well as pure quantitative growth, the paper determines the effects upon three strategic variables:

(1) the present net worth per physical unit of producers' goods,

(2) the internal rate of return ('marginal efficiency of capital'), and

(3) the optimal number of physical units of producers' goods to be held by the firm.

In all cases examined, (1) and (2) moved together, but in some cases (3) moved in the opposite direction of (1) and (2). Hence, as a measure of the inducement to invest (1) or (2) alone will not do. A more satisfactory measure of the inducement to invest would seem to be one which included net worth *as well as* optimal capital stock. One such measure would be the flow of earnings on the net worth of the entire capital stock. Statistical data on this measure are not readily available, but perhaps it may be represented by the amount of net profits per annum. As an explanation for investment in econometric work the amount of net profits per annum *has* served well — far better than alternative explanations such as the accelerator or the rate of interest.

Theory of money,
interest, and employment

JOHN R. HICKS **13**

Mr. Keynes and the "classics"; a suggested interpretation[1]

I.

It will be admitted by the least charitable reader that the entertainment value of Mr. Keynes' *General Theory of Employment* is considerably enhanced by its satiric aspect. But it is also clear that many readers have been left very bewildered by this Dunciad. Even if they are convinced by Mr. Keynes' arguments and humbly acknowledge themselves to have been "classical economists" in the past, they find it hard to remember that they believed in their unregenerate days the things Mr. Keynes says they believed. And there are no doubt others who find their historic doubts a stumbling block, which prevents them from getting as much illumination from the positive theory as they might otherwise have got.

One of the main reasons for this situation is undoubtedly to be found in the fact that Mr. Keynes takes as typical of "Classical economics" the later writings of Professor Pigou, particularly *The Theory of Unemployment*. Now *The Theory of Unemployment* is a fairly new book, and an exceedingly difficult book; so that it is safe to say that it has not yet made much impression on the ordinary teaching of economics. To most people its doctrines seem quite as strange and novel as the doctrines of Mr. Keynes himself; so

Reprinted from *Econometrica*, Vol. 5 (April 1937), pp. 147–159, by permission of the publisher and author.

[1]Based on a paper which was read at the Oxford meeting of the Econometric Society (September, 1936) and which called forth an interesting discussion. It has been modified subsequently, partly in the light of that discussion, and partly as a result of further discussion in Cambridge.

that to be told that he has believed these things himself leaves the ordinary economist quite bewildered.

For example, Professor Pigou's theory runs, to a quite amazing extent, in real terms. Not only is his theory a theory of real wages and unemployment; but numbers of problems which anyone else would have preferred to investigate in money terms are investigated by Professor Pigou in terms of "wage-goods." The ordinary classical economist has no part in this *tour de force*.

But if, on behalf of the ordinary classical economist, we declare that he would have preferred to investigate many of those problems in money terms, Mr. Keynes will reply that there is no classical theory of money wages and employment. It is quite true that such a theory cannot easily be found in the textbooks. But this is only because most of the textbooks were written at a time when general changes in money wages in a closed system did not present an important problem. There can be little doubt that most economists have thought that they had a pretty fair idea of what the relation between money wages and employment actually was.

In these circumstances, it seems worth while to try to construct a typical "classical" theory, built on an earlier and cruder model than Professor Pigou's. If we can construct such a theory, and show that it does give results which have in fact been commonly taken for granted, but which do not agree with Mr. Keynes' conclusions, then we shall at last have a satisfactory basis of comparison. We may hope to be able to isolate Mr. Keynes' innovations, and so to discover what are the real issues in dispute.

Since our purpose is comparison, I shall try to set out my typical classical theory in a form similar to that in which Mr. Keynes sets out his own theory; and I shall leave out of account all secondary complications which do not bear closely upon this special question in hand. Thus I assume that I am dealing with a short period in which the quantity of physical equipment of all kinds available can be taken as fixed. I assume homogeneous labour. I assume further that depreciation can be neglected, so that the output of investment goods corresponds to new investment. This is a dangerous simplification, but the important issues raised by Mr. Keynes in his chapter on user cost are irrelevant for our purposes.

Let us begin by assuming that w, the rate of money wages per head, can be taken as given.

Let x, y, be the outputs of investment goods and consumption goods respectively, and N_x, N_y, be the numbers of men employed in producing them. Since the amount of physical equipment specialised to each industry is given, $x = f_x(N_x)$ and $y = f_y(N_y)$, where f_x, f_y, are *given* functions.

Let M be the *given* quantity of money.

It is desired to determine N_x and N_y.

First, the price-level of investment goods = their marginal cost =

$w(dN_x/dx)$. And the price-level of consumption goods = their marginal cost = $w(dN_y/dy)$.

Income earned in investment trades (value of investment, or simply Investment) = $wx(dN_x/dx)$. Call this I_x.

Income earned in consumption trades = $wy(dN_y/dy)$.

Total Income = $wx(dN_x/dx) + wy(dN_y/dy)$. Call this I.

I_x is therefore a given function of N_x, I of N_x and N_y. Once I and I_x are determined, N_x and N_y can be determined.

Now let us assume the "Cambridge Quantity equation" — that there is some definite relation between Income and the demand for money. Then, approximately, and apart from the fact that the demand for money may depend not only upon total Income, but also upon its distribution between people with relatively large and relatively small demands for balances, we can write

$$M = kI.$$

As soon as k is given, total Income is therefore determined.

In order to determine I_x, we need two equations. One tells us that the amount of investment (looked at as demand for capital) depends upon the rate of interest:

$$I_x = C(i).$$

This is what becomes the marginal-efficiency-of-capital schedule in Mr. Keynes' work.

Further, Investment = Saving. And saving depends upon the rate of interest and, if you like, Income. $\therefore I_x = S(i, I)$. (Since, however, Income is already determined, we do not need to bother about inserting Income here unless we choose.)

Taking them as a system, however, we have three fundamental equations,

$$M = kI, \qquad I_x = C(i), \qquad I_x = S(i, I),$$

to determine three unknowns, I, I_x, i. As we have found earlier, N_x and N_y can be determined from I and I_x. Total employment, $N_x + N_y$, is therefore determined.

Let us consider some properties of this system. It follows directly from the first equation that as soon as k and M are given, I is completely determined; that is to say, total income depends directly upon the quantity of money. Total employment, however, is not necessarily determined at once from income, since it will usually depend to some extent upon the proportion of income saved, and thus upon the way production is divided between investment and consumption-goods trades. (If it so happened that the elasticities of supply were the same in each of these trades, then a shifting of demand between them would produce compensating movements in N_x and N_y, and consequently no change in total employment.)

An increase in the inducement to invest (i.e., a rightward movement of the schedule of the marginal efficiency of capital, which we have written as $C(i)$) will tend to raise the rate of interest, and so to affect saving. If the amount of saving rises, the amount of investment will rise too; labour will be employed more in the investment trades, less in the consumption trades; this will increase total employment if the elasticity of supply in the investment trades is greater than that in the consumption-goods trades — diminish it if *vice versa*.

An increase in the supply of money will necessarily raise total income, for people will increase their spending and lending until incomes have risen sufficiently to restore k to its former level. The rise in income will tend to increase employment, both in making consumption goods and in making investment goods. The total effect on employment depends upon the ratio between the expansions of these industries; and that depends upon the proportion of their increased incomes which people desire to save, which also governs the rate of interest.

So far we have assumed the rate of money wages to be given; but so long as we assume that k is independent of the level of wages, there is no difficulty about this problem either. A rise in the rate of money wages will necessarily diminish employment and raise real wages. For an unchanged money income cannot continue to buy an unchanged quantity of goods at a higher price-level; and, unless the price-level rises, the prices of goods will not cover their marginal costs. There must therefore be a fall in employment; as employment falls, marginal costs in terms of labour will diminish and therefore real wages rise. (Since a change in money wages is always accompanied by a change in real wages in the same direction, if not in the same proportion, no harm will be done, and some advantage will perhaps be secured, if one prefers to work in terms of real wages. Naturally most "classical economists" have taken this line.)

I think it will be agreed that we have here a quite reasonably consistent theory, and a theory which is also consistent with the pronouncements of a recognizable group of economists. Admittedly it follows from this theory that you may be able to increase employment by direct inflation; but whether or not you decide to favour that policy still depends upon your judgment about the probable reaction on wages, and also — in a national area — upon your views about the international standard.

Historically, this theory descends from Ricardo, though it is not actually Ricardian; it is probably more or less the theory that was held by Marshall. But with Marshall it was already beginning to be qualified in important ways; his successors have qualified it still further. What Mr. Keynes has done is to lay enormous emphasis on the qualifications, so that they almost blot out the original theory. Let us follow out this process of development.

II.

When a theory like the "classical" theory we have just described is applied to the analysis of industrial fluctuations, it gets into difficulties in several ways. It is evident that total money income experiences great variations in· the course of a trade cycle, and the classical theory can only explain these by variations in M or in k, or, as a third and last alternative, by changes in distribution.

1. Variation in M is simplest and most obvious, and has been relied on to a large extent. But the variations in M that are traceable during a trade cycle are variations that take place through the banks — they are variations in bank loans; if we are to rely on them it is urgently necessary for us to explain the connection between the supply of bank money and the rate of interest. This can be done roughly by thinking of banks as persons who are strongly inclined to pass on money by lending rather than spending it. Their action therefore tends at first to lower interest rates, and only afterwards, when the money passes into the hands of spenders, to raise prices and incomes. "The new currency, or the increase of currency, goes, not to private persons, but to the banking centers; and therefore, it increases the willingness of lenders to lend in the first instance, and lowers the rate of discount. But it afterwards raises prices; and therefore it tends to increase discount."[2] This is superficially satisfactory; but if we endeavoured to give a more precise account of this process we should soon get into difficulties. What determines the amount of money needed to produce a given fall in the rate of interest? What determines the length of time for which the low rate will last? These are not easy questions to answer.

2. In so far as we rely upon changes in k, we can also do well enough up to a point. Changes in k can be related to changes in confidence, and it is realistic to hold that the rising prices of a boom occur because optimism encourages a reduction in balances; the falling prices of a slump because pessimism and uncertainty dictate an increase. But as soon as we take this step it becomes natural to ask whether k has not abdicated its status as an independent variable, and has not become liable to be influenced by others among the variables in our fundamental equations.

3. This last consideration is powerfully supported by another, of more purely theoretical character. On grounds of pure value theory, it is evident that the direct sacrifice made by a person who holds a stock of money is a sacrifice of interest; and it is hard to believe that the marginal principle does not operate at all in this field. As Lavington put it: "The quantity of resources which (an individual) holds in the form of money will be such that the unit of money which is just and only just worth while holding in this form yields him a return of convenience and security equal to the yield of

[2]Alfred Marshall, *Money, Credit, and Commerce* (London: Macmillan & Co., Ltd., 1923), p. 257.

satisfaction derived from the marginal unit spent on consumables, and equal also to the net rate of interest."[3] The demand for money depends upon the rate of interest! The stage is set for Mr. Keynes.

As against the three equations of the classical theory,

$$M = kI, \qquad I_x = C(i), \qquad I_x = S(i, I),$$

Mr. Keynes begins with three equations,

$$M = L(i), \qquad I_x = C(i), \qquad I_x = S(I).$$

These differ from the classical equations in two ways. On the one hand, the demand for money is conceived as depending upon the rate of interest (Liquidity Preference). On the other hand, any possible influence of the rate of interest on the amount saved out of a given income is neglected. Although it means that the third equation becomes the multiplier equation, which performs such queer tricks, nevertheless this second amendment is a mere simplication, and ultimately insignificant.[4] It is the liquidity preference doctrine which is vital.

For it is now the rate of interest, not income, which is determined by the quantity of money. The rate of interest set against the schedule of the marginal efficiency of capital determines the value of investment; that determines income by the multiplier. Then the volume of employment (at given wage-rates) is determined by the value of investment and of income which is not saved but spent upon consumption goods.

It is this system of equations which yields the startling conclusion, that an increase in the inducement to invest, or in the propensity to consume, will not tend to raise the rate of interest, but only to increase employment. In spite of this, however, and in spite of the fact that quite a large part of the argument runs in terms of this system, and this system alone, *it is not the General Theory*. We may call it, if we like, Mr. Keynes' *special theory*. The General Theory is something appreciably more orthodox.

Like Lavington and Professor Pigou, Mr. Keynes does not in the end believe that the demand for money can be determined by one variable alone — not even the rate of interest. He lays more stress on it than they

---

[3]Lavington, *English Capital Market*, 1921, p. 30. See also Pigou, "The Exchange-value of Legal-tender Money," in *Essays in Applied Economics*, 1922, pp. 179–181.

[4]This can be readily seen if we consider the equations

$$M = kI, \qquad I_x = C(i), \qquad I_x = S(I),$$

which embody Mr. Keynes' second amendment without his first. The third equation is already the multiplier equation, but the multiplier is shorn of his wings. For since I still depends only on M, I_x now depends only on M, and it is impossible to increase investment without increasing the willingness to save or the quantity of money. The system thus generated is therefore identical with that which, a few years ago, used to be called the "Treasury View." But Liquidity Preference transports us from the "Treasury View" to the "General Theory of Employment."

did, but neither for him nor for them can it be the only variable to be considered. The dependence of the demand for money on interest does not, in the end, do more than qualify the old dependence on income. However much stress we lay upon the "speculative motive," the "transactions" motive must always come in as well.

Consequently we have for the General Theory

$$M = L(I, i), \qquad I_x = C(i), \qquad I_x = S(I).$$

With this revision, Mr. Keynes takes a big step back to Marshallian orthodoxy, and his theory becomes hard to distinguish from the revised and qualified Marshallian theories, which, as we have seen, are not new. Is there really any difference between them, or is the whole thing a sham fight? Let us have recourse to a diagram (Figure 1).

Against a given quantity of money, the first equation, $M = L(I, i)$, gives us a relation between Income (I) and the rate of interest (i). This can be drawn out as a curve (LL) which will slope upwards, since an increase in income tends to raise the demand for money, and an increase in the rate of

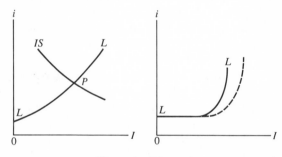

Figure 1   Figure 2

interest tends to lower it. Further, the second two equations taken together give us another relation between Income and interest. (The marginal-efficiency-of-capital schedule determines the value of investment at any given rate of interest, and the multiplier tells us what level of income will be necessary to make savings equal to that value of investment.) The curve IS can therefore be drawn showing the relation between Income and interest which must be maintained in order to make saving equal to investment.

Income and the rate of interest are now determined together at P, the point of intersection of the curves LL and IS. They are determined together; just as price and output are determined together in the modern theory of demand and supply. Indeed, Mr. Keynes' innovation is closely parallel, in this respect, to the innovation of the marginalists. The quantity theory tries to determine income without interest, just as the labour theory of value tried to determine price without output; each has to give place to a theory recognising a higher degree of interdependence.

III.

But if this is the real "General Theory," how does Mr. Keynes come to make his remarks about an increase in the inducement to invest not raising the rate of interest? It would appear from our diagram that a rise in the marginal-efficiency-of-capital schedule must raise the curve *IS*; and, therefore, although it will raise Income and employment, it will also raise the rate of interest.

This brings us to what, from many points of view, is the most important thing in Mr. Keynes' book. It is not only possible to show that a given supply of money determines a certain relation between Income and interest (which we have expressed by the curve *LL*); it is also possible to say something about the shape of the curve. It will probably tend to be nearly horizontal on the left, and nearly vertical on the right. This is because there is (1) some minimum below which the rate of interest is unlikely to go, and (though Mr. Keynes does not stress this) there is (2) a maximum to the level of income which can possibly be financed with a given amount of money. If we like we can think of the curve as approaching these limits asymptotically (Figure 2).

Therefore, if the curve *IS* lies well to the right (either because of a strong inducement to invest or a strong propensity to consume), *P* will lie upon that part of the curve which is decidedly upward sloping, and the classical theory will be a good approximation, needing no more than the qualification which it has in fact received at the hands of the later Marshallians. An increase in the inducement to invest will raise the rate of interest, as in the classical theory, but it will also have some subsidiary effect in raising income, and therefore employment as well. (Mr. Keynes in 1936 is not the first Cambridge economist to have a temperate faith in Public Works.) But if the point *P* lies to the left of the *LL* curve, then the *special* form of Mr. Keynes' theory becomes valid. A rise in the schedule of the marginal efficiency of capital only increases employment, and does not raise the rate of interest at all. We are completely out of touch with the classical world.

The demonstration of this minimum is thus of central importance. It is so important that I shall venture to paraphrase the proof, setting it out in a rather different way from that adopted by Mr. Keynes.[5]

If the costs of holding money can be neglected, it will always be profitable to hold money rather than lend it out, if the rate of interest is not greater

[5]J. M. Keynes, *The General Theory of Employment, Interest and Money* (New York: Harcourt, Brace & Co., 1936), pp. 201–202.

than zero. Consequently the rate of interest must always be positive. In an extreme case, the shortest short-term rate may perhaps be nearly zero. But if so, the long-term rate must lie above it, for the long rate has to allow for the risk that the short rate may rise during the currency of the loan, and it should be observed that the short rate can only rise, it cannot fall.[6] This does not only mean that the long rate must be a sort of average of the probable short rates over its duration, and that this average must lie above the current short rate. There is also the more important risk to be considered, that the lender on long term may desire to have cash before the agreed date of repayment, and then, if the short rate has risen meanwhile, he may be involved in a substantial capital loss. It is this last risk which provides Mr. Keynes' "speculative motive" and which ensures that the rate for loans of indefinite duration (which he always has in mind as *the* rate of interest) cannot fall very near zero.[7]

It should be observed that this minimum to the rate of interest applies not only to one curve *LL* (drawn to correspond to a particular quantity of money) but to any such curve. If the supply of money is increased, the curve *LL* moves to the right (as the dotted curve in Figure 2), but the horizontal parts of the curve are almost the same. Therefore, again, it is this doldrum to the left of the diagram which upsets the classical theory. If *IS* lies to the right, then we can indeed increase employment by increasing the quantity of money; but if *IS* lies to the left, we cannot do so; merely monetary means will not force down the rate of interest any further.

So the General Theory of Employment is the Economics of Depression.

IV.

In order to elucidate the relation between Mr. Keynes and the "Classics," we have invented a little apparatus. It does not appear that we have exhausted the uses of that apparatus, so let us conclude by giving it a little run on its own.

With that apparatus at our disposal, we are no longer obliged to make

[6]It is just conceivable that people might become so used to the idea of very low short rates that they would not be much impressed by this risk; but it is very unlikely. For the short rate may rise, either because trade improves, and income expands; or because trade gets worse, and the desire for liquidity increases. I doubt whether a monetary system so elastic as to rule out both of these possibilities is really thinkable.

[7]Nevertheless something more than the "speculative motive" is needed to account for the system of interest rates. The shortest of all short rates must equal the relative valuation, at the margin, of money and such a bill; and the bill stands at a discount mainly because of the "convenience and security" of holding money — the inconvenience which may possibly be caused by not having cash immediately available. It is the chance that you may want to discount the bill which matters, not the chance that you will then have to discount it on unfavourable terms. The "precautionary motive," not the "speculative motive," is here dominant. But the prospective terms of rediscounting are vital, when it comes to the *difference* between short and long rates.

certain simplifications which Mr. Keynes makes in his exposition. We can reinsert the missing i in the third equation, and allow for any possible effect of the rate of interest upon saving; and, what is much more important, we can call in question the sole dependence of investment upon the rate of interest, which looks rather suspicious in the second equation. Mathematical elegance would suggest that we ought to have I and i in all three equations, if the theory is to be really General. Why not have them there like this:

$$M = L(I, i), \qquad I_x = C(I, i), \qquad I_x = S(I, i)?$$

Once we raise the question of Income in the second equation, it is clear that it has a very good claim to be inserted. Mr. Keynes is in fact only enabled to leave it out at all plausibly by his device of measuring everything in "wage-units," which means that he allows for changes in the marginal-efficiency-of-capital schedule when there is a change in the level of money wages, but that other changes in Income are deemed not to affect the curve, or at least not in the same immediate manner. But why draw this distinction? Surely there is every reason to suppose that an increase in the demand for consumers' goods, arising from an increase in employment, will often directly stimulate an increase in investment, at least as soon as an expectation develops that the increased demand will continue. If this is so, we ought to include I in the second equation, though it must be confessed that the effect of I on the marginal efficiency of capital will be fitful and irregular.

The Generalized General Theory can then be set out in this way. Assume first of all a given total money Income. Draw a curve CC showing the marginal efficiency of capital (in money terms) at that given Income; a

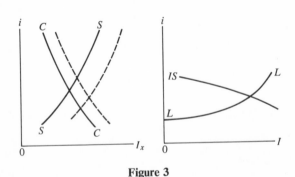

Figure 3

curve SS showing the supply curve of saving at that *given* Income (Figure 3). Their intersection will determine the rate of interest which makes savings equal to investment at that level of income. This we may call the "investment rate."

If Income rises, the curve SS will move to the right; probably CC will move to the right too. If SS moves more than CC, the investment rate of interest will fall; if CC more than SS, it will rise. (How much it rises and falls, however, depends upon the elasticities of the CC and SS curves.)

The IS curve (drawn on a separate diagram) now shows the relation between Income and the corresponding investment rate of interest. It has to be confronted (as in our earlier constructions) with an LL curve showing the relation between Income and the "money" rate of interest; only we can now generalize our LL curve a little. Instead of assuming, as before, that the supply of money is given, we can assume that there is a given monetary system — that up to a point, but only up to a point, monetary authorities will prefer to create new money rather than allow interest rates to rise. Such a generalised LL curve will then slope upwards only gradually — the elasticity of the curve depending on the elasticity of the monetary system (in the ordinary monetary sense).

As before, Income and interest are determined where the IS and LL curves intersect — where the investment rate of interest equals the money rate. Any change in the inducement to invest or the propensity to consume will shift the IS curve; any change in liquidity preference or monetary policy will shift the LL curve. If, as the result of such a change, the investment rate is raised above the money rate, Income will tend to rise; in the opposite case, Income will tend to fall; the extent to which Income rises or falls depends on the elasticities of the curves.[8]

When generalised in this way, Mr. Keynes' theory begins to look very like Wicksell's; this is of course hardly surprising.[9] There is indeed one special case where it fits Wicksell's construction absolutely. If there is "full employment" in the sense that any rise in Income immediately calls forth a rise in money wage rates; then it is *possible* that the CC and SS curves may be moved to the right to exactly the same extent, so that IS is horizontal. (I say possible, because it is not unlikely, in fact, that the rise in the wage level may create a presumption that wages will rise again later on; if so, CC will probably be shifted more than SS, so that IS will be upward sloping.) However that may be, if IS is horizontal, we do have a perfectly Wicksellian construction;[10] the investment rate becomes Wicksell's *natural rate*, for in this case it may be thought of as determined by real causes; if there is a

---

[8]Since $C(I, i) = S(I, i)$,

$$\frac{dI}{di} = -\frac{\partial S/\partial i - \partial C/\partial i}{\partial S/\partial I - \partial C/\partial I}.$$

The savings investment market will not be stable unless $\partial S/\partial i + (-\partial C/\partial i)$ is positive. I think we may assume that this condition is fulfilled.

If $\partial S/\partial i$ is positive, $\partial C/\partial i$ negative, $\partial S/\partial I$ and $\partial C/\partial I$ positive (the most probable state of affairs), we can say that the IS curve will be more elastic, the greater the elasticities of the CC and SS curves, and the larger is $\partial C/\partial I$ relatively to $\partial S/\partial I$. When $\partial C/\partial I > \partial S/\partial I$, the IS curve is upward sloping.

[9]Cf. Keynes, *General Theory, op. cit.*, p. 242.

[10]Cf. Myrdal, "Gleichgewichtsbegriff," in *Beiträge zur Geldtheorie*, ed. Hayek.

perfectly elastic monetary system, and the money rate is fixed below the natural rate, there is cumulative inflation; cumulative deflation if it is fixed above.

This, however, is now seen to be only one special case; we can use our construction to harbour much wider possibilities. If there is a great deal of unemployment, it is very likely that $\partial C/\partial I$ will be quite small; in that case *IS* can be relied upon to slope downwards. This is the sort of Slump Economics with which Mr. Keynes is largely concerned. But one cannot escape the impression that there may be other conditions when expectations are tinder, when a slight inflationary tendency lights them up very easily. Then $\partial C/\partial I$ may be large and an increase in Income tend to *raise* the investment rate of interest. In these circumstances, the situation is unstable at *any* given money rate; it is only an imperfectly elastic monetary system — a rising *LL* curve — that can prevent the situation getting out of hand altogether.

These, then, are a few of the things we can get out of our skeleton apparatus. But even if it may claim to be a slight extension of Mr. Keynes' similar skeleton, it remains a terribly rough and ready sort of affair. In particular, the concept of "Income" is worked monstrously hard; most of our curves are not really determinate unless something is said about the distribution of Income as well as its magnitude. Indeed, what they express is something like a relation between the price-system and the system of interest rates; and you cannot get that into a curve. Further, all sorts of questions about depreciation have been neglected; and all sorts of questions about the timing of the processes under consideration.

The General Theory of Employment is a useful book; but it is neither the beginning nor the end of Dynamic Economics.

FRANCO MODIGLIANI **14**

Liquidity preference and the theory of interest and money

Part I

1. Introduction

The aim of this paper is to reconsider critically some of the most important old and recent theories of the rate of interest and money and to formulate, eventually, a more general theory that will take into account the vital contributions of each analysis as well as the part played by different basic hypotheses.

The analysis will proceed according to the following plan:

I. We start out by briefly re-examining the Keynesian theory. In so doing our principal aim is to determine what is the part played in the Keynesian system by the "liquidity preference," on the one hand, and by the very special assumptions about the supply of labor, on the other. This will permit us to distinguish those results that are due to a real improvement of analysis from conclusions that depend on the difference of basic assumptions.

II. We then proceed to consider the properties of systems in which one or both Keynesian hypotheses are abandoned. We thus check our

Reprinted from *Econometrica*, Vol. 12 (January 1944), pp. 45–88, by permission of the publisher and author. [Footnotes expanded — *Eds.*]

previous results and test the logical consistency of the "classical" theory of money and the dichotomy of real and monetary economics.

III. From this analysis will gradually emerge our general theory of the rate of interest and money; and we can proceed to use this theory to test critically some recent "Keynesian" theories and more especially those formulated by J. R. Hicks in *Value and Capital*[1] and by A. P. Lerner in several articles.

IV. Finally, to make clear the conclusions that follow from our theory, we take issue in the controversial question as to whether the rate of interest is determined by "real" or by monetary factors.

In order to simplify the task, our analysis proceeds in general, under "static" assumptions; this does not mean that we neglect time but only that we assume the Hicksian (total) "elasticity of expectation" to be always unity. In Hicks's own words this means that "a change in current prices will change expected prices in the same direction and in the same proportion."[2] As shown by Oscar Lange, this implies that we assume the "expectation functions," connecting expected with present prices, to be homogeneous of the first degree.[3]

Since all the theories we examine or formulate in this paper are concerned with the determinants of equilibrium and not with the explanation of business cycles, this simplification, although it is serious in some respects, does not seem unwarranted.

2. Three alternative macrostatic systems

As a first step in the analysis, we must set up a system of equations describing the relation between the variables to be analyzed. In doing this we are at once confronted with a difficult choice between rigor and convenience; the only rigorous procedure is to set up a complete "Walrasian" system and to determine the equilibrium prices and quantities of each good: but this system is cumbersome and not well suited to an essentially literary exposition such as we intend to develop here. The alternative is to work with a reduced system: we must then be satisfied with the rather vague notions of "physical output," "investment," "price level," etc. In what follows we have chosen, in principle, the second alternative, but we shall check our conclusions with a more general system whenever necessary.

[1]J. R. Hicks, *Value and Capital* (Oxford: Oxford University Press, 1939), 331 pp.
[2]*Ibid.*, p. 205.
[3]Cf. O. Lange, "Say's Law: a Restatement and Criticism" in *Studies in Mathematical Economics and Econometrics*, edited by Lange, McIntyre, and Yntema (Chicago: The University of Chicago Press, 1942), pp. 67–68.

The equations of our system are:

$$M = L(r, Y), \tag{1}$$

$$I = I(r, Y), \tag{2}$$

$$S = S(r, Y), \tag{3}$$

$$S = I, \tag{4}$$

$$Y \equiv PX, \tag{5}$$

$$X = X(N), \tag{6}$$

$$W = X'(N)P. \tag{7}$$

The symbols have the following meaning: Y, money income; M, quantity of money in the system (regarded as given); r, rate of interest; S and I, saving and investment respectively, all measured in money; P, price level; N, aggregate employment; W, money wage rate; X, an index of physical output.[4] We may also define C, consumption measured in money, by the following identity:

$$C \equiv Y - I. \tag{8}$$

Identity (5) can be regarded as defining money income. There are so far 8 unknowns and only 7 equations; we lack the equation relating the wage rate and the supply of labor. This equation takes a substantially different form in the "Keynesian" system as compared with the "classical" systems.

In the classical systems the suppliers of labor (as well as the suppliers of all other commodities) are supposed to behave "rationally." In the same way as the supply of any commodity depends on the relative price of the commodity so the supply of labor is taken to depend not on the money wage rate, but on the real wage rate. Under the classical hypothesis, therefore, the last equation of the system takes the form:

$$N = F\left(\frac{W}{P}\right); \quad \text{or, in the inverse form:} \quad W = F^{-1}(N)P. \tag{9a}$$

The function F is a continuous function, although not necessarily monotonically increasing.

The Keynesian assumptions concerning the supply-of-labor schedule

[4]This system is partly taken from earlier writings on the subject. See especially O. Lange, "The Rate of Interest and the Optimum Propensity to Consume," *Economica*, N. S., V (Feb. 1938), 12–32, and J. R. Hicks, "Mr. Keynes and the 'Classics'; A Suggested Interpretation," *Econometrica*, V (April 1937), 147–159.

are quite different. In the Keynesian system, within certain limits to be specified presently, the supply of labor is assumed to be perfectly elastic at the historically ruling wage rate, say w_0. The limits mentioned above are given by equation (9a). For every value of W and P the corresponding value of N from (9a) gives the maximum amount of labor obtainable in the market. As long as the demand is less than this, the wage rate remains fixed as w_0. But as soon as all those who wanted to be employed at the ruling real wage rate w_0/P have found employment, wages become flexible upward. The supply of labor will not increase unless the money wage rate rises relative to the price level.

In order to write the last equation of the "Keynesian" form of our system, we must express this rather complicated hypothesis in functional form. Taking (9a) as a starting point, we may write:

$$W = \alpha w_0 + \beta F^{-1}(N)P, \qquad (9)$$

where α and β are functions of N, W, P, characterized by the following properties:

$$\alpha = 1, \qquad \beta = 0, \qquad \text{for} \qquad N \leqq N_0,$$
$$\alpha = 0, \qquad \beta = 1, \qquad \text{for} \qquad N > N_0, \qquad (10)$$

where N_0 is said to be "full employment." Equations and inequalities (10) thus state that, unless there is "full employment" ($N = N_0$), the wage rate is not really a variable of the system but a datum, a result of "history" or of "economic policy" or of both. Equation (9) then reduces to $W = w_0$. But after "full employment" has been reached at wage rate w_0, the supply of labor ceases to be perfectly elastic: W becomes a variable to be determined by the system and (9) becomes a "genuine" equation. We should add that, even in the "Keynesian" system, it is admitted that the wage rate will begin to be flexible downward before employment has reached the zero level: but in order not to complicate equation (9) still further we can, without serious harm, leave the hypothesis in its most stringent form.

For generality we may also use equation (9) as it now stands, as the "supply of labor" function of the "classical" theory. But instead of conditions (10) we have the identities (for all values of N)

$$\alpha \equiv 0, \qquad \beta \equiv 1. \qquad (11)$$

Some remarks are also necessary concerning the "demand for money" equation. According to the "quantity theory of money," the demand for money does not depend on the rate of interest but varies directly with money income. Under this hypothesis equation (1) reduces to

$$M = kY. \qquad (1a)$$

By properly combining the equations and conditions written above, we obtain three different systems which we will analyze in turn.

I.   a "Keynesian" system consisting of equations (1) to (7) and (9) and conditions (10).

II. a "crude classical" system consisting of equations (1a), (2) to (7), and (9), and identities (11).

III. a "generalized classical" system consisting of the equations listed under II but with (1a) replaced by (1).

3. A reconsideration of the Keynesian theory

In reconsidering the Keynesian system we shall essentially follow the lines suggested by J. R. Hicks in his fundamental paper, "Mr. Keynes and the 'Classics.' "[5] Our main task will be to clarify and develop his arguments, taking into account later theoretical developments.

Close consideration of the Keynesian system of equations [equations (1) to (7) and (9) to (10)] reveals that the first 4 equations contain only 4 unknowns and form a determinate system: the system of monetary equilibrium. We therefore begin by discussing its equations and its solution.

4. The transaction demand for money

In a free capitalistic economy, money serves two purposes: (a) it is a medium of exchange, (b) it is a form of holding assets. There are accordingly two sources of demand for money: the transaction demand for money and the demand for money as an asset. This is the fundamental proposition on which the theory of the rate of interest and money rests; it is therefore necessary to analyze closely each source of demand and the factors that determine it.

The transaction demand for money is closely connected with the concept of the income period. We may define the income period as the (typical) time interval elapsing between the dates at which members of the community are paid for services rendered. We shall assume for the moment that this income period is approximately the same for every individual and that it coincides with the expenditure period.[6]

Each individual begins the income period with a certain income arising out of direct services rendered or out of property and with assets (physical and nonphysical) having a certain market value. In his endeavor to reach the highest level of satisfaction he is confronted with two sets of decisions:

[5]*Econometrica*, V (April 1937), 147–159.
[6]This means, for instance, that people are required by custom or contract to pay within the income period for what they have consumed in the period (rent, grocery bill, etc.) or else must rely on "consumers' credit."

(a) he must decide what part of his income he will spend on consumption and what part he will save, (b) he must determine how to dispose of his assets.

The first set of decisions presents no special difficulty of analysis. On the basis of his tastes, his income, and market prices he will make a certain plan of expenditure to be carried out in the course of the income period. The amount of money that is necessary for individuals to carry out their expenditure plans is the *transaction demand for money by consumers*, as of the beginning of the period. The average transaction demand, on the other hand, depends on the rate at which expenditure takes place within the period.[7]

The difference between the individual's money income and the amount he decides to spend in the fashion discussed above is the money value of his savings (dissavings) for the income period. It represents the net increment in the value of his assets.

5. The demand for money as an asset

Having made his consumption-saving plan, the individual has to make decisions concerning the assets he owns. These assets, let us note, consist of property carried over from the preceding income period *plus current savings*.

There are essentially three forms in which people can keep their assets: (a) money, (b) securities,[8] and (c) physical assets.

We shall for the moment eliminate the third alternative by distinguishing between entrepreneurial and nonentrepreneurial decisions. We consider as entrepreneurs individuals who hold assets in physical form; decisions concerning the acquisition or disposal of physical assets will accordingly be treated as entrepreneurial decisions and will be analyzed in connection with the schedule of the propensity to invest [equation (3)]. An individual's decision to acquire directly physical assets (say a house) or to reinvest profits in his enterprise can be split into two separate decisions, a decision to lend (to himself) and a decision to increase his entrepreneurial risk by borrowing (from himself).

We are therefore concerned here exclusively with decisions concerning nonphysical assets and with those factors that influence the choice between the first two alternatives. Our problem is to determine whether there is any reason for individuals to wish to hold some or all of their assets in the form of money and thus to demand money over and above the quantity they need for transactions.

[7]Thus if expenditure should proceed at an approximately even rate, it would be one-half the initial demand.

[8]Under the name of securities we include both fixed-income-bearing certificates and common stocks or equities. From the strictly economic point of view, common stocks should perhaps be considered as a form of holding physical assets. For institutional reasons, however, equities have very special properties which make them in many respects more similar to bonds than to physical assets.

In this respect there is little to add to the exhaustive treatment that this subject has received in recent literature.[9]

There are two properties that all assets, whether physical or not, share in different degrees: liquidity and risk. Following a criterion particularly stressed by Jacob Marschak, we shall define liquidity of an asset in terms of the perfection of the market in which it is traded. An asset is liquid if this market is perfect, i.e., an individual's decision to buy or sell does not affect the price finitely; it is illiquid in the opposite case. It is riskless if the price at which it sells is constant or practically so; it is risky if the price fluctuates widely.

Securities clearly share with money the property of being highly liquid assets. Where there is an organized market, securities will not be significantly inferior to money in this respect. They have, however, two clear drawbacks in comparison with cash:

a. They are not a medium of exchange. Assets generally accrue in the form of money through savings, and a separate transaction is necessary to transform them into securities. This transaction involves both subjective and objective costs.

b. They are more risky than money since their market price is not constant. Even the "safest" type of securities, on which the risk of default can be neglected, fluctuates in price as the rate of interest moves. There are, it is true, some types of loans for which this last risk can be neglected, namely very-short-term loans. Let us assume, for the sake of precision, that the money market is open only on the first day of the income period; then the shortest type of loans will be those that mature at the end of said period. These types of assets will not be subject to the risk mentioned under (b) since, by assumption, the rate of interest cannot change while they are outstanding.[10]

It is just for this type of assets, however, that the disadvantage mentioned under (a), namely the cost of investment, weighs more heavily, for the yield they promise for the very short duration of the loan can only be small, so that even a moderate cost is sufficient to wipe it out. If, as is likely, the cost of investment does not rise in proportion to the amount invested, then short loans may be an interesting investment for large sums, but not so for small investors. Thus, if this were the only possible form of investment, we should expect that any fall in the rate of interest, not accompanied by a corresponding fall in the cost of investing, would induce a growing number of potential investors to keep their assets in the form of money, rather than

[9]See, for instance, J. R. Hicks, *Value and Capital, op. cit.*, Chapters 13 and 14 and *passim;* J. M. Keynes, *The General Theory of Employment, Interest and Money* (New York: Harcourt, Brace and Company, 1936), 403 pp.; Mabel Timlin, *Keynesian Economics* ([Toronto:] University of Toronto Press, 1942), Chapters 5 and 6; etc.

[10]Even if this assumption were relaxed, the possible fluctuations in the rate of interest would be negligible and the extent to which they would affect the present value of the securities mentioned above could be disregarded.

securities; that is to say, we should expect a fall in the rate of interest to increase the demand for money as an asset.

In this respect, securities of longer maturity would appear to be superior, since the yield to be gathered by holding them until maturity is larger, while the cost of acquiring them need not be different. But as the importance of the cost element decreases, the importance of the risk element grows. As is well known, a given change in the rate of interest will affect most the present value of those bonds whose maturity is furthest away. If the only reason for owning assets were to earn the income they produce, these price fluctuations would not be so important. For, as long as the owner is in a position to hold the asset until maturity, there would be only a potential loss, a loss of better opportunities. There can be little doubt, however, that for a large part of the community the main reason for holding assets is as a reserve against contingencies. A form of assets whose value is not certain must be, *ceteris paribus*, inferior to one whose value is certain, namely money.

This very fact, besides, gives an additional reason why bonds of longer maturity should be a less safe form of holding assets. For there is much less certainty about faraway income periods than there is about the near future and the possibility that one will have to realize the assets before their maturity, if any, increases accordingly; while, on the other hand, it becomes increasingly difficult to make reliable forecasts about the level of the rate of interest and the future market value of the assets.

Securities, on the other hand, are clearly superior to money in that they yield an income. The ruling rate of interest measures the remuneration to be obtained by accepting the drawbacks and assuming the risks that are characteristic of securities as compared with money. Or, to look at it from another point of view, it measures the cost of holding money instead of securities in terms of forgone income. Thus a fall in the rate of interest has, in any event, the effect of making cash cheaper and hence more attractive as a form of holding assets.

In addition, several other reasons can be mentioned that cause a low rate of interest to discourage the holding of securities. In the first place, the risk element involved in holding securities becomes more pronounced when the rate of interest is low, for a smaller fall in the capital value of the asset is sufficient to wipe out the income already earned by holding the asset. Thus, for instance, the smaller the rate of interest, the smaller is the *percentage change* in the rate itself necessary to absorb the yield obtained by holding the asset a given length of time. Again, it has been pointed out by some authors that, as the rate of interest becomes lower, there is some ground to expect that possible movements will be predominantly in the direction of an increase and therefore unfavorable to the holders of securities.

In conclusion then, the lower the rate of interest, the larger will be the number of owners of assets who will prefer to hold these assets in the form of money for the income period; the demand for money to hold (as distinguished from money to spend, previously considered) or demand for money as an asset is a decreasing function of the rate of interest. Denoting this demand by D_a, we can write

$$D_a = D_a(r)$$

for the schedule of demand for money to hold.

What can we say about the characteristics of this function? It must clearly be a monotonically decreasing function of the rate of interest; in addition, however, it must have, in the author's opinion, two important properties:

In the first place, there must be some value of r, say r', such that $D_a(r) = 0$ for $r \geqq r'$. For there must be, for every individual, some minimum net yield per income period that will induce him to part entirely with money as an asset. Hence, if he can find some type of securities such that by holding them for a given number of income periods he expects to obtain a net yield equal to or larger than the minimum, his demand for money to hold will fall to zero.[11]

Since this is true for every individual, there must also be some system of interest rates which is sufficient to reduce the aggregate demand to zero.

The second characteristic is more peculiar. Since securities are an "inferior" way of holding assets, it is generally recognized that there must be some minimum rate of interest, say r'', at which nobody will be willing to hold nonphysical assets except in the form of money. When this level is reached, the demand for money to hold becomes "absolute" and the rate of interest cannot fall any lower. Hence, $D_a'(r) = \infty$ for $r \gtreqqless r''$.

[11]Let i_0 denote the minimum yield (per income period) at which an individual is ready to hold no assets in the form of money during the period. We may also assume, without being unrealistic, that this minimum yield is the same for each income period. Suppose that the securities which, in his opinion, present the best opportunity are expected by him to produce a net yield (including capital appreciation) $i_0', i_1', \cdots, i_n'$ in periods 1, 2, $\cdots$, n. He will be induced to invest provided there is some value of n for which

$$(1 + i_0')(1 + i_1')\cdots(1 + i_n') \geqq (1 + i_0)^n.$$

From M. Timlin's treatment of this subject (*Keynesian Economics, op. cit.*, Chapter 3) it would appear that marginal holders should expect any security to yield the same net income, at least during the current period. This however is correct only if the expectations of all dealers about the future short rates of interest agree with the market expectation as shown by the forward rates established in the market. [The forward rate for the nth income period ahead can always be found by comparing the price of riskless securities maturing n periods ahead with those maturing $(n + 1)$ periods ahead.] But if an individual believes this forward rate to be too high he may acquire the security at once even though he may expect that it will yield in the current period less than some other security. For, assuming that he is right, he will be able to realize his capital gain as soon as the market recognizes its error and there is no telling when this will occur. If he should wait until the next income period and hold for the current one the asset that promises to pay a higher yield, he may lose his chance of making the expected capital gain.

6. The demand for money: conclusion

We have so far discussed the demand for money as an asset and the transaction demand for money by individuals; to complete the analysis we must consider the transaction demand by firms. In principle, the same considerations apply here as were stated in connection with individuals' transaction demand. Firms, as well as individuals, have an institutional expenditure-receipt pattern and, given this pattern, the average demand depends on the volume of transactions. We must however recognize that, in the case of firms, generalizations are less meaningful since their expenditure and receipt flows are generally less certain and uniform than for individuals.

Then, too, we must admit that we may have oversimplified the consumers' transaction demand by assuming that individuals have a rigorously defined plan of expenditure at the beginning of the income period. It may very well be that under more realistic conditions they will desire to carry some cash above the amount they plan to spend as a reserve and to avoid ending the period with a zero cash balance. This however does not substantially affect our argument. All we are interested in establishing is that, within an institutional framework, there must be for any given volume (value) of transactions a certain amount of money that is necessary to carry them out. This amount clearly depends on such institutional factors as the length of the income period and the prevailing customs as to the settlement of current purchases by firms and must therefore be substantially independent of the level of the rate of interest. The level of the rate of interest influences decisions concerning the disposition of assets, and *money needed to carry out transactions planned for the coming income period is not an asset*. In particular, there must be some level of the rate of interest that is sufficient to reduce to zero the demand for money to hold, and hence the total demand to its minimum institutional level which depends on the volume of transactions. As the rate of interest rises above this level, the demand for money will be substantially unaffected and will depend exclusively on the level of money income.

On the basis of these considerations we may, in a first approximation, split the total demand for money into two parts: the demand for money to hold, $D_a(r)$, and the demand for money to spend or for transactions, $D_T(Y)$; and write

$$L(r, Y) = D_a(r) + D_T(Y) = M. \qquad (12)$$

This is not really necessary for our argument, but is very useful since it will constantly remind us of the two sources of demand for money and it will permit us to analyze more conveniently the part played by each variable.

With this in mind we shall find it useful to consider the functioning of the money market in which decisions concerning the disposition of non-physical assets are carried out.

7. The money market and the short-run equilibrium
of the rate of interest

There are two ways of looking at this market: (a) in terms of flows (savings and net borrowing) and (b) in terms of stocks. It is from this latter point of view that we shall consider it at this moment.

The supply in this market consists of the stock that is not needed for transactions. On the basis of our first approximation (12), this supply, denoted by S_a, will be

$$S_a = M - D_T(Y),$$

and is determined for any value of the money income and the fixed supply of money.

A position of equilibrium in the money market is reached when a system of interest rates is established at which dealers are willing to hold for the income period all the available supply. Or, from a different angle, the system of interest rates is determined by the price (in terms of foregone income) that dealers are willing to pay to hold assets in the form of money for the coming income period.

This can easily be translated into the usual Marshallian supply and demand apparatus, provided we replace the system of interest rates by a single rate r, as shown in Figure 1.

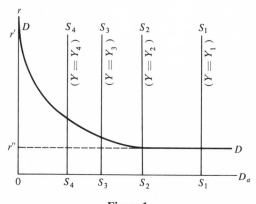

Figure 1

DD is the demand curve for money to hold, sloping downward and to the right (when the price, the rate of interest, rises, the demand falls, as in the case of ordinary commodities). The vertical lines are various supply curves corresponding to different values of Y and the fixed value of M. As the income increases, the supply falls: hence

$$Y_4 > Y_3 > Y_2 > \cdots.$$

Since a fall in supply causes a rise in price, the graph shows clearly that equation (1) gives r as an increasing function of Y.

The characteristics of the D_a function described above are shown in the graph. We noted that, for $r \geqq r'$ the demand falls to zero; hence the graph of DD joins the vertical axis and coincides with it.

On the other hand, when the rate of interest falls to the level r'', the demand for money to hold becomes infinitely elastic. Any increase in the supply of money to hold now fails to affect the rate of interest, for the owners of the extra supply will either desire to hold this in the form of cash; or else they will find some owners of securities, who, being just indifferent as to holding cash or securities, will be willing to sell without any necessity for bidding up the price of securities (lowering the rate of interest). Thus, in Figure 1, when the interest rate r'' is reached, the graph of DD becomes parallel to the D_a axis; the income corresponding to r'' cannot be more than Y_2; but if income should fall below Y_2 it would not change the interest rate.[12] This situation that plays such an important role in Keynes's *General Theory* will be referred to as the "Keynesian case."

In the diagram we have assumed that there is a single rate of interest r, instead of a whole system of rates for loans of different duration. While it may be assumed that in principle all the rates tend to move in the same direction, we must bear in mind that the extent to which a change in the supply of money changes the rates on loans of different maturities depends on the character of interest expectations.

A change in the supply will necessarily affect the short rates (unless the short rate has already reached its minimum). But the extent to which it will affect longer rates depends on the relation between the current spot rate and expected future rates.

To denote the relationship between current and expected rates we may again use the Hicksian elasticity of expectation. If this elasticity is unity, expected short rates move in the same direction and in the same proportion as the spot rate; if it is less than unity, a given percentage change in short rates leads to a smaller percentage change in expected rates; and vice versa for elasticity larger than one.

If the expectations about future short rates are based predominantly on the current shorter rates, then the elasticity of expectation tends toward one and the whole system of rates moves in close conformity. But if dealers have rigid expectations based on different elements, the elasticity of expectation will be low and a change in short rates will affect longer rates only to the extent that some of the discount rates, which determine the present value of the assets, are changed.

In practice we may expect that this elasticity will be larger than zero

---

[12]From equation (1) we obtain $dr/dY = -L_Y/L_r$ where the subscripts denote partial derivatives. Hence $dr/dY = 0$ if $|L_r| = \infty$.

and smaller than one and that it will be larger for the rates expected in the near future.[13]

To the extent that this is true there will be two reasons why rates on loans of shorter maturity should move in closer agreement with the very short rate: (a) because they are more affected by a change in the current short rate, (b) because the other future short rates (of which they are an average) are more influenced by such a change.

These necessary qualifications do not alter our previous conclusions concerning the determination of equilibrium in the money market. The equilibrium system of interest rates is determined in each period by the condition that the supply of money to hold, which (given M) depends on the transaction demand for money and hence on income, be equal to the demand for money to hold. We may therefore proceed to draw the graph of equation (1) $M = L(r, Y)$. This is the LL curve of Figure 3. Any point on this curve shows the equilibrium value of r corresponding to a value of Y and the fixed value of M: it shows therefore positions of possible equilibrium in the money market. We must prove next that only one point on this curve is consistent with the long-run equilibrium of the system.

8. Saving, investment, and the IS function

The first part of our system yields a second relationship between interest and income. Making use of equations (2) and (3) and the equilibrium condition (4) we obtain: $I(r, Y) = S(r, Y)$. In order to gain some idea of the shape of this curve we may again make use of a graphical method illustrated in Figure 2.

Figure 2-B is the graph of equation (3). Since $\partial S / \partial r$ is usually consid-

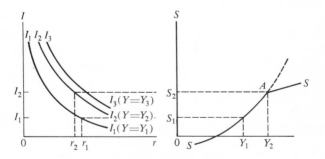

Figure 2-A   Figure 2-B

[13]Denoting by $r_1, r_2, \cdots, r_n$ the short rate of interest anticipated for periods $1, 2, \cdots, n$, we may expect that

$$\frac{\partial r_1}{\partial r_0} > \frac{\partial r_2}{\partial r_0} > \cdots > \frac{\partial r_n}{\partial r_0}.$$

ered small and of unknown sign we have simplified the drawing by eliminating r. This curve describes the relationship between money income and the proportion of it that people choose not to consume. Its position depends on the value of the fixed money wage rate w_0: given the wage rate, to any level of money income there corresponds a certain real income and price level and, therefore, a certain level of money saving. In this diagram Y_2 denotes the highest money income that can be reached with the money wage rate w_0, and A is the full employment relationship between saving and income.

The straight line beginning at A gives the relationship between money income and money saving once full employment has been reached and the second part of condition (10) replaces the first.[14] We have then what is usually called inflation: a real income cannot change but money income can rise to any level. As all prices rise simultaneously the amount of real income saved is unchanged while its money value rises in the same proportion as the price level and money income.[15] The dotted curved line, on the other hand, gives a potential relation between S and I if it were possible to raise the real income above the full employment level.

Figure 2-A is the graph of equation (2). Each curve in this graph shows the amount of investment that would be undertaken at different levels of the rate of interest and for a fixed value of the income. To larger values of Y correspond investment curves higher and to the right.

Since the vertical scale is the same in both Figure 2-A and Figure 2-B, we may use the following method to find the shape of $S(Y) = I(r, Y)$: For any value of Y, say Y_1, the corresponding amount of saving, S_1, can be read from the SS curve. But in equilibrium $S = I$, hence we can draw a line parallel to the Y axis at height S_1 and prolong it until it intersects the investment curve of Figure 2-A corresponding to the income Y_1. We may thus find the rate of interest r_1 that corresponds to the given income Y_1.

The character of the relationship between r and Y that emerges from this diagram cannot be established a priori as in the case of the LL curve discussed before. For, as Y increases, S in Figure 2-B increases too, but the corresponding value of r in Figure 2-A may increase or decrease. It all depends on the way the change in income affects the position of the investment curves. If the increase in income tends to raise the desire to save more than the desire to invest, the rate of interest will fall; in the opposite case it

---

[14]This line is the continuation of the radius vector from the origin to A.

[15]This is strictly correct only if inflation does not provoke any permanent redistribution of income; or if the redistribution does not affect the aggregate propensity to save. Since wages rise with prices we can exclude redistributions from working class to nonworking class. But we cannot exclude redistribution from fixed-income receivers (especially owners of securities) to profits. It is difficult to say whether this will change sensibly the aggregate propensity to save; it is probably a good approximation to assume that the effect will be negligible.

will rise.[16] This last possibility is, in our opinion, unlikely to occur, but it may materialize when entrepreneurs are highly optimistic and the existing equipment is already working at capacity.

The relationship between r and Y emerging from equations (2) and (3) and the equilibrium condition (4) is shown as the IS curve of Figure 3. In

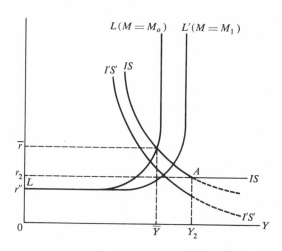

Figure 3

the normal case it will slope downward and to the right as in this diagram, but it is conceivable that, at least in a certain range, it may slope upward to the right. In this case $S_Y < I_Y$ and it is usually assumed that the equilibrium of the system will be unstable (and neutral if $S_Y = I_Y$). We shall see, however, that, with inelastic money supply, the negative slope of the IS curve is a sufficient but not necessary condition for stability.

The IS curve must also have another important property. In Figure 3, A denotes the equilibrium relationship between full-employment income (Y_2) and rate of interest (r_2). Money income cannot rise above the full-employment level denoted by Y_2 except through inflation, i.e., if wages and prices rise in the same proportion as income. As the stage of inflationary prices and wage increases is reached, the "real" value of investment that it pays to undertake at any interest rate is unchanged since yields and costs

[16]From $S(r, Y) = I(r, Y)$ we obtain $dr/dY = (S_Y - I_Y)/(I_r - S_r)$, where the subscripts denote partial derivatives. Since $I_r - S_r$ may be expected to be negative, we have $dr/dY \lesseqgtr 0$ as $S_Y \gtreqless I_Y$.

change in the same proportion.[17] The money value of profitable investments, on the other hand, rises proportionally to prices and money income. As we have seen above, the same will be true of money savings. It follows that inflationary increases in income raise saving and investment in the same proportion and must therefore leave the equilibrium value of the rate of interest unchanged at the full-employment level r_2. It is for this reason that in Figure 3, to the right of A, the IS curve becomes parallel to the income axis. The dotted curved line beyond A is again the hypothetical relationship between r and Y if it were possible to raise real income above the full-employment level (and if the wage rate should remain unchanged at the level w_0).

9. The money market and the determinants of monetary equilibrium

We may now finally proceed to consider the process by which the equilibrium of the system is established. For this purpose we must once more revert to the money market which we must, this time, consider in terms of flows rather than in terms of stocks.

In Section 5 we have seen that the rate of interest is established in the money market by the condition that supply of and demand for the stock of money to hold must be equal. This condition is sufficient to determine a position of short-run equilibrium, i.e., a position of equilibrium for the income period. We must now consider under what conditions this level of the rate of interest will also represent a position of long-run equilibrium. As in the textbook analysis of demand and supply, a position of long-run equilibrium is characterized by the fact that neither price nor quantity (demanded and supplied) tend to change any further. In the present case a position of long-run equilibrium will be reached only when the rate of interest does not tend to change from one income period to the other and this in turn is possible only if the stock of money to hold remains constant in time.

Now in each income period people increase their assets by current savings; the money thus saved, since it is not needed for transactions, constitutes an increase in the supply of money to hold. Borrowing, on the other hand, automatically decreases the supply of money to hold by taking cash out of the money market and putting it into active circulation again, through

[17]Following the example of Mr. Keynes we may define the marginal effiiency of an asset as the discount rate that makes the sum of the expected marginal discounted yields equal to the marginal cost of the asset. The expected yields need not all be equal since they depend on the expected net physical yield as well as on expected future prices; and neither is necessarily constant in time. But the expected physical yield does not depend on prices; and, owing to our "static assumption" of unit elasticity of expectation, expected prices change in the same proportion as present prices. Therefore the summation of the yields changes in the same proportion as marginal cost and so does the aggregate value of investments having marginal efficiency equal to or larger than r_2. Under unit elasticity of expectation a given change in all present prices does not modify entrepreneurs' production plans.

expenditure on investments. If net saving exceeds net borrowing then, on balance, the supply of money to hold will increase above the level of the previous period, say $D_{a \cdot 0}$. But at the old rate of interest (r_0) people will not want to hold the extra supply; they will therefore try to purchase securities and thus will lower the rate of interest. If, on the other hand, at the interest rate r_0 borrowers desire to borrow in the period more than the current amount of money savings, they must induce dealers in the money market to reduce the demand for money as an asset below the previous level $D_{a \cdot 0}$; and this is possible only if the rate of interest rises. There are then three possibilities. (The subscripts 0 and 1 denote quantities in periods zero and one, respectively.)

(1) $S_1 > I_1$: then $D_{a \cdot 1} > D_{a \cdot 0}$ and the rate of interest falls.

(2) $S_1 = I_1$: here $D_{a \cdot 1} = D_{a0}$ and the rate of interest is unchanged.

(3) $S_1 < I_1$: then $D_{a \cdot 1} < D_{a \cdot 0}$ and the rate of interest rises.

Recalling our definition of long-run equilibrium, we see at once that only situation (2) satisfies it. In equilibrium then, both demand for and supply of the stock of money to hold and demand for and supply of the flow of saving must be equal.[18] In addition, however, it is necessary that the flows of saving and of borrowing be themselves constant in time. This is possible only if two conditions hold: (a) The borrowing that occurs must be equal to the amount of investment that entrepreneurs wish to undertake at the given rate of interest and income level. The relationship between I_1, r_1, and Y_1 must be described by a point on the corresponding curve of Figure 2-A. (b) The income (and the rate of interest) must be as large as is required to induce people to go on saving an amount S_1. The relationship between Y_1, S_1, and r_1 must be described by a point lying on the curve of Figure 2-B. But if conditions (a) and (b) are satisfied the relationship between Y and r will be described by a point lying on the *IS* curve of Figure 3. Thus a position of full equilibrium must be represented by a point lying at the same time on the *LL* curve (denoting equilibrium between demand for and supply of the stock of money to hold) and on the *IS* curve (denoting equality and constancy in time of the inflow and outflow of cash in the money market); hence it must be given by the intersection of these two curves.

This is shown in Figure 3 where the equilibrium values of r and Y, thus determined, are denoted by $\bar{r}$ and $\bar{Y}$. Analytically this corresponds to the simultaneous solution of the two relationships between the income and the rate of interest obtained from equations (1), (2), (3), and (4): $M = L(r, Y)$ and $S(r, Y) = I(r, Y)$.

---

[18]The classical example of the level of water in a reservoir fits this case perfectly. The rate of interest, like the level of the water, can be constant only if inflow and outflow are equal.

10. A dynamic model of the Keynesian theory and the stability of equilibrium

So far our analysis has apparently been "timeless"[19] since it was based on the system of equations of Section 2, in which time does not appear explicitly. A close examination of the last sections, and especially Sections 7 and 9, will reveal, however, that dynamic elements have gradually slipped into our analysis, thanks to the device of "long- and short-run equilibrium," the oldest and simplest device of developing a dynamic theory with a static apparatus. Actually the criterion that distinguishes short- from long-run equilibrium is essentially a dynamic one: namely, the length of time that is required for certain decisions to be carried out, or, more generally, for certain causes to show their effects.

In our case, the equilibrium of the "money market" is a condition of short-run equilibrium (that determines the rate of interest for each period) because it is the result of decisions that can be carried into effect immediately. The condition saving = investment, on the other hand, is a condition of long-run equilibrium because the equality of *ex ante* saving and investment cannot be brought about instantaneously. This is a different way of stating the familiar proposition that the multiplier takes time to work out its full effect. This well-known fact is in turn explained essentially by the existence of a fundamental time lag: the lag between the time when income is earned and the time when it becomes available for expenditure. In the economic systems in which we live, people are usually paid for services already rendered. The income earned (or produced) in a period is the value of services rendered which will be paid for at the end of the normal income period; while the income available for expenditure represents payment for services rendered in the previous period. Decisions as to spending and saving can refer only to the disposable income, and are essentially motivated by it, even though income earned may have some influence.

This explains why the graph of the *IS* curve, unlike the *LL* curve, describes not instantaneous relationships but only possible positions of long-run equilibrium. When the two curves intersect we have a position of full equilibrium since both short- and long-run conditions are satisfied.

It will therefore be useful at this point to give explicit recognition to the dynamic elements that form the basis of our approach. This is the purpose of the following system of difference equations which may be considered as the simplest dynamic model of our theory.

$$M = L(r_t, Y_{d \cdot t}), \tag{2.1}$$

$$I_t = I(r_t, Y_{d \cdot t}), \tag{2.2}$$

$$S_t = S(r_t, Y_{d \cdot t}), \tag{2.3}$$

---

[19]The word "timeless" has been used here to avoid confusion since the word "static" has already been used to denote the assumption of homogeneity of the first degree of the "expectations functions."

$$Y_{d \cdot t} = C_t + S_t, \tag{2.4}$$

$$Y_t = C_t + I_t, \tag{2.5}$$

$$Y_{d \cdot t} = Y_{t-1}. \tag{2.6}$$

In this system Y denotes income earned and Y_d income disposable. This is a new variable to which corresponds the new equation (2.6). The remaining equations of the system are unchanged.

By repeated substitution the system reduces to the two equations

$$Y_t = Y_{t-1} - S_t + I_t = Y_{t-1} - S(Y_{t-1}, r_t) + I(Y_{t-1}, r_t),$$

$$M = L(r_t, Y_{t-1}).$$

Solving the second equation for r_t and substituting in the first, we obtain a single equation of the form: $Y_t = f(Y_{t-1})$ which determines the time path of the income. By similar procedure we obtain the time sequence of the other variables.

If the system is stable, each variable approaches some definite value which it will maintain in time until there occurs some change in the form of the functional relationship or in some parameter (M or w_0). Equation (2.1) is again the "equation of the money market" that determines the value of r for any period; but we have a position of long-run equilibrium only when $r_t = r_{t-1}$. And this implies $Y_t = Y_{d \cdot t} = Y_{t-1}$ and therefore $S_t = I_t$.

The importance of this system is not limited to the fact that it defines rigorously concepts that were loosely used in our previous analysis. It serves also another important purpose: namely it permits us to determine the conditions of stability for the system.

Following the usual method, we proceed to expand equations (2.1) to (2.3) by Taylor series around the equilibrium values neglecting all terms of degree higher than one. We then obtain:

$$0 = L_r \dot{r}_t + L_Y \dot{Y}_{t-1} + \cdots,$$

$$I_t = I(\bar{r}, \bar{Y}) + I_r \dot{r}_t + I_Y \dot{Y}_{t-1} + \cdots,$$

$$S_t = S(\bar{r}, \bar{Y}) + S_r \dot{r}_t + S_Y \dot{Y}_{t-1}.$$

Subscripts denote partial derivatives taken around the equilibrium values $(\bar{r}, Y)$ and $r_t = \dot{r}_t - \bar{r}$, $\dot{Y}_t = Y_t - \bar{Y}$. By making use of (4) and (5) and by repeated substitution we obtain the following linear difference equation with constant coefficients:

$$\dot{Y}_t = \dot{Y}_{t-1}\left[1 + \frac{L_Y}{L_r}(S_r - I_r) + I_Y - S_Y\right].$$

The solution of this equation takes the form: $\dot{Y} = \kappa \lambda^t$ or $Y = (Y_0 - \bar{Y})\lambda^t$, since $\dot{Y}_0 = Y_0 - \bar{Y} = \kappa$. Y_0 is determined by the initial conditions and

$$\lambda = 1 + \frac{L_Y}{L_r}(S_r - I_r) + I_Y - S_Y.$$

The stability condition is $|\lambda| < 1$; in the present case this reduces to

$$-\frac{L_Y}{L_r} - \frac{r}{S_r - I_r} < \frac{I_Y - S_Y}{S_r - I_r} < -\frac{L_Y}{L_r}. \tag{2.7}$$

Since the middle term is the slope of the IS curve and the right-hand term is the slope of the LL curve, the right-hand condition has a very clear graphical meaning. Stability requires that the slope of the IS curve be algebraically smaller than the slope of the LL curve. The slope of the LL curve cannot be negative ($L_Y > 0$, $L_r \geqq 0$). Also general economic considerations suggest that $S_r - I_r > 0$. Hence this condition is necessarily satisfied if $I_Y - S_Y < 0$, i.e., when the IS curve falls from left to right. But this is not necessary. Stability is also possible when the IS curve rises in the neighborhood of the equilibrium point as long as it cuts the LL curve from its concave toward its convex side.[20]

If the stability conditions are satisfied, the variables approach their equilibrium values, which are the same as those obtained by solving the static system of Section 2. In the opposite case they diverge more and more from these values in a process of cumulative contraction or expansion. In the same way, a change in some of the data will lead to a new stable equilibrium if the new functions satisfy the conditions written above.

It is interesting to note that, as long as the money supply is inelastic, the system must always have at least one stable solution since eventually the LL curve becomes perpendicular to the horizontal axis and hence its slope must become larger than the slope of the IS curve.

11. The determinants of real equilibrium

It is now time to consider the role of the second part of the system in the determination of equilibrium. Equations (5), (6), and (7) *explain* the forces that determine the real variables of the system: physical output, employment, real wage rate.[21]

The most important of these equations is (7), which states the conditions of equilibrium in the production of goods whether for consumption or for investment.[22] Production will be extended up to the point at which the given and fixed money wage rate w_0 is equal to the marginal net product of labor, or, if we prefer, up to the point at which price equals marginal labor

[20]It is only as $L_r \to \infty$ (demand for money to hold infinitely elastic, LL curve parallel to the horizontal axis) that the condition $I_Y - S_Y < 0$ becomes necessary for equilibrium. This holds equally if the supply of money is infinitely elastic for this has the same effect as $L_r = \infty$.

[21]The price level is also necessary to determine the real wage rate, given the money wage rate W.

[22]The equilibrium price of each type of physical asset is found by capitalizing a series of expected marginal yields at the current rate of interest. The expected yields of the marginal unit need not be equal in each period.

cost.[23] This assumes that the only variable factor is labor and the quantity of equipment is fixed; a condition that is approximately satisfied in the case we are considering. Eliminating equation (5) by substitution into (7) we can reduce this part of the system to two equations in the two unknowns X and N, where X' is used for dX/dN:

$$W_0 = X'(N) \frac{Y}{X}, \qquad X = X(N).$$

Since the money income is determined exclusively by the *monetary* part of the system, the price level depends only on the amount of output. If, at any given price level, the fixed wage is less than the marginal product of labor, the forces of competition lead to an expansion of employment and output which forces prices down. This lowers the marginal product of labor until it becomes equal to the wage rate. If the wage rate exceeded the marginal product of labor, output and employment would contract, which would force prices up. We see clearly from Figure 3 that the amount of employment thus determined will, in general, not be "full employment"; that is, unless the LL curve intersects the IS curve at (Y_2, r_2) or to the right of it.

12. Underemployment equilibrium and liquidity preference

This last result deserves closer consideration. It is usually considered as one of the most important achievements of the Keynesian theory that it explains the consistency of economic equilibrium with the presence of involuntary unemployment. It is, however, not sufficiently recognized that, except in a limiting case to be considered later, this result is due entirely to the assumption of "rigid wages"[24] and not to the Keynesian liquidity preference. Systems with rigid wages share the common property that the equilibrium value of the "real" variables is determined essentially by monetary conditions rather than by "real" factors (e.g., quantity and efficiency of existing equipment, relative preference for earning and leisure, etc.). The monetary conditions are sufficient to determine money income and, under fixed wages and given technical conditions, to each money income there corresponds a definite equilibrium level of employment. This equilibrium level does not tend to coincide with full employment except by mere chance, since there is no economic mechanism that insures this coincidence. There may be unemployment in the sense that more people would be willing to work at the current real wage rate than are actually employed; but in a free capitalistic economy production is guided by prices and not by desires and since the

---

[23]This is a sufficient condition under assumption of perfect competition; the modifications necessary in the case of monopolies cannot be considered here.

[24]The expression "rigid wages" refers to the infinite elasticity of the supply curve of labor when the level of employment is below "full."

money wage rate is rigid, this desire fails to be translated into an economic stimulus.

In order to show more clearly that wage rigidities and not liquidity preference explain underemployment equilibrium we may consider the results to be obtained by giving up the liquidity-preference theory and assuming instead the crudest quantity-of-money theory while keeping the assumption of rigid wages. This can be done by merely replacing equation (1) of our system by the equation

$$M = kY. \tag{1a}$$

Since M and k are constant this equation is sufficient to determine money income. Equations (5), (6), and (7) determine directly physical output and employment as we saw in Section 10. Once more there is no reason to expect that the level of employment thus determined will be "full employment"; and yet the system will be in equilibrium since there will be no tendency for income, employment, and output to change.

It is very interesting to see what part is played under these conditions by

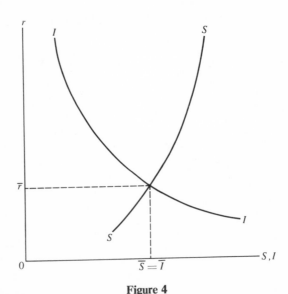

Figure 4

equations (2) and (3), the savings and investment equations that have been so much stressed by all the Keynesians. Since the income is determined by equation (1a), equation (2) reduces to an "orthodox" supply-of-saving schedule, giving saving as a function of the rate of interest. For the same reason, equation (3) reduces to a demand-for-saving schedule. Both schedules can be represented in a Marshallian supply and demand diagram as is done in Figure 4. The intersection of these curves, i.e., the equilibrium condition, demand = supply, determines the level of the rate of interest.

Finally let us notice that, in this system also, the rate of interest depends on the quantity of money, or more exactly on the ratio M/W. A change in M (W constant) raises real income and shifts both the SS and II curves to the right. The net result will be a fall in the rate of interest, if the increase in income raises the desire to save more than the desire to invest (normal case); a rise, in the opposite case.

In spite of these significant similarities between the present system and the Keynesian system, in which we recognize the existence of liquidity demand for money, there remains one very important difference; this difference is to be found in the role played by the rate of interest in the determination of equilibrium. In both cases the level of employment depends on the quantity of "active" money. But in the Keynesian system this depends on the rate of interest and consequently also on the propensities to save and invest. In the present case the quantity of active money is fixed and independent of the rate of interest. Hence the propensities to save and invest are not a part of the mechanism determining employment; they merely determine the amount of resources devoted to the improvement of the means of production.

We now proceed to consider the determinants of equilibrium in a system in which we do away not only with the liquidity-preference theory but also with the assumption of rigid wages.

13. The logical consistency of the quality theory of money and the dichotomy of monetary and real economics

In order to discuss the quantity theory of money we substitute equation (1a) for (1) and replace conditions (10) by the identities (11).

It was shown in Section 8 that a given change in prices will change income, investment, and saving in the same proportion. Consequently, after Y in equations (2) and (3) is replaced by the expression given in (5), the saving and investment equations may be written in the form

$$\frac{I}{W} = I\left(r, \frac{P}{W}X\right),$$

(3.2)

$$\frac{S}{W} = S\left(r, \frac{P}{W}X\right).$$

(3.3)

Next we divide both members of equations (4) and (5) by W obtaining

$$\frac{S}{W} = \frac{I}{W}, \tag{3.4}$$

$$\frac{Y}{W} \equiv \frac{P}{W}X, \tag{3.5}$$

$$X = X(N), \tag{3.6}$$

$$\frac{W}{P} = X'(N), \tag{3.7}$$

$$N = F\left[\frac{W}{P}\right], \tag{3.9}$$

$$\left[\frac{Y}{W} \equiv \frac{I}{W} + \frac{C}{W}. \tag{3.8}\right]$$

Equations (3.2) to (3.7) and (3.9) form a system of 7 equations in the 7 unknowns I/W, S/W, P/W, Y/W, r, X, N. These unknowns are therefore determined. Next we can write equation (1a) in the form $M = kPX = Wk(P/W)X$. But since P/W and X have already been determined, this equation determines the money wage rate and hence the price level, money income, etc. This is essentially the "classical" procedure, and we can only repeat the classical conclusions to the effect that the real part of the system, namely, employment, *interest rate*, output, or real income, do not depend on the quantity of money. The quantity of money has no other function than to determine the price level.

This result does not, of course, depend on any special feature of our system. It will always follow, provided all the supply and demand functions of commodities[25] and labor are homogeneous of the zero degree; and since we are proceeding under "static" assumptions, all the supply and demand functions must be homogeneous of zero degree, if people behave rationally.[26]

This conclusion, which is very old indeed, has some interest since it has been recently challenged by Oscar Lange. Of all the recent attacks against the traditional dichotomy of monetary and real economics, Lange's criticism is by far the most serious because it maintains that "the traditional procedure of the theory of money involves a [logical] contradiction."[27] We propose to show, however, that, while Lange's criticism of Say's law cannot be

[25]"Commodities" are, in this context, all goods except money.

[26]For a proof of this statement see O. Lange, "Say's Law: A Restatement and Criticism," *op. cit.*, pp. 67 and 68. Professor Lange shows that the homogeneity of first degree of all expectation functions is a sufficient condition for all demand and supply equations for "commodities" to be homogeneous of zero degree.

[27]*Ibid.*, p. 65.

questioned, it does not invalidate the logical consistency of the procedure of the quantity theory of money.

According to Lange, Say's law implies that the amount of cash people desire to hold is always identically equal to the quantity in existence: denoting by D_n and S_n the demand and supply of money respectively, we can write this as $S_n \equiv D_n$. Lange then states that "a proportional change of all prices does not induce a substitution between different commodities"[28] and concludes that "the demand and supply functions of commodities are, *when Say's law holds*, homogeneous of zero degree."[29] But the homogeneity of the supply and demand functions for commodities does not depend on Say's law: it depends on the assumption of rationality and the homogeneity of the expectation functions. Since a proportional change in all prices does not change the price ratios it also does not change the marginal rate of substitution, and therefore does not induce a substitution between different commodities.

Let us now consider a system in which there are n goods ($n - 1$ commodities and money). As is well known, there are only $n - 1$ prices to be determined, the price of money being unity, and $n - 1$ independent supply and demand equations, for one follows from the rest. Since the supply and demand functions for commodities are homogeneous of zero degree, the quantities demanded of the $n - 1$ commodities are functions of the $n - 2$ price ratios $p_i/p_{n-1}(i = 1, 2, \cdots, n - 2)$, where p_{n-1} is chosen arbitrarily.[30] At the same time the demand and supply function to be eliminated is also arbitrary; we may, if we choose, eliminate one of the $n - 1$ referring to commodities; we are then left with $n - 2$ equations for commodities to determine the $n - 2$ price ratios. Hence the price ratios are determined. To determine the actual prices we use the demand and supply equation for money as was done above. In Lange's system this is written:

$$k \sum_{i=1}^{n} p_i S_i = M, \qquad \text{or also} \qquad k p_{n-1} \sum_{i=1}^{n} \frac{p_i}{p_{n-1}} S_i = M,$$

where S_i denotes the equilibrium quantity supplied and demanded of the ith commodity. Since k is a constant this equation determines p_{n-1} and consequently all other prices.

As long as Say's law is not assumed, this procedure is perfectly legitimate; and we cannot escape the classical conclusion that money is "neutral," just a "veil." If, however, Say's law holds, the demand and supply of money are identically equal. The nth equation is therefore not a genuine equation. Thus we have only $n - 2$ independent equations to determine

[28] *Ibid.*, p. 63.
[29] *Ibid.*, p. 63. Italics ours.
[30] In our own system p_{n-1} was arbitrarily chosen as the wage rate.

$n - 1$ prices: the system is not determinate. In Lange's own formulation, the nth equation degenerates into the identity

$$kp_{n-1} \sum_{i=1}^{n} \frac{p_i}{p_{n-1}} S_i \equiv M,$$

which is satisfied by any value of p_{n-1} whatever; the price level is thus indeterminate.[31]

Hence one of Lange's conclusions, namely that "Say's law precludes any monetary theory,"[32] is perfectly justified. But Lange goes on to draw a conclusion which does not follow, namely that "the traditional procedure of the theory of money involves a contradiction. Either Say's law is assumed and money prices are indeterminate, or money prices are made determinate — but then *Say's law and hence the neutrality of money* must be abandoned."[33] But the traditional theory of money is not based on Say's law. The necessary condition for money to be neutral is that the $n - 1$ "real" demand and supply equations be homogeneous of order zero and this homogeneity does not "disappear when Say's law is abandoned."[34] Under "static" assumptions money is neutral even without assuming Say's law, if only people are assumed to behave "rationally"; this is all that the classical theory assumes and needs to assume.[35]

The most serious charge against the classical dichotomy can thus be dismissed, as long as we maintain our "static" assumptions.

14. Liquidity preference and the determinants of the rate of interest under the assumption of flexible wages[36]

With this in mind we may now proceed to analyze our third system consisting of equations (1) to (7), (9), and identities (11). In this system we recognize that there are two sources of demand for money, the transaction demand and the liquidity demand. But, as in the case just analyzed, we make no restrictive assumptions as to the supply-of-labor equation. The suppliers of labor as well as the suppliers of all other commodities are supposed to behave "rationally." It follows that the only difference between the present case and the case just considered is in equation (1). As in the previous case,

[31]Then k changes in inverse proportion to p_{n-1} instead of being a constant.
[32]O. Lange, *op. cit.*, p. 66.
[33]*Ibid.*, p. 65. Italics ours.
[34]*Ibid.*, p. 66.
[35]Lange's result seems due to a failure to distinguish between necessary and sufficient conditions. Say's law is a sufficient condition for the neutrality of money but not a necessary one. Lange asks me to inform the reader that he agrees with my conclusion. This conclusion, however, does not invalidate his result that under Say's law the money prices are indeterminate.
[36]The expression "flexible wages" is used here and in the following pages for brevity in place of the more exact expression "homogeneity of zero degree of the supply-of-labor function."

the last 7 equations form a determinate system which is sufficient to determine the 7 unknowns it contains, namely *the "real" variables of the system and the rate of interest.*

By use of equation (5) or (3.5) equation (1) takes the form

$$M = L\left(r, \, W \frac{P}{W} X\right). \tag{3.1}$$

Since r and P/W are already determined, this equation determines the 8th unknown of the system, the wage rate: and therefore also the price level, money, income, etc.[37]

We thus reach the conclusion that under "static" assumptions and "flexible" wages, *the rate of interest and the level of employment do not depend on the quantity of money.*

Two questions arise at once: (a) what determines the rate of interest and (b) what part do the rate of interest and liquidity demand for money play in the determination of equilibrium.

Strictly speaking, the rate of interest is determined by all the equations of a Walrasian system *except the supply-of-and-demand-for-money equation.* But it is clear that in the first approximation of partial-equilibrium analysis, the determination of the rate of interest must be associated with equations (3.2) and (3.3), the saving and investment schedules. To explain the level of the rate of interest we could use once more Figure 4, changing the variables measured on the horizontal axis from S or I into S/W or I/W. We must add at once, however, that these two schedules should in no way be confused with the schedules of supply of and demand for savings (or supply of and demand for securities) used in the textbook explanation of the determination of the rate of interest.

Equation (3.3) only tells us what part of their income people wish to devote to increasing their assets rather than to consumption, at different levels of the rate of interest.

In a similar fashion equation (3.2) shows that by devoting output worth I/W to the improvement of the means of production, it is possible to increase real income by an amount $(I/W)(1 + r)$ per unit of time. The value of r depends on the given technical conditions, on the quantity I/W and $(P/W)X$ according to the relation expressed by equation (3.2). This shows clearly the fundamental factors that determine the rate of interest. The given technical conditions, expressed by the production function [equation (3.6)], together with *tastes* of people for earning and leisure, expressed by the supply-of-labor function [equation (3.9)], give the level of real income that can be reached.[38] The saving schedule, equation (3.3), tells us what part

---

[37]Except in the Keynesian case considered later (Section 16).

[38]Under flexible wages there is, of course, always full employment under the conditions mentioned in Section 16.

of this income the community desires to save. The technical conditions (inventions, quantity of capital already in existence, etc.) expressed by the marginal-efficiency-of-investment function (3.2), determine the marginal efficiency of the amount of investment that the giving up of consumption permits undertaking: this is the equilibrium rate of interest.

Let us now examine what part is played by liquidity preference in the present system. On the basis of the given rate of interest determined in the fashion discussed above, people decide what quantity of money they want to hold as an asset. Hence, provided the liquidity demand is finite, the rate of interest, together with the supply of money, determines the quantity of active money and therefore the price level. Thus under "flexible" wages, *the desire to hold assets in liquid form does not determine the rate of interest, but determines the price level.* It follows that any factor that influences the demand for money as an asset, either directly or through the rate of interest, will have a repercussion on the price level, unless it is counteracted by an appropriate change in the quantity of money. This will in particular be the case with changes in the propensities to save and to invest.

15. Liquidity preference under rigid and flexible wages—an example

In order to see clearly the different implications of the liquidity-preference theory under different hypotheses as to the supply of labor we may briefly consider the effects of a shift in the investment schedule [equation (2) or (3.2)].

Suppose that the system is in equilibrium at money income Y_0: the flow of investments is I_0, and its marginal efficiency, r_0, is the equilibrium rate of interest. Now let us assume that for some reason the rate of investment that seems profitable at any level of the rate of interest falls. In particular the marginal efficiency of the rate of investment I_0 falls to the level $r_1 < r_0$. In order for the system to reach a new position of equilibrium, it is necessary that the rate of interest fall to this level. Except under special circumstances, to be considered later, as the rate of interest falls, the demand for money as an asset rises, and a certain amount of current money savings remains in the *money market* to satisfy the increased demand. If the supply of money is not properly increased, this, in turn, implies a fall in money income.

Under the conditions of our last model (flexible wages) the fall is brought about by an all-around reduction in wages and prices. The price level reaches its new equilibrium position when the supply has been increased sufficiently to satisfy the liquidity demand for money associated with the interest rate r_1.[39] The net effect of the shift is then to depress the interest

---

[39]The rate of interest must necessarily fall to the level r_1, for the real income and therefore the amount of real savings will be unchanged, and the marginal efficiency of this amount of real savings is r_1, by hypothesis.

rate, the money income, and money wages without affecting the real variables of the system, employment, output, real wage rate.[40]

But if money wages are rigid downward, the reduction in money income, made necessary by the fall in the rate of interest, becomes a reduction in real income and employment as well. The effect of the shift in the investment schedule is now to start a typical process of contraction so frequently described in Keynesian literature. As producers of investment goods make losses, they have no other choice than to dismiss workers, even though their physical productivity is unchanged. This, in turn, reduces the demand for consumption goods and causes unemployment to spread to this sector. Real income falls along with money income (the price level is likely to fall to a smaller extent). The fall in money income increases the supply of money to hold; the fall in real income decreases saving and raises its marginal efficiency above the level r_1.[41] This double set of reactions leads finally to a new equilibrium, with a smaller money and real income, less employment, higher real wages (since the price level falls) and a rate of interest somewhere below r_0 and above the new "full employment interest" r_1.[42] In terms of our graphic apparatus, a decreased marginal efficiency of capital (or increased propensity to save), shifts the IS curve to the left, as shown by the curve $I'S'$, and lowers interest rate and income, money as well as real income.

16. Two limiting cases

A. The Keynesian case. There is one case in which the Keynesian theory of liquidity preference is sufficient by itself to explain the existence of under-employment equilibrium without starting out with the assumption of rigid wages. We have seen (Section 5) that, since securities are inferior to money as a form of holding assets, there must be some positive level of the rate of interest (previously denoted by r'') at which the demand for money becomes infinitely elastic or practically so. We have the Keynesian case when the "full-employment equilibrium rate of interest" is less than r''. Whenever this situation materializes, the very mechanism that tends to bring about full-employment equilibrium in a system with "flexible" wages breaks down, since there is no possible level of the money wage rate and price level that can establish full-employment equilibrium.

From the analytical point of view the situation is characterized by the

[40]The real wage rate clearly cannot fall. If the real wage rate had fallen, entrepreneurs would try to expand employment while the supply of labor would, if anything, contract. If it had risen, the opposite situation would occur, and neither of these situations is compatible with equilibrium.

[41]Except if the IS curve is not monotonic decreasing, in which case the process of contraction will be more pronounced.

[42]If there was no full employment in the initial situation, then r_1 is simply the rate of interest that would maintain the old level of employment. This conclusion is also subject to the qualification mentioned in footnote 41.

fact that we must add to our system a new equation, namely $r = r''$. The system is therefore overdetermined since we have 9 equations to determine only 8 unknowns.

Equations (3.2) and (3.3) are sufficient to determine the value of the real income (since r is already determined). But this value will in general not be consistent with the value of the real income determined by the last four equations. More workers would be willing to work at the ruling real wage rate than are employed, but efforts at reducing real wages and increasing employment are bound to fail. For any fall in wages and prices increases the supply of money to hold but cannot lower the rate of interest below the level r'' since the demand for money as an asset is infinitely elastic. As Keynes would say, labor as a whole will not be able to fix its own real wage rate.

It appears clearly that, in this case, equilibrium is determined by those very factors that are stressed in the typical Keynesian analysis. In particular, real income and employment is determined by the position and shape of the saving and investment function, and changes in the propensity to invest or to save change real income without affecting the interest rate.

The price level on the other hand is in neutral equilibrium (at least for a certain range of values). It will tend to fall indefinitely as long as workers attempt to lower money wages in an effort to increase employment; and it can only find a resting place if and when money wages become rigid.

In this case the Keynesian analysis clearly departs from the classical lines and it leads to conclusions that could scarcely have been reached by following the traditional line of approach.

Whether the situation we have characterized as the "Keynesian case" is typical of some or all modern economic systems is a factual question which we cannot attempt to answer here. It is beyond doubt however that its interest is not purely theoretical.[43]

B. THE CLASSICAL CASE.   We have the classical case when the equilibrium rate of interest is sufficiently high to make the demand for money to hold zero or negligible. Graphically, the *IS* curve of Figure 3 intersects the *LL* curve in the range in which *LL* is perpendicular to the income axis. Under these conditions changes in the rate of interest (except possibly if they are of considerable size) tend to leave the demand for money unchanged or prac-

[43]In the *General Theory* Keynes explicitly recognizes that the situation described as the "Keynesian case" does not seem, so far, normally to prevail in any economic system. This situation, on the other hand, certainly plays an important part in some phases of the business cycle, when a great feeling of uncertainty and the anticipation of price reductions increase the attractiveness of liquidity and, at the same time, decreases the propensity to invest. Besides, it may also soon become a normal feature of some economies if there should come to prevail a real scarcity of investment outlets that are profitable at rates of interest higher than the institutional minimum. Modifying a well-known statement of Hicks we can say that the Keynesian case is either the Economics of Depression or the Economics of Abundance. (Hicks's original statement: "The General Theory of Employment is the Economics of Depression" is found in "Mr. Keynes and the 'Classics,' " *op. cit.*, p. 155.)

tically so; $L_r = 0$ or negligible and $M = L(Y)$. The properties of a system satisfying this condition have already been sufficiently analyzed in Sections 11 and 12.[44]

17. Preliminary conclusions

This brings to an end the first part of our analysis which aimed principally at distinguishing, as far as possible, to what extent the results of the Keynesian analysis are due to a more refined theoretical approach (liquidity preference) and to what extent to the assumption of rigid wages. We may summarize the results of our inquiry in the following propositions:

I. The liquidity-preference theory is not necessary to explain underemployment equilibrium; it is sufficient only in a limiting case: the "Keynesian case." In the general case it is neither necessary nor sufficient; it can explain this phenomenon only with the additional assumption of rigid wages.

II. The liquidity-preference theory is neither necessary nor sufficient to explain the dependence of the rate of interest on the quantity of money. This dependence is explained only by the assumption of rigid wages.

III. The result of the liquidity-preference theory is that the quantity of active money depends not only on the total quantity of money but also on the rate of interest and therefore also on the form and position of the propensities to save and to invest. Hence in a system with flexible wages the rate of interest and the propensities to save and to invest are part of the mechanism that determines the price level. And in a system with rigid wages they are part of the mechanism that determines the level of employment and real income.

We proceed now to make use of our results for two purposes: (a) To examine critically some of the theories that have their logical foundation in the Keynesian analysis. (b) To state some general conclusions about the determinants of the rate of interest.

Part II.

18. General remarks about the assumption of wage rigidity in the Keynesian theories

In the *General Theory* Keynes does of course recognize the fundamental importance of the relation between money wages and the quantity of money as is shown by his device of the wage units. This very fact, on the other

[44]To what extent the "classical case" is met in practice is again a factual question. In our opinion a moderately high rate of interest is sufficient to make it unattractive to hold assets in the form of cash and therefore to induce members of the community to limit their holdings to the amount necessary for transactions (which is determined by the institutional set-up). It is perhaps not unreasonable to expect that under normal conditions a "pure" rate of interest (i.e., net of default risk) in the neighborhood of 5 per cent might be sufficient to reduce the demand for money to hold to negligible proportions.

hand, has had the effect of obscuring the part played by wage rigidities in the determination of economic equilibrium. This can be clearly seen in a large body of literature based on the Keynesian analysis, and will be illustrated with a few examples.

A. Let us first consider the role of investment.

The statement that unemployment is caused by lack of investment, or that a fall in the propensity to invest or an increase in the propensity to save will decrease employment, has become today almost a common-place.

As we have seen, however, lack of investment is sufficient to explain under-employment equilibrium only in the "Keynesian case," a situation that is the exception and not the rule.

It is true that a reduced level of employment and a reduced level of investment go together, but this is not, in general, the result of causal relationship. It is true instead that the low level of investment and employment are both the effect of the same cause, namely a basic maladjustment between the quantity of money and the wage rate. It is the fact that money wages are too high relative to the quantity of money that explains why it is unprofitable to expand employment to the "full employment" level. Now to each level of employment and income corresponds a certain distribution of the employment between the production of consumption and investment goods determined by the saving pattern of the community. Hence, when the over-all level of employment is low there will be a reduced level of investment as well as a reduced level of consumption. And the level of investment is low because employment is low and not the other way around.

What is required to improve the situation is an increase in the quantity of money (and not necessarily in the propensity to invest); then employment will increase in every field of production including investment. Again, it is true that, in general, a fall in the propensity to invest (the propensity to save being constant) tends to decrease employment (and that an increase in the same propensity has the opposite effect), but this occurs only because it decreases (or increases) the quantity of money available for transactions relative to the money wage rate and therefore makes it profitable to contract (or expand) employment. Exactly the same result could be obtained by deflating (or inflating) the quantity of money directly. That a change in the marginal efficiency of investment has no direct influence on aggregate employment can be clearly seen in the "classical case" when the demand for money to hold is zero or negligible. In this case the change mentioned above does not affect employment, but only the rate of interest and therefore, at most, the distribution of the unchanged amount of employment between consumption and investment.

In conclusion, then, the statement that unemployment is caused by lack of investment assumes implicitly that every possible economic system works under the special conditions of the "Keynesian case"; and this is clearly unwarranted. In general the reduced level of investment is not a cause, but just a symptom of unemployment, which in turn is due to essentially monetary disturbances.

This formulation is not only more correct but carries also important implications about the concrete form of economic policies necessary to relieve unemployment.

B. Another typical result of understressing the assumption of rigid wages is to be found in connection with the concepts of a "natural rate of interest" and of "cumulative inflation" and "deflation" of Wicksellian analysis.[45]

This "natural rate" is the equilibrium (and therefore full-employment) interest rate of a system with flexible wages and not of a Keynesian system with rigid wages. Under "flexible" wages, as we know, the equilibrium rate of interest does not depend on the quantity of money. But, because of the time required for a new position of equilibrium to be reached when some of the conditions change, it will depend on the rate of change of M. Thus the money authority will be able to keep r below (or above) its equilibrium value by increasing (or decreasing) the quantity of money without limit; we thus get a process of cumulative inflation or deflation. Under Keynesian assumptions this ceases to be true; but only because wages are assumed rigid and in this condition, as we have seen, it is in general possible to change the rate of interest with a finite change in the quantity of money.[46]

C. As a last example, we may quote Lange's "optimum propensity to consume."[47] This concept, outside of its theoretical interest, is only of practical importance if for some reason, money wages and money supply are absolutely inelastic. In general all that is required to increase employment is to expand the quantity of money (or at worst reduce wages) without any necessity for interfering with the propensity to consume.[48]

[45]See J. Marschak, "Wicksell's Two Interest Rates," *Social Research*, VIII (Nov. 1941), 469–478.

[46]The case is more complicated if the relation between Y and r described by the IS curve is not monotonic decreasing in the relevant range. It might then appear that an attempt of the money authority at reducing the interest rate will result in a fall in income and employment. This is the result reached by Marschak. Actually as the money authority expands the quantity of money by open-market policy it finds that the rate of interest eventually rises along with income and employment instead of falling. If the money authority insists on keeping the interest rate at the planned level it will have to go on expanding the quantity of money. This will either push the system to some new equilibrium if the planned rate is equal to or larger than the full-employment rate, or it will cause inflation if the planned rate is below this level. But in no event will an initial attempt at lowering r by open-market policy lead to a contraction of income.

[47]Oscar Lange, "The Rate of Interest and the Optimum Propensity to Consume," *Economica*, N. S., V (Feb. 1938), 12–32.

[48]If the demand for money is infinitely elastic the propensity to consume plays an important role in the determination of employment. In this case the optimum level of consumption C' would clearly be $C' = Y' - I(r'', Y')$, where Y' is full-employment income and r'' the critical level of the rate of interest for which $L_r = \infty$.

19. Lerner's theory of the rate of interest

We proceed now to consider the typically "Keynesian" theory of the rate of interest and money due to A. P. Lerner. We choose Lerner's theory, because its extremism and its clear-cut formulation permit of a useful criticism.

The substance of Lerner's argument, as far as we can make out, is this: The "classical theory" that saving and investment determine the rate of interest must be rejected: saving and investment, being identically equal, cannot determine interest. This is instead determined by the quantity of money according to a demand-for-money function, say $M = f(r)$.[49]

The first argument is clearly unimportant since it is based on definitions. If one accepts the Keynesian definitions then, of course, actual (or *ex post*) saving and investment are identical; and clearly the *ex post* identity, saving $\equiv$ investment, cannot determine either the rate of interest or income. This however does not prove that the propensities to save and to invest are irrelevant to the determination of interest.

We know on the contrary, that, under assumption of flexible wages, neither of Lerner's arguments holds. In this case the rate of interest is independent of the quantity of money and, except in limiting cases, is determined only by the propensities to save and to invest [equations (3.2) and (3.3)].

Let us stress, in order to avoid misunderstandings, that we perfectly agree with Lerner and with all the Keynesians that saving and lending are the result of two independent decisions; our equation (3.3) is a saving schedule and not a schedule of supply of loanable funds. However we cannot agree with Lerner that to treat saving as a "demand-for-securities schedule" is, without qualifications, a serious blunder, or that the classical analysis as to the effect of shifts in the desire to invest or to save is right by pure chance. We must remember that saving and lending coincide when the demand for money to hold is zero or constant. The quantity theory of money starts out with the assumption that the demand for money to hold is identically zero: $D_a'(r) \equiv 0$ or $M = L(Y)$. Now this assumption is unsatisfactory for a general theory, but may be fully justified under certain conditions.

We know that, when the equilibrium rate of interest is sufficiently high, the demand for money to hold does become zero, even if it is not assumed to be identically zero. And, under historically realized conditions, the equilibrium rate of interest may be sufficiently high to make the demand for money to hold so negligible and so scarcely affected by observed changes in the interest rate that this demand can, safely, be neglected. Interest becomes a factor

[49]See especially, "Alternative Formulations of the Theory of Interest," *Economic Journal*, XLVIII (June 1938), 211–230; and "Interest Theory — Supply and Demand for Loans or Supply and Demand for Cash?" This latter paper has been recently made available to me by Mr. Lerner in manuscript form; [*Review of Economics and Statistics*, XXVI (May 1944), 88–91]. The present criticism is also the result of a long personal discussion and correspondence.

of secondary importance and can be dropped along with many others which certainly do influence the demand for money but are not sufficiently relevant to warrant separate consideration. Under these conditions, the assumption $M = L(Y)$ will give a satisfactory approximation to economic reality.[50] Under changed historical conditions this assumption is no longer justified and it becomes necessary to take into account new factors to avoid over-simplifications.[51]

When we recognize that the demand for money to hold need not be zero (and as long as it is finite), saving and lending coincide only when the demand for money to hold is constant, that is to say, in equilibrium. The equality of money savings and lending becomes an equilibrium condition which, under flexible wages, *determines the price level, not the rate of interest.* And this in turn may explain the traditional lack of attention to the demand for money to hold in connection with the theory of interest.

Thus Lerner's theory cannot explain the rate of interest in a system with "flexible" wages. Let us then see whether it holds within the limits of his (tacit) assumption of rigid wages. We will agree at once that under this assumption the rate of interest depends on the quantity of money, but this is true only in a very special sense. If we look at our "Keynesian" model we find that we have 7 equations in 7 unknowns and two arbitrary quantities or "parameters," M and W_0. The solution of the system gives each of the 7 variables as functions of these arbitrary parameters: $\bar{r} = r(M, W)$, $\bar{Y} = Y(M, W)$, $\bar{N} = N(M, W)$, etc. On the basis of previous considerations these can be written:

$$\bar{r} = r\left(\frac{M}{W}\right), \tag{5.1}$$

$$\bar{Y} = Y\left(\frac{M}{W}\right), \text{ etc.} \tag{5.2}$$

If this is the sense in which Lerner states that r is a function of M, his statement is formally correct. But in the first place it is not very helpful for understanding the determinants of the rate of interest. In a system with rigid wages practically every economic variable depends on the quantity of money (and the money wage). The rate of interest depends on M as much as the price of shoes or employment in ice-cream manufacturing. In the second place it has nothing to do with Keynes's liquidity preference: r depends on

[50]The fact that hoarding and unemployment have always developed in certain phases of the business cycle is not an objection to that. For these are features for a theory of business cycles to explain. Here we are only comparing static theories.

[51]Thus for example, the outcome of a certain physical experiment may be influenced, to a slight extent, by changes in humidity. Then, if the experiment is carried out in a place in which the observed variations in humidity are not sufficient to affect the outcome sensibly, it is perfectly justifiable to neglect it. If the same experiment were conducted somewhere else, where humidity is known to be highly unstable, precautions should be taken in interpreting the results.

M even if we neglect the liquidity demand for money (see Section 11). Hence if Lerner's equation, $M = f(r)$, corresponds to our equation (5.1), then it is not a demand-for-money schedule, but an empirical relationship obtained by previous solution of a system of equations of which the demand for money itself is one. And his approach certainly throws no light on the determinants of the rate of interest.

The only alternative is to consider Lerner's equation as a true demand for money corresponding to our equation (1): $M = L(r, Y)$. But why has the second variable been omitted? The answer is clear; by concentrating attention on the liquidity preference and the demand for money to hold, sight has been lost of the demand for money to spend. Thus, we go from one extreme to the other; instead of neglecting the influence of the rate of interest as in the "quantity theory," we neglect the part played by income in determining the demand for money. The results of this unjustified omission are serious in many respects. The most serious is that it leads to the conclusion (reached by Lerner) that saving and investment play no part in the determination of the rate of interest.[52] Figure 3 shows on the contrary that equations (2) and (3) play as vital a role as the demand-for-money equation. It is clear also that changes in the propensity to save or to invest or in the wage rate, lead directly to changes in the interest rate.

To defend his point Lerner is forced to say that changes in these propensities affect the rate of interest *because* they change the demand for money, i.e., because they shift the graph of $M = f(r)$.[53] But this is true and by definition only if Lerner identifies $M = f(r)$ with our equation (5.1). Since this equation is obtained by previously solving the whole system, it contains the relevant parameters of the functions which determine the rate of interest. A change in any of these parameters changes or shifts the function $r = r(M/W)$ accordingly. But, as we have already seen, equation (5.1) cannot possibly help us in understanding the determinants of the rate of interest.[54]

Another consequence of Lerner's formulation is that it leads to the

[52]In "Alternative Formulations of the Theory of Interest," Lerner writes: "For the first, easy step [from the classical to the modern theory of interest] is the insinuation of Liquidity Preference as a junior partner in the old established one-man firm in the business of interest-determination, and the second . . . step is to put Saving-Investment, the senior partner, to sleep, as a preliminary to kicking him out" (*op. cit.*, p. 221).

[53]That this is Lerner's point of view may be seen for instance in the following passage from a letter written to me in June, 1943. Discussing the effects of an increase in the propensity to invest in the "classical case" (demand for money to hold equal zero) he writes: "Even in that case there must be a fall in income which decreases the need for cash which lowers the rate of interest so that the investors have a signal that they should increase investment, but an infinitesimal decrease in employment is sufficient to bring about any necessary fall in the rate of interest. . . ."

[54]To give another example, we can solve the system to obtain, say, the equilibrium output of shoes (Q) as a function of the quantity of money: $Q = f(M, W)$ or $M = F(Q, W)$. But to say that a change in tastes changes the output *because* it shifts this function is formally correct but perfectly useless as a tool of analysis.

conclusion that the interest rate can always be lowered by increasing the quantity of money, at least to the point where the demand becomes infinitely elastic; while the truth is that no finite change in the quantity of money can hold the interest rate below the full-employment level.[55]

Let us finally note that Lerner's theory is not fully satisfactory even in the "Keynesian case." It is true that in this case saving and investment do not determine the rate of interest, but it is equally clear that the rate of interest does not depend on the quantity of money.

In conclusion, to say that the rate of interest is determined by the schedule $M = f(r)$ is useless and confusing if this schedule is arrived at by previous solution of the entire system; it is an unwarranted simplification, full of serious consequences, if this function is treated as an ordinary demand function. And the statement that the propensity to save and invest plays no part in determining the rate of interest is true only in a limiting case: the Keynesian case.

20. Hicks's theory—the rate of interest and the cost of investing in securities

In *Value and Capital* Hicks has developed what is probably the most daring attempt at reducing the rate of interest to a purely monetary phenomenon.

In Hicks's own words the rate of interest is explained by the "imperfect moneyness" of securities. "The imperfect moneyness of those bills which are not money is due to their lack of general acceptability: it is this lack of general acceptability which causes the trouble of investing in them"[56] and it is this trouble, namely "the trouble of making transactions [i.e., of purchasing securities] which explains the short rate of interest."[57] And these same factors also explain the long rate since the long rate is some average of the short rates plus a premium to cover the risk of (unanticipated) movements in the future short rates.[58]

Thus the rate of interest is explained by the fact that securities are not a medium of exchange and is determined essentially by the cost of making loan transactions. This is certainly an unusual theory of interest and an astonishing one, to say the least; it appears irreconcilable with the theory we have developed throughout this paper.

Hicks's theory finds its origin in an attempt to answer a question posed by the Keynesian analysis. The reason that induces people to hold assets in the form of cash rather than securities is that the value of even the safest type of securities is not certain: it is subject to changes due to movements in the rate of interest. Now, as we have seen, this risk decreases as the duration

[55]Proper qualifications must be made for the case in which the *IS* curve is not monotonic decreasing.

[56]*Value and Capital, op. cit.*, p. 166.

[57]*Ibid.*, p. 165.

[58]*Ibid.*, Chapter 11.

of the loan transaction becomes shorter: and it disappears entirely on loans that last only one "Hicksian week" (or one income period in our model) since by hypothesis the rate of interest cannot change. There must then be some other reason to stop people from holding all of their assets in the form of securities and thus reducing their demand for "money to hold" to zero; this reason can only be the cost of investing in this riskless type of loans. This is Hicks's starting point: and so far there seems to be no difference from our own approach as developed in Section 5. But from these correct premises Hicks draws the wrong conclusion: namely *that it is the cost of investing that explains the rate of interest.* To say that the cost of investing is necessary to explain *why* the demand for money to hold is not always zero and to say that it *explains* the rate of interest are quite different statements. There is a logical gap between the two. Thus, for example, from the correct premise that the cost of automobiles in New York cannot fall to zero because they have to be transported from Detroit, there does not logically follow the conclusion that the cost of cars in New York is explained or determined by the cost of transporting them.

There is a different way of explaining the rate of interest, which is not less satisfactory for the fact of being obvious: namely that for certain categories of people (entrepreneurs as well as spendthrifts) it is worth while to pay a premium to obtain spot cash against a promise to pay cash in the future. This is the course we have followed: and it is clearly all that is necessary to explain the existence of the rate of interest. The cost of investing continues to play an important part in our theory: (a) it explains why the demand for money to hold is not identically zero; (b) it explains why the rate of interest can never fall below a certain level in a free capitalistic economy; and hence it explains the peculiarities of the Keynesian case. But it is clear that it is not necessary to explain the rate of interest.

Our next task is to show that the cost of investing is also not sufficient to explain the nature of interest. To this end we must disprove Hicks's statement that if people were to be "paid in the form of bills . . . there would be no cost of investment and therefore . . . no reason for the bills to fall to a discount,"[59] i.e., no rate of interest. It is easy to show that, even if "bills" were to be used as a medium of exchange, there would be no reason for the rate of interest to fall to zero.

Let us consider first the case of a "stationary state." It is well known that the stationary state is characterized by the fact that the rate of change of the quantity of capital is zero; the marginal efficiency of the existing quantity of capital is equal to the rate of interest, say r_0, that makes net saving equal to zero.[60] Now it is theoretically conceivable that, in this state,

[59]*Ibid.*, p. 165.

[60]For a more detailed description of the conditions that give rise to a stationary state see, for instance, M. Timlin, *Keynesian Economics, op. cit.*, Chapter 4.

securities might replace money as a medium of exchange;[61] their purchasing power would be objectively determined by their discounted value since, by hypothesis, the future rate of interest is known and constant. Their aggregate value would also be constant but, since individual savings need not be zero, there would be a net flow from dissavers to savers. Under these conditions it is clear that securities would continue to yield the rate of interest r_0, even though they would be performing the function of a medium of exchange. Thus, as far as the stationary state goes, Hicks's conclusion does not follow: the interest rate would be zero only in the special case $r_0 = 0$.

Next let us consider an expanding economy, in which the net level of saving and investment is not zero, and let us assume again that it is technically possible for securities to be accepted as a medium of exchange.[62]

In this economy, if there is to be no inflation, it is necessary that the rate of money investment be not larger than the rate of (*ex ante*) saving. Now there are two possibilities:

a. There exists some mechanism by which the net increase in outstanding securities cannot exceed net savings. Then the competition of borrowers to obtain loans will automatically determine the level of the rate of interest.

b. There is no limitation as to the issuance of new securities per unit of time. Then, of course, the rate of interest would be zero, since there would be no necessity for borrowers to compete. But the result would clearly be a situation of unending and progressive inflation. In the first case the stability of the quantity of active money and therefore of the price level is assured by the fact that savers would increase their "hoards" of securities-money, at a rate equal to the net increase in the value of outstanding securities. But in the second case there is nothing to stop the price level from rising indefinitely, except if it so happens that the "full employment" rate of interest is zero or negative.[63]

We may therefore safely conclude that the rate of interest is not explained by the fact that securities are not money. Once we recognize this, the complicated and confusing Hicksian theory about the imperfect moneyness of securities becomes unnecessary and should, in our opinion, be abandoned.

To say that different assets share in different degrees the quality of "moneyness" either has no meaning or it is based on a confusion between liquidity and the properties of a medium of exchange. It is true that different

[61]See, for instance, *ibid.*, p. 53.

[62]This would require that all people agree at all times on the present value of every security.

[63]We are well aware of the fact that the excess of money investment over (*ex ante*) saving does not lead to inflation, unless there is full employment to begin with, or until full employment is reached. It remains true however that, except in the case mentioned in the text, a zero rate of interest must eventually lead to inflation.

assets have different degrees of liquidity, since the liquidity depends on the perfection of the market in which a good is traded. And it is also true that money is probably, under normal conditions, the most liquid of all assets. But the property of money is that it is accepted (freely or by force of law) as a medium of exchange: and liquidity does not make money out of something that is not money. Whatever one's definition of liquidity, to say that a government bond, a speculative share, a house, are money in different degrees, can at best generate unnecessary confusion. It is true that money and securities are close substitutes, but this connection is to be found elsewhere than in degrees of moneyness; it depends on the fact that both money and securities are alternative forms of holding assets in nonphysical form. Securities are thus close substitutes for money, but not for money as a medium of exchange, only for money as an asset.

Having shown that the cost of investment neither explains nor determines the rate of interest, we will agree with Hicks that "the level of that [short] rate of interest measures the trouble involved in investing funds . . . to the marginal lender."[64] One cannot disagree with this statement any more than with the statement that the price of butter measures the marginal utility of butter to each member of the community.[65] Both statements are either tautologies or definitions of rational behavior. They are tautologies if they mean that all those who found it convenient to perform a certain transaction have done so. They are definitions of rational economic behavior if they state the conditions under which economic agents will maximize their satisfaction.[66] But it is clear that whether these statements are tautologies or definitions they are not sufficient to explain either the price of butter or the level of the rate of interest.

To conclude, the, we agree with Hicks that the rate of interest is at least equal to the cost of investing to the marginal lender, but this statement is not very helpful for understanding the rate of interest. But the Hicksian theory that the rate of interest is determined or simply explained by the imperfect moneyness of securities must be discarded as faulty.

21. Saving and investment or supply of and demand for cash?—conclusions

It will now be useful, in concluding this paper, to restate in brief form the general theory of interest and money that emerges from our analysis.

We believe that the best way of achieving this aim is to show how, by means of our theory, we can answer the controversial question that has caused so much discussion in recent economic literature.

---

[64]*Op. cit.*, p. 165.

[65]More exactly: the ratio of the price of butter to that of any other commodity measures the ratio of their respective marginal utilities.

[66]If anything, Hicks's statement is less illuminating, since there is, at least theoretically, the possibility that the rate of interest may exceed the cost of lending idle funds to the marginal lender: it is this very possibility that gives rise to the "classical case."

Is the rate of interest determined by the demand for and supply of cash? Or is it determined by those "real factors," psychological and technological, that can be subsumed under the concepts of propensity to save and marginal efficiency of investment?

We consider it to be a distinct advantage of our theory that we can answer both questions affirmatively. We do not have to choose between these two alternatives any more than between the following two: Is the price of fish determined by the daily demand and the daily supply; or is it determined by the average yearly demand and the cost of fishing?

Since we have maintained throughout this paper that, in general, saving and lending are independent decisions, we must clearly agree that the "daily" rate of interest is determined by the demand for and supply of money to hold (or, for that matter, by demand for and supply of loanable funds).[67] It is this very principle that has formed the base of our analysis of the money market (Section 7). But we cannot stop at this recognition and think that this is sufficient for a general theory of the rate of interest.

To come back to our example, it is certainly true that the daily price of fish is entirely explained by the daily catch of fish. But if we want to understand why the daily price fluctuates around a certain level and not around a level ten times as high, we must look for something more fundamental than the good or bad luck of the fishermen on a particular day. We shall then discover that the number of fishermen and the amount of equipment used does not change daily but is determined by the condition that the average returns, through good and bad days, must be sufficiently high to make the occupation of fishing (and investment in fishing equipment) as attractive as alternative ones.

What is obviously true for the price of fish must also hold for the price of loans. The statement that the "daily" rate is determined by the "daily" demand for and supply of money (or, more exactly, of money to hold) does not greatly advance us in the understanding of the true determinants of the rate of interest. This theory by itself is insufficient to explain, for instance, why in countries well-equipped and of great saving capacity, like England or the United States, the system of rates of interest fluctuates around low levels (2 or 3 per cent for the pure long rate and much less for short rates); while it fluctuates around much higher levels (5 or 6 per cent or more for the long rate) in countries poor in savings or rich but scarcely developed. Is that because in the last-mentioned countries the supply of cash is insufficient? Clearly not. The explanation for this difference can only run in terms of those more fundamental factors, technological and psychological, that are included in the propensity to save and the marginal efficiency of investment.

As we have shown in our model the equality of demand and supply of loanable funds is the equilibrium condition for the week (or for our income

---

[67]In this respect we have nothing to add to the arguments developed by Hicks in Chapter 12 of *Value and Capital*. There are enough equations to determine all the prices on each Monday and it makes no difference which equation is eliminated.

period) and determines the equilibrium rate of interest (or system of rates) for the week. It corresponds to the short-run equilibrium condition of the Marshallian demand and supply analysis: price equals marginal cost. But the stock of money to hold (the supply) tends itself to change and thus push the "daily" rate toward the level at which the flow of money saving equals the flow of money investment. The condition, (*ex ante*) saving = (*ex ante*) investment, corresponds to the long-run Marshallian condition (under perfect competition): price = average cost including rent.

The first condition is satisfied even in the short period since it is the result of decisions that can be carried out instantaneously (see Section 5). The second is a long-run condition and therefore may actually never be satisfied: but it is necessary to explain the level toward which the weekly rate tends (even though this level may never be reached since the long-run equilibrium rate of interest itself changes).

Thus, to complete our theory, we must be able to explain what determines the level of long-run equilibrium. At this point we find that our answer is not unique since it depends on the assumptions concerning the form of the supply-of-labor schedule.

I. As long as wages are flexible, the long-run equilibrium rate of interest is determined exclusively by real factors, that is to say, essentially by the propensity to save and the marginal efficiency of investment. The condition, money saving = money investment, determines the price level and not the rate of interest.

II. If wages are rigid it is still true that the long-run equilibrium rate of interest is determined by the propensities to save and to invest; but the situation is now more complicated, for these propensities depend also on money income and therefore on the quantity of active money which in turn depends itself on the level of the rate of interest. Thus, unless wages are perfectly flexible or the supply of money is always so adjusted as to assure the maintenance of full employment, the long-run equilibrium rate of interest depends also on the quantity of money and it is determined, together with money income, by equations (1), (2), and (3) of our model. We want however to stress again that the dependence of the rate of interest on the quantity of money does not depend on liquidity preference. In a system with rigid wages not only interest but also almost every economic variable depends on the quantity of money.

III. Finally our theory of the rate of interest becomes even less uniform when we take into account the "Keynesian case." In this case clearly the long-run equilibrium rate of interest is the rate which makes the demand for money to hold infinitely elastic. The economic theorist here is forced to recognize that under certain conditions the rate of interest is determined exclusively by institutional factors.

JAMES TOBIN **15**

Liquidity preference as behavior towards risk[1]

One of the basic functional relationships in the Keynesian model of the economy is the liquidity preference schedule, an inverse relationship between the demand for cash balances and the rate of interest. This aggregative function must be derived from some assumptions regarding the behavior of the decision-making units of the economy, and those assumptions are the concern of this paper. Nearly two decades of drawing downward-sloping liquidity preference curves in textbooks and on classroom blackboards should not blind us to the basic implausibility of the behavior they describe. Why should anyone hold the non-interest bearing obligations of the government instead of its interest bearing obligations? The apparent irrationality of holding cash is the same, moreover, whether the interest rate is 6%, 3% or ½ of 1%. What needs to be explained is not only the existence of a demand for cash when its yield is less than the yield on alternative assets but an inverse relationship between the aggregate demand for cash and the size of this differential in yields.[2]

Reprinted from *The Review of Economic Studies*, Vol. 25 (February 1958), pp. 65–86, by permission of the publisher and author. [Footnotes renumbered and expanded — *Eds.*]
[1] I am grateful to Challis Hall, Arthur Okun, Walter Salant, and Leroy Wehrle for helpful comments on earlier drafts of this paper.
[2] " ... in a world involving no transaction friction and no uncertainty, there would be no reason for a spread between the yield on any two assets, and hence there would be no difference in the yield on money and on securities ... in such a world securities themselves would circulate as money and be acceptable in transactions; demand bank deposits would bear interest, just as they often did in this country in the period of the twenties." Paul A. Samuelson, *Foundations of Economic Analysis* (Cambridge: Harvard University Press, 1947), p. 123. The section, pp. 122–124, from which the passage is quoted makes it clear that liquidity preference must be regarded as an explanation of the existence and level not of the interest rate but of the differential between the yield on money and the yields on other assets.

1. Transactions balances and investment balances

Two kinds of reasons for holding cash are usually distinguished: transactions reasons and investment reasons.

1.1 Transactions balances: size and composition

No economic unit — firm or household or government — enjoys perfect synchronization between the seasonal patterns of its flow of receipts and its flow of expenditures. The discrepancies give rise to balances which accumulate temporarily, and are used up later in the year when expenditures catch up. Or, to put the same phenomenon the other way, the discrepancies give rise to the need for balances to meet seasonal excesses of expenditures over receipts. These balances are *transactions balances*. The aggregate requirement of the economy for such balances depends on the institutional arrangements that determine the degree of synchronization between individual receipts and expenditures. Given these institutions, the need for transactions balances is roughly proportionate to the aggregate volume of transactions.

The obvious importance of these institutional determinants of the demand for transactions balances has led to the general opinion that other possible determinants, including interest rates, are negligible.[3] This may be true of the size of transactions balances, but the composition of transactions balances is another matter. Cash is by no means the only asset in which transactions balances may be held. Many transactors have large enough balances so that holding part of them in earning assets, rather than in cash, is a relevant possibility. Even though these holdings are always for short periods, the interest earnings may be worth the cost and inconvenience of the financial transactions involved. Elsewhere[4] I have shown that, for such transactors, the proportion of cash in transactions balances varies inversely with the rate of interest; consequently this source of interest-elasticity in the demand for cash will not be further discussed here.

1.2 Investment balances and portfolio decisions

In contrast to transactions balances, the investment balances of an economic unit are those that will survive all the expected seasonal excesses of cumulative expenditures over cumulative receipts during the year ahead. They are

[3]The traditional theory of the velocity of money has, however, probably exaggerated the invariance of the institutions determining the extent of lack of synchronization between individual receipts and expenditures. It is no doubt true that such institutions as the degree of vertical integration of production and the periodicity of wage, salary, dividend, and tax payments are slow to change. But other relevant arrangements can be adjusted in response to money rates. For example, there is a good deal of flexibility in the promptness and regularity with which bills are rendered and settled.

[4]"The Interest Elasticity of the Transactions Demand for Cash," *Review of Economics and Statistics*, XXXVIII (Aug. 1956), 241–247.

balances which will not have to be turned into cash within the year. Conse-quently the cost of financial transactions — converting other assets into cash and vice versa — does not operate to encourage the holding of invest-ment balances in cash.[5] If cash is to have any part in the composition of investment balances, it must be because of expectations or fears of loss on other assets. It is here, in what Keynes called the speculative motives of investors, that the explanation of liquidity preference and of the interest-elasticity of the demand for cash has been sought.

The alternatives to cash considered, both in this paper and in prior discussions of the subject, in examining the speculative motive for holding cash are assets that differ from cash only in having a variable market yield. They are obligations to pay stated cash amounts at future dates, with no risk of default. They are, like cash, subject to changes in real value due to fluctuations in the price level. In a broader perspective, all these assets, including cash, are merely minor variants of the same species, a species we may call monetary assets — marketable, fixed in money value, free of default risk. The differences of members of this species from each other are negligible compared to their differences from the vast variety of other assets in which wealth may be invested: corporate stocks, real estate, unincorpo-rated business and professional practice, etc. The theory of liquidity prefer-ence does not concern the choices investors make between the whole species of monetary assets, on the one hand, and other broad classes of assets, on the other.[6] Those choices are the concern of other branches of economic theory, in particular theories of investment and of consumption. Liquidity preference theory takes as given the choices determining how much wealth is to be invested in monetary assets and concerns itself with the allocation of these amounts among cash and alternative monetary assets.

Why should any investment balances be held in cash, in preference to other monetary assets? We shall distinguish two possible sources of liquidity preference, while recognizing that they are not mutually exclusive. The first is inelasticity of expectations of future interest rates. The second is uncertainty about the future of interest rates. These two sources of liquidity preference will be examined in turn.

2. Inelasticity of interest rate expectations

2.1 Some simplifying assumptions

To simplify the problem, assume that there is only one monetary asset other than cash, namely consols. The current yield of consols is r per "year." $1

---

[5]Costs of financial transactions have the effect of deterring changes from the existing portfolio, whatever its composition; they may thus operate against the holding of cash as easily as for it. Because of these costs, the *status quo* may be optimal even when a different composition of assets would be preferred if the investor were starting over again.

[6]For an attempt by the author to apply to this wider choice some of the same theoretical tools that are here used to analyze choices among the narrow class of monetary assets, see "A Dynamic Aggregative Model," *Journal of Political Economy*, LXIII (April 1955), 103–115.

invested in consols today will purchase an income of $r per "year" in perpetuity. The yield of cash is assumed to be zero; however, this is not essential, as it is the current and expected differentials of consols over cash that matter. An investor with a given total balance must decide what proportion of this balance to hold in cash, A_1, and what proportion in consols, A_2. This decision is assumed to fix the portfolio for a full "year."[7]

2.2 Fixed expectations of future rate

At the end of the year, the investor expects the rate on consols to be r_e. This expectation is assumed, for the present, to be held with certainty and to be independent of the current rate r. The investor may therefore expect with certainty that every dollar invested in consols today will earn over the year ahead not only the interest $r, but also a capital gain or loss g:

$$g = \frac{r}{r_e} - 1 \tag{2.1}$$

For this investor, the division of his balance into proportions A_1 of cash and A_2 of consols is a simple all-or-nothing choice. If the current rate is such that $r + g$ is greater than zero, then he will put everything in consols. But if $r + g$ is less than zero, he will put everything in cash. These conditions can be expressed in terms of a critical level of the current rate r_c, where:

$$r_c = \frac{r_e}{1 + r_e} \tag{2.2}$$

At current rates above r_c, everything goes into consols; but for r less than r_c, everything goes into cash.

2.3 Sticky and certain interest rate expectations

So far the investor's expected interest-rate r_e has been assumed to be completely independent of the current rate r. This assumption can be modified so long as some independence of the expected rate from the current rate

[7]As noted above, it is the costs of financial transactions that impart inertia to portfolio composition. Every reconsideration of the portfolio involves the investor in expenditure of time and effort as well as of money. The frequency with which it is worth while to review the portfolio will obviously vary with the investor and will depend on the size of his portfolio and on his situation with respect to costs of obtaining information and engaging in financial transactions. Thus the relevant "year" ahead for which portfolio decisions are made is not the same for all investors. Moreover, even if a decision is made with a view to fixing a portfolio for a given period of time, a portfolio is never so irrevocably frozen that there are no conceivable events during the period which would induce the investor to reconsider. The fact that this possibility is always open must influence the investor's decision. The fiction of a fixed investment period used in this paper is, therefore, not a wholly satisfactory way of taking account of the inertia in portfolio composition due to the costs of transactions and of decision making.

is maintained. In Figure 2.1, for example, r_e is shown as a function of r, namely $\varphi(r)$. Correspondingly $\dfrac{r_e}{1 + r_e}$ is a function of r. As shown in the figure, this function $\dfrac{\varphi}{1 + \varphi}$ has only one intersection with the 45° line, and at this intersection its slope $\dfrac{\varphi'}{(1 + \varphi)^2}$ is less than one. If these conditions

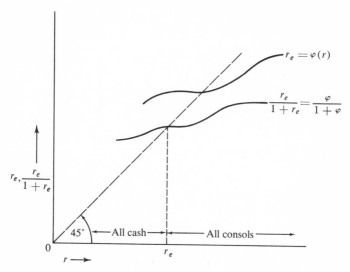

Figure 2.1
Stickiness in the relation between expected and current interest rate

are met, the intersection determines a critical rate r_c such that if r exceeds r_c the investor holds no cash, while if r is less than r_c he holds no consols.

2.4 Differences of opinion and the aggregate demand for cash

According to this model, the relationship of the individual's investment demand for cash to the current rate of interest would be the discontinuous step function shown by the heavy vertical lines $LMNW$ in Figure 2.2. How then do we get the familiar Keynesian liquidity preference function, a smooth, continuous inverse relationship between the demand for cash and the rate of interest? For the economy as a whole, such a relationship can be derived from individual behaviour of the sort depicted in Figure 2.2 by assuming that individual investors differ in their critical rates r_c. Such an aggregate relationship is shown in Figure 2.3.

At actual rates above the maximum of individual critical rates the aggregate demand for cash is zero, while at rates below the minimum critical rate it is equal to the total investment balances for the whole economy. Between these two extremes the demand for cash varies inversely with the

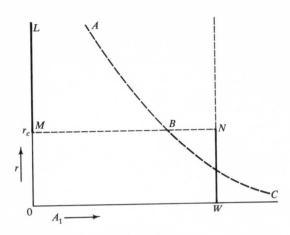

Figure 2.2
Individual demand for cash assuming certain but inelastic interest rate expectations

rate of interest r. Such a relationship is shown as $LMN\Sigma W$ in Figure 2.3. The demand for cash at r is the total of investment balances controlled by investors whose critical rates r_c exceed r. Strictly speaking, the curve is a step function; but, if the number of investors is large, it can be approximated by a smooth curve. Its shape depends on the distribution of dollars of investment balances by the critical rate of the investor controlling them; the shape of the curve in Figure 2.3 follows from a unimodal distribution.

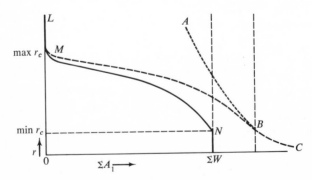

Figure 2.3
Aggregate demand for cash assuming differences among individuals in interest rate expectations

2.5 Capital gains or losses and open market operations

In the foregoing analysis the size of investment balances has been taken as independent of the current rate on consols r. This is not the case if there are already consols outstanding. Their value will depend inversely on the current rate of interest. Depending on the relation of the current rate to the previously fixed coupon on consols, owners of consols will receive capital gains or losses. Thus the investment balances of an individual owner of consols would not be constant at W but would depend on r in a manner illustrated by the curve ABC in Figure 2.2.[8] Similarly, the investment balances for the whole economy would follow a curve like ABC in Figure 2.3, instead of being constant at ΣW. The demand for cash would then be described by $LMBC$ in both figures. Correspondingly the demand for consols at any interest rate would be described by the horizontal distance between $LMBC$ and ABC. The value of consols goes to infinity as the rate of interest approaches zero; for this reason, the curve BC may never reach the horizontal axis. The size of investment balances would be bounded if the monetary assets other than cash consisted of bonds with definite maturities rather than consols.

According to this theory, a curve like $LMBC$ depicts the terms on which a central bank can engage in open-market operations, given the claims for future payments outstanding in the form of bonds or consols. The curve tells what the quantity of cash must be in order for the central bank to establish a particular interest rate. However, the curve will be shifted by open market operations themselves, since they will change the volume of outstanding bonds or consols. For example, to establish the rate at or below $min \ r_c$, the central bank would have to buy all outstanding bonds or consols. The size of the community's investment balances would then be independent of the rate of interest; it would be represented by a vertical line through, or to the right of, B, rather than the curve ABC. Thus the new relation between cash and interest would be a curve lying above LMB, of the same general contour as $LMN\Sigma W$.

2.6 Keynesian theory and its critics

I believe the theory of liquidity preference I have just presented is essentially the original Keynesian explanation. The *General Theory* suggests a number of possible theoretical explanations, supported and enriched by the experience and insight of the author. But the explanation to which Keynes gave the greatest emphasis is the notion of a "normal" long-term rate, to which

[8]The size of their investment balances, held in cash and consols may not vary by the full amount of these changes in wealth; some part of the changes may be reflected in holdings of assets other than monetary assets. But presumably the size of investment balances will reflect at least in part these capital gains and losses.

investors expect the rate of interest to return. When he refers to uncertainty in the market, he appears to mean disagreement among investors concerning the future of the rate rather than subjective doubt in the mind of an individual investor.[9] Thus Kaldor's correction of Keynes is more verbal than substantive when he says, "It is . . . not so much the *uncertainty* concerning future interest rates as the *inelasticity* of interest expectations which is responsible for Mr. Keynes' 'liquidity preference function,' . . ."[10]

Keynes' use of this explanation of liquidity preference as a part of his theory of underemployment equilibrium was the target of important criticism by Leontief and Fellner. Leontief argued that liquidity preference must necessarily be zero *in equilibrium*, regardless of the rate of interest. Divergence between the current and expected interest rate is bound to vanish as investors learn from experience; no matter how low an interest rate may be, it can be accepted as "normal" if it persists long enough. This criticism was a part of Leontief's general methodological criticism of Keynes, that unemployment was not a feature of equilibrium, subject to analysis by tools of static theory, but a phenomenon of disequilibrium requiring analysis by dynamic theory.[11] Fellner makes a similar criticism of the logical appropriateness of Keynes' explanation of liquidity preference for the purposes of his theory of underemployment equilibrium. Why, he asks, are interest rates the only variables to which inelastic expectations attach? Why don't wealth owners and others regard pre-depression price levels as "normal" levels to which prices will return? If they did, consumption and investment demand would respond to reductions in money wages and prices, no matter how strong and how elastic the liquidity preference of investors.[12]

These criticisms raise the question whether it is possible to dispense with the assumption of stickiness in interest rate expectations without losing the implication that Keynesian theory drew from it. Can the inverse relationship of demand for cash to the rate of interest be based on a different set of assumptions about the behaviour of individual investors? This question is the subject of the next part of the paper.

[9]J. M. Keynes, *The General Theory of Employment, Interest, and Money* (New York: Harcourt Brace, 1936), Chapters 13 and 15, especially pp. 168–172 and 201–203. One quotation from p. 172 will illustrate the point: "It is interesting that the stability of the system and its sensitiveness to changes in the quantity of money should be so dependent on the existence of a *variety* of opinion about what is uncertain. Best of all that we should know the future. But if not, then, if we are to control the activity of the economic system by changing the quantity of money, it is important that opinions should differ."

[10]N. Kaldor, "Speculation and Economic Stability," *Review of Economic Studies*, VII ([Oct.] 1939), 15.

[11]W. Leontief, "Postulates: Keynes' General Theory and the Classicists," Chap. 19 in S. Harris, editor, *The New Economics* (New York: Knopf, 1947), pp. 232–242. Section 6, pp. 238–239, contains the specific criticism of Keynes' liquidity preference theory.

[12]W. Fellner, *Monetary Policies and Full Employment* (Berkeley: University of California Press, 1946), p. 149.

3. Uncertainty, risk aversion, and liquidity preference

3.1 The locus of opportunity for risk and expected return

Suppose that an investor is not certain of the future rate of interest on consols; investment in consols then involves a risk of capital gain or loss. The higher the proportion of his investment balance that he holds in consols, the more risk the investor assumes. At the same time, increasing the proportion in consols also increases his expected return. In the upper half of Figure 3.1, the vertical axis represents expected return and the horizontal axis risk. A line such as OC_1 pictures the fact that the investor can expect more return if he assumes more risk. In the lower half of Figure 3.1, the left-hand vertical axis measures the proportion invested in consols. A line like OB shows risk as proportional to the share of the total balance held in consols.

The concepts of expected return and risk must be given more precision.

The individual investor of the previous section was assumed to have, for any current rate of interest, a definite expectation of the capital gain or loss g (defined in expression (2.1) above) he would obtain by investing one dollar in consols. Now he will be assumed instead to be uncertain about g but to base his actions on his estimate of its probability distribution. This probability distribution, it will be assumed, has an expected value of zero and is independent of the level of r, the current rate on consols. Thus the investor considers a doubling of the rate just as likely when rate is 5% as when it is 2%, and a halving of the rate just as likely when it is 1% as when it is 6%.

A portfolio consists of a proportion A_1 of cash and A_2 of consols, where A_1 and A_2 add up to 1. We shall assume that A_1 and A_2 do not depend on the absolute size of the initial investment balance in dollars. Negative values of A_1 and A_2 are excluded by definition; only the government and the banking system can issue cash and government consols. The return on a portfolio R is:

$$R = A_2(r + g) \qquad 0 \leq A_2 \leq 1 \tag{3.1}$$

Since g is a random variable with expected value zero, the expected return on the portfolio is:

$$E(R) = \mu_R = A_2 r. \tag{3.2}$$

The risk attached to a portfolio is to be measured by the standard deviation of R, σ_R. The standard deviation is a measure of the dispersion of possible returns around the mean value μ_R. A high standard deviation means, speaking roughly, high probability of large deviations from μ_R, both positive and negative. A low standard deviation means low probability of large deviations from μ_R; in the extreme case, a zero standard deviation would indicate certainty of receiving the return μ_R. Thus a high-σ_R portfolio offers the investor the chance of large capital gains at the price of equivalent chances of large capital losses. A low-σ_R portfolio protects the investor from capital loss, and likewise gives him little prospect of unusual gains. Although it is intuitively clear that the risk of a portfolio is to be identified with the dispersion of possible returns, the standard deviation is neither the sole measure of dispersion nor the obviously most relevant measure. The case for the standard deviation will be further discussed in section 3.3 below.

The standard deviation of R depends on the standard deviation of g, σ_g, and on the amount invested in consols:

$$\sigma_R = A_2 \sigma_g \qquad 0 \leq A_2 \leq 1. \qquad (3.3)$$

Thus the proportion the investor holds in consols A_2 determines both his expected return μ_R and his risk σ_R. The terms on which the investor can obtain greater expected return at the expense of assuming more risk can be derived from (3.2) and (3.3):

$$\mu_R = \frac{r}{\sigma_g} \sigma_R \qquad 0 \leq \sigma_R \leq \sigma_g \qquad (3.4)$$

Such an *opportunity locus* is shown as line OC_1 (for $r = r_1$) in Figure 3.1. The slope of the line is r_1/σ_g. For a higher interest rate r_2, the opportunity locus would be OC_2; and for r_3, a still higher rate, it would be OC_3. The relationship (3.3) between risk and investment in consols is shown as line OB in the lower half of the Figure. Cash holding $A_1(= 1 - A_2)$ can also be read off the diagram on the right-hand vertical axis.

3.2 Loci of indifference between combinations of risk and expected return

The investor is assumed to have preferences between expected return μ_R and risk σ_R that can be represented by a field of indifference curves. The investor is indifferent between all pairs (μ_R, σ_R) that lie on a curve such as I_1 in Figure 3.1. Points on I_2 are preferred to those on I_1; for given risk, an investor always prefers a greater to a smaller expectation of return. Conceivably, for some investors, *risk-lovers*, these indifference curves have negative slopes. Such individuals are willing to accept lower expected return in order to have the chance of unusually high capital gains afforded by high values of σ_R. *Risk-averters*, on the other hand, will not be satisfied to accept more risk unless they can also expect greater expected return. Their indifference curves will be positively sloped. Two kinds of risk-averters need to be distinguished. The first type, who may be called *diversifiers* for reasons that will become clear below, have indifference curves that are concave upward, like those in Figure 3.1. The second type, who may be called *plungers*, have indifference curves that are upward sloping, but either linear or convex upward.

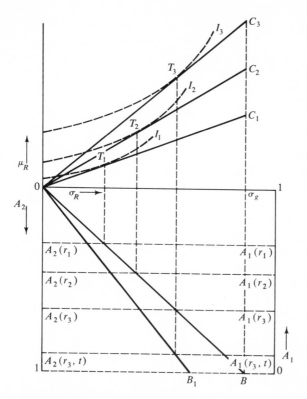

Figure 3.1
Portfolio selection at various interest rates and before and after taxation

3.3 Indifference curves as loci of constant expected utility of wealth

The reader who is willing to accept the indifference fields that have just been introduced into the analysis may skip to section 3.4 without losing the main thread of the argument. But these indifference curves need some explanation and defence. Indifference curves between μ_R and σ_R do not necessarily exist. It is a simplification to assume that the investor chooses among the alternative probability distributions of R available to him on the basis of only two parameters of those distributions. Even if this simplification is accepted, the mean and standard deviation may not be the pair of parameters that concern the investor.

3.3.1 One justification for the use of indifference curves between μ_R and σ_R would be that the investor evaluates the future of consols only in terms of some two-parameter family of probability distributions of g. For example, the investor might think in terms of a range of equally likely gains or losses, centered on zero. Or he might think in terms that can be approximated by a normal distribution. Whatever two-parameter family is assumed — uniform, normal, or some other — the whole probability distribution is determined as soon as the mean and standard deviation are specified. Hence the investor's choice among probability distributions can be analyzed by μ_R-σ_R indifference curves; any other pair of independent parameters could serve equally well.

If the investor's probability distributions are assumed to belong to some two-parameter family, the shape of his indifference curves can be inferred from the general characteristics of his utility-of-return function. This function will be assumed to relate utility to R, the percentage growth in the investment balance by the end of the period. This way of formulating the utility function makes the investor's indifference map, and therefore his choices of proportions of cash and consols, independent of the absolute amount of his initial balance.

On certain postulates, it can be shown that an individual's choice among probability distributions can be described as the maximization of the expected value of a utility function.[13] The ranking of probability distributions with respect to the expected value of utility will not be changed if the scale on which utility is measured is altered either by the addition of a constant or by multiplication by a positive constant. Consequently we are free to choose arbitrarily the zero and unit of measurement of the utility function $U(R)$ as follows: $U(0) = 0$; $U(-1) = -1$.

Suppose that the probability distribution of R can be described by a two-parameter density function $f(R; \mu_R, \sigma_R)$. Then the expected value of utility is:

$$E[U(R)] = \int_{-\infty}^{\infty} U(R) f(R; \mu_R, \sigma_R) \, dR. \tag{3.5}$$

Let $z = \dfrac{R - \mu_R}{\sigma_R}$.

$$E[U(R)] = E(\mu_R, \sigma_R) = \int_{-\infty}^{\infty} U(\mu_R + \sigma_R z) f(z; 0, 1) \, dz. \tag{3.6}$$

[13]See Von Neumann, J. and Morgenstern, O., *Theory of Games and Economic Behavior*, (3rd ed., Princeton: Princeton University Press, 1953), pp. 15–30, pp. 617–632; Herstein, I. N. and Milnor, J., "An Axiomatic Approach to Measurable Utility," *Econometrica*, XXIII (April 1953), 291–297; Marschak, J., "Rational Behavior, Uncertain Prospects, and Measurable Utility," *Econometrica*, XVIII (April 1950),111–141; Friedman, M. and Savage, L. J., "The Utility Analysis of Choices Involving Risk," *Journal of Political Economy*, LVI (Aug. 1948), 279–304, and "The Expected Utility Hypothesis and the Measurability of Utility," *Journal of Political Economy*, LX (Dec. 1952), 463–474. For a treatment which also provides an axiomatic basis for the subjective probability estimates here assumed, see Savage, L. J., *The Foundations of Statistics* (New York: Wiley, 1954).

An indifference curve is a locus of points (μ_R, σ_R) along which expected utility is constant. We may find the slope of such a locus by differentiating (3.6) with respect to σ_R:

$$0 = \int_{-\infty}^{\infty} U'(\mu_R + \sigma_R z)\left[\frac{d\mu_R}{d\sigma_R} + z\right] f(z; 0, 1)\, dz.$$

$$\frac{d\mu_R}{d\sigma_R} = -\frac{\displaystyle\int_{-\infty}^{\infty} z\, U'(R) f(z; 0, 1)\, dz}{\displaystyle\int_{-\infty}^{\infty} U'(R) f(z; 0, 1)\, dz} \tag{3.7}$$

$U'(R)$, the marginal utility of return, is assumed to be everywhere non-negative. If it is also a decreasing function of R, then the slope of the indifference locus must be positive; an investor with such a utility function is a risk-averter. If it is an increasing function of R, the slope will be negative; this kind of utility function characterizes a risk-lover.

Similarly, the curvature of the indifference loci is related to the shape of the utility function. Suppose that (μ_R, σ_R) and $[\mu'_R, \sigma'_R]$ are on the same indifference locus, so that $E(\mu_R, \sigma_R) = E(\mu_R, \sigma_R)$. Is$\left(\dfrac{\mu_R + \mu'_R}{2}, \dfrac{\sigma_R + \sigma'_R}{2}\right)$ on the same locus, or on a higher or a lower one? In the case of declining marginal utility we know that for every z:

$$\tfrac{1}{2}\, U(\mu_R + \sigma_R z) + \tfrac{1}{2}\, U(\mu_R + \sigma_R z)$$

$$< U\left(\frac{\mu_R + \mu'_R}{2} + \frac{\sigma_R + \sigma'_R}{2}\, z\right)$$

Consequently $E\left(\dfrac{\mu_R + \mu'_R}{2}, \dfrac{\sigma_R + \sigma'_R}{2}\right)$ is greater than $E(\mu_R, \sigma_R)$ or $E(\mu'_R, \sigma'_R)$, and $\left(\dfrac{\mu_R + \mu'_R}{2}, \dfrac{\sigma_R + \sigma'_R}{2}\right)$, which lies on a line between (μ_R, σ_R) and (μ'_R, σ'_R), is on a higher locus than those points. Thus it is shown that a risk-averter's indifference curve is necessarily concave upwards, provided it is derived in this manner from a two-parameter family of probability distributions and declining marginal utility of return. All risk-averters are diversifiers; plungers do not exist. The same kind of argument shows that a risk-lover's indifference curve is concave downwards.

3.3.2   In the absence of restrictions on the subjective probability distributions of the investor, the parameters of the distribution relevant to his choice can be sought in parametric restrictions on his utility-of-return function. Two parameters of the utility function are determined by the choice of the utility scale. If specification of the utility function requires no additional parameters, one parameter of the probability distribution summarizes all the information relevant for the investor's choice. For example, if the utility function is linear $[U(R) = R]$, then the expected value of utility is simply the expected value of R, and maximizing expected utility leads to the same behaviour as maximizing return in a world of certainty. If, however, one additional parameter is needed to specify the utility function, then two parameters of the probability distribution will be relevant to the choice; and so on. Which parameters of the distribution are relevant depends on the form of the utility function.

Focus on the mean and standard deviation of return can be justified on the assumption that the utility function is quadratic. Following our conventions as to utility scale, the quadratic function would be:

$$U(R) = (1 + b) R + bR^2 \tag{3.8}$$

Here $0 < b < 1$ for a risk-lover, and $-1 < b < 0$ for a risk-averter. However (3.8) cannot describe the utility function for the whole range of R, because marginal utility cannot be negative. The function given in (3.8) can apply only for:

$$(1 + b) + 2\,b\,R \geqq 0;$$

that is, for:

$$R \geqq -\left(\frac{1 + b}{2b}\right)(b > 0) \quad \text{(Risk-lover)} \tag{3.9}$$

$$R \leqq -\left(\frac{1 + b}{2b}\right)(b < 0) \quad \text{(Risk-averter).}$$

In order to use (3.8), therefore, we must exclude from the range of possibility values of R outside the limits (3.9). At the maximum investment in consols $(A_2 = 1)$, $R = r + g$. A risk-averter must be assumed therefore, to restrict the range of capital gains g to which he attaches non-zero probability so that, for the highest rate of interest r to be considered:

$$r + g \leqq -\left(\frac{1 + b}{2b}\right). \tag{3.10}$$

The corresponding limitation for a risk-lover is that, for the lowest interest rate r to be considered:

$$r + g \geqq -\left(\frac{1 + b}{2b}\right). \tag{3.11}$$

Given the utility function (3.8), we can investigate the slope and curvature of the indifference curves it implies. The probability density function for R, $f(R)$, is restricted by the limit (3.10) or (3.11); but otherwise no restriction on its shape is assumed.

$$E[U(R)] = \int_{-\infty}^{\infty} U(R) f(R) \, dR = (1 + b)\mu_R + b(\sigma_R^2 + \mu_R^2). \quad (3.12)$$

Holding $E[U(R)]$ constant and differentiating with respect to σ_R to obtain the slope of an indifference curve, we have:

$$\frac{d\mu_R}{d\sigma_R} = \frac{\sigma_R}{-\dfrac{1+b}{2b} - \mu_R} \quad (3.13)$$

For a risk-averter, $-\dfrac{1+b}{2b}$ is positive and is the upper limit for R, according to (3.9); $-\dfrac{1+b}{2b}$ is necessarily larger than μ_R. Therefore the slope of an indifference locus is positive. For a risk-lover, on the other hand, the corresponding argument shows that the slope is negative.

Differentiating (3.13) leads to the same conclusions regarding curvature as the alternative approach of section 3.3.1, namely that a risk-averter is necessarily a diversifier.

$$\frac{d^2\mu_R}{d\sigma_R} = \frac{1 + \left(\dfrac{d\mu_R^2}{d\sigma_R}\right)}{\left(-\dfrac{1+b}{2b} - \mu_R\right)^2} \quad (3.14)$$

For a risk-averter, the second derivative is positive and the indifference locus is concave upwards; for a risk-lover, it is concave downwards.

3.4 Effects of changes in the rate of interest

In section 3.3 two alternative rationalizations of the indifference curves introduced in section 3.2 have been presented. Both rationalizations assume that the investor (1) estimates subjective probability distributions of capital gain or loss in holding consols, (2) evaluates his prospective increase in wealth in terms of a cardinal utility function, (3) ranks alternative prospects according to the expected value of utility. The rationalization of section 3.3.1 derives the indifference curves by restricting the subjective probability distributions to a two-parameter family. The rationalization of section 3.3.2 derives the indifference curves by assuming the utility function to be quadratic within the relevant range. On either rationalization, a risk-averter's indifference curves must be concave upwards, characteristic of the diversifiers of section 3.2, and those of a risk-lover concave downwards.

If the category defined as *plungers* in 3.2 exists at all, their indifference curves must be determined by some process other than those described in 3.3.

The opportunity locus for the investor is described in 3.1 and summarized in equation (3.4). The investor decides the amount to invest in consols so as to reach the highest indifference curve permitted by his opportunity-locus. This maximation may be one of three kinds:

I. Tangency between an indifference curve and the opportunity locus, as illustrated by points T_1, T_2, and T_3 in Figure 3.1. A regular maximum of this kind can occur only for a risk-averter, and will lead to diversification. Both A_1, cash holding, and A_2, consol holding, will be positive. They too are shown in Figure 3.1, in the bottom half of the diagram, where, for example, $A_1(r_1)$ and $A_2(r_1)$ depict the cash and consol holdings corresponding to point T_1.

II. A corner maximum at the point $\mu_R = r$, $\sigma_R = \sigma_g$, as illustrated in Figure 3.2. In Figure 3.2 the opportunity locus is the ray OC, and point

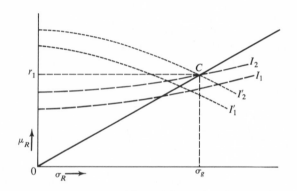

Figure 3.2
"Risk-lovers" and "diversifiers": optimum portfolio
at maximum risk and expected return

C represents the highest expected return and risk obtainable by the investor, i.e., the expected return and risk from holding his entire balance in consols. A utility maximum at C can occur either for a risk-averter or for a risk-lover. I_1 and I_2 represent indifference curves of a diversifier; I_2 passes through C and has a lower slope, both at C and everywhere to the left of C, than the opportunity locus. I_1' and I_2' represent the indifference curves of a risk-lover, for whom it is clear that C is always the optimum position. Similarly, a plunger may, if his indifference curves stand with respect to his opportunity locus as in Figure 3.3 (OC_2) plunge his entire balance in consols.

III. A corner maximum at the origin, where the entire balance is held in cash. For a plunger, this case is illustrated in Figure 3.3 (OC_1). Conceivably it could also occur for a diversifier, if the slope of his indifference curve at the origin exceeded the slope of the opportunity locus. However, case III is entirely excluded for investors whose indifference curves represent the constant-expected-utility loci of section 3.3. Such investors,

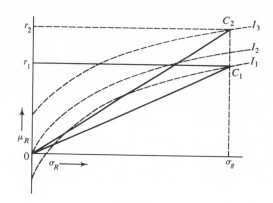

Figure 3.3
"Plungers" — optimum portfolio at minimum
or maximum risk and expected return

we have already noted, cannot be plungers. Furthermore, the slope of all constant-expected-utility loci at $\sigma_R = 0$ must be zero, as can be seen from (3.7) and (3.13).

We can now examine the consequences of a change in the interest rate r, holding constant the investor's estimate of the risk of capital gain or loss. An increase in the interest rate will rotate the opportunity locus OC to the left. How will this affect the investor's holdings of cash and consols? We must consider separately the three cases.

I. In Figure 3.1, OC_1, OC_2, and OC_3 represent opportunity loci for successively higher rates of interest. The indifference curves I_1, I_2, and I_3 are drawn so that the points of tangency T_1, T_2, and T_3, correspond to successively higher holdings of consols A_2. In this diagram, the investor's demand for cash depends inversely on the interest rate.

This relationship is, of course, in the direction liquidity preference theory has taught us to expect, but it is not the only possible direction of relationship. It is quite possible to draw indifference curves so that the point of tangency moves left as the opportunity locus is rotated counter-clockwise. The ambiguity is a familiar one in the theory of choice, and reflects the ubiquitous conflict between income and substitution effects. An increase in the rate of interest is an incentive to take more risk; so far as the substitution effect is concerned, it means a shift from security to yield. But an increase in the rate of interest also has an income effect, for it gives the opportunity to enjoy more security along with more yield. The ambiguity is analogous to the doubt concerning the effect of a change in the interest rate on saving; the substitution effect argues for a positive relationship, the income effect for an inverse relationship.

However, if the indifference curves are regarded as loci of constant expected utility, as derived in section 3.3, part of this ambiguity can be resolved. We have already observed that these loci all have zero slopes at $\sigma_R = 0$. As the interest rate r rises from zero, so also will consul holding A_2. At higher interest rates, however, the inverse relationship may occur.

This reversal of direction can, however, be virtually excluded in the case of the quadratic utility function (section 3.3.2). The condition for a maximum is that the slope of an indifference locus as given by (3.13) equal the slope of the opportunity locus (3.4).

$$\frac{r}{\sigma_g} = \frac{A_2 \, \sigma_g}{-\dfrac{1+b}{2b} - A_2 \, r}; \qquad A_2 = \frac{r}{r^2 + \sigma_g^2}\left(-\frac{1+b}{2b}\right) \qquad (3.15)$$

Equation (3.15) expresses A_2 as a function of r, and differentiating gives:

$$\frac{dA_2}{dr} = \frac{\sigma_g^2 - r^2}{(\sigma_g^2 + r^2)^2}\left(-\frac{1+b}{2b}\right); \qquad \frac{r}{A_2}\frac{dA_2}{dr} = \frac{\sigma_g^2 - r^2}{\sigma_g^2 + r^2} \qquad (3.16)$$

Thus the share of consols in the portfolio increases with the interest rate for r less than σ_g. Moreover, if r exceeds σ_g, a tangency maximum cannot occur unless r also exceeds g_{max}, the largest capital gain the investor conceives possible (see 3.10).[14] The demand for consols is less elastic at high interest rates than at low, but the elasticity is not likely to become negative.

II and III. A change in the interest rate cannot cause a risk-lover to alter his position, which is already the point of maximum risk and expected yield. Conceivably a "diversifier" might move from a corner maximum to a regular interior maximum in response either to a rise in the interest rate or to a fall. A "plunger" might find his position altered by an increase in the interest rate, as from r_1 to r_2 in Figure 3.3; this would lead him to shift his entire balance from cash to consols.

[14]For this statement and its proof, I am greatly indebted to my colleague Arthur Okun. The proof is as follows:
If $r^2 \geqq \sigma_g^2$, then by (3.15) and (3.10):

$$1 \geqq A_2 \geqq \frac{r}{2r^2}\left(-\frac{1+b}{2b}\right) \geqq \frac{1}{2r}(r + g_{max}).$$

From the two extremes of this series of inequalities it follows that $2r \geqq r + g_{max}$ or $r \geqq g_{max}$. Professor Okun also points out that this condition is incompatible with a tangency maximum if the distribution of g is symmetrical. For then $r \geqq g_{max}$ would imply $r + g_{min} \geqq 0$. There would be no possibility of net loss on consols and thus no reason to hold any cash.

3.5 Effects of changes in risk

Investor's estimates σ_g of the risk of holding monetary assets other than cash, "consols," are subjective. But they are undoubtedly affected by market experience, and they are also subject to influence by measures of monetary and fiscal policy. By actions and words, the central bank can influence investors' estimates of the variability of interest rates; its influence on these estimates of risk may be as important in accomplishing or preventing changes in the rate as open-market operations and other direct interventions in the market. Tax rates, and differences in tax treatment of capital gains, losses, and interest earnings, affect in calculable ways the investor's risks and expected returns. For these reasons it is worth while to examine the effects of a change in an investor's estimate of risk on his allocation between cash and consols.

In Figure 3.4, T_1 and $A_2(r_1, \sigma_g)$ represent the initial position of an investor, at interest rate r_1 and risk σ_g. OC_1 is the opportunity locus (3.4), and OB_1 is the risk-consols relationship (3.3). If the investor now cuts his

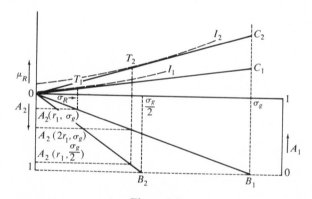

Figure 3.4

Comparison of effects of changes in interest rate (r) and in "risk" (σ_g) on holding of consols

estimate of risk in half, to $\sigma_g/2$, the opportunity locus will double in slope from OC_1 to OC_2, and the investor will shift to point T_2. The risk-consols relationship will have also doubled in slope, from OB_1 to OB_2. Consequently point T_2 corresponds to an investment in consols of $A_2(r_1, \sigma_g/2)$. This same point T_2 would have been reached if the interest rate had doubled while the investor's risk estimate σ_g remained unchanged. But in that case, since the risk-consols relationship would remain at OB_1, the corresponding investment in consols would have been only half as large, i.e., $A_2(2r_1, \sigma_g)$. In general, the following relationship exists between the elasticity of the demand for consols with respect to risk and its elasticity with respect to the interest rate:

$$\frac{\sigma_g}{A_2}\frac{dA_2}{d\sigma_g} = -\frac{r}{A_2}\frac{dA_2}{dr} - 1. \tag{3.17}$$

The implications of this relationship for analysis of effects of taxation may be noted in passing, with the help of Figure 3.4. Suppose that the initial position of the investor is T_2 and $A_2(2r_1, \sigma_g)$. A tax of 50% is now levied on interest income and capital gains alike, with complete loss offset provisions. The result of the tax is to reduce the expected net return per dollar of consols from $2r_1$ to r_1 and to reduce the risk to the investor per dollar of consols from σ_g to $\sigma_g/2$. The opportunity locus will remain at OC_2, and the investor will still wish to obtain the combination of risk and expected return depicted by T_2. To obtain this combination, however, he must now double his holding of consols, to $A_2(r_1, \sigma_g/2)$; the tax shifts the risk-consols line from OB_1 to OB_2. A tax of this kind, therefore, would reduce the demand for cash at any market rate of interest, shifting the investor's liquidity preference schedule in the manner shown in Figure 3.5. A tax on interest income only, with no

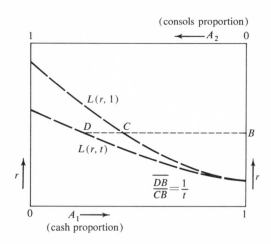

Figure 3.5
Effect of tax (at rate $1-t$) on liquidity preference function

tax on capital gains and no offset privileges for capital losses, would have quite different effects. If the Treasury began to split the interest income of the investor in Figure 3.4 but not to share the risk, the investor would move from his initial position, T_2 and $A_2(2r_1, \sigma_g)$, to T_1 and $A_2(r_1, \sigma_g)$. His demand for cash at a given market rate of interest would be increased and his liquidity preference curve shifted to the right.

3.6 Multiple alternatives to cash

So far it has been assumed that there is only one alternative to cash, and A_2 has represented the share of the investor's balance held in that asset, "consols." The argument is not essentially changed, however, if A_2 is taken to be the aggregate share invested in a variety of non-cash assets, e.g. bonds and other debt instruments differing in maturity, debtor, and other features. The return R and the risk σ_g on "consols" will then represent the average return and risk on a composite of these assets.

Suppose that there are m assets other than cash, and let $x_i (i = 1, 2, \ldots, m)$ be the amount invested in the ith of these assets. All x_i are non-negative, and $\sum_{i=1}^{m} x_i = A_2 \leqq 1$. Let r_i be the expected yield, and let g_i be the capital gain or loss, per dollar invested in the ith asset. We assume $E(g_i) = 0$ for all i. Let v_{ij} be the variance or covariance of g_i and g_j as estimated by the investor.

$$v_{ij} = E(g_i g_j) \qquad (i, j, = 1, 2, \ldots, m) \qquad (3.18)$$

The over-all expected return is:

$$\mu_R = A_2 r = \sum_{i=1}^{m} x_i r_i \qquad (3.19)$$

The over-all variance of return is:

$$\sigma_R^2 = A_2^2 \sigma_g^2 = \sum_{i=1}^{m} \sum_{j=1}^{m} x_i x_j v_{ij}. \qquad (3.20)$$

A set of points x_i for which $\sum_{i=1}^{m} x_i r_i$ is constant may be defined as a constant-return locus. A constant-return locus is linear in the x_i. For two assets x_1 and x_2, two loci are illustrated in Figure 3.6. One locus of combinations of x_1 and x_2 that give the same expected return μ_R is the line from μ_R/r_2 to μ_R/r_1, through C; another locus, for a higher constant, μ_R', is the parallel line from μ_R'/r_2 to μ_R'/r_1, through C'.

A set of points x_i for which σ_R^2 is constant may be defined as a constant-risk locus. These loci are ellipsoidal. For two assets x_1 and x_2, such a locus is illustrated by the quarter-ellipse from $\dfrac{\sigma_R}{\sqrt{v_{22}}}$ to $\dfrac{\sigma_R}{\sqrt{v_{11}}}$, through point C. The equation of such an ellipse is:

$$x_1^2\, v_{11} + 2\, x_1\, x_2\, v_{12} + x_2^2\, v_{22} = \sigma_R^2 = \text{constant.}$$

Another such locus, for a higher risk level, σ_R', is the quarter-ellipse from $\dfrac{\sigma_R'}{\sqrt{v_{22}}}$ to $\dfrac{\sigma_R'}{\sqrt{v_{11}}}$ through point C'.

From Figure 3.6, it is clear that C and C' exemplify *dominant* combinations of x_1 and x_2. If the investor is incurring a risk of σa, somewhere on the ellipse through C, he will have the highest possible expectation of return

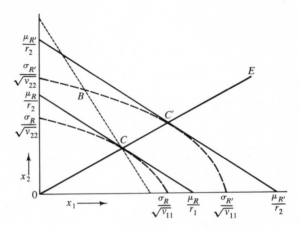

Figure 3.6
Dominant combinations of two assets

available to him at that level of risk. The highest available expected return is represented by the constant-expected-return line tangent to the ellipse at C. Similarly C' is a dominant point: it would not be possible to obtain a higher expected return than at C' without incurring additional risk, or to diminish risk without sacrificing expected return.

In general, a dominant combination of assets is defined as a set x_i which minimizes σ_R^2 for μ_R constant:

$$\sum_i \left(\sum_j v_{ij}\, x_j \right) x_i - \lambda \left(\sum_i r_i x_i - \mu_R \right) = \min \qquad (3.21)$$

where λ is a Lagrange multiplier. The conditions for the minimum are that the x_i satisfy the constraint (3.19) and the following set of m simultaneous linear equations, written in matrix notation:

$$[v_{ij}]\, [x_i] = [\lambda\, r_i]. \qquad (3.22)$$

All dominant sets lie on a ray from the origin. That is, if $[x_i^{(0)}]$ and $[x_i^{(1)}]$ are dominant sets, then there is some non-negative scalar κ such that $[x_i^{(1)}] = [\kappa\, x_i^{(0)}]$. By definition of a dominant set, there is some $\lambda^{(0)}$ such that:

$$[v_{ij}]\,[x_i^{(0)}] = [\lambda^{(0)}\, r_i]\,,$$

and some $\lambda^{(1)}$ such that:

$$[v_{ij}]\,[x_i^{(1)}] = [\lambda^{(1)}\, r_i]\,.$$

Take $\kappa = \dfrac{\lambda^{(1)}}{\lambda^{(0)}}$. Then:

$$[v_{ij}]\,[\kappa x_i^{(0)}] = [\kappa \lambda^{(0)} r_i] = [\lambda^{(1)} r_i] = [v_{ij}]\,[x_i^{(1)}]\,.$$

At the same time, $\displaystyle\sum_i r_i\, x_i^{(0)} = \mu_R^{(0)}$ and $\displaystyle\sum_i r_i\, x_i^{(1)} = \mu_R^{(1)}$.

Hence, $\mu_R^{(1)} = \kappa \mu_R^{(0)}$. Conversely, every set on this ray is a dominant set. If $[x_i^{(0)}]$ is a dominant set, then so is $[\kappa x_i^{(0)}]$ for any non-negative constant κ. This is easily proved. If $[x_i^{(0)}]$ satisfies (3.19) and (3.22) for $\mu_R^{(0)}$ and $\lambda^{(0)}$, then $[\kappa x_i^{(0)}]$ satisfies (3.19) and (3.22) for $\lambda^{(\kappa)} = \kappa\lambda^{(0)}$ and $\mu_R^{(\kappa)} = \kappa\mu_R^{(0)}$. In the two dimensional case pictured in Figure 3.6, the dominant pairs lie along the ray $OCC'E$.

There will be some point on the ray (say E in Figure 3.6) at which the investor's holdings of non-cash assets will exhaust his investment balance $(\sum_i x_i = 1)$ and leave nothing for cash holding. Short of that point the balance will be divided among cash and non-cash assets in proportion to the distances along the ray; in Figure 3.6 at point C for example, OC/OE of the balance would be non-cash, and CE/OE cash. But the convenient fact that has just been proved is that the proportionate composition of the non-cash assets is independent of their aggregate share of the investment balance. This fact makes it possible to describe the investor's decisions as if there were a single non-cash asset, a composite formed by combining the multitude of actual non-cash assets in fixed proportions.

Corresponding to every point on the ray of dominant sets is an expected return μ_R and risk σ_R; these pairs (μ_R, σ_R) are the opportunity locus of sections 3.1 and 3.4. By means of (3.22), the opportunity locus can be expressed in terms of the expected return and variances and covariances of the non-cash assets: Let:

$$[V_{ij}] = [V_{ij}]^{-1}\,.$$

Then:

$$\mu_R = \lambda \sum_i \sum_j r_i\, r_j\, V_{ij} \tag{3.23}$$

$$\sigma_R^2 = \lambda^2 \sum_i \sum_j r_i\, r_j\, V_{ij}\,. \tag{3.24}$$

Thus the opportunity locus is the line:

$$\mu_R = \sigma_R \sqrt{\sum_i \sum_j r_i\, r_j\, V_{ij}} = \sigma_R \frac{r}{\sigma_g} \qquad (3.25)$$

This analysis is applicable only so long as cash is assumed to be a riskless asset. In the absence of a residual riskless asset, the investor has no reason to confine his choices to the ray of dominant sets. This may be easily verified in the two-asset case. Using Figure 3.6 for a different purpose now, suppose that the entire investment balance must be divided between x_1 and x_2. The point (x_1, x_2) must fall on the line $x_1 + x_2 = 1$, represented by the line through BC in the diagram. The investor will not necessarily choose point C. At point B, for example, he would obtain a higher expected yield as well as a higher risk; he may prefer B to C. His opportunity locus represents the pairs (μ_R, σ_R) along the line through BC $(x_1 + x_2 = 1)$ rather than along the ray OC, and is a hyperbola rather than a line. It is still possible to analyze portfolio choices by the apparatus of (μ_R, σ_R) indifference and opportunity loci, but such analysis is beyond the scope of the present paper.[15]

It is for this reason that the present analysis has been deliberately limited, as stated in section 1.2, to choices among monetary assets. Among these assets cash is relatively riskless, even though in the wider context of portfolio selection, the risk of changes in purchasing power, which all monetary assets share, may be relevant to many investors. Breaking down the portfolio selection problem into stages at different levels of aggregation — allocation first among, and then within, asset categories — seems to be a permissible and perhaps even indispensable simplification both for the theorist and for the investor himself.

4. Implications of the analysis for liquidity preference theory

The theory of risk-avoiding behaviour has been shown to provide a basis for liquidity preference and for an inverse relationship between the demand for cash and the rate of interest. This theory does not depend on inelasticity of expectations of future interest rates, but can proceed from the assumption that the expected value of capital gain or loss from holding interest-bearing assets is always zero. In this respect, it is a logically more satisfactory foun-

---

[15][Harry Markowitz, [*Portfolio Selection: Efficient Diversification of Investments* (New York: John Wiley & Sons, Inc., 1959), treats] the general problem of finding dominant sets and computing the corresponding opportunity locus, for sets of securities all of which involve risk. Markowitz's main interest is prescription of rules of rational behaviour for investors; the main concern of this paper is the implications for economic theory, mainly comparative statics, that can be derived from assuming that investors do in fact follow such rules. For the general nature of Markowitz's approach, see his article, "Portfolio Selection," *Journal of Finance*, VII, No. 1 (Mar. 1952), 77–91.

dation for liquidity preference than the Keynesian theory described in section 2. Moreover, it has the empirical advantage of explaining diversification — the same individual holds both cash and "consols" — while the Keynesian theory implies that each investor will hold only one asset.

The risk aversion theory of liquidity preference mitigates the major logical objection to which, according to the argument of section 2.6, the Keynesian theory is vulnerable. But it cannot completely meet Leontief's position that in a strict stationary equilibrium liquidity preference must be zero unless cash and consols bear equal rates. By their very nature consols and, to a lesser degree, all time obligations contain a potential for capital gain or loss that cash and other demand obligations lack. Presumably, however, there is some length of experience of constancy in the interest rate that would teach the most stubbornly timid investor to ignore that potential. In a pure stationary state, it could be argued, the interest rate on consols would have been the same for so long that investors would unanimously estimate σ_g to be zero. So stationary a state is of very little interest. Fortunately the usefulness of comparative statics does not appear to be confined to comparisons of states each of which would take a generation or more to achieve. As compared to the Keynesian theory of liquidity preference, the risk aversion theory widens the applicability of comparative statics in aggregative analysis; this is all that need be claimed for it.

The theory, however, is somewhat ambiguous concerning the direction of relationship between the rate of interest and the demand for cash. For low interest rates, the theory implies a negative elasticity of demand for cash with respect to the interest rate, an elasticity that becomes larger and larger in absolute value as the rate approaches zero. This implication, of course, is in accord with the usual assumptions about liquidity preference. But for high interest rates, and especially for individuals whose estimates σ_g of the risk of capital gain or loss on "consols" are low, the demand for cash may be an increasing, rather than a decreasing, function of the interest rate. However, the force of this reversal of direction is diluted by recognition, as in section 2.5, that the size of investment balances is not independent of the current rate of interest r. In section 3.4 we have considered the proportionate allocation between cash and "consols" on the assumption that it is independent of the size of the balance. An increase in the rate of interest may lead an investor to desire to shift towards cash. But to the extent that the increase in interest also reduces the value of the investor's consol holdings, it automatically gratifies this desire, at least in part.

The assumption that investors expect on balance no change in the rate of interest has been adopted for the theoretical reasons explained in section 2.6 rather than for reasons of realism. Clearly investors do form expectations of changes in interest rates and differ from each other in their expectations. For the purposes of dynamic theory and of analysis of specific market situations, the theories of sections 2 and 3 are complementary rather than competitive. The formal apparatus of section 3 will serve just as well for a non-zero expected capital gain or loss as for a zero expected value of g. Stickiness of interest rate expectations would mean that the expected value of g is a function of the rate of interest r, going down when r goes down and rising when r goes up. In addition to the rotation of the opportunity locus due to a change in r itself, there would be a further rotation in the same direction due to the accompanying change in the expected capital gain or loss. At low interest rates expectation of capital loss may push the opportunity locus into the negative quadrant, so that the optimal position is clearly no consols, all cash. At the other extreme, expectation of capital gain at high interest rates would increase sharply the slope of the opportunity locus and the frequency of no cash, all consols positions, like that of Figure 3.3. The stickier the investor's expectations, the more sensitive his demand for cash will be to changes in the rate of interest.

*Theory of the price level,
money wage rates, and employment*

A. C. PIGOU **16**

The classical stationary state

1. In his *Fiscal Policy and Business Cycles* Professor Hansen writes: "The classicals were quite right when they argued that without technological progress,[1] the price system, including the rate of interest, would progressively drive the economy to the point at which there would be no net investment. They were wrong in assuming that the price system could also ensure a propensity to consume compatible with this investment situation, so as to provide full employment" (p. 288). The reason is that, before the stimulus to investment, associated, say, with the development of some invention, peters out, "customs, habits and institutional arrangements . . . have become embodied in the social structure and set up powerful resistances" to the establishment of a full-employment equilibrium. Nor are these resistances merely frictional, impeding the establishment of this kind of equilibrium. On account of them the economic system is directed towards a *different kind of equilibrium*. "Thus total expenditures decline and the economy falls towards an *equilibrial* self-perpetuating income level far short of full employment" (p. 306). This argument, the reader will understand, is conducted on the level of abstraction where perfect homogeneity and complete mobility of labour are assumed, so that "full employment" signifies a state of things in which everybody seeking employment at the ruling (uniform) rate of

Reprinted from *The Economic Journal*, Vol. 53 (December 1943), pp. 343–351, by permission of the publisher. [Footnotes renumbered and expanded — *Eds.*]

[1] On the assumption, of course, that there is no increase of population or expansion into new territory.

wages is able to obtain it. It does not have that esoteric meaning, which is given to it in much current writing, where full employment is allowed to prevail alongside of large masses of "frictional unemployment." In this article also I shall stand on that level of abstraction.

2. It is, of course, true, as Professor Hansen says, that the "classicals" were accustomed to think of the stationary state as one of full employment. Nevertheless, I suggest, the *essential* difference between his view and theirs should be stated in terms somewhat different from those he uses. The classicals, if pressed, would not have denied that, should wage-earners not act competitively, but contrive, by means of combination or otherwise, to set the real rate of wages "too high," the stationary state would not be one of full employment. Their essential contention is that in *all* circumstances a full-employment stationary state is possible and, if an appropriate wage policy is adopted, will be secured; Professor Hansen's contention is that in *some* circumstances a full-employment stationary state is not possible and cannot be secured through the adoption of *any* wage policy; and, which is not the same thing, that a less-than-full-employment is possible and will be secured. This is the issue that I propose to discuss.

3. Define savings and investment in accordance with Lord Keynes' practice in his *General Theory* and my own in *Employment and Equilibrium*, so that they are both equal to real income minus real consumption, and, therefore, as aggregates in a closed community, in all circumstances equal to one another. Then, in respect of the representative man,[2] let x be real income; r the expected net rate of return from investment, *i.e.*, the rate after allowing for incidental expenses connected with making the investment. In equilibrium this rate is necessarily equal to the net rate of interest, and is the same no matter in terms of what commodity it is measured. Let C be the physical stock of capital equipment. We have in Professor Hansen's manner an investment-income function,[3] which might equally well be called a supply function for real investment, with the amount of real investment written $f(C, x, r)$. Of the characteristics of this function we know that $\Delta x \frac{\partial f}{\partial x}$ is positive and less than Δx for all values of x and r — this is Lord Keynes' "psy-

[2]The argument of this paper is not affected by the precise way in which the representative man is defined. It is natural, perhaps, to think of him as a private person external to State activities. But he may, alternatively, be defined in such a way that account is taken, not only of what he does in his private capacity, but also of what he does as a constituent element in the State, so that, if, for example, consumption is cut down by State rationing, the representative man has *chosen* to reduce his own consumption. With this definition there can be no difference between what he desires to do and what under the suasion of the State he does do. Thus what he desires to save in given circumstances and what he does save are the same thing, and there can be no question of "forced" saving.

[3]The reader will understand that the investment-income function is here represented in a truncated form, variables which are not important for our immediate problem being neglected. In a full expression there would have in particular to be a variable indicative of the distribution of income.

chological law" (cf. *General Theory*, p. 114); while $\Delta r \dfrac{\partial f}{\partial r}$ is probably, though not certainly, positive and small; and $\Delta C \dfrac{\partial f}{\partial C}$ is negative and small — since, the more accumulated wealth people have, the less keen they are to get more.[4] We also have a demand function for real investment with the amount of real investment written $\phi(C, r)$ in which it is obvious that, given the technical situation, $\partial\phi/\partial r$ and $\partial\phi/\partial C$ are both negative. Some authorities would write here $\phi\{C, x, r\}$ with $\partial\phi/\partial x$ positive. The choice between these two forms does not affect the issues discussed here save only as regards a secondary problem to be mentioned in the concluding paragraph. Therefore I shall not argue the matter but simply adopt the form $\phi(C, r)$.

4. In the long-period equilibrium of the stationary state investment must, of course, be nil. We have, therefore, two equations: —

$$f\{C, x, r\} = 0 \tag{1}$$

$$\phi(C, r) = 0 \tag{2}$$

If, then, X be the real income appropriate to full employment, there is also, according to the "classicals," a third equation, $x = X$ (3); and the three equations together determine x, C and r.

5. The classicals tacitly assumed that investment (*i.e.*, saving) is made solely for the sake of the income that it is expected to yield in the future. On this assumption it is easy to see that in the long-period equilibrium of the stationary state the rate of interest must be equal to the representative man's rate of discounting future satisfactions. For, if this were not so, investment could not be nil, but would be either positive or negative. Write ρ for this latter rate and $\rho = \psi(C, x)$ to represent the relation between it and the amount of the representative man's real income. Then, since, as we have seen, $r = \rho$, we have, as it appears, two new equations in addition to those set out in the last section, and only one new unknown: so that the system appears *prima facie* to be over-determined. But this is not really so. For the equations

$$f(C, x, r) = 0, \qquad r = \rho \qquad \rho = \psi(C, x)$$

[4]For an *individual* there are both theoretical and statistical reasons for thinking that, as real income increases, not only the absolute amount of investment but also the proportionate amount will increase, *i.e.*, that not only $\partial f/\partial x$ but also $\dfrac{\partial}{\partial x}\left\{\dfrac{\partial f/\partial x}{f}\right\}$ is positive. On the other hand, when income increases for the representative man of a group on account of a larger part of the group finding employment, *prima facie* we should expect the proportionate amount of income saved to be unaltered. It must be remarked, however, that, when more people in a group find employment, a shift in the distribution of disposable income takes place, less than hitherto having to be transferred for the upkeep of unemployed persons, who presumably save nothing. This shift of distribution is evidently favourable to investment. Hence it may well be that, in this case, as well as with the isolated individual, increasing real income entails, other things being equal, an increasing proportion of income saved.

are not independent. On the contrary, the two last govern the functional form f in such wise as to compel the first to be valid. Thus there is no over-determination. It follows — and this is the essential point to note here — that, since the rate at which the representative man discounts future satis-factions can obviously never be <0, no matter how large his real income, the functional form f is necessarily such that, for all possible values of x and C, the equation $f\{C, x, r\} = 0$ must yield a positive value for r.

6. The assumption that investment (*i.e.*, saving) is made solely for the sake of the income that it is expected to yield, is, however, clearly not in accordance with the facts. People save (*i.e.*, invest) partly from other motives, the desire for possession as such, conformity to tradition or custom and so on. This entails that the rate of interest is less than the rate at which the representative man discounts future satisfactions. The fact that this latter rate cannot be nil or negative does not, therefore, imply that the rate of interest cannot be nil or negative. The functional form f need not, there-fore, be such that the equation $f\{C, x, r\} = 0$ yields a positive value for r for all values of x and C. On the contrary, for some values of x it may yield a negative value for r. Thus, it appears that a situation not contemplated by the classicals may arise, in which full employment and stationary state equilibrium can only be attained together on condition that the rate of interest is negative.

7. But in stationary state equilibrium, as already indicated, the rate of interest must be the same, no matter in terms of what commodity it is expressed. For this type of equilibrium implies that the future relative values of different commodities are expected to be the same as their present relative values. Some commodities, of which the most obvious is money, do not suffer appreciable wear and tear and can be held at trifling cost. In these commodities, therefore, the rate of interest in a stationary state cannot be negative in any serious degree — broadly speaking, cannot be negative. It follows that the rate of interest cannot be negative in terms of any com-modity. Hence the condition, *i.e.*, the existence of a negative rate of interest, which *in some circumstances* we have seen to be necessary in order that full employment shall be compatible with stationary state equilibrium, cannot be satisfied. When these circumstances occur, therefore, the classical thesis that full employment in a stationary state can always be brought about by competition among wage-earners in the matter of wage-rates fails. Unless, therefore, it can be shown that the circumstances contemplated above *cannot occur*, Prof. Hansen is so far right and the classicals stand convicted of error.

8. Before we debate this ultimate issue there is, however, some-thing else that should be said. To grant, if we do grant, that in certain circum-stances a full-employment stationary state is impossible is not necessarily to grant that the less-than-full-employment stationary state contemplated by

Prof. Hansen is possible and will be secured. We have a set-up containing three equalities, one inequality, and three unknowns:

$$f(C, x, r) = 0 \tag{1}$$

$$\phi(C, r) = 0 \tag{2}$$

$$x = X \tag{3}$$

$$r > 0 \tag{4}$$

This system obviously may be over-determined. The classicals and Prof. Hansen both in effect provisionally accept equations (1) and (2). Prof. Hansen then points out that, in some circumstances, (3) is incompatible with (4), so that the classicals' solution of a full-employment stationary state cannot be right. But it is open to the classicals to retort that in these same circumstances (4) is incompatible with (3), so that the alternative solution of a less-than-full-employment stationary state cannot be right. Unless, therefore, cause can be shown for rejecting equation (3), the logical outcome is that Prof. Hansen is right in what he denies but wrong in what he affirms.

9. The assertion $x = X$ derives from the proposition that work-people are able to reduce as much as they like the rate of real wages for which they ask, and, by reducing it far enough, are able to secure employment for as many people as desire it.[5] Is there any way in which this proposition can be contested with any degree of plausibility? In an economy in which wages were contracted for in kind clearly there is not. But those who think with Prof. Hansen are entitled to claim that in the economy with which they are interested wages are contracted for in money. In such an economy suppose that a less-than-full-employment stationary state is established at a net rate of interest approaching nil. Then, the argument will run, it is out of the power of wage-earners to make cuts in the rate of real wages for which they ask, and so to secure additional employment, because every cut in money wage-rates will automatically bring about an equi-proportionate reduction in prices. This argument is sometimes found in popular expositions of what the expositors mistakenly believe to be Lord Keynes' views. It is not necessary, I think, to examine it at any length. With any known type of banking system, and equally under an arrangement in which the stock of money is rigidly fixed, money income must be a function of the rate of interest, being lower or higher according as that rate is lower or higher. This follows from the fact that, for equilibrium, the convenience and so on yielded to the representative man by the marginal

---

[5]The suggestion that the rate may possibly have to be negative may reasonably be ignored over the range of our present problem.

unit of resources held in the form of money must be equally attractive with the interest yielded by the marginal unit invested in real capital. For the degree of this convenience is greater or less according as real income divided into the real value of the stock of money is less or greater; *i.e.*, according as money income divided into the stock of money (*i.e.*, the Marshallian *k*, which is the inverse of the income velocity of money), is less or greater, *i.e.*, when the stock of money is given, according as money income is greater or less. We may express this, writing T for the real value of the stock of money, by the equation $r = g(T/x)$, where T/x is always positive, and the functional form g is such that $\dfrac{d}{d(T/x)}\{g(T/x)\}$ is negative and $g(T/x)$ is positive, for all possible (*i.e.*, all positive) values of T/x; whence it follows that, as T/x increases towards infinity, $g(T/x)$ falls asymptotically towards, but never reaches 0. Thus, monetary arrangements being given, money income cannot fall unless the rate of interest falls. Since, however, in our supposed less-than-full-employment stationary state, the rate of interest is already at the minimum admissible level, it cannot fall any farther. Therefore the acceptance of lower money wage-rates by wage-earners cannot cause money income to fall. Therefore, with given employment, it cannot cause prices to fall. It follows that by cutting money wage-rates workpeople *can* cut real wage-rates, and so *can* expand employment above the amount proper to any less-than-full-employment stationary state. The attempted rebuttal of the classicals' attack fails. The logical outcome is that in circumstances where a full-employment stationary state is impossible a less-than-full-employment stationary state is also impossible; in other words, that no position of long-period equilibrium can be attained.

10. Escape from this *impasse* can be achieved if and only if it can be shown that the circumstances we have been contemplating, out of which the *impasse* is generated, are such as cannot in fact occur. I have now, resuming the main argument as it was left in § 7, to maintain that this can be shown. The stock of money being given, r is a function of money income, in such wise that, as the one tends towards nothing so also does the other, but neither can ever actually reach nothing. Suppose, then, that we start from a condition of full employment in which some investment is taking place. As time passes — on the assumption, of course, that technique remains unchanged — profitable openings for investment gradually get filled up. In our symbolism C increases, and, consequently, for any given value of r, $\phi(C, r)$ contracts; till finally no investment is demanded even at a nil rate of interest. Suppose that at this rate, with the real income proper to full employment, people still wish to supply some investment — to save something. Since, for the reasons given above, the rate of interest cannot fall below nothing, the only way in which demand and supply can be brought into equilibrium is by workpeople being forced out of employment, till a new and lower level of real income is established, in respect of which the

representative man does not desire to invest (*i.e.*, save) anything at a nil (or small positive) rate of interest. What, then, happens? To resist this movement and maintain themselves in work, wage-earners offer to accept lower rates of money wages, and go on doing this so long as the pressure to reduce employment is maintained. At first sight it seems as though this process must land us in an endless state of disequilibrium with money wage rates falling for ever. But this is not so. As money wage-rates fall money income must fall also and go on falling. Employment, and so real income, being maintained, this entails that prices fall and go on falling; which is another way of saying that the stock of money, as valued in terms of real income, correspondingly rises. But the extent to which the representative man desires to make savings otherwise than for the sake of their future income yield depends in part on the size, in terms of real income, of his existing possessions. As this increases, the amount that he so desires to save out of any assigned real income diminishes and ultimately vanishes; so that we are back in the situation described in § 5, where a negative rate of interest is impossible. Thus, through the decline of money income, the investment-income function is modified in such wise that a set-up emerges in which no condition incompatible with full employment is embodied.

11. This may be expressed symbolically by writing the investment-income function in the form $f(C, x, r, T)$; where T is the real value of the stock of money, $\partial f/\partial T$ is negative and, with r at its minimum, $f(C, x, r, T)$ can assume a nil value, if T is sufficiently large, for no matter what values of C and x and r. Our set-up then is

$$\phi(C, r) = 0 \tag{1}$$

$$f(C, x, r, T) = 0 \tag{2}$$

$$x = X \tag{3}$$

$$r = g\left(\frac{T}{x}\right). \tag{4}$$

Here there are four equations and four unknowns, so that the system is not over-determined, while our knowledge of the form of the function g, as set out in § 9, assures us that r, while it falls towards zero as T/x rises towards infinity, can never fall to zero. Thus the "some circumstances," in which it seemed, according to § 7, that the classicals' full-employment stationary state was impossible, have been found to be such as cannot, in fact, occur. That type of stationary state, provided that wage-earners adopt a competitive wage policy, is always possible; indeed it is the goal to which, granted this proviso, the economic system necessarily tends.

12. As was indicated in § 2, it is quite consistent with the classicals' general position, as it is with this conclusion, that, if wage-earners do *not*

follow a competitive wage policy, but hold money wage-rates "unduly" high, nil investment will be associated not with full, but with less than full employment. In place of equations (3) and (4) in the foregoing set-up, we have equations relating the rate of interest to money income and to the rate of money-wages, such as were developed in my book on *Employment and Equilibrium*. In this case the possibility of a negative rate of interest cannot be excluded in the manner described in the last section, because, the money rate of wages being maintained, and, therefore, prices (approximately) maintained, the value of the stock of money in terms of real income cannot be expanded. It is excluded through employment being cut down in the manner contemplated by Prof. Hansen until real income is so low that people do not desire to save or invest anything, and a less-than-full-employment stationary state is attained.

13. In conclusion a point should be noticed which was raised by Mr. Kaldor in his review of Prof. Hansen's book in the *Economic Journal* for September 1943. He maintains that the state of nil investment with less than full employment contemplated by Prof. Hansen, and, as is maintained here, realised if, and only if, money wage-rates are held above the competitive level, may not — indeed, is unlikely to — satisfy the conditions of *stable* equilibrium; in which case it can hardly claim to be a stationary state in a strict sense (*loc. cit.*, p. 110). This conclusion depends on his view that the demand function for investment ought to be written $\phi(C, x, r)$, not, as I have written it, $\phi(C, r)$. If it is $\phi(C, x, r)$, one of the conditions of stable equilibrium is that $\partial f/\partial x > \partial \phi/\partial x$, and this condition need not be satisfied; whereas with the function $\phi(C, r)$, it must be satisfied, since $\partial f/\partial x$ is positive and $\partial \phi/\partial x$ is then nil.[6] As already indicated, I do not propose to debate this matter here, for it is off the track of this discussion.[7] I have been concerned to show that, in given conditions of technique and so on, if wage-earners follow a competitive wage policy, the economic system must move ultimately to a full-employment stationary state; which is the essential thesis of the classicals. There can be no question at all that in this event the equilibrium attained is stable. This is so equally whether it is correct to represent the demand function as $\phi(C, r)$ or as $\phi(C, x, r)$. For, the equation $x = X$ having determined x, from the standpoint of the other equations in the set-up x is not a variable.

[6]Since both $\partial \phi/\partial C$ and $\partial f/\partial C$ are negative, there is no *a priori* necessity for the other stability condition, $\partial f/\partial C > \partial \phi/\partial C$ is positive, to be satisfied. Common sense tells us, however, that $\Delta C \dfrac{\partial f}{\partial C}$ is likely to be a very small negative quantity, while $\Delta C \dfrac{\partial \phi}{\partial C}$ may wel. be a considerable one; so that there is a strong probability that the condition will be satisfiedl

[7]Cf. *Economic Journal*, [LII] June–Sept. 1942, p. 250. It should be noticed that the form $\phi(C, x, r)$ cannot be defended by reference to the so-called "acceleration principle"; for this connects investment, not with consumption, but with rate of change in consumption, which in equilibrium situations is necessarily nil.

LLOYD A. METZLER **17**

Wealth, saving, and
the rate of interest

I.

The fundamental thesis of classical economics, that a free-market economy
has an automatic tendency to approach a state of full employment, has been
a subject of heated controversy in recent decades. Indeed, after the publication of Keynes's *General Theory* there were many economists who
rejected the classical thesis completely on the ground that it contained
internal inconsistencies. Today, however, we are witnessing a renaissance
of the classical doctrines. In part, the renaissance is attributable to world-
wide economic developments since the end of the war, which have been
characterized by a high level of demand and by full employment in almost
all industrial countries. But the rebirth of classical theory is also attributable, in part, to attempts to reconstruct the classical doctrines along lines
which make them immune to the Keynesian criticisms.

   The principal architect of the reconstruction is Pigou,[1] but the basic
idea of the remodeled classical theory can be found in the works of other

   Reprinted from Lloyd A. Metzler, "Wealth, Saving, and the Rate of Interest," *The
Journal of Political Economy*, Vol. 59 (April 1951), pp. 93–116, by permission of The University of Chicago Press. Copyright 1951 by The University of Chicago Press. [Footnotes
expanded — *Eds.*]
   [1]A. C. Pigou, *Employment and Equilibrium* (London: [Macmillan & Co.,] 1941), chap. 7;
"The Classical Stationary State," *Economic Journal*, LIII (Dec. 1943), 342–351.

economists as well, particularly in the works of Scitovszky[2] and Haberler.[3] The innovation which these economists introduced was a reconsideration, or perhaps I should say an elaboration, of the forces determining the quantity of real saving. In the classical theory the amounts of saving and investment out of a full-employment level of income were regarded as functions of the interest rate alone, and the latter was thus the primary governing force of the economic system as a whole. Equilibrium was attained, according to the classical theory, only when the interest rate was such that the quantity of real saving out of a full-employment income was equal to the quantity of real investment.[4] Scitovszky, Pigou, and Haberler retained this basic concept of equilibrium but argued that saving depends upon the real value of privately held wealth as well as upon the interest rate. Other things remaining the same, they said, real saving tends to be smaller and real expenditure for consumption tends to be larger, the larger is the real value of private wealth. For convenience, I shall hereafter use the expression "saving-wealth relation" to designate such a functional connection between current saving and private wealth.

The saving-wealth relation was employed by Pigou and Haberler to defend the classical theory against the criticism of Keynesian economics. In particular, the relation was employed to show that a flexible-wage economy has an automatic tendency to approach a state of full employment, as postulated in the classical theory. On account of the special purpose which it originally served, the saving-wealth relation is now widely considered to be a modification, but not a fundamental change, in the classical theory. Indeed, Haberler even suggests that some sort of functional connection between saving and wealth is implicit in works on economics which preceded the explicit recognition of the saving-wealth relation.[5]

I do not share these views. In my opinion the saving-wealth relation is more nonclassical in its implications than any of the contributions to the subject would lead one to believe. Although the Scitovszky-Pigou-Haberler system resembles the classical system in its tendency toward a state of full employment, it is quite unlike the classical system in other respects, and

[2]T. Scitovszky, "Capital Accumulation, Employment and Price Rigidity," *Review of Economic Studies*, VIII (1940–41), 69–88.

[3]G. Haberler, *Prosperity and Depression* (3d ed.; Geneva: [League of Nations,] 1941), pp. 491–503.

[4]Consider, for example, the following remark of J. S. Mill: "There must be, as in other cases of value, some rate [of interest] which . . . may be called the natural rate; some rate about which the market rate oscillates, and to which it always tends to return. This rate partly depends on the amount of accumulation going on in the hands of persons who cannot themselves attend to the employment of their savings, and partly on the comparative taste existing in the community for the active pursuits of industry, or for the leisure, ease, and independence of an annuitant" (*Principles* [5th ed.], Book III, chap. 13, § 1). Although Mill does not specify in this passage that the saving and investment which govern the interest rate are full-employment saving and full-employment investment, the tenor of his work strongly suggests that this is what he had in mind (see, e.g., *ibid.*, Book III, chap. 14).

[5]*Op. cit.*, p. 499, n. 2.

these other respects have generally been overlooked. The most striking difference between the new system and the classical concerns the interest rate, and this is the subject which I wish to explore in the present paper.

The distinguishing feature of the classical theory of the interest rate is its emphasis upon so-called "real" conditions of demand and supply and its' denial of the influence of monetary policy or banking policy. The classical economists believed that there exists a unique interest rate, or a unique pattern of long-term and short-term rates, at which the economic system is in equilibrium and that this unique interest rate cannot be influenced by changes in the quantity of money. The following quotation from Ricardo is representative of the classical opinion:

> Interest for money . . . is not regulated by the rate at which the bank will lend, whether it be 5, 4, or 3 per cent, but by the rate of profits which can be made by the employment of capital, and which is totally independent of the quantity or of the value of money. Whether a bank lent one million, ten million, or a hundred millions, they would not permanently alter the market rate of interest; they would alter only the value of money which they thus issued. In one case, ten or twenty times more money might be required to carry on the same business than what might be required in the other.[6]

In contrast to the classical doctrine, the theory of the interest rate implicit in the Scitovszky-Pigou-Haberler system is at least partly a monetary theory, as I shall demonstrate below. In this system there is no single interest rate and no single pattern of rates at which the economy is in equilibrium. Rather, there are an infinite number of different rates capable of performing the equilibrating function, and the particular rate that prevails at any given time depends to a considerable extent upon the policy of the banking authorities. Thus, in salvaging one feature of classical economics — the automatic tendency of the system to approach a state of full employment — Pigou and Haberler have destroyed another feature, namely, the real theory of the interest rate. In this respect Pigou, the archdefender of classical economics, has deserted Mill and Marshall and joined Schumpeter and Keynes![7] Although remnants of the classical, real theory of the interest rate remain, these are overshadowed, I believe, by the monetary feature

[6]David Ricardo, *Principles of Political Economy* ("Everyman's ed." [London: J. M. Dent & Sons, Ltd., 1911]), p. 246.

[7]Although Pigou is usually considered to be a defender of classical or neoclassical economic theory, his ideas concerning the interest rate were somewhat nonclassical even before the publication of his *Employment and Equilibrium*. He believed, in particular, that the banking system has a limited influence upon the equilibrium interest rate as well as upon the market rate. If the banks establish a market rate below the equilibrium rate, for example, prices and costs tend to rise, and the real expenditures of fixed-income groups are reduced. The resources thus freed are available for capital development, and the increased supply of capital reduces the equilibrium interest rate. Apart from this reservation, Pigou's earlier conception of the interest rate seems to be largely classical in its implications (see A. C. Pigou, *Industrial Fluctuations* [2d ed.; London: [Macmillan & Co.,] 1929], *passim*, but esp. p. 277).

which has been added. Moreover, the added feature which transforms the interest rate into a monetary rate is not liquidity preference, as in Keynesian economics, but the saving-wealth relation.

The subsequent analysis will be more understandable, I believe, if I digress from my principal theme long enough to indicate briefly the way in which the saving-wealth relation became prominent in economic theory. For this purpose consider an economic system in which the demand for investment is so low and the supply of saving so high that potential full-employment saving exceeds potential full-employment investment at all positive interest rates. In this event, there is no achievable interest rate which fulfils the classical condition of equilibrium. Whatever the interest rate may be, the demand for goods and services as a whole falls short of productive capacity. This is the Keynesian system in its simplest form. And the outcome of this situation, as envisaged by Keynes, is a cumulative reduction in output and employment, the reduction continuing until potential saving is reduced to the level of potential investment through a reduction in real income.

Suppose, however, that wages and other factor costs tend to fall when unemployment develops. To what extent will the reduction in costs stimulate output and move the system back toward full employment? Keynes argued that a general wage reduction affects output primarily through its influence on the interest rate. Any decline in wages and other costs is likely to result, he asserted, in a corresponding decline in other prices. In real terms, then, the only significant effect of the reduction in wages and other costs is an increase in the real value of money balances which tends, through liquidity preference, to reduce the interest rate. If full-employment saving exceeds full-employment investment at all possible interest rates, however, the reduction in the interest rate cannot conceivably eliminate all the deflationary gap and restore output to the full-employment level. Keynes's theory thus leads to the conclusion that wage-and-cost reductions are not an effective remedy for deficient demand.[8]

Pigou attempted to refute this Keynesian view concerning wage-and-cost reductions, and in doing so he introduced the saving-wealth relation. He suggested that, as wages and prices decline, the resulting increase in the real value of money balances will stimulate demand in a way which is independent of the change in the interest rate. Money balances constitute a part of private wealth, and the increase in the former accordingly implies an increase in the latter. As the real value of private wealth increases, the amount of saving out of a full-employment level of real income tends to

---

[8]J. M. Keynes, *General Theory of Employment, Interest and Money* (New York: [Harcourt, Brace & Co.,] 1936), chap. 19. On p. 267 of this chapter, Keynes says: "There is, therefore, no ground for the belief that a flexible wage policy is capable of maintaining a state of continuous full employment; . . . The economic system cannot be made self-adjusting along these lines."

decline. In this manner the excess of potential saving over potential invest-ment which accounted for the initial unemployment is eventually eliminated. In the absence of barriers to price-and-cost reductions, the system thus has an automatic tendency to approach a state of full employment, as envisaged in the classical theory. Saving is brought into line with investment not primarily through a reduction of the interest rate but rather through a general deflation and a corresponding increase in the real value of the money supply.

I do not wish to discuss the relevance of the saving-wealth relation to the arguments frequently heard for a policy of over-all flexibility of wages and prices. Other economists have pointed out that the portion of cash balances whose real value is increased by a general deflation normally constitutes a relatively small part of total assets and that an enormous reduction of prices would therefore be required to increase the real value of a country's total wealth by any substantial amount. They have argued, further, that the general increases or decreases in prices and costs required for the successful operation of such a system might easily lead to expec-tations of additional price increases or decreases which would upset the stability of the whole system.[9] Such questions of economic policy, however, are not the immediate concern of this paper. I mention them here only to avoid a possible misunderstanding of what I shall say later. In what follows, I shall make the most favorable assumptions possible as to the effects of price movements upon the demand for goods and services; I shall ignore the adverse influence of fluctuating prices upon expectations and assume that there is a substantial tendency for saving to decline when the real value of private wealth rises. Given these favorable assumptions, I shall then ask how an economic system containing the saving-wealth relation is related to classical theory.

II.

Before describing the theory of interest implicit in the Scitovszky-Pigou-Haberler system, I wish to say something about the meaning of a "mone-tary" theory of interest rates. A theory is usually regarded as a monetary theory if the economic system envisaged is one in which the equilibrium interest rate, or the equilibrium pattern of rates, can be altered by a change in the quantity of money. Although this definition is satisfactory for most purposes, it is not sufficiently accurate to characterize an economic system containing the saving-wealth relation. It is inadequate, in particular, because it does not indicate the manner in which the quantity of money is altered.

[9]M. Kalecki, "Professor Pigou on 'The Classical Stationary State,' a Comment," *Economic Journal*, LIV (April 1944), 131–132; D. Patinkin, "Price Flexibility and Full Employment," *American Economic Review*, XXXVIII (Sept. 1948), 543–564.

As I shall demonstrate below, the influence of a change in the quantity of money in the Scitovszky-Pigou-Haberler system depends not only upon the magnitude of the change but also upon the way in which it is brought about. Some changes in the quantity of money will alter the equilibrium interest rate while others will not.

We may distinguish, I believe, between two fundamentally different types of increase or decrease in the quantity of money. The first type is a change which takes place through open-market transactions of the central bank. The significant feature of this type of change is that it consists of an exchange of one form of asset for another. When money holdings are increased through central-bank purchase of securities, for example, holdings of securities outside the central bank are reduced by a corresponding amount. The second type of change consists of a direct increase or decrease in the money supply without any off-setting changes in private holdings of other assets. The supply of money may be reduced, for example, by a currency reform in which one unit of new money is exchanged for two units of old. Or the supply of money may be reduced by means of a governmental budgetary surplus, provided that the excess monetary receipts are impounded. In both these examples the supply of money is altered without altering private holdings of other assets, and it is this characteristic which distinguishes the second type of monetary change from the first.

I intend to show in subsequent parts of this paper that the theory of interest implicit in the Scitovszky-Pigou-Haberler system is a monetary theory if the change in the quantity of money is of the first type and a real theory if the change is of the second type. This means that open-market transactions of the central bank will have a *permanent* influence on the interest rate at which the system is in equilibrium, even after the bank has stopped its purchases or sales of securities. If the change in the quantity of money does not affect the private holdings of other assets, however, it will have no lasting influence on the interest rate. With respect to the rate of interest, the Scitovszky-Pigou-Haberler theory thus occupies an intermediate position between the classical theory and the Keynesian. The classical theory is a real theory of the interest rate from the point of view of both types of monetary change. According to the classical doctrine, neither a central-bank purchase or sale of securities nor an arbitrary increase or decrease in the quantity of money can have any effect upon the interest rate at which the economic system returns to equilibrium. As I have indicated above, the equilibrium interest rate of the classical theory is the rate at which full-employment potential saving is equal to full-employment potential investment, and this equilibrium rate is independent of both the quantity of money and the policy of the central bank. The classical theory, then, is a nonmonetary or real theory of the interest rate, regardless of whether the monetary disturbance is of the first type or the second type.

At the other extreme is Keynes's theory, which is a purely monetary theory from the point of view of either type of monetary disturbance. According to Keynes, the rate of interest is governed largely by the decisions of asset-holders concerning the proportions in which they wish to hold money and securities; that is, in Keynes's terminology, the rate is determined by liquidity preference.[10] Other things remaining unchanged, the desired ratio between money and securities tends to rise with a fall in the interest rate, and the equilibrium interest rate is the one at which the desired ratio of money to securities corresponds to the actual ratio. From this it follows that any monetary or banking policy which increases the actual quantity of money relative to the actual quantity of securities will reduce the interest rate at which the system is in equilibrium. Thus, both an arbitrary increase in the quantity of money (a disturbance of the second type) and an increase in the quantity of money through a limited and temporary purchase of securities by the central bank (a disturbance of the first type) will reduce the equilibrium interest rate in Keynes's system.

This brief and somewhat elliptical summary of the Keynesian and classical theories of the interest rate is intended to emphasize the polar positions which the two theories occupy, relative to the theory implicit in the Scitovszky-Pigou-Haberler system. The equilibrium interest rate in the classical theory is independent of monetary disturbances, regardless of whether such disturbances are of the first type or the second type. The equilibrium interest rate in Keynes's theory, on the other hand, can be permanently altered by a monetary disturbance of either type. In short, the classical theory is a real theory from the point of view of either type of disturbance, while the Keynesian theory is a monetary theory from the point of view of either type. The polar positions of the two theories explain, I believe, why no distinction has been made in the past between the two types of monetary disturbance. As I shall demonstrate below, however, the theory of the interest rate implicit in the Scitovszky-Pigou-Haberler system is intermediate between the classical theory and the Keynesian theory. It is a monetary theory from the point of view of the first type of monetary disturbance and a real theory from the point of view of the second type. But all this will, I hope, become clear as we proceed.

III.

The economic system which will be investigated below is one in which the capital market is subject to three main influences: (1) the influence of current saving and investment, as in the classical or neoclassical theory; (2) the influence of decisions concerning the holding of cash or securities, as in Keynes's doctrine of liquidity preference; and (3) the influence of wealth on current saving, as in the Scitovszky-Pigou-Haberler reconstruction of the

[10]Keynes, *op. cit.*, chaps. 13, 15, and 18.

classical theory. I assume that the equilibrium rate of interest, or the equilibrium pattern of rates, is determined by the interplay of these three influences.

At the outset I wish to make a number of simplifying assumptions. Although these assumptions are somewhat unrealistic, few of them are absolutely essential, and most of them could be substantially modified without altering any of my principal results. I assume, in the first place, that the economy with which we are dealing is a closed economy with a fixed amount of labor. Second, I assume that the wage rate tends to rise whenever the demand for labor is greater than the fixed supply and to fall whenever the demand is smaller than the fixed supply. Third, I assume that all agents of production except labor are produced means of production and that all production is carried on at constant returns to scale. Under these conditions the relative prices of all commodities and services are determinate and independent of the commodity composition of the national income. We can therefore speak unambiguously of a rate of total output, or of a level of national income, at which the economy's resources are fully employed. Fourth, I assume that owners of private wealth hold such wealth in only two forms, money (including demand deposits) and common stock, and that all common stock involves approximately the same degree of risk.[11] Fifth, I assume that the central bank is legally authorized to buy and sell the common stock held by the owners of private wealth and that this common stock constitutes the only nonmonetary asset of the banking system.

Given these assumptions, one can readily construct a simple geometric interpretation of the forces governing the interest rate. These forces will operate in two different markets: a market for goods and services as a whole and a market for securities. Consider, first, the market for goods and services. Stability of the general price level in the goods-and-services market obviously requires that the total demand arising from a full-employment

[11]Common stock has been selected as the typical security in order to avoid the difficulties associated with bonds during periods of inflation or deflation. Throughout the paper I assume that, in the absence of movements in interest rates, common-stock prices rise or fall to the same extent that other prices rise or fall, so that a general inflation or deflation does not affect the real value of securities. This means that the real value of a given quantity of securities is a function of the rate of interest alone. (See below.) Although the theory is simplified in this respect by regarding common stock as the typical security, two new problems are thereby introduced, and these must not be overlooked. Perhaps most important, when all investment is financed by issuing common stock, the idea of a functional relation between the rate of interest and the real volume of investment becomes somewhat vague. Under these circumstances businessmen do not commit themselves, as they do when they issue bonds, to the payment of fixed capital charges. Saying that investment depends upon the rate of interest when all securities are common stocks is equivalent to saying that businessmen undertake more investment when stock prices are high than when they are low.

Apart from the problem of defining an investment function, the use of common stock in our argument presents the further problem of separating risk payments from interest payments per se. I have attempted to avoid this second problem by assuming that the degree of risk is about the same for one stock as for another. I realize, however, that such an assumption does not meet the basic difficulty and that, in a more extended treatment of the subject, allowance should be made for differences in risk.

level of real income shall be equal to the economy's productive capacity; and this is equivalent to the requirement that potential saving out of a full-employment level of income shall be equal to potential investment. If potential investment at full employment exceeds potential saving, the demand for goods and services as a whole exceeds full-employment output; prices and costs accordingly tend to rise. If potential full-employment investment falls short of potential full-employment saving, on the other hand, this implies that the demand for goods and services as a whole falls short of full-employment output. Hence prices and costs tend to fall.

In the classical theory real saving and real investment were functions of a single variable — the interest rate — and the economy was assumed to be in equilibrium at only one rate. In the theory now being investigated, however, the amount of real saving at full employment is regarded as a function of two variables — the interest rate and the real value of wealth in the hands of the savers. As soon as the second variable is introduced, the concept of a single interest rate at which the goods-and-services market is in equilibrium loses its meaning. In place of the equilibrium rate of classical theory, we now have a schedule of rates, or a functional relation between the interest rate and the real value of private wealth.

In order to see how such a schedule can be derived, suppose that on a certain date the total of all privately held wealth — money and securities combined — has a certain real value. If the value of private wealth is fixed, saving may be regarded as a function of the rate of interest alone, and I shall assume that with this given saving schedule a rate of interest can be found at which full-employment saving is equal to full-employment investment. Consider, now, what would happen if the interest rate were arbitrarily increased above its equilibrium level. At the higher interest rate potential saving out of a full-employment income would exceed potential investment, which means that, other things remaining the same, the community's demand for goods and services would fall short of its capacity to produce. In other words, the increase in the rate of interest, taken by itself, would bring about a deflationary gap. But if the community's combined holdings of money and securities were increased in some manner at the same time that the rate of interest were raised, then the deflationary gap might be avoided. The increase in asset holdings would tend to reduce the amount of saving corresponding to any given rate of interest, thereby offsetting, or perhaps more than offsetting, the tendency toward excessive saving attributable to the rise in the rate of interest. The rise in the rate of interest would reduce investment, but the increase in the value of private wealth would reduce saving; and it is thus conceivable that full-employment potential saving might equal potential investment at the higher interest rate as well as at the lower rate.

Many other combinations of the interest rate and the real value of private wealth will fulfil the condition that full-employment saving equals full-employment investment, and we may accordingly conceive of a schedule or a functional relation indicating what the real value of private wealth would have to be, for many different interest rates, in order to make the community's demand for goods and services as a whole equal its capacity to produce. The real value of private wealth which fulfils this condition will be an increasing function of the rate of interest. Such a function is plotted as the line WW in Figure 1. For convenience, WW will be called the "wealth-

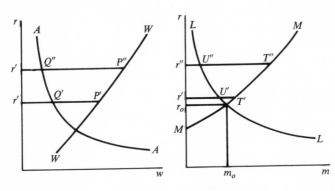

Figure 1   Figure 2

requirements schedule." At any point on this line potential saving out of full-employment income is equal to potential investment. But, as we move upward and to the right along the line, both saving and investment decline. Investment declines because of the rise in the interest rate, while saving declines because of the increase in the real value of private wealth. Any point below WW in Figure 1 represents a point of inflationary potential. At such a point the rate of interest is too low, given the value of private wealth, to bring about an equality between full-employment saving and investment. The demand for goods and services thus exceeds capacity, and prices tend to rise. In the same way one can show that any point *above* WW represents a point of *de*flationary potential. It follows that the demand for goods and services is equal to the economy's productive capacity only for combinations of the interest rate and the value of private wealth lying on WW.

The wealth-requirements schedule has been developed, above, in terms of the real value of private wealth as a whole, and no distinction has been made between private holdings of money and private holdings of securities. Such a distinction has thus far been unnecessary because saving was assumed to be a function of *total* asset holdings and not of the *composition* of these assets. When we later discuss the securities market, however, we shall find that the division of total assets between money and securities is the decisive factor in this market. Our later task will accordingly be simplified if the wealth-requirements schedule can be broken down into its two component parts, namely, money and common stock.

If the community holds a given amount of common stock, the real value of these stock holdings will obviously depend upon the interest rate. Indeed, the interest rate itself is nothing more than the yield of the stock, and this yield, in turn, is the ratio of the income earned by the stock to its market price. In the short run the income earned by the common stock is a given amount, determined by the fixed supplies of the various agents of production; and this means that the yield, or the rate of interest, varies inversely with the real value of the stock. To put the matter the other way round, we may say that the real value of the given common stock is inversely related to the prevailing rate of interest. The higher the rate of interest, the lower the real value of common-stock holdings and conversely. In Figure 1 the value of the community's security holdings is expressed as such a function of the interest rate by the line AA.

I wish to show, now, how the wealth-requirements schedule, WW, can be expressed in terms of money and interest rates rather than in terms of total wealth and interest rates. For this purpose, suppose that the interest rate is temporarily set at r'' in Figure 1. The wealth-requirements schedule tells us that, in order to prevent an excess or deficiency of demand from developing in the goods-and-services market at this interest rate, the community's holdings of money and securities combined will have to be $r''P''$. But the value of securities alone, at an interest rate of r'', is the distance $r''Q''$ in Figure 1. If the community is to have a sufficient amount of total assets to maintain a balance between demand and supply in the goods-and-service market, its holdings of money will therefore have to equal the difference between $r''P''$ and $r''Q''$, or $Q''P''$. This difference is plotted in Figure 2 as the line $r''T''$. A similar construction for a rate of interest r' carries over the distance $Q'P'$ of Figure 1 to $r'T'$ of Figure 2. The line MM of Figure 2 is the locus of all such points as T' and T''. Given the community's private holdings of securities, MM indicates the amount of money which will have to be held, at any particular interest rate, in order to keep the amount of saving out of full-employment income equal to the amount of investment. For brevity, MM will be called the "money-requirements schedule." The money-requirements schedule is thus the horizontal difference between the wealth-requirements schedule, WW, and the schedule of the real value of securities, AA.

IV.

The line MM of Figure 2, like WW of Figure 1, indicates the conditions needed to maintain a balance between supply and demand in the market for currently produced goods and services. In addition to this goods-and-services market, the market for securities must also be taken into account. The entire economic system cannot be in equilibrium unless the latter market, as well as the former, has reached a balanced position. The market for *new* securities has already been allowed for, by implication, in the preceding discussion of saving and investment; in the absence of hoarding, equality between saving and investment implies equality between the supply of and the demand for new securities. But this new-securities market is usually a relatively small part of the total securities market; in many countries, indeed, the value of new securities offered on the market in a given year is an exceedingly small fraction of the value of previously issued, or old, securities. This means that decisions of asset-holders to augment or reduce their stocks of old securities will frequently exert a much greater influence on the rate of interest than will discrepancies between current saving and current investment. The old-securities market must therefore be taken into account, along with the market for goods and services as a whole, in order to complete the description of interest rates given by Figures 1 and 2.

The existing stock of securities will influence security prices and the rate of interest only if asset-holders, on balance, decide to increase or decrease their holdings of securities, that is, only if the typical asset-holder wishes to substitute additional money for part of his security holdings or additional securities for part of his money holdings. Decisions of this sort depend largely upon the *composition* rather than the size of asset portfolios. Thus, in deciding whether to buy or sell securities, the typical asset-holder compares the existing ratio between his money holdings and his security holdings with the ratio which he regards as satisfactory under the given economic conditions. The degree of his actual liquidity, compared with a sort of optimum liquidity, governs his actions in the securities market.

I shall follow Keynes in assuming that, other things remaining the same, the typical asset-holder wishes to increase his liquidity as the rate of interest falls. Unless the banking authorities intervene, however, private asset-holders cannot, on balance, increase or decrease their holdings of old securities; as of a given moment of time, both the number of shares of stock and the quantity of money in private hands are fixed quantities. This means that, if the prevailing money-securities ratio differs from the desired ratio, security prices and the rate of interest must continue to change until the desired ratio is brought into line with the prevailing ratio; in short, the demand must be adjusted to the existing supply through appropriate movements in the rate of interest.

The influence of liquidity preference may be examined from another direction, and for present purposes this alternative point of view is more convenient. Instead of starting with a fixed amount of securities and a fixed quantity of money and asking how the rate of interest will be adjusted so that demand will equal supply, we may start with a fixed amount of securities and a fixed interest rate and ask what the total money holdings would have to be in order to satisfy the typical asset-holder with his money-securities ratio. By assuming a number of different interest rates and making similar calculations for each, a liquidity-preference schedule, or a demand-for-money schedule, can thus be built up. Suppose, for example, that, at an interest rate of r'' (Fig. 1), the typical asset-holder wishes to hold money in an amount equal to two-thirds the value of his security holdings. At this interest rate the security holdings of the community as a whole have a real value of $r''Q''$, as shown in Figure 1. It follows that asset-holders as a group will attempt to alter their security holdings and hence alter the rate of interest, unless the real value of money holdings amounts to two-thirds of $r''Q''$. Let the point U'' in Figure 2 be chosen so as to make $r''U''$ equal to two-thirds of $r''Q''$. Suppose, now, that, when the interest rate falls to r', the typical asset-holder wishes to hold money equal to the full value of his securities. The value of total securities at an interest rate of r' is $r'Q'$ (Fig. 1), and the condition of equilibrium in the old-securities market requires that money holdings shall equal this same amount. We may therefore select a point, U', in Figure 2 such that $r'U'$ is equal to $r'Q'$. The liquidity-preference schedule, LL, in Figure 2 is the locus of all such points as U'' and U'; it shows what the community's holdings of money would have to be, at any given interest rate, in order to create a proper balance between cash and securities.

From the construction of the diagram it is apparent that there are two reasons why the demand for money, LL (Fig. 2), tends to rise as the rate of interest falls. First, the typical asset-holder usually wants to hold a larger ratio of cash to securities at low interest rates than at high rates. And, second, the real value of securities, the denominator of the cash-securities ratio, is increased by a fall in the interest rate. In most discussions of liquidity preference only the first of these reasons is taken into account, but the second may be equally important.[12]

V.

I have now discussed two different functional relations between the rate of interest and the real quantity of money; the first of these I called a money-requirements schedule, while the second is the usual liquidity-preference schedule. The money-requirements schedule represents all combinations of money balances and the rate of interest for which the community's demand for goods and services as a whole is exactly equal to its capacity to produce. At any point not on this schedule there is either an excess or a deficiency of demand consequently a tendency for prices and costs to rise or fall. The

[12]The best account I have found of the second reason for the negative slope of the liquidity-preference schedule is by E. Solomon in "Money, Liquidity, and the Long-Term Rate of Interest: An Empirical Study, 1909–38" (University of Chicago dissertation, 1950).

money-requirements schedule, MM, thus indicates the possible combinations of the interest rate and the quantity of real cash balances which will maintain over-all price equilibrium in the goods-and-services market. The liquidity-preference schedule, on the other hand, describes the conditions of price equilibrium in the *securities* market. If the actual quantity of real cash balances lies on LL, there will be no tendency for asset-holders as a whole to attempt to shift from securities to cash or from cash to securities and, accordingly, no tendency for the price of securities or the rate of interest to change. At any point *not* on LL, however, the price of securities will either rise or fall, depending upon whether the demand for cash at the prevailing interest rate is smaller or greater than the actual amount.

From Figure 2 it is now apparent that only one combination of the interest rate and the real value of money balances will satisfy the conditions of equilibrium in both the goods-and-services market and the securities market. I have denoted this combination by the two letters r_0 and m_0. If all prices, including wages and the costs of other agents of production, tend to rise when demand exceeds supply and to fall when supply exceeds demand, the combination r_0 and m_0 is the one toward which the economic system will gravitate. The nature of this market mechanism will be clarified, I believe, if we consider what happens to the system when the interest rate and the real value of money balances differ from the equilibrium combination r_0 and m_0.

This is done in Figure 3, where I have reproduced the essential features of Figure 2. The points B, C, D, and E in Figure 3 represent four points which do not lie on either the liquidity-preference schedule or the money-requirements schedule. Suppose, first, that the actual situation with regard to the rate of interest and the real value of cash balances at a given moment of time can be represented by the point B. What happens, in this event, to the variables of our system? The liquidity-preference schedule shows that, at the rate of interest represented by B, the community's demand for real money balances falls short of actual money holdings. Asset-holders accordingly attempt to substitute securities for their excess cash holdings, thereby forcing up security prices and reducing the rate of interest. Moreover, in the situation B the goods-and-services market as well as the securities market is out of balance. The diagram shows that, at the prevailing interest rate, money holdings are too large to bring about an equality between full-employment saving and full-employment investment. Saving is below the equilibrium level because of the excessive cash holdings, and the demand for goods and services thus exceeds the economy's capacity to produce. As a result, prices tend to rise, and the real value of money balances is reduced. The movements in the rate of interest and in the real value of money balances are indicated by the short arrows emanating from point B.

By similar reasoning one can demonstrate that, at point C, security prices tend to fall, and the interest rate is correspondingly increased, while the prices of goods and services rise and the real value of cash balances is reduced. Likewise, at D, security prices fall, the rate of interest is increased, commodity prices and wages fall, and the real value of cash balances tends

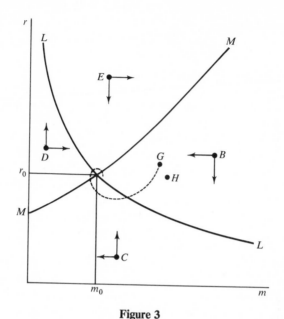

Figure 3

to rise. Finally, if the actual position of the variables is at E, security prices rise, the interest rate is reduced, commodity prices fall, and the real value of cash balances is thus increased. Movements of the variables in the neighborhood of the points C, D, and E have again been indicated by arrows.

Figure 3 demonstrates that when the economic system is out of balance at least one force is always operating to bring the variables of the system closer to the equilibrium point, r_0, m_0. The other fórce, indicated by the second of the two arrows at each of the points B, C, D, and E, operates in such a way as to impart a circular or cyclical movement to the variables. This suggests that, if the rate of interest and the quantity of real cash balances were initially at some nonequilibrium point such as G, the approach to equilibrium might be a spiral or damped cycle like the one depicted in Figure 3. Although such a damped cycle is possible, it is not inevitable, as I shall demonstrate in the Appendix. In any event, I believe it is highly unlikely that the cyclical movement implied by Figure 3 bears any close resemblance to the typical observed business cycle. Most observed cycles are cycles of output and employment, whereas the cycle depicted in Figure 3 is largely a cycle of prices and interest rates.[13] I have presented the dynamic problem concerning the movements of prices and interest rates merely to show the tendency of the system to approach an equilibrium position and not as a contribution to the theory of business cycles.

VI.

I have now shown that the market for goods and services and the market for securities can be in equilibrium simultaneously only at the point r_0, m_0 and that the economic system has an automatic tendency to approach this equilibrium. Superficially, this suggests a close analogy between the rate of interest, r_0, and the classical concept of the equilibrium rate. Like the equilibrium rate of classical theory, the rate r_0 is the only one compatible, under the assumed conditions, with equilibrium of the economic system as a whole; that is, r_0 is the only rate which satisfies both the liquidity-preference requirement and the requirement that full-employment saving shall be equal to full-employment investment. Why, then, does r_0 not have as much claim to be regarded as a real rate as does the classical concept of the real rate of interest?

Whether the rate r_0 is a real rate or a monetary rate depends, as I have indicated earlier, upon the nature of the monetary disturbance. If the disturbance is of the first type — that is, if it is a change in the quantity of money associated with the purchase or sale of securities by the central bank — it will alter some of the functional relations of Figures 1 and 2 and will accordingly change the equilibrium interest rate. The rate r_0 must therefore be regarded as a monetary rate from the point of view of monetary disturbances of this sort. On the other hand, if the monetary disturbance is of the second type, which consists of an increase or decrease in the quantity of money without any offsetting changes in other assets, then it will not alter the functional relations of Figures 1, 2, and 3 and will not permanently change the interest rate. The rate r_0 is thus a real rate from the point of view of monetary disturbances of the second type. Because it is simple to describe, I shall first consider a monetary disturbance of the second type.

Suppose that the economic system is initially in equilibrium at a rate of interest r_0 and a quantity of real cash balances m_0. And suppose that, while other things initially remain unchanged, the quantity of money is arbitrarily

[13]Superficially, the cycle of interest rates and prices described above seems to be somewhat like the monetary part of Hicks's business-cycle theory. In reality, however, the two cyclical processes are quite different. The process envisaged by Hicks involves movements of output and employment rather than movements of prices and costs; and savings in Hicks's theory depend upon the rate of interest and real income, whereas savings in the present paper depend upon the rate of interest and the real value of private wealth (J. R. Hicks, *A Contribution to the Theory of Business Cycles* [London: Oxford University Press, 1949], chaps. 11 and 12).

doubled by giving to each holder of money an additional quantity equal to the amount he already holds. Temporarily, the variables of the system will then be at point H of Figure 3; except for the increase in the quantity of money, nothing in the system will have changed. As I have shown above, however, there will be an automatic tendency for the variables of the system to return eventually to the former equilibrium position, r_0 and m_0. At point H both the securities market and the goods-and-services market will be out of balance, and changes will therefore occur in the interest rate and in the level of prices. The changes in prices, in turn, will affect the real value of cash balances.

Consider, first, the securities market. After the initial monetary disturbance, the quantity of money held by the typical asset-holder is larger than he would like to hold at the prevailing interest rate, r_0. Asset-holders as a group therefore attempt to convert some of their excess cash into securities. As a result, security prices rise, which means that the interest rate falls. The fall in the interest rate increases investment, while the initial increase in the real value of cash balances reduces saving. The demand for goods and services as a whole thus exceeds productive capacity, so that commodity prices and costs begin to rise. The rise in prices tends to reduce the real value of cash balances and thereby initiates a movement of the variables back toward the original equilibrium position. The details of this dynamic process need not concern us here. Suffice it to say that the system as a whole will not be restored to equilibrium until the real value of cash balances is reduced to m_0 and the rate of interest is restored to its former level, r_0.

If the central bank does not acquire or dispose of any assets during the period of adjustment, the real value of money balances can be reduced only by an increase in the price level. Since the real value of cash balances is ultimately restored to its former level, m_0, we know that the increase in prices, in the final position of equilibrium, must be as large as the original increase in the quantity of money. In other words, doubling the nominal quantity of money must result eventually in doubling all money prices and costs, including the money prices of securities as well as the money prices of goods and services. The real variables of the system all return to their former equilibrium levels. The rate of interest, the real value of saving and investment, and the real value of securities, as well as the real value of cash balances, are all the same in the new equilibrium as before the monetary disturbance occurred. The only permanent effect of increasing the quantity of money is a proportionate increase in the general level of prices and costs.[14]

---

[14]Using a model more complex than the one I have been considering, D. Patinkin previously demonstrated that if both the saving-wealth relation and liquidity-preference are active forces, monetary disturbances of the second type will not affect the equilibrium interest rate (see "The Indeterminacy of Absolute Prices in Classical Economic Theory," *Econometrica*, XVII [Jan. 1949], 23–27). Patinkin did not examine the effects of monetary disturbances of the first type and accordingly concluded that the model he had constructed was closer to the classical model than to the Keynesian.

With respect to monetary disturbances of the second type, such as the one I have just described, the economic system embodying both a saving-wealth relation and a liquidity-preference schedule is evidently quite similar to the classical system. In both the classical system and the system depicted in Figure 3 the values of all real variables are independent of the quantity of money. But this is true of the system in Figure 3 only if the monetary disturbances are of the second type, whereas it is true of the classical system for both types of monetary disturbance. If the disturbance is of the first type, which consists of open-market transactions by the central bank, then the equilibrium interest rate will be altered, as I have suggested above. With respect to monetary disturbances of the first type, the equilibrium interest rate of Figure 3 is therefore a monetary rate, and in this regard it resembles the Keynesian interest rate more closely than it does the classical. In other words, by purchasing or selling securities, the banking authorities can alter not only the temporary interest rate which prevails while the open-market transactions are taking place but also the rate at which the system will return to equilibrium after the bank's transactions in securities have ceased.

The power of the banking authorities to alter the equilibrium interest rate is attributable not to their influence upon the nominal quantity of money but to their influence upon the quantity and value of privately held securities. A central-bank purchase of securities, for example, reduces the quantity of privately held securities. This means that the AA schedule of Figure 1 is shifted to the left. And since the liquidity-preference schedule, LL, and the money-requirements schedule, MM, were both derived, in part, from the AA schedule, a shift in the latter causes the former schedules to shift as well. The system as a whole therefore comes into balance, after the securities purchases have been made, at a different rate of interest.

The effect of open-market transactions upon the equilibrium of the system can be described in terms of a ratio indicating the proportion of the total supply of securities held in private hands. Let this ratio be represented by the letter λ. Consider, first, the situation in which λ has a value of 1.0. This means that the total available supply of securities is held by private asset-holders, so that the central bank's assets consist exclusively of currency. Given the holdings of securities by private asset-holders, the rate of interest at which the system is in equilibrium can be determined, as in our earlier illustration, by the intersection of a liquidity-preference schedule, LL, and a money-requirements schedule, MM. Assuming that the value of private asset holdings when $\lambda = 1.0$ is given in Figure 4 by the solid line AA and that the wealth-requirements schedule is WW, the liquidity-preference schedule and the money-requirements schedule can be derived as in my earlier illustration. These derived schedules, for $\lambda = 1.0$, are represented in Figure 5 by the solid lines LL and MM, respectively. Under the assumed conditions with respect to security holdings, the equilibrium rate of interest is r_0, and the equilibrium value of real cash balances is m_0, as shown in Figure 5.

Suppose that this equilibrium is disturbed by a substantial purchase of securities on the part of the central bank. The dynamic process by which the economy adapts itself to such open-market transactions will probably be

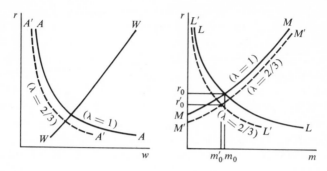

Figure 4   Figure 5

highly complicated. The securities will be purchased at many different prices from the various asset-holders, and this means that we cannot predict exactly how the open-market transactions will affect the cash balances of all asset-holders together. In any event, the real value of cash balances will be influenced by price movements as well as by the central bank's dealings in securities, and it is the combined effect of both influences which ultimately governs the equilibrium value of the real money supply. In view of our interest in the equilibrium of the system, we may pass over the dynamic problems and investigate, instead, the influence of the central bank's security purchases upon the schedules in Figures 4 and 5 which determine the ultimate resting places of our variables.

Suppose that the central bank continues to purchase securities until it has acquired one-third of the common stock available to the economy as a whole and that all transactions between asset-holders and the central bank cease at this point. When the securities market and the goods-and services market are once again in equilibrium, how will the rate of interest compare with the rate that prevailed before the open-market transactions began? According to the classical theory, the rate of interest should return to its former level as soon as the bank's security purchases have ceased. According to the system depicted in Figures 4 and 5, however, the security purchases by the central bank will permanently *lower* the equilibrium rate of interest.

If the bank acquires one-third of all available securities, the security holdings of private asset-holders will of course be only two-thirds as large as they formerly were, so that λ will have a value of ⅔. This means that at any given interest rate the real value of private security holdings will be two-thirds of its former value. The broken line $A'A'$ of Figure 4 is drawn at two-thirds of the horizontal distance of the solid line AA from the vertical axis, and $A'A'$ thus represents the real value of private security holdings, expressed again as a function of the rate of interest, after the central bank has acquired its securities. The wealth-requirements schedule, WW, depends upon preferences and upon the savings and investment schedules and presumably will be unaffected by the open-market transactions. Since the money-requirements schedule, MM, depends upon the value of private security holdings as well as upon WW, however, the MM schedule will be shifted. At any given rate of interest, the total assets — money and securities combined — needed to maintain equality between full-employment saving and full-employment investment will be the same as before. But the value of private security holdings has been reduced by the central bank's purchases, and this means that total assets cannot be maintained at the level needed for full employment unless private money holdings are increased by a corresponding amount. In short, the money-requirements schedule, MM, is moved to the right by the same amount that the securities schedule, AA, is moved to the left.[15] The new money-requirements schedule corresponding to $\lambda = $ ⅔ is shown in Figure 5 as the broken line $M'M'$.

The liquidity-preference schedule, as well as the money-requirements schedule, is affected by the central bank's purchase of securities. At any given interest rate, the proportions in which the typical asset-holder wishes to hold money and securities are presumably the same as in the old equilibrium. The value of private security holdings, however, is now only two-thirds of the former value at the same interest rate. The desired ratio be-

[15]In describing the consequences of open-market transactions, I assume that the securities schedule, AA, is the only schedule of Figure 4 which is *directly* influenced by the central bank's purchase or sale of securities; the other schedules (i.e., the wealth-requirements schedule, the money-requirements schedule, and the liquidity-preference schedule) are assumed to be affected only in so far as they are related to, or derived from, the securities schedule, AA. This implies that the income available to the typical asset-holder is not altered by the central bank's dealings in securities. If disposable income tended to fall or to rise with an increase or decrease in the central bank's holdings of securities, the saving and investment schedules would also be affected, and the wealth-requirements schedule, which is derived from the saving and investment schedules, would tend to shift.

Taken by themselves, however, open-market transactions may well have a slight influence on disposable income. If the central bank buys securities, for example, the income on these securities is transferred from the former owners to the bank. In the absence of offsetting transactions, the security purchases thus reduce the disposable income of private asset-holders and increase the profits of the central bank by a corresponding amount. I do not wish to discuss the complications introduced by this connection between open-market transactions and disposable income. I therefore assume throughout that any additional profits which the central bank earns by reason of its acquisition of securities are ultimately passed on to private hands in the form of reduced taxes. Under these circumstances, the security purchases by the bank will redistribute income between former asset owners and taxpayers but will not influence the total of disposable income.

tween money holdings and security holdings will thus not be maintained unless the real value of money balances is reduced to two-thirds of its former value. In other words, the LL schedule in Figure 5 is shifted to the left, the relative amount of the shift being the same as the leftward shift of the securities schedule, AA. The new liquidity-preference schedule, for $\lambda = \frac{2}{3}$, is represented in Figure 5 by the line $L'L'$.

The combined effect of the shift in the liquidity-preference schedule and of the shift in the money-requirements schedule is a reduction in the equilibrium rate of interest from r_0 to r_0', as indicated in Figure 5. Thus, the banking authorities by means of a limited purchase of securities have *permanently* reduced the interest rate at which the economic system is in equilibrium. The dynamic process of adjustment by which the equilibrium interest rate moves from r_0 to r_0' will probably be highly complex, as I have indicated earlier. Nevertheless, I believe that the influence of the central bank upon the equilibrium interest rate will stand out more clearly if we consider a greatly simplified dynamic sequence.

When the central bank begins to purchase securities, the first effect is a rise in security prices and a corresponding decline in the rate of interest. The actual security transactions themselves do not alter the total value of private asset holdings but merely change the form in which assets are held. The initial result of the bank's purchases, therefore, is a rise in the value of private asset holdings (capital gains) together with a reduction in the rate of interest and a shift on the part of asset-holders from securities to money. One may presume that at the new, lower rate of interest the asset-holders have exchanged securities for cash in such a way as to satisfy their demands for liquidity; for, if this were not true, the prices of securities would continue to rise, and the interest rate to fall, until the asset-holders were willing to part with the amount of securities that the central bank wanted to buy. Although the point representing the new quantity of private money holdings and the new, temporary rate of interest will thus lie somewhere on the liquidity-preference schedule $L'L'$, it cannot at the same time lie on the money-requirements schedule, $M'M'$, or the wealth-requirements schedule, WW. The fall in the interest rate, taken by itself, would normally lead to an excess of full-employment investment over full-employment saving and thus create an excess demand for goods and services. The inflationary pressure is further increased, however, by the capital gains, which increase the value of total private wealth holdings and thereby reduce current saving. As a result, prices and costs tend to rise, and the real value of the money supply is correspondingly reduced. The rise in prices and the reduction in the real value of private money holdings must continue until the real value of security-and-cash holdings combined is low enough to encourage a sufficient amount of saving to make full-employment saving once more equal to full-employment investment. The new equilibrium is finally achieved, as Figures 4 and 5 demonstrate, at a permanently lower rate of interest.

Now, since the new equilibrium must lie on the wealth-requirements schedule, WW, as well as on the money requirements schedule, $M'M'$, it is obvious that, when prices have finally stopped rising and the rate of interest has reached its new and lower equilibrium, the value of total private wealth must be smaller than in the old equilibrium. In short, the final result of the open-market security purchases by the central bank is a reduction in the real value of the total wealth in private hands. This reduction has occurred in two stages: the liquidity of the typical asset-holder has first been increased through the central-bank purchase of securities; and the real value of the larger liquid balances has subsequently been reduced through inflation. Thus, under a regime of flexible prices, central-bank purchase of securities is an indirect means of reducing the real value of the total assets — cash and securities combined — in private hands. The reduction in the value of privately held wealth tends, in turn, to increase saving and thereby reduces the rate of interest at which full-employment saving is equal to full-employment investment. To summarize briefly, then, we may say that the central bank is able to alter the equilibrium rate of interest through its power to alter the real value of private wealth.

VII.

Assuming that saving depends upon the real value of private wealth as well as upon the interest rate, I have now demonstrated that the equilibrium interest rate is partly a real rate, as in the classical theory, and partly a monetary rate, as in Keynes's theory. Monetary disturbances of one type affect the equilibrium interest rate of the system, while disturbances of another type do not. In general, any monetary disturbance which alters the amount of securities held by the typical asset-holder tends also to affect the interest rate at which the economic system as a whole is in equilibrium. On the other hand, any monetary disturbance which does not affect private security holdings will leave the equilibrium interest rate unchanged.

The distinction which I have made between the two types of monetary disturbance suggests that the true cause of a change in the interest rate is not a change in the quantity of money per se but a change in the amount of other assets held by the typical asset-holder. This conjecture is, indeed, correct. Open-market transactions of the central bank alter the equilibrium interest rate not because they affect the quantity of money but because they affect the quantity of privately held securities. Consider again, for example, the open-market transactions which I have described in Figures 4 and 5. In those illustrations the central bank is assumed to purchase one-third of all privately held securities. As a consequence, the level of prices is increased, the real value of private wealth declines, the propensity to save increases, and real saving finally comes into balance with real investment at a permanently lower interest rate.

Suppose, now, that the amount of privately held securities were reduced without any offsetting change in the quantity of money. Such a reduction could be brought about by a capital levy of one-third on all securities, payable only in kind. In other words, the government could require that one-third of all privately held securities be turned over to it. In what respects would the effects of such a policy differ from the effects of the open-market transactions described in Figures 4 and 5? Examination of the figures reveals that the interest rate, the volume of real investment, the real value of cash balances, and the other real variables of the system are affected in exactly the same way by a one-third levy in kind upon all securities as by a central-bank purchase of the same amount of securities. The nominal quantity of money is of course larger when the securities are acquired by purchase than when they are acquired by taxation. But the real value of bank balances is exactly the same, in the new position of equilibrium, in both cases. Thus, the only difference between the effects of the two means of acquiring the securities is a difference in the level of prices and costs. The price level is higher when the securities are acquired by purchase than when they are acquired by taxation. In all other respects the two situations are identical as far as the final results are concerned.

The foregoing example reveals the close analogy between central-bank security purchases and a capital levy on securities. In the system investigated above, a purchase of securities by the central bank is a means of reducing the real value of privately held wealth and operates just as effectively in this direction as a corresponding capital levy payable in kind. Indeed, the central bank's power to alter the equilibrium interest rate arises exclusively from its influence on the real value of privately held securities.

Through its power to change the interest rate, the central bank can also affect the rate of growth of the economy as a whole. At each different equilibrium interest rate full-employment saving is of course equal to full-employment investment, but the amount of real saving and investment varies with variations in the equilibrium interest rate. When the equilibrium rate is increased, the economic system comes into balance at a lower real value of investment and saving; and, when the equilibrium rate is reduced, the real value of saving and investment tends to increase. By purchasing securities, the central bank can reduce the real value of private wealth, thereby increasing the propensity to save and causing the system to attain a new equilibrium at a permanently lower interest rate and a permanently higher rate of capital accumulation. In a similar manner, the bank, through sales of securities, can increase the real value of private wealth, lower the propensity to save, raise the equilibrium rate of interest, and reduce the rate of capital accumulation.

Whether the bank has a substantial influence or only a negligible influence upon the rate of growth of the system depends upon its authority to buy and sell securities and upon the magnitude of the saving-wealth relation. If the saving-wealth relation is large, so that the propensity to save increases or decreases appreciably as the real value of private wealth falls or rises, and if the bank is authorized to buy and sell securities in large quantities, then the rate of growth may be affected to a considerable extent by central-bank policy. In practice, however, there will usually be an institutional barrier to the amount of securities the bank can sell; it cannot sell more securities than it owns. And this means that, when the bank has divested itself of all its securities, it has no further power to raise the equilibrium interest rate and lower the rate of growth. There may be a similar barrier to the amount of securities the bank can purchase, since only certain types of assets are eligible for the bank's portfolio. If the bank has acquired all the assets it is authorized to purchase, no further reduction of private wealth, and no further increase in private saving, can be accomplished by central-bank activity in the securities market.

In terms of the theory set out above, we may say that the central bank's power over the equilibrium interest rate and the equilibrium rate of growth will usually be determined by institutional arrangements which prevent it from purchasing more than a small fraction of private wealth or from selling more assets than it possesses. This might mean, for example, that the institutional arrangements were such that the value of λ would have to lie between 0.9 and 1.0. In most countries these institutional limits may well be so narrow that the actual power of the central bank to influence the equilibrium of the system is negligible. Nevertheless, if saving depends upon the real value of private wealth as described in the saving-wealth relation, the rate of interest must be regarded as partly a monetary rate. For, if the institutional limits to central-bank action were removed or reduced, the possible variation in the equilibrium interest rate which could be brought about by the central bank would be correspondingly increased.

APPENDIX

The geometrical methods employed in the text of this paper were not sufficiently powerful to deal with some of the more difficult problems encountered, particularly the dynamic problems. I am therefore adding an analytical appendix. The symbols used in this appendix have the following meanings:

r represents the rate of interest, or the yield on common stock

m represents the real value of private money holdings

a represents the real value of all common stock, whether held by private owners or by the central bank

λ represents the proportion of the total supply of common stock held by private owners

w represents the real value of all privately held wealth, including both money and common stock

S represents the real value of current saving

I represents the real value of current investment

The amount of real saving out of a full-employment income is assumed to depend upon the real value of private wealth as well as upon the rate of interest, and we may accordingly write $S = S(r, w)$. Investment, under conditions of full employment, is assumed to depend only upon the rate of interest, and the investment function may therefore be written as follows: $I = I(r)$. If real national income under conditions of full employment is y_0, and if a proportion, c, of this consists of business profits, the real value of all common stock will be the capitalized value of these profits, thus: $a = cy_0/r$. The only remaining functional relation to be defined is the liquidity-preference function. Let $L(r)$ be such a function, indicating the proportion in which asset-holders as a group wish to hold money and common stock. With the aid of these definitions we may now write down the following system of equations:

$$S(r, w) = I(r) \, ,$$

$$L(r) = \frac{m}{\lambda a} \, ,$$

$$w = \lambda a + m \, ,$$

$$a = \frac{cy_0}{r} \, .$$

(1)

The first of equations (1) expresses the condition that, in equilibrium, full-employment saving must equal full-employment investment. The second equation says that the rate of interest must be such that the desired proportion between money holdings and security holdings on the part of the owners of private wealth is equal to the actual proportion. The third equation is an identity, defining the real value of private wealth as the sum of private money holdings and private security holdings. Finally, the fourth of equations (1) says that the real value of all common stock is the capitalized value of business profits, where the capitalization is done at the prevailing rate of interest, r.

If the value of λ is given, equations (1) are sufficient to determine the equilibrium values of the four variables r, w, m, and a; i.e., the equations determine the rate of interest, the total real value of privately held wealth, the real value of money balances, and the real value of all common stock. The price level does not enter explicitly in equations (1), since all variables are in real terms. Nevertheless, price movements are implicitly taken into account through movements of m, the real value of the money supply. In the absence of open-market transactions, indeed, m can change only by means of general inflation or deflation.

Security purchases or sales by the central bank are indicated in equations (1) by changes in the value of λ. An increase in λ, for example, indicates a larger proportion of total securities in private hands and hence signifies security sales by the central bank. Changes in λ will obviously alter the equilibrium values of all our variables. In order to see how a central-bank sale of securities affects these equilibrium values, we may differentiate (1) with respect to λ, as follows:

$$\left.\begin{aligned}
(S_r - I_r)\frac{dr}{d\lambda} + S_w\frac{dw}{d\lambda} &= 0, \\[2mm]
-\frac{1}{\lambda a}\frac{dm}{d\lambda} + L_r\frac{dr}{d\lambda} \qquad\qquad + \frac{m}{\lambda a^2}\frac{da}{d\lambda} &= -\frac{m}{\lambda^2 a} \\[2mm]
\frac{dm}{d\lambda} \qquad\qquad -\frac{dw}{d\lambda} + \lambda\frac{da}{d\lambda} &= -a \\[2mm]
-\frac{a}{r}\frac{dr}{d\lambda} \qquad\qquad -\frac{da}{d\lambda} &= 0
\end{aligned}\right\} \tag{2}$$

Solving equations (2) for

$$\frac{dr}{d\lambda}, \qquad \frac{dm}{d\lambda}, \qquad \frac{dw}{d\lambda}, \qquad \text{and} \qquad \frac{da}{d\lambda},$$

we find

$$\left.\begin{aligned}
\frac{dr}{d\lambda} &= -\frac{S_w}{\Delta}\left(\frac{1}{\lambda} + \frac{m}{\lambda^2 a}\right), \\[2mm]
\frac{dm}{d\lambda} &= \frac{1}{\Delta}\left\{(S_r - I_r)\frac{m}{\lambda^2 a} - aS_w L_r\right\}, \\[2mm]
\frac{dw}{d\lambda} &= \frac{1}{\Delta}(S_r - I_r)\left(\frac{1}{\lambda} + \frac{m}{\lambda^2 a}\right), \\[2mm]
\frac{da}{d\lambda} &= \frac{1}{\Delta}\frac{aS_w}{r}\left(\frac{1}{\lambda} + \frac{m}{\lambda^2 a}\right).
\end{aligned}\right\} \tag{3}$$

The symbol Δ in equations (3) represents the basic determinant of the system, i.e.,

$$
\Delta \equiv
\begin{vmatrix}
0 & S_r - I_r & S_w & 0 \\[2mm]
-\dfrac{1}{\lambda a} & L_r & 0 & \dfrac{m}{\lambda a^2} \\[2mm]
1 & 0 & -1 & \lambda \\[2mm]
0 & -\dfrac{a}{r} & 0 & -1
\end{vmatrix},
$$

$$
\equiv (S_r - I_r)\frac{1}{\lambda a} + S_w L_r - \frac{S_w}{r} - \frac{m S_w}{\lambda a r}.
$$

(4)

The subscripts in equations (3) and (4) indicate differentiation of the S, I, and L functions with respect to the variable appearing in the subscript. I assume the system is stable in the classic sense that an increase in the rate of interest creates an excess of potential saving over potential investment; this implies that $S_r - I_r$ is positive. The saving-wealth relation is represented in (3) and (4) by S_w, which is negative, indicating that an increase in the real value of private wealth reduces real saving. The slope L_r of the liquidity-preference schedule is assumed to be negative, which implies that an increase in the rate of interest reduces the desired ratio between money and securities.

With the given signs of S_r, I_r, etc., one can see from (4) that Δ is a positive determinant. Moreover, the direction of change of most of the variables of the system can be readily determined. Thus, (3) shows that $dr/d\lambda$ is positive, $dw/d\lambda$ is positive, and $da/d\lambda$ is negative. This means that open-market sales of securities have increased the rate of interest, increased the real value of private wealth (cash and securities combined), and reduced the real value of the total supply of common stock. The only change whose sign is indeterminate is $dm/d\lambda$, the change in the real value of private money holdings. The reason for this indeterminacy is not far to seek: the central-bank sales of securities have reduced private money balances, but the real value of the remaining private balances have subsequently been increased through a general deflation. The final position of real money balances thus depends upon the relative strength of these opposing forces. But whatever happens to the real value of privately held money, equations (3) show that privately held wealth as a whole has been increased by the central bank's sales of securities. The increase in the real value of private wealth has reduced the rate of saving, and it is this reduction of saving which accounts for the permanent rise in the equilibrium rate of interest.

Thus far I have investigated the stationary or equilibrium values of the system without saying anything about the dynamic process of adjustment. I shall conclude this appendix with a few remarks concerning the behavior of the variables through time, during intervals when the system is not in equilibrium.

Consider, first, the behavior of prices when total demand is different from productive capacity. The difference between demand and productive capacity is measured, of course, by the difference between potential full-employment saving and potential full-employment investment. If the former exceeds the latter, demand for goods and services falls short of productive capacity, and prices and costs accordingly tend to decline. Conversely, if full-employment investment exceeds full-employment saving, total demand exceeds capacity, and both prices and costs rise. In the absence of new borrowing or lending by the banking system, however, an increase in prices is equivalent to a fall in the real value of money balances, and the time movement of the general price level may therefore be described in terms of movements in the value of money. As a first dynamic postulate, then, I write:

$$\frac{dm}{dt} = k_1[S(r, w) - I(r)]. \tag{5}$$

Equation (5) says that the price level tends to fall, and the real value of money balances tends to rise, whenever potential saving exceeds potential investment. Likewise, prices rise, and the real value of money balances falls, when potential saving falls short of potential investment. The speed of the price movement, in both cases, is assumed in (5) to be proportional to the size of the inflationary or deflationary gap, and the constant, k_1, represents this speed of adjustment.

So much for the general price level in the commodity-and-service market. Consider next the movement of prices in the securities market. I assume, as I indicated in the text, that the securities market is dominated by transactions in old securities rather than by supply-and-demand conditions in the new-securities market. Specifically, I assume that security prices tend to rise whenever asset-holders on balance attempt to shift from money to securities and that security prices fall when asset-holders attempt a shift in the opposite direction. The attempted shift, in turn, depends upon whether the actual ratio of cash to securities is higher or lower than the desired ratio, as indicated by the liquidity-preference function. Since a rise in security prices is equivalent to a fall in the rate of interest, our second dynamic postulate may be written

$$\frac{dr}{dt} = k_2\left[L(r) - \frac{m}{\lambda a} \right]. \tag{6}$$

In words, equation (6) says that the rate of interest rises, which means that security prices fall, when the desired ratio of money to securities exceeds the actual ratio. And, conversely, the rate of interest falls when the desired ratio is less than the actual ratio.

Equations (5) and (6) are the only equations of adjustment that we shall need. These two equations are the dynamic counterpart of the first two of equations (1). They do not form a complete system, however, since we have only two equations in four unknowns. Before we can solve our dynamic equations, we must have two more equations. The two missing equations are the third and fourth equations of our static system (1). These are merely definitional equations and are assumed to be satisfied at any moment of time, without lag. The third equation defines private wealth at a given moment as the sum of private security holdings and private money holdings, while the fourth equation defines the rate of interest as the yield on securities. The complete dynamic system is as follows:

$$\left.\begin{array}{l} \dfrac{dm}{dt} = k_1[S(r, w) - I(r)] , \\[2ex] \dfrac{dr}{dt} = k_2\left[L(r) - \dfrac{m}{\lambda a} \right], \\[2ex] w = \lambda a + m \\[2ex] a = \dfrac{cy_0}{r} . \end{array}\right\} \qquad (7)$$

Equations (7) cannot be explicitly solved, since we do not know the exact form of the functions S, I, and L. I shall therefore make a linear approximation of (7), which will be valid only for small deviations from the equilibrium values of the variables. If r_0, w_0, m_0, and a_0 represent the equilibrium values, we may write, as such a linear approximation,

$$\left.\begin{array}{l} \dfrac{dm}{dt} = \qquad\qquad k_1(S_r - I_r)(r - r_0) + k_1 S_w(w - w_0) , \\[2ex] \dfrac{dr}{dt} = -k_2\dfrac{1}{\lambda a}(m - m_0) + k_2 L_r(r - r_0) \qquad\qquad + k_2\dfrac{m}{\lambda a^2}(a - a_0), \\[2ex] 0 = \qquad (m - m_0) \qquad\qquad - (w - w_0) \qquad + \lambda(a - a_0), \\[2ex] 0 = \qquad\qquad -\dfrac{a}{r}(r - r_0) \qquad\qquad - (a - a_0). \end{array}\right\} (8)$$

The solution of (8) takes the form

$$m = m_0 + A_1 e^{\rho_1 t} + A_2 e^{\rho_2 t_1}, \qquad (9)$$

with similar results for r, a, and w, where A_1 and A_2 depend upon the initial values of the variables, and where ρ_1 and ρ_2 are the roots of the following equation:

$$\begin{vmatrix} -\rho & k_1(S_r - I_r) & k_1 S_w & 0 \\ -\dfrac{k_2}{\lambda a} & k_2 L_r - \rho & 0 & \dfrac{k_2 m}{\lambda a^2} \\ 1 & 0 & -1 & \lambda \\ 0 & -\dfrac{a}{r} & 0 & -1 \end{vmatrix} = 0. \tag{10}$$

Equation (10) may be expended in powers of ρ as follows:

$$\rho^2 + \left(\frac{k_2 m}{\lambda a r} - k_2 L_r - k_1 S_w\right)\rho + k_1 k_2 \Delta = 0, \tag{11}$$

where Δ is the basic determinant of the static system, (1).

The coefficients of the powers of ρ in equation (11) are positive, which means that the real parts of the roots of equation (11) are all negative. Thus the dynamic system is stable, for small deviations from equilibrium, regardless of the numerical values of L_r, S_w, etc. In other words, if the liquidity-preference function, the saving function, and the investment function do not alter their form or position as prices rise or fall, the dynamic system will eventually reach a stationary or static position. This does not mean, of course, that an economic system in which the saving-wealth relation is operative will always be a stable system in reality; for equations (7) and (8) have made no allowance for expectations, and such expectations may exert a strongly destabilizing influence on the system. If prices of commodities are rising, for example, consumers and producers may anticipate further price increases; if so, saving will probably decline and investment will increase, thereby widening the inflationary gap and accelerating the price rise. Likewise, if security prices are rising, asset-holders may revise downward their estimate of what constitutes a normal ratio between money and securities; and, if they do, the resulting attempt to shift from money to securities will cause a further rise in securities prices. These possibilities suggest that equations (7) and (8) are stable only in a narrow sense.

Assuming that the system is stable, we may inquire, in conclusion, about the nature of the approach toward equilibrium. Is the solution of equation (8) cyclical or noncyclical? The answer to this question depends upon the roots of equation (10) or (11). The dynamic system will not be cyclical unless these roots are complex numbers. This means that $b^2 - 4c$ is negative, where b is the coefficient of ρ in (11) and c is the constant term. I leave it to the reader to prove the following propositions: (1) the roots of equation (11) may be either real or complex, which means that the dynamic system may or may not have a cyclical solution. (2) If k_1 and k_2, the speeds of adjustment in the commodity market and the securities market, respectively, are decidedly different in magnitude, the roots are likely to be real and the dynamic system is thus likely to be a noncyclical system. (3) If $S_r - I_r$ is large, so that a small rise in the rate of interest creates a substantial deflationary gap, the system will probably be cyclical.

JAMES TOBIN **18**

Money wage rates and employment

What is the effect of a general change in money wage rates on aggregate employment and output?[1] To this question, crucial both for theory and for policy, the answers of economists are as unsatisfactory as they are divergent. A decade of Keynesian economics has not solved the problem, but it has made clearer the assumptions concerning economic behavior on which the answer depends. In this field, perhaps even more than in other aspects of the *General Theory*, Keynes' contribution lies in clarifying the theoretical issues at stake rather than in providing an ultimate solution.

Pre-Keynesian solutions to the money wage problem

How considerable this contribution is can be appreciated from a brief review of pre-Keynesian attempts to solve the problem.[2] These solutions

From THE NEW ECONOMICS: KEYNES' INFLUENCE ON THEORY AND PUBLIC POLICY, edited by Seymour E. Harris. Copyright 1947 by Alfred A. Knopf, Inc. Reprinted by permission. Pp. 572–587. [Footnotes expanded — *Eds.*]

[1]This question concerns the effects of a general change in money wage rates which is expected to be permanent. A fall in money wage rates which is expected to be followed by further reductions will discourage output and employment, and a rise which is expected to continue will stimulate output and employment. On these propositions there is no disagreement.

[2]It should be noted that R. F. Harrod ("Review of Professor Pigou's *Theory of Unemployment*," *Economic Journal*, XLIV [March 1934], 19) anticipated the Keynesian solution.

rested on one of the following assumptions: (a) that the price level is unchanged,[3] (b) that aggregate money demand (MV) is unchanged,[4] or (c) that some component of aggregate money demand, e.g., non-wage-earners' expenditure, is unchanged.[5] Naturally, if money demand is assumed to be maintained in any of these ways, the conclusion follows easily that a money wage cut will increase, and a money wage rise diminish, total employment and output. These assumptions, or any variant of them, beg the central question raised by the fact that money wage-rate changes are double-edged. They change money costs, but they change at the same time money incomes and hence money expenditures. Even the money expenditures of non-wage-earners cannot be assumed unchanged, for their incomes depend in part on the expenditures of wage-earners.

The rôle of the consumption function in Keynes' solution

Keynes replaced these assumptions with a proposition which, whatever its shortcomings, is certainly a more plausible description of actual economic behavior. This proposition is his consumption function: that *real* consumption expenditure is a unique function of *real* income, with the marginal propensity to consume positive but less than unity. So far as consumption expenditure alone is concerned, therefore, Keynes concluded that a change in money wage rates could not affect the volume of employment and output. Because the marginal propensity to consume is less than unity, any increase in output and real income would fail to generate enough of an increase in real consumption expenditure to purchase the additional output. Any decrease in output and real income would cause, for the same reason, an excess of aggregate real demand over supply. The result of a change in money wage rates would be, still considering only reactions via consumption expenditure, a proportionate change in prices and money incomes and no change in employment, output, real incomes, or real wage rates.

These are the implications of Keynes' systematic theory. In the course

[3] J. R. Hicks, *The Theory of Wages* (London: Macmillan, 1936), pp. 211–212.

[4] Cf. Hicks, "Mr. Keynes and the Classics: A Suggested Interpretation," *Econometrica*, V (April 1937), 147.

[5] A. Smithies, "Wage Policy in the Depression," *Economic Record*, [XI] Dec. 1935, p. 249.

A. C. Pigou, *Theory of Unemployment* (London: Macmillan, 1933), pp. 100–106.

In "Real and Money Wage Rates in Relation to Unemployment" (*Economic Journal*, XLVII [Sept. 1937], 405), Pigou relaxed this assumption to provide in effect that non-wage-earners' money expenditure, although not constant, is uniquely determined by the volume of employment. This variant has the same significance as the three assumptions discussed in the text. Later, under the prodding of Nicholas Kaldor ("Professor Pigou on Money Wages in Relation to Unemployment," *Economic Journal*, XLVII [Dec. 1937], 745), Pigou in "Money Wages and Unemployment" (*Economic Journal*, XLVIII [March 1938], 134), accepted in essence the Keynesian position.

of remarks which are, from the standpoint of his systematic theory, *obiter dicta*, Keynes considered two possible effects of a money wage cut on the propensity to consume: "redistribution of real income (a) from wage-earners to other factors entering into marginal prime cost whose remuneration has not been reduced, and (b) from entrepreneurs to rentiers to whom a certain income fixed in terms of money has been guaranteed."[6] The effects on consumption of the second type of transfer, (b), Keynes throught doubtful and apparently unimportant. The first type of transfer, (a), from wage-earners to other prime factors, would, if it occurred, be likely to diminish the propensity to consume; it would, therefore, be unfavorable to employment. However, Keynes over-estimated the likelihood of such a redistribution of income. Maintenance of the prices of other variable factors in the face of a wage cut would encourage substitution of labor for these factors; such substitution would not only be directly favorable to employment of labor but would also diminish or reverse the transfer of income from labor to non-wage-earners. On the other hand, if the owners of other variable factors sought to avoid such substitution, they would, as Lerner has shown, reduce their prices in the same proportion as the wage rate and consequently would not gain income at the expense of labor.[7]

Effects of money wage rate changes on investment

The possibility remains that a change in money wage rates may induce a change in the other component of Keynes' effective demand, real investment. So far as real investment is itself dependent on the level of real income or the volume of real consumption expenditure, there is clearly no reason for such a change. Likewise, the marginal efficiency of capital, so far as it is objectively determined by the amount of additional output which can result from an increment of capital, is not altered by a change in money wage rates. Three types of reactions on the rate of real investment are left:

    a. Conceivably, a change in money wage rates may affect that delicate phenomenon, the state of business confidence. However, the direction of this influence cannot be predicted in a general theory.[8] Individual business men making investment decisions may be impressed chiefly by the fact that a money wage cut reduces their costs. On the other hand, a fall in wages and prices embarrasses entrepreneurs by increasing the real burden of their debt. Without underrating the importance of these types of reactions,

    [6]*General Theory, op. cit.*, p. 262.
    [7]Problems raised by the existence of variable factors other than labor are discussed below, pp. 371, 374–375.
    [8]Except in the case discussed in footnote 1 above, or in the opposite case when wage expectations are inelastic.

therefore, Keynes had to exclude them from his theoretical structure.[9]

b. In an open economy, a change in the general wage rate and price level will affect the balance of trade. A reduction of money wage rates and prices will stimulate demand for exports and shift domestic demand to home goods in preference to imports. Such a change in the balance of trade is equivalent to an increase in real investment and has a multiplied effect on home real income and employment. This effect may be strengthened by a worsening of the terms of trade, which increases the employment necessary to obtain the equilibrium level of real income and real saving. A rise in money wage rates would have the opposite effects. On this score there is little dispute. These effects may be nullified, however, by similar wage adjustments in other countries or by changes in exchange rates.

c. A change in the level of money wage rates, prices, and money incomes alters in the same direction the demand for cash balances for transactions purposes. With an unchanged quantity of money, a reduction of money wage rates leaves a larger supply of money to satisfy the demand for cash balances from precautionary and speculative motives. The result is a reduction in the rate of interest, which should lead to an increase in the rate of real investment. Similarly a rise in money wage rates increases the interest rate and restricts real investment. It was only by this circuitous route that Keynes found any generally valid theoretical reason for expecting in a closed economy a relationship between money wage rates and employment.

The central thesis of the *General Theory*

Such is the Keynesian solution to the money wage problem. It is important to view it in the broad setting of the *General Theory*. Keynes set himself the goal of establishing, first, that there may be involuntary unemployment of labor and, second, that there may be no method open to labor to remove such unemployment by making new money wage bargains. There may be involuntary unemployment because additional labor would be offered at the going money wage rate at the same or lower real wage rates.[10] Labor, beset by a "money illusion," will permit its real wage to be reduced by price rises without leaving the market, even when it will not accede to the same reduction in its real wage by a money wage cut. At the same time, labor is powerless to take advantage of the potential demand for its services at lower real wage rates, because a reduction in the money wage may not lead to a reduction in the real wage.

The linkage between money wage rates and employment via the rate of interest appears to destroy the second half of this central thesis. For, if

[9]He considered the various possibilities in detail. *General Theory, op. cit.,* Chap. 19, especially pp. 262–264.

[10]*General Theory, op. cit.,* chap. 2. See footnote 18 below.

money wage rates were flexible, they could presumably fall enough to lower the rate of interest to a level which would induce the volume of investment necessary to maintain full employment. This linkage is, however, extremely tenuous. It can be broken at either of the following points: (a) The interest elasticity of the demand for cash balances may be infinite; (b) the interest elasticity of the demand for investment may be zero.[11] Condition (a) is likely to be approximated at low interest rates, and condition (b) is supported by the evidence that interest calculations play an insignificant part in business investment decisions. The Keynesian thesis that labor cannot erase unemployment by revising its money wage bargains is, therefore, not seriously damaged by admitting the effect of money wage rates on the demand for cash balances.

Assumptions of Keynesian money wage theory

It is damaged, however, by removal of certain of the restrictive assumptions of the Keynesian model; and their removal is logically necessary because they clash with other basic assumptions. To demonstrate this, the main assumptions of Keynesian money wage theory will be examined. They are: (1) that real wages are a decreasing function of the volume of employment, (2) that labor is the only variable factor of production, (3) that pure competition exists throughout the economy or that the degree of monopoly is constant, (4) that "money illusion" affects the supply function for labor, and (5) that "money illusion" does not occur in other supply and demand functions.

1. Diminishing marginal productivity

Adopting the traditional postulate of diminishing marginal productivity, Keynes assumed that real wage rates and employment are inversely related. Consequently, an increase in employment at the same money wage can occur only if there is a rise in prices sufficient to compensate business firms for the increase in marginal costs associated with an expansion of output. For this reason, the question whether labor will accept increased employment at a reduced real wage brought about by such a price rise becomes Keynes' criterion for the existence of involuntary unemployment. Keynes ventured the guess that real wages and money wages would usually be found to move in opposite directions, since money wages usually rise in periods of increasing employment and fall when employment is decreasing.[12] This

---

[11]F. Modigliani ("Liquidity Preference and the Theory of Interest and Money," *Econometrica*, XII [Jan. 1944], 45–89) emphasizes that except when condition (a), which he calls the "Keynesian case," is satisfied, unemployment is attributable to an improper relationship between the quantity of money and the money wage rate, i.e., to rigid wages. He does not mention that condition (b) would constitute another and very important exception to the wage rigidity explanation of unemployment.

[12]*General Theory, op. cit.*, pp. 9–10.

conjecture provoked several statistical investigations designed to check the traditional postulate.[13] Statistically these investigations were inconclusive;[14] in any case the issue, though of great interest in itself, is not crucial for Keynes' central thesis. Equilibrium with decreasing marginal costs throughout most of the economy is conceivable in a world of monopolies. In such an economy, the involuntary nature of unemployment at a given money wage would be even clearer than on Keynes' definition. Increased employment would not be purchased at the expense of a higher cost of living but would yield higher real wages. The question raised by the second proposition of Keynes' central thesis — can unemployment be removed by a money wage cut? — remains the same whether increasing or decreasing marginal productivity prevails.

2. No variable factors other than labor

The assumption that labor is the only variable factor is more serious. By this simplification, Keynes rules out the possibility of substitution as a result of money wage rate changes. If the possibility of substitution between labor and other factors is admitted, the Keynesian solution of the money wage problem can be saved only by introducing another assumption. Paradoxically, this postulate is that all factors other than labor are fully employed and that their prices are completely flexible. Then their prices will always change in the same direction and proportion as the money wage rate.[15] If the money wage rate increases, business firms will attempt to economize on labor by substituting other factors. But since these other factors are already fully employed, attempted substitution can only result in bidding their prices up until the incentive to substitute vanishes. Likewise, if there is a cut in the money wage rate, business firms will attempt to substitute labor and reduce the employment of other factors. But since the prices of these factors are perfectly flexible, this substitution will be prevented by a lowering of the prices of these factors to keep them fully employed. If the price of any other factor were rigid, a change in the money wage rate would cause substitution between labor and that factor. A money wage cut would increase the employment of labor and a money wage rise reduce it.

[13]J. T. Dunlop ("The Movement of Real and Money Wages," *Economic Journal*, XLVIII, Sept. 1938, 413) and L. Tarshis ("Changes in Real and Money Wages," *Economic Journal*, XLIX [March 1939], 150) concluded, from English and U. S. experience respectively, that Keynes was wrong in his conjecture and that real and money wage rates generally moved in the same direction. J. H. Richardson ("Real Wage Movements," *Economic Journal*, XLIX, [Sept. 1939], 425) supported the traditional, here also the Keynesian, position. M. Kalecki (*Essays in the Theory of Economic Fluctuations* [London: Allen & Unwin, 1939]) held that approximately constant marginal costs prevail.

[14]Cf. R. Ruggles, "Relative Movements of Real and Money Wage Rates," *Quarterly Journal of Economics*, LIV (Nov. 1940), 130–149.

[15]Cf. A. P. Lerner, "Mr. Keynes' *General Theory of Employment, Interest, and Money*," ILR, XXXIV, (Oct. 1936), 435; "The Relation of Wage Policies and Price Policies," *American Economic Review, Supplement*, (March 1939), 158; *The Economics of Control* (New York: Macmillan, 1946), Chap. 23, especially pp. 287–288.

3. Pure competition or constant degree of monopoly

Under conditions of pure competition, prices would be free to move up or down in the same ratio as the money wage rate, as Keynesian theory requires. Under monopolistic conditions, these proportionate price movements can occur only if the degree of monopoly — the ratio of the difference between price and marginal cost to price — remains the same. Monopolistic conditions lead to price rigidity and stickiness. Consequently a cut in the money wage rate will increase the degree of monopoly. Disregarding other results of the money wage cut, the increase in the degree of monopoly will increase the relative share of the national income going to non-wage-earners. Since non-wage-earners may be assumed to have a lower marginal propensity to consume than wage-earners, this redistribution of income reduces the real demand for consumption goods. In this respect, a money wage cut is detrimental to employment and output. A money wage rise has the opposite effect. This is presumably the *rationale* of the arguments of proponents of raising wages as an anti-depression policy.[16]

Rigidities in the prices of other factors of production, including unfinished goods and services, also lead to the substitution effects discussed in the previous section. The substitution effects of a money wage cut not only tend to increase employment directly, but also limit or prevent entirely the adverse effects on consumption expenditure from redistribution of income. Even though the degree of monopoly is increased, the increase in employment due to substitution tends to maintain labor's relative share. Monopolists in the finished and near-finished goods markets gain, possibly at the expense of labor but certainly at the expense of the sellers of factors with rigid prices, including the monopolists of unfinished products. Between the marginal propensities to consume of these two groups of non-wage-earners — monopolists in the final stages of production and monopolists in the early stages plus landlords and other property-owners — there is little to choose. Taking substitution effects into account weakens the argument that because of price rigidities a money wage cut redistributes income adversely to consumption expenditure. Indeed, if the elasticity of substitution is high enough, the redistribution of income may be favorable to consumption.

4. "Money illusion" in the supply of labor

Economic theory is usually predicated on the premise that, given their schedules of preferences for goods and services and leisure, individuals behave consistently and "rationally." A consumer is not supposed to alter his expenditure pattern when his income doubles, if the prices of the things he buys all double at the same time. Nor is a business firm expected to change its output, if the price of its product and the prices of all factors it employs

[16]Kalecki, *op. cit.* Chap. 3, especially pp. 80–86.

change in the same proportion. Generalized, this premise is what Leontief calls the "homogeneity postulate," namely, that all supply and demand functions, with prices taken as independent variables, are homogeneous functions of the zero degree.[17] Applied to the supply of labor, this postulate means that a proportionate change in the money wage and in all current prices will leave the supply of labor unchanged. Considering the real wage rate as the ratio between the money wage rate and the current price level of goods consumed by wage-earners, the postulate means that a given real wage rate will bring forth the same amount of labor whatever the level of the money wage rate — that labor will react in the same way towards a 10 per cent cut in its real wage whether this cut is accomplished by a reduction of its money wage rate or by a rise in current prices. Any other behavior seems inconsistent and "non-rational," based on a "money illusion" attributing importance to dollars *per se* rather than on an understanding of their real value.

Clearly one of Keynes' basic assumptions — Leontief calls it *the* fundamental assumption — is that "money illusion" occurs in the labor supply function.[18] Labor does attach importance to the money wage rate *per se*, and more labor will be supplied at the same real wage the higher the money wage. This assertion concerning the behavior of wage-earners is indispensable to Keynes in establishing the existence of involuntary unemployment.

What are the reasons for such "non-rational" behavior on the part of labor? First, high money wage rates are a concrete and immediate accomplishment of the leadership of individual unions. The object of individual labor groups in wage bargaining is to protect and if possible to advance their wages relative to other groups. Each union will resist a cut in money wages in order to avoid a relative reduction in real wages. The cost of living is a remote phenomenon, apparently beyond the control of organized labor, certainly beyond the control of any single bargaining unit. Money wage bargains must be made for periods during which the cost of living may frequently change. Second, wage-earners have obligations fixed in terms of money: debts, taxes, contractual payments such as insurance premiums. These obligations are a greater burden when money wage rates are cut, even though all current prices may fall proportionately. Third, labor may have inelastic price expectations; a certain "normal" price level, or range of price

[17]W. Leontief, "The Fundamental Assumption of Mr. Keynes' Monetary Theory of Unemployment," *Quarterly Journal of Economics*, LI (Nov. 1936), 192.

[18]Leontief (*op. cit.*) pointed out also that the wording of Keynes' definition of involuntary unemployment does not necessarily repudiate the "homogeneity postulate" ("Men are involuntarily unemployed if, in the event of a small rise in the price of wage-goods relatively to the money wage, both the aggregate supply of labor willing to work for the current money wage and the aggregate demand for it at that wage would be greater than the existing volume of employment." *General Theory, op. cit.*, p. 15.) It could be interpreted to mean merely that the supply schedule for labor with respect to its real wage is negatively inclined. To Keynes' definition should be added the condition that the amount of labor demanded at the lower real wage must be greater than or equal to the amount supplied.

levels, may be expected to prevail in the future, regardless of the level of current prices.[19] With such price expectations, it is clearly to the advantage of wage-earners to have, with the same current real income, the highest possible current money income. For the higher their money incomes the greater will be their money savings and, therefore, their expected command over future goods. Wage-earners with inelastic price expectations will resist money wage cuts even when prices are falling, not only because they fear that wages will not rise again when prices rise but also because the expected price rise would reduce the real value of their current saving. Fourth, labor may be genuinely ignorant of the course of prices or naïvely deceived by the "money illusion." Judged by labor's consciousness of the cost of living in the United States in 1946, this explanation, if it ever was important, is not now significant. Altogether, the support for Keynes' assumption in regard to the supply of labor is convincing; his denial of the "homogeneity postulate" for the labor supply function constitutes a belated theoretical recognition of the facts of economic life.

5. Absence of "money illusion" elsewhere in the economy

Wage-earners are the only inhabitants of the Keynesian economy who are so foolish or so smart, as the case may be, as to act under the spell of the "money illusion." They are under its spell only in their capacity as suppliers of labor. The "homogeneity postulate" is denied for the labor supply function; for all other demand and supply functions it is retained. Without the retention of the "homogeneity postulate" for all supply and demand functions except the labor supply function, the Keynesian money wage doctrine cannot be maintained. The dependence of the doctrine on this procedure and the justification for the procedure will be considered for (A) the supply functions of other factors, and (B) the consumption function.

A. SUPPLY OF OTHER FACTORS.   When the existence of variable factors other than labor is admitted, Keynesian theory requires that these factors be fully employed and that their prices be perfectly flexible.[20] This is where the "homogeneity postulate" — the assumption of "rational" behavior — enters with respect to the supply functions of these factors. If the sellers of these factors were, like the sellers of labor, influenced by the "money illusion," their prices would be rigid like wages and there could be unemployment of these factors. A change in the money wage rate could then alter the employment of labor by causing substitution between labor and other factors.

Keynes, since he assumes away the existence of other factors, presents

[19]Hicks, *Value and Capital* (Oxford: [Oxford University Press,] 1939), pp. 269–272.
[20]See p. 371 above.

no reasons for this distinction between labor and other factors. Lerner, however, asserts that it is "plausible and in conformity with the assumption of rationality of entrepreneurs and capital-owners, who would rather get something for the use of their property than let it be idle, while labor has non-rational money-wage demands."[21] It is important to note what is included in "other factors:" not only the services of land, other natural agents, and existing items of capital equipment, but also services and unfinished goods which are the products of some firms but serve as inputs for other firms. The sellers of these factors have much the same reasons as wage-earners for having "non-rational" money-price demands. Perhaps to a greater extent than labor, they have obligations fixed in terms of money. If their price expectations are inelastic, they have the same interest in high money rates of remuneration, whatever their current real returns, to protect their current savings against future price rises. They too must make money bargains for the sale of their services, contracts which will last over a period of many possible price level changes. Business firms which control the supply of intermediate goods and services often attempt to stabilize money-prices, letting their output and sales fluctuate widely. Such price rigidities are money-price demands on the part of entrepreneurs analogous in effect to the "non-rational" money-wage demands of labor.

The "money illusion" will frequently influence the suppliers of other factors. Consequently there can be price rigidities in all markets and fluctuations in the use of all factors of production. In such an economy the money wage rate is an independent determinant of the volume of employment.

B. CONSUMPTION DECISIONS. The Keynesian consumption function, which is crucial to the Keynesian solution to the money wage problem,[22] is framed in real terms: real consumption expenditure is uniquely determined by real income.[23] It is not affected, for example, by a doubling of money income and of all prices. This is the application of the "homogeneity postulate" to the consumption function. If "money illusion" occurred in consumption and saving decisions, real consumption expenditure would depend on the level of money income as well as on the level of real income, just as the supply of labor depends on the money wage rate as well as on the real wage. A change in the money wage rate, changing the level of money incomes and prices, would alter the real demand for consumption goods and therefore affect the volume of both output and employment. Here again, therefore, retention of the "homogeneity postulate" is an essential assumption for Keynesian money wage doctrine.

[21]"Relation of Wage Policies and Price Policies," *American Economic Review, Supplement,* (March 1939), 163.
[22]See p. 367 above.
[23]This is the significance of Keynes' use of wage-units.

But if wage-earners are victims of a "money illusion" when they act as sellers of labor, why should they be expected to become "rational" when they come in to the market as consumers? Most of the reasons which compel them to behave "non-rationally" in making money wage bargains would logically compel them to act "non-rationally" as consumers. And if, as argued above, labor has no corner on such non-rationality, the whole body of consumers would be influenced by the "money illusion."

In which direction would the "money illusion" be expected to operate on the consumption function? With real income given, will an increase in money income cause an increase or a decrease in real consumption expenditure? The logic of the other assumptions of Keynesian theory leads to an inverse relationship between money income and real consumption expenditure, with real income constant. For wage-earners are assumed to feel worse off when their money wages are cut; and when consumers feel worse off, they are supposed to devote a greater part of their real incomes to consumption and less to saving.

Consistency with other Keynesian assumptions is not, however, the most weighty argument in favor of such a relationship. One reason for non-homogeneous behavior in the supply of labor, we have seen, is the holding of inelastic price expectations. Such price expectations will also influence current consumption expenditure. If current prices are below the "normal" level expected to prevail in the future, consumers will substitute present purchases for future purchases, save less now and plan to save more in the future. If current prices are above expected future prices, consumers will reduce present consumption expenditure in favor of future expenditure, increase current saving at the expense of future saving. From the same real income, real consumption expenditure will be less the higher the current level of money incomes and prices. Inelasticity of price expectations is, therefore, one source of an inverse relationship between money income and real consumption expenditure out of a given real income.

If price expectations are not inelastic, a different but equally effective reason for the same relationship comes into operation. It is now widely recognized that the volume of accumulated savings held by consumers affects their propensity to consume.[24] The greater the volume of such holdings, the more consumers have already satisfied their desire to save, the greater the part of a given current income which will be spent for consumption. These assets are, except for equities, fixed or very nearly fixed in money value. Now if current price changes are expected to persist, a general decline in money prices and incomes will increase the real value of accumulated savings, and a general rise in money prices and incomes will reduce their real value. An increase in the real value of these assets should increase the

---

[24]Cf., for example, A. P. Lerner, "Functional Finance and the Public Debt," *Social Research*, X (Feb. 1943), 49.

propensity to consume, and a decrease in their value reduce it.[25] Such behavior on the part of consumers is quite consistent and rational; it appears to be the consequence of a "money illusion" only when current prices and incomes are taken as the sole variables relevant to consumption decisions.

Assuming that real consumption expenditure is, for these reasons, an inverse function of the level of money income, as well as a direct function of real income à la Keynes, a decrease in money wage rates must lead to an expansion of output and employment, and an increase in money wage rates to a curtailment of output and employment. A money wage cut, for example, will cause a general decline in prices and money incomes. This decline will stimulate an increase in the real demand for consumption goods and thereby cause a general expansion of output, real income, and employment. In the new equilibrium, prices will be lower: they will fall less than the money wage if increasing marginal costs prevail, and more than the money wage if decreasing marginal costs predominate. In the latter case, the expansion of output and employment will be greater either because more substitution of present for future consumption is induced or because the increase in real value of accumulated savings is larger. A rise in the money wage rate, of course, has the opposite effects.

These effects of changes in the money wage rate are superimposed on the substitution effects already discussed and act on the employment of labor in the same direction.

Conclusion

The central thesis of the *General Theory* contains two complementary propositions: first, that because labor has "non-rational" money wage demands, involuntary unemployment of labor is possible; second, that labor is in any case powerless to remedy this unemployment by altering its money wage bargains. (The second proposition Keynes qualifies by admitting the possibilities of reactions on employment via the rate of interest, but this qualification, for reasons given above, is of limited practical importance.) The second proposition of the central thesis rests on assumptions logically

[25]Since the assets held by consumers are the debts of other economic units, price changes affecting the real value of consumers' assets will also affect the real burden of debt. Changes in the real burden of debt may influence business investment decisions. The resulting changes in investment will act in the opposite direction from the changes in consumption described in the text. (Keynes [*General Theory, op. cit.*, p. 264] and Hicks [*Value and Capital, op. cit.*, p. 264] both considered the possible depressing influence of price and wage reductions in increasing the burden of debt without mentioning the favorable effects of the increased real wealth of creditors.) But only part of consumers' assets are, directly or indirectly, business debts; the assets of private economic units exceed private debt by the total of public debt, the monetary gold reserve, and the supply of government-issued currency. Hence, a given price change will cause a greater change in the real value of consumers' assets than in the burden of business debt.

inconsistent with the assumption contained in the first; and the premises of the second proposition are as unrealistic as the assumption underlying Keynes' labor supply function is realistic. If Keynes' denial of the "homogeneity postulate" is extended to supply and demand functions other than the labor supply function — if, in other words, "money illusion" operates elsewhere than on the sellers' side of the labor market — then employment is inversely affected by money wage rate changes. Labor is not powerless to reduce unemployment by reducing its money wage demands. Changes in employment follow from changes in the money wage because of substitution between labor and other factors and because of the effects of "money illusion" on real consumption expenditure. The substitution effect can be avoided only by assuming, as in the *General Theory*, that labor is the only variable factor or, if other factors are considered, by assuming that the suppliers of these factors, unlike labor, have no "non-rational" money-price demands. The consumption effect can be avoided only by assuming that wage-earners — and the suppliers of other factors if they are admitted to behave like wage-earners — act "rationally" as buyers even though they are "non-rational" as sellers, and by neglecting the effect of inelastic price expectations or accumulated savings on the propensity to consume. These two effects, or either one of them alone, make the money wage rate a determinant of the volume of employment. The consumption effect makes it also a determinant of the level of output and real income.

To summarize, a change in the money wage rate may alter the level of employment in the following ways:

1. By its effect on business confidence, which is not theoretically predictable, a change in the money wage rate may alter the volume of real investment.

2. In an open economy, a wage cut will have an effect equivalent to an expansion of investment by increasing the balance of trade. A wage rise will have the opposite results and affect employment adversely.

3. By reducing the demand for cash balances, a wage cut *may* reduce the rate of interest; reduction of the interest rate *may* stimulate investment and employment. A wage rise may have the opposite effects.

4. A wage cut may induce substitution of labor for other factors, and a wage rise may diminish employment by causing substitution of other factors for labor.

5. A wage cut may cause an increase in the real demand for consumption goods and therefore in both output and employment. Increased consumption demand would result either from substitution of present consumption for future consumption, when price expectations are inelastic, or from the increased real value of accumulated savings. A wage rise would have the contrary effect.

6. An effect contrary in direction to the four preceding possibilities is that a money wage cut will, because of price rigidities, redistribute income

adversely to labor and thereby reduce the propensity to consume. For similar reasons, a money wage rise would be favorable to employment. This effect will be the stronger the weaker is the substitution effect; if substitution is considerable, it may be entirely absent.

Solution of the money wage problem was greatly advanced by replacing arbitrary assumptions concerning the price level or the level of money expenditure with Keynes' analysis of effective demand. Further progress towards a solution, and ultimately towards a quantitative solution, depends on refinement and extension, both theoretical and statistical, of the basic Keynesian system. What are the variables other than real rates of remuneration affecting the supply of labor and of other factors of production, and what effects do these variables have? What variables other than real income determine real consumption expenditure, and how? What variables lie behind the marginal efficiency of capital, and how do they enter business investment calculations? Only when economists have more satisfactory answers to these broader questions will they be able to give an acceptable solution to the money wage problem.

DON PATINKIN **19**

Price flexibility and full employment[*]

At the core of the Keynesian polemics of the past ten years and more is the relationship between price flexibility and full employment. The fundamental argument of Keynes is directed against the belief that price flexibility can be depended upon to generate full employment automatically. The defenders of the classical tradition, on the other hand, still insist upon this automaticity as a basic tenet.

During the years of continuous debate on this question, the issues at stake have been made more precise. At the same time, further material on the question of flexibility has become available. This paper is essentially an

Reprinted from American Economic Association, *Readings in Monetary Theory*, F. A. Lutz and L. W. Mints (eds.) (Homewood, Ill.: Richard D. Irwin, Inc., 1951), pp. 252–283. An earlier version of this article appeared in *American Economic Review*, Vol. 38 (September 1948), pp. 543–564. Reprinted by permission of the publisher and author. [Footnotes expanded — *Eds.*]

*In the process of writing this paper the author acknowledges having benefited from stimulating discussions with Milton Friedman, University of Chicago, and Alexander M. Henderson, University of Manchester. (Advantage has been taken of this reprinting to correct and modify several parts of the article. The major changes are the following: the addition of the latter part of the last paragraph of § 5, as a result of discussions with Milton Friedman; the addition of paragraphs three and four of § 6, as a result of comments by Donald Gordon, Franco Modigliani and Norman Ture; the correction of the last paragraph of § 6 and Table 1 of § 11 in accordance with Herbert Stein's comment on the original article in the *American Economic Review*, XXXIX ([June] 1949), 725–26; and the addition of the last three paragraphs of § 14, in the attempt to clarify some points left ambiguous in the original article. All significant additions are enclosed in brackets.)

attempt to incorporate this new material, and, taking advantage of the perspective offered by time, to analyze the present state of the debate.

In Part I, the problem of price flexibility and full employment is presented from a completely static viewpoint. Part II then goes on to discuss the far more important dynamic aspects of the problem. Finally, in Part III, the implications of the discussion for the Keynesian-classical polemic are analyzed. It is shown that over the years these two camps have really come closer and closer together. It is argued that the basic issue separating them is the rapidity with which the economic system responds to price variations.

I. Static analysis

1. The traditional interpretation of Keynesian economics is that it demonstrates the absence of an automatic mechanism assuring the equality of desired savings and investment at full employment. The graphical meaning of this interpretation is presented in a simplified form in Figure 1. Here

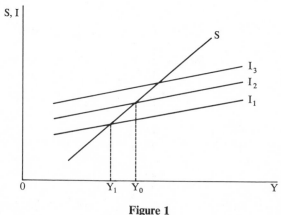

Figure 1

desired real savings (S) and investment (I) are each assumed to depend only on the level of real income (Y). I_1, I_2, and I_3 represent three possible positions of the investment schedule. Y_0 is the full employment level of real income. If the investment desires of individuals are represented by the curve I_1, desired savings at full employment are greater than desired investment at full employment. This means that unemployment will result: the level of income will drop to Y_1, at which income desired savings and investment are equal. Conversely, if I_3 is the investment curve, a situation of overemployment or inflation will occur: people desire to invest more at full employment than the amount of savings will permit. Only if the investment schedule happened to be I_2 would full employment desired investment and savings be equal. But since investment decisions are independent of savings decisions, there is no reason to expect the investment schedule to coincide with I_2; Hence there is no automatic assurance that full employment will result.

2. The classical answer to this attack is that desired savings and investment depend on the rate of interest, as well as the level of real income, and that, granted flexibility, variations in the interest rate serve as an automatic mechanism insuring full employment.

The argument can be interpreted as follows: the savings and investment functions (representing what people desire to do) are written as

$$S = \Omega(r, Y) \qquad I = \Psi(r, Y)$$

where r represents the rate of interest.

Consider now Figure 2. On this graph there can be drawn a whole family of curves relating savings and investment to the rate of interest — one pair for each level of real income. In Figure 2, these pairs of curves are

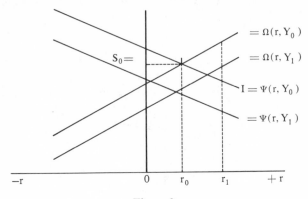

Figure 2

drawn for the full employment income, Y_0, and for the less than full employment income, Y_1. On the assumption that for a given rate of interest people will save and invest more at a higher level of income, the investment curve corresponding to $Y = Y_0$ is drawn above that corresponding to $Y = Y_1$; similarly for the two savings curves. The curves also reflect the assumption that, for a given level of real income, people desire to save more and invest less at higher rates of interest.

Consider now the pair of curves corresponding to the full employment income Y_0. If in Figure 2 the interest rate were r_1, then it would be true that individuals would desire to save more at full employment than they would desire to invest. But, assuming no rigidities in the interest rate, this would present no difficulties. For if the interest rate were to fall freely, savings would be discouraged, and investment stimulated until finally desired full employment savings and investment would be equated at the level $S_0 = I_0$. Similarly, if at full employment desired investment is greater than desired savings, a rise in the interest rate will prevent inflation. In this way variations in the rate of interest serve automatically to prevent any discrepancy between desired full employment investment and savings, and thus to assure full employment.

This argument can also be presented in terms of Figure 1: assume for simplicity that desired investment depends on the rate of interest as well as the level of real income, while desired savings depends only on the latter. Then downward variations in the interest rate can be counted on to raise the investment curve from, say, I_1 to I_2. That is, at any level of income people can be encouraged to invest more by a reduction in the rate of interest. Similarly, upward movements of the interest rate will shift the investment curve from, say, I_3 to I_2. Thus desired full employment savings and investment will always be equated.

3. The Keynesian answer to this classical argument is that it greatly exaggerates the importance of the interest rate. Empirical evidence has accumulated in support of the hypothesis that variations in the rate of interest have little effect on the amount of desired investment. (That savings are insensitive to the interest rate is accepted even by the classical school.) This insensitivity has been interpreted as a reflection of the presence of widespread uncertainty.[1] The possible effect of this insensitivity on the ability of the system automatically to generate full employment is analyzed in Figure 3. For simplicity the savings functions corresponding to different

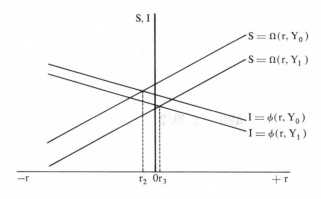

Figure 3

levels of income are reproduced from Figure 2. But the investment functions are now represented as being much less interest-sensitive than those in Figure 2. If the situation in the real world were such as represented in Figure 3, it is clear that interest rate variations could never bring about full employment. For in an economy in which there are negligible costs of storing

[1] *Cf.* Oscar Lange, *Price Flexibility and Employment* (Bloomington, Indiana: Principia Press, 1945), p. 85 and the literature cited there. For an excellent theoretical discussion of this insensitivity, *cf.* G. L. S. Shackle, "Interest Rates and the Pace of Investment," *Economic Journal*, LVI ([March] 1946), 1–17.

money, the interest rate can never be negative.[2] But from Figure 3 we see that the only way the interest rate can equate desired full employment savings and investment is by assuming the negative value r_2. Hence it is impossible for the full employment national income Y_0 to exist: for no matter what (positive) rate of interest may prevail, the amount people want to save at full employment exceeds what they want to invest. Instead there will exist some less than full employment income (say) Y_1 for which desired savings and investment can be brought into equality at a positive rate of interest, (say) r_3 (cf. Figure 3).

Thus once again the automaticity of the system is thrown into question. Whether the system will generate full employment depends on whether the full employment savings and investment functions intersect at a positive rate of interest. But there is no automatic mechanism to assure that the savings and investment functions will have the proper slopes and positions to bring about such an intersection.[3]

4. Sometimes attempts are made to defend the classical position by arguing that the investment function is really higher (or the savings function lower) than represented by the Keynesians — so that desired full employment savings and investment can be equated at a positive rate of interest (cf. Figure 3). But this is beside the point. [The fundamental disagreement between Keynesian and classical economics lies in the former's denial of the automaticity of full employment posited by the latter.] Hence a successful restatement of the classical position must demonstrate the existence of some automatic mechanism which will always bring about full employment. Thus to argue that if the investment or saving function is at a certain level, full employment will be brought about is irrelevant; what must be shown is that there exist forces which will *automatically* bring the investment or saving functions to the required level. In other words, the issue at stake is not the *possible*, but the *automatic*, generation of full employment. APR 4 1972

5. [To the Keynesian negative interest rate argument replies have been made by both Haberler and Pigou.[4] Just as the crude Keynesian argument of § 1 was answered by introducing a new variable — the rate of interest — into the savings function, so the more refined argument of § 3 is

---

[2]Note that in a dynamic world of rising prices, the effective rate of interest may become negative. But even here the *anticipated* effective rate cannot be negative. For in that event there would again be an infinite demand for money.

[3][I have discussed this whole question of the contrast between the classical and Keynes-ian positions in greater detail elsewhere. Cf. "Involuntary Unemployment and the Keynesian Supply Function," *Economic Journal* LIX (1949), 376–78.]

[4][G. Haberler, *Prosperity and Depression* (League of Nations, Geneva, 1941), 3rd ed., pp. 242, 389, 403, 491–503.]

A. C. Pigou, "The Classical Stationary State," *Economic Journal*, LIII ([Dec.] 1943), 343–351; "Economic Progress in a Stable Environment," *Economica*, n.s. XIV ([Aug.] 1947), 180–190. Although these articles deal only with a stationary state, their basic argument can readily be extended to the case in which net investment is taking place.

[In the subsequent text, I shall follow the exposition of Pigou; but the argument holds also with respect to Haberler.]

countered by the introduction of yet another variable — the real value of cash balances held by the individuals in the economy. Thus, denoting the amount of money in the economy M_1 (assumed to remain constant) and the absolute price level by p, Pigou's saving schedule is written as

$$S = \Gamma\left(r, Y, \frac{M_1}{p}\right)]$$

His argument is as follows: if people would refuse to save anything at negative and zero rates of interest, then the desired savings schedule would intersect the desired investment schedule at a positive rate of interest regardless of the level of income (*cf.* Figure 3). The willingness to save even without receiving interest, or even at a cost, must imply that savings are not made solely for the sake of future income (*i.e.*, interest) but also for "the desire for possession as such, conformity to tradition or custom and so on."[5] But the extent to which an individual wishes to save out of current income for reasons other than the desire of future income is inversely related to the real value of his cash balances.[6] If this is sufficiently large, all his secondary desires for saving will be fully satisfied. At this point the only reason he will continue to save out of current income is the primary one of anticipated future interest payments. In other words, if the real value of cash balances is sufficiently large, the savings function becomes zero at a positive rate of interest, regardless of the income level.

A graphical interpretation of this argument is presented in Figure 4. Here S and I are the full-employment savings and investment curves of Figure 3 (*i.e.*, those corresponding to $Y = Y_0$), and r_2 is again the negative rate of interest at which they are equal. Pigou then argues that by increasing the real value of cash balances, the full employment savings curve shifts to

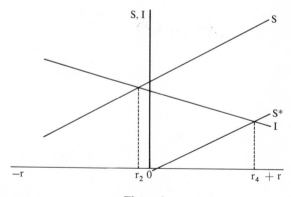

Figure 4

[5]*Ibid.*, p. 346.
[6]And all his other assets too. But the introduction of these other assets does not change Pigou's argument; while concentration on money assets brings out its (the argument's) basic aspect. *Cf.* below, § 6.

the right until it is in such a position that no savings are desired except at positive rates of interest. This is represented by the savings curve S*, which becomes zero for a positive rate of interest. (In fact, S* shows dissaving taking place for sufficiently low rates of interest.) The full employment savings curve S* clearly intersects the full employment investment curve I at the positive rate of interest r_4. Thus by changing the real value of cash balances, desired full employment savings and investment can always be equated at a positive rate of interest.

How can we be sure that real cash balances will automatically change in the required direction and magnitude? Here Pigou brings in his assumptions of flexible wage and price levels, and a constant stock of money in circulation. If full employment saving exceeds investment, national income begins to fall, and unemployment results. If workers react to this by decreasing their money wages, then the price level will also begin to fall. As the latter continues to fall, the real value of the constant stock of money increases correspondingly. Thus, as the price level falls, the full employment saving function continuously shifts to the right until it intersects the full employment investment function at a positive rate of interest.[7]

This is the automatic mechanism on which Pigou relies to assure full employment. It is essential to notice that it will operate regardless of the interest-elasticities of the savings and investment functions — provided they are not both identically zero. [It should also be emphasized, as Haberler does, that although this argument has been presented above as an answer to Keynes, it is of much older origin. In particular, it is implicit in classical theorizing on the quantity theory of money. The crucial step in this analysis, it will be recalled, comes at the point where it is argued that as a result of increasing the amount of money in the economy, individuals' cash balances are larger than desired at the existing price level, so that they will attempt to

---

[7]The exact price level is determined when to our preceding four equations is added the liquidity preference equation $M_0 = \Lambda (r, Y, p)$, where M_0 represents the given amount of money in the system. (As will be shown in the next section, the "stock of money" relevant for the liquidity equation is completely different from the "stock of money" relevant for the Pigou analysis of the savings function; hence the use of two different symbols — M_0 and M_1.) We then have the complete system of five equations in five variables:

$$I = \Phi (r, Y)$$
$$S = \Gamma (r, Y, Y\frac{M_1}{p})$$
$$I = S$$
$$Y = Y_0$$
$$M_0 = \Lambda (r, Y, p).$$

Under the Pigovian assumptions this system is consistent; its equations are satisfied for a positive rate of interest.

[The workings of a more general system of equations under the Pigovian assumption are described in detail in Parts IV and V of the reference cited in footnote 3 above. In this more detailed treatment, the full employment level, Y_0, is not arbitrarily defined — as is done in the present paper — but emerges instead from the economic behavior functions themselves.]

reduce these real balances by increasing their money expenditures. The main contribution of Haberler and Pigou is to show how this set of forces must, and can, be introduced into the Keynesian analytical apparatus.]

6. The inner mechanism and distinctive characteristic of the Pigou analysis can be laid bare by considering it from a larger perspective. It is obvious that a price reduction has a stimulating effect on creditors. But, restricting ourselves to the private sector of a closed economy, to every stimulated creditor there corresponds a discouraged debtor. Hence from this viewpoint the net effect of a price reduction is likely to be in the neighborhood of zero. The neatness of the Pigou approach lies in its utilizing the fact that although the private sector considered in isolation is, on balance, neither debtor nor creditor, when considered in its relationship to the government, it *must be* a net "creditor." This is due to the fact that the private sector always holds money, which is a (non-interest bearing) "debt" of government. If we assume that government activity is not affected by the movements of the absolute price level,[8] then the net effect of a price decline must always be stimulatory.[9] The community gains at the "expense" of a gracious government, ready, willing, and able to bear the "loss" of the increased value of its "debt" to the public.

More precisely, not every price decline need have this stimulating effect. For we must consider the effect of the price decline on the other assets held by the individual. If the decline reduces the real value of these other assets (*e.g.*, houses and other forms of consumer capital; stock shares; etc.) to an extent more than offsetting the increased value of real cash balances,[10] then the net effect will be discouraging. But the important point is that no matter what our initial position, *there exists* a price level sufficiently low so that the total real value of assets corresponding to it is greater than the original real value. Consider the extreme case in which the value of the other assets becomes arbitrarily small.[11] Clearly even here the real value of the fixed stock of money can be made as large as desired by reducing the price level sufficiently. Thus, to be rigorous, the statement in the preceding paragraph should read: "There always exists a price decline such that its effect is stimulatory." From this and the analysis of the preceding section, we can derive another statement which succinctly summarizes the results of the Pigou analysis: "In the static classical model, regardless of the position of the investment schedule, there always exists a sufficiently low price

---

[8]Pigou makes this assumption when he writes the investment function (which presumably also includes government expenditure) as independent of the absolute price level. *Cf.* footnote 7 above.

[9]It must be emphasized that I am abstracting here from all dynamic considerations of the effect on anticipations, etc. These will be discussed in Part II of the paper.

[10]A necessary (but not sufficient) condition for this to occur is that the price level of assets falls in a greater proportion than the general price level.

[11]I am indebted to M. Friedman for this example.

level such that full employment is generated." In any event, it is clearly sufficient to concentrate (as Pigou has done) on cash balances alone.[12]

[This analysis is subject to at least two reservations, neither one of which has been considered by Haberler or Pigou. First of all, we have tacitly been assuming that the depressing effect of a price decline on a debtor is roughly offset by its stimulating effect on a creditor; hence the private sector, being on balance a creditor with respect to the government, can ultimately be stimulated by a price decline. But allowance must be made for the possibility of a differential reaction of debtors and creditors. That is, if debtors are discouraged by a price decline much more than creditors are encouraged, it may be possible that there exists no price decline which would have an encouraging effect on expenditures. In brief, the Keynesian aggregative analysis followed by Pigou overlooks the possibility of microeconomic "distribution effects."

Secondly we have so far considered only the effects of a change in real balances on household behavior; that is, on the consumption (or, its counterpart, the savings) function. It seems only natural to extend the analysis to include the influence of real cash balances on firms, and, hence, on the investment function as well. However, this extension cannot be made automatically, inasmuch as the respective motivations of firms and households are not necessarily the same. Nevertheless, it does seem reasonable to assume that investment decisions of firms are favorably influenced by a higher level of real balances. Once we take account of firms, the differential reactions mentioned in the preceding paragraph become increasingly significant. If firms are, on balance, debtors with respect to households and government, then a persistent price decline will cause a wave of bankruptcies. This will have a seriously depressing effect upon the economy which may not be offset by the improved status of creditors. Furthermore, in most cases of bankruptcy the creditors also lose. For these reasons it is not at all certain that a price decline will result in a positive net effect on the total expenditures (consumption plus investment) function. On this point much further investigation — of a theoretical as well as an empirical nature — is required.]

From the preceding analysis we can also see just exactly what constitutes the "cash balance" whose increase in real value provides the stimulatory effect of the Pigou analysis. This balance clearly consists of the net obligation of the government to the private sector of the economy. That is, it consists primarily of the total interest- and non-interest-bearing

---

[12]*Cf.* above, footnote 6. Another possible reason for Pigou's emphasis on cash balances to the exclusion of other assets is that the relative illiquidity of the latter makes them less likely to be used as a means of satisfying the "irrational" motives of saving. Hence the inverse relationship between other assets and savings out of current income might not be so straightforward as that between real cash balances and savings.

government debt held outside the treasury and central bank, [plus the net amount owed by the central bank to member banks]. Thus, by excluding demand deposits and including government interest-bearing debt and member bank reserves, it differs completely from what is usually regarded as the stock of money.

These same conclusions can be reached through a somewhat different approach. Begin with the ordinary concept of the stock of money as consisting of hand-to-hand currency and demand deposits. Consider now what changes must be made in order to arrive at the figure relevant for the Pigou analysis. Clearly, government interest-bearing debt must be added, since a price decline increases its value. Now consider money in the form of demand deposits. To the extent that it is backed by bank loans and discounts, the gains of deposit holders are offset by the losses of bank debtors.[13] Thus the net effect of a price decline on demand deposits is reduced to its effect on the excess of deposits over loans, or (approximately) on the reserves of the banks held in the form of hand-to-hand currency [and deposits in the central bank]. Finally, hand-to-hand currency held by individuals outside the banking system is added in, and we arrive at exactly the same figure as in the preceding paragraph.

For convenience denote the stock of money relevant for the Pigou analysis by M_1. Note that this is completely different from the M_0 of footnote 7: for M_0 is defined in the usual manner as hand-to-hand currency plus demand deposits. This distinction is of fundamental importance. [One of its immediate implications is that central bank open market operations which do not change the market price of government bonds affect the economic system only through the liquidity preference equation]. Since such operations merely substitute one type of government debt (currency) for another (bonds), they have no effect on M_1 and hence no direct effect on the amount of savings. [Even when open market purchases do cause an increase in the price of government bonds, the changes in M_0 and M_1 will not, in general, be equal. The increase in M_0 equals the total amount of money expended for the purchase of the bonds; the increase in M_1 equals the increase in the value of bonds (both of those bought and those not bought by the central bank) caused by the open-market operations.[14] Corresponding statements can be made for open-market sales.]

7. How does the Pigou formulation compare with the original

---

[13]*Cf.* M. Kalecki, "Professor Pigou on 'The Classical Stationary State' — A Comment," *Economic Journal*, LIV ([April] 1944), 131–132.

[14][It might be argued that through its effect on the interest rate, open market purchases affect the value of assets other than government securities; hence, this change in value should also be included in the change in M_1. This is a point which deserves further investigation. The main question is whether there exists an offset to this improvement in the position of bondholders of private corporations.]

classical theory?[15] Although both Pigou and the "classics" stress the importance of "price flexibility," they mean completely different things. The "classics" are talking about flexibility of relative prices; Pigou is talking about flexibility of absolute prices. The classical school holds that the existence of long-run unemployment is *prima facie* evidence of rigid wages. The only way to eliminate unemployment is, then, by reducing *real* wages. (Since workers can presumably accomplish this end by reducing their *money* wage, this position has implicit in it the assumption of a constant price level — [or at least one falling relatively less than wages].) Pigou now recognizes that changing the relative price of labor is not enough, and that the absolute price level itself must vary. In fact, a strict interpretation of Pigou's position would indicate that unemployment can be eliminated even if real wages remain the same or even rise (namely, if the proportionate fall in prices is greater than or equal to that of wages); for in any case the effect of increased real value of cash balances is still present.[16]

The Pigou analysis also differs from those interpretations of the classical position which, following Keynes, present the effect of a wage decrease as acting through the liquidity preference equation to increase the real value of M_0 and thereby reduce the rate of interest; this in turn stimulates both consumption and investment expenditures — thus generating a higher level of national income. To this effect, Pigou now adds the direct stimulus to consumption expenditures provided by the price decline and the accompanying increase in real balances. Consequently, even if the savings and investment functions are completely insensitive to changes in the rate of interest (so that the effect through the liquidity equation is completely inoperative), a wage decrease will still be stimulatory through its effect on real balances and hence on savings.

8. Before concluding this part of the paper, one more point must be clarified. The *explicit* assumption of the Pigou analysis is that savings are directly related to the price level, and therefore inversely related to the size of real cash balances. This assumption by itself is, on *a priori* grounds, quite reasonable; [indeed, in a money economy it is a direct implication of utility maximization (above, note 15)]. But it must be emphasized that even if we disregard the reservations mentioned in the preceding sections, this assumption is insufficient to bring about the conclusion desired by Pigou.

[15]Pigou, of course, introduces the absolute price level into the analysis of the real sector of the economy, whereas classical economics insists that this sector must be considered on the basis of relative prices alone. [As I have shown elsewhere, on this point classical economics is definitely wrong. For, in a money economy, the demand for any good must, in general, depend on the absolute price level, as well as on relative prices. This is a direct result of utility maximization. *Cf.* "Money in General Equilibrium Theory: Critique and Reformulation," *Econometrica*, XVIII (1950), and references cited there.]

[16]The role of real wages in Pigou's system is very ambiguous. At one point (p. 348, bottom) he assumes that reduced money wages will also decrease real wages. At another (p. 349, lines 20–38) no such assumption seems to be involved. ("As money wage-rates fall . . . prices fall and go on falling." *Ibid.*)

For this purpose he *implicitly* makes an additional, and possibly less reasonable, assumption. Specifically, in addition to postulating explicitly the *direction* of the relationship between savings and the price level, he also implies something about its *intensity*.

The force of this distinction is illustrated by Figure 5. Here S and I are the full employment savings and investment curves of Figure 3 (*i.e.*,

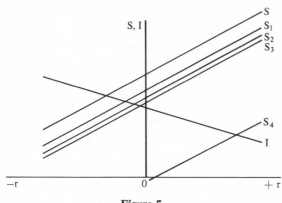

Figure 5

those corresponding to $Y = Y_0$) for a fixed price level, p_0. The other savings curves, S_1, S_2, S_3, S_4, represent the full employment savings schedules corresponding to the different price levels p_1, p_2, p_3, p_4, respectively. In accordance with the Pigou assumption, as the price level falls, the savings function shifts over to the right. (That is p_1, p_2, p_3, p_4 are listed in descending order.) But it may well be that as the real value of their cash balances continues to increase, people are less and less affected by this increase. That is, for each successive increase in real balances (for each successive price level decline) the savings function moves less and less to the right, until eventually it might respond only infinitesimally, no matter how much prices fall. In graphical terms, as the price decline continues, the savings function might reach S_3 as a limiting position. That is, no matter how much the price level might fall, the savings function would never move to the right of S_3.[17] In

[17]Mathematically this may be stated as follows. Write the savings function as
$$S = \Gamma(r, p, Y).$$
(*Cf.* footnote 7, above.) Pigou's explicit assumption is
$$\Gamma_p(r, p, Y) > 0$$
where Γ_p is the partial derivative of S with respect to p. Let $Y = Y_0$ represent the full employment income. Then the argument here is that the savings function, Γ, may still be of a form such that
$$\lim_{p \to 0} \Gamma(r, p, Y_0) = \Gamma^*(r, Y_0)$$
for any fixed r — where Γ^* is any curve which intersects the investment curve at a negative rate of interest. (In the argument of the text, Γ^* is taken to be S_3 in Figure 5.) Pigou tacitly assumes that the savings function approaches no such limit; or that if it does, the limiting function intersects the investment function at a positive rate of interest.

such an event the declining price level would fail to bring about full employment. The validity of the Pigou argument thus depends on the additional assumption that the intensity of the inverse relationship between savings and real cash balances is such that it will be possible to shift over the savings function to a position where it will intercept the investment function at a positive rate of interest: say, S₄ (*cf.* Figure 5).

What is at issue here is the reaction of individuals with already large real balances to further increases in these balances. Consider an individual with a cash balance of a fixed number of dollars. As the price falls, the increased real value of these dollars must be allocated between the alternatives of an addition to either consumption and/or real balances.[18] How the individual will actually allocate the increase clearly depends on the relative marginal utilities of these two alternatives. If we are willing to assume that the marginal utility of cash balances approaches zero with sufficient rapidity relative to that of consumption, then we can ignore the possibility of the savings curve reaching a limiting position such as in Figure 5. That is, we would be maintaining the position that by increasing the individual's balances sufficiently, he will have no further incentive to add to these balances; hence he will spend any additional real funds on consumption, so that we can make him consume any amount desired. If, on the other hand, we admit the possibility that, for sufficiently large consumption, the decrease in the marginal utility of cash balances is accompanied by a much faster decrease in the marginal utility of consumption, then the individual will continuously use most of the additional real funds (made available by the price decline) to add to his balances. In this event, the situation of Figure 5 may well occur.

9. I do not believe we have sufficient evidence — either of an *a priori* or empirical[19] nature — to help us answer the question raised in the preceding paragraph. The empirical evidence available is consistent with the hypothesis that the effect of real balances on savings is very weak. But even granted the truth of this hypothesis, it casts no light on the question raised here. What we want to know is what happens to the effect of real balances on savings as these real balances increase in size. Even if the effect were arbitrarily small, but remained constant regardless of the size of real balances, there could be no convergence of savings functions like that pictured in Figure 5. In the face of this lack of evidence, we have to be satisfied with the conclusion that, subject to the [reservations of §§ 6 and 8, Haberler and Pigou have] demonstrated the automaticity of full employment within the framework of the classical static model[20] — the main mechanism by which this is brought about being the effect of a price decline on cash balances.

[18]I am abstracting here from the possible third alternative, investment.

[19]Empirical studies on the effect of real balances on savings have been made by L. R. Klein, "The Use of Econometric Models as a Guide to Economic Policy," *Econometrica*, XV ([April] 1947), 122–125. Klein's procedure was incorrect in that he used a series for M₀, instead of M₁ in fitting his equations (*cf.* last paragraph of § 6 above).

[20]It must be re-emphasized that this conclusion holds only for static analysis. The modifications that must be introduced once dynamic factors enter are discussed in Part II.

The statement of this conclusion immediately raises the interesting question of how this set of forces [emphasized by Haberler and Pigou] could have been overlooked by Keynesian economists, in general, and Keynes himself, in particular. Questions of this type can rarely be answered satisfactorily — and perhaps should not even be asked. Nevertheless, I think it is both possible and instructive to trace through the exact chain of errors in Keynes's reasoning which caused him to overlook these factors.

I submit the hypothesis that Keynes recognized the influence of assets on saving (consumption), but unfortunately thought of this influence only in terms of physical capital assets. This was his fundamental error.[21] From it immediately followed that in his main discussion of the (short-run) consumption function, where he assumed a *constant* stock of capital, the possible influence of assets was not (and could not) even be considered.[22] But as soon as Keynes discussed a period sufficiently long for noticeable capital growth, the influence of assets on savings was immediately recognized.[23] Even here Keynes could not come to the same conclusion as Pigou. For Keynes restricted himself to physical assets, and thus rightfully pointed out that it would be "an unlikely coincidence" that just the correct amount of assets should exist — i.e., that amount which would push over the savings function to such a position where full employment could be generated. Compare this with the determinate process by which just exactly the "correct amount" of real cash balances is brought into existence in the Pigou analysis. (See above, § 5, paragraph 4.)

This exclusion of physical assets from the short-run consumption function was subconsciously extended to all kinds of assets. Here was the last link in the chain of errors. For later when Keynes began to examine the effects of increased real cash balances (brought about either by price declines or increases in the amount of money), he did not even consider their possible influence on consumption. Instead, he concentrated exclusively on their tendency, through the liquidity function, to lower interest rates.[24] (*Cf.* above, § 7, last paragraph.)

Looking back on the nature of these errors, we cannot but be struck

[21]Note that there are really two distinct errors involved here. The first is the obvious one of the exclusion of monetary assets. The second is that what is relevant for the influence on saving is not the *physical* asset, but its *real* value in terms of some general price level.

[22]J. M. Keynes, *The General Theory of Employment, Interest, and Money* (New York: Harcourt, Brace, and Co., 1936), Chap. 8. See especially pp. 91–95, where Keynes considers the possible influence of other factors besides income on consumption, and does not even mention assets.

[23]*Ibid.*, p. 218, second paragraph.

[24]*Ibid.*, pp. 231–234, 266. The following passage is especially interesting: "It is, therefore, on the effect of a falling wage- and price-level on the *demand for money* that those who believe in the self-adjusting quality of the economic system must rest the weight of their argument; though I am not aware that they have done so. If the quantity of money is itself a function of the wage- and price-level, there is, indeed, nothing to hope for in this direction. But if the quantity of money is virtually fixed, it is evident that its quantity in terms of wage-units can be indefinitely increased by a sufficient reduction in money wages. . . ." (*Ibid.*, p. 266. Italics not in original.)

by the irony that they should have emanated from the man who did most to demonstrate the fundamental inseparability of the real and monetary sectors of our economy.

II. Dynamic analysis: the question of policy

10. [The Haberler-Pigou analysis discussed in Part I makes two contributions. First, in its emphasis on the effects of a price on savings *via* its effects on real balances, it introduces into the Keynesian analytical apparatus a set of forces hitherto overlooked by the latter. (For convenience this will be referred to as the Pigou effect — though, as mentioned at the end of § 5 above, it is of much older origin.) Secondly, it proceeds to draw the implications of this new set of forces for static analysis, and summarizes its results in the following theorem (*cf*.§§ 5 and 6): *There always exists a sufficiently low price level such that, if expected to continue indefinitely,*[25] *it will generate full employment.*[26] (For convenience this will be referred to as the Pigou Theorem.) The purpose of this part of the paper is to accomplish a third objective: *viz.*, to draw the implications of the Pigou effect for dynamic analysis and policy formulation. It must be emphasized that the Pigou Theorem tells us nothing about the dynamic and policy aspects which interest us in this third objective.(This point is discussed in greater detail in § 12.)

Specifically, consider a full employment situation which is suddenly terminated by a downswing in economic activity. The question I now wish to examine is the usefulness of a policy which consists of maintaining the stock of money constant, allowing the wage and price levels to fall, and waiting for the resulting increase in real balances to restore full employment.

At the outset it must be made clear that the above policy recomendation is *not* to be attributed to Pigou. His interest is purely an intellectual one, in a purely static analysis. As he himself writes: ". . . The puzzles we have been considering . . . are academic exercises, of some slight use perhaps for clarifying thought, but with very little chance of ever being posed on the chequer board of actual life."[27]

In reality, Pigou's disavowal of a deflationary policy (contained in the paragraph from which the above quotation is taken) is not nearly as thoroughgoing as might appear on the first reading. The rejection of a price decline as a practical means of combatting unemployment may be due to:

---

[25]This qualifying phrase incorporates in it the restriction of the Pigou argument to static analysis.

[26]I am overlooking here the reservations discussed in §§ 6 and 8 above.

[27]"Economic Progress in a Stable Environment," *Economica*, n.s. XIV (1947), 188.

(a) the conviction that dynamic considerations invalidate its use as an immediate policy, regardless of its merits in static analysis; (b) the conviction that industrial and labor groups, sometimes with the assistance of government, prevent the price flexibility necessary for the success of a deflationary policy. A careful reading of Pigou's disclaimer indicates that he had only the second of these alternatives in mind; *i.e.*, that he felt that the policy would not work because it would not be permitted to work. What I hope to establish in this part of the essay is the first alternative: namely, that even granted full flexibility of prices, it is still highly possible that a deflationary policy will not work, due to the dynamic factors involved.

Nevertheless, nothing in this part of the paper is intended (or even relevant) as a criticism of Pigou, since the latter has clearly abstained from the problem of policy formulation. If sometimes the terms "Pigou effect" and "Pigou Theorem" are used in the following discussion, they should be understood solely as shorthand notations for the concepts previously explained.

11. The analysis of this section is based on the following two assumptions: (a) One of the prerequisites of a successful anti-depression policy is that it should be able to achieve its objective rapidly (say, within a year). (b) Prices cannot fall instantaneously; hence, the larger the price level fall necessary to bring about full employment *via* the Pigou effect, the longer the time necessary for the carrying out of the policy. (If no price fall can bring about full employment, then we can say that an infinite amount of time is necessary for the carrying out of the policy.)

There are at least two factors which act toward lengthening the period necessary to carry out a policy based on the Pigou effect. The first is the possibility that the effect of an increase in cash balances on consumption is so small, that very large increases (very great price declines) will be necessary. [Certainly there is a burden of proof on the supporters of a policy of absolute price flexibility to show that this is not so;] that the economic system is sufficiently responsive to make the policy practical. So far, no one has presented the required evidence.

The second factor is a result of the price decline itself. In dynamic analysis we must give full attention to the role played by price expectations and anticipations in general. It is quite possible that the original price decline will lead to the expectation of further declines. Then purchasing decisions will be postponed, aggregate demand will fall off, and the amount of unemployment increased still more. In terms of Figures 1 and 3, the savings function will rise (consumption will be decreased) and the investment function fall, further aggravating the problem of achieving full employment. This was the point on which Keynes was so insistent.[28] Furthermore,

[28]See his discussion of changes in money wages, *op. cit.*, pp. 260–269, especially p. 263. *Cf.* also J. R. Hicks, *Value and Capital* (Oxford: Oxford University Press, 1939), and O. Lange, *op. cit.*

the uncertainty about the future generated by the price decline will increase the liquidity preference of individuals. Thus if we consider an individual possessing a fixed number of dollars, and confronted with a price decline which increases the real value of these dollars, his uncertainty will make him more inclined to employ these additional real funds to increase his real balances, than to increase his expenditures.[29] In other words, the uncertainty created by the price decline might cause people to accumulate indefinitely large real cash balances, and to increase their expenditures very little, if at all. [Finally, the bankruptcies caused by the inability of creditors to carry the increased real burden of their debt (above, § 6) will strengthen the pessimistic outlook for the future. The simultaneous interaction of these three forces] will further exacerbate these difficulties. For as the period of price decline drags itself out, anticipations for the future will progressively worsen, and uncertainties further increase. The end result of letting the Pigou effect work itself out may be a disastrous deflationary spiral, continuing for several years without ever reaching any equilibrium position. Certainly our past experiences should have sensitized us to this danger.

Because of these considerations I feel that it is impractical to depend upon the Pigou effect as a means of policy: the required price decline might be either too large (factor one), or it might be the initial step of an indefinite deflationary spiral (factor two).

On this issue, it may be interesting to investigate the experience of the United States in the 1930's. In Table I, net balances are computed for the period 1929–32 according to the definition in § 6. As can be seen, although there was a 19 per cent *increase* in real balances from 1930 to 1931, real national income during this period *decreased* by 13 per cent. Even in the following year, when a further increase of 19 per cent in real balances took place, real income proceeded to fall by an additional 18 per cent. For the 1929–1932 period as a whole there was an increase in real balances of 46 per cent, and a decrease in real income of 40 per cent.

It will, of course, be objected that these data reflect the presence of "special factors," and do not indicate the real value of the Pigou effect. But the pertinent question which immediately arises is: To what extent were these "special factors" necessary, concomitant results of the price decline itself! If the general feeling of uncertainty and adverse anticipations that marked the period is cited as one of these "special factors," the direct relationship between this and the decline in price level itself certainly cannot be overlooked. Other proposed "special factors" must be subjected to the same type of examination. The data of the preceding table are not offered as conclusive evidence. But they are certainly consistent with the previously

[29]*Cf.* above, § 8, last paragraph.

Table 1

	MARKET VALUE OF GOVERNMENT INTEREST-BEARING DEBT HELD OUTSIDE GOVERNMENT AND FEDERAL RESERVE SYSTEM				RESERVE BANK CREDIT OUTSTANDING EXCLUDING THAT BASED ON RESERVE BANK HOLDINGS OF U.S. GOVERNMENT SECURITIES					NET REAL BALANCES	
MONEY IN CIRCULATION OUTSIDE TREASURY AND FEDERAL RESERVE SYSTEM		MEMBER BANK DEPOSITS IN THE FEDERAL RESERVE SYSTEM	NON-MEMBER BANK DEPOSITS IN THE FEDERAL RESERVE SYSTEM	OTHER FEDERAL RESERVE ACCOUNTS		TREASURY DEPOSITS IN MEMBER AND NON-MEMBER BANKS	POSTAL SAVINGS	NET BALANCES (M_1) $(1)+(2)+(3)+(4)+(5)-(6)-(7)+(8)$	COST OF LIVING INDEX (p)	$\frac{M_1}{p}$ $(9)\div(10)$	REAL NATIONAL INCOME
YEAR	(1)	(2)	(3)	(4)	(5)	(6)	(7)	(8)	(9)	(10)	(11)	(12)
1929	4.5	14.5	2.4	0.0	0.4	1.3	0.4	0.2	2.02	1.22	16.6	89.9
1930	4.2	13.9	2.4	0.0	0.4	0.5	0.3	0.2	20.4	1.19	17.1	76.3
1931	4.7	15.1	2.3	0.1	0.4	0.6	0.4	0.6	22.1	1.09	20.3	66.3
1932	5.3	16.0	2.1	0.1	0.4	0.6	0.4	0.9	23.7	.98	24.2	54.2

All money figures are in billions of dollars.

Data for series (1), (3), (4), (5), (6) were obtained from *Banking and Monetary Statistics*, p. 368. On pp. 360–67 of this book their interrelationships are discussed. For (7) see *ibid.*, pp. 34–5. For (8) see *Statistical Abstract of the United States*, 1947, p. 419.

Being unable to find an official series for (2), I used the following procedure: Total outstanding government debt at face value was classified according to maturities (0–5 years, 5–10, and over 10) on the basis of *Banking and Monetary Statistics*, p. 511. These classifications were multiplied by price indexes for government bonds with maturities of more than 3 and less than 4 years, more than 6 and less than 9, and more than 10, respectively (Standard and Poor, *Statistics: Security Price Index Record*, 1948 edition, pp. 139–44). The sum of these products was used as an estimate of the market value of the total debt. The ratio of this to the face value of the total government debt was computed, and this ratio applied to the face value of government debt held outside the Treasury and Federal Reserve System (*Banking and Monetary Statistics*, p. 512) to yield an estimate of the required series.

Series (10): Bureau of Labor Statistics, cost of living index *Survey of Current Business*, Supplement, 1942, p. 16.

Series (12): National income in billions of 1944 dollars. J. Dewhurst and Associates, *America's Needs and Resources* (New York: The Twentieth Century Fund, 1947), p. 697.]

stated hypothesis of the impracticability of using the Pigou effect as a means of policy; and they certainly throw the burden of proof on those who argue for its practicality.

12. The argument of the preceding section requires further explanation on at least one point. In the discussion of the "second factor" there was mentioned the possibility of an indefinitely continuing spiral of deflation and unemployment. But what is the relation between this possibility and the Pigou Theorem (*cf.* § 10) established in Part I? The answer to this question may be expressed as follows:

On the downswing of the business cycle it might be interesting to know that there exists a sufficiently low price level which, if it were expected to continue existing indefinitely, would bring about full employment. Interesting, but, for policy purposes, irrelevant. For due to perverse price expectations and the dynamics of deflationary spirals, it is impossible to reach (or, once having reached, to remain at) such a position.

The implication of these remarks can be clarified by consideration of the cobweb theorem for the divergent case. Assume that a certain market can be explained in terms of the cobweb theorem. It is desired to know whether (assuming unchanged demand and supply curves) the designated market will ever reach a stationary position; that is, whether it will settle down to a unique price that will continue indefinitely to clear the market. This question is clearly divided into two parts: (a) does there exist such a

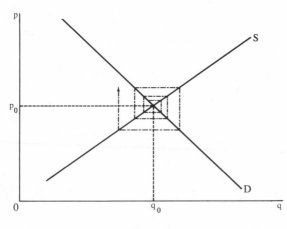

Figure 6

price, and (b) if it does exist, will the market be able to attain it. In the case of the cobweb presented in Figure 6 it is clear that such a price does exist. For if the price p_0 had always existed and were expected to exist indefinitely, it would continuously clear the market. But Figure 6 represents the case of a divergent cobweb; hence the market will never be able to reach the price p_0. In brief, even though p_0 exists, it is irrelevant to the workings of the market. The analogy to the argument of the preceding paragraph is obvious.[30]

III. Conclusions

13. The conclusions of this paper can be summarized as follows: in a static world with a constant stock of money,[31] price flexibility assures full employment. (I abstract here again from the difficulties raised in §§6 and 8.) But in the real dynamic world in which we live, price flexibility with a constant stock of money might generate full employment only after a long period; or might even lead to a deflationary spiral of continuous unemployment. On either of these grounds, a full employment policy based on a constant stock of money and price flexibility does not seem to be very promising.

[30]The distinction of this section can be expressed in rigorous mathematical form using the dynamic system which has become familiar through the work of Samuelson and Lange (P. A. Samuelson, "The Stability of Equilibrium: Comparative Statics and Dynamics," *Econometrica*, IX ([April] 1941), 97–120. Lange, *op. cit.*, pp. 91ff.) Consider a single market and let D, S, and p represent the demand, supply and price of the particular good, respectively. Let t represent time. Then we can write this system as

(a)	$D = f(p)$	demand function
(b)	$S = g(p)$	supply function
(c)	$\dfrac{dp}{dt} = h(D - S)$	market adjusting function

The last equation has the property that

$$\text{(d)} \qquad \text{sign } \frac{dp}{dt} = \text{sign } (D - S)$$

i.e., price rises with excess demand and falls with excess supply. Consider now the static system identical with (a)—(c), except that it replaces (c) by

$$\text{(e)} \qquad\qquad D = S$$

As long as (e) is not satisfied, we see from (d) that the system will not be in stationary equilibrium, but will continue to fluctuate. Thus the existence of a solution to the static system (a), (b), (e) (*i.e.*, the consistency of (a), (b), (e) is a *necessary* condition for the existence of a stationary solution for the dynamic system (a), (b), (c). But this is not a sufficient condition. For the static system (a), (b), (e) may have a consistent solution which, if the dynamic system is not convergent, will never be reached.

Thus Pigou has completed only half the task. Setting aside the difficulties of § 8, we can accept his proof of the *consistency* of the *static* classical system. But that still leaves completely unanswered the question of whether the classical *dynamic* system will converge to this consistent solution. In this and the preceding section I have tried to show why such convergence may not occur in the real world. (I have discussed these issues in greater detail elsewhere. *Cf.* footnote 3, above.)

[31]Throughout Part III, unless otherwise indicated, "stock of money" is to be understood in the M_1 sense of the last paragraph of § 6.

All that this means is that our full employment policy cannot be the fairly simple one of maintaining a constant stock of money and waiting for the economic system to generate full employment automatically through price declines. Other policies will be required. One possible alternative policy can be inferred from the Haberler-Pigou analysis itself: there are two ways to increase real balances. One is to keep the money stock constant and permit prices to fall. An equally effective way is to maintain the price level constant, and increase the stock of money by creating a government deficit.[32] This method of increasing real balances has the added advantage of avoiding one of the difficulties encountered previously (§ 11), for a policy of stabilizing the price level by increasing money stocks avoids some of the dangers of uncertainty and adverse anticipation accompanying general price declines. Nevertheless, there still remains the other difficulty — that individuals may not be very sensitive to increases in real balances. If this turned out to be true, we would have to seek still other policies.

14. [On the basis of the analysis presented in this paper it is possible to re-examine the question which has been a favorite one of economists these past years: namely,] What is the distinctive characteristic of Keynesian analysis? It certainly cannot be the claim to have demonstrated the possibility of the coexistence of underemployment equilibrium and flexible prices. This, in its day, served well as a rallying cry. But now it should be definitely recognized that this is an indefensible position. For flexibility means that the money wage falls with excess supply, and rises with excess demand; and equilibrium means that the system can continue on through time without change. Hence, by definition, a system with price flexibility cannot be in equilibrium if there is any unemployment;[33] [but, like any other proposition that must be true by definition, this one, too, is

[32]Considered from this perspective, the Pigou analysis presents in a rigorous fashion part of the theoretical framework implicit in the fiscal-monetary policy of the Simons-Mints position. *Cf.* the recently published collection of essays of Henry C. Simons, *Economic Policy for a Free Society* (Chicago: University of Chicago Press, 1948); and Lloyd W. Mints, "Monetary Policy," *Review of Economics and Statistics*, XXVIII ([May] 1946), 60–69.

[33]This can be expressed mathematically in the following way: let N^S and N^D be the amounts of labor supplied and demanded, respectively; w, the money wage rate; and t, time. Then a flexible dynamic system will, by definition, contain an equation of the general type

$$\frac{dw}{dt} = f(N^D - N^S)$$

where

$$\text{sign } \frac{dw}{dt} = \text{sign } (N^D - N^S).$$

If by equilibrium is meant a situation such that

$$\frac{dw}{dt} = 0$$

then clearly this system cannot be in equilibrium unless

$$N^D - N^S = 0$$

i.e., unless there is full employment.

uninteresting, unimportant, and uninformative about the real problems of economic policy].

Nor should Keynesian economics be interpreted as asserting that just as an underemployment equilibrium is impossible, so, too, in a static system may a full-employment equilibrium be impossible. That is, the static system may be at neither an underemployment equilibrium, nor a full-employment equilibrium. In other words, the static system may be inconsistent. (This is the negative interest rate argument of § 3.) For Pigou's and Haberler's discussion of the effect of a declining price level on real balances shows how this inconsistency is removed. It is, of course, still possible to maintain this interpretation of Keynes on the basis of the reservations of §§ 6 and 8. But I think this is neither necessary nor advisable. For the real significance of the Keynesian contribution can be realized only within the framework of *dynamic* economics. Whether or not an underemployment equilibrium exists; whether or not full-employment equilibrium always will be generated in a static system — all this is irrelevant. The fundamental issue raised by Keynesian economics is the *stability of the dynamic system:* its ability to return automatically to a full-employment equilibrium within a reasonable time (say, a year) if it is subjected to the customary shocks and disturbances of a peacetime economy. In other words, what Keynesian economics claims is that the economic system may be in a position of underemployment *dis*-equilibrium (in the sense that wages, prices, and the amount of unemployment are continuously changing over time) for long, or even indefinite, periods of time.

But this is not sufficient to characterize the Keynesians. Everyone agrees that there exist dynamic systems which will not automatically generate full employment. What distinguishes one economic school from the other is the system (or systems) to which this lack of automaticity is attributed. If the Keynesian message is applied to an economic system with no monetary policy (if such a thing is possible to define), then it is purely trivial. For few would claim automaticity of full employment for such a system. Keynesian theory acquires meaning only when applied to systems with more intelligent monetary policies. Here an element of arbitrariness is introduced; for what is termed "Keynesian" depends entirely on the choice of the monetary policy to be used as a criterion.

On the basis of Keynes' writings, I believe it is clear that he was primarily interested in attacking the policy of assuring full employment by manipulation of the interest rate through open market operations.[34] But to Keynes, this policy was equivalent to one of wage flexibility; [35] for (he

---

[34]*Cf.* Keynes, *op. cit.*, pp. 231–234; 266–267.

[35]"There is, therefore, no ground for the belief that a flexible wage policy is capable of maintaining a state of continuous full employment; — any more than for the belief that an open market monetary policy is capable, unaided, of achieving this result. The economic system cannot be made self-adjusting along these lines." (*Ibid.*, p. 267.)

erroneously thought) the only effect of a wage decline was to increase the real value of the stock of money (in the M_0, not M_1, sense; *cf.* above, last paragraph of § 6) and thereby decrease the rate of interest — just as in open market operations. As we have pointed out above (end of §§ 6 and 7), these policies are really not equivalent. For open market operations change only M_0, whereas a wage and price decline change the real value of M_1 as well. Hence, open market operations act only through the liquidity preference equation, whereas a policy of price flexibility acts also through the savings function (*cf.* above, footnote 7 and end of § 6).

Let us now assume that even if Keynes had recognized the distinction between open market and wage flexibility policies (*i.e.*, if he had recognized the Pigou effect) he still would have continued to reject the latter as a means of assuring full employment. This is not an unreasonable assumption; for most of the objections cited above (§ 11) against the use of a policy based on the Pigou effect, are the very same ones that Keynes uses in arguing against open market operations.[36]

Granted this assumption, I believe it is useful to identify the Keynesian position against one which maintains that full employment can be automatically achieved *via* the Pigou effect by maintaining a constant stock of money, and providing for wage and price flexibility. It is now possible to delineate three distinct theoretical formulations of the Keynesian position — differing in varying degrees from the classical one: (a) Most opposed to the classical position is the Keynesian one which states that even if there were no problem of uncertainty and adverse anticipations (that is, even if there were a static system), and even if we were to allow an infinite amount of time for adjustment, a policy of price flexibility would still not assure the generation of full employment. (This is the negative interest rate argument of §§3 and 8; [or the argument based on differential creditor-debtor responses of § 6].)

(b) Then there is the position which states that, in a static world, price flexibility would always assure full employment. But in a dynamic world of uncertainty and adverse anticipations, even if we were to allow an infinite adjustment period, there is no certainty that full employment will be generated. That is, we may remain indefinitely in a position of underemployment disequilibrium. (c) Finally, there is the Keynesian position, closest to the "classics," which states that even with uncertainty full employment would eventually be generated by a policy of price flexibility; but the length of time that might be necessary for the adjustment makes the policy impractical.

Although these positions are quite distinct theoretically, their policy implications are very similar. (In what way would the policies of a man

---

[36]*Cf.* the passages cited in footnote 34, above.

advocating position (a) differ from those of a man advocating (c) and stating that the adjustment would take ten years?) The policies would in general be directed at influencing the consumption and investment functions themselves, in addition to manipulating the amount of money. Thus the policies may advocate tax reductions to stimulate consumption and investment (the Simons-Mints school); or may insist on direct government investment to supplement private investment (Hansen, *et al.*). In this way we could cross-classify Keynesian positions according to their advocated policies, as well as their theoretical foundations.

[Finally, it should be noted that none of the preceding three formulations of the Keynesian position is dependent upon the assumption of wage rigidities. This assumption is frequently, and erroneously, attributed to Keynesian economics as a result of two related misconceptions as to its nature. First of all, as we have seen, the attempt to interpret Keynes' analysis of unemployment within a static equilibrium framework makes it mandatory, by definition, to assume the existence of wage rigidities. The dynamic approach followed in this paper obviates this necessity.

A second implication of restricting ourselves to static equilibrium analysis is that *involuntary* unemployment can, *by definition*, exist only if there are wage rigidities. For if there were no wage rigidities, the wage level could assume any value; and for each such value there would be a corresponding, and presumably different, amount of labor supplied. Thus at the intersection point of the demand and supply curves — the only point of interest in static equilibrium analysis — workers are providing all the labor they wish to at the equilibrium wage. There can be no question of involuntary unemployment. Only if there are wage rigidities — a minimum wage w_0, below which the workers refuse to go — can the situation be different. For then the supply curve of labor is parallel to the quantity axis at the height w_0 until a certain point (say) N_1, is reached; only afterwards does the curve begin to rise. If the demand curve is now assumed to intersect the supply curve in its horizontal portion at, say, the quantity N_0, then we can say that *involuntary* unemployment to the extent $N_1 - N_0$ exists; for at the equilibrium wage rate, w_0, workers desire to provide a maximum of N_1 units of labor, and are instead providing only N_0.

However, once we throw off the restrictions of static equilibrium analysis, we also free ourselves of the necessity of assuming wage rigidity as a necessary precondition of involuntary unemployment. For, during any given period of time, the dynamic workings of the system may well keep the workers at a point *off their supply curve*. In this departure from the supply curve lies the *involuntariness* of the unemployment. The important point here is that this situation can exist regardless of the shape of the supply curve; that is, even if wages are not rigid. One's view on the length of time such a situation can continue clearly depends on one's choice of the three alternative Keynesian positions delineated above. All this has been dealt with at length elsewhere, [37] and there is no need for any further repetition here.[38]]

[37]Cf. reference cited in footnote 3 above.

[38]It might be added that in the light of Chapter 19 of the *General Theory* — the chapter which provides the climax to Keynes' argument, and which explicitly examines the effects of wage flexibility — it is difficult to understand how wage rigidities can be considered a basic assumption of the Keynesian theory of unemployment. From this chapter it is quite clear that wage rigidities are *not* an *assumption* of Keynes' analysis, but rather a policy conclusion that follows from his investigation of the probable effects of *wage flexibility*.

Further explicit evidence that Keynes, in his theory of unemployment, was concerned with a regime of flexible prices is provided by the following passage from the *General Theory* (p. 191): "in the extreme case where money wages are assumed to fall without limit in face of involuntary unemployment . . . there will, it is true, be only two possible long period positions — full employment and the level of employment corresponding to the rate of interest at which liquidity preference becomes absolute (in the event of this being less than full employment)."

THREE

*Theory of Economic
Growth*

EVSEY D. DOMAR **20**

Expansion and employment[1]

"A slow sort of a country," said the Queen. "Now, *here*, you see, it takes all the running *you* can do, to keep in the same place. If you want to get somewhere else, you must run at least twice as fast as that."

Lewis Carroll: *Through the Looking Glass*

In these days of labor shortages and inflation, a paper dealing with conditions needed for full employment and with the threat of deflation may well appear out of place. Its publication at this time is due partly to a two-year lag between the first draft and the final copy; also to the widely held belief that the present inflation is a temporary phenomenon, and that once it is over, the old problem of deflation and unemployment may possibly appear before us again.

Our comfortable belief in the efficacy of Say's Law has been badly shaken in the last fifteen years. Both events and discussions have shown that supply does not automatically create its own demand. A part of income

Reprinted from *American Economic Review*, Vol. 37 (March 1947), pp. 34–55, by permission of the publisher and author. [Footnotes expanded — *Eds.*]
[1]This paper forms a sequence to my earlier article on "The 'Burden' of the Debt and the National Income," published in this *Review*, XXXIV, No. 5 (Dec. 1944), pp. 798–827. Though their titles seem different, the two papers are based on the same logical foundation and treat a common subject: the economic rôle of growth.

generated by the productive process may not be returned to it; this part may be saved and hoarded. As Keynes put it, "Unemployment develops . . . because people want the moon; men cannot be employed when the object of desire (*i.e.*, money) is something which cannot be produced. . . ."[2] The core of the problem then is the public's desire to hoard. If no hoarding takes place, employment can presumably be maintained.

This sounds perfectly straight and simple; and yet it leaves something unexplained. Granted that absence of hoarding is a *necessary* condition for the maintenance of full employment, is it also a *sufficient* condition? Is the absence of hoarding *all* that is necessary for the avoidance of unemployment? This is the impression *The General Theory* gives. And yet, on a different plane, we have some notions about an increasing productive capacity which must somehow be utilized if unemployment is to be avoided. Will a mere absence of hoarding assure such a utilization? Will not a continuous increase in expenditures (and possibly in the money supply) be necessary in order to achieve this goal?

The present paper deals with this problem. It attempts to find the conditions needed for the maintenance of full employment over a period of time, or more exactly, *the rate of growth of national income* which the maintenance of full employment requires. This rate of growth is analyzed in Section I. Section II is essentially a digression on some conceptual questions and alternative approaches. It may be omitted by the busy reader. Section III is concerned with the *dual* character of the investment process; that is, with the fact that investment not only generates income but also increases productive capacity. Therefore the effects of investment on employment are less certain and more complex than is usually supposed. In Section IV a few examples from existing literature on the subject are given, and Section V contains some concluding remarks. The most essential parts of the paper are presented in Sections I and III.

As in many papers of this kind, a number of simplifying assumptions are made. Most of them will become apparent during the discussion. Two may be noted at the outset. First, events take place simultaneously, without any lags. Second, income, investment and saving are defined in the *net* sense, *i.e.*, over and above depreciation. The latter is understood to refer to the cost of replacement of the depreciated asset by another one of *equal* productive capacity. These assumptions are not entirely essential to the argument. The discussion could be carried out with lags, and, if desired, in gross terms or with a different concept of depreciation. Some suggestions along these lines are made in Section II. But it is better to begin with as simple a statement of the problem as possible, bearing in mind of course the nature of assumptions made.

---

[2]John M. Keynes, *The General Theory of Employment, Interest and Money* (New York: [Harcourt, Brace & Co.,] 1936), p. 235.

I. The rate of growth

It is perfectly clear that the requirement that income paid out should be returned to the productive process, or that savings be equal to investment, or other expressions of the same idea, are simply formulas for the retention of the income *status quo*. If underemployment was present yesterday, it would still remain here today. If yesterday's income was at a full employment level, that *income level* would be retained today. It may no longer, however, correspond to full employment.

Let yesterday's full employment income equal an annual rate of 150 billion dollars, and let the average propensity to save equal, say, 10 per cent. If now 15 billions are annually invested, one might expect full employment to be maintained. But during this process, capital equipment of the economy will have increased by an annual rate of 15 billions — for after all, investment *is* the formation of capital.[3] Therefore, the productive capacity of the economy has also increased.

The effects of this increase on employment will depend on whether or not *real income* has also increased. Since money income has remained, as assumed, at the 150 billion annual level, an increase in real income can be brought about only by a corresponding fall in the general price level. This indeed has been the traditional approach to problems of this kind, an approach which we shall have to reject here for the following reasons:

1. The presence of considerable monopolistic elements (in industry and labor) in our economy makes unrealistic the assumption that a falling *general* price level could be achieved without interfering with full employment. This of course does not exclude *relative* changes among prices. As a matter of fact, if industries subject to a faster-than-average technological progress do not reduce their prices to some extent, a constant general price level cannot be maintained.

2. For an economy saddled with a large public debt and potentially faced (in peacetime) with serious employment problems, a falling price level is in itself undesirable.

3. A falling price level can bring about a larger real income only in the special case when prices of consumers' goods fall more rapidly than those of investment goods. For otherwise (with a constant propensity to save) money income will be falling as fast or faster than the price level, and real income will be falling as well. To prevent money income from falling

---

[3]The identification of investment with capital formation is reasonably safe in a private economy where only a small part of resources is disposed of by the government. When this part becomes substantial, complications arise. This question will be taken up again in Section II. Meanwhile, we shall disregard it and divide total national income, irrespective of source, into investment (*i.e.*, capital formation) and consumption.

The term "national income" is understood here in a broad sense, as total output minus depreciation, and does not touch on current controversies regarding the inclusion or exclusion of certain items. Perhaps "net national product" would be more appropriate for our purposes.

so rapidly, the volume of real investment would have to keep rising — a conclusion which will be presently reached in the more general case.

4. Finally, the assumption of a falling general price level would obscure — and I believe quite unnecessarily — the main subject we are concerned with here.

For these reasons, a *constant general price level* is assumed throughout this paper. But, from a theoretical point of view, this is a convenience rather than a necessity. The discussion could be carried on with a falling or a rising price level as well.

To come back to the increase in capacity. If both money and real national income thus remain fixed at the 150 billion annual level, the creation of the new capital equipment will have one or more of the following effects: (1) The new capital remains unused; (2) The new capital is used at the expense of previously constructed capital, whose labor and/or markets the new capital has taken away; (3) The new capital is substituted for labor (and possibly for other factors).

The first case represents a waste of resources. That capital need not have been constructed in the first place. The second case — the substitution of new capital for existing capital (before the latter is worn out, since investment is defined here in the net sense) — takes place all the time and, in reasonable magnitudes, is both unavoidable and desirable in a free dynamic society. It is when this substitution proceeds on a rather large scale that it can become socially wasteful; also, losses sustained or expected by capital owners will make them oppose new investment — a serious danger for an economy with considerable monopolistic elements.

Finally, capital may be substituted for labor. If this substitution results in a *voluntary* reduction in the labor force or in the length of the work week, no objections can be raised. Such a process has of course been going on for many years. But in our economy it is very likely that at least a part of this substitution — if carried on at an extensive scale — will be involuntary, so that the result will be unemployment.

The tools used in this paper do not allow us to distinguish between these three effects of capital formation, though, as will appear later, our concepts are so defined that a voluntary reduction in the number of man-hours worked is excluded. In general, it is not unreasonable to assume that in most cases all three effects will be present (though not in constant proportions), and that capital formation not accompanied by an increase in income will result in unemployed capital and labor.

The above problems do not arise in the standard Keynesian system because of its explicit assumption that employment is a function of national income, an assumption which admittedly can be justified only over short periods of time. Clearly, a full employment income of 1941 would cause considerable unemployment today. While Keynes' approach — the treatment of employment as a function of income — is a reasonable first approximation, we shall go a step further and assume instead that *the percentage of labor force employed is a function of the ratio between national income and productive capacity.* This should be an improvement, but we must admit the difficulties of determining productive capacity, both conceptually and statistically. These are obvious and need not be elaborated. We shall mean by productive capacity the total output of the economy at what is usually called full employment (with due allowance for frictional and seasonal unemployment), such factors as consumers' preferences, price and wage structures, intensity of competition, and so on being given.

The answer to the problem of unemployment lies of course in a growing income. If after capital equipment has increased by (an annual rate of) 15 billions an income of 150 billions leaves some capacity unused, then a higher magnitude of income can be found — say 155 or 160 billions — which will do the job. There is nothing novel or startling about this conclusion. The idea that a capitalist economy needs growth goes back, in one form or another, at least to Marx. The trouble really is that the idea of growth is so widely accepted that people rarely bother about it. It is always treated as an afterthought, to be added to one's speech or article if requested, but very seldom incorporated in its body. Even then it is regarded as a function of some abstract technological progress which somehow results in increasing productivity per man-hour, and which takes place quite independently of capital formation. And yet, our help in the industrialization of undeveloped countries will take the form not only of supplying technical advice and textbooks, but also of actual machinery and goods. Certainly the 80 odd billion dollars of net capital formation created in the United States in the period 1919–29 had a considerable effect on our productive capacity.[4]

A change in productive capacity of a country is a function of changes in i s natural resources (discovery of new ones or depletion of others), in its labor force (more correctly, man-hours available), capital and the statte of technique.[5] Since changes in natural resources and technique are ver y difficult concepts, we can express changes in total capacity via changes in the quantity and productivity of labor or of capital. The traditional approach builds around labor. The several studies of the magnitude of total output corresponding to full employment, made in the last few years, consisted in multiplying the expected labor force (subdivided into several classes) by its expected average productivity.[6] This procedure did not imply that the other three factors (natural resources, technology and capital) remained constant; rather that their variations were all reflected in the changes in productivity of labor.

It is also possible to put capital in the center of the stage and to estimate

---

[4]This figure, in 1929 prices, is taken from Simon Kuznets, *National Income and Its Composition*, Vol. I (New York: [National Bureau of Economic Research,] 1941), p. 268. The actual figure was 79.1 billion dollars.

[5]Taking other conditions listed on p. 410 as given.

[6]See for instance E. E. Hagen and N. B. Kirkpatrick, "The National Output at Full Employment in 1950," *American Economic Review*, Vol. XXXIV, No. 4 (Sept. 1944), pp. 472–500.

variations in total capacity by measuring the changes in the quantity of capital and in its productivity, the latter reflecting changes currently taking place in natural resources, technology and the labor force. From a practical point of view, the labor approach has obvious advantages, at least in some problems, because labor is a more homogeneous and easily measurable factor. But from a theoretical point of view, the capital approach is more promising and for this reason: the appearance of an extra workman or his decision to work longer hours *only* increases productive capacity without, however, generating any income to make use of this increase. But the construction of a new factory has a *dual* effect: *it increases productive capacity and it generates income.*

The emphasis on this dual character of the investment process is the essence of this paper's approach to the problem of employment. If investment increases productive capacity and also creates income, what should be the magnitude of investment, or at what rate should it grow, in order to make the increase in income equal to that of productive capacity?[7] Couldn't an equation be set up one side of which would represent the increase (or the rate of increase) of productive capacity, and the other — that of income, and the solution of which would yield the required *rate of growth?*

We shall attempt to set up such an equation. It will be first expressed in symbolic form, and later (on p. 414) illustrated by a numerical example.

Let investment proceed at an annual rate of I, and let annual productive capacity (net value added) per dollar of newly created capital be equal on the average to s. Thus if it requires, say, 3 dollars of capital to produce (in terms of annual net value added) one dollar of output, s will equal one-third or 33.3 per cent per year. It is not meant that s is the same in all firms or industries. It depends of course on the nature of capital constructed and on many other factors. Its treatment here as a given magnitude is a simplification which can be readily dispensed with.

The productive capacity of I dollars invested will thus be Is dollars per year. But it is possible that the operation of new capital will take place, at least to some extent, at the expense of previously constructed plants, with which the new capital will compete both for markets and for factors of production (mainly labor). If as a result, the output of existing plants must be curtailed, it would be useless to assert that the productive capacity of the *whole economy* has increased by Is dollars per year.[8] It has actually increased by a smaller amount which will be indicated by $I\sigma$.[9] σ may be called the *potential social average productivity of investment.* Such a long name calls for an explanation.

[7]This statement of the problem presupposes that full employment has already been reached and must only be maintained. With a small extra effort we could begin with a situation where some unemployment originally existed.

[8]These comparisons must of course be made at a full employment level of national income. See also pp. 416–419.

[9]We are disregarding here external economies obtained by existing plants from the newly constructed ones.

1. As stated above, σ is concerned with the increase in productive capacity of the whole society and not with the productive capacity per dollar invested in the new plants taken by themselves, that is with s. A difference between s and σ indicates a certain misdirection of investment, or — more important — that investment proceeds at too rapid a rate as compared with the growth of labor and technological progress. This question will be taken up again in Section II.

2. σ should not be confused with other related concepts, such as the traditional marginal productivity of capital. These concepts are usually based on a *caeteris paribus* assumption regarding the quantity of other factors and the state of technique. It should be emphasized that the use of σ does not imply in the least that labor, natural resources and technology remain fixed. It would be more correct therefore to say that σ indicates the increase in productive capacity which *accompanies* rather than which is caused by each dollar invested.

3. For our purposes, the most important property of σ is its *potential character*. It deals not with an increase in national income but with that of the *productive potential* of the economy. A high σ indicates that the economy *is capable* of increasing its output relatively fast. But whether this increased capacity will actually result in greater output or greater unemployment, depends on the behavior of money income.

The expression $I\sigma$ is the supply side of our system; it is the increase in output which the economy *can* produce. On the demand side we have the multiplier theory, too familiar to need any elaboration, except for the emphasis on the obvious but often forgotten fact that, with any given marginal propensity to save, to be indicated by α, an increase in national income is not a function of investment, but of the *increment* in investment. If investment today, however large, is equal to that of yesterday, national income of today will be just equal and not any larger than that of yesterday. All this is obvious, and is stressed here to underline the lack of symmetry between the effects of investment on productive capacity and on national income.

Let investment increase at an absolute annual rate of ΔI (*e.g.*, by two billion per year), and let the corresponding absolute annual increase in income be indicated by ΔY. We have then

$$\Delta Y = \Delta I \frac{1}{\alpha}, \tag{1}$$

where $1/\alpha$ is of course the multiplier.

Let us now assume that the economy is in a position of a full employment equilibrium, so that its national income equals its productive capacity.[10] To retain this position, income and capacity should increase at the same rate. The annual increase in potential capacity equals $I\sigma$. The annual

[10]See note 7.

increase in actual income is expressed by $\Delta I(1/\alpha)$. Our objective is to make them equal. This gives us the fundamental equation

$$\Delta I \frac{1}{\alpha} = I\sigma. \tag{2}$$

To solve this equation, we multiply both sides by α and divide by I, obtaining

$$\frac{\Delta I}{I} = \alpha\sigma. \tag{3}$$

The left side of expression (3) is the absolute annual increase (or the absolute rate of growth) in investment — ΔI — divided by the volume of investment itself; or in other words, it is the relative increase in investment, or the annual percentage rate of growth of investment. Thus the maintenance of full employment requires that investment grow at the annual percentage rate $\alpha\sigma$.

So much for investment. Since the marginal propensity to save — α — is assumed to be constant, an increase in income is a constant multiple of an increase in investment (see expression [1]). But in order to remain such a constant multiple of investment, income must also grow at the same annual percentage rate, that is at $\alpha\sigma$.

To summarize, the maintenance of a continuous state of full employment requires that *investment and income grow at a constant annual percentage (or compound interest) rate* equal to the product of the marginal propensity to save and the average (to put it briefly) productivity of investment.[11]

This result can be made clearer by a numerical example. Let $\sigma = 25$ per cent per year, $\alpha = 12$ per cent, and $Y = 150$ billions per year. If full employment is to be maintained, an amount equal to $150 \times 12/100$ should be invested. This will raise productive capacity by the amount invested times σ, *i.e.*, by $150 \times 12/100 \times 25/100$, and national income will have to rise by the same annual amount. But the relative rise in income will equal the absolute increase divided by the income itself, *i.e.*,

$$\frac{150 \times \dfrac{12}{100} \times \dfrac{25}{100}}{150} = \frac{12}{100} \times \frac{25}{100} = \alpha\sigma = 3 \text{ per cent.} \tag{4}$$

11The careful reader may be disturbed by the lack of clear distinction between increments and rates of growth here and elsewhere in the text. If some confusion exists, it is due to my attempt to express these concepts in non-mathematical form. Actually they all should be stated in terms of rates of growth (derivatives in respect to time). For a more serious treatment of this point, as well as for a more complete statement of the logic of the paper, see my article "Capital Expansion, Rate of Growth, and Employment," *Econometrica*, XIV (April 1946), 137–147.

These results were obtained on the assumption that α, the marginal propensity to save, and σ, the average productivity of investment, remain constant. The reader can see that this assumption is not necessary for the argument, and that the whole problem can be easily reworked with variable α and σ. Some remarks about a changing α are made on pp. 421–422.

The expression (3) indicates (in a very simplified manner) conditions needed for the maintenance of full employment over a period of time. It shows that it is not sufficient, in Keynesian terms, that savings of yesterday be invested today, or, as it is often expressed, that investment offset saving. Investment of today must always exceed savings of yesterday. A mere absence of hoarding will not do. An injection of new money (or dishoarding) must take place every day. Moreover, this injection must proceed, in absolute terms, at an accelerated rate. The economy must continuously expand.[11a]

II. The argument re-examined

The busy reader is urged to skip this section and proceed directly to Section III. The present section is really a long footnote which re-examines the concepts and suggests some alternative approaches. Its purpose is, on the one hand, to indicate the essential limitations of the preceding discussion, and on the other, to offer a few suggestions which may be of interest to others working in this field.

It was established in Section I that the maintenance of full employment requires income and investment to grow at an annual compound interest rate equal to $\alpha\sigma$. The meaning of this result will naturally depend on those of α and σ. Unfortunately neither of them is devoid of ambiguity.

The marginal propensity to save — α — is a relatively simple concept in a private economy where only a small part of resources is handled by the government. National income can be divided, without too much trouble, into investment and consumption, even though it is true that the basis for this distinction is often purely formal.[12] But on the whole it sounds quite reasonable to say that if marginal propensity to save is α, then an α fraction of an increase in income is saved by the public and invested in income-producing assets.

When a substantial part of the economy's resources is disposed of by the government, two interpretations of the marginal propensity to save, or of savings and investment in general, appear possible. The first is to continue dividing the total output, whether produced by government or by

[11a]After this paper was sent to the printer, I happened to stumble on an article by R. F. Harrod, published in 1939, which contained a number of ideas similar to those presented here. See "An Essay in Dynamic Theory," *Economic Journal*, XLIX (April 1939), 14–33.

[12]Thanks are due to George Jaszi for his persistent efforts to enlighten me on this subject. The division of national income into investment and consumption is really a more difficult task than my text might imply.

private business, into consumption and investment. This method was implicitly followed in this paper. But a question arises regarding the meaning and stability of α. It makes sense to say that a person or the public save, in accordance with the size of their incomes, their habits, expectations, etc., a certain, though not necessarily constant, fraction of an increment in their *disposable* (*i.e.*, after income and social security taxes) income, but can a similar statement be made regarding total national income, a good part of which is not placed at the disposal of the public? Also it is not easy to divide government expenditures into consumption and investment.

The other method would limit α to disposable income only, and then provide for government expenditures separately. It would be necessary then to find out the effects of these expenditures on productive capacity.

Depreciation raises another problem. Since all terms are defined here in the net sense, the meaning and magnitude of α will also depend on those of depreciation, irrespective of the choice between the above two methods. Depreciation has been defined here (see page 408) as the cost of replacement of a worn out asset by another one with an equal productive capacity. While this approach is about as bad or as good as any other, the difficulty still remains that businesses ordinarily do not use this definition, and therefore arrive at a different estimate of their net incomes, which in turn determine their propensity to save.

I do not have ready answers to these questions, though I do not consider them insurmountable. I am mentioning them here partly in order to indicate the limitations of the present argument, and also as obstacles which will have to be overcome if a more exact analysis is undertaken.

σ is even more apt to give rise to ambiguities. s, from which it springs, has been used, in one form or another, in economic literature before, particularly in connection with the acceleration principle.[13] Here it indicates the annual amount of income (net value added) which can be produced by a dollar of newly created capital. It varies of course among firms and industries, and also in space and time, though a study recently made seems to indicate that it has been quite stable, at least in the United States and Great Britain, over the last 70 years or so.[14] Whether s has or has not been relatively stable is not essential for our discussion. The real question is whether such a concept has meaning, whether it makes sense to say that a given economy or a plant has a certain capacity. Traditional economic thinking would, I fear, be against such an approach. Unfortunately, it is impossible to discuss this question here. I believe that our actual experience during the last depression

---

[13]See for instance Paul A. Samuelson, "Interactions between the Multiplier Analysis and the Principle of Acceleration," *Review of Economics and Statistics*, XXI (May 1939), 75–79; also R. F. Harrod, *The Trade Cycle* (Oxford: [The Clarendon Press,] 1936). These authors, however, used not the ratio of income to capital, but of consumption to capital, or rather the reciprocal of this ratio.

[14]See Ernest H. Stern, "Capital Requirements in Progressive Economies," *Economica*, n.s. XII (Aug. 1945), 163–171.

and this war, as well as a number of empirical studies, show that productive capacity, both of a plant and of the whole economy is a meaningful concept, though this capacity, as well as the magnitude of *s*, should be treated as a *range* rather than as a single number.

In some problems *s* may be interpreted as the minimum annual output per dollar invested which will make the investment worth undertaking. If this output falls below *s*, the investor suffers a loss or at least a disappointment, and may be unwilling to replace the asset after it has depreciated.

All these doubts apply to σ even more than to *s*. As explained on pages 410–411, σ differs from *s* by indicating the annual increment in capacity of the *whole economy* per dollar invested, rather than that of the newly created capital taken by itself. The possible difference between *s* and σ is due to the following reasons:

1. The new plants are not operated to capacity because they are unable to find a market for their products.

2. Old plants reduce their output because their markets are captured by new plants.

As productive capacity has no meaning except in relation to consumers' preferences, in both of the above cases productive capacity of the country is increased by a smaller amount than could be produced by the new plants; in the limiting case it is not increased at all, and $\sigma = 0$, however high *s* may be. But it must be made clear that the test of whether or not σ is below *s* can be made only under conditions (actual or assumed) of full employment. If markets are not large enough because of insufficiency of effective demand due to unemployment, it cannot yet be concluded that σ is below *s*.

3. The first two cases can take place irrespective of the volume of current investment. A more important case arises when investment proceeds at such a rapid rate that a shortage of other factors relative to capital develops. New plants may be unable to get enough labor, or more likely, labor (and other factors) is transferred to new plants from previously constructed ones, whose capacity therefore declines. In its actual manifestation, case 3 can hardly be separated from cases 1 and 2, because to the individual firm affected the difference between *s* and σ always takes the form of a cost-price disparity. The reason why we are trying to separate the first two cases from the third lies in the bearing of this distinction on practical policy. The first two cases arise from an error of judgment on the part of investors (past or present) which is, at least to some extent, unavoidable and not undesirable. The struggle for markets and the replacement of weaker (or older) firms and industries by stronger (or newer) ones is the essence of progress in a capitalist society. The third case, on the other hand, may result from poor fiscal policy. It constitutes an attempt to invest too much, to build more capital than the economy can utilize even at full employment. Such a situation can develop if an economy with a high propensity to save tries to maintain full employment by investing all its savings into capital goods. But it should be made

clear that the expressions "too much capital" or "high propensity to save" are used in a relative sense — in comparison with the growth of other factors, that is, natural resources, labor and technology.

The use of σ certainly does not imply that these factors remain fixed. As a matter of fact, it would be very interesting to explore the use of a more complex function as the right side of expression (2) instead of $I\sigma$, a function in which the growth of labor, natural resources, and technology would be presented explicitly, rather than through their effects on σ.[15] I did not attempt it because I wished to express the idea of growth in the simplest possible manner. One must also remember that in the application of mathematics to economic problems, diminishing returns appear rapidly, and that the construction of complex models requires so many specific assumptions as to narrow down their applicability.

And yet it may be interesting to depart in another direction, namely to introduce lags. In this paper both the multiplier effect and the increase in capacity are supposed to take place simultaneously and without any lag. Actually, the multiplier may take some time to work itself out, and certainly the construction of a capital asset takes time. In a secular problem these lags are not likely to be of great importance, but they may play an essential rôle over the cycle. We shall return to this question on pages 422–423.

Finally, it is possible to approach the problem of growth from a different point of view. It was established here that the rate of growth required for a full employment equilibrium to be indicated by r is equal to

$$r = \alpha\sigma, \tag{5}$$

so that if α and σ are given, the rate of growth is determined. But the equation (5) can also be solved for α in terms of r and σ, and for σ in terms of r and α. Thus if it is believed that r should be treated as given (for instance by technological progress), and if it is also decided to keep σ at a certain level, perhaps not too far from s, then it is possible to determine $\alpha = r/\sigma$, as being that marginal propensity to save which can be maintained without causing either inflation or unemployment. This approach was actually used by Ernest Stern in his statistical study of capital requirements of the United Kingdom, the United States and the Union of South Africa.[16] I also understand from Tibor de Scitovszky that he used the same approach in a study not yet published.

It is also possible to treat r and α as given and then determine what $\sigma = r/\alpha$ would have to be. Each approach has its own advantages and the choice depends of course on the nature of the problem in hand. The essential point to be noticed is the relationship between these three variables r, α,

---

[15]Some work along these lines has been done by J. Tinbergen. See his "Zur Theorie der langfristigen Wirtschaftsentwicklung" in the *Weltwirtschaftliches Archiv*, LV (May 1942), 511–549.

[16]Stern, *op. cit.*, pp. 163–171.

and σ, and the fact that if any two of them are given, the value of the third needed for the maintenance of full employment is determined; and if its actual value differs from the required one, inflation in some cases and unused capacity and unemployment in others will develop.

III. The dual nature of the investment process

We shall continue the discussion of growth by returning to expression (2) on page 414.

$$\Delta I \frac{1}{\alpha} = I\sigma,$$

which is fundamental to our whole analysis. As a matter of fact, the statement of the problem in this form (2) appears to me at least as important as its actual solution expressed in (3). To repeat, the left part of the equation shows the annual increment in national income and is the demand side; while the right part represents the annual increase in productive capacity and is the supply side. Alternatively, the left part may be called the "multiplier side," and the right part the "σ side."

What is most important for our purposes is the fact that investment appears on both sides of the equation; that is, it has a *dual effect:* on the left side it generates income via the multiplier effect; and on the right side it increases productive capacity — the σ effect. The explicit recognition of this dual character of investment could undoubtedly save much argument and confusion. Unless some special assumptions are made, the discussion of the effects of investment on profits, income, employment, etc., cannot be legitimately confined to one side only. For the generation of income and the enlargement of productive capacity often have diametrically opposed effects, and the outcome in each particular case depends on the special circumstances involved.[17]

Analyzing expression (2) further, we notice that even though investment is present on both its sides, it does not take the same form: for on the σ side we have the *amount* of investment as such; but on the multiplier side we have not the amount of investment but its annual increment, or its absolute *rate of increase.*

The amount of investment (always in the net sense) may remain constant, or it may go up or down, but so long as it remains positive (and

[17]The effects of labor-saving machinery on employment of labor is a good case in point. Some economists, particularly those connected with the labor movement, insist that such machines displace labor and create unemployment. Their opponents are equally sure that the introduction of labor-saving devices reduces costs and generates income, thus increasing employment. Both sides cite ample empirical evidence to prove their contentions, and neither side is wrong. But both of them present an incomplete picture from which no definite conclusion can be derived.

except for the rare case when $\sigma \leq 0$) productive capacity increases. But if income is to rise as well, it is not enough that just any amount be invested: *an increase in income is not a function of the amount invested; it is the function of the increment of investment.* Thus the whole body of investment, so to speak, increases productive capacity, but only its very top — the increment — increases national income.

In this probably lies the explanation why inflations have been so rare in our economy in peacetime, and why even in relatively prosperous periods a certain degree of underemployment has usually been present. Indeed, it is difficult enough to keep investment at some reasonably high level year after year, but the requirement that it always be rising is not likely to be met for any considerable length of time.

Now, if investment and therefore income do not grow at the required rate, unused capacity develops. Capital and labor become idle. It may not be apparent why investment by increasing productive capacity creates unemployment of labor. Indeed, as was argued on page 410, this need not always be the case. Suppose national income remains constant or rises very slowly while new houses are being built. It is possible that new houses will be rented out at the expense of older buildings and that no larger rents will be paid than before; or that the new houses will stand wholly or partly vacant with the same result regarding the rents.[18] But it is also possible, and indeed very probable, that the complete or partial utilization of the new buildings which are usually better than the old ones, will require the payment of larger rents, with the result that less income will be left for the purchase of, say clothing; thus causing unemployment in the clothing trades. So the substitution of capital for labor need not take the obvious form of labor-saving machinery; it may be equally effective in a more circuitous way.

The unemployment of men is considered harmful for obvious reasons. But idle buildings and machinery, though not arousing our humanitarian instincts, can be harmful because their presence inhibits new investment. Why build a new factory when existing ones are working at half capacity? It is certainly not necessary to be dogmatic and assert that no plant or house should ever be allowed to stand idle, and that as soon as unused capacity develops the economy plunges into a depression. There is no need, nor is it possible or desirable, to guarantee that every piece of capital ever constructed will be fully utilized until it is worn out. When population moves from Oklahoma to California, some buildings in Oklahoma will stand idle; or when plastics replace leather in women's handbags, the leather industry may suffer. Such changes form the very life of a free dynamic society, and should not be interfered with. The point is that there be no

---

[18]It is worth noticing that in both cases the construction of the new houses represents a misdirection of resources, at least to some extent. But a complete avoidance of such misdirection is perfectly impossible and even undesirable.

vacant houses while prospective tenants are present but cannot afford to live in them because they are unemployed. And they are unemployed because income and investment do not grow sufficiently fast.

The extent to which unused capacity, present or expected, inhibits new investment greatly depends on the structure of industry and the character of the economy in general. The more atomistic it is, the stronger is competition, the more susceptible it is to territorial, technological and other changes, the smaller is the effect of unused capacity on new investment. One firm may have an idle plant, while another in the same industry builds a new one; steel may be depressed while plastics are expanding. It is when an industry is more or less monopolized, or when several industries are financially connected, that unused capacity presents a particularly serious threat to new investment.

Strictly speaking, our discussion so far, including equation (2), was based on the assumption that α remained constant. If α varies within the time period concerned, the relation between investment and income becomes more involved. What the left side of the equation (2) requires is that *income* increase; and investment must grow only in so far as its growth is necessary for the growth of income. So if α declines sufficiently fast, a growing income can be achieved with a constant or even falling investment. But years of declining α have evidently been offset by others of rising α, because whatever information is available would indicate that over the last seventy years or so prior to this war the percentage of income saved was reasonably constant, possibly with a slight downward trend.[19] Therefore, in the absence of direct government interference, it would seem better not to count too much on a falling α, at least for the time being.

In general, a high α presents a serious danger to the maintenance of full employment, because investment may fail to grow at the required high rate, or will be physically unable to do so without creating a substantial difference between s and σ. This difference indicates that large numbers of capital assets become unprofitable and their owners suffer losses or at least disappointments (see pages 417–418). Space does not permit me to develop this idea at greater length here.[20] But it must be emphasized that what matters is not the magnitude of α taken by itself, but its relation to the growth of labor, natural resources, and technology. Thus a country with new resources, a rapidly growing population, and developing technology is able to digest, so to speak, a relatively large α, while absence or at least a very slow growth of these factors makes a high α a most serious obstacle to full employment.[21] But the problem can be attacked not only by lowering

[19]See Simon Kuznets, *National Product since 1869*, National Bureau of Economic Research (mimeographed, 1945), p. II–89. I do not mean that we must always assume a constant α; rather that we lack sufficient proof to rely on a falling one.

[20]See my paper, *Econometrica*, Vol. XIV, particularly pp. 142–145.

[21]*Cf.* Alvin H. Hansen, *Fiscal Policy and the Business Cycle* (New York, [W. W. Norton & Co.,] 1941), particularly Part IV.

α, but also by speeding up the rate of technological progress, the latter solution being much more to my taste. It must be remembered, however, that technological progress makes it *possible* for the economy to grow, without guaranteeing that this growth will be realized.

In a private capitalist society where α cannot be readily changed, a higher level of income and employment at any given time can be achieved only through increased investment. But investment, as an employment creating instrument, is a mixed blessing because of its σ effect. The economy finds itself in a serious dilemma: if sufficient investment is not forthcoming today, unemployment will be here today. But if enough is invested today, still more will be needed tomorrow.

It is a remarkable characteristic of a capitalist economy that while, on the whole, unemployment is a function of the difference between its actual income and its productive capacity, most of the measures (*i.e.*, investment) directed towards raising national income also enlarge productive capacity. It is very likely that the increase in national income will be greater than that of capacity, but the whole problem is that the increase in income is temporary and presently peters out (the usual multiplier effect), while capacity has been increased for good. So that as far as unemployment is concerned, investment is at the same time a cure for the disease and the cause of even greater ills in the future.[22]

IV. An economic excursion

It may be worth while to browse through the works of several economists of different schools of thought to see their treatment of the σ and of the multiplier effects of investment. It is not suggested to make an exhaustive study, but just to present a few examples.

Thus in Marshall's *Principles* capital and investment are looked upon as productive instruments (the σ effect), with little being said about monetary (that is, income or price) effects of investment.[23] The same attitude prevails in Fisher's *Nature of Capital and Income*,[24] and I presume in the great majority of writings not devoted to the business cycle. It is not that these writers were unaware of monetary effects of investment (even though they

[22]That income generating effects of investment are temporary and that new and larger amounts must be spent to maintain full employment, has been mentioned in economic and popular literature a number of times. Particular use has been made of this fact by opponents of the so-called deficit financing, who treat government expenditures as a "shot in the arm" which must be administered at an ever increasing dose. What they fail to realize is that exactly the same holds true for private investment.

[23]Marshall was very careful, however, to distinguish between the substitution of a particular piece of machinery for particular labor, and the replacement of labor by capital in general. The latter he regarded impossible, because the construction of capital creates demand for labor, essentially a sort of a multiplier effect. See *Principles of Economics*, 8th ed. (London, 1936), p. 523.

[24]Irving Fisher, *The Nature of Capital and Income* (New York: [The Macmillan Co.,] 1919).

did not have the multiplier concept as such), but such questions belonged to a different field, and the problem of aggregate demand was supposed to be taken care of by some variation of Say's Law.

In the business cycle literature we often find exactly an opposite situation. The whole Wicksellian tradition treated economic fluctuations as a result of monetary effects of excessive investment. It is curious that all this investment did not lead to increased output which would counteract its inflationary tendencies. Indeed, as one reads Hayek's *Prices and Production*, one gets an impression that these investment projects never bear fruit and are, moreover, abandoned after the crisis. The σ effect is entirely absent, or at least appears with such a long lag as to make it inoperative. Prosperity comes to an end because the banking system refuses to support inflation any longer.[25]

σ fares better in the hands of Aftalion.[26] His theory of the cycle is based upon, what I would call, a time lag between the multiplier and the σ effects. Prosperity is started by income generated by investment in capital goods (the multiplier effect), while no increase in productive capacity has taken place as yet. As investment projects are completed, the resulting increase in productive capacity (the σ effect) pours goods on the market and brings prosperity to an end.

A similar approach is used by Michal Kalecki. The essence of his model of the business cycle consists in making profit expectations, and therefore investment, a function (with appropriate lags) of the relation between national income and the stock of capital. During the recovery, investment and income rise, while the accumulation of capital lags behind. Presently, however, due to the structure of the model, the rise of income stops while capital continues to accumulate. This precipitates the downswing.[27]

Space does not allow us to analyze the works of a number of other writers on the subject, among whom Foster and Catchings should be given due recognition for what is so clumsy and yet so keen an insight.[28] I am also

[25]Friedrich A. Hayek, *Prices and Production* (London: [G. Routledge & Sons,] 1931). I don't mean to say that Professor Hayek is not aware that capital is productive; rather that he did not make use of this fact in his theory of the business cycle. See, however, his "The 'Paradox' of Saving," *Economica*, XI (May, 1931), 125–169.

[26]Albert Aftalion, "The Theory of Economic Cycles Based on the Capitalistic Technique of Production," *Review of Economics and Statistics*, IX (Oct. 1927), 165–170. This short article contains a summary of his theory.

[27]Michal Kalecki, *Essays in the Theory of Economic Fluctuations* [London: Allen & Unwin, Ltd.,] 1939). See particularly the last essay "A Theory of the Business Cycle," pp. 116–149. What Mr. Kalecki's model shows in a general sense is that accumulation of capital cannot proceed for any length of time in a trendless economy (*i.e.*, an economy with a secularly constant income). His other results depend upon the specific assumptions he makes.

[28]William T. Foster and Waddill Catchins, *Profits* (Boston and New York: [Houghton Mifflin Co.,] 1925). This book is the most important of their several published works. It is interesting to note that they did come to the conclusion that "... as long as capital facilities are created at a sufficient rate, there need be no deficiency of consumer income. To serve that purpose, however, facilities must be increased at a constantly accelerating rate" (p. 413). This they regarded quite impossible.

omitting the whole Marxist literature, in which capital accumulation plays such an important rôle, because that would require a separate study. The few remaining pages of this section will be devoted to Hobson and Keynes.

Hobson's writings contain so many interesting ideas that it is a great pity he is not read more often.[29] Anti-Keynesians probably like him not much more than they do Keynes, while Keynesians are apt to regard the *General Theory* as the quintessence of all that was worth while in economics before 1936, and may not bother to read earlier writings. I may say that Keynes's own treatment of Hobson, in spite of his generous recognition of the latter's works, may have substantiated this impression.[30]

Even though both Keynes and Hobson were students of unemployment, they actually addressed themselves to two different problems. Keynes analyzed what happens when savings (of the preceding period) are not invested. The answer was — unemployment, but the statement of the problem in this form might easily give the erroneous impression that if savings were invested, full employment would be assured. Hobson, on the other hand, went a step further and stated the problem in this form: suppose savings are invested. Will the new plants be able to dispose of their products? Such a statement of the problem was not at all, as Keynes thought, a mistake.[31] It was a statement of a different, and possibly also a deeper problem.

Hobson was fully armed with the σ effect of investment, and he saw that it could be answered only by growth. His weakness lay in a poor perception of the multiplier effect and his analysis lacked rigor in general. He gave a demonstration rather than a proof. But the problem to which he addressed himself is just as alive today as it was fifty and twenty years ago.[32]

This discussion, as I suspect almost any other, would be obviously incomplete without some mention of Keynes's treatment of the σ and of the multiplier effects. Keynes's approach is very curious: as a matter of fact, he has two: the familiar short-run analysis, and another one which may be called a long-run one.[33]

Keynes's short-run system (later expressed so admiringly by Oscar Lange[34]) is based on ". . . given the existing skill and quantity of available

[29]I am particularly referring to his *Economics of Unemployment* (London: [Allen & Unwin, Ltd.,] 1922) and *Rationalization and Unemployment* (London: [Allen & Unwin, Ltd.,] 1930).

[30]See *The General Theory, op. cit.,* pp. 364–371.

[31]*Ibid.,* pp. 367–368.

[32]Contrary to popular impression, Hobson does not advocate a maximum reduction in the propensity to save. What he wants is to reduce it to a magnitude commensurable with requirements for capital arising from technological progress — an interesting and reasonable idea.

[33]This whole discussion is based on *The General Theory* and not on Keynes's earlier writings.

[34]Oscar Lange, "The Role of Interest and the Optimum Propensity to Consume," *Economica,* n.s. V (Feb. 1938), 12–32. This otherwise excellent paper has a basic defect in the assumption that investment is a function of consumption rather than of the rate of change of consumption.

labor, the existing quality and quantity of available equipment, the existing technique, the degree of competition, the tastes and habits of the consumer . . ."[35] Productive capacity thus being given, employment becomes a function of national income, expressed, to be sure, not in money terms but in "wage units." A wage unit, the remuneration for "an hour's employment of ordinary labor" (page 41), is of course a perfect fiction, but some such device must be used to translate real values into monetary and *vice versa*, and one is about as good or as bad as another. The important point for our purposes is the assumption that the amount of equipment (*i.e.*, capital) in existence is given.

Now, the heart of Keynesian economics is the argument that employment depends on income, which in turn is determined by the current volume of investment (and the propensity to save). But investment (in the net sense) is nothing else but the rate of change of capital. Is it legitimate then first to assume the quantity of capital as given, and then base the argument on its rate of change? If the quantity of capital changes, so does (in a typical case) productive capacity, and if the latter changes it can be hardly said that employment is solely determined by the size of national income, expressed in wage units or otherwise. Or putting it in the language of this paper, is it safe and proper to analyze the relation between investment and employment without taking into account the σ effect?

The answer depends on the nature of the problem in hand. In this particular case, Keynes could present two reasons for his disregard of the σ effect. He could assume that the latter operates with at least a one period lag, the period being understood here as the whole time span covered by the discussion.[36] Or he could argue that over a typical year the net addition (*i.e.*, net investment) to the stock of capital of a society, such as England or the United States, will hardly exceed some 3 or 5 per cent; since this increment is small when compared with changes in income, it can be disregarded.[37]

Both explanations are entirely reasonable provided of course that the period under consideration is not too long. A five-year lag for the σ effect would be difficult to defend, and an increase in the capital stock of some 15 or 20 per cent can hardly be disregarded. I am not aware that Keynes did present either of these explanations; but there is just so much one can do in four hundred pages at any one time.

It would be perfectly absurd to say that Keynes was not aware of the productive qualities of capital. In the *long run* he laid great stress on it, possibly too great. All through *The General Theory* we find grave concern

[35]*The General Theory, op. cit.*, p. 245. See also pp. 24 and 28.

[36]This again is not quite safe unless some provision for investment projects started in preceding periods and finished during the present period is made.

[37]The second assumption is specifically made by Professor Pigou in his *Employment and Equilibrium* (London: [Macmillan and Co.,] 1941), pp. 33–34.

for the diminishing marginal efficiency of capital due, in the long run, to its increasing quantity.[38] There is so much of this kind of argument as to leave the reader puzzled in the end. We are told that marginal efficiency of capital depends on its scarcity. Well and good. But scarcity relative to what? It could become less scarce relative to other factors, such as labor, so that the marginal productivity of capital in the real sense (*i.e.*, essentially our σ) declined. But then on page 213 we read: "If capital becomes less scarce, the excess yield will diminish, without its having become less productive — at least in the physical sense."

Why then does the marginal efficiency of capital fall? Evidently because capital becomes less scarce relative to income.[39] But why cannot income grow more rapidly if labor is not the limiting factor? Could it be only a matter of poor fiscal policy which failed to achieve a faster growing income? After all we have in investment an income generating instrument; if investment grows more rapidly, so does income. This is *the* multiplier effect of investment on which so much of *The General Theory* is built.

I don't have the answer. Is it possible that, while Keynes disregarded the σ effect in the short-run analysis, he somehow omitted the multiplier effect from the long-run?

V. Concluding remarks

A traveller who sat in the economic councils of the United States and of the Soviet Union would be much impressed with the emphasis placed on investment and technological progress in both countries. He would happily conclude that the differences between the economic problems of a relatively undeveloped socialist economy and a highly developed capitalist economy are really not as great as they are often made to appear. Both countries want investment and technological progress. But if he continued to listen to the debates, he would presently begin to wonder. For in the Soviet Union investment and technology are wanted in order to enlarge the country's productive capacity. They are wanted essentially as labor-saving devices which would allow a given task to be performed with less labor, thus releasing men for other tasks. In short, they are wanted for their σ effects.

In the United States, on the other hand, little is said about enlarging productive capacity. Technological progress is wanted as the creator of investment opportunities, and investment is wanted because it generates income and creates employment. It is wanted for its multiplier effect.

Both views are correct and both are incomplete. The multiplier is not just another capitalist invention. It can live in a socialist state just as well

---

[38]See for instance pp. 31, 105–106, 217, 219, 220–221, 324, and 375.

[39]There is a third possibility, namely, that income is redistributed against the capitalists, but Keynes makes no use of it.

and it has been responsible for the inflationary pressure which has plagued the Soviet economy all these years, since the first five-year plan. And similarly, σ is just as much at home in one country as in another, and its effect — the enlarged productive capacity brought about by accumulation of capital — has undoubtedly had much to do with our peacetime unemployment.

But what is the solution? Shall we reduce σ to zero and also abolish technological progress thus escaping from unemployment into the "nirvana" of a stationary state? This would indeed be a defeatist solution. It is largely due to technology and savings that humanity has made the remarkable advance of the last two hundred years, and now when our technological future seems so bright, there is less reason to abandon it than ever before.

It is possible that α has been or will be too high as compared with the growth of our labor force, the utilization of new resources, and the development of technology. Unfortunately, we have hardly any empirical data to prove or disprove this supposition. The fact that private investment did not absorb available savings in the past does not prove that they could not be utilized in other ways (*e.g.*, by government), or even that had private business invested them these investments would have been unprofitable; the investing process itself might have created sufficient income to justify the investments. What is needed is a study of the magnitudes of s, of the difference between s and σ which can develop without much harm and then of the value of α which the economy can digest at its full employment rate of growth.

Even if the resulting magnitude of α is found to be considerably below the existing one, a reduction of α is only one of the two solutions, the speeding up of technological progress being the other. But it must be remembered that neither technology, nor of course saving, guarantee a rise in income. What they do is to place in our hands the *power* and the ability of achieving a growing income. And just as, depending upon the use made of it, any power can become a blessing or a curse, so can saving and technological progress, depending on our economic policies, result in frustration and unemployment or in an ever-expanding economy.

ROY F. HARROD 21

Fundamental dynamic theorems

At the conclusion of the last lecture I discussed two approaches to the problem of what might govern the market rate of interest in a steadily advancing community. I hasten to add that both these approaches, though at first sight appropriate to the problem in hand and conformable with economic analysis generally, were totally unrealistic.

On the one hand we considered the possibility that the market having looked forward and in its wisdom assessed that fundamental conditions required a falling rate of interest in the coming period, so marked the values of gilt-edged securities of various maturities that, with expectations unchanged, a steady fall in the rate of yield would eventuate between the present and the dates of maturity. It appeared clearly that this was to attribute far too much foresight to the market and that any assessment of this sort implies a valuation of securities of various maturities which is altogether in conflict with the whole mass of our market experience. It is also very difficult to see what, on this basis, the market could do with securities without redemption date.

The other line of approach went to the opposite extreme and supposed that the market in long-dated securities would be governed by the current balance between supply and demand for new capital.[1] Shortsighted though

Reprinted from Roy F. Harrod, *Towards a Dynamic Economics,* Lecture 3 (London: Macmillan, 1948), pp. 63–100, by permission of Macmillan & Co. Ltd., The Macmillan Company of Canada Ltd., and St. Martin's Press, Inc. This selection embodies the formulations in Harrod's pathbreaking article published in the *Economic Journal* (March, 1939). [Footnotes renumbered — *Eds.*]

[1]It is not implied that the doctrine in this extreme form has been held by recent writers.

the market may be it is not as shortsighted as all this. An adjustment of the security values to the monthly balance between the supply of and the demand for new capital would surely mean variations of at least the order of 1 or 2 per cent in the rate of interest, *i.e.* of 50 or 100 per cent in the value of irredeemable securities. The idea that the market will, in the course of a short period, mark perfectly good British Government securities, now at 140, now at 70, is quite wide of the mark. Such a procedure would be wrong from every point of view. Especially is this so when one recalls that according to this theory the alleged changes in the market prices of these securities should occur even if there were no change in expectations as regards the future. Changes of expectation may cause big changes in Stock Exchange values, albeit probably not changes big enough to secure the monthly balance in the supply and demand for new capital; but there is no reason whatever to suppose that such changes of expectation will occur, indeed it would be quite fantastic to suppose that they would occur every time there was a need, from the point of view of the monthly balance, to get a big change in prices. I class this method of approach, therefore, as being quite as unrealistic as the other.

The approach by Keynes to the problem of the market rate of long-term interest, whatever criticisms one may bring against it, is much more realistic than either of these. The future is not left out of account, although Keynes did not think that the Stock Exchange took a very long view! Still there is no question in the Keynes analysis of the market fixing present values at levels that are widely different from what they judge the future will have in store. On the other hand no definite curve of future prices is deemed to be foreseen. On the contrary, it is the essence of the theory that the market is very largely uncertain as to what is to happen in the future. In Dynamics we must not, any more than in Statics, think away uncertainty. Even if we postulate that the fundamental conditions are changing steadily, so as to determine, if all could be assessed accurately, a steady rate of advance and therewith a steady fall of interest, we must not postulate that it is known that these conditions will be such.

In Keynes interest is reduced to nothing more than a risk premium against fluctuations, about which we are uncertain. Is the rate of interest unduly high, if it is deemed to serve no other function than that of being a risk premium? After all a change of ½ per cent may mean a change of some 20 per cent in capital values, and 2½ per cent is perhaps a not unduly high premium to charge for bearing this risk.

Criticisms have been made of this theory on the ground that it leaves interest suspended, so to speak, in a void, there being interest because there is interest. Professor Robertson's subtle thoughts on economics have for long solaced the hearts of economists, and great weight is due to any criticism he makes. I quote from page 25 of his *Essays in Monetary Theory:*

Thus the rate of interest is what it is because it is expected to become other than it is; if it is not expected to become other than it is there is nothing left to tell us why it is what it is. The organ which secretes it has been amputated, and yet it somehow still exists — "a grin without a cat." Mr. Plumptre of Toronto, in an unpublished paper, has aptly compared the position of the lenders of money under this theory with that of an insurance company which charges its clients a premium, the only risk against which it insures them being the risk that its premium will be raised. If we ask what ultimately governs the judgments of wealth owners as to why the rate of interest should be different in the future from what it is to-day, we are surely led straight back to the fundamental phenomena of productivity and thrift.

Or again, Mr. Hicks writes: "But to say that the rate of interest on perfectly safe securities is determined by nothing else but uncertainty of future interest rates seems to leave interest hanging by its own boot straps; one feels an obstinate conviction that there must be more in it than that." Mr. Hicks, however, does not base himself upon productivity and thrift but upon the cost incurred by the marginal transferer of money into short-dated securities, long-term interest being on this view ultimately governed by short-term interest.

These criticisms suggest that the Keynes theory of interest is circular; there is interest because the rate of interest is expected to change; in fine, there is interest, because there is expected to be interest. But why is there expected to be interest? And so, why is there interest?

I do not think that this criticism is decisive. Surely there are some phenomena of the mind — and interest is nothing but a phenomenon of the mind, the resultant of thoughts and opinions, hopes and fears, itself only a promise, finally indeed an act, but one solely originating in the will of the two parties, not a physical phenomenon at all — surely there are mental phenomena to which the dictum may correctly be applied that there is nothing true but thinking makes it so.

And I am inclined to think that this account of interest hanging by its own boot straps is an exaggeration. Consider a security with a certain par value due in twenty years, carrying 2½ per cent. Without interest the present value of £100 of such stock would be £150. This is a definite sum of money. But the market does not value the stock at £150, but at some lower figure, say, £100, to allow for the fact that the holder cannot be sure of getting the exact calculated sum, whatever it may be, between £150 and £100 at a date of his own choosing in the next twenty years. But, it will be objected that if there is no interest, and known that there will not in any case be any interest, will he not have a certainty of getting this appropriate sum? But this assumption is too far-reaching. In fairness to Keynes, I do not think we are entitled to assume, in rebutting the theory of liquidity preference, a world in which it was known that there never could be any interest, presumably a world in which there never had been any interest! And are not the critics going a little far? Did Keynes anywhere say that liquidity preference was the sole and only reason why there ever had been or could be interest? Or did he not rather merely say that liquidity preference was the sole determinant of the level of the interest rate?

I am not prepared to reject Keynes's theory, even in the stripped form in which his critics present it, as untenable. It is certainly much more realistic than the other two possible theories I have touched on. On the other hand I do not think that Keynes compels us to suppose that the market in brooding upon future prices, and on the uncertainties thereof, pays no regard whatever to Professor Robertson's productivity and thrift.

And I would add this in defence of Keynes. Some critics imply, perhaps Keynes himself implied, that he was substituting his theory for some well-established orthodox theory, so that, if we reject Keynes, there is something to fall back on. I deny the existence of the alleged orthodox theory, and claim that the Keynes theory ought properly to be regarded as an attempt to fill a void.[2] If we reject the Keynes theory in whole or in part, we must offer something in its place (as Mr. Hicks does) or acknowledge that we are so far without any theory of interest. It surely cannot be maintained that dealers in the market acting for their own advantage are in a position to evaluate long period trends in the manner described in the last lecture and to mark stocks in such a way as to imply that the yield on them due to interest and appreciation (or depreciation) will move during future years along a curve — if there is a redemption date the curve will often have to rise and fall alternately. Nor is it in the least degree feasible to hold that values are adjusted so as to balance the contemporary increments of demand and supply regardless of the future.

In the case of commodity markets contemporary disequilibrium can be made good by absorption into or release from stocks. Now it might at first blush be supposed that jobbers or other dealers by holding stocks and shares on speculative account or taking up bear positions perform a function precisely analogous to that of dealers in commodity markets. This is an illusion. The operations of dealers in the two kinds of market are similar in that they both tend (or should tend) to iron out fluctuations of prices. But the great difference is that whereas physical commodities can be carried forward through time by storage, it is impossible to do this with "waiting" or "saving"; it cannot be put into a bottle and transferred from time A to time B. Real assets can, of course, be carried forward through time, pending their use; commodity stocks are indeed a particular example of this. But this carry forward is *after* saving has been taken up and embodied in something real. It cannot be carried forward prior to such embodiment.

In the cases both of particular commodities and saving in general, price oscillation would probably have to be extremely violent to equate output to use day by day. In the former case this oscillation is reduced by the

2I do not imply that his was the first attempt!

device of storing output for future use. In the case of saving this device is not available and the *modus operandi* of the security markets is different. By preventing these heroic rises in interest changes which might be necessary from time to time to confine investment plans to saving available on that day, they allow those plans to go forward. This progress is achieved, not by the release of stored up "saving" nor as a direct result of the speculators' purchases, but indirectly by reduction of real stocks in some other part of the economy. Conversely when interest rates would be required to fall to zero or below it in order to get a day to day adjustment of the provision of saving to its use, security dealers allow the saving to go forward despite the lack of adequate investment plans, and this is effected through the unwanted accumulation of capital stocks in some other part of the economy.

But the matter does not rest there. To trace its ramifications Keynes brought forward his multiplier theory. What is it that prevents that large oscillation in the value of interest, which would be needed to equate the provision to the use of savings from time to time? According to Keynes, variations in employment and income. What is the orthodox theory in regard to what limits oscillations in the rate of interest? I submit with respect that there is no established traditional theory to be pitted against Keynes's specific theory.

There is a somewhat different line of criticism of Keynes's liquidity preference theory of interest which I confess I have always thought to have substance. Keynes insists that interest is solely the reward for parting with liquidity and not in any sense the reward for waiting. This insistence has appeared to me to be one-sided and not necessary for his case. It must be agreed, surely he would have to agree, that two activities are necessary before capital can be provided, namely (1) waiting and (2) parting with liquidity. Both activities, anyhow in certain circumstances, have to be rewarded if they are to take place. If a reward for waiting is necessary in order that there shall be waiting, those who want to enjoy the benefit of it will have to pay that reward, the liquidity preference question apart.

A promising line of analysis might seem to be that when there are two activities of this sort both necessary, the user of the end product (viz. capital disposal) will have to pay the price necessary to satisfy the lender in his capacity of waiter or the price necessary to satisfy him in his capacity of parter with liquidity, whichever is higher. There seems to be an assumption in Keynes that the second will be higher, and, in circumstances in which this is so and those only, it is the second that will determine the rate of interest; in those circumstances and those only the whole of Keynes's argument follows as set out. Keynes would not, I think, have accepted this limitation. He would rest himself on the view that income, the source of saving, is a dependent variable in the whole picture and that the supply schedule of saving will so adjust itself as to conform to the rate of interest established in the market to satisfy liquidity preference whatever that rate might be.

We may grapple with this problem in another way. Accepting the liquidity preference theory of the market rate, there are two possibilities in regard to the relation of this to the supply of saving, only one of which Keynes appears to have considered. And to that extent his *General Theory* may be deemed to lack generality. One case, the case he treated, is where the liquidity preference rate is higher than that rate of interest which would make capital outlay equal to all the saving that would occur at that rate of interest in conditions of full employment. That being so, insufficient capital outlay occurs, and by consequence there is not full employment. But what of the case in which the market rate of interest, as determined by the forces defined by Keynes, established itself at a level at which capital outlay exceeded the volume of saving forthcoming at that rate at full employment? Then we should have an inflationary condition — such as we have now! The present is precisely a situation in which the efforts of the Chancellor of the Exchequer are holding the liquidity preference rate of interest far below the level at which capital outlay would balance saving forthcoming at full employment. Hence the need for controls. If Keynes did not deal with this other case, it may be that at the time of writing he deemed it so far removed from actuality as to have no practical interest. Formally one may say that he has only tackled half his subject.

There is a fundamental difference, however, between the state of affairs as outlined in the Keynesian analysis which arises when the liquidity preference rate is too high and that which — at least in the absence of Keynes to analyse this other half of the field! — we must deem to arise should the liquidity preference rate of interest be too low. In the former case Keynes presents us with what in the absence of fresh disturbing causes can be regarded as a stable equilibrium with involuntary unemployment present. On the other side of the line one would have, it appears, not any kind of equilibrium, but an inflationary condition, an unstable condition of expansion, destined ultimately to be terminated. Capital outlay exceeding saving at full employment, there would be an inflationary pressure with rising prices, an expansion beyond the rate that could be sustained, and in the end some kind of breakdown. Thus we are confronted with asymmetry.

In this connection I should like to remind you of the main difference between Keynes's *Treatise on Money* and his *General Theory*. As you are well aware, he altered his definitions of saving and investment between the two treatises, a matter about which we need not complain too much! In the *Treatise* his concepts of saving and investment, though not identical with, are first cousins to, the concepts of ex-ante saving and investment. In the *Treatise* he envisages two alternative conditions, one in which investment is greater than saving and the other the opposite. The former of these is roughly analogous to the case where the liquidity preference rate of interest is below the level at which capital outlay would be equal to the saving as it then was; capital outlay is thus stimulated. The *General Theory* concentrates attention on the other case. But there is a great difference between the two treatments. In the *Treatise* we get an unstable condition on both sides of the line, viz., progressive expansion on the one side and progressive contraction on the other. In the *General Theory*, on the other hand, Keynes provides for the possibility of a stable equilibrium on the lower side, namely where the liquidity preference rate of interest is above the level required to secure full-employment-capital-outlay. In this, of course, the *General Theory* breaks new ground. It was this to which he attached great importance. It was important. It was in order to get what he thought would be a convenient apparatus for demonstrating this possibility of stable equilibrium on the low side that he abandoned the ex-ante and went over to the ex-post concepts of saving and investment.

I suggest that the *Treatise* may be regarded as his diagnosis of the trade cycle, and the *General Theory* as his diagnosis of chronic unemployment or under production. The *Treatise* does not provide a satisfactory account of chronic unemployment, because there the conditions in which the liquidity preference rate (to anticipate his later terminology) is too high are essentially conditions of instability, of growing depression. And the opposite conditions are essentially those of gathering momentum. There is no notion of stability at a certain level when the rate of interest is above its proper height, however that may be defined. Thus there is nothing arising from the analysis of the *Treatise* to suggest that in certain circumstances the rate of interest may be chronically too high, that we may have a permanent unemployment problem, over and above that caused by the cycle itself. But the circumstances at the time were such as to suggest that there is in fact a problem of chronic unemployment, needing analysis. The *General Theory* was Keynes's answer. Until that the greater number of economists had lulled themselves with the idea that unemployment, bad as it might be, was a function of frictions, rigidities and the trade cycle. This assumption was first seriously challenged by the *General Theory* and that was itself important. In the light of this it is not perhaps of great moment that Keynes did not in the *General Theory* embark upon an analysis of the other possibility, where the rate as determined by liquidity preference tended chronically to over-stimulate capital outlay.

There is a more important line of criticism on which I wish to dwell briefly. In the *General Theory* the goal of our endeavours, so to speak, is full employment. Management of the rate of interest is to be directed to this goal. But there is another concept, quite different from though not necessarily inconsistent with the idea of full employment, namely a steady rate of progress conformable with fundamental conditions. Of course we wish for a steady rate of progress with full employment, using that expression in not too exaggerated a sense, all along the line. But what of the analysis? Full employment is one thing and a steady rate of progress quite another. To secure full employment in the short period without regard to what may be necessary for securing a steady rate of progress is shortsighted. We shall not have a very sound policy if we envisage treating the problem of unemployment *ad hoc* from month to month without regard to what sustained level of capital outlay is necessary for an advance of the economy in line with what fundamental conditions allow. I am not suggesting that there is anything radically wrong with the Keynesian remedies, but only that they must ultimately be based upon a somewhat different analytical approach and judged by a different criterion.

An interesting point may be noted in passing. If we start from a condition of severe unemployment, some pump-priming — I will not bother about the precise form, but for the moment we may think of that old-fashioned remedy of public works — may be necessary. If we have success, and conditions improve, at some point the acceleration principle must surely come into play, I will not say with precisely what force. As we move forward to full employment capital outlay may well exceed, almost must exceed, the normal level appropriate to the fundamental conditions of our steadily advancing economy. For in this upward phase we are advancing much more rapidly than at the normal steady rate. Therefore if we carry our policy through and approach full employment, there must be a falling off of the capital outlay associated with the abnormal rate of advance, an abnormal rate which may proceed over a year or two. Thus, still speaking in terms of this old-fashioned remedy of public works, the point at which it will be above all necessary to have a large volume of public works to turn on, perhaps a larger volume than in the original pump-priming phase, is when we approach full employment.

Having criticized Keynes for his lack of a dynamic principle, we must return to the consideration of that principle. In our earlier lecture we reached the conclusion that fundamental conditions might require a steadily falling rate of interest. We found great difficulties in envisaging how the capital market could ever succeed in providing such a steady decline.

Static theory does two things. It defines the positions of rate of output and price at which everyone will be willing to carry on. Each person, if you like, is on the most favoured indifference curve which he can reach, and no one sees any means of self-improvement in the circumstances prevailing. Secondly, it has something to say as to how these positions are reached. In this uncertain world we have to proceed by trial and error. A producer tries producing so much. Experience and observation may then suggest that he could enlarge his profit by producing more. If a man is not doing the best for himself the pricing mechanism gives him guidance; it beckons him on or shows him the red light. It does so anyhow in cases in which the preferred position is a stable equilibrium. Of course we know from static theory that there may be more than one position of stable equilibrium, of which one may be better than the other, but will not necessarily be reached if the agent happens to have got into the other; we know that there may be ranges of indeterminacy. These matters are being ever more intensively examined. In a very broad sense, however, we believe that on the assumptions required for static analysis there is a tendency for the various members of the economy to work towards and stay in the best available positions. If demand exceeds supply, the price will rise, and so forth.

The most difficult problem in the static analysis is probably the general level of output — Keynes's problem in fact. Relative levels of the output of each article are well catered for, subject to the secondary difficulties already mentioned. For the general level of output we have had to rely on the balancing of the marginal utility of income with the marginal disutility of work. It is rightly felt to be disturbing to the structure of this theory if long continued "involuntary" unemployment is possible.

The decision by an entrepreneur to increase output has a twofold effect: it alters his relative position and it alters the general level of output. If he is but one unit in a large economy the second-mentioned effect may be unimportant. But may it entail some tendency to set up a cumulative process of expansion? A harvest variation, because widespread, may have more important effects in that direction than changes by an individual.

I will not pause, however, to consider possibilities within the static conditions, but proceed directly to dynamic assumptions. Growth is the aggregated effect of a great number of individual decisions. In the foregoing treatment I have attempted to analyse the main elements in growth, and to indicate the nature of possible lines of advance. This corresponds to the representation of what the positions would be in the equilibrium of a stationary state. But what of the analysis of the stability of that equilibrium? If the rate of growth entailed by the aggregated individual decisions based on trial and error is different from the rate of growth required by the fundamental conditions, are there forces tending to correct that rate and bring it into line with the growth required by the fundamental conditions?

It will not be possible in what follows to keep our minds altogether free of the trade cycle problem. I am afraid that a proper understanding of the relation between the requirements of a steady advance and what the market can provide is very much mixed up with the trade cycle problem. But there are various aspects of that problem which I propose to leave entirely on one side, particularly those connected with lags. I wish to concentrate attention on one or two aspects that seem to me very closely related to the general dynamic problem.

I propose, if you will allow me, to seek to push forward by reverting to a method of analysis suggested in an article which I wrote in the *Economic Journal* of March 1939, in particular to the fundamental equation there set out. Pending any damaging criticism of that equation, I feel that it is a powerful tool for sorting out the factors involved and would therefore ask you to give attention to it. I shall slightly, but only slightly, alter the notation.

This fundamental equation has two forms. In one it is a truism, in the other a statement of the rate of growth which will leave the various parties satisfied. Neither is directly related to the growth made possible by continuing changes in fundamental conditions. First we may look at the truism. For this purpose I write the equation as follows:

$$GC = s.$$

G, which stands for growth, is the increment of total production in any unit period expressed as a fraction of total production. Thus if the line of steady advance meant an increase in output of 2 per cent per annum, G would be $\frac{1}{50}$; or if the unit period chosen was a month, G would be $\frac{1}{600}$.

C (capital) is the increase in the volume of goods of all kinds outstanding at the end over that outstanding at the beginning of the period divided by the increment of production in that same period. This seems a somewhat complicated concept, but I hope that you will feel, as the argument proceeds, that it is really a very simple one.

The value of GC is independent of the unit period chosen. Consider one standard unit period and another unit period n times the length of the standard unit. The numerator of G measured for the second-named unit period is n^2 times that of the standard unit period, while the denominator is n times that of the standard unit period (*e.g.* income per annum is twelve times income per month); therefore the value of G measured for the second-mentioned unit period is n times its value mentioned for the standard unit period. The numerator of C for the second-mentioned unit period is n times its numerator measured for the standard unit period, while the denominator of the former is n^2 times the denominator of the latter. Thus the value of C for the second-mentioned period is $1/n$ times that of the latter. Thus the value of GC is independent of the unit period chosen.

s is the fraction of income saved. It is not necessary for the following argument to assume that s is constant as G changes. The long analysis in the last lecture did not, I think, yield a more convenient way of expressing the value of saving likely to be volunteered than as a fraction of income. On the whole that seemed to be the most probable value for the saving required if an advance was to be steady at constant interest. It was recognized, however, that in crucial cases saving as a fraction of income might not be constant.

All that is required for the argument immediately to follow is that any changes in s, *i.e.* saving expressed as a fraction of income, should be small by comparison with experimental changes in G. And this requirement is clearly fulfilled. Without any great revolution G might easily change from 2 to 6 per cent. This clearly could not cause saving to be trebled. The extreme case of saving being as low as 2 per cent of income and all extra income, due to a rise of G, being saved may be ruled out. If saving is greater than 2 per cent then for saving as a fraction of income to increase by as much as G, consumption would have to be cut (in all probable cricumstances by large amounts) as income rose, and this, too, may be ruled out.

To meet the criticism that this equation gives too much emphasis to the acceleration principle, we may insert a term which may be interpreted as liberally as you wish. Let us write the equation

$$GC = s - k,$$

where k consists of current additions to capital (the value thereof to be expressed as a fraction of current income) the worth-whileness of which is not deemed to have any immediate relation to current requirements. k is in fact the capital outlay of a long-range character, capital outlay which no one expects to see justified or not justified within a fairly short period. In the long run k must disappear, for in the long run all capital outlay is justified by the use to which it is put. But it may be very important to separate it out in the short period. In the short period make k as large as you please. Units of equipment, etc., which are included in k must be omitted in the computation of C. If k is very large (as in war) and exceeds s, C may become negative, and we shall then have an inflationary situation.

C is the addition to capital, but need not consist exclusively or even mostly of capital goods. It is merely the accretion during the period of all goods (less those goods which are included in k). This equation does not make any explicit reference to goods in process. The varying level of these is no doubt important, but I deliberately do not distinguish them because I believe that we are on the way to certain basic truths, which are independent of complications that have to be introduced when we seek to build up a more detailed picture of the whole process. I emphasize that this equation is necessarily true. It follows from the definitions of the terms.[3] It is a dynamic equation since it contains G, which refers to the rate of increase. I also commend to you its extreme simplicity. I should like to think that it might serve as a target for frequent attack, like Fisher's famous truism $MV = PT$. I will only say this. Do not seek to criticize it by reference to alternative equations or formulae which do not contain a dynamic term such as G. That would not be playing the game. I feel that I shall have achieved something really important if in the discussion and criticism of this formula I can habituate the critics to thinking in dynamic terms. I know of no alterna-

---

[3] It can easily be seen, by the cancellation of common terms, that it is reducible to the truism that ex-post "investment" is equal to ex-post saving.

Let Y stand for income, I for investment and S for saving.

$$GC = \frac{\Delta Y}{Y} \cdot \frac{I}{\Delta Y} \text{ and } s = \frac{S}{Y}.$$

tive formulation, in the world of modern economic theory, of any dynamic principle of comparable generality. We must start with some generality however imperfect. We shall never go ahead if we remain in a world of trivialities or fine points. It is useless to refine and refine when there are no basic ideas present at all.

We now come to the form of the equation which expresses the equilibrium of a steady advance. I write this:

$$G_w C_r = s.$$

Repeating the terminology of my earlier article I call G_w the warranted rate of growth. This has nothing whatever to do with the rate of growth determined by the fundamental conditions of population increase, etc., which was discussed earlier. This equation expresses the condition in which producers will be content with what they are doing.

How are we to compare the equilibrium of a steady advance with a static equilibrium? In the static equilibrium producers remain content with their existent rate of output. They look upon their work and they see that it is good. On a broad definition this need not preclude variations in particular commodities. We may suppose that some producers find that the demand is falling off and others that it is increasing, in fact that not all individuals are content to rest in their present condition, but are subject to forces requiring them to adjust upwards or downwards. But if the fundamental conditions as a whole are stationary, the amount of contraction suggested by this condition of markets for various specialities should be equal to the amount of expansion suggested by other markets. An adjustment is made, and the static equilibrium equations prescribe the new values at which the various kinds of output will eventually settle down after a shorter or longer period.

The same circumstances apply to a steady advance. This concept need not preclude the more rapid advance in certain sectors, lower advances or even declines in others. In this case, however, there will be an over-all tendency to advance somewhat, namely, if the short period conditions are right for a steady advance, at the rate G_w. The decision by each entrepreneur to continue producing at the rate he has produced or to produce something more is no doubt determined both by the satisfactory or unsatisfactory character of the results of his previous decisions as experienced to date — a point upon which the lag analysis lays primary stress — and also by a reasonable prognostication of what is to come based on a survey of the particular markets. I define G_w as that over-all rate of advance which, if executed, will leave entrepreneurs in a state of mind in which they are prepared to carry on a similar advance. Some may be dissatisfied and have to adjust upwards or downwards, but the ups and downs should balance out and, in the aggregate, progress in the current period should be equal to progress in the last preceding period.

The equation before us sets out to define the rate of advance which will give satisfaction and lead to its own perpetuation.

C_r is the term for capital requirements. Whereas in the truistic equation there was an ex-post term expressing the amount of capital goods actually produced per period, C_r is an equilibrium term expressing requirements for new capital. C_r is defined analogously with C, namely as the requirement for new capital divided by the increment of output to sustain which the new capital is required. C_r is thus the required capital coefficient.

This definition is based on the idea that existing output can be sustained by existing capital and that additional capital is only required to sustain additional output. This follows from the assumption that the capital/income ratio is constant, *i.e.* that the length of the production process is unchanged and this follows from the two assumptions on which we are at present working, namely, (1) that inventions are neutral and (2) that the rate of interest is constant. The equation must be modified in a way that I shall presently describe when we have to deal with the case of the production processes getting more roundabout.

Of course this does not imply that all inventions are neutral. There is no need to make such a rigid requirement, which would of course be altogether unrealistic. In the case of certain goods an invention may come forward greatly raising the amount of capital required for the more efficient production of a given quantum of goods. In other cases the "invention" may take the form of an improvement in managerial methods — the point in which some say we are much further behind the Americans than in our physical capital equipment — whereby a given plant is made to yield a higher output of goods. What we are postulating in our dynamic approach to these problems is that on average all the various inventions and improvements accruing in a unit period are neutral, those requiring more capital per unit of output balancing the effect of those which require less. On this assumption the existing capital of the country, always of course changing its precise form in all the different sectors, can sustain the existing output. New capital is required in relation to new output (whether the new output is due to an increase of population or an increase of output per head). C_r is of course a marginal notion; it is the new capital required to sustain the output which will satisfy the demands for consumption arising out of consumers' marginal addition to income.[4] Thus C_r, the marginal requirement for new capital, may not be equal to the capital coefficient in the economy as a whole. But as a condition for a steady advance we have to assume that C_r does not change over the range of income increase that occurs during the postulated period of steady advance. You may think that all these assumptions involved in the definition of C_r taken together are rather large, but I suggest that they define the simplest possible case from which we can well proceed to develop various complications.

[4]After a recession, when there is much redundant capacity, C_r is temporarily reduecd to a low level.

It may suggest itself to your minds that the frequent occurrence of inventions or frequent changes of taste would lead to demands for fresh saving even although both kinds of change were on balance of neutral character. Will not new installations be required in consequence of the changes, and new savings, in order to finance them? In general this does not appear to be the case. Provided that the tempo of change is recognized by entrepreneurs, they will fix their depreciation allowances accordingly. These will be higher in a progressive than in a stagnant economy. In particular cases, however, unforeseen changes might be so great as to throw whole firms into liquidation before they had had time to write down the obsolete sector of their assets to zero, and it could be argued that this loss of real capital will not be offset by the longevity, in other firms, of assets which last beyond expectation, since assets cannot be written down below zero. Strictly, losses such as these should be deducted from positive savings in fixing the value of s. Alternatively new installations of a value equal to the loss of incompletely written off assets in the hands of bankrupt firms might be included in k. The existence of such losses does not affect the argument which follows.

I now ask you to look closely at the two equations set out. The former, you remember, is a truistic equation which must be satisfied whatever advance or recession takes place. The latter expresses the fact that if the advance is to be maintained, C, the quantity of the addition to capital actually accruing, must be what is needed. This capital, as I have already pointed out, covers both equipment and stock-in-trade. I am not at present basing myself upon the distinction between durable and non-durable goods or upon that between producer and consumer goods. C consists in part of consumer goods, including non-durable consumer goods. In an advancing community goods in the pipe-line, shops, warehouses, transit, and producers' stores, have to increase in proportion to turnover. All these goods are part of capital. The rise or fall of goods in the pipe-line above or below the required level may be just as big a factor as the margins of unwanted equipment or shortage of equipment in depressing or stimulating the system.

Taking these two equations together, we can see a relation of the utmost simplicity, and I ask you to join with me in thinking it extraordinarily impressive. The greater G, the lower C. That can hardly be questioned. Consequently if G has a value above G_w, C will have a value below C_r. I see no way of escape from that. If C has a value below C_r, this means that on balance producers and traders find the goods in the pipe-line or the equipment insufficient to sustain existing turnover. Let me repeat: if the value G is above that of G_w, the value of C must be below that of C_r; there will be insufficient goods in the pipe-line and/or insufficient equipment, and orders will be increased. If the value G is above the value G_w, that is if the actual growth is above the line of growth consistent with a steady advance, orders will be increased, And, of course, conversely. This strikes me as an extraordinarily simple and notable demonstration of the instability of an advancing system. Around the line of advance, which, if adhered to, would alone give satisfaction, centrifugal forces are at work, causing the system to depart farther and farther from the required line of advance.

G is a quantity determined from time to time by trial and error, by the collective trials and errors of vast numbers of people. It would be great luck if their collective appraisals caused them to hit precisely upon the value G_w. But if they do not do so their experience will tend to drive them farther and farther from it. This kind of instability has nothing to do with the effect of lags, and strikes me as more fundamental. The only way in which this conclusion could be upset would be by the suggestion that variations in G would cause equally large variations in the value of s. But this is clearly unacceptable for reasons already stated. It is not thinkable, for instance, that saving as a fraction of income could be multiplied by 4 in consequence of a change in the increase of income from 1 per cent to 4 per cent. The only case in which anything of this sort could possibly happen would be if the value of k was almost as great as that of s, that is if almost all savings were absorbed in capital outlay which had no relation to the requirements of current demand.

So far then we have two propositions. (i) There is a line of advance which, if adhered to, would leave producers content with what they had done. A small point that will readily occur to you is that perhaps C_r should be deemed to have a value slightly lower than the required amount of capital, lower, that is, by the amount necessary to keep producers moving forward on the line of advance. If C_r were precisely equal to requirements they might lapse into a stationary condition.

(ii) If the aggregated result of trial and error by numerous producers gives a value of G which is different from G_w, there will not be any tendency to adapt production towards G_w, but, on the contrary, a tendency to adapt production still farther away from it, whether on the higher or lower side.

Next it is desirable to relate these two equations to that steady rate of advance determined by fundamental conditions, which has been so much discussed already. We may set this out in the form of an equation as follows:

$$G_n C_r = \text{or} \neq s.$$

G_n ($_n$ for natural) is the rate of advance which the increase of population and technological improvements allow. It has no direct relation to G_w.

G_n represents the line of output at each point on which producers of all kinds will be satisfied that they are making a correct balance between work and leisure; it excludes the possibility of "involuntary" unemployment. G_w is the entrepreneurial equilibrium; it is the line of advance, which, if achieved, will satisfy profit takers that they have done the right thing; in Keynesian fashion it contemplates the possibility of growing "involuntary" unemployment. Thus the plot thickens. We have not only to consider divergences of G and G_w but also those of G_w from G_n.

In the first place it is to be observed that G_n sets a limit to the maximum average value of G over a long period. After a recession G may attain a higher value than G_n for a considerable period. But it is not possible to maintain growth at a greater rate for an indefinite period than the increase of population and technological improvements (both being expressed in G_n) allows.

Secondly, the relation of G_n to G_w is clearly of crucial importance in determining whether the economy over a term of years is likely to be preponderatingly lively or depressed. A paradox is involved. Whenever G exceeds G_w there will be a tendency for a boom to develop; and conversely. Now if G_n exceeds G_w there is no reason why G should not exceed G_w for most of the time. Consequently there is no reason why the economy should not enjoy a recurrent tendency to develop boom conditions. But if G_w exceeds G_n, then G must lie below G_w for most of the time, since the average value of G over a period cannot exceed that of G_n. Therefore in such circumstances we must expect the economy to be prevailingly depressed. This is paradoxical, since, at first blush, one would suppose it to be a good thing that the line of entrepreneurial contentment should be one implying an attempt to push forward always at a greater rate than fundamental conditions allow. Would not this make for a constantly buoyant economy, a tendency always towards full employment? Analysis reveals the opposite to be the case. It is the departures from G_w, not the value of G_w itself, which have paramount influence in producing boom and slump. If the value of G_w is too great (greater than that of G_n) there will be a prevailing tendency for departures to be in a downward direction. From that there is no escape. I believe that this paradox is very near the heart of the contrast between Keynesian economics and classical economics. Saving *is* a virtue and beneficial so long as G_w is below G_n. While it is disastrous to have G_w above G_n, it is not good to have it too far below, for in that case, although we may have plenty of booms and a frequent tendency to approach full employment, the high employment will be of an inflationary and thereby unhealthy character. In these circumstances saving is a virtue since, by raising G_w, it enables us to have good employment without inflation. But if G_w is above G_n saving is a force making for depression.

It is far from my purpose to give a finished theory of the trade cycle. Lags, psychological, monetary and other factors, no doubt play their part. I should suggest that no theory can be complete which neglects the fundamental causes of instability expressed in the equations which have been set out.

The following points are, however, tentatively advanced.

1. In a revival, in which unemployed resources are brought back

to work, G stands above G_n. When full employment is reached it must be reduced to G_n. If G_n stands below G_w then a slump is inevitable at that point, since G has to fall below G_w and will, for the time being, be driven progressively downwards.

2. G_w itself fluctuates in the trade cycle. Even if saving as a fraction of income is fairly steady in the long run, it is not likely to be so in the short run. There is some tendency for saving in the short period to be a residual between earnings and normal habits of consumption. Companies are likely to save a large fraction of short period increases of net receipts. Thus even if G_w is normally below G_n it may rise above it in the later stages of an advance, and, if it does so, a vicious spiral of depression is inevitable when full employment is reached. If G_w has not been raised above G_n during the course of the advance and there is continued pressure to expand when full employment is reached, then the consequent inflation of prices and profit will sooner or later raise G_w above G_n and thus precipitate the vicious spiral of depression.

3. Before full employment is reached G may have to be reduced owing to the increasing difficulty of transferring labour and other resources to their required uses as employment gets better. If G_w is substantially above G_n, the G curve may intersect the G_w curve some time before full employment is reached, thus making a vicious spiral of depression inevitable at this point.

4. If G_w is very substantially above G_n, G may never rise very far above G_w during the revival owing to mobility difficulties, and in this case maintenance of the revival may be precarious, and a vicious spiral of depression may be precipitated long before full employment is reached.

While the equations clearly show the instability of an advancing economy, they do not in themselves provide very good tools for analysing the course of the slump. It is probably necessary for that purpose to draw a distinction between durable and non-durable capital. It should be noticed that C is positive if the quantity of capital is moving in the same direction as the level of income. In a slump what matters is that circulating capital should be reduced. The existence of surplus fixed equipment in those trades whose output is shrinking — the output of some may continue to expand under longer period influences in a slump — is not in itself a force making for a further downward adjustment, since orders cannot be reduced below zero. On the other hand a pipe line filled fuller than appropriate to a falling turnover will cause a further contraction of orders.

Consequently in a slump the value of C_r will be lower than usual, being confined to the requirements for circulating capital. Thus the negative value to which $s - k$ has to fall in order to check a certain rate of recession is not nearly so great as the positive value to which it has to rise in order to check the same rate of upward movement.

It is well known that in trade-cycle study gross capital outlay and gross saving are more serviceable concepts than net outlay and saving.

During a decline gross outlay on durable plant over part of the field may be nil. A sort of equilibrium of decline would thus be reached in which the negative value of s (gross) minus k minus such capital (considered as a fraction of income) as was required for that part of industry which was still expanding despite the slump, was equal to the rate of decline multiplied by a much reduced capital coefficient consisting of the amount of circulating capital that could be dispensed with in consequence of the decline.

Gross capital requirements, however, do not, like net requirements, depend primarily on the rate of increase of output, but to some extent also on the total level of output. In the early part of the slump these may be reduced to nil (in the contracting sectors), because the old machines or other fixed equipments need not be replaced at the end of their working life owing to reduced output. But sooner or later the requirements for replacements must become positive, if any output at all is to be maintained. The consequent reduction in C_r (a rise in the numerical value of its numerator reduces its algebraic value) may reduce it below C. The actual reduction of capital stock becomes greater than what is convenient. This will arrest the downward movement and turn it into an upward one.

This account of the complete cycle makes no claim to be fully satisfactory. It requires supplementing by the findings of other methods of approach to cycle study.

Thus there are two distinct sets of problems both for analysis and policy, namely: (1) the divergence of G_w from G_n; and (2) the tendency of G to run away from G_w. The former is the problem of chronic unemployment, the latter the trade cycle problem.

First as regards analysis. According to classical doctrine, if there is general unemployment owing to any cause, wages will tend to fall; if wages are none the less maintained in these circumstances, continuance of unemployment is thereby rendered inevitable. This is tantamount to saying that a reduction of wages would be a cure for the unemployment.

You are all familiar with Keynes's views about the effect of wage reduction. I may remind you in passing that his theory and the practical recipes that flow from it relate to a closed system, that being the problem on which he was concentrating his mind. Now that the problem of our foreign trade has become such a predominant one, we have to temper Keynesian policy by reference to it. Keynes's diagnosis may have introduced some measure of levity about the harm that might be done by money wage increases not warranted by the situation.

Of course under the Bretton Woods régime unjustified increases in money wages may be offset by reductions in the foreign exchange rates. None the less they will not be helpful. The working of the International Monetary Fund will in any case bristle with problems, and it is most undesirable that Britain, one of its main pillars, should add to its problems by frequent requests that the value of sterling be reduced. Nor, I think, is the progressive deterioration of the goods value of a currency desirable on other grounds. We do not want savings to go down the drain, especially at this time when they have become more widely diffused and when we hope that the savings of all citizens will grow progressively.

The wage-reduction remedy should be considered under the two heads set out. First as regards the excess of G_w over G_n. It must be remembered that in this investigation of trends, a once-over reduction has no meaning. Does the situation require a year-by-year reduction? This would have no direct effect on G_n. Would it tend to depress G_w? There is no reason to suppose that it would. Unless output per head is actually falling through time, it does not seem natural to suppose that a steady reduction of money wages is required. On the contrary it seems that a steady reduction of money wages would inflame the difficulties. An upward tendency in the goods value of money certainly increases corporate saving for the reasons stated in the first lecture, and probably increases surplus corporate saving. A steady reduction in money wages would entail an upward movement in the goods value of money. The effect of the reduction would therefore be to raise G_w and so take it still further away from G_n. Thus the chronic tendency to depression would be intensified. We conclude that in an economy tending predominantly to depression a steady reduction of money wages would be injurious.

How does this alleged remedy stand in relation to the trade cycle problem of a run-away of G from G_w? There are two questions: (1) Would a once-over wage reduction give a fillip to output? (2) Would output be sustained at a higher level in consequence of the fillip?

The answer to the second question depends on the nature and causes of the recession. If before the set-back an advance had been proceeding at a rate not too much in excess of G_n and with perhaps some slack of resources still to be taken up, and the set-back was due to some particular adverse event which had sent the system into a downward spin, then a fillip — due to a wage reduction or any other cause — might be useful. It might serve to restore the system to where it was before and thus enable it to proceed on a healthy line of advance. Even if the fillip had in itself no tendency to raise the marginal efficiency of capital or to reduce the propensity to save, it might be of benefit to employment, since on this hypothesis the marginal efficiency of capital before the set-back was sufficient to maintain employment, the present low marginal efficiency being merely due to the decline in activity consequent on the set-back.

But if before the set-back G and G_w were both considerably in excess of G_n and the system approaching full employment, a mere fillip will be in vain. If the system is jerked up to a higher level of employment, it will merely relapse again. If the trouble is an excessive G_w, the wage reduction can do no good even if it does give a fillip. I am of the opinion that an analysis of the effects of a wage reduction which does not use the growth factor as a tool can throw no light on such a situation.

Would a wage reduction have any tendency to give a fillip (in a closed system)? It is important to stress that the fillip, if any, which it might give would be due entirely to the increased consumption by rentiers. In a closed economy in which income could be exhaustively classified as wages (including salaries and fees of all kinds) and profits, a reduction of wages would entail a fully proportional reduction of prices and profits.[5] This would be so unless the profit-taking class accompanied their wage reductions by an increase of personal consumption. In practice, having tender consciences, they would be more likely to do the opposite. Since the economy would receive an equal fillip by an increase of profit-takers' consumption, without any wage reduction, the fillip in question should not be attributed to the wage reduction. The rentiers, on the other hand, will receive a higher goods income in consequence of the fall of money wages and prices and it would be natural for them to increase their consumption; to the extent that they do so the goods income of profit takers will also be enlarged. Thus the fillip given by wage reduction consists in essence of the provision of more purchasing power to the rentiers. In so far as they are an important element, this may be of substantial importance. The effectiveness of the fillip depends on the causes of the recession, as already explained.[6]

Whether it is desirable to list such a remedy as a standing order to be applied from time to time, even if it were practical to do so, is doubtful. While I have already urged that we should not wish to destroy the purchasing power of past savers by monetary inflation, it is another matter to raise that purchasing power artificially from time to time. An enlargement of the purchasing power of rentiers at the expense of other sharers in the national dividend is not warranted in equity and tends to reduce the incentive to the more active elements in the community, whether the enlarged payments in terms of goods have to be charged onto the receipts of industry or predominantly, as when the national debt is very large, onto the taxpayers.

We must now turn to the question of interest rates. That a reduction of these would tend to produce the desired effect is agreed, although there may be doubt whether the weapon would be potent enough to cause revival in all circumstances. Where there is disagreement is whether in circumstances of falling employment there is any natural tendency for the rates of interest to move down, for instance under the pressure of an excess of loanable funds, to the level required to restore employment.

It must be remembered that there are two problems, the divergence of G_w from G_n and the runaway of G from G_w. If G_w implies a steeper gradient than G_n what will be the position of the rate of interest? Certainly a progres-

[5]For a proof of this proposition, see *Economic Journal*, [XLIV] Mar. 1934, 23.

[6]It is also possible, of course, that the wage reduction might give a fillip by inducing entrepreneurs to increase capital outlay, whether there was any observed increase in consumption or not. It seems more probable that they would wait for some tangible profit to accrue before embarking on this course.

sive fall in the rate of interest is the appropriate remedy, vouchsafed by classical and Keynesian economics alike.

Hitherto we have been working on the assumption that inventions have been neutral. To meet the case of their not being so, we may introduce another term into the equilibrium equation. Let d (for deepening) stand for the value of new capital installations during the unit period, expressed for convenience as a fraction of income, involved in the lengthening of the production process. If inventions are "capital saving," d is negative. Thus,

$$G_w C_r = s - d.$$

It may seem artificial to separate d from C_r. But it is logically possible; and it is right in principle. We want to keep C_r segregated as that capital requirement which essentially belongs to the growth of output as such, from the requirement for increased capital per unit of output.

d may have a positive value because of the nature of the inventions occurring. It may also have a positive value because the rate of interest is falling. Our aim should be to get such a progressive reduction in the rate of interest that

$$G_w C_r = s - d = G_n C_r.$$

If d is positive, C_r will increase through time, and may eventually become so great as to enable us to dispense with d. At that point interest need fall no further. A positive value for d incidentally serves to raise G_n. A falling rate of interest may also — and this is of course important if it so turns out — reduce s.

The question we now have to ask is whether there will be any natural tendency for the rate of interest to come down sufficiently. This is the crux of the matter, the crux, perhaps, of that modern economic situation to which we shall revert, when the post-war shortages cease. This is where the lack of adequate dynamic theory is particularly unfortunate. That theory tells us that a falling rate of interest is necessary if the economy is to advance at its potential rate and reasonably full employment is to be maintained. But whereas static theory not only defines a position of equilibrium but indicates how, through the laws of supply and demand, the economy tends to move into that position, dynamic theory has not so far shown how or whether the market, as subject to the forces that normally operate upon it, will tend to mark the rate of interest down at an appropriate pace.

Keynes's theory, with all its imperfections upon it, does definitely point to a negative answer. Even if the market could form a fairly clear view as to the future trend — which it cannot, since inventions which may be capital requiring, are in essence unpredictable — none the less the lack of certainty would make it demand a risk premium (measuring liquidity preference) for long-term loans. Thus the present rate would be somewhat above the level appropriate to the present situation and to the changing level most likely to be required in future; and, as each future period will in due course become a present one, this liquidity factor which affects the present rate will also affect future rates to an unknown extent and so prevent the right levels of future rates being made the basis of an argument now. And so we get back again to a rate of interest which is hanging by its own bootstraps. How escape from this?

The long-term problem is also complicated by the short-term problem. Getting G_w into equality with G_n over the long period would not by itself prevent a run-away of G downwards from G_n from time to time. Changes in the market rate due to natural forces clearly will not prevent this; and I shall argue in the next lecture that no Bank Rate policy, however heroic, would be likely to prevent it. (It does not follow that we need despair of an effective contra-cyclical policy.) During the periods in which G is low and unemployment high, clearly less saving will accrue than would otherwise. The loss of savings, which in the aggregate will be large, must affect the long-run course of the interest rate. Thus it would be relevant for an all-wise market to ask how great and how prolonged the downward run-aways of G in future are likely to be. But it will not get an answer.

Critics of Keynes, disliking the divorce which his theory seems to entail between the forces affecting the rate of interest and the supply and demand for savings, have urged that we must consider the stream of loanable funds coming into the market and their tendency to depress the rate of interest as activity falls off. They have to call time-lags to their aid. Strictly in Keynesian theory the effect of the multiplier on activity is instantaneous. But there is no doubt an interval in which there is a discrepancy between ex-ante and ex-post investment. If those involved in unintended investment — accumulation of stocks — do not come into the capital market for the loan of funds — they may have had a cash balance at the expense of which they can hold the unwanted stocks — there may be an excess of the supply of funds over the demand. Or again income may continue to be distributed after output has fallen — presumably also at the expense of the cash of firms — and individuals may supply funds to the market accordingly, or may reckon what they will save on the basis of their income in the last preceding period instead of the present. I am most reluctant to enter this field of thought. Let it be that at the onset of recession there is a greater presentation of funds in the capital market than the strict doctrine of the multiplier would suggest and a consequent downward movement in the rate of interest.

It is not usually sufficient to prevent the onward movement of the recession. So what does it matter? In due course the multiplier will have its full effect in reducing income and savings. At the end of a depression aggregated savings will be less than they would otherwise have been. The rate of interest as governed by the supply of and demand for savings will be higher than if a steady advance had been maintained. Natural forces will not have served to secure that fall in the rate of interest necessary to absorb all savings accruing through time with the community advancing steadily at reasonably full employment.

I am bound to conclude negatively. It does not appear to be shown that the system will of its own secure a sufficient fall in the rate of interest. There is general agreement that this is the true remedy for unemployment. Unemployment has persisted for years and not been remedied. There is therefore a *prima facie* case for a planned reduction in the rate of interest.

Keynes proposed an assault on it by the methods now being used by the Chancellor of the Exchequer, namely by increasing the amount of liquidity available. This has not proved altogether unsuccessful. It is an unfortunate irony that we should have had a spurt in the policy, no doubt justified by the National Debt position and long-run considerations, just at a time when the short-period situation considered in itself would require an exceedingly high rate of interest.

Of course there may be limits to the success of this policy, limits which may appear even before, from a long-range point of view, $G_w C_r$ is reduced to the required level. Ultimately the market may refuse to believe that the rate of interest ought to be any lower, and may absorb an unlimited amount of liquidity rather than mark security prices up further. I shall have to return to this.

It may also be that this assault method will not achieve a steady rate of fall but only a series of bumps. That, however, is not fatal, because there will in any case also be a trade cycle problem requiring separate treatment. This is due to the fact that, quite apart from any failure to get the rate of interest down at the required steady rate, there are bound to be exogenous shocks tending to make G diverge from G_w and setting the trade cycle processes going. There will, for instance, be times in which inventions are not neutral. And there will be other shocks.

For this reason, quite apart from our long-range policy of acting upon the rate of interest, we shall have to have a separate contra-cyclical policy. But of this more hereafter.

ROBERT M. SOLOW **22**

A contribution to the theory of economic growth

I. Introduction

All theory depends on assumptions which are not quite true. That is what makes it theory. The art of successful theorizing is to make the inevitable simplifying assumptions in such a way that the final results are not very sensitive.[1] A "crucial" assumption is one on which the conclusions do depend sensitively, and it is important that crucial assumptions be reasonably realistic. When the results of a theory seem to flow specifically from a special crucial assumption, then if the assumption is dubious, the results are suspect.

I wish to argue that something like this is true of the Harrod-Domar model of economic growth. The characteristic and powerful conclusion of the Harrod-Domar line of thought is that even for the long run the economic system is at best balanced on a knife-edge of equilibrium growth. Were the magnitudes of the key parameters — the savings ratio, the capital-output ratio, the rate of increase of the labor force — to slip ever so slightly from dead center, the consequence would be either growing unemployment or prolonged inflation. In Harrod's terms the critical question of balance boils down to a comparison between the natural rate of growth which depends,

Reprinted by permission of the publishers from Robert Solow THE QUARTERLY JOURNAL OF ECONOMICS Cambridge, Mass.: Harvard University Press, Copyright, 1956, by the President and Fellows of Harvard College. Vol. 70 (February 1956), pp. 65–94. [Footnotes expanded — *Eds.*]

[1]Thus transport costs were merely a negligible complication to Ricardian trade theory, but a vital characteristic of reality to von Thünen.

in the absence of technological change, on the increase of the labor force, and the warranted rate of growth which depends on the saving and investing habits of households and firms.

But this fundamental opposition of warranted and natural rates turns out in the end to flow from the crucial assumption that production takes place under conditions of *fixed proportions*. There is no possibility of substituting labor for capital in production. If this assumption is abandoned, the knife-edge notion of unstable balance seems to go with it. Indeed it is hardly surprising that such a gross rigidity in one part of the system should entail lack of flexibility in another.

A remarkable characteristic of the Harrod-Domar model is that it consistently studies long-run problems with the usual short-run tools. One usually thinks of the long run as the domain of the neoclassical analysis, the land of the margin. Instead Harrod and Domar talk of the long run in terms of the multiplier, the accelerator, "the" capital coefficient. The bulk of this paper is devoted to a model of long-run growth which accepts all the Harrod-Domar assumptions except that of fixed proportions. Instead I suppose that the single composite commodity is produced by labor and capital under the standard neoclassical conditions. The adaptation of the system to an exogenously given rate of increase of the labor force is worked out in some detail, to see if the Harrod instability appears. The price-wage-interest reactions play an important role in this neoclassical adjustment process, so they are analyzed too. Then some of the other rigid assumptions are relaxed slightly to see what qualitative changes result: neutral technological change is allowed, and an interest-elastic savings schedule. Finally the consequences of certain more "Keynesian" relations and rigidities are briefly considered.

II. A model of long-run growth

There is only one commodity, output as a whole, whose rate of production is designated $Y(t)$. Thus we can speak unambiguously of the community's real income. Part of each instant's output is consumed and the rest is saved and invested. The fraction of output saved is a constant s, so that the rate of saving is $sY(t)$. The community's stock of capital $K(t)$ takes the form of an accumulation of the composite commodity. Net investment is then just the rate of increase of this capital stock dK/dt or $\dot{K}$, so we have the basic identity at every instant of time:

$$\dot{K} = sY. \tag{1}$$

Output is produced with the help of two factors of production, capital and labor, whose rate of input is $L(t)$. Technological possibilities are represented by a production function

$$Y = F(K,L). \tag{2}$$

Output is to be understood as net output after making good the depreciation of capital. About production all we will say at the moment is that it shows constant returns to scale. Hence the production function is homogeneous of first degree. This amounts to assuming that there is no scarce nonaugmentable resource like land. Constant returns to scale seems the natural assumption to make in a theory of growth. The scarce-land case would lead to decreasing returns to scale in capital and labor and the model would become more Ricardian.[2]

Inserting (2) in (1) we get

$$\dot{K} = sF(K,L). \tag{3}$$

This is one equation in two unknowns. One way to close the system would be to add a demand-for-labor equation: marginal physical productivity of labor equals real wage rate; and a supply-of-labor equation. The latter could take the general form of making labor supply a function of the real wage, or more classically of putting the real wage equal to a conventional subsistence level. In any case there would be three equations in the three unknowns K, L, real wage.

Instead we proceed more in the spirit of the Harrod model. As a result of exogenous population growth the labor force increases at a constant relative rate n. In the absence of technological change n is Harrod's natural rate of growth. Thus:

$$L(t) = L_0 e^{nt}. \tag{4}$$

In (3) L stands for total employment; in (4) L stands for the available supply of labor. By identifying the two we are assuming that full employment is perpetually maintained. When we insert (4) in (3) to get

$$\dot{K} = sF(K,L_0 e^{nt}) \tag{5}$$

we have the basic equation which determines the time path of capital accumulation that must be followed if all available labor is to be employed.

Alternatively (4) can be looked at as a supply curve of labor. It says that the exponentially growing labor force is offered for employment completely inelastically. The labor supply curve is a vertical line which shifts to the right in time as the labor force grows according to (4). Then the real wage rate adjusts so that all available labor is employed, and the marginal productivity equation determines the wage rate which will actually rule.[3]

---

[2]See, for example, Haavelmo: *A Study in the Theory of Economic Evolution* (Amsterdam, 1954), pp. 9–11. Not all "underdeveloped" countries are areas of land shortage. Ethiopia is a counterexample. One can imagine the theory as applying as long as arable land can be hacked out of the wilderness at essentially constant cost.

[3]The complete set of three equations consists of (3), (4) and $\dfrac{\partial F(K,L)}{\partial L} = w$.

In summary, (5) is a differential equation in the single variable $K(t)$. Its solution gives the only time profile of the community's capital stock which will fully employ the available labor. Once we know the time path of capital stock and that of the labor force, we can compute from the production function the corresponding time path of real output. The marginal productivity equation determines the time path of the real wage rate. There is also involved an assumption of full employment of the available stock of capital. At any point of time the pre-existing stock of capital (the result of previous accumulation) is inelastically supplied. Hence there is a similar marginal productivity equation for capital which determines the real rental per unit of time for the services of capital stock. The process can be viewed in this way: at any moment of time the available labor supply is given by (4) and the available stock of capital is also a datum. Since the real return to factors will adjust to bring about full employment of labor and capital we can use the production function (2) to find the current rate of output. Then the propensity to save tells us how much of net output will be saved and invested. Hence we know the net accumulation of capital during the current period. Added to the already accumulated stock this gives the capital available for the next period, and the whole process can be repeated.

III. Possible growth patterns

To see if there is always a capital accumulation path consistent with any rate of growth of the labor force, we must study the differential equation (5) for the qualitative nature of its solutions. Naturally without specifying the exact shape of the production function we can't hope to find the exact solution. But certain broad properties are surprisingly easy to isolate, even graphically.

To do so we introduce a new variable $r = K/L$, the ratio of capital to labor. Hence we have $K = rL = rL_0e^{nt}$. Differentiating with respect to time we get

$$\dot{K} = L_0e^{nt}\dot{r} + nrL_0e^{nt}.$$

Substitute this in (5):

$$(\dot{r} + nr)L_0e^{nt} = sF(K,L_0e^{nt}).$$

But because of constant returns to scale we can divide both variables in F by $L = L_0e^{nt}$ provided we multiply F by the same factor. Thus

$$(\dot{r} + nr)L_0e^{nt} = sL_0e^{nt}F\left(\frac{K}{L_0e^{nt}}, 1\right)$$

and dividing out the common factor we arrive finally at

$$\dot{r} = sF(r,1) - nr. \qquad (6)$$

Here we have a differential equation involving the capital-labor ratio alone.

This fundamental equation can be reached somewhat less formally. Since $r = K/L$, the relative rate of change of r is the difference between the relative rates of change of K and L. That is:

$$\frac{\dot{r}}{r} = \frac{\dot{K}}{K} - \frac{\dot{L}}{L}.$$

Now first of all $\dot{L}/L = n$. Secondly $\dot{K} = sF(K,L)$. Making these substitutions:

$$\dot{r} = r\frac{sF(K,L)}{K} - nr.$$

Now divide L out of F as before, note that $L/K = 1/r$, and we get (6) again.

The function $F(r,1)$ appearing in (6) is easy to interpret. It is the total product curve as varying amounts r of capital are employed with one unit of labor. Alternatively it gives output per worker as a function of capital per worker. Thus (6) states that the rate of change of the capital-labor ratio is the difference of two terms, one representing the increment of capital and one the increment of labor.

When $\dot{r} = 0$, the capital-labor ratio is a constant, and the capital stock must be expanding at the same rate as the labor force, namely n. (The warranted rate of growth, warranted by the appropriate real rate of return

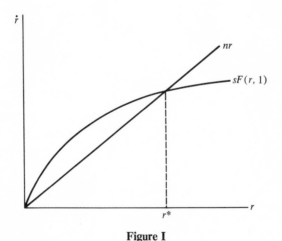

Figure I

to capital, equals the natural rate.) In Figure I, the ray through the origin with slope n represents the function nr. The other curve is the function $sF(r,1)$. It is here drawn to pass through the origin and convex upward: no output unless both inputs are positive, and diminishing marginal productivity of capital, as would be the case, for example, with the Cobb-Douglas function. At the point of intersection $nr = sF(r,1)$ and $\dot{r} = 0$. If the capital-labor ratio r^* should ever be established, it will be maintained, and capital and labor will grow thenceforward in proportion. By constant returns to scale, real output will also grow at the same relative rate n, and output per head of labor force will be constant.

But if $r \neq r^*$, how will the capital-labor ratio develop over time? To the right of the intersection point, when $r > r^*$, $nr > sF(r,1)$ and from (6) we see that r will decrease toward r^*. Conversely if initially $r < r^*$, the graph shows that $nr < sF(r,1)$, $\dot{r} > 0$, and r will increase toward r^*. Thus the equilibrium value r^* is *stable*. Whatever the initial value of the capital-labor ratio, the system will develop *toward* a state of balanced growth at the natural rate. The time path of capital and output will not be exactly exponential except asymptotically.[4] If the initial capital stock is below the equilibrium ratio, capital and output will grow at a faster pace than the labor force until the equilibrium ratio is approached. If the initial ratio is above the equilibrium value, capital and output will grow more slowly than the labor force. The growth of output is always intermediate between those of labor and capital.

Of course the strong stability shown in Figure I is not inevitable. The steady adjustment of capital and output to a state of balanced growth comes about because of the way I have drawn the productivity curve $F(r,1)$. Many other configurations are a priori possible. For example in Figure II

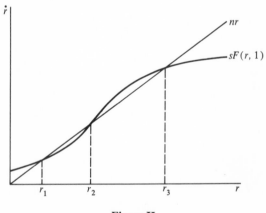

Figure II

there are three intersection points. Inspection will show that r_1 and r_3 are stable, r_2 is not. Depending on the initially observed capital-labor ratio, the system will develop either to balanced growth at capital-labor ratio r_1 or r_3.

[4]There is an exception to this. If $K = 0$, $r = 0$ and the system can't get started; with no capital there is no output and hence no accumulation. But this equilibrium is unstable: the slightest windfall capital accumulation will start the system off toward r^*.

In either case labor supply, capital stock and real output will asymptotically expand at rate n, but around r_1 there is less capital than around r_3, hence the level of output per head will be lower in the former case than in the latter. The relevant balanced growth equilibrium is at r_1 for an initial ratio anywhere between 0 and r_2, it is at r_3 for any initial ratio greater than r_2. The ratio r_2 is itself an equilibrium growth ratio, but an unstable one; any accidental disturbance will be magnified over time. Figure II has been drawn so that production is possible without capital; hence the origin is not an equilibrium "growth" configuration.

Even Figure II does not exhaust the possibilities. It is possible that no balanced growth equilibrium might exist.[5] *Any* nondecreasing function $F(r,1)$ can be converted into a constant returns to scale production function simply by multiplying it by L; the reader can construct a wide variety of such curves and examine the resulting solutions to (6). In Figure III are shown two

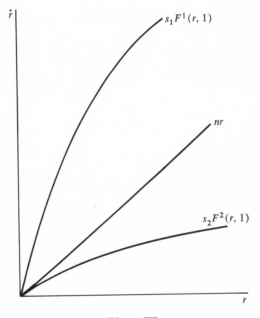

Figure III

possibilities, together with a ray nr. Both have diminishing marginal productivity throughout, and one lies wholly above nr while the other lies

[5]This seems to contradict a theorem in R. M. Solow and P. A. Samuelson: "Balanced Growth under Constant Returns to Scale," *Econometrica*, XXI ([July] 1953), 412–424, but the contradiction is only apparent. It was there assumed that every commodity had positive marginal productivity in the production of each commodity. Here capital cannot be used to produce labor.

wholly below.[6] The first system is so productive and saves so much that perpetual full employment will increase the capital-labor ratio (and also the output per head) beyond all limits; capital and income both increase more rapidly than the labor supply. The second system is so unproductive that the full employment path leads only to forever diminishing income per capita. Since net investment is always positive and labor supply is increasing, aggregate income can only rise.

The basic conclusion of this analysis is that, when production takes place under the usual neoclassical conditions of variable proportions and constant returns to scale, no simple opposition between natural and warranted rates of growth is possible. There may not be — in fact in the case of the Cobb-Douglas function there never can be — any knife-edge. The system can adjust to any given rate of growth of the labor force, and eventually approach a state of steady proportional expansion.

IV. Examples

In this section I propose very briefly to work out three examples, three simple choices of the shape of the production function for which it is possible to solve the basic differential equation (6) explicitly.

Example 1:
Fixed proportions

This is the Harrod-Domar case. It takes a units of capital to produce a unit of output; and b units of labor. Thus a is an acceleration coefficient. Of course, a unit of output can be produced with *more* capital and/or labor than this (the isoquants are right-angled corners); the first bottleneck to be reached limits the rate of output. This can be expressed in the form (2) by saying

$$Y = F(K,L) = \min\left(\frac{K}{a}, \frac{L}{b}\right)$$

where "min (. . .)" means the smaller of the numbers in parentheses. The basic differential equation (6) becomes

$$\dot{r} = s \min\left(\frac{r}{a}, \frac{1}{b}\right) - nr.$$

Evidently for very small r we must have $r/a < 1/b$, so that in this range $\dot{r} = sr/a - nr = (s/a - n)r$. But when $r/a \geq 1/b$, i.e., $r \geq a/b$, the equa-

[6]The equation of the first might be $s_1F^1(r,1) = nr + \sqrt{r}$, that of the second $s_2F^2(r,1) = \frac{nr}{r+1}$.

tion becomes $\dot{r} = s/b - nr$. It is easier to see how this works graphically. In Figure IV the function $s \min (r/a, 1/b)$ is represented by a broken line: the ray from the origin with slope s/a until r reaches the value a/b, and then

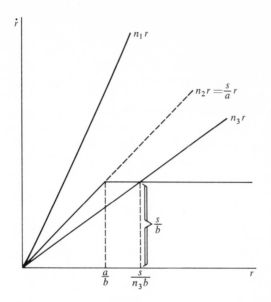

Figure IV

a horizontal line at height s/b. In the Harrod model s/a is the warranted rate of growth.

There are now three possibilities:

      a. $n_1 > s/a$, the natural rate exceeds the warranted rate. It can be seen from Figure IV that $n_1 r$ is always greater than $s \min (r/a, 1/b)$, so that r always decreases. Suppose the initial value of the capital-labor ratio is $r_0 > a/b$, then $\dot{r} = s/b - n_1 r$, whose solution is $r = \left(r_0 - \dfrac{s}{n_1 b} \right) e^{-n_1 t} + \dfrac{s}{n_1 b}$. Thus r decreases toward $s/n_1 b$ which is in turn less than a/b. At an easily calculable point of time t_1, r reaches a/b. From then on $\dot{r} = (s/a - n_1) r$, whose solution is $r = \dfrac{a}{b} e^{\left(\frac{s}{a} - n_1 \right) \left(t - t_1 \right)}$. Since $s/a < n_1$, r will decrease toward zero. At time t_1, when $r = a/b$ the labor supply and capital stock are in balance. From then on as the capital-labor ratio decreases labor becomes redundant, and the extent of the redundancy grows. The amount of unemployment can be calculated from the fact that $K = rL_0 e^{nt}$ remembering that, when capital is the bottleneck factor, output is K/a and *employment is* $b\dfrac{K}{a}$.

    b. $n_2 = s/a$, the warranted and natural rates are equal. If initially $r > a/b$ so that labor is the bottleneck, then r decreases to a/b and stays there. If initially $r < a/b$, then r remains constant over time, in a sort of neutral equilibrium. Capital stock and labor supply grow at a common rate n_2; whatever *percentage* redundancy of labor there was initially is preserved.

    c. $n_3 < s/a$, the warranted rate exceeds the natural rate. Formally the solution is exactly as in case (a) with n_3 replacing n_1. There is a stable equilibrium capital output ratio at $r = s/n_3b$. But here capital is redundant as can be seen from the fact that the marginal productivity of capital has fallen to zero. The proportion of the capital stock actually employed in equilibrium growth is an_3/s. But since the capital stock is growing (at a rate asymptotically equal to n_3) the absolute amount of excess capacity is growing, too. This appearance of redundancy independent of any price-wage movements is a consequence of fixed proportions, and lends the Harrod-Domar model its characteristic of rigid balance.

    At the very least one can imagine a production function such that if r exceeds a critical value r_{max}, the marginal product of capital falls to zero, and if r falls short of another critical value r_{min}, the marginal product of labor falls to zero. For intermediate capital-labor ratios the isoquants are as usual. Figure IV would begin with a linear portion for $0 \leqq r \leqq r_{min}$, then have a phase like Figure I for $r_{min} \leqq r \leqq r_{max}$, then end with a horizontal stretch for $r > r_{max}$. There would be a whole *zone* of labor-supply growth rates which would lead to an equilibrium like that of Figure I. For values of n below this zone the end result would be redundancy of capital, for values of n above this zone, redundancy of labor. To the extent that in the long run factor proportions are widely variable the intermediate zone of growth rates will be wide.

Example 2:
The Cobb-Douglas function

The properties of the function $Y = K^a L^{1-a}$ are too well known to need comment here. Figure I describes the situation regardless of the choice of the parameters a and n. The marginal productivity of capital rises indefinitely as the capital-labor ratio decreases, so that the curve $sF(r,1)$ must rise above the ray nr. But since $a < 1$, the curve must eventually cross the ray from above and subsequently remain below. Thus the asymptotic behavior of the system is always balanced growth at the natural rate.

    The differential equation (6) is in this case $\dot{r} = sr^a - nr$. It is actually easier to go back to the untransformed equation (5), which now reads

$$\dot{K} = sK^a(L_0 e^{nt})^{1-a}. \qquad (7)$$

This can be integrated directly and the solution is:

$$K(t) = \left[K_0^b - \frac{s}{n} L_0^b + \frac{s}{n} L_0^b\, e^{nbt} \right]^{1/b}$$

where $b = 1 - a$, and K_0 is the initial capital stock. It is easily seen that as t becomes large, $K(t)$ grows essentially like $(s/n)^{1/b} L_0 e^{nt}$, namely at the same rate of growth as the labor force. The equilibrium value of the capital-labor ratio is $r^* = (s/n)^{1/b}$. This can be verified by putting $\dot{r} = 0$ in (6). Reasonably enough this equilibrium ratio is larger the higher the savings ratio and the lower the rate of increase of the labor supply.

It is easy enough to work out the time path of real output from the production function itself. Obviously asymptotically Y must behave like K and L, that is, grow at relative rate n. Real income per head of labor force, Y/L, tends to the value $(s/n)^{a/b}$. Indeed with the Cobb-Douglas function it is always true that $Y/L = (K/L)^a = r^a$. It follows at once that the equilibrium value of K/Y is s/n. But K/Y is the "capital coefficient" in Harrod's terms, say C. Then in the long-run equilibrium growth we will have $C = s/n$ or $n = s/C$: the natural rate equals "the" warranted rate, not as an odd piece of luck but as a consequence of demand-supply adjustments.

Example 3

A whole family of constant-returns-to-scale production functions is given by $Y = (aK^p + L^p)^{1/p}$. It differs from the Cobb-Douglas family in that production is possible with only one factor. But it shares the property that if $p < 1$, the marginal productivity of capital becomes infinitely great as the capital-labor ratio declines toward zero. If $p > 1$, the isoquants have the "wrong" convexity; when $p = 1$, the isoquants are straight lines, perfect substitutability; I will restrict myself to the case of $0 < p < 1$ which gives the usual diminishing marginal returns. Otherwise it is hardly sensible to insist on full employment of both factors.

In particular consider $p = \frac{1}{2}$ so that the production function becomes

$$Y = (a\sqrt{K} + \sqrt{L})^2 = a^2 K + L + 2a\sqrt{KL}.$$

The basic differential equation is

$$\dot{r} = s(a\sqrt{r} + 1)^2 - nr. \tag{8}$$

This can be written:

$$\dot{r} = s[(a^2 - n/s)r + 2a\sqrt{r} + 1] = s(A\sqrt{r} + 1)(B\sqrt{r} + 1)$$

where $A = a - \sqrt{n/s}$ and $B = a + \sqrt{n/s}$. The solution has to be given implicitly:

$$\left(\frac{A\sqrt{r} + 1}{A\sqrt{r_0} + 1}\right)^{1/A} \left(\frac{B\sqrt{r} + 1}{B\sqrt{r_0} + 1}\right)^{-1/B} = e^{\sqrt{n}st} \tag{9}$$

Once again it is easier to refer to a diagram. There are two possibilities, illustrated in Figure V. The curve $sF(r,1)$ begins at a height s when $r = 0$.

If $sa^2 > n$, there is no balanced growth equilibrium: the capital-labor ratio increases indefinitely and so does real output per head. The system is highly productive and saves-invests enough at full employment to expand very

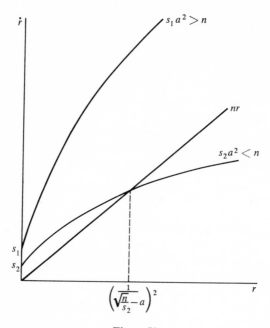

Figure V

rapidly. If $sa^2 < n$, there is a stable balanced growth equilibrium, which is reached according to the solution (9). The equilibrium capital-labor ratio can be found by putting $\dot{r} = 0$ in (8); it is $r^* = (1/\sqrt{n/s} - a)^2$. It can be further calculated that the income per head prevailing in the limiting state of growth is $1/(1 - a\sqrt{s/n})^2$. That is, real income per head of labor force will rise to this value if it starts below, or vice versa.

V. Behavior of interest and wage rates

The growth paths discussed in the previous sections can be looked at in two ways. From one point of view they have no causal significance but simply indicate the course that capital accumulation and real output would have to take if neither unemployment nor excess capacity are to appear. From another point of view, however, we can ask what kind of market behavior will cause the model economy to follow the path of equilibrium growth. In this direction it has already been assumed that both the growing labor force and the existing capital stock are thrown on the market inelastically, with the real wage and the real rental of capital adjusting instantaneously so as to clear the market. If saving and investment decisions are made independently, however, some additional marginal-efficiency-of-capital conditions have to be satisfied. The purpose of this section is to set out the price-wage-interest behavior appropriate to the growth paths sketched earlier.

There are four prices involved in the system: (1) the selling price of a unit of real output (and since real output serves also as capital this is the transfer price of a unit of capital stock) $p(t)$; (2) the money wage rate $w(t)$; (3) the money rental per unit of time of a unit of capital stock $q(t)$; (4) the rate of interest $i(t)$. One of these we can eliminate immediately. In the real system we are working with there is nothing to determine the absolute price level. Hence we can take $p(t)$, the price of real output, as given. Sometimes it will be convenient to imagine p as constant.

In a competitive economy the real wage and real rental are determined by the traditional marginal-productivity equations:

$$\frac{\partial F}{\partial L} = \frac{w}{p} \tag{10}$$

and

$$\frac{\partial F}{\partial K} = \frac{q}{p}. \tag{11}$$

Note in passing that with constant returns to scale the marginal productivities depend only on the capital-labor ratio r, and not on any scale quantities.[7]

The real rental on capital q/p is an own-rate of interest — it is the return on capital in units of capital stock. An owner of capital can by renting

[7]In the polar case of pure competition, even if the individual firms have U-shaped average cost curves we can imagine changes in aggregate output taking place solely by the entry and exit of identical optimal-size firms. Then aggregate output is produced at constant cost; and in fact, because of the large number of relatively small firms each producing at approximately constant cost for small variations, we can without substantial error define an aggregate production function which will show constant returns to scale. There will be minor deviations since this aggregate production function is not strictly valid for variations in output smaller than the size of an optimal firm. But this lumpiness can for long-run analysis be treated as negligible.

One naturally thinks of adapting the model to the more general assumption of universal monopolistic competition. But the above device fails. If the industry consists of identical firms in identical large-group tangency equilibria then, subject to the restriction that output changes occur only via changes in the number of firms, one can perhaps define a constant-cost aggregate production function. But now this construct is largely irrelevant, for even if we are willing to overlook its discontinuity and treat it as differentiable, the partial derivatives of such a function will not be the marginal productivities to which the individual firms respond. Each firm is on the falling branch of its unit cost curve, whereas in the competitive case each firm was actually producing at locally constant costs. The difficult problem remains of introducing monopolistic competition into aggregative models. For example, the value-of-marginal-product equations in the text would have to go over into marginal-revenue-product relations, which in turn would require the explicit presence of demand curves. Much further experimentation is needed here, with greater realism the reward.

and reinvesting increase his holdings like compound interest at the *variable* instantaneous rate q/p, i.e., like $e^{\int_0^t q/p\,dt}$. Under conditions of perfect arbitrage there is a well-known close relationship between the money rate of interest and the commodity own-rate, namely

$$i(t) = \frac{q(t)}{p(t)} + \frac{\dot{p}(t)}{p(t)}. \tag{12}$$

If the price level is in fact constant, the own-rate and the interest rate will coincide. If the price level is falling, the own-rate must exceed the interest rate to induce people to hold commodities. That the exact relation is as in (12) can be seen in several ways. For example, the owner of \$1 at time t has two options: he can lend the money for a short space of time, say until $t + h$ and earn approximately $i(t)h$ in interest, or he can buy $1/p$ units of output, earn rentals of $(q/p)h$ and then sell. In the first case he will own $1 + i(t)h$ at the end of the period; in the second case he will have $(q(t)/p(t))h + p(t + h)/p(t)$. In equilibrium these two amounts must be equal

$$1 + i(t)h = \frac{q(t)}{p(t)}\,h + \frac{p(t + h)}{p(t)}$$

or

$$i(t)h = \frac{q(t)}{p(t)}\,h + \frac{p(t + h) - p(t)}{p(t)}.$$

Dividing both sides by h and letting h tend to zero we get (12). Thus this condition equalizes the attractiveness of holding wealth in the form of capital stock or loanable funds.

Another way of deriving (12) and gaining some insight into its role in our model is to note that $p(t)$, the transfer price of a unit of capital, must equal the present value of its future stream of net rentals. Thus with perfect foresight into future rentals and interest rates:

$$p(t) = \int_t^\infty q(u)e^{-\int_t^u i(z)dz}\,du.$$

Differentiating with respect to time yields (12). Thus within the narrow confines of our model (in particular, absence of risk, a fixed average propensity to save, and no monetary complications) the money rate of interest and the return to holders of capital will stand in just the relation required to induce the community to hold the capital stock in existence. The absence of risk and uncertainty shows itself particularly in the absence of asset preferences.

Given the absolute price level $p(t)$, equations (10)–(12) determine the other three price variables, whose behavior can thus be calculated once the particular growth path is known.

Before indicating how the calculations would go in the examples of section IV, it is possible to get a general view diagrammatically, particularly when there is a stable balanced growth equilibrium. In Figure VI is drawn the ordinary isoquant map of the production function $F(K,L)$, and some possible kinds of growth paths. A given capital-labor ratio r^* is represented

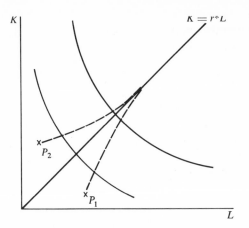

Figure VI

in Figure VI by a ray from the origin, with slope r^*. Suppose there is a stable asymptotic ratio r^*; then all growth paths issuing from arbitrary initial conditions approach the ray in the limit. Two such paths are shown, issuing from initial points P_1 and P_2. Since back in Figure I the approach of r to r^* was monotonic, the paths must look as shown in Figure VI. We see that if the initial capital-labor ratio is higher than the equilibrium value, the ratio falls and vice versa.

Figure VII corresponds to Figure II. There are three "equilibrium"

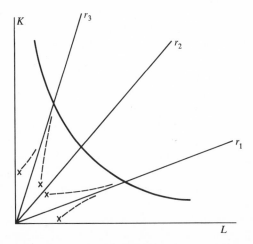

Figure VII

rays, but the inner one is unstable. The inner ray is the dividing line among initial conditions which lead to one of the stable rays and those which lead to the other. All paths, of course, lead upward and to the right, without bending back; K and L always increase. The reader can draw a diagram corresponding to Figure III, in which the growth paths pass to steeper and steeper or to flatter and flatter rays, signifying respectively $r \to \infty$ or $r \to 0$. Again I remark that K and L and hence Y are all increasing, but if $r \to 0$, Y/L will decline.

Now because of constant returns to scale we know that along a ray from the origin, the slope of the isoquants is constant. This expresses the fact that marginal products depend only on the factor ratio. But in competition the slope of the isoquant reflects the ratio of the factor prices. Thus to a stable r^* as in Figure VI corresponds an equilibrium ratio w/q. Moreover, if the isoquants have the normal convexity, it is apparent that as r rises to r^*, the ratio w/q rises to its limiting value, and vice versa if r is falling.

In the unstable case, where r tends to infinity or zero it may be that w/q tends to infinity or zero. If, on the other hand, the isoquants reach the axes with slopes intermediate between the vertical and horizontal, the factor price ratio w/q will tend to a finite limit.

It might also be useful to point out that the slope of the curve $F(r,1)$ is the marginal productivity of capital at the corresponding value of r. Thus the course of the real rental q/p can be traced out in Figures I, II, and III. Remember that in those diagrams $F(r,1)$ has been reduced by the factor s, hence so has the slope of the curve. $F(r,1)$ itself represents Y/L, output per unit of labor, as a function of the capital-labor ratio.

In general if a stable growth path exists, the fall in the real wage or real rental needed to get to it may not be catastrophic at all. If there is an initial shortage of labor (compared with the equilibrium ratio) the real wage will have to fall. The higher the rate of increase of the labor force and the lower the propensity to save, the lower the equilibrium ratio and hence the more the real wage will have to fall. But the fall is not indefinite. I owe to John Chipman the remark that this result directly contradicts Harrod's position[8] that a perpetually falling rate of interest would be needed to maintain equilibrium.

Catastrophic changes in factor prices do occur in the Harrod-Domar case, but again as a consequence of the special assumption of fixed proportions. I have elsewhere discussed price behavior in the Harrod model[9] but I there described price level and interest rate and omitted consideration of factor prices. Actually there is little to say. The isoquants in the Harrod case are right-angled corners and this tells the whole story. Referring back to Figure IV, if the observed capital-labor ratio is bigger than a/b, then capital

[8]In his comments on an article by Pilvin, *Quarterly Journal of Economics*, [LXVII] Nov. 1953, p. 545.

[9]R. M. Solow, "A Note on Price Level and Interest Rate in a Growth Model," *Review of Economic Studies*, [XXI] No. 54 (1953–54), pp. 74–78.

is absolutely redundant, its marginal product is zero, and the whole value of output is imputed to labor. Thus $q = 0$, and $bw = p$, so $w = p/b$. If the observed r is less than a/b labor is absolutely redundant and $w = 0$, so $q = p/a$. If labor and capital should just be in balance, $r = a/b$, then obviously it is not possible to impute any specific fraction of output to labor or capital separately. All we can be sure of is that the total value of a unit of output p will be imputed back to the composite dose of a units of capital and b units of labor (both factors are scarce). Hence w and q can have any values subject only to the condition $aq + bw = p$, $aq/p + bw/p = 1$. Thus in Figure IV anywhere but at $r = a/b$ either capital or labor must be redundant, and at a/b factor prices are indeterminate. And it is only in special circumstances that $r = a/b$.

Next consider the Cobb-Douglas case: $Y = K^a L^{1-a}$ and $q/p = a(K/L)^{a-1} = ar^{a-1}$. Hence $w/q = \dfrac{1-a}{a} r$. The exact time paths of the real factor prices can be calculated without difficulty from the solution to (7), but are of no special interest. We saw earlier, however, that the limiting capital-labor ratio is $(s/n)^{1/1-a}$. Hence the equilibrium real wage rate is $(1 - a)(s/n)^{a/1-a}$, and the equilibrium real rental is an/s. These conclusions are qualitatively just what we should expect. As always with the Cobb-Douglas function the share of labor in real output is constant.

Our third example provides one bit of variety. From $Y = (a\sqrt{K} + \sqrt{L})^2$ we can compute that $\partial Y/\partial L = a\sqrt{K/L} + 1 = a\sqrt{r} + 1$. In the case where a balanced growth equilibrium exists (see end of section IV) $r^* = \left(\dfrac{1}{\sqrt{n/s} - a}\right)^2$; therefore the limiting real wage is $w/p = \dfrac{1}{\sqrt{n/s} - a} + 1 = \dfrac{1}{1 - a\sqrt{s/n}}$. It was calculated earlier that in equilibrium growth $Y/L = \left(\dfrac{1}{1 - a\sqrt{s/n}}\right)^2$. But the relative share of labor is $(w/p)(L/Y) = 1 - a\sqrt{s/n}$. This is unlike the Cobb-Douglas case, where the relative shares are independent of s and n, depending only on the production function. Here we see that *in equilibrium growth* the relative share of labor is the greater the greater the rate of increase of the labor force and the smaller the propensity to save. In fact as one would expect, the faster the labor force increases the lower is the real wage in the equilibrium state of balanced growth; but the lower real wage still leaves the larger labor force a greater share of real income.

VI. Extensions

Neutral technological change

Perfectly arbitrary changes over time in the production function can be contemplated in principle, but are hardly likely to lead to systematic conclusions. An especially easy kind of technological change is that which simply multiplies the production function by an increasing scale factor. Thus we alter (2) to read

$$Y = A(t)F(K,L). \tag{13}$$

The isoquant map remains unchanged but the output number attached to each isoquant is multiplied by $A(t)$. The way in which the (now ever-changing) equilibrium capital-labor ratio is affected can be seen on a diagram like Figure I by "blowing up" the function $sF(r,1)$.

The Cobb-Douglas case works out very simply. Take $A(t) = e^{gt}$ and then the basic differential equation becomes

$$\dot{K} = se^{gt}K^a(L_0e^{nt})^{1-a} = sK^aL_0{}^{1-a}e^{(n(1-a)+g)t},$$

whose solution is

$$K(t) = \left[K_0{}^b - \frac{bs}{nb + g} L_0{}^b + \frac{bs}{nb + g} L_0{}^b e^{(nb+g)t} \right]^{1/b}$$

where again $b = 1 - a$. In the long run the capital stock increases at the relative rate $n + g/b$ (compared with n in the case of no technological change). The eventual rate of increase of real output is $n + ag/b$.* This is not only faster than n but (if $a > \frac{1}{2}$) may even be faster than $n + g$. The reason, of course, is that higher real output means more saving and investment, which compounds the rate of growth still more. Indeed now the capital-labor ratio never reaches an equilibrium value but grows forever. The ever-increasing investment capacity is, of course, not matched by any speeding up of the growth of the labor force. Hence K/L gets bigger, eventually growing at the rate g/b. If the initial capital-labor ratio is very high, it might fall initially, but eventually it turns around and its asymptotic behavior is as described.

Since the capital-labor ratio eventually rises without limit, it follows that the real wage must eventually rise and keep rising. On the other hand, the special property of the Cobb-Douglas function is that the relative share of labor is constant at $1 - a$. The other essential structural facts follow from what has already been said: for example, since Y eventually grows at rate $n + ag/b$ and K at rate $n + g/b$, the capital coefficient K/Y grows at rate $n + g/b - n - ag/b = g$.

The supply of labor

In general one would want to make the supply of labor a function of the real wage rate and time (since the labor force is growing). We have made

---

*[Professor Solow has corrected this as follows:

"This is simply an arithmetical slip. As is now well-known, the eventual rate of increase of output is the same as that of the capital stock, $n + g/b$. Hence the capital-output ratio is asymptotically constant. The real wage grows at the same ultimate rate as output per worker, namely g/b" — Eds.]

the special assumption that $L = L_0 e^{nt}$, i.e., that the labor-supply curve is completely inelastic with respect to the real wage and shifts to the right with the size of the labor force. We could generalize this somewhat by assuming that whatever the size of the labor force the proportion offered depends on the real wage. Specifically

$$L = L_0 e^{nt} \left(\frac{w}{p}\right)^h. \tag{14}$$

Another way of describing this assumption is to note that it is a scale blow-up of a constant elasticity curve. In a detailed analysis this particular labor supply pattern would have to be modified at very high real wages, since given the size of the labor force there is an upper limit to the amount of labor that can be supplied, and (14) does not reflect this.

Our old differential equation (6) for the capital-labor ratio now becomes somewhat more complicated. Namely if we make the price level constant, for simplicity:

$$\dot{r} = sF(r,1) - nr - h\frac{\dot{w}}{w}. \tag{6a}$$

To (6a) we must append the marginal productivity condition (10) $\partial F/\partial L = w/p$. Since the marginal product of labor depends only on r, we can eliminate w.

But generality leads to complications, and instead I turn again to the tractable Cobb-Douglas function. For that case (10) becomes

$$\frac{w}{p} = (1 - a)r^a$$

and hence

$$\frac{\dot{w}}{w} = a\frac{\dot{r}}{r}.$$

After a little manipulation (6a) can be written

$$\dot{r} = (sF(r,1) - nr)\left(1 + \frac{ah}{r}\right)^{-1},$$

which gives some insight into how an elastic labor supply changes things. In the first place, an equilibrium state of balanced growth still exists, when the right-hand side becomes zero, and it is still stable, approached from any initial conditions. Moreover, the equilibrium capital-labor ratio is *unchanged;* since $\dot{r}$ becomes zero exactly where it did before. This will not always happen, of course; it is a consequence of the special supply-of-labor schedule (14). Since r behaves in much the same way so will all those quantities which depend only on r, such as the real wage.

The reader who cares to work out the details can show that over the long run capital stock and real output will grow at the same rate n as the labor force.

If we assume quite generally that $L = G(t,w/p)$ then (6) will take the form

$$\dot{r} = sF(r,1) - \frac{r}{G}\left(\frac{\partial G}{\partial t} + \dot{w}\,\frac{\partial G}{\partial\left(\dfrac{w}{p}\right)}\right) \tag{6b}$$

If $\dot{r} = 0$, then $\dot{w} = 0$, and the equilibrium capital-labor ratio is determined by

$$sF(r,1) = \frac{r}{G}\frac{\partial G}{\partial t}.$$

Unless $1/G\,(\partial G/\partial t)$ should happen always to equal n, as in the case with (14), the equilibrium capital-labor ratio *will* be affected by the introduction of an elastic labor supply.

Variable saving ratio

Up to now, whatever else has been happening in the model there has always been growth of both labor force and capital stock. The growth of the labor force was exogenously given, while growth in the capital stock was inevitable because the savings ratio was taken as an absolute constant. As long as real income was positive, positive net capital formation must result. This rules out the possibility of a Ricardo-Mill stationary state, and suggests the experiment of letting the rate of saving depend on the yield of capital. If savings can fall to zero when income is positive, it becomes possible for net investment to cease and for the capital stock, at least, to become stationary. There will still be growth of the labor force, however; it would take us too far afield to go wholly classical with a theory of population growth and a fixed supply of land.

The simplest way to let the interest rate or yield on capital influence the volume of savings is to make the fraction of income saved depend on the real return to owners of capital. Thus total savings is $s(q/p)Y$. Under constant returns to scale and competition, the real rental will depend only on the capital-labor ratio, hence we can easily convert the savings ratio into a function of r.

Everyone is familiar with the inconclusive discussions, both abstract and econometrical, as to whether the rate of interest really has any independent effect on the volume of saving, and if so, in what direction. For the purposes of this experiment, however, the natural assumption to make is that the savings ratio depends positively on the yield of capital (and hence inversely on the capital-labor ratio).

For convenience let me skip the step of passing from q/p to r via marginal productivity, and simply write savings as $s(r)Y$. Then the only modification in the theory is that the fundamental equation (6) becomes

$$\dot{r} = s(r)F(r,1) - nr. \tag{6c}$$

The graphical treatment is much the same as before, except that we must allow for the variable factor $s(r)$. It may be that for sufficiently large r $s(r)$ becomes zero. (This will be the case only if, first, there is a real rental so low that saving stops, and second, if the production function is such that a very high capital-labor ratio will drive the real return down to that critical value. The latter condition is not satisfied by all production functions.) If so, $s(r)F(r,1)$ will be zero for all sufficiently large r. If $F(0,1) = 0$, i.e., if no production is possible without capital, then $s(r)F(r,1)$ must come down to zero again at the origin, no matter how high the savings ratio is. But this is not inevitable either. Figure VIII gives a possible picture. As usual r^*, the equilibrium capital-labor ratio, is found by putting $\dot{r} = 0$ in (6c). In Figure VIII the equilibrium is stable and eventually capital and output will grow at the same rate as the labor force.

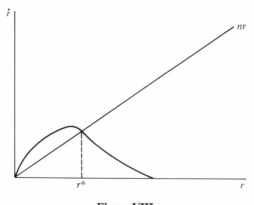

Figure VIII

In general if $s(r)$ does vanish for large r, this eliminates the possibility of a runaway indefinite increase in the capital-labor ratio as in Figure III. The savings ratio *need* not go to zero to do this, but if it should, we are guaranteed that the last intersection with nr is a stable one.

If we compare any particular $s(r)$ with a constant saving ratio, the two curves will cross at the value of r for which $s(r)$ equals the old constant ratio. To the right the new curve will lie below (since I am assuming that $s(r)$ is a decreasing function) and to the left it will lie above the old curve. It is easily seen by example that the equilibrium r^* may be either larger or smaller than it was before. A wide variety of shapes and patterns is possible, but the net effect tends to be stabilizing: when the capital-labor ratio is high, saving is cut down; when it is low, saving is stimulated. There is still no possibility of a stationary state: should r get so high as to choke off saving and net capital formation, the continual growth of the labor force must eventually reduce it.

Taxation

My colleague, E. C. Brown, points out to me that all the above analysis can be extended to accommodate the effects of a personal income tax. In the simplest case, suppose the state levies a proportional income tax at the rate t. If the revenues are directed wholly into capital formation, the savings-investment identity (1) becomes

$$\dot{K} = s(1 - t)Y + tY = (s(1 - t) + t)Y.$$

That is, the effective savings ratio is *increased* from s to $s + t(1 - s)$. If the proceeds of the tax are directly consumed, the savings ratio is *decreased* from s to $s(1 - t)$. If a fraction v of the tax proceeds is invested and the rest consumed, the savings ratio changes to $s + (v - s)t$ which is larger or smaller than s according as the state invests a larger or smaller fraction of its income than the private economy. The effects can be traced on diagrams such as Figure I: the curve $sF(r,1)$ is uniformly blown up or contracted and the equilibrium capital-labor ratio is correspondingly shifted. Nonproportional taxes can be incorporated with more difficulty, but would produce more interesting twists in the diagrams. Naturally the presence of an income tax will affect the price-wage relationships in the obvious way.

Variable population growth

Instead of treating the relative rate of population increase as a constant, we can more classically make it an endogenous variable of the system. In particular if we suppose that $\dot{L}/L$ depends only on the level of per capita income or consumption, or for that matter on the real wage rate, the generalization is especially easy to carry out. Since per capita income is given by $Y/L = F(r,1)$ the upshot is that the rate of growth of the labor force becomes $n = n(r)$, a function of the capital-labor ratio alone. The basic differential equation becomes

$$\dot{r} = sF(r,1) - n(r)r.$$

Graphically the only difference is that the ray nr is twisted into a curve, whose shape depends on the exact nature of the dependence between population growth and real income, and between real income and the capital-labor ratio.

Suppose, for example, that for very low levels of income per head or the real wage population tends to decrease; for higher levels of income it begins to increase; and that for still higher levels of income the rate of population

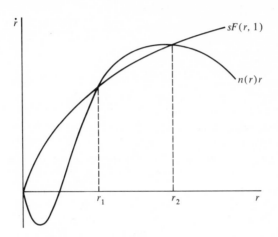

Figure IX

growth levels off and starts to decline. The result may be something like Figure IX. The equilibrium capital-labor ratio r_1 is stable, but r_2 is unstable. The accompanying levels of per capital income can be read off from the shape of $F(r,1)$. If the initial capital-labor ratio is less than r_2, the system will of itself tend to return to r_1. If the initial ratio could somehow be boosted above the critical level r_2, a self-sustaining process of increasing per capita income would be set off (and population would still be growing). The interesting thing about this case is that it shows how, in the total absence of indivisibilities or of increasing returns, a situation may still arise in which small-scale capital accumulation only leads back to stagnation but a major burst of investment can lift the system into a self-generating expansion of income and capital per head. The reader can work out still other possibilities.

VII. Qualifications

Everything above is the neoclassical side of the coin. Most especially it is full employment economics — in the dual aspect of equilibrium condition and frictionless, competitive, causal system. All the difficulties and rigidities which go into modern Keynesian income analysis have been shunted aside. It is not my contention that these problems don't exist, nor that they are of no significance in the long run. My purpose was to examine what might be called the tightrope view of economic growth and to see where more flexible assumptions about production would lead a simple model. Under-employment and excess capacity or their opposites can still be attributed to any of the old causes of deficient or excess aggregate demand, but less readily to any deviation from a narrow "balance."

In this concluding section I want merely to mention some of the more elementary obstacles to full employment and indicate how they impinge on the neoclassical model.[10]

Rigid wages

This assumption about the supply of labor is just the reverse of the one made earlier. The real wage is held at some arbitrary level $(\bar{w}/p)$. The level of employment must be such as to keep the marginal product of labor at this level. Since the marginal productivities depend only on the capital-labor ratio, it follows that fixing the real wage fixes r at, say, $\bar{r}$. Thus $K/L = \bar{r}$. Now there is no point in using r as our variable so we go back to (3) which in view of the last sentence becomes

$$\bar{r}\dot{L} = sF(\bar{r}L,L),$$

or

$$\frac{\dot{L}}{L} = \frac{s}{\bar{r}} F(\bar{r},1).$$

This says that *employment* will increase exponentially at the rate $(s/r)F(\bar{r},1)$. If this rate falls short of n, the rate of growth of the labor force, unemployment will develop and increase. If $s/\bar{r}F(\bar{r},1) > n$, labor shortage will be the outcome and presumably the real wage will eventually become flexible upward. What this boils down to is that if $(\bar{w}/p)$ corresponds to a capital-labor ratio that would normally tend to decrease $(\dot{r} < 0)$, unemployment develops, and vice versa. In the diagrams, $s/\bar{r}F(\bar{r},1)$ is just the slope of the ray from the origin to the $sF(r,1)$ curve at $\bar{r}$. If this slope is flatter than n, unemployment develops; if steeper, labor shortage develops.

Liquidity preference

This is much too complicated a subject to be treated carefully here. Moreover the paper by Tobin just mentioned contains a new and penetrating analysis of the dynamics connected with asset preferences. I simply note here, however crudely, the point of contact with the neoclassical model.

Again taking the general price level as constant (which is now an unnatural thing to do), the transactions demand for money will depend on real

[10]A much more complete and elegant analysis of these important problems is to be found in a paper by James Tobin in the *Journal of Political Economy*, LXII ([April] 1955), 103–115.

output Y and the choice between holding cash and holding capital stock will depend on the real rental q/p. With a given quantity of money this provides a relation between Y and q/p or, essentially, between K and L, e.g.,

$$\bar{M} = Q\left(Y, \frac{q}{p}\right) = Q(F(K,L), F_K(K,L)) \tag{15}$$

where now K represents capital *in use*. On the earlier assumption of full employment of labor via flexible wages, we can put $L = L_0 e^{nt}$, and solve (15) for $K(t)$, or employed capital equipment. From $K(t)$ and L we can compute $Y(t)$ and hence total saving $sY(t)$. But this represents net investment (wealth not held as cash must be held as capital). The given initial stock of capital and the flow of investment determine the available capital stock which can be compared with $K(t)$ to measure the excess supply or demand for the services of capital.

In the famous "trap" case where the demand for idle balances becomes infinitely elastic at some positive rate of interest, we have a rigid factor price which can be treated much as rigid wages were treated above. The result will be underutilization of capital if the interest rate becomes rigid somewhere above the level corresponding to the equilibrium capital-labor ratio.

But it is exactly here that the futility of trying to describe this situation in terms of a "real" neoclassical model becomes glaringly evident. Because now one can no longer bypass the direct leverage of monetary factors on real consumption and investment. When the issue is the allocation of asset-holdings between cash and capital stock, the price of the composite commodity becomes an important variable and there is no dodging the need for a monetary dynamics.

Policy implications

This is hardly the place to discuss the bearing of the previous highly abstract analysis on the practical problems of economic stabilization. I have been deliberately as neoclassical as you can get. Some part of this rubs off on the policy side. It may take deliberate action to maintain full employment. But the multiplicity of routes to full employment, via tax, expenditure, and monetary policies, leaves the nation *some* leeway to choose whether it wants high employment with relatively heavy capital formation, low consumption, rapid growth; or the reverse, or some mixture. I do not mean to suggest that this kind of policy (for example: cheap money and a budget surplus) can be carried on without serious strains. But one of the advantages of this more flexible model of growth is that it provides a theoretical counterpart to these practical possibilities.[11]

[11]See the paper by Paul A. Samuelson in *Income Stabilization for a Developing Democracy*, ed. Millikan (New Haven: [Yale University Press,] 1953), p. 577. Similar thoughts have been expressed by William Vickrey in his essay in *Post-Keynesian Economics*, ed. Kurihara (New Brunswick: [Rutgers University Press,] 1954).

Uncertainty, etc.

No credible theory of investment can be built on the assumption of perfect foresight and arbitrage over time. There are only too many reasons why net investment should be at times insensitive to current changes in the real return to capital, at other times oversensitive. All these cobwebs and some others have been brushed aside throughout this essay. In the context, this is perhaps justifiable.

T. W. SWAN **23**

Economic growth and
capital accumulation

1. From Adam Smith to Arthur Lewis

"The design of the book is different from that of any treatise on Political
Economy which has been produced in England since the work of Adam
Smith." "The last great book covering this wide range was John Stuart
Mill's *Principles of Political Economy.*" The first sentence is from Mill's
preface, the second from the preface to Lewis' *The Theory of Economic
Growth.* It would be rash to conclude from this sequence that one might
keep up-to-date in economics by reading a new book every century. Lewis'
remark is partly a warning that his book is about applications as well as
theories, and partly a reminder that he is taking up an old theme of English
economic thought. When Keynes solved "the great puzzle of Effective
Demand," he made it possible for economists once more to study the
progress of society in long-run classical terms — with a clear conscience,
"safely ensconced in a Ricardian world."

The aim of this paper is to illustrate with two diagrams a theme common to Adam Smith, Mill, and Lewis, the theory of which is perhaps best
seen in Ricardo: namely, the connexion between capital accumulation and
the growth of the productive labour force. The neoclassical economists were
in favour of productivity and thrift, but never found a way to make much

Reprinted from *The Economic Record*, Vol. 32 (November 1956), pp. 334–343 (excludes
appendix), by permission of the publisher and author. [Footnotes expanded — *Eds.*]

use of them. Earlier views were much more specific: for example, Adam Smith's industry "proportioned to capital," Ricardo's Doctrine of Unbalanced Growth, Mill's "Irish peasantry, only half fed and half employed," now so familiar in the work of Harrod, Nurkse, or Lewis, and in a hundred United Nations reports. Nevertheless, our illustration takes a neo-classical form, and enjoys the neo-classical as well as the Ricardian vice.[1]

2. An unclassical case

In the first instance, capital and labour are the only factors of production. In a given state of the arts, the annual output Y depends on the stock of capital K and the labour force N, according to the constant-elasticity production function $Y = K^\alpha N^\beta$. With constant returns to scale, $\alpha + \beta = 1$. The annual addition to the capital stock is the amount saved[2] sY, where s is given ratio of saving to output (or income). Therefore the annual relative rate of growth of capital is $s\dfrac{Y}{K}$. The symbols y and n stand for the annual relative rates of growth of output and labour respectively. In these terms the production function implies the basic formula for the rate of growth of output:[3]

$$y = \alpha s \frac{Y}{K} + \beta n \tag{1}$$

Effective demand is so regulated (*via* the rate of interest or otherwise) that all savings are profitably invested, productive capacity is fully utilized, and the level of employment can never be increased merely by raising the level of spending. The forces of perfect competition drive the rate of profit or interest r and the (real) wage rate w into equality with the marginal productivities of capital and labour, derived from the production function:

$$r = \alpha \frac{Y}{K} \tag{2}$$

$$w = \beta \frac{Y}{N} \tag{3}$$

[1]An appendix discusses some of the questions — especially those raised by Joan Robinson — concerning the role of Capital as a factor of production in the neo-classical theory. However, the appendix makes no attempt to discuss or defend the use of this or other concepts in a dynamic analysis, except by indicating some very artificial assumptions by which the main difficulties might be dodged. [Appendix omitted — *Eds.*]

[2]A given amount of saving, in terms of output, has a constant productive equivalent in terms of the capital stock. In Joan Robinson's language, the Wicksell effect is assumed to be zero. Part IV of the appendix argues that Joan Robinson is mistaken in her view that a rule can be laid down regarding the direction of the Wicksell effect.

[3]The formula is obtained after logarithmic differentiation of the production function. All variables are treated as continuous functions of time, which is measured in years. For example, "annual output" is the instantaneous rate of output per annum. The words "growth," "rate of growth," etc. always refer to instantaneous relative rates of growth per annum, subject to instantaneous compounding.

Thus the profit rate is proportional to output per unit of capital, Y/K, or the *output-capital ratio;* the wage rate is proportional to output per unit of labour, Y/N, or *output per head.* The relative shares of total profits and total wages in income are constants, given by the production elasticities α and β.

In Figure 1, look first at the three heavy lines. That rate of growth of capital $s\dfrac{Y}{K}$ is shown as a function of the output-capital ratio by a line through the origin with a slope equal to the saving ratio ($s = 10$ per cent).[4] This

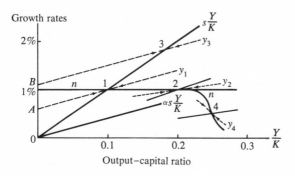

Figure 1

may be called the *growth line* of capital. The resulting contribution of capital to the growth of output, $\alpha sY/K$, is another line through the orgin, of slope αs ($\alpha = 0\cdot 4$), and may be called the *contribution line* of capital.[5]

The growth line of labour is horizontal, the rate of growth of the labour force being assumed for the present to be constant ($n = 1$ per cent). The distance OA on the vertical axis is βn ($\beta = 1 - \alpha = 0\cdot 6$), which is labour's contribution to the growth of output. Adding the contributions of capital and labour gives the growth line of output, y_1. Since $\alpha + \beta = 1$, the geometry of the diagram implies that the three growth lines (of capital, labour, and output) must intersect at the same point (1), where growth in each case is 1 per cent per annum. The growth line of output is the intermediate between the growth lines of labour and capital, and divides the vertical distance between them in the proportion $\alpha : \beta$. Anywhere west of (1) output is growing faster than capital, so the output-capital ratio is rising — moving eastward. Anywhere east of (1), capital is growing faster than output, so the movement of the output-capital ratio is westward. Only at (1) is there a

[4]Numerical plottings are used merely to help fix ideas.

[5]According to the marginal productivity formula (2) above, $\alpha s\dfrac{Y}{K} = sr$. The rate of profit may therefore be read directly from Figure 1 by multiplying the contribution line of capital by 10.

resting-place. *At any other point the economy is always in motion towards (1),*[6] as shown by the arrows on the line y_1.

The point (2) is another equilibrium point like (1), except that it corresponds with a saving ratio of 5 per cent, instead of 10 per cent at (1). The (unlabelled) continuous line is the new growth line of capital, with a slope through the origin of 5 per cent. The line y_2 is the new growth line of output, which if extended would meet the vertical axis at A as before. (The new contribution line of capital is not drawn.) At (2) economic growth is uniformly 1 per cent, just as at (1), because the three growth lines must still intersect somewhere on the horizontal line n. The given rate of growth of labour thus determines the equilibrium growth rate of the whole economy, while the saving ratio determines the output-capital ratio at which equilibrium will occur.

Suppose the economy is at (2), and that a thrift campaign suddenly raises the saving ratio from 5 per cent to 10 per cent. The growth line of output shifts from y_2 to y_1. Output per head begins to improve (as shown by the height of y_1 above n near (2)), and the wage rate rises in the same proportion. The output-capital ratio gradually sinks westward, and the profit rate sinks in the same proportion. The improvement of output per head continues at an ever-slackening pace down the slope of y_1, towards (1). At (1) output per head and the wage rate are higher than at (2), while the output-capital ratio and the profit rate are lower. These are permanent changes, but the rate of economic growth is faster only in the course of transition from (2) to (1).

Suppose next that the state of the arts, hitherto assumed constant, continually improves. "Neutral" technical progress contributes to the growth of output an annual m per cent beyond the contributions of capital and labour. In Figure 1 the distance AB on the vertical axis is m, at an assumed rate of ½ per cent. The new growth line of output y_3 shows this amount added on top of y_1 (for a 10 per cent saving ratio), and it cuts the growth line of capital at the point (3). This will now be the equilibrium point. In some respects the transition from (2) to (1) is reversed by the introduction of technical progress, since the output-capital ratio and the rate of profit are both higher at (3) than at (1). But the main change is that

---

[6]Figure 1 is in effect the "phase portrait" of a first-order differential equation in the variable Y/K (cf. Andronow & Chaikin, *Theory of Oscillations*, Chapter 4). A similar device is used by R. M. Solow ("A Contribution to the Theory of Economic Growth," *Quarterly Journal of Economics*, [LXX] Feb. 1956, [165–194]). The approach to the point (1) along y, is asymptotic — i.e., (1) is reached only in infinity, the speed of travel towards it being directly related to the distance remaining to be travelled. (The time taken for Y/K to move any given distance towards equilibrium is not revealed by the diagram, and can be discovered only by integrating the differential equation.) A point such as (1) is a *stable* equilibrium point because the growth line of capital cuts the growth line of labour (and so the growth line of output) from below. If over a certain range the saving ratio s were a decreasing function of Y/K, the growth line of capital might cut the growth line of labour from above, and this second intersection would be an *unstable* equilibrium point (the arrows would be directed away from it on either side).

output per head is not only permanently higher, but perpetually rising (as shown by the height of y_3 above n at (3)). Its rate of increase is actually greater than the m per cent contributed directly by technical progress, because the contribution of capital is also sustained by technical progress at a higher level (as shown by the height of y_1 above n at (3)).

The effect of a change in thrift, assuming constant technical progress, is not shown in the diagram. If another situation were depicted, combining the 5 per cent saving ratio of (2) with the ½ per cent technical progress of (3), its equilibrium point would be found to lie well to the east of (3), but on exactly the same parallel of economic growth. So long as technical progress and the rate of growth of labour are taken as *data*, they jointly determine the equilibrium growth rate of output and capital.[7] After a transitional phase, the influence of the saving ratio on the rate of growth is ultimately absorbed by a compensating change in the output-capital ratio.

This conclusion is not really surprising. It is in fact the counterpart in our present unclassical model of the classical proposition that capital accumulation leads *ultimately* to the stationary state. A rise in the saving ratio does mean that the level of output per head is permanently higher at any time thereafter than it would have been otherwise. Further, the "transitional phase" is never literally completed; the "transitional" acceleration-deceleration of growth might be visible for centuries, depending entirely on the numerical assumptions. However, only extreme assumptions could produce such a result. It is at first sight disconcerting to find that "plausible" figuring suggests that even the impact effect of a sharp rise in the saving ratio may be of minor importance for the rate of growth: for example, the maximum amount added to the rate of growth, at the beginning of the transition from (2) to (1) in Figure 1, is only 0·4 per cent, though the thrift campaign doubles the saving ratio at a point where the yield on capital is 8 per cent.

To this anti-accumulation, pro-technology line of argument there are at least two possible answers. First, the rate of technical progress may not be independent of the rate of accumulation, or (what comes to much the same thing) accumulation may give rise to external economies, so that the true social yield of capital is greater than any "plausible" figure based on common private experience.[8] This point would have appealed to Adam

[7]Equation (1) on page 478, with the addition of m per cent technical progress, becomes

$$y = \alpha s \frac{Y}{K} + \beta n + m \qquad (1')$$

from which it follows that when $y = s\dfrac{Y}{K}$ (i.e., at an equilibrium point where the output-capital ratio is stationary) $y = \dfrac{\beta n + m}{1 - \alpha}$. For $\alpha + \beta = 1$ this is simply $y = n + \dfrac{m}{1 - \alpha}$.

[8]In Figure 1, allowing for external economies, $\alpha + \beta$ would exceed unity and so y_1 would cut the growth line of capital above the level of n, just as y_3 does. If the external economies were concentrated on the side of capital (rather than labour), this elevation would take the form of a steeper slope for the contribution line of capital, which of course would no longer correspond with the rate of profit.

Smith, but it will not be pursued here. Second, the rate of growth of labour may not be independent of the rate of accumulation. This is the distinctively classical answer.

In Figure 1 the sloping branch of the growth line of labour represents a situation in which the supply of labour is "elastic" in the vicinity of a certain level of output per head (and wage rate). This situation may be given a Malthusian interpretation, as the response of population to an improvement in the means of subsistence; it may be a situation of "disguised unemployment," with unproductive labour kept in reserve (by sharing with relatives, etc.) at a minimum living standard; it may be the result of Trade Union resistance or some other kind of institutional or conventional barrier, expressed in real terms; or it may reflect a potential supply of migrant labour, available if satisfactory living standards are offered. In any of these situations, "demand for commodities is not demand for labour" (if only Mill had understood his own doctrine): the growth, or productive employment, of the labour force depends directly on the rate of accumulation. In the neighbourhood of the point (4), which is drawn for a saving ratio of 2 per cent, a higher saving ratio will evidently raise the rate of economic growth almost in proportion — and not only "transitionally," but in equilibrium as well. On the other hand, the wage rate and output per head (of *productively employed* labour) will not be much improved; nor will the rate of profit and the output-capital ratio suffer much decline.

This last fact is of course one of the reasons why capital accumulation appears so much more effective in raising the rate of economic growth when faster growth means primarily a faster expansion of productive employment, rather than a faster improvement of output per head. But the main reason is that accumulation is justly credited with the productive contribution of the additional labour that it "sets in motion."

It is now possible to look at Figure 1 in a new light. What is the maximum rate of labour growth consistent with the maintenance of a given standard of output per head? The answer (assuming no technical progress) is that for any such standard — i.e., at any given level of the output-capital ratio — the maximum rate of growth is directly proportional to the saving ratio. In fact, the growth line of capital $s(Y/K)$, wherever it lies, is the locus of all growth rates at which output per head is constant.

This is a more classical view of the problem, and also, unfortunately perhaps more relevant to many contemporary problems of population pressure and economic growth. However, to see its implications in either context, it is necessary to introduce a characteristic feature of the classical model — namely, the limited "powers of the soil."

3. A classical case

A fixed factor of production, which may be called land, can be introduced very simply. Let its production elasticity be γ. Then, assuming constant returns to scale, $\alpha + \beta + \gamma = 1$. However, since land is fixed in supply, it does not appear in the basic formula for the growth of output, $y = \alpha s \dfrac{Y}{K}$ $+ \beta n$, but makes its presence felt by reducing the sum of α and β below unity. With this interpretation, the former marginal productivity relationships for r and w remain unchanged, and there is now a third, of similar form, to determine the rent of land. α, β, and γ are now the constant relative shares of the three factors in income.

If Figure 1 were drawn for $\alpha + \beta < 1$, the growth line of output would cut the growth line of capital below the horizontal growth line of labour. The only possible equilibrium with constant labour growth (and no technical progress) would be one in which output per head and the wage rate were perpetually falling. However, an answer can be given to the question: what rate of labour growth will maintain constant output per head? This condition can be expressed by putting $y = n$ in the formula repeated in the last paragraph, which gives $n = \dfrac{\alpha}{1 - \beta}\, s\dfrac{Y}{K}$. In Figure 2 the constants are assumed to be $\alpha = 0 \cdot 3$, $\beta = 0 \cdot 5$, $\gamma = 0 \cdot 2$ and $s = 10\%$. The coincident values of y and n that satisfy the condition of constant output per head are

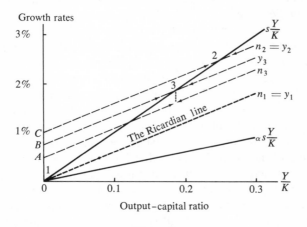

Figure 2

shown as a function of the output-capital ratio by the growth line $n_1 = y_1$, and this *locus classicus* is called the Ricardian line.

Along the Ricardian line labour is growing as fast as is compatible with a given living standard — keeping pace with the growth of output. Except at the origin, the growth line of capital lies above the Ricardian line, for capital must always grow faster than labour in order to sustain output per head in the face of continually diminishing returns on the land. But since capital is therefore also growing faster than output, the output-capital ratio is continually falling; the profit rate is falling the same proportion, the wage rate is stable, while rent per acre is rising in proportion with output. As the output-capital ratio falls, the growth rate of labour and output gradually recedes down the slope of the Ricardian line, retreating from the unequal struggle against niggardly nature. In this manner the natural progress of society continues indefinitely towards the origin, where at last the growth line of capital and the Ricardian line intersect, at the point (1), in a stationary state.

If "long indeed before this period the very low rate of profit" has "arrested all accumulation," the change will have been seen in Figure 2 in the form of a decline in the saving ratio, reducing the slopes of the growth lines down to zero. On the other hand, a higher saving ratio would proportionally raise the growth rates at every point, but only temporarily interrupt the inevitable progress towards stationariness.

Suppose that this "gravitation . . . is happily checked at repeated intervals" by a constant rate of technical progress ($m = \frac{1}{2}$ per cent, as before). The new version of the Ricardian line $n_2 = y_2$ will lie above the old by the distance OC, which is $\frac{m}{1 - \beta}$.[9] At the point (2) where the new line intersects the growth line of capital, technical progress is exactly balanced against diminishing returns, and output per head is constant with a growth rate of about 2½ per cent. So instead of gravitating towards the origin, the economy if necessary levitates to this stable equilibrium point. Ricardo would no doubt object that if population is supposed to grow for ever at 2½ per cent, it is very likely that at some point diminishing returns will set in with a violence not allowed for in our production function.

Given the proposition that at *some* standard of living (for the purpose of the foregoing argument it may be low or high) population will multiply fully in proportion with output, there is perhaps something to be said for the classical "law" of historically diminishing returns. It is in relation to the Malthusian postulate that the classical vision failed most signally. Suppose then that each generation demands something better for its children: population is regulated so as to achieve, not a given living standard, but a progressive annual improvement of q per cent. The new element q affects the growth line of labour (now the locus of all labour growth rates consistent with q per cent improvement in output per head) exactly as if q were subtracted from the rate of technical progress, m.[10] Assuming q to be as little as ¼ per cent, the new growth lines n_3 and y_3 determine an equilibrium growth rate of labour of about 1½ per cent at the point (3).

Growth lines such as n_1, n_2, and n_3 can be considered, not as timepaths which on various improbable assumptions the economy would follow towards an equilibrium point, but rather as a grid that divides the economic

[9]This is obtained by putting $y = n$ in $y = \alpha s \dfrac{Y}{K} + \beta n + m$.

[10]This is obtained by putting $y = n + q$ in the formula of the last footnote.

map into characteristic zones of improvement or determination in output per head. Every point on the map represents a particular conjunction of a labour growth rate with an output-capital ratio. In Figure 2, any point to the south and east of n_1 is a situation in which output per head is rising even if there is no technical progress. Between n_1 and n_3 output per head in the absence of technical progress would be falling, but with the assumed ½ per cent technical progress it is rising by more than ¼ per cent. Between n_3 and n_2 the rise is less than ¼ per cent. A labour growth rate that strays to the north and west of n_2 incurs a decline in output per head, unless technical progress is greater than ½ per cent.

A higher saving ratio, even though it does not change the growth rate at any of the so-called equilibrium points, swings the whole grid to the north and west. As a result, there is a larger area of desirable situations to the south and east of any given criterion of improvement, and a smaller area of undesirable situations to the north and west.

4. The Harrod model

The model used above differs from Harrod's model of economic growth only in that it systematizes the relations between the "warranted" and "natural" rates of growth, and introduces land as a fixed factor.

Any point on the growth line of capital, $s\dfrac{Y}{K}$, is Harrod's warranted rate of growth $G_w = s/C_r$, since the output-capital ratio Y/K at any given level is the reciprocal of Harrod's capital coefficient C_r. The corresponding point on the growth line of output is Harrod's natural rate of growth G_n. At an equilibrium point, where the two growth lines intersect, the warranted and natural rates of growth are equal. At any other point the wage rate and the profit rate are moving in such a way as to induce entrepreneurs to adjust the output-capital ratio in the direction which will bring the warranted and natural rates of growth together. Specifically, a reduction in the output-capital ratio (an increase in Harrod's C_r) always involves a decline in the rate of profit, and this automatically implies the appropriate movement of the wage rate.

Harrod envisages exactly the same mechanism of adjustment, *via* the "deepening" factor, d, which "may have a positive value because the rate of interest is falling." He argues that natural market forces cannot be expected to achieve the desired results, but does not despair that Keynesian policies may be successful. Nevertheless some of his readers seem to have been misled into the belief that in Harrod's model equality between the warranted and the natural rates of growth can occur only "by a fluke."[11] Harrod's own view is stated very clearly:

[11]Joan Robinson, *The Accumulation of Capital* (London: Macmillan and Co., Ltd., 1956), p. 405.

"Our aim should be to get such a progressive reduction in the rate of interest that $G_wC_r = s - d = G_nC_r$. If d is positive, C_r will increase through time, and may eventually become so great as to enable us to dispense with d. At that point interest need fall no further."[12]

The mechanism of Figures 1 and 2 merely makes explicit what this statement implies.

[12]Roy Harrod, *Towards A Dynamic Economics* (London: Macmillan and Co., Ltd., 1948), p. 96.

JAMES TOBIN **24**

A dynamic aggregative model[1]

Contemporary theoretical models of the business cycle and of economic growth typically possess two related characteristics: (1) they assume production functions that allow for no substitution between factors, and (2) the variables are all real magnitudes; monetary and price phenomena have no significance. Because of these characteristics, these models present a rigid angular picture of the economic process: straight and narrow paths from which the slightest deviation spells disaster, abrupt and sharp reversals, intractable ceilings and floors. The models are highly suggestive, but their representation of the economy arouses the suspicion that they have left out some essential mechanisms of adjustment.

The purpose of this paper is to present a simple aggregative model that allows both for substitution possibilities and for monetary effects. The growth mechanism in the model is not radically different from the accelerator mechanism that plays the key role in other growth models. But it is unlike the accelerator mechanism in that there is not just one tenable rate of growth.

Reprinted from James Tobin, "A Dynamic Aggregative Model," *The Journal of Political Economy*, Vol. 63 (April 1955), pp. 103–115, by permission of The University of Chicago Press. Copyright 1955 by The University of Chicago Press.

[1]I wish to acknowledge with gratitude helpful discussions of this subject with graduate students and colleagues at Yale University. In particular, Henry Bruton, Thomas F. Dernburg, William Fellner, Challis A. Hall, and Arthur Okun read the paper and made valuable comments. So did Robert M. Solow of M.I.T. But it is not their fault if I have failed to follow all their advice. The paper was written while I was holding a Social Science Research Council Faculty Fellowship.

As in accelerator models, growth is limited by the availability of factors other than capital. But here these limitations do not operate so abruptly, and they can be tempered by monetary and price adjustments that the accelerator models ignore.

The cyclical behavior of the model is similar to the nonlinear cyclical processes of Kaldor, Goodwin, and Hicks.[2] But the cycle in the present model depends in an essential way on the inflexibility of prices, money wages, or the supply of monetary assets.

Furthermore, the model to be described here does not restrict the economic process to two possibilities, steady growth or cycles. An alternative line of development is continuing underemployment — "stagnation" during which positive investment increases the capital stock and possibly the level of real income. This outcome, like the cycle, depends on some kind of price or monetary inflexibility.

In Part I the structure of the model will be described, and in Part II some of its implications will be examined.

I.

The building blocks from which this model is constructed are four in number: (1) the saving function; (2) the production function; (3) asset preferences; and (4) labor-supply conditions.

The saving function

At any moment of time output is being produced at a rate Y, consumption is occurring at a rate C, and the capital stock, K, is growing at the rate $\dot{K}$, equal to $Y - C$. The saving function tells how output is divided between consumption and net investment:

$$\dot{K} = S(Y). \tag{1}$$

This relationship is assumed to hold instantaneously. That is, consumption is adjusted without lag to the simultaneous level of output; any output not consumed is an addition to the capital stock. Whether or not it is a welcome addition is another matter, which depends on the asset preferences of the community, discussed below.

Of the saving function, it is assumed that $S'(Y)$ is positive and that $S(Y)$

---

[2]N. Kaldor, "A Model of the Trade Cycle," *Economic Journal*, L (March, 1940), 78–92; R. Goodwin, "The Nonlinear Accelerator and the Persistence of Business Cycles," *Econometrica*, XIX (Jan. 1951), 1–17, and "Econometrics in Business Cycle Analysis," in A. H. Hansen, *Business Cycles and National Income* (New York: W. W. Norton & Co., 1951), chap. 22; J. R. Hicks, *A Contribution to the Theory of the Trade Cycle* (Oxford: Oxford University Press, 1950).

is zero for some positive Y. Otherwise the shape of the saving function is not crucial to the argument. Variables other than Y — for example, W, total real wealth — could be assumed to affect the propensity to save without involving more than inessential complications.

The production function

The rate of output, Y, depends jointly on the stock of capital in existence, K, and the rate of input of labor services, N:

$$Y = P(K, N). \tag{2}$$

The production function is assumed to be linear homogeneous. It follows that the marginal products are homogeneous functions of degree zero of the two factors; in other words, the marginal products depend only on the proportions in which the two inputs are being used. The real wage of labor, w, is equated by competition to the marginal product of labor; and the rent, r, per unit of time earned by ownership of any unit of capital is equated to the marginal product of capital:

$$w = P_N(K, N), \tag{3}$$

$$r = P_K(K, N). \tag{4}$$

If labor and capital expand over time in proportion, then output will expand in the same proportion, and both the real wage and the rent of capital will remain constant. If capital expands at a faster rate than labor, its rent must fall, and the real wage must rise.

A production function with constant returns to scale, both at any moment of time and over time, is a convenient beginning assumption. In judging the appropriateness of this kind of production function to the model, it should be remembered that, if it ignores technical improvement, on the one hand, it ignores limitations of other factors of production, "land," on the other. In the course of the argument the consequences of technological progress will be briefly discussed.

Asset preferences

Only two stores of value, physical capital and currency, are available to owners of wealth in this economy. The own rate of return on capital is its rent, r, equal to its marginal product. Currency is wholly the issue of the state and bears an own rate of interest legally and permanently established. This rate will be assumed to be zero. The stock of currency, M, is exogenously determined and can be varied only by budget deficits or surpluses. The counterpart of this "currency" in the more complex asset structure of an actual economy is not money by the usual definition, which includes bank deposits corresponding to private debts. It is, for the United States, currency in circulation plus government debt plus the gold stock.[3]

If p is the price of goods in terms of currency, the community's total real wealth at any moment of time is

$$W = K + \frac{M}{p}.$$ (5)

Given K, M, and p, the community may be satisfied to split its wealth so that it holds as capital an amount equal to the available stock, K, and as currency an amount equal to the existing real supply, M/p. Such a situation will be referred to as "portfolio balance."

Portfolio balance is assumed to be the necessary and sufficient condition for price stability ($\dot{p} = 0$). If, instead, owners of wealth desire to hold more goods and less currency, they attempt to buy goods with currency. Prices are bid up ($\dot{p} > 0$). If they desire to shift in the other direction, they attempt to sell goods for currency ($\dot{p} < 0$). These price changes may, in turn, be associated with changes in output and employment; but that depends on other parts of the model, in particular on the conditions of labor supply.

What, then, determines whether an existing combination of K and M/p represents a situation of portfolio balance or imbalance? Portfolio balance is assumed in this model to be defined by the following functional relationship:

$$\frac{M}{p} = L(K, r, Y),$$ (6)

$$L_K \gtreqless 0, \qquad L_r < 0, \qquad L_Y > 0.$$

Requirements for transactions balances of currency are assumed, as is customary, to depend on income; this is the reason for the appearance of Y in the function. Given their real wealth, W, owners of wealth will wish to hold a larger amount of capital, and a smaller amount of currency, the higher the rent on capital, r. Given the rent on capital, owners of wealth will desire to put some part of any increment of their wealth into capital and some part into currency. It is possible that there are levels of r (e.g., negative rates) so low that portfolio balance requires all wealth to be in the form of currency and that there is some level of r above which wealth owners would wish to hold no currency. But the main argument to follow in Part II concerns ranges of r between those extremes.

[3]This is the same concept developed in connection with discussions of the "Pigou effect"; see Herbert Stein, "Price Flexibility and Full Employment: Comment," *American Economic Review*, XXXIX (June 1949), 725–726, and Don Patinkin, "Price Flexibility and Full Employment: Reply," *American Economic Review*, XXXIX (June 1949), 726–728.

The assumption about portfolio balance has now been stated, and the reader who is more interested in learning its consequences than its derivation can proceed to the next section. But since this is the one of the four building blocks of the model that introduces possibly unconventional and unfamiliar material into the structure, it requires some discussion and defense.

The theory of portfolio balance implicit in most conventional aggregative economic theories of investment implies that rates of return on all assets must be equal. Applied to the two assets of the mythical economy of this paper, this theory would go as follows: Owners of wealth have a firm, certain, and unanimous expectation of the rate of price change, $\dot{p}_e$. This may or may not be the same as the actual rate of price change $\dot{p}$ at the same moment of time.[4] The rate at which a unit of wealth is expected to grow if it is held in the form of currency is, therefore, $-\dot{p}_e/p$. Similarly, owners of wealth have a firm and unanimous view of the rate at which wealth will grow if it is held as physical capital. This rate is r_e, the expected market rent, which may or may not be the same as r. Owners of wealth will choose that portfolio which makes their wealth grow at the fastest rate. If $-\dot{p}_e/p$ were to exceed r_e, they would desire to hold all currency and no capital; if r_e were greater than $-\dot{p}_e/p$, they would desire to hold all capital and no currency. Only if the two rates are equal will they be satisfied to hold positive amounts of both assets; and, indeed, in that case, they will not care what the mix of assets is in their portfolios. On this theory of asset preferences the relative supplies of the assets do not matter. Whatever the supplies, portfolio balance requires that the real expected rates of return on the assets be equal. In particular, if $r_e = r$ and $\dot{p}_e = 0$, equilibrium requires that $r = 0$.

Keynes departed from this theory in his liquidity-preference explanation of the choice between cash balances and interest-bearing monetary assets. He was able to show that, given uncertainty or lack of unanimity in the expectations of wealth owners, the rate of interest that preserves portfolio balance between cash and "bonds" is not independent of the supplies of the two kinds of assets. But he did not apply the same reasoning to the much more important choice between physical goods or capital, on the one hand, and monetary assets, on the other. His theory of investment was orthodox in requiring equality between the marginal efficiency of capital and the rate of interest.

The assumptions behind the portfolio-balance equation in the present model, equation (6), may be briefly stated. Each owner of wealth entertains as possibilities numerous values of both r_e and $-\dot{p}_e/p$, and to each possible pair of values he attaches a probability. The expected value of r_e, that is,

---

[4]An individual may be assumed to know the historical course of prices $p(t)$ up to the present (for $t \gtrless t_0$) and to expect a future course of prices $p_e(t)$ (for $t \gtrless t_0$). Presumably the expected course starts at the same price at which the historical course ends ($p[t_0] = p_e[t_0]$). But there is no reason that one should start with the same slope with which the other ends: $p'(t_0)$, referred to in the text as $\dot{p}$, is not necessarily the same as $p_e'(t_0)$, referred to in the text as $\dot{p}_e$.

the mean of its marginal probability distribution, is assumed to be r. The expected value of $-\dot{p}_e/p$ is assumed to be zero. In other and less precise words, the owner of wealth expects *on balance* neither the rent of capital nor the price level to change. But he is not sure. The dispersions of possible rents and price changes above and below their expected values constitute the risks of the two assets.

Owners of wealth, it is further assumed, dislike risk. Of two portfolios with the same expected value of rate of return, an investor will prefer the one with the lower dispersion of rate of return.[5] The principle of "not putting all your eggs in one basket" explains why a risk-avoiding investor may well hold a diversified portfolio even when the expected returns of all the assets in it are not identical. For the present purpose it explains why an owner of wealth will hold currency in excess of transactions requirements, even when its expected return is zero and the expected return on capital is positive. It also explains why, given the risks associated with the two assets, an investor may desire to have more of his wealth in capital the larger is r. The higher the prospective yield of a portfolio, the greater is the inducement to accept the additional risks of heavier concentration on the more remunerative asset.[6]

Labor supply

The behavior of the model depends in a crucial way on assumptions regarding the relations of the supply of labor to the real wage, to the money wage, and to time. It will be convenient, therefore, to introduce alternative assumptions in the course of the argument of Part II.

II.

Stationary equilibrium

The model would be of little interest if its position of stationary equilibrium were inevitably and rapidly attained, but, for the sake of completeness, this position will be described first. There are any number of combinations of labor and capital that can produce the zero-saving level of output. To each combination corresponds a marginal productivity of labor, to which the real wage must be equal; this marginal productivity is higher the more capital-intensive the combination. Suppose there is a unique relation between the supply of labor and the real wage. An equilibrium labor-capital combination is one that demands labor in an amount equal to the supply

[5]Risk aversion in this sense may be deduced from the assumption of generally declining marginal utility of income. Here, however, it is not necessary to go into the question of the usefulness of the concept of cardinal utility in explaining behavior under uncertainty.

[6]There is an "income effect" working in the opposite direction. The portfolio-balance function, equation (6), assumes the substitution effect to be dominant.

forthcoming at the real wage corresponding to that combination. The equilibrium absolute price level is then determined by the portfolio-balance equation. Given the rent and amount of capital in the equilibrium combination and the supply of currency, portfolio balance must be obtained by a price level that provides the appropriate amount of real wealth in liquid form.

Balanced growth

Proportional growth of capital, income, and employment implies, according to the assumed production function, constancy of capital rent, r, and the real wage, w. Maintenance of portfolio balance requires, therefore, an increase in M/p. Given the supply of currency, the price level must fall continuously over time. Balanced growth requires an expanding labor supply, available at the same real wage and at an ever decreasing money wage.

Growth with capital deepening

In this model, unlike those of Harrod, Hicks, and others, failure of the labor supply to grow at the rate necessary for balanced growth does not mean that growth at a slower rate is possible. If the real wage must rise in order to induce additional labor supply, the rent of capital must, it is true, fall as capital grows. Portfolio balance requires, therefore, that a given increment of capital be accompanied by a greater price decline than in the case of balanced growth. But there is some rate of price decline that will preserve portfolio balance, even in the extreme case of completely inelastic labor supply. Although the rate of price decline per increment of capital is greater the less elastic the supply of labor with respect to the real wage and with respect to time, the time rate of price decline is not necessarily faster. The growth of income, saving, and capital is slower when labor is less elastic, and it takes longer to achieve the same increment of capital.

Technological progress and price deflation

The preceding argument has assumed an unchanging production function with constant returns to scale. In comparison with that case, technological progress is deflationary to the extent that a more rapid growth of income augments transactions requirements for currency. But technological progress has offsetting inflationary effects to the extent that it raises the marginal productivity of capital corresponding to given inputs of capital and labor. Conceivably technical improvement can keep the rent on capital rising even though its amount relative to the supply of labor is increasing. This rise might even be sufficient to keep the demand for real currency balances from rising, in spite of the growth of the capital stock and of transactions requirements. At the other extreme, it is possible to imagine technological progress that fails to raise or even lowers the marginal productivity of capital corresponding to given inputs of the two factors. Progress of this kind contains nothing to counteract the deflationary pressures of a growing capital stock, declining capital rent, and increasing transactions needs.

Monetary expansion as an alternative to price deflation

Growth with continuous price deflation strains the assumption that wealth owners expect, on balance, the price level to remain constant. The process itself would teach them that the expected value of the real return on currency is positive, and it would perhaps also reduce their estimates of the dispersion of possible returns on currency. This lesson would increase the relative attractiveness of currency as a store of value and thus force an ever faster rate of price decline.

An alternative to price deflation is expansion of the supply of currency. As noted above, monetary expansion cannot, in this model, be accomplished by monetary policy in the conventional sense but must be the result of deficit financing.[7] Assume that the government deficit $\dot{M}$ takes the form of transfer payments. Then equation (1) must be changed to read:

$$\dot{K} + \frac{\dot{M}}{p} = S\left(Y + \frac{\dot{M}}{p}\right). \tag{7}$$

The normal result is that consumption will be a larger and investment a smaller share of a given level of real income. Thus, the greater is $\dot{M}$, the slower will be the rate of capital expansion. At the same time the growth of the currency supply meets growing transactions requirements and satisfies the desire of wealth owners to balance increased holdings of capital, possibly yielding lower rents, with enlarged holdings of liquid wealth.

That there is a time path of M compatible with price stability may be seen by considering the inflationary consequences of large values of $\dot{M}$. There is presumably a value of $\dot{M}$ large enough so that the desire of the community to save at the disposable income level $Y + \dot{M}/p$ would be satisfied by saving at the rate $\dot{M}/p$. Then the capital stock would remain constant, its marginal product would stay constant, and transactions requirements would remain unchanged. Portfolio balance could then be maintained only by inflation at the same rate as $\dot{M}/M$. Somewhere between this value of $\dot{M}$ and zero there is a rate of growth of the currency supply compatible with price stability.

Wage inflexibility as an obstacle to growth

If the currency supply grows too slowly, the necessity that price deflation — probably an ever faster price deflation — accompany growth casts consider-

[7]The implications of the approach of this paper concerning the effects of conventional monetary policy are left for discussion elsewhere. Clearly such a discussion requires the introduction of additional types of assets, including bank deposits and private debts.

able doubt on the viability of the growth processes described above. This doubt arises from the institutional limits on downward flexibility of prices, in particular money wage rates, characteristic of actual economies. The purpose of this and the two following sections is to analyze the behavior of the system when money wage rates are inflexible.

For this analysis it is convenient to work with two relationships between the price level, p, and employment of labor, N. Both relationships assume a constant capital stock, K. The first, called the "labor market balance" (LMB) relation, gives for any level of employment, N, the price level, p, that equates the marginal productivity of labor to the real wage. Given the money wage, this p is higher for larger values of N, because the marginal product of labor declines with employment with a given capital stock. This relation is shown in Figure 1 as curve LMB. The level of employment N_f is

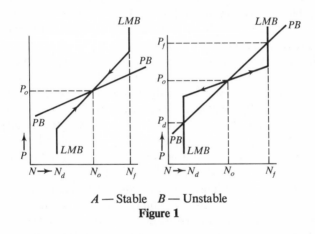

A — Stable B — Unstable
Figure 1

the maximum labor supply that can be induced at the given money wage. At that level of employment the money wage becomes flexible upward. If the money wage is raised or lowered, the LMB curve will shift up or down proportionately. If the capital stock is expanded, the LMB curve will shift downward, because an addition to capital will raise the marginal product of labor at any level of employment.

The second relation between the same two variables, p and N, is the "portfolio balance" relation PB, also shown in Figure 1. As the name indicates, it shows for any level of employment the price level required for portfolio balance between the given stock of capital K and the given supply of currency M. Its slope may be either positive or negative. The marginal productivity of the given stock of capital, and hence the rent of capital, is greater the higher the volume of employment. Currency is thus a relatively less attractive asset at higher levels of employment; so far as this effect is concerned, the price level must be higher at higher levels of employment in order to reduce the real supply of currency. The transactions relation of demand for currency to the level of real income works, however, in the opposite direction. Whatever its slope, the *PB* curve will, for obvious reasons, shift upward if currency supply *M* is expanded, and downward if capital expands.

It is not possible to establish a priori which curve, *LMB* or *PB*, has the greater slope. The two possibilities are shown in Figures 1*A* and 1*B*. In Figure 1*A* the *LMB* curve has the greater slope; both curves are drawn with positive slopes, but the *PB* curve could equally well have a negative slope. In Figure 1*B* the *PB* curve has the greater slope. As indicated by the arrows, the intersection (p_0, N_0) is a stable short-run equilibrium in Figure 1*A* but an unstable one in Figure 1*B*. This follows from the assumption that $\dot{p}$ will be positive, zero, or negative, depending on whether wealth owners regard their currency holdings as too large, just right, or too small.[8] In Figure 1*B* (p_f, N_f) is a stable short-run equilibrium. And there may be another stable intersection (p_d, N_d). Here N_d would be a level of employment so low and, correspondingly, a real wage so high that the rigidity of the money wage breaks down.

Capital expansion shifts both the *LMB* and the *PB* curve downward. How does capital expansion affect the point (p_0, N_0)? The following results are proved in the Appendix: When the intersection (p_0, N_0) is an unstable point (Fig. 1*B*), capital expansion increases both N_0 and p_0. The *PB* curve shifts more than the *LMB* curve, and their intersection moves northeast. The qualitative effect of capital expansion may be depicted graphically by imagining the *PB* curve to shift downward while the *LMB* curve stays put. The same argument shows that capital accumulation moves a point like (p_f, N_f) or (p_d, N_d) in Figure 1*B* downward, while capital decumulation moves it upward. When the intersection (p_0, N_0) is a stable point (Fig. 1*A*), the argument of the Appendix indicates that capital expansion necessarily lowers p_0 but may either increase or decrease N_0; the intersection may move either southeast or southwest. It is, in other words, not possible to say which curve shifts more as a consequence of a given change in the capital stock.

These results permit consideration of the question whether growth with full employment of labor is compatible with a floor on the money wage rate. Except in the case where labor supply grows as rapidly as capital or more rapidly, the growth process brings about an increase of the real wage. A certain amount of price deflation is therefore compatible with rigidity of the money wage. But, according to the results reported in the previous paragraph, certainly in the unstable case and possibly in the stable case, too, the amount of price deflation needed to maintain portfolio balance is too

---

[8]Employment has been assumed always to be at the point where the marginal product of labor equals the real wage. But the conclusions on the stability of (p_0, N_0) in the two parts of Figure 1 would not be altered if it were assumed instead that $\dot{N}$ is positive, zero, or negative depending on whether the marginal product of labor exceeds, equals, or is less than the real wage.

much to enable employment to be maintained at a rigid money wage. Capital growth shifts the *PB* curve down more than the *LMB* curve. However, it is also possible in the stable case that the *LMB* curve shifts more than the *PB* curve, so that employment could be maintained and even increased while the money wage remains rigid and prices fall. But even this possibility depends on the assumption that wealth owners balance their portfolios on the expectation that the price level will remain the same. As noted above, it is only realistic to expect that a process of deflation would itself teach owners of wealth to expect price deflation rather than price stability. Such expectations would inevitably so enhance the relative attractiveness of currency as an asset that the process could not continue without a reduction of the money-wage rate.

Wage inflexibility and cyclical fluctuations

It is the situation depicted in Figure 1*B* that gives rise to the possibility of a cycle formally similar to those of Kaldor, Goodwin, and Hicks. Suppose the economy is at point (p_f, N_f). Capital expansion will sooner or later cause this point to coincide with (p_0, N_0) at a point like *R* in Figure 2. This day will

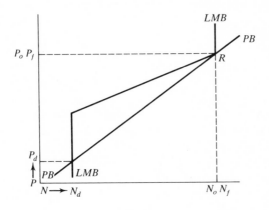

Figure 2

be hastened by any inflation in the money-wage floor fostered by full employment; it may be that, once having enjoyed the money wage corresponding to (p_f, N_f) in Figure 1*B*, labor will not accept any lower money wage. Once *R* is reached, any further capital expansion will require a price decline that will push the real wage of labor, given that the money wage cannot fall, above its marginal productivity. Employers will therefore contract employment. But this does not obviate the necessity of price deflation. Indeed, it aggravates it, because the reduction of employment lowers the marginal productivity of capital. Balance cannot be restored both in the labor market and in wealth holdings until a level of employment is reached at which the wage rate becomes flexible downward (N_d in Fig. 2).

The permanence of this "floor" equilibrium depends upon the saving function. If positive saving occurs at the levels of income produced by labor supply N_d, capital expansion will continue; and so also will price and wage deflation. Increase of employment then depends on the willingness of labor to accept additional employment at the low level to which severe unemployment has driven the money wage. Willingness to accept additional employment at this money wage may be encouraged by the increase in the real wage due to continued capital accumulation. A sufficient lowering of the money-wage rate demanded for increased employment would result in a situation like that represented by point S in Figure 3, and full employment could be restored.

Alternatively, the "floor" may correspond to a level of income at which there is negative saving. The gradual attrition of the capital stock will then move the PB curve up relative to the LMB curve. As capital becomes scarcer, its marginal product rises; and for both reasons its attractiveness relative to that of currency increases. Whatever happens to the money-wage terms on which labor will accept additional employment, the decumulation of capital will eventually lead to a position like S in Figure 3.

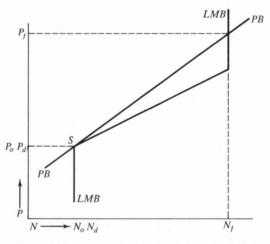

Figure 3

Once S is reached, any further reduction in the money wage, or any further decumulation of capital, will lead to an expansion of employment. But increasing employment only enhances the relative attractiveness of the existing stock of capital, causing the price level to rise and employment to be still further increased. As Figure 3 shows, the only stopping point is (p_f, N_f). Once N_f is reached, the money wage becomes flexible upward and follows the price level upward until portfolio balance is restored at the price level p_f. The cycle then repeats itself.

The floor in this model is provided by a level of employment so low, and a real wage correspondingly so high, that money-wage rates become flexible downward. The breakdown of money-wage rigidity may also be interpreted as a function of time; as Leontief has suggested, money-wage rigidity may not reflect any persistent "money illusion" on the part of workers and their organizations but only a lag in their perception of the price level to use in reckoning their real wage.[9] Trouble occurs at full employment, even when real wages are increasing, because the time rate of price deflation becomes too fast in relation to this lag. Likewise, contraction of employment can be stopped and even reversed when money-wage demands have had time to catch up with what has been happening to the price level.

In this discussion of the floor it has been assumed that the rate of capital decumulation is controlled by the saving function. An interesting question arises when the saving function indicates dissaving at a rate higher than that at which the capital stock can physically decumulate. In the models of Goodwin and Hicks, in fact, the floor is the level of income at which dissaving equals the maximum possible rate of capital decumulation.

A physical limit on the rate of capital decumulation cannot really be handled within the framework of an aggregative model that takes account of only one industry, one commodity, and one price level. Such a model assumes that the output of the economy is essentially homogeneous and can equally well be consumed or accumulated in productive stocks, from which it can be withdrawn at will. If capital goods and consumers' goods are regarded as less than perfect substitutes, it is necessary to imagine that they have different price levels. Encountering a Goodwin-Hicks floor would then mean that the two price levels diverge. At any lower level of income the community would be unable to consume capital at the rate at which it wished to dissave. Consequently, the community would dissave from its holdings of currency. This would stop the fall in the price level of consumption goods and make the Goodwin-Hicks floor an equilibrium level of employment and income. The price of capital goods would continue to fall as owners of wealth attempted to convert capital into either currency or consumption. This fall in the value of capital goods would restore portfolio balance — even though consumers' goods prices ceased to fall and money-wage rates remained rigid — by making capital a smaller proportion of the community's wealth.

With the model thus amended, the physical limit on capital decumulation provides a floor that will stop and eventually reverse a contraction

[9]W. Leontief, "Postulates: Keynes' *General Theory* and the Classicists," in S. E. Harris (ed.), *The New Economics* (New York: Alfred A. Knopf, 1947), chap. 19.

even if the money-wage rate is intractable. But the contraction need not proceed to this extreme, if the wage-flexibility floor described above occurs at a higher level of employment and output.

Wage inflexibility and stagnation

The cycle just described arises from the situation depicted in Figure 1B. But the situation of Figure 1A, where the LMB curve has an algebraically greater slope than the PB curve and the intersection (p_0, N_0) is a stable equilibrium, also is a possibility. In this case the intersection may move to the left as the capital stock increases. Growth of capital is accompanied by reduction of employment, so long as the money-wage rate is maintained. This process may end in a stationary equilibrium position if it entails such a reduction in output (or, if wealth is relevant to the saving function, such an increase in wealth) as to reduce saving to zero. But it is also possible that a process with positive saving, growth of capital, and increasing unemployment will continue indefinitely.

Summary

The simple aggregative model that has been presented here differs from others used in discussions of growth and cycles in two main respects. The production function allows for substitution between capital and labor. The willingness of the community to hold physical capital depends on its rate of return and on the value of the liquid wealth held by the community. These two assumptions provide a link, generally absent in other models, between the world of real magnitudes and the world of money and prices. This link provides the model with some adjustment mechanisms ignored in other growth and cycle models. The following conclusions result:

1. Growth is possible at a great variety of rates and is not necessarily precluded when the labor supply grows slowly or remains constant.

2. The course of the price level as capital grows depends on (a) the accompanying rate of expansion of the labor force, (b) the rate at which the supply of currency is augmented by government deficits, and (c) the rate of technological progress. The first two factors are both inflationary. Technological progress has mixed effects. In the absence of monetary expansion and technological progress, price deflation is a necessary concomitant of growth even when the labor supply is increasing just as rapidly as capital. In these circumstances, therefore, growth with stable or increasing employment cannot continue if the money-range rate is inflexible downward.

3. Given wage inflexibility, the system may alternate between high and low levels of employment and, concurrently, between periods of price inflation and deflation. The ceiling to this cyclical process is provided by inelasticity of the labor supply. The floor may be provided either by the

breakdown of the rigid money wage or by physical limits on the rate of consumption of capital. Alternatively, the system may "stagnate" at less than full employment, quite conceivably with capital growth and reduction of employment occurring at the same time. Whether the system behaves in this manner or with cyclical fluctuations depends on the relation between the conditions of portfolio balance and the rate of return on capital. The greater the shift in portfolios that owners of wealth wish to make when the rate of return on capital changes, the more likely it is that the system will have a cyclical solution.

APPENDIX

The equation of the labor-market-balance curve, for given K, is

$$pP_N (K, N) = w_0 , \tag{1}$$

where w_0 is the rigid money-wage rate. The slope of this curve is

$$\left(\frac{dp}{dN}\right)_{LMB} = \frac{-p^2 P_{NN}}{w_0} . \tag{2}$$

Since $P_{NN} < 0$, this slope is positive.

The equation of the portfolio-balance curve, for given K and M, is

$$\begin{aligned} M &= pL(K, r, Y) \\ &= pL(K, P_K[K, N], P[K, N]) . \end{aligned} \tag{3}$$

The slope of this curve is

$$\left(\frac{dp}{dN}\right)_{PB} = \frac{-p^2}{M} (L_r P_{KN} + L_Y P_N) . \tag{4}$$

Since $L_r < 0$, $P_{KN} > 0$, and $L_Y > 0$, this slope may be either positive or negative.

The point (p_0, N_0) is determined by the intersection of (1) and (3). The problem is to find the changes in p_0 and N_0 associated with an increase in K.

Differentiating (1) and (3) with respect to K gives

$$\frac{\partial p_0}{\partial K}\left(\frac{w_0}{p_0}\right) + \frac{\partial N_0}{\partial K} (p_0 P_{NN}) = -p_0 P_{NK} , \tag{5}$$

$$\frac{\partial p_0}{\partial K}\left(\frac{M}{p_0}\right) + \frac{\partial N_0}{\partial K} (p_0 L_r P_{KN} + p_0 L_Y P_N) = -p_0 L_K - p_0 L_r P_{KK} - p_0 L_Y P_K . \tag{6}$$

Equations (5) and (6) give the following solutions:

$$\frac{\partial p_0}{\partial K} = -\frac{p^2}{D}(P_{NK}^2 L_r - P_{NN}P_{KK}L_r - L_K P_{NN} + P_{NK}P_N L_Y - P_{NN}P_K L_Y), \quad (7)$$

$$\frac{\partial N_0}{\partial K} = -\frac{1}{D}(w_0 L_K + w_0 L_r P_{KK} - M P_{NK} + w_0 L_Y P_K), \quad (8)$$

where

$$D = w_0 L_r P_{KN} - M P_{NN} + w_0 L_Y P_N. \quad (9)$$

From (2), (4), and (9), it can be concluded that D will be positive, zero, or negative according as the slope of the LMB curve is greater than, equal to, or less than the slope of the PB curve. In the stable case (Fig. 1A), D is positive. In the unstable case (Fig. 1B), D is negative.

The production function is assumed to be homogeneous of degree one. Consequently,

$$P_N N + P_K K = P.$$

Differentiating this with respect to N and K gives

$$P_{NN} N + P_{KN} K = 0, \quad (10)$$

$$P_{NK} N + P_{KK} K = 0. \quad (11)$$

Using (10) and (11) in (7) gives

$$\frac{\partial p_0}{\partial K} = \frac{-p_0^2}{D}(P_{NN} L_K + P_{NK} P_N L_Y - P_{NN} P_K L_Y). \quad (12)$$

Since P_{NN} is negative, this derivative has the opposite sign of D. Consequently, in the stable case it is negative, and in the unstable case it is positive.

Using (9), (10), and (11) in (8) gives

$$\frac{\partial N_0}{\partial K} = \frac{1}{D}\left(\frac{N}{K} D - w_0 L_K - w_0 L_Y \frac{Y}{K}\right), \quad (13)$$

where L_K and L_Y are positive. Consequently, if D is negative — the unstable case — $\partial N_0/\partial K$ must be positive. But if D is positive — the stable case — the derivative may have either sign.

A point like (p_f, N_f) represents the intersection of the portfolio-balance curve (3) with a vertical labor-market-balance curve. To find out whether employment can be maintained at N_f when K is increased, it is necessary only to find $\partial w_0/\partial K$ for fixed N_f from (1) and (3). If this $\partial w_0/\partial K$ is negative, then maintenance of employment is not consistent with maintenance of portfolio balance unless the money-wage floor w_0 is lowered. If the derivative is zero or positive, then employment can be maintained or indeed increased even though the money-wage rate remains fixed or rises. Differentiating (1) and (3) with respect to K, for fixed N, gives:

$$\frac{\partial w_0}{\partial K} - \frac{\partial p_f}{\partial K}\left(\frac{w_0}{p_f}\right) = p_f P_{NK},$$ (14)

$$\frac{\partial p_f}{\partial K}\left(\frac{M}{p_f}\right) = -p_f L_K - p_f L_r P_{KK} - p_f L_Y P_K.$$ (15)

Therefore:

$$\frac{\partial w_0}{\partial K} = \frac{-w_0 L_K - w_0 L_r P_{KK} - w_0 L_Y P_K + M P_{NK}}{M/p_f}.$$ (16)

Comparing (8) and (16),

$$\left(\frac{\partial w_0}{\partial K}\right)_{N_{\text{const.}}} = \frac{D}{M/p_f}\left(\frac{\partial N_0}{\partial K}\right)_{w_{0_{\text{const.}}}}$$ (17)

From the conclusions previously reached with the aid of (13), it follows that, when D is negative (unstable case), $\partial w_0/\partial K$ is negative. But when D is positive (stable case), $\partial w_0/\partial K$ may have either sign.

NICHOLAS KALDOR
JAMES A. MIRRLEES

25

A new model of economic growth

I.

The purpose of this paper is to present a "Keynesian" model of economic growth which is an amended version of previous attempts put forward by one of the authors in three former publications.[1] This new theory differs from earlier theories mainly in the following respects:

1. It gives more explicit recognition to the fact that technical progress is infused into the economic system through the creation of new equipment, which depends on current (gross) investment expenditure. Hence the "technical progress function" has been re-defined so as to exhibit a relationship between the rate of change of gross (fixed) investment per operative and the rate of increase in labour productivity on *newly installed* equipment;

Reprinted from *The Review of Economic Studies*, Vol. 29 (June 1962), pp. 174–192, by permission of the publisher and authors. [Footnotes expanded — *Eds.*]

[1]Cf. N. Kaldor, "Alternative Theories of Distribution," *Review of Economic Studies*, XXIII (1955–56), 83–100 [reprinted in *Essays on Value and Distribution* (Glencoe, Ill.: Free Press of Glencoe, 1960), pp. 228–236]. "A Model of Economic Growth," *Economic Journal*, LXVII (Dec. 1957), 591–624 [reprinted in *Essays in Economic Stability and Growth* (Glencoe, Ill.: Free Press of Glencoe, 1960), pp. 256–300] and "Capital Accumulation and Economic Growth," (presented in Corfu, September 1958 and published in F. A. Lutz and D. C. Hague, *The Theory of Capital* [New York: St. Martin's Press, Inc., 1961], pp. 177–220). N. Kaldor's ideas in connection with the present model were worked out during his tenure as Ford Research Professor in Economics in Berkeley, California.

2. It takes explicit account of obsolescence, caused by the fact that the profitability of plant and equipment of any particular "vintage" must continually diminish in time owing to the competition of equipment of superior efficiency installed at subsequent dates; and it assumes that this *continuing obsolescence is broadly foreseen by entrepreneurs* who take it into account in framing their investment decision. The model also assumes that, irrespective of whether plant and equipment has a finite physical life-time or not, its *operative* life-time is determined by a complex of economic factors which govern the rate of obsolescence, and not by physical wear and tear;

3. In accordance with this, the behavioural assumptions concerning the investors' attitudes to uncertainty in connection with investment decisions and which are set out below, differ in important respects from those made in the earlier models;

4. Account is also taken, in the present model, of the fact that some proportion of the existing stock of equipment disappears each year through physical causes — accidents, fire, explosions, etc. — and this gives rise to some "radioactive" physical depreciation in addition to obsolescence;

5. Since, under continuous technical progress and obsolescence, there is no way of measuring the "stock of capital" (measurement in terms of the historical cost of the surviving capital equipment is irrelevant; in terms of historical cost *less* accrued "obsolescence" is question-begging, since the allowance for obsolescence, unlike the charge for physical wear and tear, etc., depends on the share of profits, the rate of growth, etc., and cannot therefore be determined independently of all other relations), the model avoids the notion of a quantity of capital, and its corollary, the rate of capital accumulation, as variables of the system; it operates solely with the value of current gross investment (gross (fixed) capital expenditure per unit of time) and its rate of change in time. The macro-economic notions of income, income per head, etc., on the other hand are retained.

II.

The present model is analogous to the earlier models in the following main features:

1. Like all "Keynesian" economic models, it assumes that "savings" are passive — the level of investment is based on the volume of investment decisions made by entrepreneurs, and is independent of the propensities to save; it postulates an economy in which the mechanism of profit and income generation will create sufficient savings (at any rate within certain limits or "boundaries") to balance the investment which entrepreneurs decide to undertake;

2. The model relates to an isolated economy with continuous

technical progress, and with a steady rate of increase in the working population, determined by exogeneous factors;

3. The model assumes that investment is primarily *induced* by the growth in production itself, and that the underlying conditions are such that growth-equilibrium necessarily carries with it a state of continuous full employment. This will be the case when the purely 'endogeneous' growth rate (as determined by the combined operation of the accelerator and the multiplier) which is operative under conditions of an unlimited supply of labour, is appreciably higher than the "natural rate of growth," which is the growth of the "labour potential" (i.e., the *sum* of the rate of growth of the labour force and of (average) labour productivity). In that case, starting from any given state of surplus labour and underemployment, continued growth, as determined by these endogeneous factors, will necessarily lead to full employment sooner or later; and once full employment rules, continued growth involves that the "accelerator-multiplier" mechanism becomes "tethered" (through variations in the share of profits and through the imposition of a quasi-exogeneous growth rate in demand) to the natural rate of growth.

III.

In a situation of continuing full employment the volume of investment decisions for the economy as a whole will be governed by the number of workers who become available, per unit period, to "man" new equipment, and by the amount of investment per operative. It may be assumed that each entrepreneur, operating in imperfectly competitive markets, aims at the maximum attainable growth of his own business (subject as we shall explain below, to the maintenance of a satisfactory rate of return on the capital employed) and for that reason prefers to maintain an appreciable amount of excess capacity so as to be able to exploit any chance increase in his selling power either by increasing his share of the market or by invading other markets. However, when gross investment per period is in excess of the number of workers becoming available to "man" new equipment, the degree of excess capacity must steadily rise; hence whatever the desired relationship between capacity and output, sooner or later a point will be reached when the number of workers available for operating new equipment exerts a dominating influence (via the mechanism of the accelerator) on the volume of investment decisions in the economy.[2]

We shall assume that the equipment of any given vintage is in "limita-

[2]We may assume that for the average, or representative, firm, sales grow at the same rate as production in the economy as a whole. But there will always be of course the exceptional firms who grow at a higher rate, and sub-average firms who grow at a lower rate. Investment in all cases serves the purpose of keeping productive capacity in some desired relationship with expected sales.

tional" relationship to labour — i.e. that it is not possible to increase the productivity of labour by reducing the number of workers employed in connection with already existing equipment (though it is possible that productivity would, on the contrary, be *reduced* by such a reduction, on account of its being associated with a higher ratio of overhead to prime labour). This does not mean that the equipment of any vintage requires a fixed amount of labour to keep it in operation. The latter would assume the case not only of "fixed coefficients" but of complete indivisibility of the plant and equipment as well.

Writing n_t for the number of workers available to operate new equipment per unit period and i_t for the amount of investment per operative on machines of vintage t, and I_t for gross investment in fixed capital

$$i_t \equiv \frac{I_t}{n_t} \tag{1}$$

We shall use the symbols Y_t for the gross national product at t, N_t for the working population, and y_t for output per head, so that

$$y_t \equiv \frac{Y_t}{N_t}$$

IV.

We shall assume that "machines" of each vintage are of constant physical efficiency during their lifetime, so that the growth of productivity in the economy is entirely due to the infusion of new "machines" into the system through (gross) investment.[3] Hence our basic assumption is a technical progress function which makes the annual rate of growth of productivity per worker *operating on new equipment* a function of the rate of growth of investment per worker, i.e., that

$$\dot{p}_t/p_t = f(\dot{i}_t/i_t) \text{ with } f(0) > 0, \qquad f' > 0, f'' < 0 \tag{2}$$

This function is illustrated in Figure 1. It is assumed that a constant rate of investment per worker over time will itself increase productivity per worker; but that the rate of growth of productivity will also be an increasing function

[3] It is probable that in addition to "embodied" technical progress there is some "disembodied" technical progress as well, resulting from increasing know-how in the use of existing machinery. On the other hand it is also probable that the physical efficiency of machinery declines with age (on account of higher repair and maintenance expenditures, etc.); our assumption of constant physical efficiency thus implies that these two factors just balance each other.

of the rate of growth of investment per worker, though at a diminishing rate.[4]

Both output per operative and investment per operative are measured in terms of money values deflated by an index of the prices of "wage goods" (i.e., consumption goods which enter into the wage-earners' budget). This

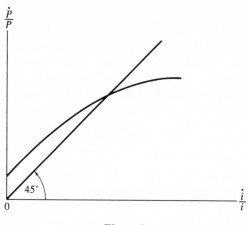

Figure 1

means that changes in the prices of equipment goods in terms of wage-goods (and also of such consumption goods which only enter into consumption out of profits) will in general cause shifts in the f-function. Provided, however, that there is a reasonably stable trend in the prices of these latter goods in terms of wage goods, we can still conceive of the function as stable in time for any particular value of I_t/Y_t in money terms, and the system may still possess a steady growth equilibrium with a constant (equilibrium) value of I_t/Y_t. A full demonstration of this would require, however, a fully fledged 2-sector model in which the technical progress functions of the consumption goods sector and the capital goods sector, the distribution of employment and of savings between the two sectors, etc., are all treated separately. Since this would go far beyond the scope of this paper, it is better to assume, for the present purposes, that the rate of technical progress, as

[4]It should be noted that the "technical progress function" in this model relates to the rate of growth of output per man-hour of the workers operating newly installed equipment (the equipment resulting from the investment of period t), *not* to the rate of growth of productivity in the economy in general (though in full steady growth equilibrium, as we shall see, the two will correspond to each other); and to the rate of growth of gross investment per worker from year to year, not the rate of accumulation of capital (which may not be a meaningful or measurable quantity). It is plausible that, with technical progress, the same investment per operative should yield a higher output per operative in successive years; and that this rate of growth will be enhanced, within limits, when the value of investment per operative is increasing over time.

measured by productivity growth, is the same in all sectors, and hence that relative prices remain constant; bearing in mind, however, that the model could probably be extended to cover a wider range of possibilities.

V.

With regard to the manner in which entrepreneurs meet risk and uncertainty, we shall make two important assumptions. In the first place we shall assume that entrepreneurs will only invest in their own business in so far as this is consistent with maintaining the earning power of their fixed assets above a certain minimum, a minimum which, in their view, represents the earning power of fixed assets in the economy in general. This is because, if the earnings of a particular firm are low in relation to the capital employed, or if they increase at a lower rate than the book value of the fixed assets, fixed assets will take up an increasing proportion of the total resources of the firm (including its potential borrowing power) at any given rate of growth, with the result that the financial position of the firm will become steadily weaker, with enhanced risks of bankruptcy or take-over bids. Hence we may assume that the sum of the expected profits anticipated from operating the equipment during its anticipated period of operation (or lifetime), T, will earn after full amortisation, a rate of profit that is at least equal to the assumed rate of profit on new investment in the economy generally. Hence for any particular investor

$$i_t \leq \int_t^{t+T} e^{-(\rho+\delta)(\tau-t)}(p_t - w_\tau^*)\, d\tau \tag{3}$$

where ρ stands for what the entrepreneur assumes the general rate of profit to be, w_τ^* for the expected rate of wages which is a rising function of future time[5] and δ is the rate of "radioactive" decay of machines (we take it that the investor assumes his machine is an average machine).[6]

In the second place, under conditions of continuing technical progress, the expectations concerning the more distant future (whether in regard to

[5]In a golden age equilibrium, the inequality (3) should be replaced by an equality, and since all the variables will be determined independently by the other equations, (3) can then be taken as determining the rate of profit on investment. Cf. p. 513 below.

[6]Our equation (3) thus postulates conditions under which the amount of "finance" available to the firm is considerably greater than its fixed capital expenditure, so that the firm is free to vary its total investment expenditure per unit of time; and that it will adopt projects which pass the tests of adequacy as indicated by (3) even though it could earn a higher *rate* of profit on projects involving a smaller volume of investment and yielding a smaller *total* profit. (In other words we assume that the firm is guided by the motive of maximising the rate of profit on the shareholders' equity, which involves different decisions from the assumption of maximising the rate of profit on its fixed investment.)

money wages or in regard to the prices — or demands — of the particular products produced by a firm, both of which are projected in w_τ^*) are regarded as far more hazardous or uncertain than the expectations for the near future, where the incidence of unforseeable major new inventions or discoveries is less significant. Hence investment projects which qualify for adoption must pass a further test — apart from the test of earning a satisfactory rate of profit — and that is that the cost of the fixed assets must be "recovered" within a certain period — i.e., that the gross profit earned in the first h years of its operation must be sufficient to repay the cost of investment. Hence

$$i_t \le \int_t^{t+h} (p_t - w_\tau^*) \, d\tau \tag{4}$$

VI.

We shall assume, for the purposes of this model, that (3) is satisfied whenever (4) is satisfied — hence in (4) the = sign will apply, i.e., the undiscounted sum of profits over h periods must be equal to i_t. There is plenty of empirical evidence that the assumption underlying (4) is a generally recognised method of meeting the uncertainty due to obsolescence in modern business, though the value of h may vary with the rate of technical progress, and also as between different sectors. (In the U.S. manufacturing industry h is normally taken as 3 years; but in other sectors — e.g., public utilities — it is much higher.)[7]

VII.

It is assumed, as in the earlier Keynesian growth models, that the savings which finance business investment come out of profits, and that a constant

[7]The assumptions represented by these two equations should be contrasted with the assumptions made in "Capital Accumulation and Economic Growth," according to which

$$\frac{P}{K} = r + \rho$$

$$\rho = \xi(v)(\xi' > 0)$$

where P/K the rate of profit, r the money rate of interest, ρ the risk premium, v the capital/output ratio. ρ was assumed to be a rising function of v, because v reflects the ratio of fixed to circulating capital, and investment in the former is considered far more risky or "illiquid" than investment in the latter. The present assumptions are not inconsistent with the former hypothesis concerning the higher returns demanded on fixed investments; but they also take into account that the "riskiness" of the investment in fixed capital will be all the greater the longer the period over which the cost of the investment is 'recovered' out of the profits — a matter which depends not only on the capital/output ratio (or rather, the investment/output ratio) but also on the share of gross profits in output. "Gross profits" should for this purpose be calculated net of other charges, including a notional interest charge on the 'liquid' business assets (i.e., the investment in circulating capital associated with the investment in fixed capital).

proportion, s, of *gross* profits are saved.[8] Hence (dividing income into two categories, profits and wages, which comprise all forms of non-business income) the share of (gross) profits, π_t, in the gross national product will be given by the equation

$$\pi_t = \frac{1}{s}\frac{I_t}{Y_t} \tag{5}$$

which, in virtue of equation (1), reduces to

$$\pi_t = \frac{r}{s}\frac{i_t}{y_t} \tag{5a}$$

where r is defined by

$$r_t = n_t/N_t$$

where N_t is the total labour force at time t and n_t, as earlier defined, is the number of workers available to operate new equipment per unit period.

We shall assume that once equipment is installed the number of workers operating it will only fall in time by the physical wastage of equipment, caused by accidents, fires, etc. — until the whole of the residual equipment is scrapped on account of obsolescence. Writing δ for the rate of (radioactive) depreciation per unit period, and $T(t)$ for the age of the equipment which is retired at t (i.e., the lifetime of equipment as governed by obsolescence), we have the following relationship for the distribution of the labour force:

$$N_t = \int_{t-T}^{t} n_\tau e^{-\delta(t-\tau)} \, d\tau \tag{6}$$

and for total output

$$Y_t = \int_{t-T}^{t} p_\tau n_\tau e^{-\delta(t-\tau)} \, d\tau \tag{7}$$

Since output Y_t is divided into two categories of income only, wages and profits, the residue left after profits is equal to the total wages bill. Writing w_t for the rate of wages at t, we further have

$$Y_t(1 - \pi_t) = N_t w_t \tag{8}$$

Finally, since equipment will only be employed so long as its operation more than covers prime costs, the profit on the oldest yet surviving machinery must be zero. Hence

$$p_{t-T} = w_t \tag{9}$$

[8]Savings out of wages are ignored — i.e., they are assumed to be balanced by non-business (personal) investment (i.e., residential construction). The assumption that business savings are a constant proportion of *gross* profits (after tax) is well supported by data relating to gross corporate savings.

We shall assume that population grows at the constant rate λ, hence

$$\dot{N}_t = \lambda N_t \tag{10}$$

We shall also assume that businessmen anticipate that wages in terms of output units will rise in the foreseeable future at the same rate as they have been rising during the past l periods.

Hence the expected wage rate at a future time T will be

$$w_T^* = w_t \left(\frac{w_t}{w_{t-l}} \right)^{(T-t)/l} \tag{11}$$

Finally, the model is subject to two constraints (or "boundary conditions") which are known from earlier models:

$$w_t \geq w_{min} \qquad \pi \geq m$$

In other words, the wage rate resulting from the model must be above a certain minimum (determined by conventional subsistence needs) and at the same time the share of profits resulting from the model must be higher than a certain minimum (the so-called "degree of monopoly" or "degree of imperfect competition").

VIII.

The above system gives 10 independent equations (regarding (3) only as a boundary condition) which are sufficient to determine the 10 unknowns; I_t, i_t, n_t, p_t, w_t, w_t^*, π_t, T, y_t, N_t, given the parameters, s, h, δ and λ, and the function f.

We shall investigate whether this system yields a solution in terms of a steady growth (or golden age) equilibrium where the rate of growth of output per head is equal to the rate of growth of productivity on new equipment and both are equal to the rate of growth of (fixed) investment per worker, and to the rate of growth of wages; i.e., where

$$\dot{p}/p = \dot{y}/y = \dot{i}/i = \dot{w}/w$$

and where the share of investment in output I/Y, the share of profits in income π, and the period of obsolescence of equipment, T, remain constant. Finally we shall show that there is a unique rate of profit on investment in a steady growth equilibrium.

The assumptions about the technical progress function imply that there is *some* value $\dot{p}/p$ (let us call it γ) at which

$$\dot{p}/p = \dot{i}/i = \gamma$$

Equilibrium is only possible when this holds.

If we integrate equation (4) using (11), we see that

$$i_t = hp_t - w_t \frac{e^{vh} - 1}{v} \qquad (12)$$

where v is the expected rate of growth of w. Hence p could only grow faster than i in the long run if w was growing faster than p: that would imply a continuous reduction in T, which would lead to unemployment and stagnation before T fell to h (at which point the rate of profit would be negative). On the other hand, p cannot grow more slowly than i in the long run, since w cannot fall below w_{min} (and there would in fact be an inflation crisis before that point was reached).

It is clear too that, so long as $\dot{w}/w$ does not diverge too far from $\dot{p}/p$, i/i would increase if it were less than $\dot{p}/p$, and decrease if it were greater than $\dot{p}/p$. For if $\dot{p}/p$ were less than γ, it would breed, by equation (4), a rate of growth of investment, $\dot{i}/i$ that would require higher $\dot{p}/p$, and so on, until the equilibrium position is reached. A similar mechanism would be at work if $\dot{p}/p$ were greater than γ. Thus the equilibrium would in general be stable; but instability cannot be excluded, and a movement away from equilibrium would be possible in either of the two ways described above. For example a downward drift of the technical progress function might allow the rate of growth of p to fall off, and remain below the rate of growth of w (which reflects the rate of growth of y over the recent past) sufficiently long until with falling investment, unemployment and stagnation set in.[9] Conversely an upward shift in the technical progress function might lead to an inflationary situation at which investment, by one means or another, would be compressed below that indicated by (4) and (3).

Hence, excluding the case where $\dot{p}/p$ is significantly different from $\dot{w}/w$, when

$$\dot{p} > i \qquad p < i$$

there will be a convergent movement until (12) is obtained.

IX.

It will be convenient to deduce two further relations from the above equations. The first one relates to n_t, the amount of labour available for new equipment: it is obtained by differentiating (6) with respect to t.

$$n_t = \dot{N}_t + \delta N_t + n_{t-T}\left(1 - \frac{dT}{dt}\right)e^{-\delta T} \qquad (13)$$

[9]For example, a slowing down of technical progress in the late 1920's may have been responsible for that "sudden collapse of the marginal efficiency of capital" which led to the crisis and stagnation of the 1930's.

This equation says that n_t will be composed of three elements: (i) the growth in working population, $\dot{N}_t$; (ii) the labour released by physical wastage of equipment all vintages, which is δN_t; (iii) and finally the labour released by the retirement of obsolete equipment.

Differentiating equation (7) in the same way we obtain

$$\dot{Y}_t = p_t n_t - p_{t-T} n_{t-T}\left(1 - \frac{dT}{dt}\right)e^{-\delta T} - \delta Y_t$$

Substituting w_t for p_{t-T} in accordance with (9) and using (13) this becomes

$$\dot{Y}_t = p_t n_t - w_t(n_t - \dot{N}_t - \delta N_t) - \delta Y_t$$

Dividing both sides by $Y_t = N_t y_t$ we obtain

$$\frac{\dot{Y}_t}{Y_t} = r\frac{p_t}{y_t} - \frac{w_t}{y_t}(r - \lambda - \delta) - \delta$$

Using

$$\frac{\dot{Y}_t}{Y_t} = \frac{\dot{y}_t}{y_t} + \lambda$$

and re-arranging we finally obtain

$$\frac{\dot{y}_t}{y_t} + \lambda + \delta = r\frac{p_t}{y_t} - (r - \lambda - \delta)\frac{w_t}{y_t} \qquad (14)$$

X.

In order that entrepreneurial expectations should be fulfilled, it is necessary that wages should grow at constant rate in time, β.

$$\frac{\dot{w}_t}{w_t} = \beta \text{ (constant)} \qquad (15)$$

We shall now proceed to demonstrate that when β is constant, T will also be constant, provided that

$$\gamma < (s/h) - \lambda - \delta$$

It follows from (9) that

$$\frac{\dot{w}_t}{w_t} = \frac{\dot{p}_{t-T}}{p_{t-T}}\left(1 - \frac{dT}{dt}\right)$$

Hence

$$1 - \frac{dT}{dt} = \frac{\beta}{\gamma}, \text{ a constant}$$

Integrating with respect to t we obtain

$$T = T_0 + \left(1 - \frac{\beta}{\gamma}\right)t \tag{16}$$

where T_0 is the lifetime of equipment at some initial date, $t = 0$.

Substituting (16) into (13) and remembering that $r_t = n_t/N_t$, we obtain

$$r_t = \lambda + \delta + r_{t-T}e^{-(\lambda+\delta)T}\frac{\beta}{\gamma} \tag{17}$$

In order to show that, in a state of steady growth equilibrium $T = T_0$ and $\beta = \gamma$, we shall first consider the cases where $\beta \neq \gamma$.

(i) When $\gamma < \beta$, clearly steady growth cannot continue since entrepreneurs' profits would become negative sooner or later.

(ii) When $\gamma > \beta$, it follows from equation (16) that T becomes indefinitely large with time (and perhaps this is enough to dispose of this case, since for most goods there may be a maximum physical lifetime, quite apart from obsolescence). In any case this implies, in accordance with (17), that r ultimately tends to $\lambda + \delta$; and since w/y must tend to zero, so that the share of profits, π, tends towards unity.

$$i/y \text{ tends to } \frac{s}{\lambda + \delta} \tag{18}$$

Also from (4):

$$i/p \text{ tends to } h$$

Hence from (14):

$$\dot{y}/y \text{ tends to } \frac{s}{h} - \lambda - \delta$$

(18) shows that y ultimately grows at the same rate as i, which grows at the rate γ.

Therefore

$$\gamma = \frac{s}{h} - \lambda - \delta \tag{19}$$

which implies, in Harrod's terms, that the "natural rate" (here, $\gamma + \lambda + \delta$) is equal to what the "warranted rate" would be if wages were zero and profits absorbed the whole output (since then s would equal the proportion of Y saved, and $h = i/p$).

XI.

It is easy to see that in fact the rate of growth of output per head cannot in the long run be greater than this quantity $(s/h) - \lambda - \delta$. By (5), i/y can rise no higher, ultimately, than s/r; hence by (4), even if (as might happen ultimately) the wage rate were negligible in relation to output per head, p/y could not be greater than $s/(rh)$. Turning to equation (14), we see that it implies the inequality

$$\dot{v}_t/y_t + \lambda + \delta \leq r.\frac{s}{rh} = \frac{s}{h}$$

Hence there can be no steady growth equilibrium unless

$$\gamma \leq \frac{s}{h} - \lambda - \delta$$

Normally we would not expect to have to worry about this constraint, for the quantity s/h will be large — especially when we remember that h will be small when there is a high rate of growth. If it is asked what would happen if the equilibrium growth rate given by the technical progress function really did fail to satisfy this inequality, the answer must be that the wage rate would be driven down to its minimum level and entrepreneurs would then find themselves unable to invest as much as the prospects would warrant: the equality (4) would become an inequality again. The rest of the discussion will be carried on under the assumption that the equilibrium rate of growth γ does satisfy this inequality.

We can see that, quite apart from the unrealistic value of γ implied by equation (19), equilibrium with $\gamma > \beta$ is a freak case; the slightest shift in γ would either render equilibrium impossible, or make it possible only with $\beta = \gamma$.

XII.

(iii) It is clear from the above that steady growth equilibrium will involve

$$\beta = \gamma$$

in which case it also involves a constant T. (17) has now become

$$r_t = \lambda + \delta + r_{t-T}e^{-(\lambda+\delta)T}$$

where T is constant, so that r_t will tend to the equilibrium value

$$r = \frac{\lambda + \delta}{1 - e^{-(\lambda+\delta)T}} \tag{20}$$

From equation (5)

$$y_t = w_t + \frac{r}{s}i_t$$

so that, since r is constant in equilibrium, y_t also grows at the equilibrium growth rate γ. It is convenient to write this last equation as

$$\frac{r}{s}\frac{i}{y} + \frac{w}{y} = 1 \tag{21}$$

In equilibrium, expectations are fulfilled, so that $w_t^* = w_t$. Since $w_t = w_0 e^{\beta t} = w_0 e^{\gamma t}$ (where w_0 is the wage rate at some initial time), the integral in equation (4) can be evaluated, so that

$$i_t = hp_t - \frac{e^{\gamma h} - 1}{\gamma} w_t$$

which we can write

$$\frac{1}{h}\frac{i}{y} + \frac{e^{\gamma h} - 1}{\gamma h}\frac{w}{y} - \frac{p}{y} = 0 \tag{22}$$

(14) can now be rewritten

$$(r - \lambda - \delta)\frac{w}{y} - r\frac{p}{y} = -(\gamma + \lambda + \delta) \tag{23}$$

Equations (21), (22), (23) can be treated as three simultaneous equations for i/y, w/y, and p/y (which are all constants in a state of steady growth).

Now equation (9) provides an equation for T:

$$e^{\gamma T} = \frac{p}{w} = \frac{p/y}{w/y} \tag{24}$$

Using the values of r, p/y, w/y found by solving (21), (22) and (23), we obtain:

$$e^{\gamma T} = \frac{1 - \dfrac{h(\gamma + \lambda + \delta)}{s}\dfrac{e^{\gamma h} - 1}{\gamma h} + \dfrac{\gamma}{r}}{1 - \dfrac{h(\gamma + \lambda + \delta)}{s}} \tag{25}$$

And from (20), since

$$e^{\gamma T} = [e^{-(\lambda+\delta)T}]^{-\gamma/(\lambda+\delta)}$$

$$e^{\gamma T} = \left[1 - \frac{\lambda + \delta}{r}\right]^{-\gamma/(\lambda+\delta)} \tag{26}$$

(25) and (26) determine T and r simultaneously in terms of the parameters λ, δ, h, s, and the steady growth rate γ (which was determined by the technical

progress function). Equation (20) is not valid when $\lambda + \delta = 0$. In that case we go back to equation (6); integration gives

$$rT = 1 \qquad (27)$$

which replaces (26) in this particular case.

XIII.

Although (25) and (26) are rather cumbersome equations, numerical solution for particular values of the parameters presents no particular difficulty. Once T and r are calculated, simultaneous solution of (23) and (24) yields the values of p/y and w/y (the share of wages). Then i/y is found from (22). A demonstration of the existence of a unique meaningful solution to the equations is given in the Appendix.

If capital stock were valued at historic cost, without any allowance for reduction in value through obsolescence, we should have

$$K = \int_{t-T}^{t} i_\tau n_\tau e^{-\delta(t-\tau)} \, d\tau$$

and

$$Y = \int_{t-T}^{t} p_\tau n_\tau e^{-\delta(t-\tau)} \, d\tau \qquad (28)$$

so that the aggregate capital-output ratio,

$$\frac{K}{Y} = \frac{i}{p},$$

since this latter is constant.

However, when obsolescence is *foreseen* the knowledge of the share of profits, π, and of the historical cost of invested capital as shown by (28), does not enable us to calculate either net profits or the rate of profit on capital. The value of capital at any one time will be lower than K_t by the accrued provision made for obsolescence, and the appropriate obsolescence provision — which must take into account the annual reduction in the profits earned on equipment of a given vintage, as well as the retirement of equipment when it becomes T years old — cannot be calculated without knowing the capital on which the profit is earned, which in turn cannot be known without knowing the rate of profit.

XIV.

In a state of fully-fledged golden age equilibrium, where (1) expectations are (in general) fulfilled and the expected profit on new investments is therefore the same as the realised profit, and (2) the rate of profit earned on all investment will be the same, the inequality (3) above can be replaced by an equality and regarded as an additional equation determining ρ (since i_t, p_t, w_t and T are all determined by the other equations of the system).

$$i_t = \int_0^T e^{-(\rho+\delta)\tau} (p_t - W_{t+\tau}) \, d\tau \tag{3a}$$

ρ is constant, so the familiar relation

$$\gamma + \lambda = \rho\sigma \tag{29}$$

where σ is the proportion of *net* profits saved, holds; for it is easy to check that the value of capital — in terms of output to come — grows at the equilibrium growth rate $\gamma + \lambda$, and that ρ defined by (3a) is equal to the ratio of net profit to the stock of capital. In general, of course, σ depends on ρ, and is best calculated from the relation (29). But when $s = 1$, i.e., when all (gross) profits are invested, σ must also be equal to unity, so that the rate of profit is equal to the rate of growth of output: $\rho = \gamma + \lambda$. On the face of it, it is not clear that this value of ρ satisfies (3a): yet it must do. To show that it does, we use the fact that total output,

$$Y_t = \int_0^T p_{t-\tau} n_{t-\tau} e^{-\delta\tau} \, d\tau$$

$$= p_t n_t \int_0^T e^{-(\gamma+\lambda+\delta)\tau} \, d\tau$$

Thus, when we put $\rho = \gamma + \lambda$ in the right hand side of (3a), we get:

$$\frac{y_t}{r_t} - w_t \int_0^T e^{-(\lambda+\delta)\tau} \, d\tau$$

This last integral $=$

$$(1 - e^{-(\lambda+\delta)T})/(\lambda + \delta) = 1/r$$

by equation (20). Hence the right hand side of equation (3a) is equal to $(y_t - w_t)/r$, which is equal to i_t when $s = 1$ (by equation (21)).

If $s \neq 1$, we must find ρ from equation (3a). If we perform the integration (which we can do, since p and w are growing exponentially), we get the following relation, which can be solved numerically for $\rho + \delta$:

$$\frac{i}{v} = \frac{1 - e^{-(\rho+\delta)T}}{\rho + \delta} \frac{p}{y} - \frac{1 - e^{-(\rho+\delta-\gamma)T}}{\rho + \delta - \gamma} \frac{w}{y} \tag{30}$$

Outside a golden age equilibrium a rate of profit on investment does not exist except in the sense of an *assumed* rate of profit, based on a mixture of convention and belief, which enables entrepreneurs to decide whether any particular project passes the test of adequate profitability.

XV. Some numerical results

The following are the solutions of the equations for various arbitrarily selected values of the parameters.[10]

For the U.S. in the 1950's, reasonable values of the parameters are $\gamma = 2$ to $2\frac{1}{2}$ percent, $\lambda + \delta = 2 - 4$ percent, $s = .66$, $h = 4$ to 5 years. The average lifetime of equipment in manufacturing industry has been estimated at 17 years. π as indicated by the ratio of gross corporate profit after tax to the gross income originating in corporations after corporation tax has been 21 percent, and the ratio of business fixed capital to business gross product around 1.5. These, as the table shows, are close to the results

For $s = 0.66$:

h YEARS	$\lambda + \delta\%$	$\gamma\%$	T YEARS	r	$\pi\%$	$I/Y\%$	i/p	$\rho + \delta\%$
3	2	2	8.03	.135	8.0	5.3	.367	21.7
		2.5	8.15	.133	10.1	6.7	.459	22.1
		3	8.27	.131	12.2	8.1	.551	22.4
	4	2	8.68	.136	8.9	5.9	.401	23.0
		2.5	8.82	.135	11.2	7.5	.501	23.4
		3	8.97	.133	13.5	9.0	.601	23.7
4	2	2	11.20	.100	11.2	7.5	.672	17.0
		2.5	11.44	.098	14.1	9.6	.839	17.3
		3	11.68	.096	17.1	11.4	1.006	17.6
	4	2	12.54	.101	12.9	8.6	.759	18.2
		2.5	12.84	.100	16.3	10.9	.948	18.6
		3	13.15	.098	19.8	13.2	1.136	18.9
5	2	2	14.69	.078	14.6	9.7	1.080	14.1
		2.5	15.10	.077	18.5	12.3	1.348	14.4
		3	15.53	.075	22.4	14.9	1.615	14.7
	4	2	17.13	.081	17.8	11.9	1.267	15.4
		2.5	17.71	.079	22.5	15.0	1.579	15.7
		3	18.34	.077	27.4	16.4	1.888	16.0

[10]We are indebted to Mr. D. G. Champernowne for programming these calculations, and to the Director of the Mathematical Laboratory of Cambridge University for making the computer available.

Some representative values for different s:

s	h	$\lambda + \delta\%$	$\gamma\%$		T	r	$\pi\%$	$I/Y\%$	i/p	$\rho + \delta\%$
.33	3	2	$\lbrace$	2	20.66	.059	20.4	6.8	.955	30.6
				2.5	21.26	.058	25.6	8.5	1.169	30.8
.50	4	4	$\lbrace$	2	19.98	.073	20.7	10.3	1.207	21.7
				2.5	20.66	.071	26.2	13.1	1.490	22.0
				3	21.42	.070	31.8	15.9	1.765	22.3
	5	2	$\lbrace$	2	22.61	.055	22.2	11.1	1.655	17.0
				2.5	23.47	.053	28.1	14.0	2.038	17.3
				3	24.41	.052	34.1	17.0	2.407	17.6
1.00	4	4	$\lbrace$	2.5	6.08	.185	7.7	7.7	.387	6.5
				3	6.22	.182	9.4	9.4	.474	7.0
	5		2	$\lbrace$ 2.5	7.28	.148	9.0	9.0	.561	4.5
				3	7.49	.144	11.1	11.1	.691	5.0
			4	$\lbrace$ 2.5	8.20	.143	10.4	10.4	.662	6.5
				3	8.44	.140	12.7	12.7	.812	7.0

Of the model when $s = .66$, $h = 5$, $\lambda + \delta = 4$ percent, and when γ is $2 - 2.5$ percent.[11]

The rate of profit on investment, on the other hand, appears rather high. However it must be remembered that our equation (3) derives the rate of (net) profit from the stream of gross profit *after* tax, and not (as is usually done) from the gross profit before tax. This involves a smaller provision for obsolescence, and consequently a higher net profit, than in the usual method of calculation. It also implies that in "grossing up" for tax, the relevant rate is the effective tax charge on profits before depreciation, and not the rate of tax on profits net of depreciation. Hence, if the tax on corporation profits is one third of gross profits before tax, a rate of net profit (net of tax) of 12.5 percent (assuming $\lambda = 1$ percent, $\delta = 3$ percent) corresponds a to rate of net profit *before* tax of 18.5 percent.[12]

It can be seen from the figures, too, that π and i/p are quite sensitive to changes in the technical progress function (i.e. in γ), and highly sensitive to changes in s and h, but stable for changes in λ and δ. T is only sensitive to changes in s and h, but *not* to γ. These results may sound surprising at first.

[11]It should be borne in mind, of course, that no allowance was made in the model for net investment in working capital (inventory accumulation) which would affect the values of T, π, I/Y and i/p, but the effect of which can be subsumed in h. Equally, the model assumes that government savings and investment are equal — i.e., that there is no financial surplus or deficit arising out of government operations, and that personal savings and personal investments (mainly in housing) are equal.

[12]U.S. estimates put the average rate of profit on (business) investment 16 percent before tax and 8 percent after tax.

One would expect T to be inversely related to γ, and one would also expect $r(=n_t/N_t)$ to be positively correlated with $(\lambda + \delta)$. However, a rise in γ leads to a rise in i/p, and hence of π, which more than compensates for the rise in γ in determining the associated change in T; a rise in $(\lambda + \delta)$ reduces (as between one steady growth equilibrium and another) the amount of labour released through obsolescence in relation to the current labour force (since the labour force T years ago was that much smaller, when λ is larger; and of the equipment built T years ago so much less survives to be scrapped when δ is larger) so that it compensates for the increase in $(\lambda + \delta)$, leaving the value of r pretty much the same.

XVI. General conclusions

The model shows technical progress — in the specific form of the rate of improvement of the design, etc., of newly produced capital equipment — as the main engine of economic growth, determining not only the rate of growth of productivity but — together with other parameters — also the rate of obsolescence, the average lifetime of equipment, the share of investment in income, the share of profits, and the relationship between investment and potential output (i.e., the "capital/output ratio" on new capital).

    The model is Keynesian in its mode of operation (entrepreneurial expenditure decisions are primary; incomes, etc., are secondary) and severely *non*-neo-classical in that technological factors (marginal productivities or marginal substitution ratios) play no role in the determination of wages and profits. A "production function" in the sense of a single-valued relationship between *some* measure of capital, K_t, the labour force N_t and of output Y_t (all at time t) clearly does not exist. Everything depends on past history, on how the collection of equipment goods which comprises K_t has been built up. Thus Y_t will be greater for a given K_t (as measured by historical cost) if a greater part of the existing capital stock is of more recent creation; this would be the case, for example, if the rate of growth of population has been accelerating.

    Whilst "machines" earn quasi-rents which are all the smaller the older they are (so that, for the oldest surviving machine, the quasi-rents are zero) it would be wrong to say that the position of the marginal "machine" determines the share of quasi-rents (or gross profits) in total income. For the total profit is determined quite independently of the structure of these "quasi-rents" by equation (5), i.e., by the factors determining the share of investment in output and the proportion of profits saved and therefore the position of the "marginal" machine is itself fully determined by the other equations of the system. It is the macro-economic condition specified in (5), and not the age-and-productivity structure of machinery, which will determine what the (aggregate) share of quasi-rents will be.

This technical progress function is quite consistent with a technological "investment function", i.e., a functional relationship (shifting in time) between investment per worker and output per worker.[13] However, owing to anticipated obsolescence and to uncertainty, it would not be correct to say that the "marginal product" of investment, dp_t/di_t, plays a role in determining the amount per man. Since the profitability of operating the equipment is expected to diminish in time, the marginal addition to the stream of profits (which we may call the "marginal value productivity") will be something quite different from the marginal product in the technological sense, and unlike the latter, it will not be a derivative of a technological function alone but will depend on the whole system of relationships. Further, owing to the prevailing attitude to uncertainty, it would not even be correct to say that "profit-maximising" will involve adding to investment per man until the marginal increment in anticipated profits, discounted at the ruling rate of interest or at some "assumed" rate of profit becomes equal to the marginal addition to investment. Whenever the desire to recover the cost of investment within a certain number of years — owing to the greater uncertainty of the more distant future — becomes the operative restriction (as is assumed in equation (4)), investment per man will be cut short before this marginal condition is satisfied.

The inequality (3) together with equation (4) enables us to specify an investment function in terms of the parameters of the system which determine both n_t and i_t without regard to the relationship between the expected rate of profit on investment and the rate of interest. In previous "Keynesian" models the existence of an independent investment function was closely tied to the postulate of some relationship between the "marginal efficiency" of investment and — an independently determined — rate of interest. This was a source of difficulty, since it either caused such models to be "overdetermined"[14] or else it required the postulate that the capital/output ratio (or the amount of investment per worker) itself varied with the excess of the rate of profit over the money rate of interest.[15] The weakness of this latter approach has been that it assigned too much importance to the rate of interest. So long as one could assume that the rate of interest was a constant, determined by some psychological minimum (the "pure" liquidity prefer-

---

[13]On the relationship of a technical progress function and a production function cf. John Black, "The Technical Progress Function and The Production Function," *Economica*, May 1962. Whilst it is possible to make assumptions under which a technical progress function is merely one way of representing an (ex-ante) production function of constant elasticity which shifts at some pre-determined rate in time, the postulate of a technical progress function is also consistent with situations in which the rate of technical progress does not proceed at some pre-determined rate (where the shift of the "curve" is bound up with the movement *along* the "curve") and where therefore one cannot associate a unique production function with a given "state" of knowledge.

[14]Cf. R. C. O. Matthews, "The Rate of Interest in Growth Models," *Oxford Economic Papers*, [XII] Oct. 1960, pp. 249–268.

[15]Cf. Kaldor, "Capital Accumulation and Economic Growth," *op. cit.*, pp. 217 ff.

ence of Keynesian theory), this did not matter very much. But it was unsatisfactory to rely on the *excess* of the rate of profit over the rate of interest as an important element — determining the chosen capital/output ratio and through that, the other variables — considering that this excess is under the control of the monetary authorities; if the authorities were to follow a policy of keeping the money rate of interest in some constant relationship to the rate of profit — which they may be easily tempted to do — this would have endowed them with an importance in the general scheme of things which is quite contrary to common experience.

The present model, by contrast allows the money rate of interest to move up and down, without the slightest effect on investment decisions, provided such movements do not violate certain constraints.[16] This is in much better accord with the oft-repeated assertions of business men (both in the U.K. and the U.S.) that the rate of interest has *no* influence on their investment decisions at least as far as investment in fixed capital is concerned.

Finally there is the question how far the postulate of a "technical progress function" as specified in (2) implies some restraint on the *nature* of technological change. Every change in the rate of investment per worker implies a change in the extent to which new ideas ("innovations") are actually exploited. Since the "capital saving" innovations — which increase the output/capital ratio as well as the output/labour ratio — are much more profitable to the entrepreneur than the "labour-saving" ones that yield the same rate of increase in labour productivity, clearly the former are exploited first and the balance of technological change will appear more "capital-using" (all the less "capital-saving") the greater the rate of increase in investment per man. There is therefore always *some* rate of increase in investment per worker which allows output per man to grow at the same rate as investment per man and in that sense takes on the appearance of "neutral" technical progress; to assume that this rate of increase in investment per man remains unchanged over time implies also assuming that the relative importance of "capital saving" and "capital using" innovations in the total flow of innovations remains unchanged. To assume this is really implied in the assumption that the rate of technical progress is *constant;* since a growing incidence of "capital saving" innovations is the same thing as an upward drift in the technical progress function, and *vice versa*. Therefore the only sense in which the technical progress function postulates some "neutral" technical progress is the sense in which "unneutral" technical progress necessarily involves either a continuous acceleration or deceleration in the rate of increase in productivity for any given value of i/i.

The main "practical" conclusion for economic policy that emerges

[16]For it must still remain true, of course, that the expected rate of profit on (fixed) investment must exceed the rate of interest by more than some minimum compensation for the "illiquidity" or other risks.

from this model is that any scheme leading to the accelerated retirement of old equipment (such as a tax on the use of obsolete plant and equipment) is bound to accelerate for a temporary period the rate of increase in output per head $\dot{y}/y$, since it will increase n_t (the number of workers "available" for new machines) and hence I_t; and will thus involve a reduction in p_t/y_t. A more permanent cure, however, requires stimulating the technical dynamism of the economy (*raising* the technical progress function) which is not only (or perhaps mainly) a matter of more scientific education and more expenditure on research, but of higher quality business management which is more alert in searching for technical improvements and less resistant to their introduction.

Appendix

We must enquire whether the solution of the equations for a state of steady growth is unique. Equation (25) is a linear equation for $e^{\gamma T}$ in terms of $1/r$; it can be represented on a diagram, with $1/r$ measured along one axis and $e^{\gamma T}$ along the other, by a straight line.

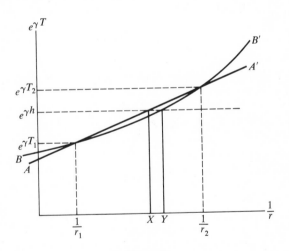

Figure 2

Equation (26), on the other hand, represents a curve of increasing slope (as shown in the diagram). The curve representing equation (26), BB', passes through the point $e^{\gamma T} = 1$, $1/r = 0$; AA', which represents equation (25), has $e^{\gamma T} < 1$ when $1/r = 0$.

We shall prove that (1) AA', in fact cuts BB', and cuts it in two points, to which correspond the values r_1 and r_2 of r, and T_1 and T_2 of T; (2) $T_1 < h$, so that this case is in fact impossible (for entrepreneurs will make losses). It follows that there is a single possible steady growth state.

1. To prove that AA' does not fail to cut BB', we show that there are points of BB' lying *below* AA'. Let x be the value of $1/r$ corresponding to $T = h$ on the curve AA' (i.e., found by solving equation (25)); and let y be the value of $1/r$ corresponding to $T = h$ on the curve BB' (i.e., found by solving equation (26)).

Then

$$\gamma x = e^{\gamma h}\left[1 - \frac{h(\gamma + \lambda + \delta)}{s}\right] + \frac{h(\gamma + \lambda + \delta)}{s}\frac{e^{\gamma h} - 1}{\gamma h} - 1$$

$$= e^{\gamma h} - 1 - \frac{(\gamma + \lambda + \delta)}{\gamma s} \times [\gamma h \cdot e^{\gamma h} - e^{\gamma h} + 1]$$

$$= \gamma h + \tfrac{1}{2}(\gamma h)^2 + \tfrac{1}{6}(\gamma h)^3 + \cdots - \frac{\gamma + \lambda + \delta}{\gamma s}[\tfrac{1}{2}(\gamma h)^2$$

$$+ \tfrac{1}{3}(\gamma h)^3 + \tfrac{1}{8}(\gamma h)^4 + \cdots]$$

$$= \gamma h + \tfrac{1}{2}(\gamma h)^2\left[1 - \frac{\gamma + \lambda + \delta}{\gamma s}\right] + \tfrac{1}{6}(\gamma h)^3\left[1 - 2\frac{\gamma + \lambda + \delta}{\gamma s}\right]$$

$$+ \tfrac{1}{24}(\gamma h)^4\left[1 - 3\frac{\gamma + \lambda + \delta}{\gamma s}\right] + \cdots$$

Clearly $\gamma + \lambda + \delta > \gamma s$, so that all the terms in square brackets are negative. Hence:

$$\gamma x < \gamma h - \tfrac{1}{2}(\gamma h)^2\left[\frac{\gamma + \lambda + \delta}{\gamma s} - 1\right]$$

so that

$$\gamma x < \gamma h - \tfrac{1}{2}\gamma h^2 \cdot (\lambda + \delta) \tag{31}$$

since $s \leq 1$. Also,

$$\gamma y = \frac{\gamma}{\lambda + \delta}(\lambda + \delta)y = \frac{\gamma}{\lambda + \delta} \times [1 - e^{-(\lambda+\delta)h}]$$

$$> \frac{\gamma}{\lambda + \delta}[(\lambda + \delta)h - \tfrac{1}{2}(\lambda + \delta)^2 h^2]$$

$$= \gamma h - \tfrac{1}{2}\gamma h^2(\lambda + \delta)$$

which, as we have just shown, $> \gamma x$. Hence $y > x$; which is to say, that when $T = h$, the curve BB' lies to the right of AA'. Hence AA' meets BB'; for AA' cuts the $e^{\gamma T}$-axis below BB', and BB' eventually rises above AA'.

2. It also follows from the fact that BB' lies to the right of AA' when $T = h$ that one of the points at which AA' and BB' cut has $t < h$; i.e., $T_1 < h$. Thus only T_2 (which is $> h$) is a possible value for T.

What we have shown is that there exists a single possible solution to our equations for the state of steady growth at rate γ. [The case $\lambda + \delta = 0$ follows in the same way; from (31), $\gamma x < \gamma h$; and $h = y$ in this case.]